"I chose *Communication Law: Practical Applications in the Digital Age* because the textbook is accessible for my undergraduate law students. My students like the fact that the authors are able to clearly communicate often dense legalese, while still maintaining the integrity of the material."

David J. Weinert, *University of Miami, USA*

"When I was assigned to teach Media Law, I approached it with great trepidation – then I found *Communication Law* and realized I knew a lot more about media law than I thought I did. *Communication Law* and my teaching reflected how the law is used in media instead of the other texts I reviewed which were like books for lawyers rather than journalists."

Cliff Brockman, *Wartburg College, USA*

COMMUNICATION LAW

This fully revised 4th edition brings a fresh approach to the fundamentals of mass media and communication law in an engaging and accessible way, keeping legal jargon to a minimum and highlighting real-life examples of legal conflicts.

Designed for students of communication that are new to law, this volume presents key principles and emphasizes the impact of timely, landmark cases on today's media world. Providing an applied learning experience, this new edition offers expanded coverage of telecommunications, digital media law, and social media. It presents discussions of contemporary political, social, and cultural issues such as artificial intelligence, surveillance, cybersecurity, revenge porn, deepfakes, and disinformation campaigns. To encourage critical thinking, chapters include "From the Trenches" vignettes written by practitioners, "Global View" pieces comparing U.S. status to that in other countries, and "Ethical Dilemmas" ideal for class discussion.

Communication Law serves as a core textbook for undergraduate courses in communication and mass media law.

Online resources for instructors, including an Instructor's Manual, Test Bank, PowerPoint slides, and Timelines are available at: www.routledge.com/9781032612980.

Dom Caristi is a professor emeritus of media at Ball State University, USA.

William R. Davie is a professor of communication at the University of Louisiana at Lafayette, USA.

Laurie Thomas Lee is a professor of broadcasting at the University of Nebraska-Lincoln, USA.

COMMUNICATION LAW
PRACTICAL APPLICATIONS IN THE DIGITAL AGE

4th Edition

Dom Caristi,
William R. Davie,
and Laurie Thomas Lee

Routledge
Taylor & Francis Group
NEW YORK AND LONDON

Designed cover image: Shutterstock

Fourth edition published 2025
by Routledge
605 Third Avenue, New York, NY 10158

and by Routledge
4 Park Square, Milton Park, Abingdon, Oxon, OX14 4RN

Routledge is an imprint of the Taylor & Francis Group, an informa business

First edition published by Taylor & Francis 2012
Third edition published by Routledge 2022

ISBN: 978-1-032-61299-7 (hbk)
ISBN: 978-1-032-61298-0 (pbk)
ISBN: 978-1-003-46298-9 (ebk)

DOI: 10.4324/9781003462989

Typeset in Times New Roman
by Apex CoVantage, LLC

Access the Support Material: www.routledge.com/9781032612980

Contents

Preface

This textbook's fourth edition is not only noteworthy in terms of updated materials but also the approach we take to business and commercial law, an emphasis missing in our competition. These facets include attention to labor law that came to the fore in the recent strikes in Hollywood. The new approach to artificial intelligence due to its rapid diffusion and impact on intellectual property rights raised new questions in this text. The principal questions posed here – perhaps the most obvious ones – who is the rightful owner of a work created by an anonymous computer scraping the internet? If a machine is taught to creatively fix verbal and visual transcriptions online without direct human manipulation, then who holds the rights to the IP? Shall we look to the designer of the AI programming, the AI business interest involved, the content users, or the original creators of the scraped images and words? Where exactly does this content enter the public domain? Beyond those tricky questions there are others involving cybersecurity and disinformation. And most significantly, we took a renewed focus on our ancillary materials by adding two specialists in media and education to our team to create test banks, lecture slides, and instruction activities for the adopters of this textbook.

Boxed Material

In this book we provide material set apart from the main text to help students better organize material. You will find

- Definitions

  Instead of a glossary at the back of the book, we have provided definitions for key terms in the margins where the terms are used, which we believe to be more user-friendly.
- Bedrock Law

  Bedrock quite literally means foundation. In the margins we identify several foundational rules that are fundamental to our understanding of free expression and our U.S. legal system.
- Global View

  This text focuses on U.S. law, but our system does not operate in a vacuum. Throughout the book we provide information about systems in other countries and their similarities and differences from our own.
- Ethical Dilemmas

  Because so many communication law courses also consider ethics, each chapter ends with a discussion of an unresolved ethical issue. Law and ethics are related but not analogous. That which is legal is not always ethical and vice versa.
- From the Trenches

  For this feature we have invited practitioners to talk about their own experiences in dealing with legal issues. As professors we have noticed that students appreciate hearing from practitioners in class, and we have attempted to replicate that experience with guest essays.

Foreword

By Dr. Kevin Johnson, Professor and Director of the Center for First Amendment Studies at California State University, Long Beach. A version of this essay first appeared on the Center's website September 26, 2023.

Frank Snepp: Learning Media Law and the First Amendment May Save Your Life

Frank Snepp is a Peabody Award winning journalist and has lived an interesting life spanning from CIA spy, to being left penniless, to being a university teacher and esteemed journalist. He spoke about his experiences as a young member of the CIA and his defeat in the Supreme Court in the case of *Snepp v. United States*.

His message to students is that the lessons learned in media law and First Amendment courses are essential and may even save your life one day. Many students who take First Amendment and media law courses think they tend to be idealistic until they are radically confronted with legal realities in their careers and personal lives. He noted how he has had many great teachers in his own life, and how he learned many of the lessons the hard way.

His case that made it to the Supreme Court pertained to the nature and scope of security agencies to maintain power over prior restraint. In his specific case, what power does the CIA have to review works to judge whether certain material may be published by those with access to classified information?

Snepp maintains that the CIA should not have the power to review materials by former employees about the CIA if all the materials in the publication are a matter of public knowledge. In other words, leaking classified information may be a crime and that should be punished, but if a former CIA official publishes material that is not classified then the CIA should not have the power to review and/or censor that material.

The Supreme Court disagreed with Snepp's argument and ruled that he had breached his contractual agreement with the agency to "not . . . publish . . . any information or material relating to the Agency, its activities or intelligence activities generally, either during or after the term of [his]employment . . . without specific prior approval by the Agency." Snepp believes that contract requirement violates his First Amendment right to publish material on matters of public concern so long as he is not sharing classified information.

The Supreme Court disagreed and ruled against Snepp. That left him penniless. He lost all the money from his book publishing, and nobody would hire him because he was perceived as an enemy of the United States. He was shunned from all jobs immediately following the decision.

He does not believe he is an enemy of the United States. He maintains he kept all classified information classified (and still does to this day). He also maintains that he is very much an American, and even advocated for students to consider joining the intelligence community because we need smart and responsible people in the agencies to protect it from some of its negative impulses.

He is haunted by the way the U.S. exited Vietnam. He recalled barely escaping Saigon and being one of the fortunate and believes that the U.S. failed to have a viable exit strategy. As a result, "During the last day, we played God . . . We determined who would be saved and who wouldn't, and it was heart-wrenching. You would get one person in the family, but not the child, not the mother, not the father. We separated families in a wink . . . because we hadn't planned adequately."

Those who support the Supreme Court's ruling against Snepp argue that security agencies ought to have review powers even if there isn't any classified material because their review may prevent any accidental releases of classified information that may be otherwise released and the damage already done.

Snepp believes that as a trained spy, he knows better than to disclose classified information, the U.S. government entrusted him with that information, and that he should retain his First Amendment rights that other citizens are entitled to. In other words, he argues that if he is publishing based on information already available to the public, then he should have the First Amendment right to do so just like any other American.

Perhaps the best lesson is that which is passed on to the students, particularly those in the field of journalism – take the media law and First Amendment courses seriously. The stakes and the consequences are far from abstract. They are real and may save your life.

1

Sources of Law and Systems of Justice

LEARNING OBJECTIVES

After reading this chapter, you should know

- how different sources serve to create laws
- what judicial review can do to uphold acts of law or strike them down
- how courts proceed when neither legislative acts nor legal precedents apply
- what cases are assigned to courts by legal and regional jurisdiction
- the way in which administrative agencies design and apply their regulations
- how landmark rulings compare with other forms of precedent
- the terms and procedures of civil and criminal law
- the research process for legal scholarship

The Rule of Law

Americans regard the rule of law as an essential foundation to safeguard their freedoms, especially important rights of religion, speech, press, assembly, and petition. Under this principle, state and local governments must act fairly, justly, and equally respectful of the rights of the people.

Whenever laws are enacted and orders granted that threaten to undermine these guarantees, courts may be asked to review the legislation to see if what lawmakers crafted upholds the Constitution. For example, when cybersecurity concerns were raised by politicians over TikTok, offices of government at different levels moved to ban its use, relying on various sources of law.

In 2020, an executive order came from the White House to ban all U.S. transactions with the corporate parents of a messaging app, WeChat, and TikTok, a social media platform. The company Tencent that owns WeChat and TikTok is under ByteDance's control, but both are under the watchful eye of the Chinese government.

Lawsuits were filed challenging the president's authority to order the ban based on differing interpretations of the International Emergency Economic Powers Act (IEEPA), which was the authority cited for his action. Lawyers for the tech firms argued the order violated IEEPA's stated prohibition on the regulation of informational materials. Injunctions were

DOI: 10.4324/9781003462989-1

granted against the executive order enabling TikTok and WeChat to continue business in the United States despite the executive order. U.S. lawmakers had other ideas about how to stop this Chinese threat to U.S. cybersecurity.

Republicans and Democrats dispensed with partisan rivalries in the Senate and united their forces on a cybersecurity bill. The RESTRICT Act's sponsor Sen. John Thune (R-South Dakota) claimed this law was an imperative since ByteDance could be used as a tool of espionage in service to the Chinese Communist Party. Other members of Congress agreed but also realized TikTok was popular among their constituents, about 100 million U.S. users.

The American Civil Liberties Union and Electronic Frontier Foundation filed their opposition to the RESTRICT Act on constitutional grounds. Some critics decried it as the Patriot Act of the digital age.

Movement on the bill slowed as opposing sides wrangled over the issue. Several senators called on the Federal Trade Commission – a U.S. administrative agency – to launch an investigation. Rather than wait on Congress, though, lawmakers in several states drafted their anti-TikTok bills.

In Montana, Gov. Greg Gianforte signed a law making it a crime for TikTok to operate in his state based on the belief the Chinese government would be harvesting American data from the popular app. This argument was aimed at a national intelligence law in China requiring domestic companies to cooperate with the government in its data collection activities. So could that law serve its purpose to effectively ban TikTok in Montana?

A trade group representing tech giants Apple and Google had their doubts. TechNet told reporters their app stores lacked the ability to "geofence" platforms by state or region. Then there is the larger question raised by TikTok advocates – First Amendment rights. More than one question was left for the courts to decide. Nonetheless, both legislative and executive branches of government come under scrutiny from the judicial branch as this case illustrates.

Other new laws have been enacted to protect personal information online by requiring *reasonable security* measures. California's Consumer Privacy Act (CCPA), for example, gave residents the right to file a complaint if a business failed to guard personal information with reasonable security measures. New York's SHIELD law imposed a similar standard enacted for personal data protection, as did Massachusetts that included encryption coding.

So where do these sources of law come from in the first place?

Sources of Law

Legislative Source
The representative branch of government was established in Article I of the U.S. Constitution. It holds authority to pass laws through acts of Congress. In state government, elected assemblies of lawmakers perform the same function.

As the TikTok example illustrates, laws affecting media institutions come from different sources. The major sources of American law are statutes, administrative regulations, executive orders, common law, and constitutions.

Federal and state statutory laws are enacted by elected lawmakers, while regulations may be passed by federal administrative agencies such as the Federal Trade Commission; presidents, governors, and mayors can issue executive orders; and courts of equity may issue injunctions.

Legal challenges may then be brought to the state and federal courts that hand down decisions also having the force of law known as the common law. Of course, the highest or supreme source of law is found in the constitutions of state and federal government, including provisions for freedom of expression like the First Amendment.

Any introduction to the origins of law should include both ancient and contemporary sources. Laws of contract, for instance, can be traced to Plato's second book of the Law where it was written binding agreements are subject to tribal courts for enforcement. Roman law recognized for the ownership of property promises must be kept (*pacta sunt servanda*). It spelled out contracts as agreements between citizens for temporary and permanent ownership.

Religion also gave meaning to contracts. Ancient scriptures cite specific covenants – both man-made and providential – for the exchange of oaths, the trade of items, and security for debts. Some strictures are common to all forms of contract law. Participants must enter into agreements voluntarily without coercion; they cannot be enforced for illegal or immoral ends, and a remedy must exist whenever there is a breach of contract, leaving the terms unfulfilled.

In media law, contracts are routinely forged in terms of employment, purchases of technology and property, and for commercial or advertising promotions. Communication professionals are likely to encounter contracts for content and program licensing, trademark registration, and copyright ownership.

In the age of artificial intelligence, intellectual property ownership can produce charges of infringement for algorithmic scraping of images from a multitude of digital sources to create a composite work without consent or even acknowledgment of the original owners of the repurposed content. There is another source of law where these concepts are becoming more significant – international law.

Global sources of law originate with world trade and communications among nations where treaties and agreements are forged in conventions like the International Telecommunications Convention of 1982 (ITC). Special agencies hosted by the United Nations serve to protect global media interests.

The International Telecommunications Union traces its origin to the International Telegraph Union of 1865. Its mission now is to oversee the shared uses of electromagnetic spectrum and facilitate international cooperation in technical standards, satellite telecommunications, and broadband deployment.

The advent of the Internet also produced treaties to protect intellectual property. The World Intellectual Property Organization (WIPO) headquartered in the United Nations advances the provisions of 26 international treaties covering a range of interests from audiovisual media to literary and artistic ownership.

Constitutional Structure

Although influenced by Anglo-Saxon law, the American legal system is unique in establishing a federal charter – the U.S. Constitution – to empower three branches of national government. In the beginning its passage met with some resistance, and in 1791 time was pressing for the Constitution's adoption.

Judicial Branch
Established in Article III of the U.S. Constitution, this part oversees the court system. In the federal government, legal authority resides both in the Supreme Court and the lower federal courts that Congress may establish.

If the vote was postponed "it may occasion suspicions, which though not well founded, may tend to influence or prejudice the public mind, against our decisions," wrote James Madison as he pleaded for "wise and liberal men to make such alterations as shall produce that effect"[1] and move for its passage. Figure 1.1 is a portrait of Madison.

The three branches were given their respective powers in the first three articles of the Constitution with legislative first, followed by executive, and then judiciary. The last four articles subsequently dealt with states' rights and relations, constitutional amendments, qualifications for public office and treaties, and the means for ratification. The first ten amendments were added in 1791 to establish a Bill of Rights to protect essential freedoms and set the boundaries of federal government.

The judicial branch exercised its power of oversight in a landmark case, *Marbury v. Madison* (1803), that showed how the Supreme Court would interpret the Constitution. From that case comes the principle that courts interpret laws and have the power to strike down ones in violation of the Constitution.

1. James Madison, "Debate in the First Congress," June 8, 1789, as cited by Neil H. Cogan, *Contexts of the Constitution* 812 (New York: Foundation Press, 1999). Twelve amendments were proposed originally, but the first two were not ratified.

Figure 1.1 Portrait of James Madison

Source: By Chester Harding, National Portrait Gallery, Washington, DC

One Baltimore financier, William Marbury, wanted his place among the federal elite, and President Adams tried to accommodate him with a justice of the peace appointment in 1801. However, President Jefferson, an anti-Federalist, refused to grant his commission, saying the deadline had passed before his appointment.

Marbury stubbornly sought to have the office he felt was rightfully his and took his case to the Supreme Court. He sought a *writ of mandamus*, a court order that would force Secretary of State James Madison to confirm his appointment. No such luck.

In a unanimous 4–0 ruling, Chief Justice John Marshall claimed the Court held no jurisdiction because it was beyond its constitutional authority to grant such a writ. But the ruling addressed another question over whether the Court had the power to review any act of Congress, or those of lesser bodies of law, to see if they conformed to the dictates of the Constitution.

The answer was yes, "it is emphatically the province and duty of the judicial department to say what the law is" since the Constitution is the "supreme law of the land" (*Art. VI, Clause 2*). Thus, any "legislative act contrary to the Constitution is not law," and Marshall's ruling held.[2] As for Marbury, his story ended well despite this denial of a federal appointment. After losing his bid to become a U.S. justice of the peace, he became director of a Maryland bank.

2. *Marbury v. Madison*, 5 U.S. (1 Cranch) 137; 2 L. Ed. 60 (1803).

Executive Branch

The enforcement wing of the U.S. government headed by the president. It is defined in Article II of the U.S. Constitution as holding authority for execution of the laws. In the states, governors hold that same authority.

Judicial review by an appeals process allows courts an opportunity to correct errors in the judgment of lower courts. Such a review took place after a protest captured headlines during a public demonstration against police in Baton Rouge, Louisiana.

Civil rights activist DeRay Mckesson organized the protest after the shooting death of Alton Sterling, 37, a Black resident killed by white police officers. His demonstrators marched on the city police department and blocked the highway by police headquarters under Mckesson's supervision. One angry demonstrator hurled a piece of concrete, striking a police officer in the jaw, smashing his face, knocking him to the ground, and breaking some of his teeth.

The officer registering the complaint was granted anonymity as John Doe after suing the out-of-state activist for allegedly leading his followers into a criminal activity – blocking the highway – knowing full well police would have to respond to the obstruction and violence might ensue.

At his trial, Mckesson sought protection under the First Amendment maintaining he should suffer no liability for the actions of others based on Supreme Court precedent (*NAACP v. Claiborne Hardware*, 1982).[3]

On appeal, the federal Fifth Circuit Court sided with the police officer ruling the First Amendment does not offer immunity for protesters who lead followers to perpetrate illegal actions. Reversing his opinion in the case, Judge Don R. Willett had a judicial change of heart. After first siding with "Doe," he dissented from his earlier decision and summoned the memory of Martin Luther King, Jr. who led protests and saw demonstrators break store windows in Memphis before his assassination.

The U.S. Supreme Court responded by vacating the Fifth Circuit's opinion based on a disputed "negligent protest" view of liability; after which the officer's lawsuit was dismissed in district court.

Bill of Rights

The first ten amendments of the U.S. Constitution.

Separation of powers and the checking function of the three coequal branches are central to our republican form of government. The role of the courts is to ensure that the executive and legislative branches do not overreach their authority.

Even though the mechanism creating this balance of branches, separate and equal, is inefficient, it stands as a safeguard against dictatorial rule under a relatively stable constitution that has been amended only 27 times since its ratification in 1787.

Constitutional Law

Bedrock Law

The legal authority of the U.S. government is subject to a system of checks and balances that is exercised by the executive, legislative, and judicial branches.

All 50 states have a **constitution**, and many resemble the federal charter with respect to individual rights and freedom within the states. Even though the national charter remains fundamentally unchanged since 1791, most state constitutions have been rewritten one or more times.[4]

Article IV of the Constitution charts certain provisions concerning state government, and the Tenth Amendment in the Bill of Rights reserves for the states those powers not delegated to the federal government.

The "supreme law of the land" means that all other laws must fall in line with the Constitution's guiding provisions. Article VI, paragraph 2, affirms this fact through the **supremacy clause**. The Constitution further empowered the legislative branch to oversee

3. 458 U.S. 886 (1982).
4. Massachusetts is one of the few states operating under its original charter, which was formed in 1780.

communications through Article I, Sec. 8, which gave Congress the power to regulate interstate commerce.

For example, Congress created in 1914 an executive agency, the Federal Trade Commission, which protects consumers and prevents monopolies. It has the authority to draft and proclaim rules covering advertising and marketing so long as they are legally consistent with constitutional principle. The FTC, for example, offers guidance on everything from brand disclosures by social media influencers to false and deceptive advertising on television.

Supremacy Clause
Article VI, paragraph 2, of the U.S. Constitution mandates that federal law is supreme whenever a conflict arises between federal and state law.

Global View

The United States declared its independence from England in 1776, but it wasn't until 1788 before the United States had an official constitution ratified by the necessary nine states. There are some countries that have never had a constitution.

Our legal heritage from the United Kingdom offers no *codified* constitution. Uncodified means that a constitution is not formally collected into a single document but is instead "understood" to exist from among various legal documents and actions. The United Kingdom's laws continue to evolve since the Magna Carta in 1215 established some basic premises, but unlike the United States, there is not a single repository for the "supreme law of the land."

Britain, like Canada and Israel, continues to function smoothly without a codified constitution. Acts of Parliament are considered the supreme laws, and the U.K. judiciary does not review them to determine their constitutionality.

Perhaps the most significant difference is judicial review, the doctrine under which the judiciary is the final arbiter of the constitutionality of executive and legislative acts, first established in *Marbury v. Madison*. Constitutions usually have high bars set for amendments. In the United States, we've only seen 27 amendments in two centuries, and ten of those all came at once. Countries without codified constitutions are able to pass laws, changing their system under the same rules as passing any other law, although a constitution gives definitive guidance to resolve disputes about the appropriate rule of law.

Statutory Law

Approved laws or statutes are organized into codes and indexed by titles, with rules bound together by common topics. Title 17 of the U.S. Code, for example, covers copyright ownership protecting music, videos, books, movies, and valuable intellectual property. These codes are compilations of legislative actions, and they delineate the rule of law from diverse sources.

Imagine separate branches of government diverging like a river's distributaries transporting laws in different directions. At the state level, streams of **statutory law** flow from state legislatures, city councils, and legislative bodies of local government.

At the headwaters is the state legislature, where lawmakers gather in chambers generally modeled after the U.S. Congress representing constituent districts and passing bills to govern their citizens. Serving below the state legislatures are county and parish offices, followed by municipalities where ordinances are enforced by local officials.

A law's creation at any tier is a study in political compromise requiring negotiation and agreements within and between different branches of government.

A bill's passage is impossible without politicians who are willing to move it over all the hurdles of committees and debate to reach the chief executive official who signs it into law. Sponsors bring their bill to an open hearing, so subcommittees can study it before the floor debates.

Writ of Mandamus
Issued by courts to command lower courts or government officials to perform specific duties.

Statutory Law
Law that is enacted into statute by a legislative body.

Even if a proposed law moves beyond that vote by committee to win passage on the floor, does the legislature's approval guarantee success? If the bill survives in both legislative chambers, a conference committee irons out key differences, which then demands another vote before the chief executive can either sign or veto it.

Overriding a veto usually takes a two-thirds majority of both houses of the legislature, although that does vary by state. Seven states – including the unicameral legislature of Nebraska – require a three-fifths majority to override the governor's signature against the bill. Six states require only a majority vote to override a veto.

Statutory laws may be created and enforced for years before they are legally challenged and for different reasons. There can be a clarity issue.

For criminal statutes, a lack of clarity is itself considered unconstitutional, but other issues such as earlier regulation might be involved. Suppose a city adopted a billboard law limiting the placement and size of roadside advertising. It would not have to be consistent with prior statutes and ordinances if it was the most recent rule, but it would prevail only so long as it clearly conformed with state and federal constitutions.

Overbroad or Vague
Phrases and wording of a law considered too general or indefinite to give people fair notice of when and whether their conduct constitutes a violation of the rule of law.

In *Reed v. Town of Gilbert* (2015),[5] for example, the Supreme Court unanimously held an Arizona community's signage law was unconstitutional due to restrictions it imposed on a church pastor's signs specifying their content and display without a compelling reason.

If the law's wording is deemed as **vague** or **overbroad**, then that might spell trouble ahead. Anyone should be able to distinguish right from wrongful acts after reading a law.

For example, which billboards are legal and which ones are illegal should be discernible from the text. The law cannot, for instance, prohibit billboards described as "too big" or "too close" to the road. Such vague rules would be impossible to consistently define.

The rule of law means the law is equally enforced for everyone, and all can understand what is allowed or not under its terms. Lawyers call this requirement *fair notice*, which means the terms are so clear the average reader can distinguish wrongful activities from lawful ones.

Grandfather
When a regulation goes into effect, preexisting violations are not governed by the new law.

Complicating matters is the fact that laws can be created allowing existing activities to continue even though they might conflict with the new law. Using our earlier example, a city might restrict the size of new billboards to 200-square feet but then **grandfather** existing, larger billboards – meaning the new law would not be enforced against pre-existing billboards.

What happens when two states pass similar bills, but different federal appeals courts disagree on the constitutionality of the laws? Even though both legislative acts mirror one another, if the appellate courts disagree on their lawfulness a **diversity of opinion** might exist. When legislatures in Florida and Texas passed sweeping measures to mitigate social media's power to censor and tag users posting online content a conflict emerged in legal interpretation.

In *NetChoice v. Attorney General of Florida* (2022), a federal appeals court put a halt to the "Stop Social Media Censorship Act" by declaring it violated the First Amendment right of social media companies when it "de-platformed" politicians and removed their content containing suspect information.

In its ruling, the federal appeals court in Atlanta supported the "content-moderation" decisions of social media platforms like Facebook and Twitter (now known as X), describing their editorial functioning as a prerogative protected by the First Amendment. The Eleventh Circuit further held it would be onerous for Florida to demand a report of the rationale of each decision made on content, as well as impractical and unconstitutional.

Meanwhile the Fifth Circuit Court of Appeals in New Orleans took the opposite approach and found no constitutional issue with Texas House Bill 20 ("Relating to complaint procedures and disclosure requirements for and censorship of user's expressions by social media

5. 576 U.S. 155 (2015).

platforms"). This federal appeals court frowned on the social media's challenge to the law, finding it to be a "rather odd inversion of the First Amendment," giving the corporate platforms an "unenumerated right to muzzle speech."[6] These two cases were not the first time this issue had been raised before the courts.

During President Trump's first administration, the Supreme Court took up something similar after he blocked users critical of his tweets. A group of seven followers sued the president because they felt Twitter, now known as X, should be viewed as a public forum, which meant they deserved access to his tweets to learn of his presidential actions. The Second Circuit Court held Twitter's use by the president was different than a personal account since it had become a designated public forum, where viewers should not be blocked just because of their opinions.[7]

The U.S. Supreme Court subsequently stepped in to settle the controversy. It vacated the earlier decision since the case was deemed moot after President Trump left office after his first term. What remained relevant in this instance was a dissenting opinion that held digital platforms like X should be viewed as *common carriers* subject to certain government restrictions.[8]

A common carrier is a channel or platform offering its services to the general public without discrimination but usually with the authority of a regulatory body or licensing agency. For example, telephone services are regulated under Title II of the Communications Act of 1934 as common carriers, considered to be like public utilities that must be available to everyone at a reasonable price and only carry content rather than originate it. In the United States, the FCC exercised authority over Internet Service Providers by redefining them as common carriers authorized to afford services for the public's convenience and necessity.

The Common Law

Common Law
Jurisprudence based on adherence to rulings established in previous and similar cases.

Another source of law is called the **common law** or *judge-made law*, which comes from judicial decisions and a respect for case precedents. U.S. reliance on traditions dates back to the colonial period and even before then as early American lawyers from the nation's founding pored over Sir William Blackstone's four volumes covering British trials.

Blackstone's *Commentaries on the Laws of England* were drafted by an eighteenth-century legal scholar who taught at Oxford, and some of our nation's founding fathers were in his classroom. In the nineteenth century, Abraham Lincoln began preparing for his legal career by borrowing Blackstone's volumes to become well versed on the common laws of England.

It was Blackstone's theory that the "rights of all mankind" should be shared, including "the right of personal security, the right of personal liberty, and the right of private property."[9] This viewpoint echoed the Enlightenment thinking of French magistrate and writer Charles, Baron de Montesquieu, who believed strongly in the separation of powers and the need for checks and balances in government.[10] Blackstone also held government authority should be regarded as absolute in cases at court.

6. *See NetChoice v. Paxton*, 2022.
7. *See Knight First Amendment Institute v. Trump*, 928 F.3d 226 (2019).
8. *See Biden v. Knight First Amendment Institute at Columbia University* 593 U.S. _____ (2021).
9. W. Blackstone, *Commentaries on the Laws of England* 125, ed. Thomas M. Cooley (Clark, NJ: Lawbook Exchange Ltd., 1769). *See* Amir Paz-Fuchs, *Constitutions and the Classics: Coke, Blackstone, and Rousseau* (Oxford: The Foundation for Law, Justice, and Society in association with the Centre for Socio-Legal Studies: Wolfson College, University of Oxford, October 4, 2012), *at* www.fljs.org/sites/www.fljs.org/files/publications/Coke-Blackstone-Rousseau.pdf.
10. Charles de Secondat, baron de Montesquieu, 1689–1755, *The Spirit of Laws* (London: Printed for J. Collingwood, 1823).

Setting Precedent

Stare Decisis
The legal doctrine requiring judges to follow earlier authorities in case precedent to direct the outcome of legal dilemmas based on similar issues.

Blackstone's commentaries on the laws of England afford a historic understanding of the U.S. system's reliance on case precedent whereby lawyers can cite earlier rulings to resolve disputes.

A Latin phrase describes this approach as ***stare decisis***, which should be interpreted to mean, "let the decision stand."[11] This common-law tradition means the case law of the United States can spell the outcome at trials with similar issues and/or sets of facts.

This collection of case precedents form what we think of as our *jurisprudence*. That also applies to a broader philosophy undergirding theories of *natural law* and legal *positivism*. In practical terms, case precedent is how the courts interpret the historical rule of law.

If a legal principle was previously interpreted in a special way, then subsequent rulings must follow that interpretation unless the court adjusts its reasoning to fit new circumstances. When judges ignore precedent, however, their rulings become vulnerable to reversal on appeal.

Landmark Ruling
Case used to establish a new legal principle.

One of two forms of authority illustrate how legal precedent comes into play. When a principle is binding to an earlier decision, it is a *must-follow rule*. *Must-follow* precedent presumes the previous ruling directly relates to the issue(s) at hand, and its relevance makes it a binding precedent.

A different sort of precedent will serve an advisory function, which is *persuasive authority*. That is not binding precedent, especially if the previous ruling is found in a different state or district.

If one state legislature opts to ban violent video games for minors, for example, the game manufacturer's lawyers might cite an appellate ruling from another jurisdiction freeing up their sale as a point of persuasive reference. If a higher court has yet to rule on a controversial issue, then nonbinding precedent might be applied until a binding rule is found to settle the point at the appellate level of the same jurisdiction.

Bedrock Law
Courts must follow legal principles established by either statute or precedent until a higher court holds the rule or precedent to be unconstitutional or otherwise unlawful.

Some legal systems follow an alternative form of law classified as civilian code or civil law, not to be confused with civil lawsuits that are grouped together under tort law. This form of jurisprudence is unlike *stare decisis* and prevails in countries where the magistrate's interpretation of the legal code prevails over any prior ruling on the case books.

By citing legislative acts and codes drafted by civilian representatives, the court's ruling is reached. Courts refer to statutes and codes drawing from brief texts rather than pointing to a prior ruling illustrating how justice had been served. Louisiana, however, provides an unusual example – relying in part on its civilian law code and common law in other places.

The bayou state's jurisprudence is a mixture of common law and civilian code from French and Spanish traditions. Of course, federal courts in every state use only the common law rule of *stare decisis* in setting precedent, such as for First Amendment cases.

Executive Orders

Executive power is embedded in Article II (Sections 1 and 3) of the U.S. Constitution, which gives the president military preeminence as "Commander in Chief of the Army and Navy." The Constitution requires the president to faithfully execute all U.S. laws, and like any citizen, the office holder can recommend legislative acts such as the annual budget bill.

Only Congress can introduce actual bills for legislative action, it must be noted. But the president does hold the power of veto and can either sign or refuse to sign bills brought to their desk by Congress.

11. The complete Latin phrase is actually *stare decisis et non quieta movere*, which means "stand by the decision and don't move what has been settled."

Executive Orders
Directives issued by the president on how to execute a particular act. These signed papers can carry the force of statutory law by way of congressional consent, but they also can be limited by the executive's term in office and be subject to removal by the successor to that office.

As noted in the TikTok example, executive power comes in both orders and memoranda the president chooses to authorize, sometimes used as an alternative to congressional action when the passage of preferred legislation appears unlikely. Executive orders may be for such special purposes as the desegregation of schools, the protection of civil rights, emergency declarations, or even to halt federal funding of abortions. A city's mayor or a state's governor can issue executive orders, proclaim curfews or civil emergencies, and declare free speech zones at political events.

When these executive orders are issued from the White House they serve as a means for directing administrative agencies and can even substitute for more sweeping directives. President Truman issued an order to classify federal documents and communiqués as "TOP SECRET" and in effect established secrecy levels for security documents.

A president's executive order can be overturned through the passage of legislation contradicting its provisions or by stripping away its funding. It also can be overturned if a federal court finds it's unlawful. Executive orders must conform with constitutional provisions.

Administrative Law

Administrative Law
The regulations set out by executive branch agencies that come in the form of rules, inquiries, opinions, and reports.

This source of law comes from administrative oversight covering a wide berth of federal and state agencies. Administrative law owes its origination to the nation's railroads when in the late nineteenth century, the federal government began shaping the law to govern their operations, creating the Interstate Commerce Commission in 1887 for this purpose.

When U.S. financial agencies and businesses began growing in the early twentieth century, sources of legal control also sprouted up around Washington, DC, such as the Federal Trade Commission (FTC, 1914) and the Securities and Exchange Commission (SEC, 1934). The Federal Radio Commission (FRC, 1927) and later the Federal Communications Commission (FCC, 1934) supervised the electromagnetic order of the radiating airwaves.

Administrative agencies take sweeping actions in regulation and oversight given their special offices of authority. The president nominates agency commissioners and appoints the chair to preside over meetings and agendas. The U.S. Senate advises and confirms the president's nomination of commissioners and chairs to these agencies.

Bedrock Law
Federal agencies have legal powers that include drafting rules, enforcing them, and deciding appeals to their enforcement.

Federal agencies are directed by statutes, which define the extent of an agency's authority, including their powers and procedures for issuing rules. For example, the Federal Communications Commission gains its authority from the Communications Act of 1934, which distinguishes what the FCC can and cannot do in regulation terms.

Statutes can't possibly be written in anticipation of every eventuality or to address every detail, so federal bureaus following the agency's authorizing U.S. legislation will draft regulations that are published in the Code of Federal Regulations (CFR). For example, the FCC has rules in the CFR specifying in detail the height and effective radiated power of broadcast station antennas. If a dispute arises over an agency's use of its authority, the dispute is often resolved using the federal agency's interpretation of the law.

Federal Communications Commission (FCC)
The U.S. administrative agency established by the Communications Act of 1934 to regulate interstate communications by radio, television, wire, satellite, and cable.

In a 1984 decision, the Supreme Court established the *Chevron Rule*, holding that "if the statute is silent or ambiguous with respect to the specific issue, the question for the court is whether the agency's answer is based on a permissible construction of the statute."[12] Forty years later, in 2024, the Supreme Court reversed direction saying that courts must arbitrate independently when the rules are ambiguous. Writing for the majority, Chief Justice Roberts asserted that the Administrative Procedures Act requires courts to apply their own judgment rather than deferring to agencies' interpretations.[13]

12. *Chevron USA v. Natural Resources Defense Council*, 467 U.S. 837 (1984) at 843. This decision involved the Environmental Protection Agency's interpretation of the Clean Air Act giving Chevron greater latitude on federal permits for its facilities and equipment.
13. *Loper Bright Enterprises v. Raimondo*, 603 U.S. ___ (2024).

The laws passed on Capitol Hill are fewer in number than those enacted by federal agencies, yet agency decisions are rarely challenged in a courtroom outside their own internal system of appeals. They may be enforced for years before they are legally challenged.

At some point, they may be invalidated for reasons of *arbitrary and capricious* enforcement, or they might be deemed violative of our constitutional rights. For example, broadcasters are warned from time to time that they might be punished for airing indecent content in violation of federal law.[14]

One U.S. court of appeals found the FCC's actions were arbitrary and capricious because federal agencies should be consistent and logical in their rule enforcement.[15] This form of judicial review – sometimes called "the hard look" review – requires an adequate explanation be given for enforcing a rule, including proof of evidence and reasoning for the punishment.

The Administrative Procedure Act (APA) set this standard in 1946.[16] Consequently, federal agencies are responsible for making certain their administrative actions are well reasoned and can withstand a challenge on the grounds their actions indicate arbitrary or capricious decision-making.

If an FCC decision is to be challenged, a plaintiff can take the petition to the U.S. Court of Appeals for the District of Columbia. The D.C. Circuit covers the smallest area of any federal court of appeals hearing cases from administrative agencies in Washington, DC.[17]

Spectrum Auctions: An Example of Administrative Law and Congressional Oversight

In 2023, the Federal Communications Commission found itself in somewhat of a predicament. For decades, the agency had held spectrum auctions raising an estimated $233 billion dollars for investment in technology and communications. These auctions moved bandwidth to 5G wireless carriers and made way for new applications; however, the competitive bidding process needed congressional authorization to take place.

The last such authorization, the Spectrum Act of 2012, expired on March 9, 2023, and the Commission lacked the necessary authority to transfer any more bandwidth for use by other carriers. For the first time in spectrum history, nearly 30 years since Congress first authorized the FCC to hold auctions, it had failed to pass the legislation necessary for it to continue.

In this case, the consequences occurred as soon as the lapse in authority had taken place: T-Mobile had no licenses necessary for 5G transmission.

So why was the administrative delay in congressional action necessary in the first place?

It was due to lawmaker inquiries about the impact of spectrum transfer on the nation's military after the Pentagon shared concerns over the switch to commercial use of bandwidth between 3.1–3.45 GHz at its disposal for the nation's defense.

Senators also wanted more time to study the impact because NASA and the National Oceanic and Atmospheric Administration also had bandwidth reserved for their use in that spectrum space in anticipation of competitive bidding. Congressional committees reported out the legislation necessary to authorize the spectrum auctions.

14. 18 U.S.C. § 1464.
15. 5 U.S. Code § 706 (2)(A).
16. The Administrative Procedure Act (APA), Public Law 79–404, 60 Stat. 237 (1946). For a federal agency action to be reversed by this standard, the APA specifies its enforcement must be "arbitrary and capricious, an abuse of discretion, or otherwise not in accordance with the law."
17. Several U.S. Supreme Court justices served in the D.C. Circuit before their confirmation, including Chief Justice John Roberts and Associate Justices Ketanji Brown Jackson, Clarence Thomas, and Brett Kavanaugh.

Equity Law
U.S. courts are a unified system with access to both equitable and legal remedies. Historically, courts of equity granted remedies by decreeing orders for rival parties either to perform or refrain from certain actions. Rather than requiring payment of monetary damages, an injunction or restraining order would be decreed as an equitable remedy.

Bedrock Law
Equity law allows a court to create a just and fair remedy to resolve a civil dispute in circumstances including instances where a statute or common law does not apply.

Injunctive Relief
A court order requiring a legal remedy other than damages to require action or prevent it. An equity order can be a temporary or permanent injunction.

Once the next auction is held, it would yield the FCC proceeds necessary for implementing new technologies and expanding broadband service, in addition to distributing bandwidth for use to commercial carriers like T-Mobile to do business with their customers.

Actions in Equity

"Oyez, Oyez, Oyez!" (Hear ye, Hear ye, Hear ye), a bailiff proclaims when the judge enters the courtroom and takes their seat. "This court now presides in law and **equity**." Equity is the source of law that often takes up where the common law and statutory law leaves off, but it does not rely on a jury's discretion since it is only a judge who presides in equity law.

This form of law defines cases in which justice is served although not in monetary terms. It is by means of a court order necessary to apply a particular remedy. This solution can come in cases of family law, bankruptcy petitions, or contractual disputes, but judges cannot simply make up a remedy in the absence of black letter law.

What the court rules in equity puts in place a proactive solution to prevent an anticipated harm or set in motion a necessary act to be performed. But in all cases, the order must be constitutional.

Certain statutes specify necessary equitable remedies in the form of injunctions. This form of relief can serve as a remedy until a larger issue is resolved. For example, there may be a law that specifies who has the rights of ownership to a particular piece of intellectual property – say a recording.

A court in equity will issue an injunction to stop the performance or release of the recording until the ownership can be determined. In equity law, judges can choose to offer **injunctive relief**, which stops someone or some group from pursuing a particular course of action. Celebrity stalkers may be enjoined from pursuing their targets under equity law.

The paparazzi photographer who famously harassed former First Lady Jacqueline Kennedy Onassis by jumping out of bushes and popping flash bulbs in her and her family's faces was enjoined from engaging in this sort of offensive behavior. The judge granting an **injunction** to prevent Ron Galella from coming within a specified distance of Ms. Onassis or her children issued a decree in equity.[18]

Systems of Justice

The contest of law requires all facts and evidence to be shared to determine which side has been harmed, suffered loss, or will be held accountable in a legal dispute. Using strategies somewhat akin to a chess master, lawyers for both sides choose the best moves for their client based on an established set of rules and procedures.

Courts in civil actions resolve the differences between plaintiffs and defendants, while in criminal court the contest is between prosecutors and defendants. Civil suits deal with complaints between individuals or groups, whereas in a criminal trial, justice is sought for offenses caused by the commission of crimes. A simplified comparison of civil and criminal trials is Table 1.1.

Sometimes a defendant can be acquitted in a criminal court, and then after the criminal trial is over, they face a separate action as a lawsuit filed in civil court. The O.J. Simpson trials of the 1990s found him to be *not guilty* of murder in a criminal court, and yet he was held *liable* for causing a wrongful death in civil court. In both civil and criminal cases, whether a conviction or a settlement is reached, specific procedures are followed.

18. *Galella v. Onassis*, 487 F.2d 986 (2d Cir. 1973).

Civil Law
The body of law that regulates disputes between private parties.

Criminal Law
The body of law that defines conduct prohibited and punished by the state.

Burden of Proof
The threshold of certainty a party in court must meet to prove a matter in a dispute.

Beyond a Reasonable Doubt
The burden of proof in criminal cases.

Preponderance of Evidence
The burden of proof in civil cases.

Because a criminal trial involves the potential deprivation of liberty by incarceration, the standard for conviction is higher than in civil court where legal remedies are usually monetary damages. A criminal conviction must be "beyond a reasonable doubt" and requires a unanimous jury (in felony cases). That means all jurors must agree there is no reasonable likelihood that the defendant is not guilty of charges.

In a civil lawsuit, a majority of jurors must agree on the verdict, and the common standard of proof is "a preponderance of the evidence," which generally means a 50% + 1 chance that the defendant is responsible for the harm. That is why a defendant may be acquitted in a criminal trial, which has a higher standard of proof, yet still be held liable in a civil lawsuit, where it is sometimes easier for the plaintiff to win damages than a criminal conviction.

Civil suits deal with complaints between individuals or groups, whereas in a criminal case justice is sought for harms caused by violent or unlawful behavior. These acts also include crimes against the state, such as sedition and treason, which will be further discussed in Chapter 3.

There are times when some of the same evidence used in a criminal trial can be brought forth in a civil court, depending on the nature of the offense. In both civil and criminal cases, whether a trial is held to resolve the dispute or a settlement is reached, specific procedures must be followed as spelled out by law.

If a crime is committed, the nature of the act determines the level of the offense and the severity of the punishment. An offense is categorized as either a *misdemeanor* or a *felony*. Felony acts are crimes against a person, such as assault, rape, and murder, but they also can be for nonviolent offenses such as drug possession or thefts above a certain dollar amount.

Misdemeanors usually cover lesser crimes against property, such as theft and burglary, but also can be charges against violent behavior such as in domestic abuse cases. Charges may lead to criminal trials at the municipal, county, or even federal levels based on which court is given *jurisdiction* in the case. Jurisdiction is determined by both location and statute.

Criminal judgments are made on evidentiary elements, and the defendant is entitled to a presumption of innocence prior to trial. As noted, the defendant is either found to be *guilty* or *not guilty*. Civil offenses are judged to be lesser harms not requiring jail time.

The term *innocent* is too broad for criminal charges that must be narrowly defined in scope, and courts avoid characterizing any defendant beyond the specific crime(s) alleged. The accused may be tried for multiple crimes, or *counts*, and so the prosecutor should prove to a jury that *guilt beyond a reasonable doubt* exists before the defendant's freedom can be taken away or before fines can be imposed for punishment.

Lesser standards of proof in lawsuits, such as *clear and convincing evidence* – a medium standard, or *preponderance of the evidence* – the lightest burden of proof, are brought to bear in civil trials. These proofs are necessary when the question is not one of guilt but *liability*.

Suppose, for example, that a reporter is accused of defamation, and the person whose reputation is under scrutiny seeks damages for a story that was written with false information. An employer may be sued, along with the reporter.

If the court finds either a preponderance of the evidence or clear and convincing proof – depending on the standard – the defendant and employer might have to pay restitution in an award of *damages* to the plaintiff.

Criminal Procedures

Courts for civil actions and criminal cases vary in other ways besides just procedures and penalties. Criminal cases, for example, arrive at court through a variety of portals, sometimes as a police citation, an arrest, or even a **grand jury indictment**.

Small crimes are classified as *misdemeanors*, including day-to-day infractions such as shoplifting, traffic infractions, disorderly conduct, and other minor offenses. They produce smaller fines and shorter jail times.

Felony crimes, such as assaults, armed robberies, and murders, endanger public safety and security and need to be punished more harshly. The term felony defines high-dollar crimes or conspiracies handed down by grand jury indictment after a closed-door hearing of witnesses or charges are issued before a judge.

Once the court accepts the charges, the defendant will be asked to answer a question of guilt. It is important to understand felony charges do not necessarily emanate from grand juries, and preliminary hearings can be used to present evidence with certain exceptions. Connecticut and Pennsylvania only use grand juries for investigating crimes but not for indictments.

Indictment
A formal accusation that a person has committed a felony or serious crime. After a hearing, the grand jury issues either a true bill, in which case the person is charged, or a no bill, in which case the person is not charged.

Pretrial Phase

Any viewer of American TV courtroom drama has heard actors in police uniform advise suspects of their rights during an arrest. "You have the right to remain silent and refuse to answer questions. If you give up the right to remain silent, anything you can and will be used against you in a court of law."

Arraignment
A hearing where formal charges are read against a criminal defendant and the defendant is expected to enter a plea.

This warning was the result of a 1966 Supreme Court case, *Miranda v. Arizona*,[19] where the suspect was unaware of his constitutional rights. Under the Fifth and Sixth Amendments, Americans have a right to remain silent to avoid self-incrimination and a right to a trial by jury with legal counsel.

Suspected criminals cannot be held for long without charges – usually 24 hours – and bail must be set for the accused to secure freedom in exchange for the financial promise to show up in court on their trial date. The problem with bail is that it advantages the wealthy who can afford to "make their bail" and go free during the interim while impoverished suspects are forced to stay behind bars awaiting trial.

Discovery
Pretrial phase in which each party is entitled to request and gain access to evidence possessed by the other side.

One point of clarification is the difference between bail and bond especially for lesser crimes. Unlike bail, a bond is posted on a defendant's behalf to keep the accused out of jail and may involve the services of a bail bondsman.

If the defendant fails to make a court appearance or violates other conditions of their release, the bond is often forfeited. In some jurisdictions, the clerk of the court keeps 10% of the bond and the rest is returned at trial.

The criminal case enters the pretrial phase of **discovery**, which is when attorneys have a chance to review police reports, videos, photographs, and other physical evidence from the other side related to the crime. This stage is when lawyers review witness statements and take **depositions** from those with first-hand knowledge of the crime.

Nolo Contendere
A plea entered by the defendant in a criminal case that admits neither guilt nor innocence but does not contest the charge.

The official charge of the crime is read at the **arraignment**, where the defendant can plead either guilty, not guilty, or ***nolo contendere*** (no contest) in response to the charges. Pretrial hearings also can determine what is *not* allowed for admission into the court record. Evidence seized without a proper warrant, for example, can be ruled out of bounds, including videos, audio recordings, and photos. Even depositions can be ruled inadmissible if improperly taken without notice.

Defense attorneys make motions to quash *subpoenas* for items like the defendant's arrest record or medical history that might yield more incriminating evidence. Lawyers may move to entirely dismiss a case against their client at the pretrial hearing. The state prosecution can also drop charges at the hearing and offer a plea agreement, especially if a lesser charge is available to avoid the time and expense of an unpredictable trial. Otherwise, a trial date must be set.

Miranda Warning
Requirement to apprise suspects of their constitutional rights arising from the Supreme Court case *Miranda v. Arizona* (1966).

19. 384 U.S. 436.

Voir Dire
The pretrial process of jury selection based on a term that means speak the truth.

Continuance
Postpones proceedings until a later date.

Peremptory Challenge
A challenge to a juror in *voir dire* but not for cause – most jurisdictions afford lawyers multiple "strikes" without giving a reason for excusing the prospective juror.

Change of Venire
Importing jurors from a different geographical location.

Depositions
Out-of-court sworn oral testimony transcribed for use at trial.

Change of Venue
Moving a trial to a different geographical location.

Trial Phase

The right to a trial by jury once charged with a crime draws from both the body of the U.S. Constitution (Art. III, Sec. 2) and the Bill of Rights (Sixth Amendment). At first, the Constitution did not require a jury for civil trials, but the Seventh Amendment granted that right in federal court in cases where the disputed sum was larger than 20 dollars. Under the law or constitution of most states, civil jury trials are guaranteed for large claims, especially relevant to personal injury trials.

The jury selection or ***voir dire*** (French term meaning "to speak the truth") opens the trial, with attorneys from both parties questioning the jury panel. Each prospective juror's capacity to render a fair and impartial verdict is evaluated at the ***voir dire***.

Lawyers for both sides either accept or refuse to seat jurors during this selection process. Attorneys can *strike for cause* if a prospective juror seems biased or has impaired judgment for some reason. If there is no clear reason why a juror should *not* be seated, a **peremptory challenge** can be given, and the lawyer need not disclose the reason for it.

Most jurisdictions afford one or more unexplained strikes, but jurors cannot be struck based on their gender or race. If a jury cannot be impaneled to faithfully serve justice, then three options are available: A **change of venue** would move the case to a distant locale, a **change of venire** would import jurors from another community, and a **continuance** would postpone the trial until a more suitable time.

After the jury is seated, lawyers for the government and the accused may present opening statements. This introduction is followed by their examination and cross-examination of the witnesses.

The prosecution presents its case first and calls its witnesses. The defense counsel cross-examines each state witness after their testimony is given. After the prosecution rests its case, the defense presents its witnesses, and the examination process is reversed. After that, closing arguments are given.

The prosecution reminds the jury they must find the defendant is guilty beyond a reasonable doubt. The judge's charge to the jury requires them to consider in their deliberations if the level of proof has been met. If a guilty verdict is returned, the sentencing phase follows where witnesses testify under more relaxed rules.

Posttrial Phase

If a guilty verdict is reached or a judge finds the defendant guilty, the decision can be appealed and overturned on the grounds a **reversible error** was made. Such an error means a mistake was made thwarting the fair administration of justice. It can be the misapplication of a pertinent law, or it can rise to the level of a constitutional violation. In either case, the terms and procedures for finding such an error require something more significant than a mere oversight or inaccuracy, which though regrettable would not constitute reversible error.

What can reverse a conviction, *vacate a verdict*, or *remand a case* is the denial of the defendant's constitutional rights. A remand sends the case back to the lower court for further action but *setting aside a judgment* would be the action taken to avoid requiring a new trial in civil matters, especially if fraud is perpetrated in the case.[20]

Suppose the owner of a local video arcade in your community was convicted and fined for violating a city ordinance prohibiting teenagers 17 and younger from playing video games depicting extreme violence – bloodshed, decapitation, dismemberment, or explicit sexual activities without an accompanying parent or guardian. The merchant then appeals the conviction, and the higher court rules in the defendant's favor. What happens next?

20. *See* Rule 60 of Federal Rules of Civil Procedure: Relief from a Judgment or Order.

Tort
From the Latin "break," a tort is a civil wrong that involves the breach of a duty to someone else, resulting in foreseeable harm.

Plaintiff
In a civil trial, it is the party bringing the cause of action.

Respondent
The responding party in a legal proceeding, particularly in appellate proceedings or proceedings initiated by petition.

Defendant
The accused party in a criminal proceeding or the respondent in civil lawsuit.

Interrogatories
Written questions to witnesses posed by attorneys for both sides in the discovery phase of a trial.

Summary Judgment
A final judgment for one party without trial when a court finds no material fact is in dispute and the law alone clearly establishes one party's claim.

The appellate court can reverse and remand the case citing the lower court's error in not recognizing First Amendment rights for video games as a form of expression.[21] The term *remand* is used because it means further action is needed since the higher court requires a *new mandate* from the lower court consistent with its ruling.

Civil Procedures

Civil lawsuits are either based on contracts or *torts*, covering laws intended to resolve legal promises or duties to others gone wrong. The principal concern of torts is determining who is to blame and who should pay, which might require describing what *fault* exists that created this offense and who should be held liable.

The harmed party is called the *plaintiff*, who submits a *complaint* (otherwise known as a lawsuit) to the clerk of court citing key elements of the offense, including the court's *jurisdiction*, *facts of the case*, *cause of action*, *damages*, and a "prayer for relief." The relief may be sought in damages or a declaratory judgment. The party receiving the complaint is the *respondent* or *defendant*, who must either answer the lawsuit in a set period, around 20 days, or risk suffering a default.

The respondent or defendant answers by agreeing to facts or claiming certain ones to be false. They can challenge the legal grounds for the cause of action by citing points relevant to the complaint. Anyone can *file* a suit, but whether the suit makes it to trial is another matter.

The vast majority of civil lawsuits never make it to court and are settled by attorneys outside the courtroom. Most lawyers prefer these settlements outside of court and for two good reasons: it is less expensive and less risky for both parties involved.[22]

Pretrial Phase

A number of motions can be entered in the pretrial phase of a lawsuit, including one for *discovery*, *dismissal*, or *summary judgment*. Once a civil complaint enters the *discovery phase*, witnesses give their *depositions*, answer **interrogatories** – questions pertinent to the case posed by attorneys on both sides – and sign affidavits.

If a pretrial motion seeks a dismissal or **summary judgment**, the attorney asks the judge to prevent the lawsuit from coming to trial. A summary judgment is granted in instances where the facts are not held in dispute and the judge concludes the *movant* (side entering the motion) is entitled to a ruling based on the law.

Otherwise, the judge must respond by either trying the case, dismissing it, or in lieu of summary judgment asking the disputing parties to agree to an alternative dispute resolution (ADR) where a mediator serves to resolve their issues. Parties cannot be ordered to settle out of court, but they can be directed to confer about the matter with a magistrate judge.

Either side can file a legal brief, a summary of decisions supporting a favorable decision. If third parties wish to become involved, they file what is called an *amicus curiae* – friend of the court brief. The American Civil Liberties Union (ACLU), for example, files supporting briefs of this sort when it finds constitutional rights are involved in important cases.

21. *See*, for example, *American Amusement Machine Assoc., et al., v. Teri Kendrick, et al.*, 244 F.3d 954 (7th Cir. 2001).
22. *See* T. Eisenberg & C. Lanvers, "What Is the Settlement Rate and Why Should We Care?" *Cornell University Law School Faculty Publications*, Paper 203, 2009, *at* https://scholarship.law.cornell.edu/cgi/viewcontent.cgi?article=1202&context=facpub.

Demurrer or Motion to Dismiss
A challenge to the legal sufficiency of a claim set forth in a filing by an opposing party.

If the respondent thinks the plaintiff has no **standing**,[23] then the pretrial motion called a **demurrer** (also called a motion to dismiss) is filed. By filing a demurrer, the respondent admits the facts of the complaint but claims nothing illegal happened.

It may be thought of as the "Yeah, so what?" motion. If the rival parties reach an agreement about the financial terms or other compensation, then a settlement is reached, but such agreements generally avoid any admission of fault or liability and are forged largely to bring the legal dispute to a close.

Of course, lawyers also can file a motion to dismiss for other reasons including violations of the defendant's rights, insufficient evidence, errors found in the complaint, and filing past the statute of limitations, just to name a few.

Trial Phase

Vacated
A lower court decision that is voided because it is in error.

If the lawsuit makes it to trial, lawyers for both the plaintiff and defendant give opening statements announcing what they believe to be the key issues in the dispute and what facts are most favorable to their client. The plaintiff's case is presented first, where witnesses are called to testify on behalf of the complaint and then cross-examined by the defendant's lawyer.

Damage Award
Money awarded to the plaintiff in a civil suit, to be paid by a defendant.

Defense lawyers next bring their witnesses to the stand for questioning and cross-examination until all the evidence is brought before the court. Closing arguments precede the judge's instructions to the jury, if there are any, followed by deliberations to determine the trial's outcome.

Table 1.1 Elements in criminal cases and civil actions

Criminal cases	Civil actions
FIRST: CRIME COMMITTED How large - misdemeanor or felony?	FIRST: HARM OCCURRED Is there a cause of action, a legal claim?
SECOND: PERSON RESPONSIBLE Criminal defendant charged or indicted	SECOND: PERSON RESPONSIBLE Plaintiff sues respondent/defendant
THIRD: PRETRIAL PHASE Discovery (police reports, evidence, eyewitness depositions) Arraignment (pleas: guilty, not guilty, nolo contendere)	THIRD: PRETRIAL PHASE Discovery (affidavits, depositions, interrogatories, legal briefs, amicus briefs) Motions: dismiss, summary judgment, alternative dispute resolution (ADR)
FOURTH: TRIAL PHASE Delays (continuance, change of venue, change of venire) Opening statements Witnesses and cross-examinations Deliberations Verdict (guilty or not guilty)	FOURTH: TRIAL PHASE Motions for change of venue, venire, or move forum to different jurisdiction Opening statements Witnesses and cross-examinations Closing arguments Deliberations Verdict/Judgment (finding for plaintiff or defendant)
FIFTH: POSTTRIAL PHASE Sentencing or freedom	FIFTH: POSTTRIAL PHASE Assessment of damages

23. In civil suits, the plaintiff must show the harm done was actually "of and concerning" the plaintiff. In a 2016 suit, the Supreme Court made clear that a plaintiff must show "concrete and particularized" injury to have standing in a civil suit. *Spokeo v. Robins*, 136 S. Ct. 1540, 1545 (2016).

The judge is notified when the jury has reached a decision and in open court reads the decision. The judge also can enter a verdict from the bench if they disagree with the decision. Juries decide questions of facts, but the judge can argue against the decision and even set aside the jury verdict if it undermines the law.

Actual Damages
A form of compensatory damages, this monetary payment is designed to remedy the losses suffered by the plaintiff.

Posttrial Phase

If the plaintiff prevails at trial, the relief is calculated in several ways: **actual damages** (or **compensatory**), **special damages**, and **punitive damages**. Actual or compensatory damages are based on a dollar estimate of the actual harm done, including pain and suffering.

Special damages give relief for out-of-pocket expenses, including missing wages, special expenses, profit losses, and the like. Punitive damages are levied when the court seeks to punish the defendant regardless of the actual harm to the plaintiff.

In cases in which exorbitant damages are announced, an appeals court can reduce that amount so that it is more proportionate to the harm done. And either side may appeal the decision based on errors in fact or law. For the same matter, if a court finds no substantial harm or losses were suffered, then it may award the plaintiff only **nominal damages**, which could be as little as one dollar.

Punitive Damages
One type of damage award not intended to make the plaintiff whole but to act as an additional deterrent to the type of conduct or negligence attributed to the defendant.

Generally, lawyers are given 30 days to file a notice of appeal challenging the trial court's decision relying on questions of law rather than pointing to errors in fact. Although appeals courts will not retry cases, they can summon both sides for oral hearings and decide to either reverse or affirm the trial court's verdict.

Court System

When it comes to criminal actions, Americans are entitled to their day in court. Fifty-two court systems – one for the nation, each state, and the District of Columbia – have been established to serve them. In the federal system, there are 94 U.S. district courts (some states have more than one) that handle federal cases at the trial court level. These circuit courts also take state cases concerning constitutional matters holding jurisdiction over large regions of the country.

Reversible Error
Legal mistakes found by an appellate court to have occurred sufficiently harmful to warrant a judgment's reversal.

Appeals to circuit court decisions go to the U.S. Supreme Court for review, but thousands of petitions are filed each year and only several hundred are reviewed. Of that number, 80 or so cases are granted **certiorari**. To grant certiorari is a term taken from Latin, *certiorari volumnus*, meaning to become informed about a lower's court's decision, or as lawyers might phrase it, "granted cert" once the petitioner's request for a hearing is accepted.

A majority vote is not required to review a case since the *rule of four* prevails – only four justices must ask to bring a case before the Supreme Court including briefs, oral arguments, and deliberations before a decision is reached. So how are these jurists chosen?

Federal judges are appointed by the president and confirmed by the Senate in a process used for the Supreme Court as well as lower federal district and circuit courts. It is a lifetime appointment, subject only to removal by impeachment for a breach of duty or due to another serious infraction.[24]

Individual states use different systems to either appoint or elect their judges. Twenty-four states and the District of Columbia prefer a merit system in which a judicial commission submits qualified candidates to the governor (the mayor in the case of the District of Columbia) for appointment.

24. One public interest group calculated the impeachment rate to less than one-half of 1%, and the rate of conviction was lower still at 0.2%, http://CourtZero.org.

Six states hold elections where judicial candidates identify party affiliation on the ballot; 15 states hold judicial elections where the political party is not identified. Three states leave the appointment of judges entirely up to the governor, while two states turn it over to the legislature for their selection.

Most states follow some form of the "Missouri Plan" for judicial appointments, named after the first state to adopt it in 1940. It was designed to eliminate partisan influence in judicial offices and emphasize the candidate's merits instead. It is based on a nonpartisan commission reviewing and recommending candidates to the governor for appointment. After the appointee serves one full term (or less), then voters decide whether to retain the judge in office.

In terms of the judicial province, jurisdictions are based on geographic maps and the type of law served. These lines tend to vary from state to state. In the federal system, the original charter for the judiciary (Art. III of the Constitution) only mentions "one Supreme Court" but gives Congress authority to establish "such inferior courts" as necessary, which covers the U.S. district courts allocated by geography and population.

Each district court sends notice of disputed decisions to one of the circuit courts of appeal, including the District of Columbia, also based on geography.[25] Each of these federal appellate circuit courts serves at least three states, and the largest one is the Ninth Circuit Court in San Francisco, which is famous for some high-profile decisions, including rulings on the Pledge of Allegiance,[26] the death penalty,[27] and immigration.[28]

Its prominence is not surprising since this California bench has been a progressive court, although its record is more nuanced and mixed than its reputation.

Bedrock Law

Civil law involves rules designed to protect individuals or groups of individuals. Criminal laws are enforced to protect society at large.

De Novo

Latin for "from the beginning," refers to when an appellate court reviews a nonjury trial record, it may look from the beginning for error in the judge's findings of fact as well as law.

The Appeals Process

Imagine the legal system (both federal and state) as a courthouse with three floors (Figure 1.2). On the first floor, the trial court serves to gather the facts of a dispute or an alleged crime, which makes it the court of original jurisdiction. The record of fact is drawn from depositions, eyewitness testimony, and those items that are admitted in evidence.

It is on this first floor that judges and juries perform their roles in assessing the facts of the case. Because two parties are in contest, there is often some disagreement regarding both the facts of their dispute and the law's application to those facts.

When questions produce a disagreement of fact, the jury's or judge's discretion is used to render a decision. Once the testimony has been heard and the necessary evidence presented, a verdict is reached by applying the law to the evidence.

In most cases, a criminal conviction can be appealed but an acquittal stands without further action. Any civil case is subject to appeal if reversible errors are found at the trial level.

If an appeal is filed, the case moves to the appellate level on the "second floor" for a review. In most but not all states and in the federal system, appellate court acceptance for first level review is automatic. Map 1.1 shows the location and jurisdiction of the federal appeals courts.

Appellate courts will not hear the facts of a case up for appeal but will look only at how the law was applied to the case. An appellate court may, however, opt to review the factual record if the case was dismissed during the pretrial phase or some allegation of misconduct was made. This event might call for a *de novo review*, which indicates the case needs a fresh look.

25. The D.C. Circuit Court of Appeals handles federal agency cases, while the U.S. Court of Appeals for the Federal Circuit hears other cases, including patent claims, since it was a consolidation of the old Court of Customs and Patent Appeals and Court of Claims.
26. *Elk Grove Unified School District v. Endow*, 542 U.S. 1 (2004).
27. *Ewing v. California*, 538 U.S. 11 (2003); *Locker v. Andrade*, 538 U.S. 63 (2003).
28. *Flores v. Lynch*, No. 15–56434 (9th Cir. 2016).

Figure 1.2 Boone County (Missouri)

Source: https://commons.wikimedia.org/wiki/File:Boone_County_Courthouse_in_Columbia,_Missouri.jpg

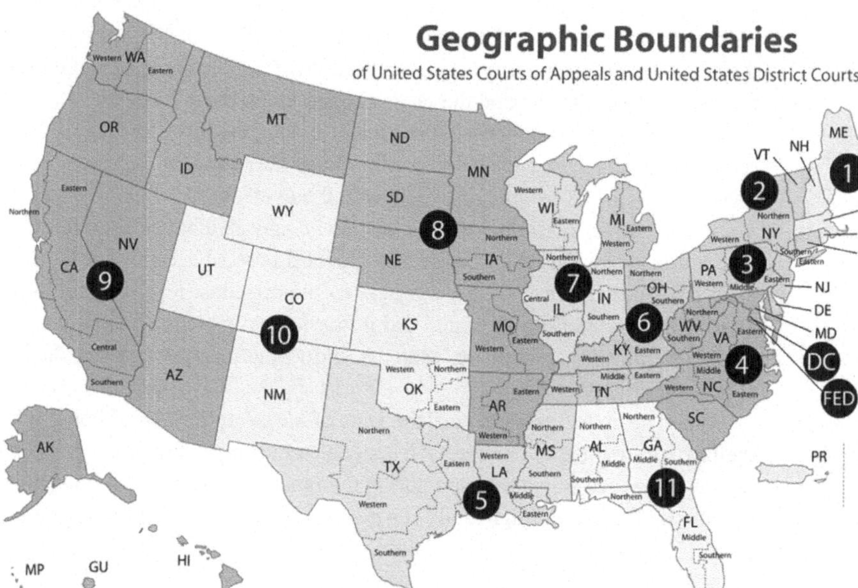

Map 1.1 The United States is divided into 13 federal appellate circuits. Each of the 11 geographic circuits has multiple district courts. The twelfth appellate court is in Washington, DC, which oversees the rulings of the federal administrative agencies, and a thirteenth circuit oversees federal cases. This federal circuit court was created in 1982 with jurisdiction over patent case appeals.

When judicial review occurs at the appellate level, judges search for material defects, for what is called *reversible error*. It is understood virtually every case produces a variety of harmless errors, but a reversible one means either someone's substantive rights were violated or a judicial mistake materially influenced the outcome of the case.

It might also mean the appellate court found pieces of evidence that either should or should not have been allowed. In those cases an error in legal procedure has taken place.

Remanded
When an appellate court sends back a case to a lower court for further action.

A common misconception is that an appeals court arrives at a separate verdict, but what happens in fact is the trial court's decision is either affirmed or it is not. If the case is returned to this imagined courthouse's first floor, it is *remanded* or *remitted*, which means the appeals court wants the lower court to reconsider its judgment based on a new interpretation or rationale.

If the lower court's ruling is affirmed or reversed, either party has the right to pursue the matter to the court of last resort. It then ascends to the third floor of justice.

Supreme Courts

In each state, a court of last resort renders the final decision in a case on appeal. After hearing the appeal, the high court passes judgment regarding issues of law and justice. It is this last tribunal where the judges are responsible for finding and correcting mistakes made at either the trial court or lower appellate courts.

The authority of this panel of jurists, often called a state supreme court, is defined by the U.S. Constitution, and lower state courts and federal courts respect it as the determinant authority. A case will only move beyond a state court's discretion if there is a federal question involved.

Most state supreme courts operate on the principle of *discretionary review*. What that means is the high court can refuse to consider cases from a lower court for any reason even if a conflict of precedent is involved. It is their discretion to do so after reviewing how the law was applied.

The same holds true at the federal level. The U.S. Supreme Court serves as the last resort in the succession of appeals to a decision, but only for those relatively few cases it accepts. As noted, of the thousands of petitions submitted each year to the high court, only hundreds are given a formal review.

Of that number only 80 or so are placed on the docket for hearing. Unless there is a vacancy due to death, resignation, or incapacitation, nine justices[29] sit on the bench to decide these cases. When an even number of justices sit on the Court, eight justices for example, and there is a tie vote, then the lower court's decision usually will stand.

The nine justices of the Supreme Court occupy the most privileged office in the U.S. government, and given their lifetime tenure, the Constitution specifies they should serve only "during good behavior."[30] Even former president William Howard Taft said he preferred his seat on the Court to the power he had held in the White House.

To achieve such a pinnacle, a presidential nomination is needed and approval by the "Advice and Consent of the Senate" (Art. II, Sec. 2, para. 2). Senate hearings for the nominee are held, which can result in a vote against confirmation to the high court.

29. The title "Justice" is reserved for a state or federal Supreme Court judge.
30. U.S. Constitution, Art. III, §1. Relatively few judges have been removed for bad behavior, but there have been several whose judicial temperament due to their "free and intemperate use of intoxicating liquors" required action, such as Judge John Pickering in 1804.

The Senate has done just that in 36 of 160 cases – 22.5% of the time. The Senate also can refuse to hold any hearings, which was the case before President Obama left office in 2016. He nominated Merrick Garland, the chief judge of the District of Columbia, Circuit Court of Appeals, to replace the late Justice Antonin Scalia.

There was a high hurdle awaiting Garland's appointment in the U.S. Senate. Majority Leader Mitch McConnell (R-Ky) announced no hearings would be held because 2016 was an election year and that it should be up to the next president to appoint the next justice.[31]

In retaliation, Democrats moved to prolong the approval process for President Trump's nominee to replace Scalia on the high court, Judge Neil Gorsuch of the Tenth Circuit Court of Appeals. Gorsuch was eventually confirmed.

The partisan divide widened in 2018 when Brett Kavanaugh, a federal judge for the D.C. Circuit, was nominated by President Trump to replace retiring Justice Anthony Kennedy. Numerous ethics complaints were filed against Judge Kavanaugh, but following days of rancorous hearings he was confirmed by a largely partisan vote of 51–49 in the U.S. Senate.

The partisan tumult barely quelled when the next Supreme Court vacancy emerged. Republicans in the Senate had claimed in 2016 it would be wrong to move on President Obama's pick with little more than nine months left in his term but saw it differently in 2020.

When President Trump had a chance to fill the seat vacated by Justice Ruth Bader Ginsberg's passing Judge Amy Coney Barrett of the Seventh Circuit Court of Appeals was nominated with less than four months before Trump's term expired and 35 days before the U.S. presidential election. The U.S. Senate moved with alacrity to confirm Judge Barrett along a largely party line vote, 52–48.

The most recent justice to be confirmed was a relatively non-controversial choice by comparison. Judge Ketanji Brown Jackson of the D.C. Circuit Court of Appeals was President Biden's nomination to succeed retiring Justice Stephen Breyer. Justice Brown Jackson was confirmed as the first Black woman and federal public defender to serve on the high court. The vote in her favor was 53–47, largely along party lines.

As the national court of last resort, the U.S. Supreme Court normally serves as the final stage for a case's appeal it is held to be of federal importance. In rare cases, it can serve as a trial court of original jurisdiction to resolve issues arising from an interpretation of the Constitution. For example, the Supreme Court twice tried a case pitting the state of New Mexico against the state of Texas[32] over state boundaries *de novo*.

Writ of Certiorari
A formal request issued by the Supreme Court to review a lower court's decision.

Granting *Certiorari*

As noted earlier, appellant lawyers who approach the U.S. Supreme Court seek a *writ of certiorari* or *grant of cert*, which is a formal request to review a lower court's decision. Even though fewer than 2% of the thousands of petitions brought before the Court are given this ultimate shot at justice, it does not mean the justices believe a lower court decision was correct.

31. R.K. Kar & J. Mazzone, "The Garland Affair: What History and the Constitution Really Say about President Obama's Powers to Appoint a Replacement for Justice Scalia," *NYU Law Review: On-Line Features*, March 21, 2016, *at* http://papers.ssrn.com/sol3/papers.cfm?abstract_id=2752287.
32. *New Mexico v. Texas*, 276 U.S. 558 (1928); *Texas v. New Mexico*, 462 U.S. 554 (1983).

It also does not necessarily mean the lower court decision was wrong. In fact, no requirement is made for the court to give any reason for its selections. Judicial biographers, legal scholars, and journalists, however, love to dissect and speculate on their rationale.

Bedrock Law

The Supreme Court accepts only a small portion of the petitions it is asked to hear based on the timing of the appeal and its significance to the rule of law.

The justices avoid certain questions in federal law and the cases raising them because they do not appear to be *ripe*. Once the issue in a petition for appeal has been allowed to become timely and significant (*ripen*), the Supreme Court may vote to hear the appeal. But sometimes the court is not prepared to hear it, perhaps because the ruling is not relevant to a pertinent question on federal grounds.

It could be that the petition is too case-specific, or the petitioner is complaining about losing in the lower court without probable evidence for *granting cert*. Because a Supreme Court ruling may be creating a precedent to guide lower courts for decades to come, the justices try to avoid disputes when shifting social norms or structural changes might render the ruling outmoded and therefore irrelevant.

Oral Arguments and Opinions

For a case to be heard before the Supreme Court, attorneys first must be admitted to the Supreme Court Bar and that requires at least three years of state practice. Each side is required to file written briefs before making their oral arguments before the high court. Lawyers prepare themselves for half-hour presentations, and justices typically zero in on the points raised in oral remarks or in the briefs.

Since judges at all levels interrupt lawyers, such spontaneous questioning at the highest court is not considered ill-mannered at all. However, what might be thought different about the justices' questions is how they evoke speculation over the court's mindset in terms of how they will finally vote, which occurs afterward behind closed doors in a conference meeting.

A certain level of secrecy adds to the mystical aura of this august tribunal. The justices gather with no one else present – not even a secretary to take notes – and discuss the key issues. In fact, if someone knocks at the door, it is the obligation of the junior justice – the one who has served for the shortest duration – to answer the door.

The importance of seniority and secrecy in the conference room extends beyond mere trivialities. When justices do begin to deliberate, the chief justice speaks first, followed by associate justices in descending order of seniority.[33] Speakers schooled in rhetoric understand that going first holds the advantage of framing the issue. When it comes time for a vote, justices go in reverse order of seniority with the chief justice voting last.

Because the Supreme Court accepts cases with an eye toward posterity and precedent, lengthy opinions are sometimes drafted to explain their rationale. These written opinions usually contain both a *holding* and *dicta*, comments explaining different elements of the case to show the reasoning.

Concurring Opinion

When a judge or justice agrees with the judicial decision reached by the majority but believes that conclusion should have been reached by a different rationale.

Dicta form the bulk of the judicial opinion but should not be confused with the holding in the case, which speaks directly to the issues involved. The holding is the specific decision reached by the court resolving the key issue and is determinative of the outcome. Dicta, on the other hand, do afford guidance about how to evaluate lesser issues involved.

A majority opinion in the U.S. Supreme Court means five or more justices are of like mind with respect to a case decision. One of them is delegated the duty of explaining their conclusion to all parties involved, including the legal community.

The justices are fully aware when they hand down a landmark decision that scholars and lawyers will cite their words for years to come, and so they write for both the present and

33. The chief justice always has the position of seniority, even though they might have served fewer years on the court than other justices.

future. Seniority affords a privilege in this duty. It is the senior justice voting with the majority who assigns the writing task.

In 1969, Justice Abe Fortas wrote for a 7–2 majority opinion in *Tinker v. Des Moines Independent Community School District*, a landmark decision establishing First Amendment rights in public schools since neither "students or teachers shed their constitutional rights to freedom of speech or expression at the schoolhouse gate."[34]

Bedrock Law
Bedrock law is a principle or custom in communication law that is widely recognized and held to be fundamentally correct based on its history and/or logic in American jurisprudence.

Justice Fortas, amid controversy, resigned from the Court in 1969 and died in 1982; yet his words written on behalf of young students' rights resonate today and underscore principles we have chosen to call *bedrock law*.

Sometimes a majority of the justices agree for different reasons, requiring the writing of a *concurring opinion*. A justice will write a special explanation to justify why their reasoning departs from the presiding opinion in the decision.

A *plurality opinion* may also exist, where no majority rules in the appeal yet several justices agree on the rationale for a specific course of action. A plurality opinion does not produce a solid precedent because the majority agree on the outcome but differ in their reasoning for the result.

The simplest and briefest way of dispensing justice is by means of a *memorandum opinion* that points to a winning side but does not explain the rationale for the decision. In such cases, the justices unanimously base their opinion on a settled principle or precedent that holds little or no special significance. Such a unanimous decision also may be attributed to the case having a fact pattern the court wishes to avoid amplifying as a precedent.

Memorandum Opinion
Unanimous judgment identifying the winning party in an appeal without explanation. Could be based on settled law or other factors unsuited for special distinction as a legal precedent.

In other rare instances, a decision is handed down with an opinion that is not signed. This type of ruling is called a *per curiam* order, which means "by the Court" as a whole. For example, when the 2000 presidential election was stymied over the recounting of ballots, the Supreme Court put an end to it by issuing a *per curiam* order in *Bush v. Gore*.

The dissenting opinions give justices voting against the majority an opportunity to explain why they took exception to the majority viewpoint in the case. While they have no legal bearing on the case at hand, these dissents may take on greater importance over time and may even figure prominently in future decisions signaling a new direction. Some appear in law reviews or legal treatises and have a long-term impact.

Studying the Law

Scholars in communication law may write from the perspective of revered judges, lawyers, or as faculty members of law schools. Their former students and colleagues use their research because their writings have a bearing on the interpretation and application of legal principles.

A well-framed analysis of a landmark case or a powerful argument of theoretical significance resonates for years. U.S. Chief Justice Oliver Wendell Holmes, Jr. observed, "[T]he life of the law has not been logic; it has been experience."[35] His colleague Justice Louis D. Brandeis added, "[T]he logic of words should yield to the logic of realities."[36] If legal logic is a form of common sense, Justice William O. Douglas's opinion is especially apt: "[C]ommon sense often makes good law."[37]

In principle, scholars employ the twin perspectives of logic and history to make key points about the context and meaning of the law. These are the elements, but how the legal scholar applies them into written documents makes all the difference.

34. *Tinker v. Des Moines Independent Community School District*, 393 U.S. 503 (1969).
35. As cited in *The Common Law* (Little, Brown, 1881).
36. *See* Brandeis's opinion in *DeSanto v. Pennsylvania*, as cited in Melvin I. Urofsky & Louis D. Brandeis, "Advocate Before and On the Bench," 30 *J. Sup. Ct. Hist.*, 31–46 (2005).
37. *Peak v. United States*, 353 U.S. 43 (1957).

Per Curiam Order
A judgment rendered with an opinion left unsigned by the court. This type of ruling is considered to be "by the Court" as a whole.

The quality of legal writing relies on several factors – the strength of the viewpoint, the soundness of the reasoning, and the depth of analysis applied through order and engaging prose. Legal researchers understand the quality of their scholarship is in proportion to their success achieving two objectives: understanding the law and applying the law.

Their writings will clearly indicate if the legal scholarship relies on one of two approaches: the *positivist* or *realist* perspective. For the positivist analysis, conventional sources of legal codes, briefs, legislative records, and case digests go a long way in addressing legal issues.[38] The legal realist, on the other hand, prefers a different type of approach to enlighten legal theory. They explore the character and context of important decisions as well as the parties involved.

Scholars also look beyond these traditional approaches on occasion to address questions with tools from the social sciences and empirical data to gauge the law through surveys, content analyses, and other methodologies. These data sets in legal analysis might be received for publication, albeit with some reservation by the legal community at large.

Research Procedures

It is best to think of time, topic, and location when searching for the best legal resource. When national laws are invoked, scholars turn to one of several resources using different formats. Lawyers who need federal statutes organized by subject heading reference the *United States Code* instead of the *United States Statutes at Large*, which orders laws chronologically.

If the point of the research involves federal regulation, then either the *Federal Register* (*Fed. Reg.*), or *Code of Federal Regulations* (CFR) will fill the bill. The CFR is organized by topics described as *Titles*, while the *Fed. Reg.* is ordered by chronology and includes proposed rules for public comment. It is somewhat cumbersome though to use for legal research.

For timely release to the legal community, newly enacted federal statutes are published as "slip pages" by the United States Code Service of the Lawyers Cooperative, or West Publishing's *United States Code Annotated*. Federal statutes also are viewed online at https://www.govinfo.gov/app/collection/uscode.

Electronic access through an administrative agency's website is another option. The Federal Communications Commission webpage (www.fcc.gov) offers indexes for electronic broadcasting media regulations. For information on legal procedures, the U.S. Government Publishing Office's website, www.gpo.gov, invites public inspection of agency rules.

If the goal of legal research calls for digging deeper into legislative activities, exploring congressional records can be accomplished online. Recent records (since 1994) are at https://www.govinfo.gov/app/collection/. For state laws, official codebooks of statutes are placed on library shelves below titles like Vernon's *Texas Civil Statutes* or *California Codes*. A search of the state government website will usually yield quick results.

Case Law Sources

At first glance, a variety of databases seem to give scholars an easy way to capture both statutes and relevant cases, but several sources are significant. Law schools and lawyers often favor the legal database Westlaw, but Lexis-Nexis, accessible to academics through its Academic Universe subscription, puts readers in touch with court decisions and commentaries.

A scholar may also search LegalTrac via subject or keywords to collect inquiry responses. Two other popular search engines are FindLaw (www.findlaw.com) and the Meta Index for Legal Research (http://hrlibrary.umn.edu/lawform-new.html).

38. Susan Dente Ross, *Deciding Communication Law: Key Cases in Context 2.1–2.2* (Mahwah, NJ: Lawrence Erlbaum Associates, 2004).

Online indexes usually guide scholars to decisions before printed versions are available. Published rulings are contained in a series of volumes called *reporters*. Rulings by the U.S. Supreme Court appear in print in the *United States Reports – the government's official reporter* – after being made available online in the legal databases of Lexis-Nexis or Westlaw.

The first printed versions of the U.S. Supreme Court decisions appear in *United States Law Week* (U.S.L.W.) along with rulings from other courts and federal agencies. The decisions from the U.S. District Court are published in *Federal Supplements* (*F. Supp.*). Once cases are taken up on appeal, West's *Federal Reporter* prints the decisions from the U.S. circuit courts.

State appellate court rulings are published in seven different *reporters* organized by geographic region, sometimes with surprising designations. Indiana's and Nebraska's federal cases, for example, appear in the *Northeastern Reporter*, while Tennessee and Kentucky are grouped in the *Southwestern Reporter* with Texas, Arkansas, and Missouri.

Briefing a Case

After the law has been digested and the text of relevant cases examined, key decisions are organized according to a consistent format. An abstract of an important decision is made concise by its basic elements: *citation, facts, issue, decision, explanation, rule of law,* and *opinions (concurring and dissenting)*. For the purposes of illustration, let's consider the landmark case, *Tinker v. the Des Moines Independent Community School District* (1969).[39]

Citation

The brief begins with the **citation** that includes the name of the case, the volume and page numbers of the legal reporter where it is published followed by the year it was decided. The Tinker family members and a friend are identified as the appellant or petitioner, and the Des Moines Independent Community School District is the respondent or appellee.

The petitioner who is appealing the lower court ruling comes first in the title, while the respondent is listed second, and "v." signifies *versus*. In *Tinker v. Des Moines Independent Community School District*, the Tinker family sued the school district for their rights of free speech after the school district suspended three students who wore armbands in protest of the Vietnam War.

"U.S." is the abbreviation for the official publication, *United States Reports*. The numeral 393 represents the volume number, and 503 marks the beginning page number. The year 1969 is when the Supreme Court handed down its decision. *Tinker v. Des Moines School District* is also found in other publications, so parallel citations may be used or added.

Facts

The second element of the brief is the **facts** section of the case. This is the summary given to report the key elements that led to the decision. This part answers the journalist's basic questions of "who, what, where, when, how, and why" in a summary that briefs the conflict.

Here, the case arose from a public school system in Des Moines, Iowa, when three students wore to class black armbands with the peace symbol silently protesting the Vietnam War. Before that day, the school principal warned the students not to conduct or express themselves in this manner because it would disrupt the learning environment.

39. A sample brief of this case is located online at *Tinker v. Des Moines Independent Community School District*, Oyez, https://www.oyez.org/cases/1968/21 (Accessed July 5, 2023).

Despite the warning, the students wore the armbands and consequently received suspension notices. The students' parents sued on First Amendment grounds claiming the suspension by a government institution – the public school system – violated freedom of speech.

The family members lost their case in the U.S. District Court for the Southern District of Iowa and appealed to the U.S. Court of Appeals for the Eighth Circuit, where they lost again. The Supreme Court granted certiorari, and the majority ruled in favor of the protesters.

Issue(s)

The third part of the briefing covers the **issue** and spells out the principal question the court was seeking to resolve. It is usually stated as a question or described in one or two declarative sentences. Do public school systems have the right to ban even silent protests to prevent a disruption to classroom learning, or do such bans violate students' First Amendment rights?

Decision

The fourth part of the case briefing abstracts the **decision** of the court, which usually begins with a one-word response to the question framed in the issue. It may be referred to as a *ruling, holding, judgment*, or sometimes *disposition.*

REVERSED. In a 7-to-2 decision, the U.S. Supreme Court reversed the lower court in ruling the Tinkers' expressive conduct was protected and the school districts' interest in safeguarding the learning environment did not override their First Amendment rights. No substantial disruption occurred in the classroom. Justice Abe Fortas wrote the majority opinion.

Rationale

The fifth part of the brief is the **rationale** where an explanation given for the ruling indicates how the decision relates to earlier case precedents and statutes, and it discusses relevant legal theory. Here, the Supreme Court ruled there was no finding or showing wearing peace symbol armbands would materially or substantially interfere with discipline in the school.

School officials had no right to ban speech just because they suspected it might disrupt the learning environment. The ruling reversed the lower court rulings on the basis that the students' First Amendment rights had been violated.

Rule of Law

The sixth part of the brief summarizes the consequences of the ruling in one or two sentences. It is called the **rule of law**. In this case the students' expressive rights were under the protection of the Free Speech Clause of the First Amendment and the Due Process Clause of the Fourteenth Amendment. Thus, a ban against students expressing their opinions without evidence the ban is necessary to prevent disruptions at school is constitutionally impermissible.

Concurring or Dissenting Opinions

Finally, if there are **dissenting** or **concurring opinions**, they may be summarized and discussed in the seventh part of the briefing. Here, the dissenting justices felt school administrators should be given legitimate responsibility to protect the learning environment and should not have to bend to the will of students who want to use their classrooms as a forum for expressive conduct.

Justice Hugo Black claimed the court was usurping authority from the teachers and administrators to control their classrooms. He also objected to the idea that symbolic speech, akin to pure speech, warrants a special dispensation in public school for adolescents. And he felt the claim this silent protest was not disruptive simply was false. "Even a casual reading of the record shows how this armband did divert students' minds from their regular lessons."

Justice Harlan wrote a separate dissent in *Tinker* basing his opinion on the proposition school officials and teachers deserve the benefit of the doubt when it comes to rules on speech in class – and the burden on overturning such a rule belongs to the students. "[I]n cases like this . . . the burden of showing that a particular school measure was motivated by other than legitimate school concerns – for example, a desire to prohibit the expression of an unpopular point of view" should be placed on the students who were punished.

Ethical Dilemmas: No Supreme Court Code of Ethics

"See there's a conflict of interest!" A provocative phrase like that might be used by politicians, pundits, and influencers to create outrage against their opponents. Sometimes overlooked though is the need to show at least two interests – one legitimate and the other not – are in fact creating a real and specific conflict leading to some alleged misconduct.

U.S. Supreme Court justices were placed under conflict-of-interest scrutiny in 2023 after reports surfaced that at least two justices accepted gifts from conservative political supporters. For decades, Texas billionaire Harlan Crow bestowed tangible acts of kindness on Justice Clarence Thomas, including a portrait of him with his wife, a $19,000 Bible once owned by the nineteenth-century abolitionist Frederick Douglass, and luxury vacations to attractive resorts. Justice Samuel Alito was also gifted with an Alaska vacation trip from business professionals.

The Senate Judiciary Committee responded to the reports of possible conflicts by drafting a legislative act that would empower a panel of five lower court judges to investigate charges of ethical misbehavior on the court, but the bill was given little chance of passage. So is merely accepting outside gifts clear evidence of a conflict of interest on the high court?

In such cases there must be a secondary interest the justice served shown in evidence coming in actual conflict with their primary interest of dispensing equal and impartial justice.

Principles of ethical conduct are self-regulated by justices unlike other U.S. office holders since there is no ethical code to serve as an oversight policy for the U.S. Supreme Court. It is left up to each justice to oversee and correct their own personal conduct and receipt of gifts.

Summary

- The character of a nation's government is measured by its *rule of law*, and American governance is a product of both the sources of law and their application throughout the system of justice. The sources of legal power in the legislative branch rely on the judiciary for interpretation and the executive branch for enforcement.
- The three branches of the federal government limit the consolidation of power by protecting rights with respect to freedom of expression and using a system of checks and balances between the executive, legislative, and judicial branches.
- The Supreme Court has the authority to strike down flawed laws, and in the process establish precedent for future cases. Appellate courts of last resort in the states and the

nation exercise the power of judicial review and can either uphold laws or strike them down. This form of common law authority is traced to the landmark case of *Marbury v. Madison* (1803), where the U.S. Supreme Court established its authority to review acts of Congress and determine if they were constitutionally valid or not.

- Courts are bound to follow precedent, known as *stare decisis*, meaning "to let the decision stand." The U.S. Supreme Court accepts only a small percentage of the appeals it is asked to consider based on the significance and timing of the case.
- Courts preside over equity actions and are empowered to offer injunctive relief. Courts can serve injunctions and issue other writs through equity law when neither the statutes nor the case precedents apply to the legal disputes at hand.
- The jurisdiction for various courts deciding cases and their appeals varies by state and the type of case heard. A legal hierarchy exists in all states, allowing higher courts to review and examine lower court rulings. Precedent-setting cases influence the common law guiding courts to resolve disputes beyond statutory construction.
- To better understand the difference between civil and criminal courts, it helps to look at the type of offense involved. While crimes against society involve harm to person or theft of property, civil cases often boil down to legal disputes over reputation, privacy, and intellectual property rights. Instead of losing personal freedom through incarceration, civil cases usually only yield monetary damages. A crime results in arrest and possible incarceration and is prosecuted by the government; a civil dispute is a lawsuit among private parties usually seeking recovery of lost finances.
- Federal agencies hold legal powers that include drafting and approving rules, enforcing them, and deciding appeals to their administration. Heads of federal agencies are appointed by the president and confirmed by the U.S. Senate.
- Attorneys in most states are required to stay abreast of changes in the law by continuing their education. Both the activities of the courts and their sources of authority provide worthy subjects of scholarly research, especially since laws and legal practitioners must adapt to the dynamic currents of society's changes.

2

First Amendment in Principle and Practice

LEARNING OBJECTIVES

After reading this chapter, you should know

- how fear often results in pressure to curtail rights of free expression
- Emerson's four values inherent in the protection of free expression
- the First Amendment protects rights of expression from *government* restrictions; it does not eliminate restrictions by nongovernment actors
- words are sometimes not speech but action, and actions can sometimes be considered protected free expression
- the First Amendment attempts to protect both the rights of the speaker and the listener, but sometimes those rights may be in conflict
- rights of free expression are never absolute; there are multiple factors considered in determining the limits
- the language of the First Amendment is brief, but the interpretation of key phrases such as "no law," "abridging freedom," and "petition for redress of grievances" has been the subject of extensive debate – and litigation

Freedom of expression is an expansive concept. As we discuss throughout this text, expression can take many forms of speech and action including burning a flag, wearing certain clothing, marching in protest, or a religious ceremony. But none of these forms is absolutely protected – there are limits. Religious expression is protected, but a ritual of worship that involved human sacrifice obviously would be prohibited.

Lorie Smith was a small business owner in Colorado doing website design. She wanted to expand her business to include wedding announcement websites but had one concern. Smith did not want to accept business from same-sex couples, something she felt her religious beliefs prevented her from doing. Instead, she planned to post a notice that she would not accept such business and then provide information on other businesses that would. She learned that doing so would put her in violation of the Colorado Anti-Discrimination Act. She decided to file a lawsuit. In 2019, a federal district court in Colorado ruled against Smith, finding Colorado's anti-discrimination law to be constitutional. The Tenth Circuit Court of Appeals agreed.

DOI: 10.4324/9781003462989-2

The U.S. Supreme Court heard the appeal and in 2023 voted 6–3 to overturn the lower courts and grant Smith the right to refuse to do business with same-sex couples.[1] The court did *not* find the anti-discrimination law unconstitutional but instead wrote that Smith's right not to "speak" in a way that was contrary to her beliefs was her First Amendment right. While free speech advocates applauded the decision, supporters of rights for the LGBTQ community were bothered by it. But what about people who support *both* free expression and LGBTQ rights? Surely every case has a winner and loser, but in many cases, observers may feel that a decision had both positive and negative outcomes.

The First Amendment to the U.S. Constitution

Congress shall make no law respecting an establishment of religion, or prohibiting the free exercise thereof; or abridging the freedom of speech, or of the press; or the right of the people peaceably to assemble, and to petition the government for a redress of grievances.

– The First Amendment to the U.S. Constitution, 1791

A (Very) Brief History

The United States Constitution was created in 1787 and went into effect in 1789, after the requisite nine states had ratified it. Ratification was not a sure thing; leading anti-Federalists like George Mason claimed the new document did not do enough to protect individual liberties. As noted in Chapter 1, James Madison fought for ratification, and one of the promises he made was that once the Constitution was ratified, he would champion amendments to enumerate personal freedoms. True to his word, in the first Congress of the United States, Madison was the main proponent behind the Bill of Rights, the first ten amendments, which were ratified and became part of the Constitution in 1791.

Understanding the history of the American colonies helps to put the First Amendment into context. The new nation had just gained independence from the British government, which had imposed a tax on publishing, jailed publishers, punished protesters, and had a king who was the head of both church and state. The First Amendment was a direct response to the limits on free expression that colonists had suffered for decades.

In theory and on paper, the United States was willing to defend free expression, but in practice there were signs that suggested otherwise. Religious freedom was denied in multiple ways: New York banned Catholics from public office; Maryland denied civil rights to Jews; and only Protestants could serve as state legislators in New Hampshire until as late as 1877.[2]

Freedom of the press was clearly violated with the passage of the **Alien and Sedition Acts of 1798**. The young nation was worried about the possibility of war with France after its war with England, and some members of Congress were frightened by press attacks on the government. The Sedition Act actually made it a crime to publicly oppose the U.S. government. Benjamin Franklin's own grandson, Benjamin Franklin Bache, was an ardent critic of Presidents George Washington and John Adams and was arrested for violation of the Sedition Act. The Sedition Act expired in 1801, but not before more than two dozen people were prosecuted. The Sedition Act serves as a painful reminder that the freedom of expression guaranteed by the First Amendment will not always be protected by the government, especially in times when the government feels vulnerable.

The American Revolution was not the only one that shook the world. The Bolshevik Revolution in Russia in 1917 brought Marxists to power and caused quite a stir, even in the

1. *303 Creative LLC v. Elenis*, 600 U.S. 570 (2023).
2. K. Davis, "America's True History of Religious Tolerance," *Smithsonian Magazine*, October 2010.

United States. Fear that a similar revolution might occur here caused our government to suppress the free expression of splinter groups that distributed pamphlets or otherwise spoke out against our leaders or system of democracy. World War I added to the uncertainty. The U.S. Congress responded with the Espionage Act in 1917 and added a set of amendments to it in 1918, creating another Sedition Act. Its constitutionality was upheld by the Supreme Court, but after the war ended, the sedition portion that prohibited "disloyal, profane, scurrilous, or abusive language" directed at the government, the Constitution, the flag, or the military was repealed.[3]

Nuclear weapons certainly cause fear among many people, and the prospect they might fall into the wrong hands understandably causes Americans concern. In 1979, *The Progressive* magazine intended to publish a kind of "how to" piece on building a nuclear weapon. When it came to the attention of the U.S. Justice Department, officials acted to stop the publication. Another magazine published essentially the same information. Because the justification for enjoining publication no longer existed (the information was already out), the case was dismissed.

These examples show how the government often attempts to suppress free expression when our nation feels threatened. Fortunately, none of these perceived threats ever materialized, and the suppressions were seen in retrospect as unnecessary. In the twenty-first century, the United States continues to face threats, real and perceived, and free expression often hangs in the balance.

Drawing the Line

The First Amendment, while referring specifically to five freedoms (religion,[4] speech, press, assembly, and petition), is generally accepted as protecting freedom of expression. All five of those individual rights are different and yet broadly reflect our freedom of expression.

Though this book focuses on the U.S. Constitution, it is worth noting all 50 states also protect free expression rights in their state constitutions. Legal actions regarding free expression usually invoke federal protection, but there have been cases where state constitutions have been the subject of free speech cases and, in some instances, extended rights even more than federal law would allow.[5] New Jersey and Connecticut have been cited as offering more protection than the U.S. Constitution,[6] and Supreme Court Justice William Brennan advocated for increased use of state constitutions to protect such rights.[7]

The right of free expression is *not* an absolute. There are limits to what the law will allow. Perhaps the most famous example of this is the pithy quote from U.S. Supreme Court Justice Oliver Wendell Holmes, Jr. Writing in *Schenck v. United States*,[8] he stated, "The most stringent protection of free speech would not protect a man in falsely shouting fire in a theatre and causing a panic."[9] Most Americans support limiting free expression in areas where it

3. Public Laws 65–150, 40 Stat. 553, enacted May 16, 1918.
4. Legal scholars distinguish religious freedom by recognizing *two* rights: freedom *of* religion, known as the free exercise clause, and freedom *from* government-dictated religion, which is the establishment clause.
5. Some scholars believe state constitutions provide more protection since at least 1951. *See* Monrad G. Paulsen, "State Constitutions, State Courts and First Amendment Freedoms" (1951), *at* https://www.repository.law.indiana.edu/facpub/2200. More recently scholars contended state constitutions hold the key for restricting offensive behavior on social media that the U.S. Constitution might permit. *See* Elijah O'Kelley, "State Constitutions as a Check on the New Governors: Using State Free Speech Clauses to Protect Social Media Users from Arbitrary Political Censorship by Social Media Platforms," 69 *Emory L. J.* 111 (2019).
6. "State Constitutional Provisions on Expressive Rights," *The First Amendment Encyclopedia*, https://www.mtsu.edu/first-amendment/encyclopedia.
7. "State Constitutions and the Protection of Individual Rights," 90 *Harv. L. Rev*. 489 (1977).
8. 249 U.S. 47 (1919).
9. *Id.* at 52.

would endanger national security, unfairly damage the reputation of individuals, or corrupt children. The difficulty lies in deciding exactly when expression does these things and how to prohibit such expressions while still protecting other communication. To engage in this line-drawing exercise, it is important to understand the reasons for protecting free expression in the first place. Knowing *why* we protect expression will help us understand *what* we protect and what we don't.

The Value of Free Expression

Yale University Law Professor Thomas Emerson identified four values inherent in the American desire to protect freedom of expression.[10] They are as follows:

- Free expression aids in the discovery of truth.
- Free expression is necessary for democratic governance.
- Free expression helps promote a stable society.
- Free expression ensures individual self-fulfillment.

Discovery of Truth

If we assume people would prefer knowing what is true rather than what may be wrong, or even worse, a lie, it is necessary for people to express their thoughts, opinions, ideas, and theories. If the only things people hear come from those in authority, then the only things people will hear are those opinions that support existing authority. Dissent will never be heard.

Marketplace of Ideas
The justification for freedom of expression that holds the best way to find truth is to allow conflicting ideas to compete. This idea is typically associated with philosopher John Stuart Mill or John Milton.

In common parlance, this concept is known as the **marketplace of ideas.**[11] Imagine an open-air marketplace with stores positioned all around. Each of these shops represents someone with a different thought, opinion, or idea. People can browse the shops, searching for just what suits them. In this metaphor, if what one merchant happens to be "selling" is too expensive or is not appealing, "buyers" can find someone else providing a satisfactory "product." Competition in the open market will result in the "buyers" making the right choices from the best vendors, forcing those with inferior "products" to either modify their wares or go out of business.

The symbolic value of the marketplace of ideas has been around for centuries. One of the best-known and most often quoted passages in support of its power comes from *Areopagitica*, a work written by English poet John Milton in 1644. In arguing that the government should do away with a law requiring authors to receive prior approval before publishing anything, he asserted that free expression would provide the best course for discovering the truth:

> And though all the winds of doctrine were let loose to play upon the earth, so Truth be in the field, we do injuriously, by licensing and prohibiting, to misdoubt her strength. Let her and falsehood grapple; who ever knew Truth put to the worse, in a free and open encounter?[12]

10. T. Emerson, *The System of Freedom of Expression* (New York: Random House, 1970).
11. *Abrams v. United States*, 250 U.S. 616 (1919). The concept appears in Justice Oliver Wendell Holmes, Jr.'s dissent at 630, "[T]he ultimate good desired is better reached by free trade in ideas – that the best test of truth is the power of the thought to get itself accepted in the competition of the market."
12. *Areopagitica* in 2 *Complete Prose Works of John Milton* 504. Ed. D. Wolfe (New Haven, CT: Yale University Press, 1975).

The belief by Milton was that in a "free and open encounter," truth would win out over all other thought. People will choose what is best. This approach to the discovery of truth has been used by scholars and philosophers for centuries[13] and has been cited by the U.S. Supreme Court in dozens of cases.

John Milton's *Areopagitica*

Best known for his epic ***Paradise Lost***, John Milton was born in London in 1608 and had a comfortable upbringing, including tutors and a Cambridge education. By the time he married in 1642, he was already an established author, not only of poems but also religious and political pamphlets – the seventeenth-century way of speaking out on the controversies of the day. Milton's marriage to a woman half his age was in trouble early on. After just a month, Mary went home to visit her family and stayed away. He then published a couple of pamphlets on divorce, advocating it as an appropriate action – rather controversial at the time. When the British Stationers, a licensed organization of printers and publishers, attempted to censor Milton's divorce writings, he responded by writing ***Areopagitica***, calling for an end of censorship and advocating a marketplace of ideas. Ironically perhaps, not even Milton adopted an absolutist view of free expression. He believed there were certain forms of expression that deserved to be censored (most notably blasphemy). As it happens, Mary did return to him after several years but died in 1652. John Milton married three times but never once divorced. What lives on as a result of this union is Milton's famous metaphor placing truth and falsity in a struggle whose outcome is ensured by truth's superior power.

Of course, the marketplace metaphor relies on a *fair* marketplace to be effective. In imagining our open-air marketplace, would our expectation of the outcome change if we knew that all the "stores" were owned by only one or two people? What if we knew some sellers had the ability to "package" their wares more attractively than their competitors? Would the consumers in the marketplace be educated enough to see through the packaging and actually analyze the product? The metaphor of the marketplace is less enticing to us if we believe that the marketplace is anything less than "fair." If certain buyers or sellers have advantages, which others do not enjoy, the likelihood that "truth" will be the "winner" in the marketplace of ideas is doubtful. Supporters of the marketplace of ideas believe that free expression needs to be protected to facilitate both the discovery of truth and the correction of error. A collection of news racks, like the one in Figure 2.1, is a more modern equivalent of a marketplace of ideas.

This implies that if we value free expression for its contribution to the discovery of truth, it also suggests that communication that intentionally and knowingly distorts the truth deserves no protection. In our current reality it's easy to think about instances where people know that what they're saying is false or highly exaggerated. Whether it is a politician lying about their past or a toothpaste advertisement promising you'll be more popular with their product, commercial messages that don't promote the discovery of truth have less constitutional protection under our system of free expression that places a premium on the discovery of truth.

13. A few well-known examples include the works of Jean-Jacques Rousseau, John Locke, and John Stuart Mill.

Figure 2.1 News racks on a Washington, DC, street offering multiple voices to choose from

Questioning the Marketplace Metaphor

A marketplace functions best when there are lots of buyers and sellers. If one or two sellers dominate the market, they can distort it. Criticizing the dominance of newspapers in the twentieth century, A.J. Liebling wryly observed, "Freedom of the press is guaranteed only to those who own one." With the proliferation of the Internet in the twenty-first century, anyone can be a publisher, but clearly there are dominant voices, and others who have yet to be heard.

A central premise of Milton's approach is that truth will win over falsehood in a free and open encounter, but we have reason to question that in our social media world. Conspiracy theories flourish online, and research shows that falsehoods may spread faster than the truth. In a study published in *Science*, more than ten years of tweets showed that false news reached more people than the truth, at least on the platform formerly known as Twitter.[14] In the twenty-first century, does truth always win?

Scholar Jared Schroeder writes that the marketplace approach was flawed centuries ago, but today it is indefensible. Internet communication creates multiple spaces where like-minded people gather and ignore other views (echo chambers). Platforms feed people increasingly inflammatory information, often created by machines, whether or not that information is true.[15]

14. S. Vosoughi, D. Roy & S. Aral, "The Spread of True and False News Online," *Science*, March 9, 2018, 1146.
15. J. Schroeder, *The Structure of Ideas: Mapping a New Theory of Free Expression in the AI Era* (Stanford: Stanford University Press, 2024).

Bedrock Law
The marketplace of ideas rationale for free expression argues in favor of the public's ability to choose good and truthful ideas over bad and false ones.

Democracy

The basic premise of representative government is that citizens elect their leaders. How do citizens make the decision about whom to elect? To make informed choices, citizens must have information about the candidates and the issues. To get this information, they must be free to express their opinions and beliefs. Without this prerequisite, the electorate cannot possibly select the best leaders. If democracy is to be at all effective, there must be a free flow of information so that the best choices can be made. Democratic government without a right of free expression is basically useless.

Legal philosopher Alexander Meiklejohn asserted that the main reason for protecting free expression in our society is its key role in support of representative government.[16] The Supreme Court has repeatedly noted how **political speech** lies at the "core of the First Amendment."[17] There are several implications of such an approach, not all of them positive for proponents of free expression. If political speech is most worthy of protection, then by implication other forms of expression are less worthy of protection, or worthy of less protection. It also creates the dilemma of distinguishing whether or not expression is political, thereby deserving of the highest level of protection. Early in his career, Meiklejohn asserted only political speech was deserving of the ultimate protection, but in later writings, he conceded that scientific and artistic expression certainly has the capacity to become political speech. Accordingly, paintings and literary works can offer political commentary. Scientific writing about abortion or secondhand smoke surely has the potential to influence political decisions regarding such issues. If any form of communication has the potential of influencing political decision-making, it does no good to assert that political speech is at the core of a free expression right because all speech is potentially political. **Commercial speech** is generally placed far from the heart of the First Amendment (advertising will be covered in Chapter 11) and therefore less worthy of protection than political speech; yet legal battles have been fought over the claim cigarette commercials raise controversial questions about smoking,[18] and whether advertising for gas-guzzling automobiles is a form of political debate involving environmental issues.[19]

Commercial Speech
Commercial speech is speech with a profit motive. The classic example of commercial speech is advertising. This type of speech is much more subject to regulation and restriction than other forms.

In spite of the difficulty of deciding whether speech is political, courts continue to differentiate expression when the connection to democracy is less ambiguous. On April 26, 1968, Paul Cohen walked into the Los Angeles County Courthouse wearing a jacket emblazoned with the phrase "Fuck the Draft" to show his displeasure with the U.S. Selective Service and the American involvement in the Vietnam conflict. When California found him guilty of disturbing the peace by "offensive conduct," he appealed his case and eventually the U.S. Supreme Court found Cohen's expression protected.[20] We don't know for certain, but it's probably a safe bet that if he had been walking the corridors of the courthouse shouting "fuck" over and over, the court would be less concerned with his rights. It was because Cohen's speech was related to a political issue that it took on a heightened value worthy of First Amendment protection. While "offensive conduct" may be punished in California, offensive political speech is another matter. Writing for the court, Justice John Harlan II quoted a decision written by Justice Felix Frankfurter. "[O]ne of the prerogatives of American citizenship is the right to criticize public men and measures – and that means not only informed and responsible criticism but the freedom to speak foolishly and without moderation."[21] Other words might not have effectively expressed his feelings. The particular verb

16. A. Meiklejohn, *Free Speech and Its Relation to Self Government* (New York: Harper, 1948).
17. The Supreme Court decisions noting political speech at the "core" of the First Amendment include *Williams v. Rhodes*, 393 U.S. 23, 32 (1968); *Buckley v. Valeo*, 424 U.S. 1, 45 (1976); and *McConnell v. FEC*, 540 U.S. 93, 264 (2003).
18. *Banzhaff v. FCC*, 405 F.2d 1082 (D.C. Cir. 1968), *cert. denied*, 396 U.S. 842 (1969).
19. *Friends of the Earth v. FCC*, 449 F.2d 1164 (D.C. Cir. 1971).
20. *Cohen v. California*, 403 U.S. 15 (1971).
21. *Id.* at 26 (citing *Baumgartner v. United States*, 322 U.S. 665, 673–674 [1944]).

stenciled on Cohen's jacket may have been crude and distasteful, but the court refused to allow him to be punished for such an indiscretion given the nature of his expression.

If promoting democracy is the value of protecting free expression, it would follow that expression that does not contribute to the debate on issues does not rise to the same level of protection. As stated earlier, however, nearly all messages can be characterized as political. Advertising can be viewed narrowly as selling a product or it can be contextualized as promoting a consumer culture. Drawing a line is a difficult exercise.

Stability of Society

Bedrock Law
Political expression is granted a higher degree of freedom because of its value to the democratic process.

To promote a stable society, individuals must have the means to complain. Allowing for dissent actually helps to quell potential problems. If individuals are restricted in their expression, their pent-up frustrations could result in far more damaging actions than merely dissent. Frustration and the inability to speak out are the prerequisites for an uprising. As Dr. Martin Luther King, Jr. said, "a riot is the language of the unheard."[22] It may seem counterintuitive, but suppressing complaints and criticisms can lead to greater societal damage than allowing them.

The metaphor to think of here is a pot of water on the stove. As the water temperature rises, if the lid on the pot is tightly sealed, eventually the steam will build up enough pressure to blow off the lid. But if the pot is allowed to "let off steam" slowly, the pot is not damaged. Our society (the pot in the metaphor) is better served by allowing the citizenry to let off steam as necessary rather than trying to prevent it.

Marxist critics of our system point out another aspect of this metaphor. Allowing steam to escape means that the pot never changes. An exploding pot at least puts an end to the constant boiling. Critics might claim rather than addressing societal problems, accepting "controlled" dissent allows those in power to maintain the status quo while never having to do anything differently.[23]

Marxist criticism aside, the right to protest in America is regarded as highly valued because it *can* lead to changes in society. Picketers spend hours carrying signs, sometimes in inclement weather and other adverse conditions, precisely because they believe their actions will result in some kind of change. The Supreme Court protected the right of protest by recognizing the importance of picketing as a way of expressing that protest. In 1988, the Court struck down a law prohibiting picketing within 500 feet of a foreign embassy.[24] Congress had passed such a law not only to protect foreign diplomats from embarrassment but also to protect officials from possible security threats. The Court was less concerned with embarrassment than it was with the importance of security and asserted such protection could be provided in a manner that was less restrictive of free expression. As with every First Amendment right, this freedom is not absolute. The Supreme Court upheld a Colorado law restricting the activity of protesters within 100 feet of the entrance to a healthcare facility.[25] While finding that protesters still had free speech rights, the Court found that restricting their communication in this specific context did not completely eliminate their ability to express themselves, and that the distance imposed by the statute fairly balanced the protesters' rights and those of the clinic's patrons.

Imminent Lawless Action
In 1969, the Supreme Court ruled that speech that merely advocated the illegal use of force was protected, but speech that was likely to incite or produce **imminent lawless action** is not protected.

The Supreme Court's use of an **imminent lawless action** standard is a further example of this adherence to the value of free expression to protect a stable society. The Court is unwilling to protect expression that constitutes a danger to society. This will be covered in

22. M.L. King Speech, "The Other America," March 14, 1968, *at* www.gphistorical.org/mlk/mlkspeech/.
23. The successful demonstrations against U.S. troops in Vietnam and the protests of the civil rights movement are used to rebut the arguments of the Marxists.
24. *Boos v. Barry*, 485 U.S. 312 (1988).
25. *Hill v. Colorado*, 530 U.S. 703 (2000).

detail later, but for now it serves to illustrate the notion that free expression serves as a stabilizing force in society. If it is destabilizing to the point of public disruption, then it is not deserving of protection. There is a bit of irony here. If the Supreme Court were to rule on the right of a crackpot to advocate violence, it might not allow the government to prohibit their speech particularly if it constituted no threat of imminent lawless action. On the other hand, the very same advocacy presented by a more believable charismatic speaker might be actionable under this rule given its greater likeliness to incite violence. Viewed in this way, the government actually is permitted to regulate speakers based on their effectiveness. Ineffective speakers bear no threat to society, but those who can whip a crowd into some sort of frenzy might be considered a lawless hazard.[26]

If we value expression only because of its contribution to a stable society, a great deal of expression would not be protected. In fact, to promote stability, the only expression needing protection would be highly emotional speech – the kind likely to lead to violence if suppressed.

Bedrock Law

Some types of communication may pose so real and imminent a danger that the courts have ruled in favor of the government's right to restrain them.

Self-Fulfillment

Some contend that the true value of free expression is that it protects a basic human right. The ability to freely communicate is part of what defines us as being human. Viewed in this light, freedom of expression is a fundamental right and deserving of protection whether or not it promotes some public good. The values of promoting democracy, discovering truth, and maintaining stability are all societal goods, but free expression viewed as a human right has both intrinsic and extrinsic value. The Supreme Court has stated the importance of self-fulfillment in First Amendment cases for more than 30 years.[27] There is a litany of philosophers from centuries past who have argued for the freedom of self-realization.[28]

After all, when we think about the kind of expression needing protection, isn't it the emotional expression a speaker uses when they are especially passionate about a topic? People who get worked up over something are often the ones who are outspoken and who may use language that offends or upsets others (as was the case with Cohen's jacket). In this chapter, we have seen how different instances of offensive speech resulted in legal action that was appealed all the way to the U.S. Supreme Court. Such expression certainly can be political, but it is also most definitely self-fulfilling. People engaged in such communication make political statements, but they also make personal statements. Their expression is likely to be far more visceral than some corporation speaking only to drive up its profits or even a candidate whose speech has been massaged by a political consultant hoping to win the most votes.

From the Trenches: Free Speech and the Right to Panhandle

By Jane Henegar

The First Amendment defends all kinds of expressive content. Following an ACLU of Indiana lawsuit, a federal court struck down a state law that would have prohibited all attempts to solicit donations, or to "panhandle," on the public streets in the state of Indiana. The court quoted Frederick Douglass in the decision:

26. See *Brandenburg v. Ohio*, 395 U.S. 444 (1969).
27. For example, *Police Department of Chicago v. Moseby*, 408 U.S. 92 (1972), at 95–96. "To permit the continued building of our politics and culture, and to assure self-fulfillment for each individual, our people are guaranteed the right to express any thought, free from government censorship."
28. The list includes such famous names as Dewey, Kant, Spinoza, Hobbes, Voltaire, and Hume. *See* 1 M. Adler, *The Idea of Freedom* 171–201 (New York: Doubleday & Co., 1961).

> No right was deemed by the fathers of the Government more sacred than the right of speech. . . . Liberty is meaningless where the right to utter one's thoughts and opinions has ceased to exist. That, of all rights, is the dread of tyrants. It is the right which they first of all strike down.
>
> *Indiana Civil Liberties Union, Inc. v. Superintendent, Indiana State Police*, 2020 WL 3546018 (7th Cir. 2020)

The ACLU filed the 2020 lawsuit on behalf of its staff members who regularly hand out copies of the Constitution and solicit donations to the organization for its work defending individuals' civil liberties, such as freedom of speech.

The courts have repeatedly stated that the First Amendment makes no distinction between whether persons are soliciting funds for recognized charities, for third parties, or for themselves. As the Second Circuit noted in striking down a New York law banning begging,

> Even without particularized speech, however, the presence of an unkempt and disheveled person holding out his or her hand or a cup to receive a donation itself conveys a message of need for support and assistance. We see little difference between those who solicit for organized charities and those who solicit for themselves in regard to the message conveyed. The former are communicating the needs of others while the latter are communicating their personal needs. Both solicit the charity of others. The distinction is not a significant one for First Amendment purposes.
>
> *Loper v. New York City Police Department*, 999 F.2d 699, 704 (2d Cir. 1993) (internal citations omitted)

Freedom of speech under the First Amendment to the U.S. Constitution clearly prohibits government restrictions that target particular speech content, such as Indiana's panhandling statute. Who expresses that content or the manner in which that content is conveyed – whether with words, an outstretched hand, an artist's image, or a sign – does not matter.

Jane Henegar is Executive Director of the ACLU of Indiana

So, Then, Which Value Is the Important One?

Obviously, this question is not to be taken seriously. *All* four values espoused by Emerson can be found in philosophical arguments, sociological data, and court decisions. If discovery of truth were the *only* reason for valuing free expression, then any expression not directly advancing the cause of truth would be undeserving of protection. A lot of advertising simply provides brand awareness rather than information and as such does not advance the discovery of truth. Advertising also might lose some protection if free speech's only purpose is to protect individual self-fulfillment, as very little advertising is motivated by the desire to express oneself.[29] If it is only necessary to uphold democracy, then political messages might be the only ones protected – and then only voices of dissent if the object is mainly to create a stable society.

Our deeply held protection of free expression encompasses all of the values Emerson identifies. The concept of free expression is rather complex and, quite frankly, misunderstood by many Americans. Surveys have shown that more Americans can identify the five

29. One exception to this might be advocacy advertising, such as the sort encouraging some sort of social cause (safe sex/abstinence, environmental issues, etc.).

members of the cartoon Simpson family than can identify the five freedoms protected by the First Amendment.[30] Opinions about free expression change based on political climate, most notably Americans' sense of security. The First Amendment Center conducts an annual survey on the state of the First Amendment. Immediately following the terrorist attacks of September 11, 2001, survey results showed a much lower level of support for the rights of free expression, but the percentages have been gradually increasing to pre-9/11 levels.[31]

Because free expression is such a complex concept, it is often frustrating for people studying the subject for the first time. Students who have spent years learning to provide the "right answers" to their teachers and professors want to be given one true answer. Yet because so many elements are involved in the analysis of free expression, the answer often must be, "It depends." There are a number of factors determining how far the First Amendment extends, and so a simple *yes* or *no* answer is often inadequate and inappropriate. In the next section, we will examine a variety of factors that affect the decision about whether the expression is protected.

Global View

Most Americans are proud of the protections provided by the First Amendment and might even boast of having the freest environment for expression in the world. Most of the rest of the world would disagree. Each year, Reporters Without Borders ranks 180 countries in its World Freedom Index. The Index is based on seven scales that include pluralism, media independence, and self-censorship. In 2023, Norway had the best overall ranking (the top nine countries were all in Europe), while North Korea had the worst score. The United States came in at 45th – dropping from 42nd the year before. Reporters Without Borders found major structural barriers to press freedoms such as declining local news and increased partisanship. For advocates of free expression, it must be disappointing that the group says the United States was "*once* considered a model for freedom of expression" (emphasis added).[32]

Deconstructing the First Amendment

To better understand the First Amendment, let's take it apart and examine the words closely.

Congress: The First Amendment begins, "Congress shall make no law. . . . " Obviously, this term applies first and foremost to the U.S. Congress, but it also applies to the president of the United States and all the executive agencies created by the government (including the Federal Communications Commission, Federal Trade Commission, etc.). Through a sequence of legal decisions, we have come to interpret "Congress" as "government." Government means all branches of government – executive, legislative, and judicial. We are told the founders used the "Congress" language because the legislature was seen as the branch responsible for making laws, but a more valid view would show that when courts interpret the law and executive agencies issue and enforce rules authorized by Congress, they, too, are engaged in governance.

At first, it may have just meant the federal government, but thanks to the Fourteenth Amendment,[33] the same restriction on the federal government also applies to state and local

30. Howard Troxler, "Even Homer Can Defend Our Nation's 5 Freedoms," *St. Petersburg Times*, March 5, 2006, at 1B.
31. The latest results can be found at https://www.freedomforum.org/first-amendment-survey-2023/.
32. The entire list, with annotations, is available at https://rsf.org/en/index.
33. Section 1 of the Fourteenth Amendment reads, "All persons born or naturalized in the United States, and subject to the jurisdiction thereof, are citizens of the United States and of the State in which they reside. No State shall make or enforce any law which shall abridge the privileges or immunities of citizens of the United States; nor shall any State deprive any person of life, liberty,

governing bodies. Whether the original intention of the framers was for the Bill of Rights to apply to only the federal government or to be extended to the states makes for a great constitutional debate, but the point is moot; the Fourteenth Amendment is now understood to make the First Amendment applicable to all states.

Incorporating the First Amendment

Americans may not realize all five of the freedoms guaranteed by the First Amendment are applied to the states through landmark rulings of the U.S. Supreme Court. This authority is based on the incorporation doctrine, where equal protection is granted in the Fourteenth Amendment that was adopted to protect the rights of newly freed slaves after the Civil War. That same provision now protects all Americans in certain areas. Free speech, for instance, was incorporated in 1925 when the Court interpreted "Congress" to mean all government bodies.[34] The facts went against the defendant but affirmed our freedom of speech.

Benjamin Gitlow was arrested for distributing pamphlets about a "Left Wing Manifesto," which New York police charged with advocating the overthrow of the government by promoting a new socialist world order. Gitlow was convicted for violating a state criminal anarchy statute, which the U.S. Supreme Court held to be constitutional under the First Amendment. Today, it is unlikely Gitlow would be convicted under such a criminal anarchy statute but sharing such radical beliefs in a pamphlet at that time cost him his freedom.

The other four rights incorporated by the U.S. Supreme Court can be found in subsequent rulings including landmark cases on newspaper censorship (*Near v. Minnesota*, 1931);[35] religious freedom (*Cantwell v. Connecticut*, 1940);[36] non-establishment of state religion (*Everson v. Board of Education*, 1947);[37] freedom of assembly (*DeJonge v. Oregon*, 1937);[38] and right of petition (*Edwards v. South Carolina*, 1963).[39]

Local jurisdictions are also included, so that city government, public schools, and local police are prohibited from restricting free expression rights. This means not only legislatures and police are barred from restricting free expression, but other government entities – like public schools and universities – are barred as well.

Note the adjective "public" in "public schools." Public schools and public universities are a part of the government because they are publicly funded. There is no question that public schools and public universities must comply with the First Amendment's free expression directive, but what about private schools? Are they bound to abide by the First Amendment? The answer is not so clear, although courts have generally taken the position that a private school's restriction of free expression would not be a violation of the First Amendment because there is no *state action* involved.[40]

or property, without due process of law; nor deny to any person within its jurisdiction the equal protection of the laws."

34. *Gitlow v. New York*, 268 U.S. 252 (1925).
35. 283 U.S. 697 (1931).
36. 310 U.S. 296 (1940).
37. 330 U.S. 1 (1947).
38. 299 U.S. 353 (1937).
39. 372 U.S. 229 (1963).
40. In 2000, a student was expelled from a New York private school because he maintained a website the school considered "inappropriate." The family's lawsuit in federal district court was dismissed because the school was not a government entity for First Amendment purposes. *Ubriaco v. Albertus Magnus High School*, 2000 U.S. Dist. LEXIS 10141 (2000).

Private actors who restrict free expression through whatever means are generally not in violation of the First Amendment. They may be guilty of other legal infractions but not limiting a constitutional right of free speech. For example, if your friend covers your mouth to keep you from speaking, it might be considered battery (unlawful touching), but it would not violate the First Amendment. If someone does not like the same political candidate you do and tears down the sign you've placed in your yard to show your support, it's probably trespassing and vandalism, but it's not a violation of the First Amendment. Newspapers that refuse to publish a story, or radio and television stations that refuse to air a program, or even social media blocking a user might all be accused of "censorship,"[41] but unless they are government-operated, they are not infringing on anyone's First Amendment rights.

In 2019, the Supreme Court decided that a private company overseeing cable public access channels in New York did not become a government actor just because it imposed restrictions on two cable performers, who felt their First Amendment rights were violated. The Manhattan Neighborhood Network (MNN) banned two activists who wanted to show a documentary about the cable access channel but were denied access. The filmmakers then filed suit claiming their First Amendment rights were violated because MNN was a traditional public forum, and this action would be discrimination against them. If MNN's parent company, the Manhattan Community Access Corp., had been ruled a state actor, the ban would be unconstitutional, but the Court majority held that providing a public forum does not automatically turn a corporation into a state actor. Overseeing cable TV access is not a "traditional, exclusive public function."[42]

Bedrock Law

The First Amendment specifies "Congress," but it applies to other lawmaking bodies that serve as tax-supported representatives of government.

While it is often easy to tell when a restriction on expression comes from the government, there are times when it can become complicated, and that's when context does matter. You don't usually think of janitors at your university as government actors, but they *could become* ones if they selectively remove posters around campus based on the poster's content. Or suppose a student at State Public University (SPU) likes to wear clothes with the brand name and logo of a rival school, Other Public State University (OPSU). Now imagine a cranky professor bans the student from class for wearing OPSU clothes, would that be a First Amendment violation because the prof is paid as a government employee? The answer is yes. So how about students who work for the Admissions Office and give tours of SPU, can they maintain their right to wear OPSU clothes while working? The answer is no because the Admissions Office just like any other employer would have the authority to refuse them that right.

Shall make no law: "Make no law" may seem less ambiguous than it really is. Despite the tautological argument claiming, "no law means no law," the Supreme Court has never adopted such an approach to the First Amendment. The First Amendment restricts government from preventing people from expressing their opinions, but what about them spreading wild conspiracy theories or dangerous misinformation? The right of free expression is *not* absolute. There are limits to what the law will allow. Perhaps the most famous example of this limit is the pithy quote from U.S. Supreme Court Justice Oliver Wendell Holmes, Jr. mentioned earlier,[43] "The most stringent protection of free speech would not protect a man in falsely shouting fire in a theatre and causing a panic."[44] Most Americans support limiting free expression in areas where it would endanger national security, unfairly damage the reputation of individuals, or corrupt children. The difficulty lies in deciding exactly

41. While the term *censorship* is sometimes used to define government restriction of expression, its colloquial use often includes other limitations that are not government action. In fact, the phrase "self-censorship," used by the Supreme Court in dozens of cases, implies that censorship can occur without state action.
42. *Manhattan Community Access Corp. v. Halleck*, 587 U.S. _ (2019).
43. *Schenck v. U.S.*, supra note 8.
44. *Id.* at 52.

when it does these things and how to prohibit those expressions while still protecting other communications.

"Make no law" translates to more than just legislation. It is necessary to incorporate other government action. Administrative rules passed by federal agencies are law, and so are city ordinances, school board regulations, and even student codes of conduct at public institutions. Sometimes a law can be ruled as constitutional, but the manner in which it is enforced is not. Thus, when a law or rule is enforced in such a way as to violate someone's right of expression, it is still a First Amendment violation, and the courts have a duty to protect that right.

In 1993, Gloria Bartnicki used her cell phone to talk with the president of a local teachers' union about the negotiations she was handling for them with a school district in Pennsylvania. The calls were intercepted by a third party, and recordings were passed among several people, including a radio talk show host, who aired a portion of the tape. Bartnicki filed a lawsuit against the broadcaster, claiming that the interception of her telephone conversation was in violation of a portion of the Omnibus Crime Control and Safe Streets Act of 1968, prohibiting forms of wiretapping and electronic surveillance. The Supreme Court refused to hold radio show host Frederick Vopper responsible for airing a confidential telephone conversation. The ruling was *not* a finding of anything constitutionally wrong with the Omnibus Crime Control and Safe Streets Act. The Court ruled that applying this law to Vopper, a third party not involved in intercepting the call, would violate his First Amendment rights.[45] A law that may or may not infringe on freedom of expression might be found unconstitutional as applied in a particular instance. That was the Supreme Court's response to Frederick Vopper's playing of the tape-recorded phone conversation on his radio program; the law itself was constitutional, but the law as applied was unconstitutional.

Respecting an establishment of religion, or prohibiting the free exercise thereof: The focus of this textbook is communication, not religion, so we will not dwell on this portion of the First Amendment. Lots of excellent texts exist on the topic. Briefly stated, government actors are prohibited from both favoring and disfavoring religion. Public schools cannot schedule time for prayer during class or a graduation ceremony (that would respect an establishment of religion), but neither can they prevent students on their own from organizing popular "prayer at the pole" activities before school,[46] or thanking God during a graduation speech by the class president (that would be prohibiting the free exercise thereof). As with any constitutional provision, the questions get complicated. Is it "respecting the establishment of a religion" for a university to allow a student religious group to use university buildings for meetings? In 1981, the Supreme Court ruled allowing secular groups to use facilities while prohibiting religious groups would be "prohibiting the free exercise of" religion.[47]

Abridging: *Abridging* freedom of speech can occur through a variety of means. The plain meaning of the term *abridge* is to diminish or reduce in scope. Thus, to abridge freedom of speech is to engage in any government action that diminishes free expression. Laws that prevent people from registering a trademark because someone will consider the term offensive are unconstitutional because they abridge freedom of speech. Laws that prohibit criticism of the government abridge freedom of speech. Public school teachers who prohibit nondisruptive protests abridge freedom of speech.

Obviously, laws that explicitly prohibit particular views or ideas would abridge this right, but so might laws or government action that discourage free expression without overtly restricting it. The Supreme Court repeatedly refers to the "chilling effect" such government

45. *Bartnicki v. Vopper*, 532 U.S. 514 (2001). Specifically, the Court claimed that the unique circumstances that protected Vopper were the facts that he had no part in the illegal interception of the phone call, that he obtained the tapes legally, and that the content of the recordings was a public concern. *Id.* at 525.
46. "See You at the Pole" has been promoted since the 1990s as an activity where students gather at the school flagpole before the school day to pray. So long as it is not sanctioned by a public school, it is protected expression.
47. *Widmar v. Vincent*, 454 U.S. 263 (1981).

actions can have on free expression, whereby speakers refrain from speaking for fear of punishment. This effect most often occurs when a law is vague and can be interpreted to apply to a wide variety of communications or behaviors, well beyond whatever is intended for regulation. In these instances, the laws are considered to have a "chilling effect" on expression that would not be deemed illegal. For example, Congress passed the Communications Decency Act (CDA) into law in 1996. It was an attempt to regulate content on the Internet to keep obscene and indecent material away from minors. As soon as the CDA became law, it was challenged in court (more than one court, actually).

The CDA was ruled to be unconstitutional for many reasons (discussed in detail in a later chapter), but one of those reasons was the vagueness of the rules. The Court stated, "The vagueness of such a regulation raises special First Amendment concerns because of its obvious chilling effect on free speech."[48] In other words, speakers might restrict themselves from saying certain things for fear that they might subsequently be punished, when in fact the speech in which they would engage would be constitutional.

Chilling Effect
The consequence of vague restrictions on speech causing speakers to restrain themselves from saying certain things for fear of punishment, when in fact their speech is constitutionally protected.

The first time the U.S. Supreme Court majority used the **chilling effect** argument to assert that a law was preventing expression that should otherwise be protected was in the landmark libel case of *New York Times Co. v. Sullivan*[49] (discussed extensively in Chapter 5). In unanimously finding that an Alabama libel law could not hold *The New York Times* responsible for libeling a public official without also showing that the paper had acted with a knowledge of falsity or a reckless disregard for the truth, the Court broke new ground in 1964 by prohibiting punishment for criticizing government officials, even if some minor parts of the criticism were later proven to be false. Those criticizing public officials must be given the "breathing room" required. Errors must be allowed so long as they are not intentional to protect the robust sort of debate that is necessary. If speakers are fearful that a single misstatement can result in punishment, they might be overly cautious and avoid any commentary that is not absolutely, 100% provable. While some people who feel they have been maligned by the media would prefer this to be the standard, our value on free expression is too great to permit such a restriction. In the *Sullivan* libel case, the Court quoted from a decision a couple years earlier that error must be protected if the First Amendment is to have the "breathing space" it requires to survive.[50]

Compelling Speech

Interestingly, one's speech also can be abridged if compelled to speak. Being made to speak if one would prefer to remain silent is another means of abridging free expression. This was the essence of the *303 Creative v. Elenis* case that opens this chapter: whether a web designer could be required by law to create websites carrying messages they didn't agree with. As already discussed, such a requirement violates the First Amendment.

The issue of compelled speech was first addressed by the Supreme Court in 1943. The West Virginia State Board of Education had made the Pledge of Allegiance a daily requirement in its classrooms for both students and teachers. Expulsion and fines were possible for those refusing to participate. A group of Jehovah's Witnesses filed suit against the law, claiming it violated their religious beliefs.[51] Somewhat surprisingly, the Court did not address the issue as much from religious grounds as from a freedom of speech perspective. In finding the requirement unconstitutional, the decision stated,

48. *Reno v. ACLU*, 521 U.S. 844 (1997), at 871–872.
49. 376 U.S. 254 (1964).
50. Quoting *N.A.A.C.P. v. Button*, 371 U.S. 415 (1962).
51. Jehovah's Witnesses believe that no "graven images" should be bowed to or served, in keeping with God's commandments as set forth in the book of Exodus. Pledging allegiance to a flag for them constitutes bowing to a graven image.

> To sustain the compulsory flag salute we are required to say that a Bill of Rights which guards the individual's right to speak his own mind, left it open to public authorities to compel him to utter what is not in his mind.[52]

The Court asserted that compelling speech is abridging speech, putting to rest an earlier Supreme Court decision upholding the pledge as necessary to create "cohesive sentiment" in support of national unity.[53]

Does this then mean that people could refuse to pay their taxes if those tax dollars were being used to support speech with which they did not agree? In 1996, some students attending the University of Wisconsin were upset because they had to pay over $300 per year in student activity fees, largely to support student organizations. They were particularly upset because some of the money went to support student associations like the Wisconsin Student Public Interest Research Group, a social activist group. The U.S. Supreme Court allowed the university to continue collecting and distributing fees providing it did so in a viewpoint-neutral manner (in other words, not favoring or disfavoring any groups based on their viewpoints).[54]

Because this type of support for the Wisconsin student organization is a viewpoint-neutral means of distribution, it was held to be constitutional, unlike the situation a few years earlier involving compelled speech and the California State Bar Association. The Bar is an organization that attorneys must belong to in California to practice law. They have no choice but to pay their dues if they want to work. Twenty-one members of the California Bar filed suit claiming that the Bar used a portion of their dues to support political and ideological causes, and thus their dues were a form of compelled speech, violating their First Amendment rights. The U.S. Supreme Court declared the Bar could not require its members to pay dues to support speech that members did not support.[55] Dues could be required of members, but that money could not then fund expressive activity.

The Court followed the precedent it had established in an earlier case dealing with labor unions and compelled speech. Michigan had authorized union representation for nonunion government employees. Rather than requiring employees to join the union, employees could opt instead to pay a "service charge" to the union. After all, nonunion government employees also benefited when the union negotiated labor contracts. Some teachers filed suit against the Detroit Board of Education, refusing to pay compulsory dues to the teachers' union. Rather than invalidate the arrangement, the Court held that the portion of the service charge used to fund expression could not be required of nonunion employees. The Court had no problem with a requirement that nonunion employees had to pay for union representation, but it refused to allow the union to assess nonmembers for the promotion of its ideology. Quoting Thomas Jefferson, the Court stated, "[T]o compel a man to furnish contributions of money for the propagation of opinions which he disbelieves is sinful and tyrannical."[56] Unlike the University of Wisconsin case, the rules for the California Bar and Michigan school teachers were unconstitutional because the ideological speech that members' fees were funding could be distinguished from the other activities of the Bar and the union.

The Beef Promotion and Research Act of 1985 contained a provision requiring cattle farmers to pay one dollar per head on the sale or import of cattle, and that money would be used for the promotion of beef (perhaps you've heard their "Beef – It's What's for Dinner" slogan). The Livestock Marketing Association challenged the law by arguing that cattle farmers were being compelled to subsidize speech. Unlike the compelled speech cases mentioned earlier, the Supreme Court did not find this law encroaching on the First Amendment.

52. *West Virginia State Bd. of Ed. v. Barnette*, 319 U.S. 624 (1943), at 634.
53. *Minersville School District v. Gobitis*, 310 U.S. 586 (1940).
54. *Board of Regents v. Southworth*, 529 U.S. 217 (2000).
55. *Keller v. State Bar of Cal.*, 496 U.S. 1 (1990).
56. *Abood v. Detroit Board of Ed.*, 431 U.S. 209 (1977), at 235.

The critical difference was it was *government* speech, and citizens have no First Amendment right not to fund government speech.[57] It would be a real Pandora's Box to permit taxpayers to refuse to pay a portion of their taxes anytime they claimed the government promoted policies with which the people did not agree.

The Curious Case of License Plates

A surprising number of First Amendment cases have dealt with automobile license plates. One controversy is how far the state can go in restricting what people choose to put on "vanity plates." People pay extra to request specific letters or numbers on their ***state-issued*** license plates. Despite legalizing marijuana, Colorado prohibits words referencing the substance.[58] On the other hand, a federal judge in Michigan ruled the First Amendment applies to messages on license plates, and a consent agreement prevents Michigan from censoring plates that it finds in "bad taste."[59] A Georgia motorist received a $24,000 settlement after he sued the state for denying him plates reading "GAYGUY" and "4GAYLIB." Vermont had a much bigger bill when it had to pay $150,000 in legal fees for denying a driver the plate JN36TN, a reference to the New Testament Bible verse John 3:16. New Hampshire had a prohibition on religious references on vanity plates, which an appeals court held was unconstitutional.[60] In 2020, California's law allowing the state to deny vanity plate applications for messages "offensive to good taste and decency" was struck down as a violation of free speech.[61]

Another interesting question is whether states can compel people to say things via a license plate. What if a state's motto is printed on a license plate, and that motto is considered offensive to some? That was the case when New Hampshire added the motto, "Live Free or Die" to its plates in 1969. Jehovah's Witnesses George and Maxine Maynard found the slogan in violation of their religious beliefs, so he first covered it up with red tape, and then cut it off the plates. Maynard was fined twice and refused to pay, for which he was sent to jail. Citing its earlier decision striking down mandatory pledges in schools, the Supreme Court stated "the right of freedom of thought protected by the First Amendment against state action includes both the right to speak freely and the right to refrain from speaking at all"[62] and allowed Maynard to cover the state slogan.

In addition to raising revenue by offering personalized plates, states often offer motorists the opportunity to purchase specialized plates to support not-for-profit organizations. The surcharge for the plates is divided between the state and the charity. Universities, arts groups, animal welfare groups, and many others have realized an added source of revenue this way. But what happens when a group wants its symbol included that the state would rather not have on its license plates? The Sons of Confederate Veterans wanted the Confederate flag used on Texas license plates purchased to support the group. In a 5–4 decision, the U.S. Supreme Court ruled that Texas had the right to deny the group a symbol it found to be objectionable. Just as New Hampshire could not force residents to display plates with messages against their beliefs, the Sons of Confederate Veterans could not force Texas to display a "message" it considered

57. *Johanns v. Livestock Mkting. Association*, 544 U.S. 550 (2005).
58. "Is Censoring Vanity License Plates: A Violation of Free Speech?" September 21, 2016, *at* http://denver.cbslocal.com/2016/09/21/vanity-license-plates-colorado-marijuana/.
59. "Judge: Free Speech Applies to Michigan Vanity Plates," September 4, 2014, *at* www.indystar.com/story/news/politics/2014/09/04/judge-free-speech-applies-michigan-vanity-plates/15058711/.
60. "Vanity License Plate Rules Lead to Free Speech Fights," July 31, 2013, *at* http://blogs.lawyers.com/2013/07/vanity-plate-free-speech/.
61. *Ogilvie v. Gordon*, 540 F. Supp. 3d 920 (N.D. Cal. 2020).
62. *Wooley v. Maynard*, 430 U.S. 705 (1977), at 714.

to be unacceptable.[63] The same group tried to raise the question when North Carolina did away with the Confederate flag on plates, but in 2023 the Supreme Court refused to take the case.

Freedom of speech: The First Amendment protects "speech," but speech takes many forms. Earlier we explained how a Texas law prohibiting burning the U.S. flag in protest violated the freedom of speech. In Chapter 4, you'll read about middle school students wearing black armbands to school, another form of protected "speech," although no words were spoken. Sometimes "actions" can be considered speech. Protesters wearing armbands, badges, or holding signs may be uttering no words, but their "actions" have meaning, and this symbolic form of speech is protected. We recognize that there are times when actions are forms of protected expression. Is it speech or action to flash a car's headlights to signal other motorists that a speed trap is ahead? Courts in both Missouri and Oregon have ruled that flashing a car's headlights (a common signal that police are near) is protected free expression. A federal district court in Missouri ruled that motorists have the right to communicate with each other on the road,[64] while a county court in Oregon said, "the government cannot enforce the traffic laws, or any other laws, to punish drivers for their expressive conduct."[65]

The reverse is also true when words are not speech, but action. Earlier we quoted the words of Justice Holmes who famously reasoned that falsely shouting "fire" in a theater would not be protected speech. The best way to understand this idea is to recognize that in this case, the speaker is not so much engaged in expression as in action. Shouting "fire" in this situation is not protected as free expression because the "speaker" isn't engaging in expression at all – the speaker is inciting a panic. The First Amendment is intended to protect expression, not action. It might seem self-evident that words are expression but that is not always the case. This concept may be even easier to see using the word *fire* in another context. Suppose for a moment a violent gang bound and gagged someone and pointed their guns at the victim. Imagine then the gang leader says, "Fire," and the gangsters shoot the victim. Would the gang leader be able to successfully defend his actions in court by claiming he was merely exercising his right of free speech? Certainly, no court would accept this argument; so, why not? The utterance was more than speech; it was action – the criminal action of inciting murder. In this instance, "speaking" was not expression. Whenever speech is mixed in with illegal activity, it can be punished as a crime, including such deeds as sexual harassment, blackmail, perjury, conspiracy, and fraud. However, other personal activities may be protected by the First Amendment.

Spending money can be a form of protected speech. When it comes to funding campaigns for public office, this question has caused a lot of controversy. When Congress was attempting to create campaign finance reform laws, the Supreme Court upheld some of the rules while finding other parts of the legislation unconstitutional.[66] The Federal Election Campaign Act of 1971 limited the amount individuals could contribute to candidates in presidential elections, and it also limited the amount they could spend on their own to express their support for candidates or the amount candidates could spend on their own campaigns. The Court upheld the limits on individual contributors, holding it was reasonable to restrict the amount to prevent improper influence or even the appearance of improper influence on a candidate. When it came to restricting how much an individual could spend on their own speech though, the Court would not allow such a limit to stand.

63. *Walker v. Texas Division, Sons of Confederate Veterans*, 576 U.S. 200 (2015).
64. *Elli v. Ellisville*, 997 F. Supp. 2d 980 (E. Dist. MO. 2014).
65. Other states, including Alaska, Arizona, and North Dakota make flashing headlights illegal. *See* Judge Rules Flashing Headlights Are Free Speech in Oregon, *at* https://www.foxnews.com/politics/judge-rules-flashing-headlights-is-free-speech-in-oregon-case.
66. *Buckley v. Valeo*, 424 U.S. 1 (1975).

> A restriction on the amount of money a person or group can spend on political communication during a campaign necessarily reduces the quantity of expression by restricting the number of issues discussed, the depth of their exploration, and the size of the audience reached. This is because virtually every means of communicating ideas in today's mass society requires the expenditure of money.[67]

After *Buckley*, restrictions could be imposed on how much candidates are allowed to accept in donations from any individual or organization, but those same individuals and organizations would be free to spend as much as they like, however they like to spend it.

As a result, the **political action committee (PAC)** became a powerful force in U.S. politics. PACs were growing more influential with each election. PACs exist to collect money from constituents in order to use those funds in support of candidates, or just as likely, to defeat candidates. PACs are organized around a particular business, trade association, or political ideology. There's usually no way to know just from the name whether a group is liberal (Onward Together) or conservative (Alliance Defending Freedom), Republican (America First) or Democrat (Midwest Values). Once satisfied just to donate money, in the twenty-first century the groups became more active in producing their own content. One well-known attack created by the PAC called Swift Boat Veterans for Truth claimed that presidential candidate Sen. John Kerry was "unfit to serve." The ads created quite a stir and may have played a role in Kerry losing the 2004 election. In 2010, a major Supreme Court ruling held PACs could not be restricted in their spending the way individuals were restricted by the Campaign Act of 1971. Unlike individuals, PACs could not appear to be corrupted by large contributions and a restriction was thus unnecessary.[68] Corporations were judged to have First Amendment rights.

Political Action Committees

Tax-exempt organizations to raise money for influencing the outcome of elections and/or legislation, PACs may lawfully collect donations from individuals, businesses, and not-for-profit organizations, including unions and volunteer groups.

The issue was the televised sponsorship of *Hillary: The Movie*, a critical look at her candidacy during the 2008 presidential campaign. Putting aside the question of how much the decision in favor of the conservative group Citizens United affects the democratic process, this 5–4 decision stands as a lesson in First Amendment law. Here is what makes the case special: first, the length of 176 pages of the Court's decision, which is unusual, especially in terms of the 90-page dissent. Second, both the majority and the dissenting justices criticize each other's use of *stare decisis*. Justice Kennedy argued it was necessary to reverse the Court's reasoning in *Austin v. Michigan Chamber of Commerce* (1990) by reminding his colleagues that if *stare decisis* was taken to mean always upholding precedent-setting cases, then "segregation would be legal, minimum wage laws would be unconstitutional, and the Government could wiretap ordinary criminal suspects without first obtaining warrants." A better understanding of *stare decisis*, concluded Justice Kennedy, requires the Court to reverse precedent when the rule of law requires it.

The dissenting opinions, on the other hand, challenged the ruling that held it was an affront to free speech to uphold the Bipartisan Campaign Reform Act of 2002 preventing spending from a corporate treasury 30 days prior to an election. Justice Stevens read part of his dissent from the bench and that too was unusual. "Relying largely on individual dissenting opinions, the majority blazes through our precedents, overruling or disavowing a body of case law." The concerns raised by *Citizens United* have moved

67. *Id.* at 19.
68. *Citizens United v. Federal Election Commission*, 558 U.S. 310 (2010).

some to call for a constitutional amendment to reverse the notion that corporations should be treated the same as people, and their independent expenditures for campaign speech must be unfettered. One last point to make about this landmark decision is a cautionary one. It would be wrong to construe it as a partisan battle between Democrats and Republicans. One of the fiercest critics of the Supreme Court's decision in *Citizens United* was Sen. John McCain (R-AZ), and one of its strongest defenders is the American Civil Liberties Union (ACLU).

Impact of *Citizens United*[69]

Not many Supreme Court decisions stir so much outrage that a U.S. president criticizes the ruling during his State of the Union Address right to the faces of the sitting justices who wrote it. Yet that was the case after the ruling was handed down in ***Citizens United v. FEC*** (2010). President Obama, after nodding to the separation of powers granted to the other two branches of government assembled before him, claimed the ruling would "open the floodgates for special interests – including foreign corporations – to spend without limit in our elections." One Supreme Court justice, Samuel Alito, responded on the floor by shaking his head and saying, "Not true." Years later, President Obama, formerly a constitutional law professor, reaffirmed his objection to allowing political action committees, Super PACS, labor unions, and corporations to invest unlimited sums on electioneering campaigns, posing "real harm to our democracy . . . dark money floods our airwaves with more and more political ads that pull our politics into the gutter."[70]

Or of the press: Whether this clause indicates a special protection for institutionalized media (versus "speech") has been debated by the high court and legal scholars for years.[71] Some commentators assert the inclusion of speech and press rights should be interpreted in general terms freeing all forms of expression and that the First Amendment, with its protections for speech and press along with religion, assembly, and petition, should be read as a general protection of expression. On the other hand, others maintain the framers chose two different words, *speech* and *press*, because they viewed the rights as distinctive and distinguishable.

While recognizing the literal argument for distinguishing between speech and press freedoms, we prefer the perspective those terms simply encompass all forms of expression – print and spoken and more – since there were no forms of electronic communication in the eighteenth century. Despite the phrase "or of the press," the Supreme Court does not treat the press differently. For example, in 1972 a reporter was required to appear before a Kentucky grand jury. Paul Branzburg reported for his newspaper on illegal drug use he observed, and the grand jury wanted to investigate the perpetrators. He attempted to avoid testifying by claiming the First Amendment shielded him from having to testify. In a 5–4 decision, the Supreme Court ruled it was unwilling to grant the press a "testimonial privilege that other citizens do not enjoy."[72] In 1974, the Court held a California law that prohibited face-to-face interviews between prison inmates and news media did not violate the First Amendment. Inmates' free speech was not violated, but the Court also concluded the press's right of access to sources of information was no greater (or less) than that of the general public.[73]

69. 558 U.S. 310.
70. White House Press Release, January 21, 2015, *at* https://obamawhitehouse.archives.gov/the-press-office/2015/01/21/statement-president.
71. Potter Stewart, "Or of the Press," 26 *Hastings L. J.* 631 (1975).
72. *Branzburg v. Hayes*, 408 U.S. 665 (1972), at 690.
73. *Pell v. Procunier*, 417 U.S. 817 (1974).

Right of Association
The constitutional right of people to affiliate with groups, or not affiliate, as they choose. It includes the right to keep those affiliations private if desired.

After all, legal language is filled with redundancies, so it's easy to see how terms such as *speech* and *press* are different manifestations of the same concept since both are communication. People speak of "texting or messaging." Is there a difference between the two forms of communication? Maybe, but not enough to change their constitutional protection.

There are times when a distinction is made in law regarding the press when it comes to prior restraint (censorship) or the watchdog role it plays in checking political power, as Justice Hugo Black observed in *New York Times v. U.S.* (1971):[74]

> In the First Amendment the Founding Fathers gave the free press the protection it must have to fulfill its essential role in our democracy. The press was to serve the governed, not the governors. The Government's power to censor the press was abolished so that the press would remain forever free to censure the Government. The press was protected so that it could bare the secrets of government and inform the people.[75]

Peaceably to Assemble: The right of the people peaceably to assemble is not a concern for most media fighting for their own First Amendment rights of free expression, but it is a concern for the many public interest groups seeking to stage parades, protests, and rallies in public spaces. What's more, this phrase has been interpreted to incorporate other rights in addition to just assembling in public places, most notably the right of *association*. Do Americans have the right to belong to any organization of their choice? What if those organizations are subversive? Do they have the right to join these groups secretly and keep their memberships confidential? The answers may appear easy at first, but those questions actually present complex issues.

In 1951, the NAACP opened a regional office in Alabama. At that time, Alabama had a law that required, among other things, organizations doing business within the state to give the government a list of their members. The NAACP had never complied with the law. After five years, Alabama filed suit. The case made it all the way to the U.S. Supreme Court, which unanimously decided the NAACP should not be required to provide the names of its members to the government.[76] This is a principle that has been upheld in a multitude of situations, often as a means of protecting both the organization and its members. The logic is that some organizations might have fewer members if they were required to make their names a matter of public record. This danger is easy to see with noxious groups like the Ku Klux Klan, but it also might be true of other "mainstream" organizations not favored by some. In the context of Alabama in the 1950s, it is easy to imagine how some people would fear that their membership in the NAACP might result in action taken against them at work or in the community if their association were to be made public. Perhaps a liberal physician might fear conservative patients would choose another doctor if they knew about those personal political leanings. The result would be fewer members for the organization and a denial of the physician's right to freely associate with the group.

In another registration case involving Seattle's maritime trade, the Supreme Court held that a member of the Communist Party could not be penalized because he did not register as a member of a "subversive" group while working at a shipyard, which the government had classified as a "defense facility." The Subversive Activities Control Act of 1950 deemed it unlawful for any member of a Communist action group to work in a defense facility. The federal government tried to assert that, as part of its war powers, it could enact a law to limit such subversive activity. The Supreme Court agreed that the government could limit subversive *activity* but to prohibit someone's employment merely because they were a *member*

74. Ashley Alman, "Barack Obama: 'The Citizens United Decision Was Wrong' Politics," *Huffington Post*, January 22, 2015, *at* www.huffingtonpost.com/2015/01/21/barackobama-citizens-united_n_6517520.html.
75. *New York Times Co. v. United States*, 403 U.S. 713 (1971), at 717.
76. *NAACP v. Alabama*, 357 U.S. 449 (1958).

of a group infringed on their right of association under the First Amendment.[77] The Court was not limiting the government's ability to regulate illegal activity, but it was limiting its interference with the freedom of association. In fact, the Supreme Court earlier upheld the Subversive Activities Control Act requirement that the Communist Party register with the government.[78]

Does an organization have the right to discriminate? Does the right of association also include the right to *exclude* members? In a rather controversial case, the Supreme Court narrowly held the Boy Scouts did not have to allow an avowed homosexual to be an assistant scoutmaster.[79] While generally the law prohibits discrimination based on sexual orientation, the 5–4 ruling affirmed the Boy Scouts had a constitutional right of expressive association allowing them to exclude from their membership individuals whose presence affects the group's ability to advocate public or private viewpoints. New Jersey's public accommodation law, which prohibits discrimination, might prevent other groups from excluding members based on sexual orientation, but the Court found the Boy Scouts' position on homosexuality to be part of its creed, and to require the group to accept as a member someone who directly contradicted those values was to violate the group's First Amendment right of *expressive* association, meaning the group engaged in expressive activity as a normal part of the organization.

Petition the government for a redress of grievances: The petition clause completes the First Amendment, and even though it comes last in order it was foremost in the minds of the framers who noted in the Declaration of Independence the royal lack of response from the monarchy to their colonial petitions. "We have petitioned for redress in the most humble terms: our repeated petitions have only been answered by repeated injury." Thomas Jefferson and his fellow revolutionists felt the king's indifference was surely the mark of a tyrant.

It is the right to petition that gives the whole of the First Amendment its teeth because it guarantees the people can sue the government to recover from the loss of civil liberties. Before the Civil War, northern abolitionists seeking to end the South's reliance on slavery used the petition clause to encourage Congress to pass a bill of abolition. This right of redress promised in the First Amendment's petition clause, however, does not guarantee satisfaction with the result. It only promises public officials shall grant some access to the people they govern who have a public issue to address. In this way, it ensures a form of public dialogue. Today, the right of petition extends to all branches of government, which is why names on a petition are often gathered to effect changes in our schools, our governments, or even our taxes. The right of petition has come to mean that we as Americans are entitled to a nonviolent means of motivating our government to action.

Speaker Rights Versus Listener Rights

Something else to consider when examining why or how we protect free expression is the distinction between the rights of speakers and the rights of listeners. In 1984, the Supreme Court struck down a regulation that prohibited public broadcasting stations from editorializing. The majority found the law not only restricted speakers but denied listeners access to commentary on matters of public importance.[80] Often the rights are complementary, and protecting one results in a benefit to the other. When we protect the rights of speakers, listeners benefit from the opportunity to hear a multiplicity of views. This is the rationale underlying the marketplace of ideas discussed previously. It is the listeners who benefit when the rights of speakers are protected.

77. *U.S. v. Robel*, 389 U.S. 258 (1967).
78. *Communist Party v. Subversive Activities Control Bd.*, 367 U.S. 1 (1961).
79. *Boy Scouts of Am. v. Dale*, 530 U.S. 640 (2000).
80. *FCC v. League of Women Voters*, 468 U.S. 364 (1984).

It is not always a given that protecting speakers' rights is to the benefit of listeners and viewers, most notably when listeners would prefer to be shielded from certain communications. When Paul Cohen was allowed to wear his offensive jacket in a California courthouse, it was with the recognition that others might find it distasteful. And Gregory Lee Johnson's burning of the American flag at the Republican Convention of 1984 was "seriously offensive" to some people. In each of these instances and in many others, the Supreme Court recognized the rights of the speakers to express themselves – even in ways that might have been objectionable to others. The Court pointed out the ones offended by Cohen's jacket could "avoid further bombardment of their sensibilities simply by averting their eyes."[81]

Offensiveness is probably not enough to silence a speaker, in most cases. For years the U.S. Patent and Trademark Office denied trademark applications that it considered "scandalous or immoral." When one artist/musician requested a trademark for his Friends U Can't Trust brand (known as FUCT), the trademark office turned him down, but the Supreme Court noted, "there are a great many immoral and scandalous ideas in the world," but it would be a First Amendment violation to prevent them from being trademarked if they are only offensive.[82] The restriction was held to be overbroad.

In most cases, listeners can avoid offensive expressions, but some situations make it almost impossible. The Court has shown more sympathy in the circumstances of a *captive audience* than it has in situations like those in the California courthouse. In a number of instances in which audiences are unable to avoid communication, their right *not* to be subjected to offensive messages may outweigh the rights of those wanting to disseminate them. The Court has stated, "The First Amendment permits the government to prohibit offensive speech as intrusive when the 'captive' audience cannot avoid the objectionable speech."[83] Of course, the term *captive* is not absolute at all. The concept has changed noticeably over time. In a 1951 decision, the Supreme Court concluded that street preachers may take advantage of what is "in a sense, a captive audience."[84] Certainly individuals who must use the street to reach their destinations are no more captive than individuals who must conduct their business in a local courthouse. Despite the shifting concept of captivity, the courts still show a willingness to protect listeners from communications they do not wish to receive in situations where they have less opportunity to avoid an unwelcome message.

One of the reasons the U.S. Supreme Court prohibited religious invocations at official graduation ceremonies for public secondary schools is precisely because the audience in attendance, most notably the students, is a captive audience.[85] The Court found such invocations at Thanksgiving Day addresses were "worlds apart" from those gatherings where students and their families are captive audiences at graduation ceremonies.

One other area where listeners' rights have outweighed the rights of speakers has been in the listeners' own homes. In *Rowan v. United States Post Office*, the Supreme Court upheld a law allowing individuals to "block" mail they found offensive and to require the vendors of such advertising to remove their addresses from future mailing lists.[86] Rejecting the argument that such a rule violated the constitutional rights of those speakers wanting to reach their target audience, the Court adhered to the ancient notion that "a man's home is his castle into which not even the king may enter."[87] The Court was unwilling to give the speaker's rights preference over the listener's rights when the listener was within their own home.

81. *Cohen v. California*, supra note 14, at 21.
82. *Iancu v. Brunetti*, 588 U.S ___ (2019).
83. *Frisby v. Shultz*, 487 U.S. 474 (1988), at 487.
84. *Kunz v. New York*, 340 U.S. 290 (1951), at 298.
85. *Lee v. Wiseman*, 505 U.S. 577 (1992). The larger First Amendment issue in this case was whether such an invocation constituted an "establishment of religion," as constitutionally prohibited. In its analysis, the Court also addressed the captive audience.
86. 397 U.S. 728 (1970).
87. *Id.* at 737.

"That we are often 'captives' outside the sanctuary of the home and subject to objectionable speech and other sound does not mean we must be captives everywhere."[88]

Global View

The First Amendment was created in the United States to protect the freedom of expression, which is regarded globally as a basic human right. The right to speak your mind in public without fear of punishment is part of the Universal Declaration of Basic Human Rights recognized by the United Nations.

China views itself today as an emerging superpower of some preeminence, but when it comes to "First Amendment" styled guarantees of freedom, its citizens supposedly enjoy "freedom of speech, of the press, of assembly, of association, of procession and demonstration" provided by Article 35 of the People's Republic of China Constitution (1982). Juxtaposed with the U.S. First Amendment, the rights appear to be comparable, but of course the reality is something quite different.

Censorship is practiced routinely in China with the help of monitors scouring the Internet for hot-button terms like Tiananmen Square 1989, independent Taiwan, freedom for Tibet, or Falun Gong. Even the term "democracy" can silence a chatroom depending on its use and context in China. Social media outlets such as Facebook, Snapchat, or Instagram are prohibited for Chinese viewers and their devices.

On the other hand, anyone in the United States who enjoys the comedy of late-night TV talk shows understands how making fun of our leaders and celebrities is a cherished freedom. In 2013 Chinese President Xi Jinping visited with President Obama, and humorists lampooned the pair strolling together with a cartoon of Winnie the Pooh walking beside Tigger the Tiger. Chinese censors were not amused by their leader's depiction as a child's toy companion, and after banning the meme, they stalled the release in China of a motion picture featuring the same characters.

This sort of government censorship would seem relatively harmless until the suppression of news in Wuhan occurred in 2020. One doctor in particular, Dr. Li Wenliang, an ophthalmologist, blogged about the emerging coronavirus (COVID-19) early in 2020 but was arrested by state police and forced to sign a statement promising not to make any more "false comments on the internet." After Dr. Li's blogging and arrest became widely known, the Chinese version of Twitter (Weibo) lit up with public outrage: "The Wuhan government owes Dr. Li Wenliang an apology," and "We want freedom of speech," were among citizen comments censored by the Chinese government.[89]

Such tributes for a doctor who was only trying to save lives came late and were not fully recognized until after Dr. Li had contracted COVID-19. Li's death at the age of 33 was reported on February 7, 2020, after which the government issued an apology.

The "Climate" for Free Expression

After closely examining the words of the First Amendment and their interpretation over the centuries, it is clear the right of free expression is not an absolute, and it is moderated by other influences and conditions. The difficulty arises in understanding all the various environmental pressures and externalities that affect free expression. It might be useful here to use an environmental example as an analogy – the weather.

88. *Id.* at 738.
89. H. Tan, "Coronavirus Whistleblower Doctor Dies, Sparking Outpouring – and Censorship – on Social Media," *CNBC.com*, February 7, 2020, *at* www.cnbc.com/2020/02/07/hashtag-censored-after-coronavirus-whistleblower-doctors-death.html.

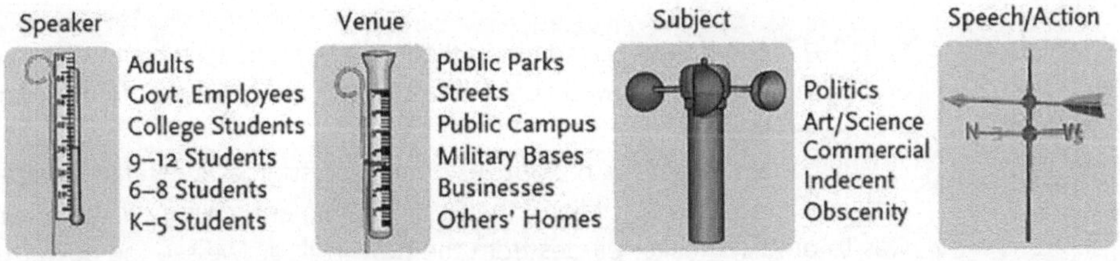

Figure 2.2 Measuring the "climate" for free expression

Bedrock Law

Weighing all the factors that could curb freedom of expression requires understanding the nature, content, and location of the communication.

Whenever someone complains about the heat, invariably someone else will add, "It's not just the heat, it's the humidity." When it's cold, meteorologists are always telling us about the "wind chill factor" because just knowing the temperature is not enough to know what it feels like outside. Each of these measures affects our "comfort level."

So it is, too, with our "free expression comfort level." There are multiple factors affecting how free we are to express ourselves. Just as an 80-degree day may "feel" warmer with 100% humidity, an adult, nongovernment speaker (highly protected) may have their speech restricted on private property. Each of the previously mentioned indicators reflects one of those factors. The higher up on each scale, the greater the free expression rights are. It is never enough to be at 100% protected on just one – the level on *all* the indicators is relevant. The illustration in Figure 2.2 provides a metaphor for the "climate" for free speech.

While a 100% level on any one of the indicators may not be enough to guarantee protected expression, it is a fair bet that a zero level on any of the indicators will result in unprotected expression. Speakers have very few rights of free expression in the privacy of other people's homes, regardless of their personal status as a speaker or the subject of their expression.

Anyone with an understanding of the First Amendment recognizes the many complexities involved in determining when expression is protected. There have been thousands of court cases involving restrictions on free expression. It would be naïve to believe that all of those could be resolved simply by asserting that free expression is constitutionally protected.

Ethical Dilemmas: Are Marginalized Groups Empowered or Oppressed by Free Expression?

The annual State of the First Amendment Survey, conducted by the First Amendment Center, found 29% of those surveyed believe the First Amendment "goes too far" in the rights it guarantees. That same study found 46% believe public institutions should revoke invitations to speak if they felt the speaker would be "likely to offend" some groups or individuals.

The First Amendment protects offensive speech, whether it's in a trademark, on a jacket, or in the expressive speech of burning a flag. But a significant portion of the public argues that expression that dehumanizes a group of people for their race, religion, sex, or sexual orientation crosses the line between speech and action and should be prohibited. A Black graduate student at Purdue University put it this way, "people with privileged identities who benefit from the oppression of marginalized people should not be allowed to determine what is crossing the line into threatening or hostile territory."[90] Even the American Civil Liberties Union, which has traditionally been a strong supporter of free speech rights, has stopped supporting First Amendment cases in which the speech can "inflict serious harm" on marginalized communities.[91]

90. U. Hester, "A Black Graduate Student's Perspective on University Speech Codes," *Diverse*, February 12, 2019, *at* https://diverseeducation.com/article/138410/.
91. W. Kaminer, "The ACLU Retreats From Free Expression," *Wall Street Journal*, June 20, 2018.

In 2017, the Knight Foundation asked college students which was more important, and 53% of those surveyed chose diversity and inclusion over free speech (only 46% chose speech).[92]

When members of the majority use free expression as a defense for attacks on marginalized groups, is that taking the First Amendment too far? If the original intention was to protect weaker parties from the powerful, do we see the powerful now using free expression to intimidate and humiliate the marginalized?

Summary

- Throughout the history of the United States, threats to national security have resulted in increased restrictions on free expression. In retrospect, most of those restrictions appear to have been unnecessary or excessive.
- In the United States, we value free expression for four reasons: because it is necessary to the discovery of truth; because a democratic system of government requires an informed electorate; because allowing free expression promotes stability in a society; and because part of what it means to be human is to be expressive.
- The First Amendment to the U.S. Constitution is a restriction on government infringement of the free speech of individuals and institutions. It does not prohibit any private restrictions on expression.
- The protection of free expression includes actions that are primarily expressive in nature, such as the burning of a flag. Conversely, not all words are necessarily deserving of protection as expression, such as ordering someone's execution.
- It's easy to understand that the First Amendment protects speakers, but it goes much further. Having the right to speak also implies the right not to be forced to speak. Protecting free expression to promote democracy implies that listeners' rights also need to be protected. There is a right to hear messages as well as the right to be free from hearing them.
- The U.S. Supreme Court has *never* held that free expression is an absolute. It must always be weighed against other rights. In determining the relative weight of free expression, courts consider factors such as the identity of the speaker, the venue, the subject of the expression, and whether the expression is more speech or more action.
- The First Amendment, like the rest of the U.S. Constitution, is a framework rather than an explicit list of rules. It has been subject to legal interpretation for more than 200 years and, as a living document, continues to evolve.

92. Free expression on campus: What college students think about First Amendment issues, *at* https://knightfoundation.org/reports/free-expression-on-campus-what-college-students-think-about-first-amendment-issues/.

3

Sedition and Censorship

LEARNING OBJECTIVES

After reading this chapter, you should know

- when government censorship is considered constitutional in the United States
- what legal restraints can be used in the United States to silence political dissent
- what forms of sedition have been historically subject to criminal law enforcement
- what the Supreme Court does to ensure First Amendment rights for dissent
- how tests such as the clear and present danger and imminent lawless action apply
- what standards of judicial review are used to evaluate controversial laws
- how the government attempts to censor speech and if prior restraint is constitutional

Until January 6, 2021, few people thought about or understood the term "sedition." The insurrection at the U.S. Capitol put the term front and center before the American people who questioned whether those involved were guilty of sedition. Eventually, militia group members and associates were charged with seditious conspiracy, and some, including members of the Oath Keepers, have been convicted.[1] But what exactly is sedition? Can words expressed to armed protesters to march to the Capitol and "fight like hell" and "take back our country" constitute sedition?[2]

Sedition
The common law crime of advocating and intending to bring about harm to the government.

Sedition generally means to incite, encourage, or promote the forceful overthrow of government. A crime of seditious conspiracy occurs when two or more people conspire to overthrow, put down, or destroy by force the government of the United States.[3] To be clear, this is different from "treason," which is a crime of intentionally committing an overt act against the United States in "levying War" or giving "Aid and Comfort" to its enemies.[4] So while treason is about actively levying war, sedition is about conspiring and inciting others to act against the state.

1. Michael Kunzelman & Alanna Durkin, "Jury Finds 4 Oath Keepers Guilty of Seditious Conspiracy in Jan. 6 Case," *PBS News*, January 23, 2023.
2. Paris Alston and Jeremy Siegel, "What Is 'Seditious Conspiracy' Could Trump Face Criminal Charges for Role in Jan, 6 Insurrection?" *GBH*, June 14, 2022, *at* https://www.wgbh.org/news/politics/2022-06-14/what-is-seditious-conspiracy-could-trump-face-criminal-charges-for-role-in-jan-6-insurrection.
3. 18 U.S.C. § 2384.
4. Art. III §3 U.S. Constitution; 18 U.S.C. § 2381.

DOI: 10.4324/9781003462989-3

Treason
Generally, it is the crime of betraying your sovereign nation. In U.S. law, treason is levying war against the United States or giving aid and comfort to its enemies.

Sedition is a Civil War-era charge that can result in 20 years behind bars, yet it is rarely charged because it is difficult to convict. Given that sedition typically occurs through speech or writings, it's not surprising that it comes in conflict with the constitutional right of free speech. Throughout history, sedition has been used as a means to criminalize political speech. The First Amendment weighs in the balance when critical views of the government are treated as sedition and may be chilled, suppressed, or otherwise censored.

Consider how offenses of treason and sedition took on new meaning after 9/11 when public sentiment favored security over censorship. In 2010, a militia group called "the Hutaree," operating in Michigan, Ohio, and Indiana, was charged with seditious conspiracy on suspicion of planning to kill law enforcement officers as a way to incite a wider rebellion against the U.S. government. The case was thrown out in 2012, however, with the judge ruling that talking about hatred of the government does not amount to sedition.[5]

Later, in the aftermath of the killing of George Floyd in 2020 by a white police officer in Minneapolis, the founder of the New York chapter of Black Lives Matter, Hawk Newsome, told a Fox News reporter, "If this country doesn't give us what we want, then we will burn down this system and replace it." President Trump reacted to Newsome's statement, tweeting, "This is Treason, Sedition, Insurrection!"[6] Did Newsome's words conspire to "overthrow, put down, or destroy by force" the government of the United States? Newsome explained "I could be speaking . . . figuratively. I could be speaking literally. It's a matter of interpretation." He was not charged.

Yet were the words leading up to the violent insurrection at the Capitol on January 6th a punishable crime of seditious conspiracy or political speech protected by the First Amendment? What exactly is the legal line between sedition and free speech? Is there a difference between seditious libel and seditious conspiracy? The answer is framed by a long history of sedition in the United States and its conflict with the constitutional right of free speech.

Seeds of Sedition

Censorship
An act of government to prevent expressions of speech or publication.

About three centuries before the Declaration of Independence was signed, the British Crown held trials to punish those accused of seditious libel for writing or speaking ill of either church or state. The British exercised control by licensing printers and demanding that their bonds be forfeited if they generated public unrest through their publications. Colonists continued promoting and protecting their subversive views of the Crown in print, despite the harsh penalties levied at printers.

Power and the press went hand in hand for those who ruled with a scepter, and they used the threat of government censorship whenever their authority was threatened. King Henry VIII, in the early sixteenth century, insisted on licensing printers to keep his critics from circulating adverse pamphlets. Acting as both head of church and state, Henry VIII consolidated his power by censoring all "errors and seditious opinions," and he discouraged "heretics" who would encourage a puritanical revolt. The king seized power over all printed materials he deemed mistaken – either political or ecclesiastical.[7] The press could still sway the people in this age, but only at the behest of the throne.

Gold was the incentive for the British printers who accepted a royal contract. The company of printers called the *Worshipful Company of Stationers and Newspaper Makers* was

5. "Christian Militia Acquitted of Sedition in US," *Al Jazeera*, March 28, 2012, *at* www.aljazeera.com/news/americas/2012/03/20123284550627577.html.
6. *See*, H. Alexander, "Donald Trump Slams Black Lives Matter Leader Hawk Newsome's Call to 'Burn Down This System' as 'Treason, Sedition, Insurrection'," *Daily Mail*, June 25, 2020, *at* www.dailymail.co.uk/news/article-8460437/Black-Lives-Matter-leader-Hawk-Newsome-says-change-doesnt-happen-burn-system.html.
7. Frederick S. Siebert, *Freedom of the Press in England, 1476–1776* (Urbana, IL: University of Illinois Press, 1952).

Bedrock Law
The theory behind freedom of the press is that truth ultimately prevails in a free marketplace of ideas.

organized to serve those interests, and they were the ones who handed over unlicensed publishers for trial at the Court of the Star Chamber. Truth was no defense for defaming a public official since such reports were inflammatory by nature and caused "not only the breach of the peace, but also the scandal of government."[8] A conviction for this crime carried severe consequences. For merely publishing a book favoring the right to rebel against a despotic ruler, printer William Twyn in 1663 was sentenced to a cruel death, to be "emasculated, disemboweled, quartered, and beheaded."[9]

A blind poet challenged the control of publications by royal licensing. When John Milton's tracts on divorce displeased the throne, he responded with a "marketplace of ideas" argument for freedom of expression (see Chapter 2). He felt it was important to allow for a struggle in "a free and open encounter" between truth and falsity, and he believed truth would ultimately prevail. Yet Milton's opinion was not the sole voice of wisdom of the day. Pamphleteer Richard Baxter felt giving all men the right "to speak both in presse and pulpit" would cause trouble because "if ten men's voices be louder than one, would the noyse of errour drown the voice of truth."[10]

Seditious Libel
The common law crime of punishing speech harmful to the government.

The licensing law of Britain was abolished in 1695, and over the next 25 years, censorship in England waned. Treason was reconceived as a crime requiring action more than words, but the lesser offense of **seditious libel**, rebellious speech against the government, was still subject to punishment by whippings, fines, or imprisonment.[11]

The American Experience

The idea of voting for lawmakers to serve the will of the people is something early Americans did not clearly envision in the nation's infancy. The prospect of a system of checks and balances for government branches was novel. Freedom of expression was not taken to mean a lack of controls; instead, censorship could occur through **prior restraint** by a colonial system of publication licensing.

Prior Restraint
A form of censorship in which the government, in advance of publication, prevents a publisher from publishing certain material.

Benjamin Franklin's older brother James exploited that system until he was arrested for lampooning the actions of the colonial legislature of Massachusetts in his unlicensed print titled *The New England Courant*.[12] The royal government's ire was provoked by Franklin's droll darts aimed at Massachusetts's frustration in stopping coastal pirates, who might be rounded up "sometime this month, wind and weather permitting."[13] Such witticisms cost J. Franklin his freedom as he was placed under confinement, preventing him from printing any pamphlet or paper that might disturb the public peace. After his release, Franklin shifted the newspaper publisher's title to his younger brother Benjamin. Royal authorities were not

8. Sir James Fitzjames Stephen, *A History of the Criminal Law of England* 304–305 (London, 1883), quoted by Leonard W. Levy, *Emergence of a Free Press* 7 (Oxford: Oxford University Press, 1985).
9. *See Id.*, Levy's abstraction of *Rex v. Twyn* as recorded by 6 Thomas Bayly Howell, *State Trials* 513, 536, 1663, in *Emergence of a Free Press*.
10. Richard Baxter, *Aphorismes of Justification* (1649), "To the Reader," as quoted in William Haller, *Liberty and Reformation in the Puritan Revolution* 171–172 (New York: Columbia University Press, 1955).
11. Today, we think of the term "libel" as someone harming a person in reputation only, but the broader term of libels (little books) once specified several crimes, including obscenity, blasphemy against religion, criticism of the government, or slandering private persons.
12. Legal historian Leonard Levy noted that "the most suppressive body by far, surpassing even the prerogative court of the (royal) governor-and-Council, was that acclaimed bastion of the people's liberties: the popularly elected Assembly." Leonard W. Levy, *Legacy of Suppression: Freedom of Speech and Press in Early American History* 20 (Cambridge, MA: Harvard University Press, 1960).
13. *Id.* at 36–37.

Bill *Ignoramus*
When a grand jury does not find enough evidence to charge a crime, it returns a no bill, or bill *ignoramus*, instead of a true bill.

amused by this ploy and brought him up on charges – only this time a grand jury signed a "**bill *ignoramus***"[14] that set him free in 1723.

For both English mainlanders and colonial Americans, a freedom-spirited move to only punish harmful expressions *after the fact* gained acceptance in 1769, when Sir William Blackstone's (Figure 3.1) common-law commentary proclaimed "*[L]iberty of the press* is indeed essential to the nature of a free state; but this consists in laying no *previous* restraints upon publications, and not in freedom from censure for criminal matter when published."[15] Blackstone's broad strokes painted the terms of what could be punished after the fact: "[I]f he publishes what is improper, mischievous, or illegal, he must take the consequences of his own temerity."[16]

The danger in uttering or publishing words of sedition meant that suspects could be prosecuted for their threats to the peace of society and public order. German immigrant John Peter Zenger splashed criticisms of the colonial governor across the pages of his paper and became press freedom's poster child in the colonial era. His *New York Weekly Journal* blistered Gov. William Cosby for a dismal record of acts perpetrated against the colonists. Zenger was tried for seditious libel, and the jury exonerated him. This surprising verdict using the defense of factual truth made news across the colonies.

Figure 3.1 Portrait of Sir William Blackstone

14. A bill *ignoramus* was an indication that the jury refused to find him guilty. Technically, the jury was unable to find him not guilty because he had in fact published the statements, and they were not being asked to judge whether the statements were libelous. It was a legal trick to keep from having to find him guilty.
15. Sir William Blackstone, *Commentaries on the Laws of England* 151–152 (London, 1765–1769), as cited by Levy, *Legacy of Suppression*, supra note 12 at 14.
16. *Id.* at 14.

Zenger and the Defense of Truth

Editor John Peter Zenger was arrested after spending less than 25 years on American soil, and his trial produced "a great noise in the world" since the paper's editorials had scandalized royal governor William Cosby. Cosby was the principal target after he began seizing lands from American colonists and gifting the property to friends and supporters. In addition to these royal acts, Cosby appointed loyal followers to lifetime commissions at salaries so high the New York General Assembly had them overturned. When the governor read in Zenger's *New York Weekly Journal* about his part in rigged elections, his failure to properly deal with Indian tribes, and ballads about "petty fogging knaves" and "scoundrel rascals," he was moved to act. Zenger was held behind bars for eight months while his wife Anna cranked out editions of the newspaper.

A Philadelphia attorney named Andrew Hamilton argued the case on Zenger's behalf, and he persuaded the jurors to consider it no crime when a journalist is "exposing and opposing arbitrary power in this part of the world at least by speaking and writing the truth."[17] As with Franklin, the jury refused to find him guilty. While Zenger's acquittal received widespread publicity and moved public sentiment against government censorship, it did not bring down the curtain on seditious libel. However, it did cause colonial Americans to consider Hamilton's point about defending truthful reporting.

Alien and Sedition Acts

After the War for Independence, the new nation's second president, John Adams, addressed the menace of sedition with a repressive law. As a Federalist party member, President Adams took aim at the opposition party, the Democratic-Republicans,[18] and one of its leaders, Vice President Thomas Jefferson, an election rival. International tensions and division were running high as France and England were at war, with Democratic-Republicans supporting France while President Adams and his Federalist party supported England. The Federalists claimed French revolutionaries were going to export terrorism to the United States. Favoring security over liberty, President Adams sought to control immigration and secure the borders as necessary war measures in the name of national unity. At the same time, he was infuriated with newspaper editors who insulted him in print, including Benjamin Franklin's grandson, Benjamin Franklin Bache, who described Adams as "old, querulous, bald, blind, crippled, toothless Adams."[19]

The result was the **Alien and Sedition Acts** of 1798. The set of laws included the Alien Act, which authorized the president to arrest and deport any alien suspected of "treasonable or secret leanings." The law also significantly lengthened the time it took for immigrants, who tended to vote Democratic-Republican, to gain citizenship and the right to vote. The Sedition Act criminalized "any false, scandalous and malicious" writings against the federal government, Congress, or the president, with intent to defame, bring into contempt, or excite hatred against. Yet it was primarily enforced against Democratic-Republicans and the press. Twenty-five people were arrested under the new law, with 14 editors brought to court, including 8 Democratic-Republican journalists. Matthew Lyon, a popular editor and member of Congress, accused Adams of "ridiculous pomp" and was fined and jailed for violating the Sedition Act.

17. James Alexander, *A Brief Narrative of the Case and Trial of John Peter Zenger* (reprint ed. Cambridge, MA: Harvard University Press, 1972) (1736).
18. The Democratic-Republican Party was founded in 1792 by Thomas Jefferson and James. In the 1820s, the party split into several factions, including the modern-day Democratic Party.
19. Ronald G. Shafer, "The Thin-Skinned President Who Made It Illegal to Criticize His Office," *The Washington Post*, September 8, 2018.

In claiming that the Alien and Sedition Acts were unconstitutional, Thomas Jefferson argued for states' rights, limited presidential power, and the First Amendment right of free speech and press. The laws were also challenged by strong public protests and riots, a unified opposition party, and internal Federalist party bickering. Federalists complained that the criticism was designed to undermine Adams's lawful election. But the sedition law was among the most hated in America and ultimately mobilized support for Jefferson and his party whose elections were seen as a rejection of the Act. As a result, President Adams lost reelection to Thomas Jefferson in 1800, who allowed the Sedition Act to expire in 1801, pardoning those convicted under the law. Yet the tables were turned when President Jefferson urged Pennsylvania's governor to prosecute a Federalist newspaper and editors for personal attacks on him. Seditious libel was not entirely repudiated – it was now left to the states. Nonetheless, the battle over the Sedition Act led to the birth of what may be viewed as the modern First Amendment.[20] The First Amendment would now be understood to mean that criticism of government officials is protected and not punishable as a crime.

Sedition During Times of War

A different form of repression emerged when the nation's peculiar institution of slavery dominated public discourse and the Civil War erupted. Governments in a democracy rely on the consent of the governed, and that calls for open debate on policies that shape the national destiny and future directions. Yet during times of war, when citizens are called upon to risk and sacrifice their lives to achieve the government's goals, the debate can become frenzied to the point of insurrection. Should free expression be curtailed during such times of violent conflict, or should the government tolerate virulent strains of dissent? This would become a recurring question throughout major conflicts in American history.

The most important consequence of the Civil War for freedom of expression was the adoption of the Fourteenth Amendment of the U.S. Constitution. It not only led to citizenship rights for former slaves but also ensured that the First Amendment would be incorporated by all of the nation's states. The Fourteenth Amendment later played a special part in the twentieth century during the "war to end all wars," where it was instrumental in preventing prior restraint of the press.

Espionage and Sedition Cases

After the United States entered World War I, the Espionage Act of 1917 was adopted by Congress and signed by President Woodrow Wilson. It dealt primarily with espionage, but parts of the bill also aimed to quell war dissenters. "When the United States is at war," the law read, whoever shall willfully obstruct or attempt to stop the recruiting or enlistment service of the United States with "language intended to incite, provoke, or encourage resistance to the United States" should be punished by a fine of up to $10,000 and imprisonment of up to 20 years.[21]

In 1918, an amendment to the **Espionage Act** informally known as the Sedition Act also made it a crime through oral or written means for anyone to encourage contempt and scorn for the U.S. government by "disloyal, profane, scurrilous, or abusive language."[22] Federal prosecutors brought almost 2,000 people to trial and secured over 900 convictions, but implementation of the Act did not stop there. In its zeal to protect the U.S. war effort, the post

20. Joseph Russomanno, "The Right and the Duty: Jefferson, Sedition and the Birth of the First Amendment's Central Meaning," 23 *Communication Law and Policy* 49–90 (2018).
21. Joseph Russomanno, "The Right and the Duty: Jefferson, Sedition and the Birth of the First Amendment's Central Meaning,"40 *Statutes at Large* 553–554 (1918).
22. *See* Pub. L 65–150, 40 Stat. 553. Sixth-Fifth Congress, Sess. II (1918) at 553.

office censored thousands of newspapers, books, and pamphlets under the Act. Entire issues of magazines went undelivered if pages appeared to cross the line into seditious territory.

The *Schenck* Case

The first of four cases[23] tried under the Sedition Act concerning sedition and the First Amendment was the U.S. Supreme Court ruling against Charles T. Schenck for his work as general secretary of the American Socialist party in Philadelphia.[24] He printed and distributed 15,000 leaflets discouraging young men from enlisting in the military by questioning what he considered the cold-blooded and ruthless venture of World War I to fatten Wall Street purses. "Assert your rights – Do not submit to intimidation," urged his circular. This outspoken socialist and one of his fellow party members were arrested, tried, and convicted for obstructing the war effort. The U.S. Supreme Court took the *Schenck* case on appeal and handed down its landmark ruling against Schenck in 1919.

Writing the unanimous decision, Justice Oliver Wendell Holmes coined a phrase that resonated in First Amendment literature for years to come. He wrote,

> The question in every case is whether the words used are used in such circumstances and are of such a nature as to create a **clear and present danger** that they will bring about the substantive evils that Congress has a right to prevent.
>
> (emphasis added)

The Court established that the First Amendment is not absolute; freedom of speech may be abridged when it rises to the level of a clear and present danger to the state.

Bad Tendency Test
Standard that allowed government to criminalize speech if found to have a bad tendency to contribute to collapse of the government.

Nonetheless, in affirming the conviction, the high court relied on the **bad tendency** test in concluding that Schenck's mailings had a "bad tendency" when it came to endangering national security. The bad tendency test was an old common law test that became the most influential standard used by the courts during WWI to assess government criticism. In this case, the Court held Schenck's printed dissent against the war up to a magnifying glass of reasonableness, showing how Schenck's words were *intended* to put readers in a mind of revolt toward the war. Context matters, where words that may ordinarily be harmless can become criminal when expressed during times of war because of the heightened danger they present. "When a nation is at war many things that might be said in time of peace are such a hindrance to its effort that their utterance will not be endured,"[25] concluded Holmes. It was also in *Schenck* that Justice Holmes made his famous analogy that "free speech would not protect a man in falsely shouting fire in a theatre and causing panic."

Abrams v. United States

The United States embarked on a serious phase of suppression during and after World War I. Public hatred for wartime protests after U.S. soldiers were killed overseas brought a group of Jewish immigrants from Russia to trial in New York City. President Wilson had dispatched American soldiers to fight on the Russian front, which concerned Jacob Abrams and his Jewish friends who secretly printed leaflets they hoped would discourage the manufacture of armaments directed at fellow Russians. Jacob Abrams, his girlfriend Molly Steimer, and three others who distributed the leaflets were found guilty of violating the law. It was unlikely those leaflets printed in English and Yiddish had any significant impact on the U.S. war effort or its wartime factories, but the "bad tendency" test was used to uphold their convictions.

23. The other three cases were *Abrams v. United States*, 250 U.S. 616 (1919); *Debs v. United States*, 249 U.S. 211 (1919); and *Frohwerk v. United States*, 249 U.S. 204 (1919).
24. *Schenck v. United States*, 249 U.S. 47 (1919).
25. *Id.* at 52.

Clear and Present Danger Test
Standard applied by courts that allows government to criminalize speech only if it presents a clear and present danger. Provides more protection for speech than the earlier "bad tendency" test.

In *Abrams v. United States*,[26] the rumblings of a movement toward a more liberal, speech-protective test could be heard. This time Justice Holmes along with Justice Brandeis broke with the majority, arguing that the "silly leaflet" of "poor and puny anonymities" posed no real threat to American efforts and failed to present the "clear and present danger" as required by law. In his dissent, Justice Holmes put forth a stricter "clear and present danger" standard that restricts and punishes "speech that produces or is intended to produce clear and imminent danger that it will bring forthwith certain substantive evils that the United States constitutionally may seek to prevent."

Debs v. United States

"Socialism is the Answer," was what Eugene Debs, (Figure 3.2) a leftist labor leader, proclaimed in Canton, Ohio, as he urged young men to resist soldiering under the U.S. flag. "I might not be able to say all that I think, but you need to know that you are fit for something better than slavery and cannon fodder."[27] Even though Debs's speech was only mildly provocative in terms of its antiwar message, the Court applied its bad tendency test to seal his conviction and 10-year sentence in a Georgia federal prison. His speech did not necessarily represent a clear and present danger to others, but it might produce a bad result. Undaunted, the 65-year-old Debs ran for president from prison. Federal Judge Charles Amidon described the reactionary mood of jurors in similar sedition cases during World War I: "[Jurors] looked

Figure 3.2 Eugene V. Debs following his release from Atlanta Federal Penitentiary in 1921

26. *Abrams v. United States*, 250 U.S. 616 (1919).
27. *Debs v. United States*, 249 U.S. 211, 214 (1919).

back into my eyes with the savagery of wild animals, saying by their manner, 'Away with the twiddling, let us get at them.'"[28]

The following year 1920, the Sedition Act was repealed, and Justice Holmes's clear and present danger test was becoming well-known. The courts continued to rely on the bad tendency test despite insistence from Justices Holmes and Brandeis that the clear and present danger test should be applied in such cases.[29] Government agents would continue to lock up antiwar dissidents and subsequently target proponents of socialism.

Criminal Syndicalism Violent insurrection and antigovernment protests.

Criminal Syndicalism and *Gitlow*

After the Sedition Act, state legislatures turned to laws against **criminal syndicalism,** another name for violent insurrection and antigovernment protests. These laws were aimed at European immigrants to whom the fashionable doctrines of Karl Marx were attractive even before their arrival in the United States. New York had already adopted its criminal syndicalism law in 1902.

Leftist New Yorker Benjamin Gitlow found himself ensnared by the criminal syndicalism law and brought his case before the U.S. Supreme Court in 1925. He was one of the founders of the Communist Party USA, and he distributed the *Left Wing Manifesto*, which urged socialism by class action in any form. Gitlow called for a nonviolent protest to cancel the draft, which he compared to a type of "involuntary servitude," banned by the Thirteenth Amendment. But Gitlow's conviction was affirmed. Justices Holmes and Brandeis dissented, again suggesting the application of the clear and present danger test. The two justices felt the conviction should be reversed and argued in support of Gitlow's freedom of speech. Justice Holmes wrote that the slight difference between an opinion and an incitement could change the fate for Gitlow. "The only difference between the expression of an opinion and an incitement in the narrower sense is the speaker's enthusiasm for the result."[30]

Whitney v. California

Anita Whitney testified she never intended to violate any law or serve as "an instrument of terrorism or violence," but the U.S. Supreme Court nonetheless considered her role in the founding of the Communist Labor Party (CLP) worthy of conviction. Whitney was a member of a prominent family in Alameda County, CA, and had been active in the local Oakland branch of the Socialist Party, which in turn switched its allegiance to the CLP.

In his concurring opinion, Justice Louis Brandeis fashioned a fuller interpretation of the clear and present danger test. "No danger flowing from speech can be deemed clear and present," he allowed, "unless the incidence of evil apprehended is so imminent that it may befall before this opportunity for full discussion."[31] Whitney was "to be punished, not for attempt, incitement or conspiracy, but a step in preparation, which, if it threatens the public order at all, does so only remotely."[32] Justice Holmes advocated a "time to answer" standard. That is, no threat should be considered imminent unless there is no time to respond to the political aggression. Legislatures should not punish offensive protests without first defining the exact danger they pose to the state.

28. Geoffrey R. Stone, "Civility and Dissent During Wartime," *Human Rights Magazine*, Winter 2006, at 4.
29. See, e.g., *Gitlow v. New York*, 268 U.S. 652 (1925); *Whitney v. California*, 274 U.S. 357 (1927).
30. *Gitlow v. New York*, at 673.
31. *Whitney v. California*, at 377.
32. *Id.* at 373.

American Civil Liberties Union (ACLU)

It is difficult to imagine how much violence Americans have encountered due to national fevers of war and labor unrest, but in the Roaring Twenties, dissent literally exploded. A box blew up in 1920 on the doorstep of U.S. Attorney General A. Mitchell Palmer, the man behind the nation's crusade to bring "Bolsheviks" to justice. Bolsheviks were a branch of working-class Marxists organized in 1905 by Vladimir Lenin and Alexander Bogdanov, ultimately forming the Communist Party of Russia. At Palmer's behest, federal agents rounded up more than 5,000 people in 33 American cities who were suspected of taking the wrong side of the Russian uprisings during World War I. The nation's top prosecutor vigorously applied the espionage law to deport foreign residents without trial. These deportees included famed anarchist, Emma Goldman, who was shipped back to the Soviet Union along with hundreds of others.

No one among the arrested immigrants was charged with the fateful bombing at Palmer's Washington townhouse, but the ruthless means for dealing with suspect newcomers did lead to the creation of a political activist group. In 1920, a small band of Eastern intellectuals headed by Roger Baldwin channeled their outrage to form a legal watchdog group: the American Civil Liberties Union (ACLU).

Elizabeth Gurley Flynn, a New England activist and cofounder of the ACLU, made speeches as a teenager on behalf of the Industrial Workers of the World (IWW or "Wobblies"). She rose as an early feminist in the United States and was appointed to serve on the ACLU board. But her tenure quickly ended after she was outed as a member of the Communist Party. The ACLU refused to seat supporters of any form of totalitarian government. Flynn went to jail for her political leanings, but after her death, the ACLU voted to restore her membership based on her important contributions to women's rights.

The Smith Act

As Axis forces began invading Europe and Asia and consolidating military might, Virginia congressman Rep. Howard W. Smith called for the Alien Registration Act for noncitizen adults in the United States. His bill made it a crime for any foreign citizen or American to teach or advocate "destroying any government in the United States by force or violence."[33] It also criminalized joining any group with such insurrections in mind. President Roosevelt signed the **Smith Act** in 1940 to ferret out wartime dissidents, including members of the Socialist Worker's Party, pro-Nazi groups, and leaders of the Communist Party USA. Individual states enacted similar measures as criminal syndicalism acts, punishing acts of rebellion and violence directed at state and local governments.

Dennis v. United States

It was the red-baiting era of the 1950s that helped produce the convictions of 12 Communists, and one of them was Eugene Dennis, secretary general of the Communist Party USA, who was a former member of the Industrial Workers of the World – nicknamed the "Wobblies" – in California. Dennis's name was a pseudonym for Francis Xavier Waldron, who had spent several years in the Soviet Union and was believed to have been a source of Russian intelligence during World War II. He was arrested with 11 other party leaders in 1948, and for months, the nation followed the proceedings against him, where evidence included passages from the *Daily Worker* newspaper and the *Communist Manifesto*. The prosecution had to prove that even though Dennis and the others had not actually called for the violent overthrow

33. Alien Registration Act of 1940, 18 U.S. Code § 2385.

of the United States in public, they had done so privately. Under the Smith Act, Communists were to be convicted for advocating the forcible overthrow of the United States.

The government won its case, and the U.S. Supreme Court upheld their convictions by a 6–2 decision, with Chief Justice Fred Vinson stating that "an attempt to overthrow the Government by force, even though doomed from the outset because of the inadequate numbers or power of the revolutionists, is a sufficient event for Congress to prevent."[34] Justice Hugo Black wrote a stirring dissent, however, concluding, "No matter how it is worded, this is a virulent form of prior censorship of speech and press, which I believe the First Amendment forbids." To Justice Black, the First Amendment did not permit the Supreme Court to suppress freedom of speech based on their notions of "reasonableness."

> Such a doctrine waters down the First Amendment so that it amounts to little more than an admonition to Congress (and) so construed is not likely to protect any but those "safe" or orthodox views which rarely need its protection.[35]

Yates v. United States

Over the next few years, dozens of Communists were prosecuted until the Supreme Court decided to take another look at the Smith Act. Following the death of Joseph Stalin, the end of the Korean conflict, and the censure of anti-Communist Sen. Joseph McCarthy, the Supreme Court chose to revisit the Smith Act in the case of *Yates v. United States*.[36] The legal question to be decided for California heiress Oleta Yates was whether the law could be used against her and 13 other Communists for simply advocating the future overthrow of the United States as an abstract idea rather than an imminent threat. In 1957, the majority ruled that teaching an idea was not the equivalent of planning its implementation and consequently deserved constitutional protection. The Court, however, did not strike down the Smith Act; it only removed its sting and left it standing.

Brandenburg v. Ohio and Imminent Lawless Action

Half a century after it was first proposed by Justice Holmes, the clear and present danger test was effectively replaced by a new three-part test that remains the standard today. In 1967, Clarence Brandenburg, a Ku Klux Klan leader, made a speech at a Klan rally on a farm in Ohio to which he had invited a Cincinnati television station reporter and cameraman to film. Portions of the films were subsequently broadcast locally and on a national network, showing a dozen hooded figures, some carrying firearms, and Brandenburg making derogatory statements about African Americans and Jews. While most of the words were incomprehensible, Brandenburg could be heard stating, "We're not a revengent organization, but if our President, our Congress, our Supreme Court, continues to suppress the white, Caucasian race, it's possible that there might have to be some revengeance taken."

Bedrock Law
The *Brandenburg* case established that only direct incitement to imminent lawless action would invalidate the First Amendment's protection for political speech.

Brandenburg was arrested and convicted under the Ohio Criminal Syndicalism Act for "advocat[ing] or teach[ing] . . . crime, sabotage, violence, or unlawful methods of terrorism as a means of accomplishing industrial or political reform." He argued the law violated the First and Fourteenth Amendments, and the U.S. Supreme Court agreed.

In *Brandenburg v. Ohio*,[37] the Court unanimously advanced a new standard known as the **imminent and lawless action** test. The Court found the syndicalism law unconstitutional because it punished "mere advocacy," stating that

34. *Dennis v. United States*, 341 U.S. 494, 509 (1951).
35. *Id.* at 508.
36. *Yates v. United States*, 354 U.S. 298 (1957).
37. *Brandenburg v. Ohio*, 395 U.S. 444 (1969).

the constitutional guarantees of free speech and free press do not permit a State to forbid or proscribe advocacy of the use of force or of law violation except where such advocacy is directed to inciting or producing imminent lawless action and is likely to incite or produce such action.

This statement formed a three-part test that could be used to assess when the advocacy of violence or unlawful activity rises to such a level that it may be punished or prohibited. The imminent lawless action test requires the government to provide a compelling argument that shows

- **intent** to incite violence or unlawful activity
- **imminence** of the violence or unlawful activity
- **likelihood** of the violence or unlawful activity.

This more demanding standard protected Brandenburg's speech that called for "revengeance" because, while ominous and disturbing, it wasn't explicitly clear that he intended violence, it wasn't contemplated as occurring immediately, and it wasn't likely to happen at the rally where there were no opposing groups around. Many people think that the Court got it wrong, however, in extending First Amendment protection to racist organizations such as the Ku Klux Klan. The decision would later apply to cases addressing a growing problem of hate speech in America and the laws created to counter it.

The *Brandenburg* case meant the government would penalize only direct incitement to imminent lawless actions in the future. The ruling invalidated state sedition laws that ignored the difference between advocacy and inciting immediate action against the government. The Court also overruled *Whitney*,[38] which had a similar syndicalism law, and made clear that "mere abstract teaching" is also "not the same as preparing a group for violent action." A law that fails to draw that distinction violates the First Amendment.

Global View

Early in 2020, a teenage girl in India began her speech with the words "Pakistan Zindabad," which in Urdu could mean, "Long live the Pure Land," or pointedly, "Victory for Pakistan!" The 14-year-old was immediately arrested. A few weeks earlier, several students raising pro-Pakistani slogans were also arrested. Their crimes? Sedition.

In India, sedition is a rare crime, but arrests have been increasing in recent years. Sedition cases have increased by 28% under the Modi government, with more than 500 sedition cases filed by Indian authorities since 2014, involving more than 7,000 people.[39] In one state, over 3,000 protesters against a citizenship law were charged with sedition, and over 3,300 farmers protesting land disputes in another state were charged with sedition. Damage to property accounts for many of the offenses, and violence by "anti-national elements" including insurgents and terrorists was added to the list of crimes in 2017.

The law of sedition in India dates back to 1870. Section 124A of the Indian Penal Code makes it a crime for dissenters to bring hatred or contempt upon the government. During the colonial period, the law was used to stifle the voices of the Indian freedom movement. A related Dramatic Performances Act of 1876 even put restrictions on plays

38. *Whitney v. California*, supra note 29.
39. Linda Lakhdhir, "Sedition Law: Why India Should Break from Britain's Abusive Legacy," *Human Rights Watch*, July 18, 2022, *at* https://www.hrw.org/news/2022/07/18/sedition-law-why-india-should-break-britains-abusive-legacy.

and artistic expressions of a "seditious, defamatory or scandalous nature," although it was repealed in 2017.

In the postcolonial era, sedition became the legal tool used by India to stifle political opposition. Yet given its constitution recognizes a right of free expression going against the prosecution of sedition, only a few cases have resulted in conviction. The Indian Supreme Court is reviewing the law's constitutionality.[40]

Globally, sedition has been increasingly viewed as a draconian law. The United Kingdom revoked it in 2010. Still in India widespread public criticism has prompted several unsuccessful attempts at repealing the British colonial-era law, most recently in 2023.[41] The government simply maintains sedition law is needed to "effectively combat anti-national, secessionist and terrorist elements."

Theories of Prior Restraint

Prior Restraint
Official control of messages designed to keep them from reaching the intended audience; sometimes called prior censorship.

Some powers seek to silence dissent or hide information before it enters the public arena. This form of censorship is called **prior restraint**. It might occur through a system of licensing as discussed earlier, or it might assume any number of different forms, such as taxation, confiscating or destroying materials, claims that information is classified, or even seizing the actual machinery of communication. By whatever means, it is most clearly the evil the First Amendment was designed to prevent. The modern use of the term prior restraint calls for careful denotation to prevent its confusion with more random encroachments on free expression. Strictly speaking, prior restraint means government oversight of expression in a systematic manner, not targeting single messengers or their messages. Prior restraint also occurs before the communication reaches the public, not during its expression or afterward. While there may be subsequent accountability and even punishment, censorship must not occur prior to dissemination. For a thriving democracy, citizens must be the arbiters of the facts and ideas expressed in the public sphere, not the government.

Arguments against censorship are certainly well-known. Society has an interest in protecting citizens from chicanery, but the government's reliance on prior restraint must be the last resort. One principle guarding against prior restraint by the government stems from the belief that more, not less, speech is best suited to advance society's interests. The people's right to know depends on it, and the idea of limited government carries with it the requirement to inform citizens of errors so they may correct their elected leaders. A government can ill afford to silence its critics, especially if it means forbidding them to share their insights and solutions.

Beyond the arena of political interest, freedom of speech and thought is critically essential for the successful search for truth. Scientists of an earlier age, for example, understood how harshly ecclesiastics punished unbelievers for simply observing the sun occupies the center of the solar system. Prior restraint tends to curb the power of unpopular sentiments. The mere act of reviewing ideas before they enter the marketplace imposes a delay that dilutes their strength. Once the authority of prior restraint is removed and the censorial role is relieved, society can afford a judicious, public hearing of the controversy. The 45 words of the First Amendment are thus essential to protecting the viewpoints of those who stand in dissent of popular opinion.

40. Ananya Bhatia, "Weaponization of Colonial-Era Sedition Law: The Future of India's Free Speech," *Columbia Undergraduate Law Review*, January 5, 2024, *at* https://www.culawreview.org/current-events-2/the-future-of-indias-free-speech.
41. Ashok Sharma, "India Moves to Replace British Colonial-Era Sedition Law with its Own Version," *Associated Press*, August 11, 2023.

Strict Scrutiny
The highest standard U.S. courts apply in reviewing laws. Strict scrutiny tests whether the law 1) serves a compelling government interest, 2) is narrowly tailored for achieving that end, and 3) uses the least restrictive means to do so.

Because prior restraint is the most abhorrent form of government intervention, the courts require **strict scrutiny** as the test of its constitutional validity. Strict scrutiny is the most stringent level of review, requiring the government to show a *compelling* public interest at stake for a law or government action to stand. As a result, a prior restraint is seldom upheld when challenged. The courts might allow a prior restraint if a compelling national security interest is at stake, but not for lesser interests such as aesthetics, convenience, or to avoid public embarrassment (see Chapter 4 for levels of scrutiny).

Twentieth-Century Landmarks

Historians of First Amendment law search for the trail of binding precedents to the point where Sir Blackstone's sentiments against "previous restraints" of expression on the press clearly emerge in the judicial record. That was not until 1931 when the landmark Supreme Court case ***Near v. Minnesota***[42] provided the necessary foundation for addressing prior restraint of the media. The case involved the criminal prosecution of a Minnesota scandal sheet featuring two ink-stained gadflies, Jay M. Near and his partner in print Howard Guilford, a failed mayoral candidate. Their typewriters at the *Saturday Press* roiled the political powers of Minneapolis and St. Paul, especially the chief of police whom they accused of taking graft from high-rolling bootleggers they smeared as the Jewish mafia. One passage revealed the anti-Semitic flavor of their yellow journalism:

> It is Jew thugs who have pulled practically every robbery in this city. . . . Practically every vendor of vile hooch, every owner of a moonshine still, every snakefaced gangster and embryonic yegg in the Twin Cities is a Jew . . . ninety percent of the crimes committed against society in this city are committed by Jew gangsters.[43]

Doctrine of Incorporation
Neither the U.S. Constitution nor its amendments apply to the states as a whole. However, specific parts of the Constitution are made applicable to the states through the Fourteenth Amendment's limitation on state government once the Supreme Court takes up a case that affords this action.

Both scandalmongers were arrested under a Minnesota statute that forbade "malicious, scandalous, or defamatory" publications. The *Saturday Press* was padlocked after nine editions, and the men were threatened with jail time if they tried to crank out more papers. This action "put the publisher under an effective censorship" through the "suppression of the offending newspaper."[44] Near and Guilford chose to slug it out though in the Minnesota courts, which handily dealt them defeats all the way up to the Supreme Court.

Near decided to take his case alone to the highest tribunal, which applied the **doctrine of incorporation**, citing the freedom of press in the First Amendment.[45] Covering state law with First Amendment freedoms meant striking down Minnesota's Public Nuisance law of 1925. Because it punished the press prior to publication, Chief Justice Charles Evans Hughes and four justices rejected the law as flawed. Yet Justice Hughes believed the press could be suppressed under certain conditions such as national security, where information about military movements and the sailing dates of ships might be restrained.[46] In his opinion, the government also has a right to censor expressions inciting acts of violence or generating obscenity. Moreover, "the constitutional guaranty of free speech does not protect a man from an injunction against uttering words that may have all the effect of force."[47]

42. *Near v. Minnesota*, 283 U.S. 697 (1931).
43. *Id.* at 738.
44. *Id.* at 697.
45. As noted in the "Doctrine of Incorporation" box, selective incorporation applied the Bill of Rights to the states as a part of the Fourteenth Amendment, which specifies due process for all Americans regardless of their state of residence.
46. *Near v. Minnesota*, supra note 42.
47. *Id.* at 716.

The 5–4 decision was a close victory for freedom of the press but underscored the freedom to print does not grant an escape from punishment.

> The fact that the liberty of the press may be abused by miscreant purveyors of scandal does not make any the less necessary the immunity of the press from previous restraint in dealing with official misconduct. Subsequent punishment for such abuses that may exist is the appropriate remedy, consistent with constitutional privilege.[48]

While *Near v. Minnesota* did not absolutely sustain the British common law, it did make clear that protection from prior restraint is not unlimited and exceptions to the rule will usually involve some visible danger. Citing *Schenck*, "When a nation is at war many things that might be said in time of peace are such a hindrance to its effort that their utterance will not be endured."[49] On similar grounds, the decency and security of the community life may be protected against obscene publications, incitements to violence, and advocacy of the violent overthrow of the government.

Doctrine of Incorporation

At first reading of the Bill of Rights, one thing becomes clear – it is designed for federal lawmakers: "Congress shall make no law . . ." declares the First Amendment. So then can state governments abridge freedoms of speech, press, religion, or assembly? For many years, the answer was a resounding "yes."

In *Barron v. Mayor of Baltimore*, Chief Justice John Marshall declared in 1833 the first ten amendments to the U.S. Constitution "contain no expression indicating an intention to apply them to the State governments."[50] Baltimore wharf owner John Barron's case was about the money he felt the city owed his business in the harbor, where he lost thousands of dollars in shipping business because the city had been dumping mounds of dirt from road construction in the water near his wharf. Barron asked the high court to honor the Fifth Amendment's guarantee against taking private property for public use without justly compensating the owner. The U.S. Supreme Court, however, ruled that the constitutional amendment applied only to the federal government in Washington, DC, and not the one in Baltimore, MD.

After the Civil War ended, the Fourteenth Amendment added to the Constitution rights for all citizens, including freed slaves. It also provided a means for the Court to incorporate the Bill of Rights for the states, although the Court strictly limited its incorporation to clauses that were applicable to particular cases and not entire amendments. The *Gitlow* case,[51] for example, incorporated only freedom of speech, and *Near v. Minnesota* (1931) did the same for the freedom of the press clause.[52]

Justice Hugo Black disagreed with this piecemeal approach and tried to convince his fellow justices to incorporate the first eight amendments all at once, but they chose instead to stick with selective incorporation.

Prior Restraint by Taxing

The threat of taxation became a widely challenged form of prior censorship used against news media in states where the press was considered a problem for the high and mighty. During the Great Depression, rural residents of Louisiana were enthralled by the bombast of

48. *Id.* at 697.
49. *Schenck v. United States*, supra note 24 at 51.
50. *Barron v. Mayor of Baltimore*, 32 U.S. 243, 250 (1833).
51. *Gitlow v. New York*, supra note 29.
52. *Near v. Minnesota*, supra note 42.

Bedrock Law
The Supreme Court has ruled that punishing the press for inflammatory political content by means of prior restraint is unconstitutional.

the "Kingfish," Governor Huey P. Long. The populist Democrat did not hold all of Louisiana under his spell, especially certain newspapers. So Long decided to relieve his exasperation by imposing a "license tax" of 2% on all dailies with a circulation of 20,000 or more. The governor felt it amounted to "two pennies per lie" and levied it against 13 papers, including the *New Orleans Times-Picayune*, well-known for criticizing Long's stylish demagoguery.

The 1936 case of *Grosjean v. American Press Co.* brought the tax question before the U.S. Supreme Court and cemented the name Alice Lee Grosjean in Louisiana legal history. Grosjean, the governor's former secretary and alleged mistress, was responsible for collecting the newspaper tax.[53] In a unanimous opinion against Louisiana's politically charged revenue scheme, the Court recalled how British rulers used similar means to silence dissent and how much of the nation's founding was based in outrage against onerous taxes and the despots who levied them. Justice George Sutherland's opinion underscored the "well known and odious" nature of censorship through financial means. He believed allowing the press to be restricted was to "fetter ourselves." Thus, Louisiana's press tax was an impermissible violation of the First Amendment.

The threat of politicians taming the news media by taxing them into submission was not buried in the bayous; it sprang to life in the laws of Arkansas and Minnesota. The Commissioner of Revenue in 1974 began levying a "use tax" on Minnesota publications spending major sums of money on paper and ink – more than $100,000 worth per year. Such a tax tightened government controls on 11 publishers, including the state's largest circulation daily, *The Minneapolis Star Tribune*, which paid roughly two-thirds of the revenue garnered by the tax.

Bedrock Law
Government attempts to exercise control over the press through discriminatory taxes have been regarded as unconstitutional prior restraints.

After the U.S. Supreme Court heard the newspaper's complaint, it became clear the state was saddling an unequal share of the burden on the paper's shoulders. In Justice Sandra Day O'Connor's opinion, that "differential treatment, unless justified by some special characteristic of the press, suggests that the goal of the regulation is not unrelated to suppression of expression, and such a goal is presumptively unconstitutional."[54]

The "intimidation-by-taxes" episode concluded in Minnesota, but magazine owners in Arkansas felt the squeeze on their pocketbooks when the legislature decided to separate general-interest magazines from newspapers, religious periodicals, and sports journals. In *Arkansas Writer's Project, Inc. v. Ragland*, the government of Arkansas felt the brunt of constitutional justice from Justice Thurgood Marshall who found the state's discriminatory tax on general-interest magazines "disturbing" and "particularly repugnant to First Amendment principles."[55]

Prior Restraint by Injunction

Injunction
A court order directing a person or organization to refrain from some act.

Injunctions are sometimes used against the media as an effective means for restraining publication. An **injunction** is a court order typically directing a person or organization to cease or refrain from a particular act. As an equitable remedy, the court issues an injunction through a written order called a *writ*, which specifies the prohibited action and binds the party by law. Injunctions are used to prohibit future actions, such as stopping a willful copyright infringement, but injunctions can also mandate that an action be taken to fix or repair a matter, such as removing an infringing trademark. Some recognized injunctions against the media have been used to restrain messages about the spread of weapons of mass destruction, racial hatred, and the reasons a nation has gone to war.

53. *Grosjean v. American Press Co.*, 297 U.S. 233 (1936).
54. *Minneapolis Star Tribune Co. v. Minnesota Comm'r of Revenue*, 460 U.S. 575, 581–585 (1983).
55. *Arkansas Writer's Project, Inc. v. Ragland*, 481 U.S. 221, 230 (1989).

Pentagon Papers Case

The most controversial and definitive example of prior restraint is the case of the "Pentagon Papers." In 1971, a secret Pentagon study fell into the hands of reporters at *The New York Times* and the *Washington Post* through an ardent anti-Communist and Harvard-trained economist, Dr. Daniel Ellsberg. Ellsberg had been working as an analyst for the RAND Corporation and the Department of Defense, which had commissioned a study on the political and military involvement of the United States from WWII to Vietnam. Ellsberg was eventually convinced the American war effort in Southeast Asia was futile and the public needed to know why Americans were sent to die there. So he secretly made photocopies of the 47-volume study that provided a history of the decision-making process on Vietnam policy, otherwise known as the Pentagon Papers.

For several months, *Times* reporter Neil Sheehan and his colleagues pored over thousands of pages. When it was time to go to press, *The New York Times* headlined their initial feature, "Vietnam Archive: Pentagon Study Traces 3 Decades of Growing U.S. Involvement." Within two days, U.S. Attorney General John Mitchell telegrammed the *Times* urging it to cease printing immediately because of the harm the series posed to the military presence.

When the *Times* refused to stop the presses, the Department of Justice asked federal Judge Murray I. Gurfein to issue a temporary restraining order, or "TRO." Judge Gurfein was serving his first day as a federal judge when he enjoined the *Times*. The *Washington Post* stepped in the breach to publish its portions of the secret report, but the U.S. attorney general quickly secured a second injunction against the *Post*.

Appeals for both newspapers quickly moved up through the courts to the U.S. Supreme Court, which responded with unusual efficiency by handing down a decision within two weeks. The outcome of *New York Times Co. v. United States*[56] was a press victory of sorts. The Court's 6–3 decision was written without a majority opinion. Instead, a *per curiam* opinion was given that was short and simple, citing precedent that any prior restraint on publication bears "a heavy presumption against its constitutional validity."[57] The Court then concluded that the government had failed to meet the "heavy burden of showing justification" for imposing such a restraint.[58]

Each of the nine justices then wrote separate opinions. Justices Black and Douglas believed federally imposed prior restraints on the press were unconstitutional – period. Justice White said disclosure of the documents could not result in "direct, immediate, and irreparable damage to our Nation or its people."[59] Justice Brennan stressed that a prior restraint can be justified only when there is proof that a publication is shown to "inevitably, directly and immediately cause the occurrence of an event kindred to imperiling the safety of a transport already at sea."[60]

Bedrock Law
Censorship of the news media to protect national security must meet a heavy burden of proof that includes direct harm to the people.

Yet the decision was not exactly a decisive win for the press. Three justices complained they did not have enough time to properly consider the legal questions. Some were in favor of subsequent criminal sanctions against the newspapers. And Justices Stewart, White, and Marshall were of the opinion that the courts lacked the authority to enjoin a publication in the absence of laws authorizing such prior restraints, leaving open the possibility that Congress could create a restrictive law that may be acceptable.

Chief Justice Warren Burger and Justices Harlan and Blackmun dissented, citing possible foreign relations and national security issues caused by the publication of the documents.

56. *New York Times Co. v. United States*, 403 U.S. 713 (1971).
57. *Id.* at 714.
58. *Id.*
59. *Id.* at 730.
60. *Id.* at 727.

Justice Blackmun gave a stern warning, outlining the possible consequences if this grant of freedom unfolded into remorse:

> [I]f, with the Court's action today, these newspapers proceed to publish the critical documents and there results therefrom "the death of soldiers, the destruction of alliances, the greatly increased difficulty of negotiation with our enemies, the inability of our diplomats to negotiate," to which list I might add the factors of prolongation of the war . . ., then the Nation's people will know where the responsibility for these sad consequences rests.[61]

Given the conflicting opinions and narrow ruling, what some considered to be the case of the century was somewhat diminished. The Court did not rule on the constitutionality of prior restraint, only that the government failed to meet the heavy burden of showing that a prior restraint was necessary in this case. Nonetheless, the Pentagon Papers case has been celebrated for its protection of press freedom and has provided guidance for subsequent courts addressing prior restraint. Indeed, *The New York Times* continued printing the series, earning a Pulitzer Prize in 1972 for public service.[62]

A Valid Claim of National Security?

In some cases, overzealous classification and claims of national security by government agencies can become a means of prior restraint by preventing the release of information for reasons other than valid national security concerns.

Misuse of the national security privilege was at issue in a tragic plane crash in 1948.[63] On October 6, an Air Force B-29 bomber took off from Robbins Air Force Base in Georgia to test secret navigation equipment. Before returning, a fire broke out in one of the engines and the plane crashed, killing nine including three engineers. The engineers' widows, including Patricia Reynolds, sued the government for wrongful death under the Federal Tort Claims Act (FTCA), a law intended for citizens to sue the U.S. government for harm caused by negligence or misconduct. Their lawyer requested a copy of the Air Force investigative report of the accident but was denied, brushed off by the claim it would not be in the "public interest" to release it. Later, the government claimed that releasing the report would seriously hamper national security. The federal district judge offered to review the report in private himself, but the Air Force contested that arrangement. When the lawyer instead entered a judgment for the widows on a negligence claim, the government appealed the case to the Supreme Court, claiming the report was privileged against disclosure.

In 1953, the Supreme Court issued its landmark "state secrets" ruling in ***United States v. Reynolds***.[64] In a 6–3 decision, the Court concluded the Air Force could withhold its accident report, stating that "the most compelling necessity cannot overcome the claim of privilege if the court is ultimately satisfied that military secrets are at stake."[65] Yet the Court chose not to rule on whether the government's national security privilege was valid. The widows ultimately settled out of court for a lesser amount.[66]

Then 47 years later, the daughter of one of the engineers, Judith Palya Loether, discovered in 2000 on the Internet the secret report had been declassified. Obtaining a copy, she was outraged to learn that it contained no military secrets. Instead, there

61. *Id.* at 763.
62. P. Kihss, "The *Times* Wins a Pulitzer for the Pentagon Papers," *The New York Times*, May 2, 1972.
63. T. Lynch, "In '48 Crash, the U.S. Hid Behind National Security," *CATO Institute*, June 22, 2003, *at* www.cato.org/publications/commentary/48-crash-us-hid-behind-national-security.
64. *United States v. Reynolds*, 345 U.S. 1 (1953).
65. *Id.* at 11.
66. Lynch, "In '48 Crash, the U.S. Hid Behind National Security," supra note 63.

Balancing
When the judiciary weighs different interests against one another to determine the outcome of a case, courts are said to be balancing. Supporters of balancing argue that rights often come into conflict and must be balanced in each case. The critics of balancing consider it a way for judges to act arbitrarily.

was incriminating evidence showing gross negligence – a protective shield to prevent engine overheating had not been installed. The families petitioned to reopen the case and sought a reversal based on a fraudulent claim of national security. But the Third Circuit Court of Appeals upheld the decision in 2005,[67] stating the technical details about the aircraft itself might have compromised national security had they fallen in the hands of the wrong party.

The decision came as a disappointment to those who know unchecked secrecy in government breeds abuse and misconduct. It also highlights the need for greater oversight of government officials who claim national security as their shield from prosecution for misconduct, civil liability, incompetence, or simply public embarrassment.

Free Speech for Former Spies Writing Books?

While pulling the plug on news media coverage is an unlikely solution for national security measures, government employees, especially those with tenure at the Central Intelligence Agency (CIA), can be easily censored. Victor Marchetti wrote a novel based on his CIA experiences, *The Rope Dancer*, after he exited the agency in 1969. It caused little difficulty, but his second book, *The CIA and the Cult of Intelligence*, was nonfiction and hundreds of passages alarmed his former agency employers. The agency asked him to delete all of them, but he resisted until a compromise was achieved where Marchetti excised only classified material. Marchetti complained the CIA "posed a particular threat to the right of Americans to be informed for the present and future by an objective knowledge of the past."[68]

When another ex-CIA employee began to write of secret matters, the U.S. government's response became quite clear. Frank Snepp served as an agent in Vietnam, but he exited Saigon with a burden of guilt for the suffering of the South Vietnamese. As all operatives in Vietnam were asked to do, he signed a secrecy order when he left his job. But he then chose to ignore the order when he began writing about his life in Vietnam for publication. After *Decent Interval* went to press, Snepp's attorneys argued the restrictive federal contract violated his constitutional rights. A trial judge disagreed and called upon Snepp to place his book profits in a trust fund for his former employer.

The ex-CIA analyst-turned-author appealed to the U.S. Supreme Court, which showed little sympathy for his claim. Upholding the federal district court's ruling based on his breach of contract, the Court enjoined him from future writings about his days at the CIA. Snepp signed away those rights, said the ruling, when he first joined the agency and again when he left it in 1976.[69]

Bedrock Law
By virtue of secrecy agreements, Americans can cede their right of free speech on the basis of contractual terms of employment.

Do not surmise that government employees have no free speech protections, however. In 2005, a police officer in Paterson, NJ, was demoted when he was seen carrying a yard sign that supported a mayoral candidate. The officer claimed he was delivering it to his bedridden mother and that he was not involved in the political campaign, but the demotion was enforced. Officer Heffernan filed a suit, which was thrown out by lower courts that found his actions were not expression protected by the First Amendment. On appeal, the U.S. Supreme Court ruled 6–2 that regardless of whether an employer was factually mistaken (that Heffernan was involved in a political campaign), a government employee who is demoted because of perceived political involvement has a First Amendment right to appeal the demotion.[70]

67. *Herring v. United States*, 424 F.3d 384 (3d Cir. 2005).
68. Victor Marchetti, "Propaganda and Disinformation: How the CIA Manufactures History," 9 *J. Hist. Rev*. 305 (1989).
69. *Snepp v. United States*, 444 U.S. 507 (1980).
70. *Heffernan v. City of Paterson*, 136 S. Ct. 1412 (2016).

Prepublication Review

Prepublication review can become a prior restraint for some authors writing books and articles that may contain secrets the government doesn't want spilled. A prepublication review system requires former military and intelligence officials turned authors to submit for review any memoirs and other writings related to their former job. The review system has its roots in the 1950s when it was imposed on a few CIA officials. It grew to cover more people and agencies in the 1970s before the *Snepp* case[71] and then mushroomed under the Reagan administration. Since then, this practice of prior restraint has proliferated around Washington, DC. Consenting to reviews is now part of the process of even gaining a security clearance.

Many lawsuits have been filed over the handling of particular manuscripts, but the first one challenging the censorship system itself was filed in 2019 by a group of former CIA officials, who argued the system is sometimes abused, with some writings critical of the government subject to delays or discriminatory treatment.[72] One of the plaintiffs said he had trouble getting his book, *Unjustifiable Means: The Inside Story of How the C.I.A., Pentagon, and U.S. Government Conspired to Torture*, cleared for publication, reporting it took eight months after which censors demanded removal of 113 passages that he claimed were already publicly available in the *Congressional Record* and elsewhere. Plaintiffs in the case also complained that the review restriction is lifelong and unjustifiably thwarted their rights of free speech and due process. While acknowledging the government has a legitimate interest in protecting bona fide national security secrets, "this system sweeps too broadly, fails to limit the discretion of government censors and suppresses political speech that is vital to informing public debate."[73]

Tell-all books, such as one by former national security adviser John Bolton, came under particular review by the Trump administration. While unflattering to the president, the administration claimed Bolton's book, *The Room Where It Happened*, would expose classified information, pitting concerns over national security with the First Amendment. After months of review, Bolton took his chances and opted out of the prepublication review process to proceed with publication. A federal judge ultimately allowed its release after multiple copies of the book were already distributed.[74]

What About Inadvertent Disclosures and Leaks?

The Supreme Court ruling in the Pentagon Papers case may have affected but did not prevent cases of court-ordered prior restraints of the news media where classified or sealed information was leaked or made available in error. Press Freedom Tracker[75] reports 39 incidents of prior restraint affecting American journalists or news organizations from 2017 through mid-2024, with nearly a dozen occurring in 2023 alone. A number of these prior restraint cases centered on reporting official content that was leaked or inadvertently made available, rather than filed under seal. In nearly all cases, the news media ultimately prevailed.[76]

71. *Snepp v. United* States, supra note 69.
72. C. Savage, "Ex-National Security Officials Sue to Limit Censorship of their Books," *New York Times*, April 2, 2019.
73. *Id.*, quoting Jameel Jaffer, executive director of the Knight First Amendment Institute at Columbia University, which jointly represented the plaintiffs with the American Civil Liberties Union.
74. "Federal Judge Says John Bolton Can Publish Memoir Trump Administration Tried to Block," *Los Angeles Times*, June 20, 2020.
75. https://pressfreedomtracker.us/prior-restraint/.
76. In incidents considered a prior restraint where the media did *not* prevail, it was not leaks but the behavior of the journalist that was at issue. In 2024, independent investigative blogger Thom

For example, in 2019, county officials in Colorado obtained an order prohibiting a local TV station from reporting on an inappropriate relationship between a sheriff's deputy and a jail inmate based on an unintentionally disclosed affidavit the government claimed should have been sealed. The judge ruled the order was an unconstitutional prior restraint. In another case, a Central California city sought an injunction to keep the local weekly newspaper from publishing leaked memos between the city council and its attorneys about the firing of its city manager. In finding for the newspaper, a Monterey Superior Court judge concluded attorney-client privilege and preventing the release of the information was not compelling enough to override the right of free speech.[77]

A case involving bribery, obstruction, police corruption, organized crime, and lying to the FBI led to a secret plea deal that was inadvertently exposed to news media. In 2018, the details of a plea deal between a narcotics officer and federal prosecutors were mistakenly posted online and reported in a story by the *Los Angeles Times*. Police detective John Saro Balian allegedly lived a double life, helping gang and Mexican mafia members with drug trafficking, a car theft ring, and tipping off criminals about police raids. His plea deal to cooperate with federal prosecutors was supposed to be filed under seal but ended up on the federal court's online records system, PACER. The *Times* promptly wrote a story for its website, and Balian immediately sought and was granted a temporary restraining order that required the *Times* to both delete elements of the article and refrain from further publishing any of the plea agreement details. The *Times* complied but filed an emergency petition for a writ of mandamus with the U.S. Court of Appeals for the Ninth Circuit. Dozens of media organizations, journalists, and others came out in support of the newspaper, submitting a letter to the federal court stating that

> the desire to correct this administrative error, . . . cannot justify the imposition of a prior restraint. . . . [O]nce information is made public, nearly 90 years of constitutional law stand in the way of using prior restraints to prevent a newspaper from communicating the information to its readers.[78]

The court agreed, vacating the restraining order and denying Balian's motion for a (more permanent) preliminary injunction against the paper. Although admonishing the paper for "exploiting an honest mistake by a docketing clerk," the decision allowed the *Times* to freely publish the full story without censorship.

Julian Assange and WikiLeaks

Australian computer programmer and journalist Julian Assange founded WikiLeaks in 2006 as a means for people to share (the "wiki" part of the name) leaked information about questionable government activity. An anonymous Dropbox folder gave contributors a way to provide source material to be vetted by WikiLeaks

Roddy was issued a no-contact and no-trespassing order in North Carolina after allegedly pinning a county official between two vehicles and yelling at her in a threatening manner. The order effectively restricts Roddy from being at the county courthouse. Another incident of prior restraint involved a journalist who recorded and livestreamed a criminal proceeding in North Carolina, despite posted signs prohibiting such recording. Davin Eldridge was found guilty of criminal contempt and was required to write an essay about respect for the court and publish it online and censor negative comments. *Id.*

77. Attorney-client privilege is the common-law right to keep certain communications between lawyers and their clients secret.
78. "Judge Orders Los Angeles Times to Delete Published Article About Plea Deal," *U.S. Press Freedom Tracker*, July 14, 2018, *at* https://pressfreedomtracker.us/all-incidents/judge-orders-los-angeles-times-remove-certain-facts-published-article/; J.M. Shepard, "Prior Restraint Still Makes Important Stories a Hassle," *Medium*, January 22, 2019, *at* https://medium.com/@jasonmshepard/prior-restraint-still-makes-important-stories-a-hassle-e8471abb7603.

volunteers. Assange said this additional anonymity would encourage people to reveal information they might otherwise keep secret due to the potential for punishment in fines, imprisonment or, in extreme cases, death. The first posting in 2006 was a document authorizing the assassination of government officials signed by a Somali sheikh.

WikiLeaks made a big impact in the United States with the release of thousands of records in 2010, including incriminating videos related to the war in Afghanistan. Those files were followed by the release of hundreds of thousands of diplomatic cables between the U.S. State Department and its embassies around the world. A U.S. soldier with security clearance, Private Chelsea Manning, was court martialed for violating the Espionage Act by releasing more than a half-million government documents to WikiLeaks. Manning was sentenced to 35 years in prison, which was later commuted to seven years by President Obama. This soldier was originally accused of aiding the enemy – a charge potentially resulting in a death sentence – but was acquitted. She was a lightning rod for discussion of leaked government secrets. She was guilty of disclosure, and many believed her sentence was too light. On the other hand, the released documents and videos clearly showed inappropriate and illegal activity by the U.S. military that was unlikely to come to light any other way. Some credited the leaks with being the catalyst for the so-called Arab Spring in late 2010, resulting in protests against government corruption in several Arab countries.[79]

In addition to Manning, the federal government chose to expand its investigation into wrongdoing by discovering whether WikiLeaks and Assange had violated U.S. law. The case against WikiLeaks would be more complicated since Assange was not an American nor was he living here. After hours of probing, federal officials declared Assange would not be prosecuted for disclosing government secrets as Manning had been, largely because of the protection afforded to journalists: the one who *leaks* the documents may be guilty of criminal activity, but the one who disseminates the information is not. "The problem the department has always had in investigating Julian Assange is there is no way to prosecute him for publishing information without the same theory being applied to journalists," said former Justice Department spokesman Matthew Miller. "And if you are not going to prosecute journalists for publishing classified information, which the department is not, then there is no way to prosecute Assange."[80]

Assange has been under attack for other WikiLeaks releases, such as video of a U.S. military helicopter killing Iraqi civilians and emails damaging to presidential candidate Hillary Clinton. After living in asylum in the Ecuadorian Embassy in London, Assange was indicted in May 2019 and again on broader charges in June 2020 for violations of the U.S. Espionage Act in recruiting and agreeing with hackers to commit computer intrusions in the Chelsea Manning case. He was detained in the United Kingdom on extradition request from the United States. Assange ultimately pleaded guilty in 2024 to one felony charge of obtaining and publishing U.S. military secrets in a plea deal that considered his time served and allowed him to return to his native Australia.[81]

79. "Amnesty International Hails WikiLeaks and Guardian as Arab Spring 'Catalysts,'" *The Guardian*, May 13, 2011.
80. "Julian Assange Unlikely to Face U.S. Charges over Publishing Classified Documents," *Washington Post*, November 25, 2013.
81. Mari Yamaguchi, et al, "WikiLeaks' Assange Pleads Guilty to Publishing US Military Secrets in Deal That Secures His Freedom," *AP*, June 25, 2024.

Edward Snowden

Edward Snowden was working for Booz Allen Hamilton, an independent consulting firm working for the U.S. National Security Agency (NSA). Snowden copied and leaked classified NSA documents in 2013 that served as the basis for dozens of news stories about U.S. spying. The documents exposed a wealth of intelligence about surveillance programs around the world, including disclosures of the United States monitoring of its allies, which proved embarrassing, to say the least.[82]

The NSA is supposed to monitor foreign communications in an effort to keep the nation safe, but monitoring Americans is a bit more controversial, even when it produces results. After a four-month investigation of the leaked materials, the *Washington Post* reported that the surveillance activities led to the capture of a Pakistan-based bomb builder, a terrorist bombing suspect in Indonesia, and those the *Post* declined to identify. And the investigation also showed that the NSA monitored many more citizens, thanks to an NSA program code-named PRISM, authorized by Congress in 2008 through amendments to the Foreign Intelligence Surveillance Act.[83] The NSA was authorized to monitor content stored in user accounts, including Americans' use of Yahoo, Facebook, Google, Microsoft, and other websites.[84] Some "extra" information is bound to be scooped up in the process, but privacy advocates question whether the NSA casts too wide a net and whether it should keep information that does not fit its investigative charge.

Snowden's release of thousands of documents showed how the federal agency was engaged in an unprecedented level of surveillance. The NSA was even monitoring popular online gaming sites, like the massive multiplayer community engaged in *World of Warcraft*. Given that the federal agency was also tracking the location of cell phones and searching individual emails, Snowden contended he was acting in the best interest of Americans by letting everyone know how far the NSA snooping had gone. The Espionage Act became a tool to quiet whistle-blowers like himself, he contended, but regardless of motivation, the consequences of his explosive revelations are felt even today.[85]

The U.S. Justice Department charged Snowden with violating the Espionage Act, although given his flight abroad, federal prosecutors have been unable to try him. Snowden was given asylum from Russia and has been in that country since 2013, being granted Russian citizenship in 2022.[86] Like Chelsea Manning and Julian Assange, Snowden is cast as either a traitor or hero, depending on your perspective.[87]

Restraint in an Age of Terrorism and Mass Shootings

It would be a mistake to say seditious libel ended with the freedom granted to Clarence Brandenburg. In 1993, federal prosecutors convicted a group of terrorists of violating the Seditious Conspiracy Act, which made it a crime to seek the violent overthrow of the U.S.

82. "Court Gave NSA Broad Leeway in Surveillance, Documents Show," *Washington Post*, June 30, 2014.
83. "U.S., British Intelligence Mining Data from Nine U.S. Internet Companies in Broad Secret Program," *Washington Post*, June 7, 2013.
84. "In NSA-Intercepted Data, Those Not Targeted Far Outnumber the Foreigners Who Are," *Washington Post*, July 5, 2015.
85. "The NSA Deputy Chief on Edward Snowden's True Motivations," *Washington Post*, October 27, 2016.
86. "Putin Grants Russian Citizenship to Former NSA Contractor and Whistleblower Edward Snowden," *CBS News*, Sept. 26, 2022.
87. "Was Snowden Hero or Traitor? Perhaps a Little of Both," *Washington Post*, January 19, 2017.

government. Ramzi Yousef of Kuwait and Sheikh Omar Abdel Rahman, a blind leader of an Egyptian Muslim group devoted to terrorist acts, along with eight others railed against the U.S. government and threatened acts against American citizens. Youssef Adel Rahman and his followers made good on those threats by bombing the World Trade Center in 1993, and their clearly present danger caused the deaths of six New Yorkers and the wounding of more than a thousand others. It was only a foretaste of the terror to come eight years later.

After the World Trade Center was destroyed and 2,977 lives lost in the attacks of September 11, 2001, President George W. Bush announced the nation was at war. Soon thereafter, his administration asked broadcasters to resist telecasting the videotaped statements of al Qaeda leader Osama bin Laden out of concern it could be his means for sending coded messages to his followers. American networks opted to comply, and so the government's power in this regard was accepted. Still, critics questioned the White House's informal use of prior restraint.

Other more intrusive post 9/11 measures alarmed Americans. Reacting to some of the president's initiatives, the town of Brewster, MA, called a town meeting to discuss the anti-terrorist **USA PATRIOT Act**. Because U.S. law enforcement agents, not local governments, enforced the PATRIOT Act's search, seizure, and detention provisions, the town hall opposition reflected an alliance of people opposing the administration's policies that would have a chilling effect on antiwar research or communications. The U.S. Department of Justice argued that such alarm over the USA PATRIOT Act was unfounded. Federal law enforcement officials rarely, if ever, applied its most controversial provisions, which would involve secretly subpoenaing library records, or "sneak-and-peek" warrants allowing investigators to conduct a secret search.

Patriot Act (USA PATRIOT Act)
Uniting and Strengthening America by Providing Appropriate Tools Required to Intercept and Obstruct Terrorism Act of 2001.

In one instance, the federal government did move to prosecute subversive television content. In 2006, Javed Iqbal was taken into custody for dealing with a Hezbollah-operated TV channel known as al-Manar. The 42-year-old Pakistani immigrant and owner of HDTV Ltd. was prosecuted under the International Emergency Economic Powers Act – a law that made it a federal crime to deal financially with terrorist groups. The U.S. government labeled the channel – al-Manar – a "Designated Global Terrorist," believing that its sources of revenue were used to fund terrorist activities. Iqbal pleaded guilty in 2008 to providing material support through Hezbollah television in exchange for thousands of dollars in payment. One consequence of Iqbal's case was New York's loss of televised reports espousing the opinions of Hezbollah, the Shiite Muslim group then at war with Israel in Lebanon.

Mass shootings in the United States have also prompted actions of prior restraint against news media. In the aftermath of the mass shooting at Marjory Stoneman Douglas High School, the South Florida *Sun-Sentinel* was barred from disclosing glimpses of a publicly released report.[88] The school board had posted it all on its website despite a judge's orders to redact facts about how the Broward County public school system failed to comply with laws governing students with disabilities. The school board charged the *Sun-Sentinel* with published the damning details knowing the court had directed them to remain private, prompting contempt proceedings against the paper and its reporters. The *Sun-Sentinel* echoed the Supreme Court's position that it is the government's burden to safeguard information, not the news media's responsibility. They also pointed out a mass shooting at school is of high public interest and that publishing it could help better understand the shooter's motivation and future response. The contempt proceedings were dismissed.

The deadliest mass shooting in the United States to date occurred in Las Vegas where local media outlets then faced an injunction preventing them from publishing information

88. S. Chen, "Court Should Not Hold *Sun-Sentinel* and Its Reporters in Contempt for Publishing Legally Obtained Information," *Reporters Committee for Freedom of the Press*, August 14, 2018, *at* www.rcfp.org/reporters-committee-and-30-media-organizations-court-should-not-hold/.

from publicly released autopsy reports of the 58 victims.[89] The wife of one of the victims obtained the injunction to prohibit the *Las Vegas Review-Journal* and the Associated Press from reporting on her deceased husband's redacted autopsy report. In reiterating that prior restraints on the press are presumptively unconstitutional, the Nevada Supreme Court struck down the injunction.

Threats in the Digital Age

In 2012, a Kent State University sophomore was arrested for tweeting a threat he would shoot up the campus. Police arrested him on felony charges for causing a panic. Authorities might have acted differently if the post on his Twitter account wasn't just five days after 12 people were shot and killed in a Colorado movie theater.[90] A grand jury refused to indict him for a felony, but the former Dean's List student was suspended and banned from campus. Was the threat real or the baseless rantings of an angry teen?

Three middle school students were expelled in 2012 when they posted threats to kill some classmates and teachers on Facebook. The school district in Griffith, IN, called the comments a "true threat," while the girls' families called the comments "complete jest" that no one would take seriously. There were more than 70 posts, including such specifics as using a box cutter, a butcher knife, and lighting someone on fire.[91] A lawsuit filed in federal court was dismissed in 2013 when the parties reached a confidential out-of-court settlement.[92]

Schools aren't the only ones dealing with threats on social media. A quick web search will yield dozens of actions initiated against someone for threats on social media. Like the Griffith, IN, case, most end in settlements rather than a court decision.

One exception occurred in 2015 when the Supreme Court weighed in on the matter in *Elonis v. United States*.[93] Anthony Douglas Elonis wrote rap lyrics, some of which were violent, and shared them on Facebook. He was indicted for separate posts that were considered threatening to an amusement park's employees and patrons, his estranged wife, law enforcement, and an unidentified kindergarten class. After his wife was given a restraining order against him, Elonis posted,

> "Fold up your [protection-from-abuse order] and put it in your pocket
> "Is it thick enough to stop a bullet?
> "Try to enforce an Order
> "that was improperly granted in the first place
> "Me thinks the Judge needs an education
> "on true threat jurisprudence
> "And prison time'll add zeros to my settlement . . .
> "And if worse comes to worse
> "I've got enough explosives
> "to take care of the State Police and the Sheriff's Department."[94]

Elonis was indicted on five separate counts of making threats, and a trial court found him guilty on four of the counts. He insisted he was exercising his free speech rights, and

89. T. Shanks, Esq, "A Review of Prior Restraints and Restraining Media Coverage of the Las Vegas Shooting," *Nevada Lawyer*, November 2018, *at* www.nvbar.org/wp-content/uploads/NevadaLawyer_Nov2018_Prior-Restraint.pdf.
90. "College Rampage Threat 5 Days after the Colorado Shooting Leads to Arrest," *Christian Science Monitor*, July 30, 2012.
91. "Griffith Public Schools: Facebook Comments Posted by 3 Girls, Expelled, Posed A 'True Threat,'" *Huffington Post*, June 15, 2012.
92. "Indiana School, Girls, Settle Facebook Threat Lawsuit," March 19, 2013, *at* http://will.illinois.edu/news/story/indiana-school-girls-settle-facebook-threat-lawsuit.
93. 575 U.S. 723, 135 S. Ct. 2001 (2015).
94. *Id.* at 2006.

several of his posts mentioned free speech (one even linked to a Wikipedia entry). When the Supreme Court granted *certiorari*, legal scholars hoped that the Court would clear up the First Amendment issues surrounding online threats. But when the decision was rendered, the majority stated that "it is not necessary to consider any First Amendment issues," deciding instead to overturn the convictions based on the principle that Elonis could not be prosecuted only if a reasonable person *felt* threatened by him. The Court ruled the instructions given to the jury were in error. Prosecutors would have to prove that Elonis *intended* to threaten others with his words for the words to rise to the level of threats under felony law. Thus, the *intention* to threaten must be present.

In 2023, the Supreme Court further clarified that in true threat cases the State must prove that the defendant was *aware* in some way of the threatening nature of the communications. In *Counterman v. Colorado*,[95] Billy Counterman had sent hundreds of Facebook messages to a local singer and musician whom he had never met. She ignored and tried to block him, but his messages increasingly suggested violent harm would befall her.[96] She contacted the authorities and Counterman was ultimately charged and convicted for violating Colorado's law against making repeated communication in "a manner that would cause a reasonable person to suffer serious emotional distress."[97] But Counterman appealed, arguing that the First Amendment requires the State to show that he was aware of the threatening nature of his statements.

The Supreme Court agreed with Counterman, although clarifying that in true threats cases, the standard of proof that the First Amendment requires of a defendant's subjective mindset or *mens rea* (guilty mind) is no more than *recklessness*. In the context of threats, this means that a speaker is aware "that others could regard his statements as" threatening violence and "delivers them anyway."[98] The Court concluded this standard of recklessness offers "enough 'breathing space' for protected speech," without sacrificing too many of the benefits of enforcing laws against true threats.[99] (See Chapter 9 for more about the *Elonis* and *Counterman* cases.)

Summary

- Government censorship today is not forbidden, but it must surmount a high hurdle when public interest or government secrets are involved. Ever since the *Brandenburg* case, the rationale of government has been to prevent imminent lawless action, which is intentional, imminent, and likely.
- In 1833, the Supreme Court ruled the Bill of Rights did not apply to state governments because nothing in the language of the first ten amendments suggested otherwise. Following the Civil War and the adoption of the Fourteenth Amendment, the Supreme Court adopted a selective incorporation approach, applying various clauses from each amendment to the states as matters of case law. The free speech clause of the First Amendment was incorporated in the case of *Gitlow v. New York*, and the free press clause came later in *Near v. Minnesota*.
- The theory behind freedom of the press is that the truth ultimately prevails in a free marketplace of ideas. In other words, the best antidote to bad speech is better speech correcting it. Democracies rely on an informed electorate, so it is imperative to inform citizens

95. 600 U.S. 66, 143 S. Ct. 2106 (2023).
96. Messages included "Fuck off permanently," "Staying in cyber life is going to kill you," and "You're not being good for human relations. Die." *Id.* at 2112.
97. Colo. Rev. Stat. § 18-3-602(1)(c).
98. 600 U.S. 66, 143 S. Ct. 2106, 2117, citing *Elonis*, 575 U.S. at 746 (Alito, J., concurring in part and dissenting in part).
99. *Id.*, at 2119.

of errors in policy and political judgment in order to have an impact on the outcome of laws and elections.

- The Supreme Court developed its bad tendency test during the twentieth century, when immigrants and left-leaning radicals were viewed as threats to the federal government, particularly during times of war. Justices Holmes and Brandeis argued in dissent, saying the Constitution protected defiant and rebellious speech. A clear and present danger meant there were both the means and opportunity for real violence and the forcible overthrow of the government. Ultimately, the *Brandenburg* test for imminent and lawless action became the standard for assessing when the advocacy of violence or unlawful activity rises to such a level that it may be punished or prohibited.
- Prior restraints are a way government attempts to exercise control over the press. One type of prior restraint is discriminatory taxes, which are considered unconstitutional. The most common legal tool censoring free expression is a court-ordered injunction. Injunctions can and have been used to stop government criticism prior to the offending information's publication. The Pentagon Papers case is the definitive example where the Supreme Court ruled that prior restraints are presumptively unconstitutional; government has the heavy burden of justifying a prior restraint. Dissenting speech has also been stopped by refusing to grant access to potentially condemning information, as the government has done in times of war.

Ethical Dilemma: Violence on Social Media

What should a social media company do when a post promotes violence? What if the post comes from a politician, such as the president of the United States?

As private businesses, social media companies such as X (formerly Twitter) and Facebook are not subject to the same First Amendment censorship constraints as the government. They have free, editorial control over the content on their sites. But how far should they go?

For years, the company formerly called Twitter had a policy against allowing posts that glorify violence. But when President Donald Trump posted a tweet that included the statement "when the looting starts, the shooting starts," the social media giant made the controversial decision to only flag the tweet as violating their policy. The flag required users to dismiss the warning before viewing the tweet, and it prohibited them from liking or retweeting it.

Twitter's action put pressure on other social media companies to do the same in dealing with posts that threaten violence. But Facebook and Twitter executives were at opposite ends of a debate when it came to accepting the president's posts. A battle over how tech companies handle violent content and controversial political content escalated.

While Facebook had a policy on "community standards on violence and incitement" that it invoked against violators, it chose not to treat the "shooting" post as violating its policy. They flagged other users' posts for violence that were copies of the president's post, but not the president's own post. The company's CEO Mark Zuckerberg explained that he did not believe that as a private technology company they should be in the business of vetting what politicians say.

Facebook and Zuckerberg then came under fire for declining to act against President Trump's posts inciting violence. Zuckerberg stood firm in his decision not to moderate posts of the president, arguing a deference for speech that it deems "newsworthy." Some Facebook employees then staged a virtual walkout to protest the company's stance, and some vowed to quit. Ultimately bowing to public pressure, employee unrest, and a burgeoning advertiser boycott, Zuckerberg announced that Facebook would remove posts that incited violence, even from political leaders.

Earlier, other Twitter flags had prompted the Trump administration to threaten to strip social media companies of their long-standing liability protection against lawsuits for the content they carry, as provided by Section 230 of the Communications Decency Act. Later, the administration called on the tech giants to act against violent posts by others calling for violent acts amid protests, including rioting and toppling of statues.

In 2023, Twitter unveiled a new policy that prohibited violent speech and expanded on its old rules, in part to comply with European Union rules that require platforms to control for material that promotes such things as terrorism and hate speech. The policy additions included a ban on "coded language," akin to "dog whistles" used to indirectly incite violence. It also added a rule that prohibited "threatening to damage civilian homes and shelters, or infrastructure."[100]

But in 2024, now X softened its rules to allow violent (and pornographic) content so users could "express themselves, show and learn about what's happening, and debate global issues, often sharing images and videos as part of the conversation." Content should not be "excessively gory or depicting sexual violence," and content that explicitly threatens or incites or glorifies violence would continue to be disallowed.[101]

If you were working for a social media company and facing violent posts, how would you respond?

Should any posts citing violence be allowed? How would you determine which posts should be removed? Apply the imminent and lawless action test? Should there be an exception for politicians, given the greater weight traditionally afforded to political speech and its news value? If you disagreed with how your company was handling violent posts, would you take a stand? Quit?

As you grapple with your ethical decision-making, you might consider philosopher Wm. David Ross's focus on outcomes and competing ethical claims or duties. Consider, on the one hand, your fidelity to your profession as a social media specialist, your own conscience and moral compass, and your interest in self-preservation in earning a living to support yourself and others. On the other hand, consider your responsibility to your employer that could be hurt by losing subscribers, advertising dollars, and even legal protections. Then there's the beneficence and welfare of the many subscribers. Where would you stand?

100. Barbara Ortutay, "Twitter's New 'Violent Speech' Policy Similar to Past Rules," *Associated Press*, March 1, 2023.

101. Chris Newbould, "X Changes Rules to Formally Allow Porn and Violent Content on its Platform," *Prolific North*, June 4, 2024, *at* https://www.prolificnorth.co.uk/news/x-changes-rules-to-formally-allow-porn-and-violent-content-on-its-platform/.

4

Forums of Freedom

LEARNING OBJECTIVES

After reading this chapter, you should know

- how U.S. law defines *public*, *designated*, *limited*, and *nonpublic forums*
- when content-neutral and content-based rules are necessary
- how time, place, and manner rules affect public communication
- what legal precedents protect communication at schools and work
- how true threats are defined under the First Amendment
- what rules restrict freedom of expression for public employees
- what protection are examples of hate speech given under the First Amendment

News events engage Americans and influence how they think in ways that are unprecedented. In 2022, the U.S. Supreme Court reversed *Roe v. Wade* (1973)[1] leading some state governments to impose bans on abortion for pre-viability pregnancies imposing gestational limits of from 6 to 22 weeks. One such law in Florida prompted the state senate minority leader and Democratic party chair to march against the new abortion restriction. Sen. Lauren Book and State Chair Nikki Fried were arrested outside Tallahassee City Hall for *trespassing*.

What happened to their First Amendment rights in what would be considered a public forum?

An estimated 1,000 protesters were arrested in Texas after the murder of George Floyd. Their message, "Black Lives Matter!", resounded in forums prompting some to ask: Who has the right to make such statements on taxpayer-supported property? Courts look to precedent-setting decisions to determine if restrictions on the content and context of forum communication are constitutional, but first they determine how to legally define the speech.

The U.S. Supreme Court took up the question of how to classify vehicle tags in *Walker v. Texas Division, Sons of Confederate Veterans* (2015) – public forums or government speech. Texas descendants of Confederate soldiers wished to show off Dixie's stars and bars on their cars. The Lone Star State's government refused the request to celebrate the defenders

1. *Dobbs v. Jackson Women's Health Organization*, 597 U.S. 215 (2022) was the landmark ruling reversing *Roe v. Wade*, 410 U.S. 113 (1973) holding that the U.S. Constitution does not confer a national right to abortion, and that it should be left up to the states to impose any legal restrictions on that medical procedure.

DOI: 10.4324/9781003462989-4

Government Speech Doctrine

U.S. Supreme Court principle giving to local, state, or federal governments the right to advance its perspective through public communication regardless of viewpoint.

of slavery on specialty license plates. Taking their case to the Supreme Court, the Confederate descendants claimed it was their constitutional right to display personal messages on license plates and asked if the First Amendment prohibits the government from censoring such messages.

The Fifth Circuit Court of Appeals in New Orleans agreed the Confederate flag was a "symbol of sacrifice, independence, and Southern heritage" deserving of access to Texas license plates as public forums.[2] The Supreme Court, however, took a decidedly different view. Personalized license plates are not *limited public forums*, but instead represent government communication subject to oversight. The high court affirmed the prior restraint except for the dissenting opinion of Justice Samuel Alito who viewed those "little mobile billboards" as *limited public forums*, which would be given freedom from censorship.[3] Such distinctions are sometimes hard to understand especially when others are allowed to express viewpoints on public property to provoke protests.[4] This chapter covers how competing interests in public forums are controlled.

A Flag Flying Forum

Flags unfurled and flying high may inspire awe and respect but seldom cause controversy. That is unless it is in Boston, where three flagpoles are designated to fly one flag for the Stars and Stripes, another one for the Commonwealth of Massachusetts, and one for the City of Boston at City Hall. This third flagpole is also designated to fly flags for other purposes – foreign nations, ceremonial events, and even special interest groups. One group, however, Camp Constitution, was denied a request to fly its flag at Boston City Hall. The "Christian flag" was meant to fly in honor of the Judeo-Christian moral heritage. One city official ruled flying that flag violated the municipal policy against religious endorsement and refused to do so. Camp Constitution sued for its rights but lost at trial and later at the U.S. First Circuit Court of Appeals.

The Supreme Court reviewed the City of Boston's decision on flag placement to see if the constitutional rights of Camp Constitution were violated by this decision. The third flagpole was made available to outside, private groups and would be considered a limited public forum. No viewpoint discrimination was practiced by the government in its oversight of a limited public forum – even against religious organizations. The Court used an approach based on history and logic – who controls the public expression on the flagpole and who would the public consider to be the speaker. Using that test, the third flagpole was not to be viewed as government speech since other banners flew there. So the Court unanimously held that refusing flag placement would be "impermissible viewpoint discrimination," and it would not be promoting a religious viewpoint to allow a group to fly a Christian flag there.[5]

Forums

The idea government has the final say over what public property is open for free speech and when areas should be shared by others can be traced to a nineteenth-century dispute in a New England municipal park. A fervent evangelist was jailed several times for sharing his gospel message without invitation or a permit on the Boston Common, a public park.

2. *Texas Div., Sons of Confederate Veterans, Inc. v. Vandergriff*, 759 F. 3d 388 (2014).
3. *Walker v. Texas Division, Sons of Confederate Veterans*, 576 U.S. 200 (2015).
4. See *Rust v. Sullivan*, 500 U.S. 173 (1991), where the Court first articulated the government speech doctrine affirming a federal rule against counseling the choice of abortion as a means of family planning.
5. *Shurtleff v. City of Boston*, 596 U.S. ___ (2022).

Rev. William F. Davis had no certificate and was not interested in getting one. His mission was to share the gospel and defend his right of religious freedom in public. The itinerant minister was cited, convicted, and jailed. He eventually lost his appeal after the U.S. Supreme Court saw his mission as subordinate to the city's power to control its public parks. This ruling likened government suppression to a private homeowner's rule over his house.[6]

This public/private homeowner analogy survived for 42 years until the Supreme Court was forced to rethink its view of public parks and streets after union members in New Jersey were confronted by police and arrested for sharing U.S. labor news in Jersey City.[7] Mayor Frank "Boss" Hague earned his nickname by ruling his town with a tight fist for over 30 years.[8] The Committee for Industrial Organizations (CIO) raised his hackles when they handed out pamphlets touting union organizing freedoms granted under the National Labor Relations Act. Boss Hague reacted with force believing unions were a step toward communism.

The mayor had the CIO pamphleteers arrested and ferried back to Staten Island, NY. Union lawyers answered the mayor's challenge by questioning his enforcement of the city's permit ordinance before the U.S. Supreme Court. The union victory in *Hague v. CIO* (1939) not only gave the union room to breathe and dispense its fliers, but it also formed the first ladder rung of the forum doctrine defining public parks, streets, and sidewalks as ***traditional public forums***.[9] This landmark ruling forced politicians and public officials to rethink their role in the use of public places by everyone for the purposes of freedom of speech.

Bedrock Law

Traditional public forums cannot exclude by government license or permit specific messages based on their subject or viewpoint.

> Wherever the title of streets and parks may rest, they have immemorially been held in trust for the use of the public and, time out of mind, have been used for purposes of assembly, communicating thoughts between citizens, and discussing public questions.[10]

With those words, Justice Owen Roberts created what would become the *forum doctrine*, although the term itself did not appear in this ruling. Years later after settling public communication disputes in education, politics, and protests, the Court came up with that term.[11]

Forums and School Expression

If a person speaks in a publicly-owned outdoor space customarily used for all purposes, it's likely to be open and deserving of full First Amendment protection. These spaces might be an outdoor gazebo, a pedestrian walkway, or the portico of a public building that are traditional public forums. The Court holding in *Hague* held "streets and parks" were to be given such a free and open status, but how would that doctrine apply to other areas? Would a public university president's office, a municipal auditorium, or public school teacher mailboxes be organized under the same principle?

6. *Davis v. Commonwealth of Massachusetts*, 167 U.S. 43, 47 (1897).
7. *Hague v. Committee for Indus. Org.*, 307 U.S. 496 (1939).
8. Another moniker for Hague was "I am the law" – the words he used to silence a subordinate who dared to question his authority.
9. In *Jamison v. Texas*, 318 U.S. 413 (1943), the U.S. Supreme Court explicitly rejected the Boston Common definition of a public homeowner after Dallas city officials cited *Davis* to support their ban upon the distribution of handbills in city streets. The public forum concept outweighs government interest unless it is substantial.
10. *Hague v. Committee for Indus. Org.*, supra note 7 at 515.
11. Legal historians attribute the classification to the 1983 ruling in *Perry Educ. Association v. Perry Local Educators' Association* although earlier cases used the term *public forum* in their decisions.

History Matters

Courts review the history of a disputed public space to see how it was used in the past. Suppose there is a controversy over what advertising can be placed on or in public buses, and a politician wants the space used for their campaign promotions. What happens next? Supreme Court Justice Harry Blackmun recommended taking a careful look in the rear-view mirror, saying "before you could say whether a certain thing could be done in a certain place you would have to know the history of the particular place."[12]

The City of Shaker Heights refused to sell a candidate for the Ohio House of Representatives space on their bus billboards for his campaign advertising. Both the location and previous use of the space determine its status under this analysis, which is how the courts have applied the *history and logic* test. In this case, the high court ruled that the rapid transit system was not a public forum, although four justices dissented given their belief commercial advertising on public transportation should be viewed as a public forum.

In judging what locations are deemed public forums, the Supreme Court's landmark decision in an Indiana teachers' union case is also pertinent. The teachers in Perry Township were voting on which collective bargaining union should represent them in negotiations over salaries, benefits, and work-related issues. Two unions vied for their representation, but the bid by Perry Education Association (PEA) won over Perry Local Educators' Association (PLEA).

A key stipulation of the new contract with PEA was that no rival union should be granted access to the teachers' mailboxes. PLEA, upset by this provision, contested it on constitutional grounds before the Supreme Court. It was a close vote (5–4), but the ruling held the public employee mailboxes could be restricted to use by PEA (and not PLEA). School mailboxes were not an *open forum*, accessible to all parties given the terms of that contract. Justice White established a classification scheme for public forums in the majority opinion.[13]

To be clear, **traditional public forums** cover the following areas: around public parks, streets and sidewalks, and certain parts of public buildings. The rules adopted for such places afford safety and reasonable access, and any legal line limiting expression at such places is subject to the highest level of protection, *strict scrutiny*. That would place the burden on the government to show a valid reason for restricting speech based on a *compelling public interest* including such concerns as public health and safety, national security, or the fundamental rights of U.S. citizenship including the rights of citizen voting.

A **limited public forum** was defined as you might expect, "property, which the state has opened for use by the public as a place for expressive activity,"[14] which might include government bulletin boards, speakers' corners on college campuses, or student-run newspapers. The test for delineating those forums requires two elements: first, the government clearly indicates a *substantial* or important interest must be served by the rule, and second, that no viewpoint is discriminated against by the government. It must be a *content-neutral* rule. Such rules require alternative channels for communication be made available. And a limited forum is subject to what's known as the *compatible use doctrine* based on its history and reasonable use for expressive activities.[15]

Justice White saw in his typology a third type of space: **nonpublic forums**. These are locations supported by taxes invested in buildings or surroundings for larger purposes, where the government may lawfully restrict or even refuse expressive activities. Any list of nonpublic forums identifies military bases, state hospitals, and prisons – places where the

12. *Lehman v. Shaker Heights*, 418 U.S. 298 (1974), at 302.
13. *Perry Educ. Association v. Perry Local Educators' Association*, 400 U.S. 37 (1983).
14. *Id.* at 45.
15. In *Grayned v. City of Rockford* (1972), the Supreme Court declared "[t]he crucial question is whether the manner of expression is basically incompatible with the normal activity of a particular place at a particular time" (at 408 U.S. 104, 116).

building's purpose necessitates this restriction on open communication. In such spaces, the primary purpose usually overrides First Amendment interests.

Several precedents in case law also pertain to constraints placed on a person's freedom of expression in personal dress, sexually oriented materials, and even correspondence.[16] The burden of challenging a *nonpublic forum* designation falls on the petitioner, who must prove it is an unreasonable rule and no *legitimate* interest is served by it.

Limited or Designated Public Forums

A fourth classification is that of a *designated public forum*. In the 1960s, city officials of Chattanooga, TN, were afraid of welcoming the rock musical *Hair* to their town knowing that some actors' nudity would appear in the city auditorium. Southeastern Productions, Ltd., a New York firm, fought this prior restraint order believing the stage production was not obscene, as the city maintained. The U.S. Supreme Court agreed and concluded Chattanooga's city officials had gone too far. Their refusal to "use this public forum accomplished a prior restraint under a system lacking in constitutionally required minimal procedural safeguards," adding that "the danger of censorship and of abridgment of our precious First Amendment freedoms is too great where officials have unbridled discretion over a forum's use."[17]

The difference between a *limited forum* and a *designated public forum* depends on how much control the government exercises over the property involved for the benefit of others. Some courts have held a limited public forum is a subcategory of a designated public forum, and the distinction is relevant when it comes to scrutinizing the specific regulations. The U.S. Supreme Court allowed advertising billboards on public buses to be viewed as a *limited* and not a *designated public forum*. The buses were in Seattle, WA, and the Ninth Circuit affirmed a district court decision based on the petitioner's request to advertise mug shots of 16 wanted terrorists, even though the public bus system refused to display the suspect Middle Eastern faces. In four other jurisdictions, public bus advertising was viewed as a designated public forum, which called for government to apply strict scrutiny, but in this case the public bus was a limited public forum, and the court was satisfied its rule against demeaning or discomfiting advertising was reasonable and viewpoint neutral.[18]

The Tinker Landmark

High school-age students and younger ages have less freedom of expression than adults, but are they left without any constitutional rights? They might be subject to a different set of standards based on how their school forum is defined in law. Recall from Chapter 1 the case of the Tinker siblings and Christopher Eckhardt, all students in Des Moines, IA, public schools. John Tinker, his sister Mary Beth Tinker, and their friend, demonstrated for peace at school in 1965. The three students prepared black armbands with peace symbols to protest the U.S. involvement in the Vietnam War.

School officials quickly chose to preempt their silent symbolic demonstration by imposing a rule against armbands. They would tell the students to remove them, and if they did not comply, each one would be suspended. John, Christopher, and Mary Beth (Figure 4.1) wore their peace symbols, were sent home, and told to stay there until they showed a personal willingness to obey the administration and return without them.

16. *Parker v. Levy*, 417 U.S. 733 (1974), at 743–749; *Goldman v. Department of Defense*, 475 U.S. 503 (1986); *General Media Communications v. Perry*, 952 F. Supp. 1072 (1997), and *Procunier v. Martinez*, 416 U.S. 396 (1974).
17. *Southeastern Productions, Ltd. v. Conrad*, 420 U.S. 546 (1975).
18. *American Freedom Defense Initiative v. King County, Washington*, 577 U.S. _____ (2016).

Figure 4.1 Mary Beth Tinker continues to advocate for free speech; here she shows her detention slip from nearly 50 years ago to a group at Ithaca College

Bedrock Law

The *Tinker* rule allows students freedom of expression on school grounds unless their communication predictably poses a material, substantial disruption to education.

The families of the three students filed a lawsuit against the school system in response. They asked for an injunction to stop the Des Moines school officials from enforcing the ban, but the Iowa district court refused to do so. The school district convinced the court schools held the type of authority over students necessary to prevent such demonstrations because to allow otherwise would adversely affect the discipline needed in the classroom environment.

An appellate court sided against the Tinker family and affirmed the school's regulation, but the Tinkers felt strongly enough about the issue to appeal to the U.S. Supreme Court. This landmark decision offered a rationale for affirming freedom of symbolic communication at schools throughout the United States.[19]

Disruption Test

School officials knew the students' reason for wearing the armbands was to protest through a symbolic act akin to "pure speech," but a more important interest also would be served. A student cannot speak out, even passively and symbolically in class, without some restraint. As Justice Abe Fortas set the rule, schools need to "forecast substantial disruption of or material interference with any school activities" before acting as censors in classrooms and on campus.[20]

19. *Tinker v. Des Moines Ind. Comm. Sch. Dist.*, 393 U.S. 503 (1969).
20. *Id.* at 514.

Tinker Rule – How to Define the Terms: "Material and Substantial Disruption"

- Is it a serious, physical disruption that would affect the educational process?
- Is there a reasonable forecast of disruption before the action is taken?
- How is the disruption defined in speech, action, or both?

The challenge for school administrators was how to strike the proper balance, considering the "need for affirming the comprehensive authority of the states and of school officials, consistent with fundamental constitutional safeguards, to prescribe and control conduct in the schools."[21]

Justice Fortas wrote a familiar passage in this case: Students do not "shed their constitutional rights to freedom of speech or expression at the schoolhouse gate."[22] No public school has absolute authority over its students to create "enclaves of totalitarianism."[23]

Justice Hugo Black dissented because to his way of thinking, the Court had gone too far since "taxpayers send children to school on the premise that at their age they need to learn, not teach."[24] Justice Black's dissent also carried some weight over time. The high court sometimes avoided the Tinker precedent until it took a social media case over 50 years later.

Online and Off Campus

The idea of teachers and administrators controlling communication by students who may be located miles away from campus seemed farfetched, but once social media became popular, things changed. What a high school student chooses to do on their personal computer at home can only become a concern for teachers or students if it materially affects what happens in class. But what happens when the posting comments go beyond teenage gossip and crushes on classmates and if the social media turns aggressive with threats or worse? Can school officials make a move to get involved? Appellate cases across the country demonstrate this fact.

In King County, WA, the Kent School District imposed a policy designed to protect students from harassment, but it was found to be unconstitutional. Officials tried to prohibit "inappropriate, harassing, offensive, or abusive" online communication when a student named Nick Emmitt constructed a malicious website styled as the "Unofficial Kentlake High Home Page" where classmates were invited to vote for the one student or teacher they most wanted to see die. Emmitt was suspended for this cyber-aggression, and in return he sued the school. In 2000, the court ruled in his favor by judging his home laptop to be "entirely outside the school's supervision or control."[25]

In a similar incident shortly after, a federal court in Pittsburgh struck down a policy targeting "inappropriate, harassing, offensive, or abusive behavior" among students after a volleyball player posted four messages on an Internet bulletin board criticizing teachers he disliked at the school. The student was punished and taken off the team, only to be reinstated

21. *Id.* at 507.
22. *Id.* at 506. The Supreme Court denied cert. in a 2013 Third Circuit decision supporting the right of two high school girls to wear "I heart boobies" bracelets to school. The Easton (PA) School District tried to argue that the bracelets were lewd, and the girls were suspended for "disrespect, defiance and disruption." The appeals court disagreed and a 107-page decision cited *Tinker* for the premise that nondisruptive speech was permissible in school. *B. H. v. Easton Area Sch. Dist.*, 827 F. Supp. 2d 392 (E.D. Pa., 2011). Cert. denied *Easton Area Sch. Dist. v. B. H.*, 134 S. Ct. 1515 (March 10, 2014).
23. *Id.* at 511.
24. *Tinker v. Des Moines Ind. Comm. Sch. Dist.*, supra note 19, at 524.
25. *Emmett v. Kent Sch. Dist.*, 92 F. Supp. 2d 1088 (W.D. Wash. 2000).

later once it became clear the supposed disruption interfering with the school day never materialized in the evidence presented against him.[26]

Yet while the National School Boards Association found some student websites to be immature and mildly offensive, others had become outright threatening. The high court of Pennsylvania dealt with the latter category in a case in which a student's off-campus website featured a gruesome image of a teacher's decapitated head dripping with blood. The site invited visitors to donate $20 to hire a hit man. The Pennsylvania Supreme Court held that even though the student created his website off campus, it was aimed at school personnel and was accessed at school by the perpetrator. As a result, the punishment was upheld even after the *Tinker* test was applied.[27]

The proliferation of social media would also present challenges. In another corner of Pennsylvania, a high school student was suspended after creating a fake Myspace profile with his principal's image on it. Justin Layshock's profile targeted the principal with absurd answers to fake questions about the principal's interests and activities, including drug use, drinking, and sex. Layshock was suspended, but a federal district judge later ruled against the disciplinary action in view of the nature of the offense.

It would be an unseemly and dangerous precedent to allow the state in the guise of school authorities to reach into a child's home and control the child's actions there to the same extent that they can control that child when they participate in school-sponsored activities. Allowing a district court to punish Layshock for conduct he engaged in using his grandmother's computer while at his grandmother's house would create just such a precedent.[28] An appeals court later affirmed, holding that the First Amendment prohibits the school from reaching beyond the schoolyard to impose what might otherwise be appropriate discipline.[29]

Yet in *Kowalski v. Berkeley County Schools II* (2011), the trial court applied *Tinker*'s test to punish a form of cyberbullying where West Virginia high school students ganged up on a classmate by posting on a webpage titled S.A.S.H. (Students Against Sluts Herpes). The webpage author was Kara Kowalski, who alleged a classmate had a sexually transmitted disease. Kowalski was suspended for five days but appealed her punishment claiming her private out-of-school speech was off-limits to authorities. The appellate court disagreed, noting that Kowalski's victim was distraught, and her school participation had been disrupted. The suspension was affirmed. "We are confident that Kowalski's speech caused interference and disruption described in *Tinker* as being immune from First Amendment protection."[30]

In 2023, the Supreme Court granted certiorari to a case to determine if school punishment in response to off-campus speech via social media was violative of the First Amendment. *Mahanoy Area School District v. B.L.* (2021) gave precedence to student freedom, and it relied on *Tinker* to do so.

It all began on a Saturday afternoon at the Cocoa Hut, a convenience store about 100 miles northwest of Philadelphia, where Brandi Levy, a high school freshman took her frustration to social media to curse over her failure to make the varsity cheerleading squad and softball team. She posted on Snapchat, "Fuck school fuck softball fuck cheer fuck everything." That message featuring Brandi's raised middle finger was captured on Snapchat and shared among classmates and teachers.

Rather than finding her words offensive, it was observed in oral arguments that just how much one curses can be viewed as a *badge of honor* among students. According to the school

26. *Flaherty v. Keystone Oaks School District*, 24 F. Supp. 2d 698 (2003).
27. *J.S., a Minor through His Parents v. Blue Mountain School District*, 650 F.3d 915 (3d Cir. 2011).
28. *Layshock v. Hermitage School District*, 496 F. Supp. 2d 587 (W.D. Pa. 2007).
29. *Layshock v. Hermitage School District*, No. 07–4465 (3d Cir. 2011) (en banc); *Layshock v. Hermitage School Dist.*, 593 F.3d 249 (3d Cir. 2010).
30. *Kowalski v. Berkeley Cnty. Sch.*, 652 F.3d 565, 567 (4th Cir. 2011), at 513.

district policy, however, Levy's use of profanity in the context of an extracurricular event was punishable by a one-year suspension – not from school – but from the junior varsity squad cheering on the Golden Bears. The Court had to decide. Would Snapchat be viewed as some sort of school forum that falls under administrative oversight?

Recall *Tinker v. Des Moines Independent Community School District* (1969) protected the rights of in-person expression protesting the Vietnam War with armbands that did not disrupt classroom activities. Levy's parents certainly did not believe their daughter's use of profanity online and on the weekend was any business of the Mahanoy Area School District, and the Supreme Court agreed. It held 8–1 against the school district's punishment of the student. Justice Stephen Breyer wrote for the majority, "Geographically speaking, off-campus speech will normally fall within the zone of parental rather than school-related responsibility." Most importantly, "America's public schools are the nurseries of democracy," declared Justice Breyer.[31]

From the Trenches: Is Hair Free Expression?

By Marjorie Esman, Former ACLU Attorney

Public schools often have dress codes that restrict hair, with different rules for girls and boys. Such rules tend to normalize the hair of White students and treat natural hairstyles among Black students as "disruptive." So far, the Supreme Court hasn't accepted a challenge to these policies, and they rarely succeed in lower courts. Courts typically defer to schools to decide what, other than free speech, is "disruptive." A significant exception is if the hair is religiously mandated.

Due to the First Amendment's "free exercise" provision, deference is given to a religious exception to a hair policy. Some Native American faiths prohibit boys and men from cutting their hair except in certain circumstances. Courts routinely rule in favor of such students if they show the long hair to be part of an established religious belief. Even the Fifth Circuit Court of Appeals in New Orleans, generally considered a conservative appellate court, ruled in favor of these students.

For example, in *A.A. v. Needville Indep. Sch. Dist.*,[32] a Native American student refused to cut his hair, which he wore in two braids in violation of school policy. The appellate court upheld his right, based on his and his family's religious beliefs, to wear his hair long and in the open. Rastafarians also believe that boys and men should not cut their hair. Often schools simply relent when a student shows that the hair is part of a sincerely held religious belief, so there are few cases that have gone to trial on this issue.

For prisoners, whose hair is also subject to regulation for security reasons, that right is now established. In *Ware v. La. Department of Corrections*,[33] Rastafarian Christopher Ware, an inmate in a Louisiana facility, was disciplined for refusing to violate his beliefs and cut his hair in accordance with prison policy. While he lost at trial, on appeal the Fifth Circuit upheld his religious right to long hair.[34]

What does this mean? The law in this area, as in many others, is constantly changing. Students can engage in free expression that isn't disruptive. Schools have wide leeway in deciding what is and isn't disruptive, but they may not force a student to violate the student's religious beliefs.

31. *Mahanoy Area School District v. B.L.*, 594 U.S. 180 (2021)
32. 611 F.3d 248 (5th Cir. 2010).
33. 866 F.3d 263 (5th Cir. 2017).
34. *Id.*

Compatible Use Doctrine Speech restrictions are allowed if the regulation is basically consistent with the normal activity for a particular place and time and prevents interference with it.

Compatible Use Doctrine

Tinker's armbands were a symbolic form of political expression, but when the protest is with bullhorns and the volume loud enough to reach the classroom students, there can be a restriction. During one school day in 1972, students upset in Rockford, IL, rallied outside classrooms loud enough for students and teachers to hear their protests and see protest signs from windows. Demonstrators carrying placards pointed to inequality in hiring teachers and counselors and when choosing their cheerleaders. The signs read "Black cheerleaders to cheer too," "Black history with black teachers," and "Equal rights, Negro counselors." Police arrested about 40 protesters carrying those signs, including organizer Richard Grayned. He was tried and convicted for violating Rockford's anti-picketing and anti-noise ordinances. He appealed his conviction and won a partial victory. The anti-picketing rule was overbroad, but the anti-noise rule met the need of protecting classes from disruption by loudspeakers near campus.

When Grayned's case went before the Supreme Court, Justice Thurgood Marshall held the nature of a public place is important, including "the pattern of its normal activities," which "dictate the kinds of regulations of time, place, and manner that are reasonable."[35] This decision formed the basis of what is known as the **compatible use doctrine**. "The crucial question is whether the manner of expression is basically incompatible with the normal activity of a particular place at a particular time."[36] In this case, picket signs protesting racial discrimination were acceptable, but loud bullhorns interrupting classroom lectures were not. *Grayned* is noted for the phrase describing content-neutral regulation by **"time, place and manner"** limits.

Explicit Speech at School

Case law has more to say on freedom of expression at public schools. The Supreme Court referenced its *Tinker* principle years later after a high school student was suspended for creating a scene at a student assembly. The action was prompted by Matthew Fraser's nominating speech that drew vividly on sexual imagery. Fraser was campaigning on behalf of his classmate Jeff Kuhlman, who was hoping to become student vice president of Bethel High School, near Tacoma, WA. Against the advice of others, Fraser used a comic approach using sexual innuendo to boost his candidate, "who is firm in his pants . . . Jeff is a man who will go to the very end – even the climax, for each and every one of you."[37] Bethel High School students hooted and acted out his wordplay. Kuhlman won the election.

The outcome for Fraser was not so victorious; he was suspended from high school for his speech made against his teachers' advice. Fraser responded with a lawsuit claiming his right to freedom of speech had been violated and sought injunctive relief for his civil rights under 42 U.S.C. § 1983. With the support of his parents and the American Civil Liberties Union, Fraser's case was appealed to the Supreme Court. By a 7–2 vote, Fraser's suspension had been revoked but was reinstated. Chief Justice Warren Burger concluded "a high school assembly or classroom is no place for a sexually explicit monologue directed towards an unsuspecting audience of teenage students."[38] *Tinker* was not applied in this case since the Court saw the speech as "offensively lewd and indecent" rather than politically symbolic. Besides, "the constitutional rights of students in public school are not automatically coextensive with the rights of adults in other settings."[39]

35. *Grayned v. City of Rockford*, 408 U.S. 104 (1972).
36. *Id.* at 116.
37. *Bethel Sch. Dist. v. Fraser*, 478 U.S. 675 (1986).
38. *Id.* at 686.
39. *Id.* at 682.

Hazelwood Landmark
Public schools are not bound by the *Tinker* rule if student speech is restricted to the context of course work and does not occur in a designated public forum.

Hazelwood Landmark

Fourteen years after the *Tinker* Court protected students' right to silently protest in class, three high school students in St. Louis, MO, protested that their words in print had been silenced. The Journalism II students reported and edited for *The Spectrum* at Hazelwood East High School. It was customary to deliver newspaper pages to the principal for approval prior to publication. With this edition, Principal Robert Reynolds took special interest in stories about sex and divorce.

One article disclosed how pregnancy had shaken three students' lives (without naming names), while another one covered the dramatic impact of a divorce. The principal felt the unpublished names of pregnant students would not be kept secret for long, and the sexual activity discussed including contraception would reach the eyes of younger students. The school principal expressed these concerns and others because the divorced parent was severely criticized by his daughter. The father in this case was left without room for his side of the story. The principal turned thumbs down on these articles due to these issues and misgivings.

The Spectrum's controversial pages were subsequently extracted and the stories deleted. The impact felt by Hazelwood's student journalists was one of betrayal since becoming convinced this censorship was wrong. When the U.S. Court of Appeals for the Eighth Circuit addressed the issue, it applied *Tinker* and sided with the students based on the lack of evidence those deleted articles were disruptive. The Hazelwood school district was not done fighting, and it appealed to the U.S. Supreme Court to protect and uphold the principal's authority.

In a 5–3 decision, the Supreme Court rejected the *Tinker* analysis holding the school administrators can exercise prior restraint when it is school-sponsored expression – such as a newspaper that is part of the curriculum because this sort of prior restraint was related to teaching journalism. In doing so, the majority concluded "educators do not offend the First Amendment by exercising editorial control over the style and content of student speech in school-sponsored expressive activities so long as their actions are reasonably related to legitimate pedagogical concerns."[40] The dissenting justices felt the promise to allow "free expression or diverse viewpoints within the rules of responsible journalism" was replaced by "a taxonomy of school censorship." Justice Brennan concluded "the young men and women of Hazelwood East expected a civics lesson, but not the one the Court teaches them today."[41]

Taking *Hazelwood* to College?

In 2005, the U.S. Court of Appeals for the Seventh Circuit revisited the rationale of *Hazelwood* for a college case. Writers for *The Innovator* at Governors State University in Illinois issued front-page criticisms of both teachers and administrators. Co-editors Margaret Hosty and Jeni Porche refused to print retractions or rebuttals. They had enjoyed freedom from censorship, but after taking aim at faculty and administrators, Dean Patricia Carter chose to withhold publication pending prior review, which the co-editors believe went against the school's stated policy. Hosty and Porche sought an injunction. An appeals court applied *Hazelwood* and held school-sponsored speech – even at the college level – is not necessarily subject to public forum analysis.

Borrowing from *Hazelwood*, the basic question became simply whether the administration was reasonably responding to pedagogical concerns.[42] The appellate decision turned on the issue of forum analysis and kept *Hazelwood* as the standard for college newspapers

40. *Hazelwood Sch. Dist. v. Kuhlmeier*, 484 U.S. 260 (1988), at 273.
41. *Id.* at 291.
42. *Hosty v. Carter*, 412 F. 3d 731(7th Cir. 2005), at 735.

by holding that the dean demanding prior review of the newspaper content would not be held liable for censorship. The legislature of Illinois and at least two other states responded by enacting bills to allow more student control of college newspapers after the Governors State case.

Nonpublic Forum
A building, space, or facility that is not open for public expression and assembly.

What happens when the speech on campus has yet to take place, but the public university anticipates the sort of disruption forecast in the *Tinker* case? In *Healy v. James* (1972),[43] the Supreme Court held public universities could impose reasonable time, place, and manner rules on student activities but could not ban political groups unless presented with evidence such groups would defy reasonable regulations. *Healy* was then cited in *Papish v. Board of Curators of the University of Missouri* (1973) when the Court warned public universities not to censor offensive ideas just because they fail to conform to prevailing norms of decency.[44]

What About Student Banners and School Mission?

Forum decisions often begin by defining the location and event. When students leave campus for extracurricular activities, another factor may be added to the disruption analysis. In *Morse v. Frederick* (2007), a high school principal was incensed by a banner reading "BONG HiTS 4 JESUS" unfurled at exactly the right moment for TV cameras to capture the image during a school-supervised outing to see the Olympic Torch Relay in Juneau, AK. Principal Deborah Morse confiscated the banner and suspended Joseph Frederick for his role in the hijinks.

Bedrock Law
Courts determine once a traditional (quintessential), designated, or nonpublic forum is involved in a challenge whether the rule is valid based on either a balancing test (nonpublic), intermediate scrutiny (limited), or strict scrutiny (traditional).

Frederick appealed the suspension and sued over his constitutional rights. He lost at the trial level but won later in the Ninth Circuit Court of Appeals. The Supreme Court ruled against the student by stating that "a principal may, consistent with the First Amendment, restrict student speech at a school event, when that speech is reasonably viewed as promoting illegal drug use"[45] – something schools may properly take steps to safeguard against.

A good example of the nonpublic forum is found in the case of *Greer v. Spock* (1976), where the famous baby physician, Dr. Benjamin Spock, chose to run for the office of U.S. president. Dr. Spock tried to access a military installation, Fort Dix in New Jersey, to hand out campaign fliers protesting the Vietnam War. He was denied entrance by the military brass, and so the doctor-turned-candidate took his case to court on First Amendment grounds. The Supreme Court felt the military was within its rights to stop him at the gate and curb his free speech rights because this nonpublic forum was designated principally for training soldiers and not campaign events.[46]

Books Banned in Boston . . . and Elsewhere

Book banning is older than the nation itself, dating to the Puritan reign in New England where in 1650 their elders set fire to a pamphlet contradicting church orthodoxy about redemption. Closer to today, censorship gained a new life in New England in the twentieth century when the phrase "Banned in Boston" was used to boost sagging sales for books needing some controversy to spark reader interest.

Book banning advocates experienced a surge of support in 2021 when they joined with special interest groups and drafted rules to remove books from school and public libraries. The American Library Association and a nonprofit group of U.S. writers called PEN America reported over 1,500 book bans targeting more than 1,100 books by

43. 408 U.S. 169 (1972).
44. 410 U.S. 667 (1973).
45. *Morse v. Frederick*, 551 U.S. 393 (2007), at 408.
46. *Greer v. Spock*, 424 U.S. 828 (1976).

2022.[47] Censorious leaders enacted rules to block librarians from having the final say on books about race, sexual identity, or other matters deemed offensive and dangerous to traditional values. One Southern state even threatened its librarians with jail time if they knowingly loaned sexually graphic books that might be later defined as obscene, although that law was blocked by a federal judge.[48]

The important issue now becomes one of whether school or city officials who remove books from school and public libraries are in some sense violating the First Amendment. The Court dealt with this question in *Island Trees School District v. Pico* in 1982 but left legal scholars in somewhat of a quandary. Three justices sided with Justice William Brennan who believed "local school boards may not remove books from school library shelves simply because they dislike the ideas contained in those books."[49] On the other hand, three justices agreed with Chief Justice Warren Burger holding the school board's actions were acceptable. The ninth vote in *Pico* came from Justice Byron White who declined to take a side.

Challenging book banning based on *Pico*'s precedent is to stand on not-so-solid ground. Even though book banning based solely on partisan or political interests is clearly censorship, the *Pico* ruling is clearer in deciding bounds for curriculum supervision. School boards can "establish and apply their curriculum in such a way as to transmit community values," ruled the Court, because "there is a legitimate and substantial community interest in promoting respect for authority and traditional values be they social, moral, or political."[50]

President Trump's Designated Forum – Twitter

Before President Trump was exiled from Twitter following the January 6th storming of the U.S. Capitol, he enjoyed an enthusiastic following as @RealDonaldTrump. There were followers who often retweeted his comments or, in some cases, took issue with them. Some not only challenged the 45th president's facts, but also his spelling and diction. "Eugene Gu, MD," posted a pointed criticism following Trump's haphazard tweet of a wrongly spelled term, *Covfefe*. "The same guy who doesn't proofread his Twitter handles the nuclear button," wrote Gu. After this post of disapproval, Gu found himself blocked from the site, but he was not the only one. Six others had been blocked by @RealDonaldTrump. In this case, a federal judge for the Southern District of New York recognized the president had taken his private platform and created a forum of sorts to discuss public officials, policy, and comment on notable issues of national importance.

Columbia University's Knight First Amendment Institute argued those blocked users should have access to such a social media space – even a private account of the president's should be kept free and open to all. The ruling in *Knight First Amendment Institute v. Trump* held the president's forum was not the same as for a private citizen.[51] Whether he realized it or not, President Trump had created a *designated public forum*, and censoring followers based on their viewpoints was out of line with the First Amendment. Such use of social media sites as a public forum allows content-neutral

47. H. Natanson, "More Books Are Banned than Ever Before as Congress Takes on the Issue," *The Washington Post*, April 7, 2022, *at* https://www.washingtonpost.com/education/2022/04/07/book-bans-congress-student-library/.
48. J. Riley, "Judge Blocks Arkansas Law to Jail Librarians for 'Harmful' Books," *Metroweekly*, August 2, 2023, *at* https://www.metroweekly.com/2023/08/judge-blocks-arkansas-law-to-jail-librarians-for-harmful-books/.
49. *Island Trees Sch. Dist. v. Pico by Pico*, 457 U.S. 853, 854 (1982).
50. *Id.* at 864.
51. 302 F. Supp.3d 541 (2018).

restrictions, but to block users for adverse views would not be content neutral and constituted unlawful government censorship.

When the Supreme Court took the appeal to the decision retitled *Biden v. Knight First Amendment Institute at Columbia University* (2021),[52] it dismissed the complaint as moot. But after vacating that decision, Justice Clarence Thomas wrote a concurring opinion to raise key issues. If Twitter had become a public forum under the president's use of it, then how was he removed from the platform by Twitter, a private firm without any public input whatsoever.

And if digital platforms have the "right to exclude" consumers and exercise power with impunity free of government oversight, then who is to protect the public interest in this space?

Faith and Limited Public Forums

In the 1981 court case *Widmar v. Vincent*, the Supreme Court redefined the rights granted to limited public forums on school grounds. The University of Missouri at Kansas City sought to prevent the Cornerstone Christian group from meeting on campus. The group was using a university room for its religious gathering. In 1977, it was advised to leave campus because its religious use of government property violated the First Amendment's establishment clause. Yet the U.S. Supreme Court ruled that granting access to a religious group to use a limited public forum does not represent the public endorsement of any religion. Also, the government would have to show a compelling reason to ban a group based on the content of its communications. In this instance, it could not.[53]

The government went one step further when it defined the money collected through university fees for student publications as a limited public forum. In *Rosenberger v. Virginia* (1995), the University of Virginia restricted the use of Student Activities Funds from publications espousing beliefs in a "deity or ultimate reality," meaning it would block any financial assistance for Wide Awake: A Christian Perspective at the University of Virginia. The student fees, however, represented a *limited public forum* at the University of Virginia, and the Christian group was entitled to its share of funding without the government violating the establishment clause of the First Amendment.[54]

Returning to the question of religion at a public university, the Supreme Court ruled 5–4 in favor of the right of the University of California's Hastings College of the Law's decision to deny official status to the Christian Legal Society (CLS) as a registered student organization because its bylaws excluded students who engage in "unrepentant participation in or advocacy of a sexually immoral lifestyle."

The administration concluded that such a membership ban would contradict the official college policy for student organizations to welcome all students regardless of their status.[55] The Court ruled it was appropriate to require open access to a limited public forum such as the one denied to this student organization because the policy affirmed the neutral viewpoint required of such a forum. The CLS argued instead that the "all comers" policy violated its exercise of freedom of association, religion, and speech. It claimed the university should differentiate between a choice in sexual activity and one's status such as race, gender, or ethnicity. The Court held sexual orientation to be a status and *not* a preference.

52. 593 U.S.______ (2021).
53. *Widmar v. Vincent*, 454 U.S. 263 (1981).
54. *Rosenberger v. Rector and Visitors of the University of Virginia*, 515 U.S. 819 (2005).
55. *Christian Legal Society v. Martinez*, 561 U.S. 661 (2011).

Shopping Malls a Public Forum?

While it might seem sensible to have privately owned property defined as something other than a public forum, there are cases when private real estate may function as a public forum. Perhaps the best example of this distinction is the shopping mall. The entire space is usually privately owned, but it serves as a public space inviting all members of society to engage in retail commerce. In 1968, the U.S. Supreme Court considered whether First Amendment rights in and around shopping malls were protected. At first, the Court ruled that one privately owned shopping center in Pennsylvania was the "functional equivalent" of a public forum, and it had to allow union members to picket on this property since their demonstration was pertinent to the area.[56] But the Court reversed itself less than a decade later, declaring that prohibitions by private shopping center owners could not be considered state action.[57]

In 1980, the Court ruled that freedom of speech should prevail at malls in California because the state of California adopted a provision allowing picketers.[58] If a state chooses to ensure the rights of freedom of expression in retail centers beyond what the case law or statute holds, it may. On the other hand, some states have chosen to prohibit handing out fliers in mall parking lots, and the authority to do so has been affirmed.[59]

Protected Speech for Public Employees

Public schools throughout the nation have imposed dress codes that have been affirmed as constitutional.[60] Of course imposing such dress codes for adult-aged college students would seem peculiar, to say the least. The "unique" mission of military employment, however, poses a condition for enforcing a dress code. One Air Force rule prohibited airmen from wearing headwear indoors, including the Jewish yarmulke and other religious headwear.[61] In 2017, the Pentagon revised its U.S. Army rules on uniform standards to allow more flexibility for religious garb like the Jewish yarmulke, the Muslim hijab, and the turban for Sikhs.[62]

Public employees might find their rights of expression curbed depending upon where they work and for whom. The first U.S. measure directed at free expression for public employees was passed in 1939, which required government employees to remove themselves from political campaigns or rallies.[63] Congress revised that rule in 1993, giving U.S. civil servants the freedom to run for nonpartisan office and campaign on behalf of candidates outside of work. Still, it did not preclude the possibility of punishment for getting involved with controversies related to their work.

Disruptions in the Workplace

Speaking out or even writing a letter to the newspaper can cause trouble as Marvin L. Pickering discovered. This high school science teacher was concerned with the school board's use of taxpayer money to improve athletics at the expense of unattended academic priorities. He complained to a local newspaper editor about how school board members found money for

56. *Amalgamated Food Employees Union Local 590 v. Logan Valley Plaza*, 391 U.S. 308 (1968).
57. *Hudgens v. NLRB*, 424 U.S. 507 (1976).
58. *Pruneyard Shopping Ctr. v. Robins*, 447 U.S. 74 (1980).
59. *Id.*; *See also State v. Felmet*, 302 N.C. 173, 273 S.E.2d 708 (1981).
60. For example, *Harper v. Poway Unified Sch. Dist.*, 445 F.3d 1166 (9th Circ. 2006), upheld public school prohibition on T-shirts that denigrate others on the basis of sexual orientation.
61. *Goldman v. Weinberger*, 475 U.S. 503 (1986).
62. M. Myers, "New Army Policy OKs Soldiers to Wear Hijabs, Turbans and Religious Beards," *ArmyTimes*, January 5, 2017, *at* www.armytimes.com.
63. An act to prevent pernicious political activities named for Senator Carl Hatch of New Mexico (5 U.S.C. §§ 7321–7326, and §§ 5001, 5008).

sodding the football field but not for teacher salaries. This assertion and similar ones resulted in Pickering getting fired from his job for acting in a manner the board deemed "detrimental" to the school district's interest. Once the case reached Washington, DC, the Supreme Court rejected that contention and supported this teacher's right to participate in the public debate. This decision created what became known as the *Pickering* balancing test,[64] which weighs the free speech rights of the public employee against the operational efficiency of the public employer. Pickering's fight for his right to protest at work came at a price. He gave up teaching for a time and took a job in a soup factory while working the appeals. After his win, he was reinstated by the district.

The Supreme Court removed the protection for employee speech in a case where an assistant prosecutor in New Orleans passed around a survey asking colleagues about their morale at work. District Attorney Harry Connick sought to remove Sheila Myers, but she refused the transfer, and so he fired her for insubordination.[65] Myers appealed her dismissal on First Amendment grounds, but the Supreme Court sided with Connick.

> When employee expression cannot be fairly considered as relating to any matter of political, social, or other concern to the community, government officials should enjoy wide latitude in managing their offices, without intrusive oversight by the judiciary in the name of the First Amendment.[66]

A nurse at an Illinois hospital was fired after she criticized the facility's training and staffing policies. Cheryl Churchill's superiors said she was acting out of spite, and her criticisms had a disruptive effect on the hospital's environment. When the case reached the Supreme Court, Justice Sandra Day O'Connor offered a test for judging a public employee's right to speak out at work. Her standard held the highest level of constitutional protection for discussion of *public issues*, but it also provided a rationale for employers to guard their interest in avoiding disruptions to efficiency and morale.

Just how far employees can go relates to the impact their speech has on those involved, as another teacher in Pennsylvania learned after blogging offensive terms about her students. The U.S. Court of Appeals for the Third District affirmed a lower court's summary judgment in applying the Pickering-Connick balancing approach. The court found Natalie Munroe's blog posts meant to be kept private "did not rise to the level of constitutional protection." The school district had the authority to discipline her for public "expressions of hostility and disgust against her students" because those blogging posts "would disrupt her duties as a high school teacher and the functioning of the School District."[67]

Bedrock Law

The case law supports public employer controls over employee expression if it is shown to disrupt workplace efficiency and morale.

There is a fine line between legitimate criticism and disruptive speech. The Supreme Court in 2006 narrowly concluded a deputy district attorney's criticisms of a local sheriff went beyond those bounds. Richard Ceballos criticized a sheriff's conduct in obtaining a search warrant. Ceballos was subsequently demoted and transferred. He filed a lawsuit to get his job back, and his case made it to the Supreme Court in *Garcetti v. Ceballos*. The Court ruled against him. "We hold that when public employees make statements pursuant to their official duties, the employees are not speaking as citizens for First Amendment purposes, and the Constitution does not insulate their communications from employer discipline."[68] The Court made a clear distinction limiting public employee speech made pursuant to their official duties. The state must prove whether the **disruptive impact** of the employee's communication outweighs constitutional protection. If the employer reasonably arrives at such a

64. Also known as the Pickering-Connick balancing test to indicate such judgments also could go against the public employee as it did in *Connick v. Myers*, 461 U.S. 138 (1983).
65. *Pickering v. Board of Educ.*, 391 U.S. 563 (1968).
66. 461 U.S. at 146 (1983).
67. *Munroe v. Central Bucks School District*, 805 F.3d 454, 476 (2015).
68. *Garcetti v. Ceballos*, 2006 U.S. LEXIS 4341.

conclusion, then punishment or dismissal is deemed to be acceptable, even if no disruption takes place. In this case, the hospital prevailed.[69]

Scrutiny Applications

Content-Based Restrictions
Laws that restrict speech based on its subject matter. Such laws are subject to strict scrutiny.

Strict Scrutiny
The highest standard of judicial review applied to pure speech and content-based regulation of speech. It requires the law 1) serve a compelling government interest, 2) be narrowly tailored to achieving that goal, and 3) use the least restrictive means to do so.

When the government passes a rule or law dealing with certain categories of communication, the level of First Amendment protection is determined by a balancing test of certain standards. For example, obscenity and true threats are both considered communication without constitutional protection. But there are other topics such as political advertising, where the rules are judged by what is known as **strict scrutiny**, meaning that the law touching that topic is held up to a sort of legal magnifying glass to see if the government has a *compelling* public interest more pressing than the freedom of expression guaranteed by the First Amendment.[70]

If, for example, a local city council deemed large, political and commercial road signs a public hazard, a rule regarding these harms would be subject to strict scrutiny to see if it is constitutional, particularly if the rule is **content-based** as opposed to **content-neutral**. A law restricting speech that is content-based rises to the level of strict scrutiny. What does this mean? The wording of the law should curb no more freedom than is necessary, and it must be narrowly tailored with no other means available to satisfy the compelling interest the law is meant to address.

In 2022, the Supreme Court was asked to decide whether an Austin, TX, law allowing digital billboards on-site but prohibiting them in other locations was content-based or content neutral. By a vote of 6–3, the Court ruled that the distinction was content neutral and thus the ordinance was not subject to strict scrutiny. The Court defined a law as content-based if it "applies to particular speech because of the topic discussed or the idea or message expressed."[71]

Intermediate Scrutiny

What happens then when the government adopts **content-neutral** rules, where *all* communication activities are controlled without regard to any specific content? Think of laws designed to protect your residence from excessive noise, or ones to afford access to the entrances and exits of public buildings, or ones that maintain order along parade routes and other public concerns. When courts turn their attention to such content-neutral rules, they rely on a test called **intermediate scrutiny** where the government's burden is to show a *substantial* or *important* interest that the law achieves without suppressing anyone's viewpoint.

Content-neutral rules provide the yardstick to measure whether a **time, place, or manner** regulation is constitutional. When speech or even non-speech elements are part of some conduct, "incidental limitations" on free expression will be justified. There are, for example, countless laws regulating the size and placement of signs, the volume of sounds, or the location of stages and arenas for public performances. The Supreme Court recognized the need for government to regulate when (time), where (place), and how (manner) expression is permitted, provided it does not exceed certain boundaries.

69. *Waters v. Churchill*, 511 U.S. 661 (1994).
70. Consider the flag-burning case, for example, where strict scrutiny was applied to the Texas law that placed Gregory Lee Johnson in custody. While the act of burning the flag was expressive conduct or symbolic speech and not "pure" speech, its ban was not content-neutral, raising the level of scrutiny to strict scrutiny. *Texas v. Johnson*, 491 U.S. 397, 414 (1989).
71. *City of Austin, Texas v. Reagan National Advertising of Texas Inc.*, 596 U.S. __ (2022).

Time, Place, and Manner
Content-neutral restrictions based only on when, where, and how expression may be limited. Subject to an intermediate scrutiny test.

When noise levels in the Central Park music band shell became a problem, the City of New York required a sound technician to oversee the volume levels and avoid disrupting nearby apartments. The ruling in *Ward v. Rock Against Racism* (1989) found the city ordinance was not a violation of the First Amendment because the rule was content-neutral and narrowly tailored to satisfy an important public interest during normal waking hours.[72] But the government was prevented from limiting the speech of a postal employee, Earl Mosely, who picketed on a public sidewalk in front of a Chicago high school for civil rights. As the law against picketing in Chicago was written, it afforded a content exception for labor picketing but not for issues of social justice, and it was therefore declared unconstitutional.[73]

Judicial review does place a burden on the government to justify its rules when challenged for violating constitutional rights. The Supreme Court stated in the landmark case *United States v. O'Brien* its belief a government regulation is sufficiently justified if it is within the constitutional power of the government; if it furthers an important or substantial governmental interest; if the governmental interest is unrelated to the suppression of free expression; and if the incidental restriction on First Amendment freedoms is no greater than is essential to the furtherance of that interest.[74] This is known as the *O'Brien test*.

U.S. Capitol Riots of January 6th

Supporters of President Donald Trump were motivated by a furious will on January 6, 2021, to "stop the steal" of the election and prevent Joe Biden from taking the oath as U.S. president. Groups identifying themselves as Proud Boys, Oath Keepers, and other vigilante associations felt the presidential contest was a "rigged election," and they responded enthusiastically when President Trump asked them to "fight like Hell" to keep him as president in the White House.

The Constitution requires after each presidential election in the United States for the vice president to count the votes of the Electoral College in a joint session of Congress and announce the outcome. President Trump wanted to make sure that protocol did not take place as planned on January 6, 2021. Acting as a type of civilian commander in chief, he urged on his followers to stop Vice President Mike Pence from certifying the electoral vote count ensuring his defeat.

The First Amendment guarantees the rights of citizens to petition for a redress of grievances and to peaceable assembly, but the men and women who followed President Trump's suggestion and made their way to the U.S. Capitol initiated a violent attack by toppling barricades, smashing TV cameras, battering windows, and assaulting police officers. Hundreds of arrests were made. At trial some Trump supporters used a First Amendment defense to justify their acts were to remedy what was a "stolen election."

Four leaders of the Proud Boys organization were tried under charges involving conspiracy and obstruction in a federal court for the District of Columbia. They claimed to be rightfully exercising their constitutional rights of freedom of expression that day. But they were charged with obstructing and interfering with police at the Capitol and conspiring to "stop, delay, or hinder Congress's certification of the Electoral College vote."[75] The free speech argument they used in court failed to win the day because the "incidental limitations on First Amendment freedoms" that were imposed in this case were necessary to protect the policy and procedures required by Congress to handle its duties, ruled Judge Timothy Kelly.

72. 491 U.S. 781 (1989).
73. *Police Dept. of the City of Chicago v. Mosley*.
74. *United States v. O'Brien*, 391 U.S. 367 (1968), at 397.
75. Title 18 U.S.C. §1512(c-2).

Protesting on Principle

The key to understanding how public debates over issues such as war, religion, and abortion can be controlled by location requires an examination of time, place, and manner rules. In a St. Louis suburb, one lettered sign appeared in a homeowner's window protesting the War in the Persian Gulf during the first Bush administration. Margaret Gilleo's message to passersby read, "For Peace in the Gulf."[76] The City of Ladue informed her of a local ordinance restricting signs to the sale of property, zoning restrictions, and safety hazards. She reminded local officials of the First Amendment and successfully defended her right to place a sign in her window. Ms. Gilleo fought her case all the way to the U.S. Supreme Court, where she won despite the acknowledgment that cities have a right to reduce visual clutter. In 2015, a unanimous Supreme Court ruled that content-based restrictions on signs must be subject to strict scrutiny, even if a regulation does not single out a specific group.[77]

The case raised the question of just exactly when the time, place, and manner of posting a sign becomes an illegal, content-based restriction. *Reed v. Town of Gilbert* made a point about how local government cannot impose content-based restrictions on signage, even if it seems to be content-neutral.[78] The case also clarified the level of constitutional scrutiny that should be applied to content-based restrictions on speech. Cities not allowing residents to place signs in the windows of their own homes may go too far, but even in outdoor areas, lawsuits over residents' symbolic rights are also subject to questions over zoning restrictions.

Viewpoint Discrimination

Door-to-door salesmen and church groups face hostile receptions in some neighborhoods when the product they're selling requires money or faith. In the late 1930s, the U.S. Supreme Court joined several First Amendment cases from Wisconsin, California, Massachusetts, and New Jersey to clarify the First Amendment protections. All four cases involved Jehovah's Witnesses who appealed convictions for either handing out leaflets on public streets or door-to-door sharing. Three towns punished the Witnesses when their fliers were thrown to the ground after being placed in the hands of passersby. Do such rules meet the Court's intermediate scrutiny test by supporting a substantial interest in clean streets? Not according to this landmark decision, which held that the government carries the burden to clean up afterward and not punish pamphleteers for what others do carelessly with their fliers.[79]

Just before World War II, other members of the Jehovah's Witness religion met with police officers as they marched single file down the streets of Manchester, NH. Sixty-eight members were arrested for failure to obtain a permit, but this time their convictions had been upheld because, as Justice Hughes pointed out, the local law justifiably regarded "considerations of time, place, and manner so as to conserve the public convenience . . . and to minimize the risk of disorder."[80] In addition, the city's license fee for such demonstrations was deemed necessary to meet the expenses of public services that the government had to provide.

Pro-Life Protests

What happens when the question is not a door-to-door visit or a flier handed out in the streets, but actual picketers standing in front of a home? In the late 1980s, a Wisconsin

76. *City of Ladue v. Gilleo*, 512 U.S. 43 (1994).
77. *Reed v. Town of Gilbert*, 576 U.S. 155 (2015).
78. 576 U.S. 155.
79. *Schneider v. State*, 308 U.S. 147 (1939).
80. *Cox v. New Hampshire*, 312 U.S. 569, 576 (1941).

Bedrock Law

The Supreme Court strikes down laws in which governments use licensing without clearly defined content-neutral rules for granting or denying permits.

abortion doctor sought to remove right-to-life advocates protesting outside his house. They effectively held the physician captive in his own home, but because one's home is one's castle, the picketers had to go.[81] This decision in *Frisby v. Schultz* served a key interest – protecting residential privacy.

While privacy at one's home is protected, the workplace is quite a different matter. In *Madsen v. Women's Health Ctr., Inc.*, the U.S. Supreme Court affirmed that injunctions could limit right-to-life protests outside of an abortion clinic.[82] Protesters in this Florida case sought to dissolve an injunction ordering them to stay at least 36 feet away from the clinic's entrance. The order also banned displaying observable signs (usually graphic) with images within the sight of pregnant patients. The Court declared the restriction on graphic signs was unreasonable, but the buffer zone of 36 feet around the clinic's doors was upheld.

One approach in the State of New York was to limit the abortion protesters' access by creating a 15-foot bubble of breathing space around women entering or leaving the clinic. That movable zone of privacy, however, was struck down in *Schenck v. Pro-Choice Network* (1997).[83] The Court did accept the footage around the clinic's entrance – as it did in *Madsen* – as 15-foot zones free of protest around the entrance and exits. However, right-to-life advocates were free to approach abortion patients on public sidewalks to impose objections beyond the zone outside the clinics.

A legal action pursued by the National Organization for Women (NOW) against a man trained as a Benedictine monk, Joseph Scheidler, and his Pro-Life Action League of Chicago became one of the longest-running courtroom dramas concerning this issue. The lawsuit first filed in 1986 produced a jury verdict that found the right-to-life activists liable for using intimidation, violence, and extortion. NOW pursued the lawsuit under the Freedom of Access to Clinic Entrances (FACE) Act, which President Clinton signed into law in 1994. It overwhelmingly passed Congress, establishing both criminal and civil penalties for anyone who used "force, threat of force or physical obstruction" to halt the use of reproductive health services.[84] Two lower court cases upheld the FACE law as constitutional.[85]

The issue of content-based regulation at crisis pregnancy centers or CPCs was at issue in the case of *National Institute of Family and Life Advocates v. Becerra* (2018). California's requirement that all patients must be advised about free and low-cost publicly funded family planning services, including contraception and abortion, violated their rights under the First Amendment. This Freedom, Accountability, Comprehensive Care, and Transparency Act (the "FACT Act" or the "Act") appeared to a 5–4 majority to be content-based law, and the lower court's decision was reversed.

Football, Faith, and Free Speech

The First Amendment involves different issues when it comes to expressive activities involving public employees. Imagine, for example, a high school coach takes a knee at the 50-yard line following a football game, and while players gather around, he starts to pray. That's what happened in Bremerton, WA, when school officials became alarmed by Coach Joseph Kennedy, who they believed violated the establishment clause of the First Amendment by his government speech.[86] School officials warned

81. *Frisby v. Schultz*, 487 U.S. 474 (1988).
82. 512 U.S. 753 (1994).
83. 519 U.S. 357 (1997).
84. See 18 U.S.C. § 248, Freedom of Access to Clinic Entrances Act of 1994.
85. The Fourth Circuit Court of Appeals considered Joyce Woodall's claim that the FACE law would restrain her and members of her group, Concerned Women of America, from praying in front of clinics to discourage women from getting abortions. The court rejected her antiabortion arguments. See *Woodall v. Reno*, 47 F.3d 656 (4th Cir. 1995).
86. *Kennedy v. Bremerton School District*, 597 U.S. 507 (2022).

against this prayer practice and after repeating their warnings chose to act against him. The coach was fired because as a government employee, he was told not to pray in his role as a coach.

What if, in fact, the coach's claims are true – he was not engaged in government speech because those prayers were offered as he was serving as a private citizen who has rights, too, including his personal freedom of speech and religion the school system also needs to respect. He sues to get his rights of faith and freedom of speech restored under the First Amendment

The Supreme Court then must separate what is government speech and what constitutes private speech. That's what the coach maintains he was expressing, although he was in public at the time serving as a football coach. How do we classify speech of a public school teacher or football coach engaged in the classroom with students or kneeling on the playing field? Coach Joseph Kennedy's prayer during the postgame period was private and not government speech within the scope of his duties as a coach. The answer is *government speech* in most cases, which cannot be challenged due to viewpoint discrimination in most cases. Coaches and teachers are expected to endorse certain ideas and best practices, but the school system's belief that he was endorsing religion as a government employee was wrong.

Symbolic Acts

Whether it's armbands, performance art, or even taking a knee during a sports event, symbolic acts raise First Amendment questions about content and context. In defining the terms of the debate, how the symbolic speech is expressed becomes important – nonverbal and not written. As long as any restriction is content-neutral, rules affecting symbolic expression are subject to intermediate scrutiny. But such rules might be limited, for example, if the expression is not peaceful or is destructive to government property. A law may be stricter and more punishing for a draft-card resister burning his military registration certificate than for a protester burning an American flag.

In 1966, David Paul O'Brien was taken into custody on the steps of a Boston courthouse. O'Brien, along with several protesters, stood before print and broadcast media members and set fire to his draft registration card, property of the government documenting draft-eligible men. The U.S. Supreme Court found that the United States had a substantial interest in protecting such records, and O'Brien had other means of protest at his disposal.[87] This standard was applied with a four-part test requiring the law be examined for its constitutionality, important public interest, and whether that interest is unrelated to the suppression of free expression, which must be achieved through the least restrictive means to curbing free speech.

The O'Brien test, however, was rejected as relevant to other symbolic speech cases, including ones involving flag burning. In *Spence v. Washington* (1974),[88] for example, the law against misuse of the flag was directly related to the symbolic act (peace symbol on the flag). What to take from both the ruling in *Spence* and the subsequent flag-burning decision in *Texas v. Johnson* (1989)[89] is that symbolic acts are judged on content, context, and communication. First, there is a two-part test to determine the speaker's intention to convey a particular message, and second, to see if that message was clearly understood by the audience. Then the courts may judge the symbolic act's lawfulness by distinguishing the elements meant to convey meaning and those items having other effects, such as the destruction

87. *United States v. O'Brien*, 391 U.S. 367 (1968).
88. 418 U.S. 405 (1974).
89. 491 U.S. 397 (1989).

of federal property as in the O'Brien draft-card burning case or disturbing the public peace as was alleged during the civil rights marches of the 1960s.

Dangerous Speech

Malicious words spoken to others that inflict injury and incite an immediate breach of the peace are not protected as free speech. The judicial precedent underscoring this point was coined early in World War II:

> [T]here are certain well-defined and narrowly limited classes of speech, the prevention and punishment of which have never been thought to cause any constitutional problems. These include . . . the insulting or **'fighting words'** – which by their very utterance inflict injury or tend to incite an immediate breach of the peace.[90]

Chaplinsky v. New Hampshire (1942) stands as the early landmark for the legal doctrine of "fighting words," where it becomes necessary to discern when and where someone has gone too far with their expressions of anger (such as Chaplinsky, who called a police officer a "damned Fascist" [sic]). Because such words lead to so little discovery of truth, the Supreme Court held they are easily outweighed by the people's interest in peace and public order, rendering this category of speech outside of First Amendment protection.

Unlike seditious speech (against the state), fighting words are typically spoken in face-to-face situations and involve personal insults that are likely to prompt the recipient to respond with violence against the speaker. The doctrine requires the "injury" be more than emotional, and its regulation must be content-neutral. Deciding what types of words and images inflict harm by their very nature, or when people should be liable for those communication harms committed, is a difficult one for courts to make.

What happens when words are not spoken in anger but emblazoned on the back of a denim jacket? The 1968 arrest of Paul Robert Cohen in a Los Angeles courthouse was prompted by a statement stenciled on his jacket by a woman he had met just the night before. He was in the courthouse to serve as a witness in another case and suddenly noticed she had decorated his jacket with the words "Fuck the Draft," a popular sentiment among young people of the era. Because there were children in the public courthouse corridor where Cohen had worn his jacket, an officer arrested him. The court found his jacket represented fighting words and declared he maliciously and willfully disturbed the peace. Cohen was convicted but pursued his appeal to the U.S. Supreme Court because he didn't want to go to jail for 30 days. He won his case by a one-vote margin. Justice Harlan wrote a landmark opinion and cited two reasons for reversing Cohen's conviction:

1. The law cannot ban particular words regardless of context.
2. Emotional expressions that are not intended to be obscene are worthy of First Amendment protection.[91]

The Cohen ruling became famous for the words, "One man's vulgarity is another one's lyric."[92] However, the ruling left unresolved the question of when angry expressions sparked by political fervor lose First Amendment protection.

The fighting words doctrine still poses a challenge for today's scholars.[93] It produces punishment of speech based on the *effectiveness* of the expression. Hurling insults at another

90. *Chaplinsky v. New Hampshire*, 315 U.S. 568, 572 (1942, emphasis added).
91. *Cohen v. California*, 403 U.S. 15 (1971).
92. *Id.* at 25.
93. See, e.g., B. Caine, "The Trouble with Fighting Words: *Chaplinsky v. New Hampshire* Is a Threat to the First Amendment and Should be Overturned," 88(3) *Marq. L. Rev* 441 (2004).

Fighting Words
Personally directed communication that by its very utterance inflicts injury or tends to incite an immediate breach of the peace.

person is not necessarily a fighting words offense unless the verbal aggression becomes threatening. It may be best to think of fighting words as something similar, if not analogous to, an assault. Note that assault is not the act of striking someone, which is battery, but the willful attempt to verbally inflict injury upon another, when coupled with an apparent present ability to do so, and any intentional display of force such that it would give the victim reason to fear or expect immediate bodily harm.[94] It is the conversion of words from expression to action (from just speech to intimidation or threat, which are actions) that removes First Amendment protection.

The Heckler's Veto

It is a strange turn of phrase – heckler's veto – but the U.S. Supreme Court has used it to describe the right to speak freely in public in the face of hostile audiences. The heckler's veto was first used to describe how a hostile crowd moves to silence a speaker's remarks. In the face of public unrest or threatened attacks against controversial speakers, the heckler's veto stands as a challenge to the First Amendment. In 1949, a fiery preacher was vindicated for a speech he gave in Chicago that caused a riot in the streets. Arthur Terminiello took his case to the Supreme Court, which deemed his conviction for causing a breach of the peace was based on a law that could not be held constitutional because speech should be allowed to stir listeners to action.[95] On the other hand, the high court two years later found police enforcing a heckler's veto to be justified. Irving Feiner was arrested and convicted for causing a disturbance of the peace in Syracuse, NY, after police asked him to stop his loudspeaker rally against racial oppression.[96] They feared violence would ensue as a result.

Bedrock Law
The fighting words doctrine developed in *Chaplinsky* evolved to curb fighting words that would tend to incite an imminent threat of violence.

In the era of cancel culture, heckler's veto has become so commonplace three of the nation's leading law schools held forums where invited speakers were either interrupted by groups opposed to a political viewpoint who felt they had a right to shout down a guest speaker because it was their form of free speech and the school was their forum. After episodes of angry disruptions upset conservative guest speakers at Yale and Stanford law schools, legal commentators began to question whether such elite institutions were opting for cancel culture rather than deliberating ideas through civil discourse and freedom of speech. Exercising heckler's veto by shouting down speakers whose previous words and deeds are deemed offensive only leads to majoritarian rule with little room for enlightened debate.

The fear of hecklers in public convinced some local governments to charge speakers a fee for police protection, which had the effect of preventing them from making their opinions known. The U.S. Supreme Court also ruled these speaker's fees would be unconstitutional.[97] It is not the controversial speaker but the hecklers who must be constrained, Justice William O. Douglas made clear in his *Terminiello* ruling:

> [F]reedom of speech, though not absolute, . . . is nevertheless protected against censorship or punishment, unless shown likely to produce a clear and present danger of a serious substantive evil that rises far above public inconvenience, annoyance, or unrest.[98]

The Supreme Court's first use of the term was a footnote in *Brown v. Louisiana* (1966) extracted from a law professor's book on the civil rights struggles of African Americans.[99] The ruling in *Brown* held that Blacks in Louisiana had a right to conduct a sit-in protest at

94. *Black's Law Dictionary* 114 6th ed. (1990).
95. 337 U.S. 1 (1949).
96. 340 U.S. 315 (1951).
97. *Forsyth County v. Nationalist Movement*, 505 U.S. 123, 125–126 (1992).
98. *Terminiello v. City of Chicago*, 337 U.S. 1 (1949).
99. Harry Kalven, Jr., *The Negro and the First Amendment* (Columbus, OH: Ohio State University Press, 1965).

Figure 4.2 Sit-in at a Florida lunch counter, 1960

a public library where they were forbidden from using the books because of their race. In a narrow win for civil rights protests, the Court held the "heckler's veto," that is, when the librarian asked protesters to leave the library to prevent public unrest, was invalid. "Participants in an orderly demonstration in a public place are not chargeable with the danger, unprovoked except by the fact of the constitutionally protected demonstration itself, that their critics might react with disorder or violence."[100]

"Getting into Good Trouble"

"Getting into Good Trouble!" was how Congressman John Lewis described his life's work. Those words apply to his civil rights demonstrations of the 1960s that laid the foundation for free speech today. Their dedication to protest prompted the Supreme Court to make it plain – trumped-up charges against demonstrators in public forums would not stand. In the South civil rights activists like Lewis convened at four places – the lunch counter (Figure 4.2), the bus station, city square, and public library. At each place, police arrested them with one crime in mind – *disturbing the peace*.

First, students from historically Black Southern University in 1960 moved on to lunch counter seats typically occupied by Whites at the state capitol during lunchtime. They were charged with trying to "disturb or alarm the public" under a state law.[101] In *Garner v. Louisiana*, the U.S. Supreme Court found no convincing proof of it, and civil rights attorney Thurgood Marshall, a future Supreme Court justice, won on the protesters' behalf.[102]

In northern Louisiana, six men were arrested for violating another breach-of-the-peace statute.[103] Noticing racial lines had been crossed in a bus depot, Shreveport's chief of police asked four men to go back to the Colored waiting room and exit the

100. *Brown v. Louisiana*, 383 U.S. 131, 133 n. 1 (1966).
101. Title 14, Article 103(7) La. Criminal Code.
102. 368 U.S. 157 (1961).
103. *Taylor v. Louisiana*, 370 U.S. 154 (1962).

"Whites Only" part of the station. Testimony at their trial showed no unruly or violent behavior. In fact, they were "quiet, orderly, and polite."[104] The Court rejected Louisiana's argument "the mere presence of Negroes in a white waiting room was likely to give rise to a breach of the peace."[105]

The third case came during Christmas shopping season in 1961 when 23 protesters started picketing a segregated restaurant in Baton Rouge. Local police charged them with illegal picketing. Congregationalist minister B. Elton Cox came to their support by securing permission to bring an estimated 2,000 protesters from Southern University to march across the street from where they were held in jail. The minister was arrested and charged with provoking a breach of the peace, picketing near the courthouse, and obstruction of a public passageway. Rev. Cox was convicted and lost appeals on all three counts at the state level. When the U.S. Supreme Court took up his case, the breach-of-peace charge was the first to fall, and the others followed suit.[106]

When the U.S. Supreme Court accepted its fourth case from Louisiana, *Brown v. Louisiana*,[107] the scene shifted to the public library. The lead plaintiff in this case Henry Brown was joined by four others who entered a segregated library branch in 1964. Brown requested "The Story of the Negro." The librarian advised it was not available and promised to request it for him. He took a seat in the small building with fellow demonstrators standing nearby. A plurality opinion from the Supreme Court concluded the disturbing the peace charge in the library came without evidence. Using breach-of-peace laws, the high court showed how segregation is just plain wrong because public spaces should be open for all races.

Global View of Hate Speech

Hate speech is a global concern, and it has been the subject of all sorts of rules based on race, gender, ethnic status, religion, or sexual orientation. Some countries – for example, Canada and France – criminalize speech leading to discrimination, hatred, or violence based on race and religion. There is greater sensitivity in Europe toward racism in general and anti-Semitism in particular. For example, any attempt to revise the history of Nazi Germany's extermination of the Jews during World War II is not tolerated by the European Court of Human Rights, which limits its protection of free speech to only those expressions consonant with "underlying values," which means sharing "racially discriminatory" ideas of any kind is forbidden according to this tribunal.[108]

The United States, however, has a different approach to hate speech. And two scholars have led the battle for stronger sanctions. Professor Richard Delgado proposed a civil solution, claiming that victims of racist words are entitled to sue for psychological, sociological, and political harms for such insults. This sort of language injures one's dignity and self-respect, and it releases a toxic message that deserves damages for recovery.[109]

Scholar Mari J. Matsuda argued the government's failure to punish racial epithets is tantamount to supporting it, she believed. Matsuda advocated adherence to a United Nations resolution calling for the countries of the world to make it a crime to appeal to ideas of "racial superiority or hatred, (and) incitement to racial discrimination."[110]

104. *Id.* at 156.
105. *Id.* at 154.
106. *Cox v. Louisiana*, 379 U.S. 536 (1965).
107. *Brown v. Louisiana*, 383 U.S. 161 (1966).
108. European Court of Human Rights, *Hate Speech*, Fact Sheet, September 2020, *at* https://www.echr.coe.int/documents/fs_hate_speech_eng.pdf.
109. R. Delgado, "Words That Wound: A Tort Action for Racial Insults, Epithets, and Name-Calling," 17 *Harv. C.R.-C.L. L. Rev*. 133 (1982).
110. M.J. Matsuda, "Public Responses to Racist Speech: Considering the Victim's Story," 87 *Mich. L. Rev* 2320 (1988–89).

Modern Hate Crime Controls

In 1952, Illinois enforced its state law against group libel by prosecuting the president of the White Circle League, who conducted a campaign against African Americans moving to Chicago. White Circle League leader Paul Beauharnais's leaflets warned of the "southern negro's" propensity for "rapes, robberies, knives, guns and marijuana." He was convicted under a group libel law that made it a crime to publish charges of "depravity, criminality, unchastity, or lack of virtue" to a class of citizens based on their race, color, creed, or religion.[111] The Supreme Court upheld his conviction by just one vote. Justice Hugo Black led four dissenters, who called the concept of group libel antithetical to American freedom and said this affirmation of the Illinois statute might further curb freedom of expression. It is for this reason that the *Beauharnais* decision has been seldom cited as precedent.

Flames of Racism

By 1992, hate crime legislation had been adopted in all but four states of the United States. Most of these statutes followed the model created by the Anti-Defamation League of B'nai B'rith calling for both criminal and civil penalties. One case that made its way to the U.S. Supreme Court to test the validity of such ordinances was *R.A.V. v. St. Paul* (1992). This landmark case was based on a municipal ordinance prohibiting "any symbol, object or graffiti including burning a cross or placing a Nazi swastika, which one knows arouses anger, alarm or resentment in others based on race, color, creed, religion or gender."[112] R.A.V. was a teenager at the time he was convicted of burning a cross inside the fenced yard of Russ and Laura Jones, an African American couple living in St. Paul, MN. The Court referred to the juvenile by his initials to conceal his identity.[113]

The Minnesota Supreme Court affirmed the bias-motivated crime ordinance applying the fighting words doctrine of *Chaplinsky*. When the case reached the U.S. Supreme Court, however, the majority struck down the ordinance because it prohibited only fighting words based on "race, color, creed, religion, or gender," while permitting hate speech motivated by other factors such as political party, union membership, disability, or homosexuality. "The First Amendment," Justice Antonin Scalia concluded, "does not permit St. Paul to impose special prohibitions on those speakers who express views on disfavored subjects."[114] The repugnant metaphor in his opinion concluded hateful acts of symbolism must be protected. "Burning a cross in someone's yard is reprehensible," he said. "But St. Paul has sufficient means at its disposal to control such behavior without adding the First Amendment to the fire."[115]

The Court returned in 2003 to consider cross burning and determine if it could be defined as protected speech or was instead an act of fear and intimidation outside the law. Virginia had a statutory ban that brought two cases to trial in 1998. The first incident took place in Virginia Beach, where teenagers tried to ignite a cross in the front yard of a mixed-race couple.[116] It was joined with a second case from Carrol County, VA, where a "cross lighting" took place at a Ku Klux Klan rally held on private property. The state law in Virginia made it a felony for "any person . . . with the intent of intimidating any person or group of persons to burn, or cause to be burned, a cross on the property of another, a highway or other public place."

111. *Beauharnais v. Illinois*, 343 U.S. 250 (1952).
112. *R.A.V. v. St. Paul*, 505 U.S. 377 (1992).
113. Viktora actually changed the spelling of his name to include a "K" for the Ku Klux Klan (KKK) and was represented by the normally liberal ACLU. He was subsequently prosecuted for criminal trespass and was convicted.
114. *Id.* at 391.
115. *Id.* at 396.
116. *Virginia v. Black*, 538 U.S. 343 (2003).

The Virginia law had declared "any such burning of a cross shall be *prima facie* evidence of an intent to intimidate a person or group of persons." The U.S. Supreme Court agreed that a state, consistent with the First Amendment, may ban cross burning carried out with intent to intimidate. But the high court did find unconstitutional the provision in the Virginia statute treating the act of cross burning as prima facie evidence of intent to intimidate. In other words, a true threat cannot be presumed from just the act of cross burning.

The landmark incitement case of *Brandenburg v. Ohio* (1969) involves a Klansman who was tried under the state's criminal syndicalism law that made it a crime to advocate violence for political reform (see Chapter 3). Clarence Brandenburg threatened there "might have to be some revengeance taken, if our President, our Congress, our Supreme Court continues to suppress the white, Caucasian race," but it was not thought to be a serious threat.[117] Even though *R.A.V. v. St. Paul* held hate speech cannot be banned, threats amounting to intentional, imminent, lawless violence are offered no First Amendment shield. Brandenburg, however, appeared to have no means to make real his words of implied violence, and unless the means for imminent lawless action exist, such empty words are protected as freedom of expression.

In some cases, the state may choose to further penalize a threat if it culminates in a violent assault prompted by racial hatred. In 1993, the vicious beating of a white male resulted in a unanimous Supreme Court decision against the assailants. After a group of black youths saw the movie *Mississippi Burning*, Todd Mitchell, 19, asked his friends, "Do you feel all hyped up to move on some white people?" He was looking at a 14-year-old youth across the street. "There goes a white boy. Go get him." The teens left their victim, who survived the attack, in a coma. Mitchell was convicted of aggravated battery, and his punishment was increased under a state law allowing penalty enhancements for hate crimes. Chief Justice William Rehnquist concluded, "A physical assault is not by any stretch of the imagination expressive conduct protected by the First Amendment."[118]

Summary

- The forum doctrine underscores constitutional rights of expression in public spaces depending on their location, history, and purpose.
- A forum is not just a physical space since the legal definition of forum has been expanded to include the digital domains of social media and internet communications.
- There are four types of forum defined by case law: traditional public forums, designated public forums, limited public forums, and nonpublic forums.
- Time, place, and manner restrictions are content-neutral limits that may be constitutionally protected.
- Narrow prohibitions on speech uphold restrictions on communications that act as a prelude to violence as in fighting words or true threats.
- Symbolic speech is speech plus action, and rules limiting symbolic speech fall under intermediate scrutiny unless content-based.
- Communication at a public school is protected constitutionally until it becomes substantially disruptive expression.
- The *Tinker* rule has not protected speech tied to curriculum in public schools or thwarted the enforcement of school rules, such as rules against indecency or advocating drug use.
- Public employees find their rights to expression curbed depending upon where they work and for whom.

117. *Brandenburg v. Ohio*, 395 U.S. 444 (1969).
118. *Wisconsin v. Mitchell*, 508 U.S. 476 (1993).

- Content-neutral rules must survive challenges using tests of judicial review including strict scrutiny, intermediate scrutiny, and a rational or reasonable basis test.
- Strict scrutiny places the burden on the government to identify the compelling public interest prompting the state to pass a law affecting the freedom of its citizens.
- Intermediate scrutiny places the government with the challenge to prove a substantial public interest is served.
- The Supreme Court has declared that "fighting words" fall beyond the umbrella of the First Amendment's protection because they either inflict injury or incite an immediate breach of the peace.
- Hate speech cannot be banned, but when an act of violence is motivated by prejudice based on race, religion, gender, or other personal traits, the First Amendment does not protect the act.[119]

Ethical Dilemmas: The Chilling Effect

It is one of the invisible enemies of free speech on college campuses – the personal fear of speaking out in public. In legal terms, it is called a "chilling effect" when the urge to communicate is suppressed whenever ideas might be judged to be suspect or offensive under vague or overbroad rules on campus, leaving students feeling isolated, powerless, and dumbstruck.

When college administrators move to adopt speech codes designed to prevent unpopular expressions for fear certain terms will provoke an adverse response or hurt feelings, they risk chilling the speech of all. Stories of radical speakers who have been forbidden a platform on campuses for fear they will engender negative reactions or even violence are quite common.

Student editors have been dismissed for challenging orthodox beliefs, and professors have been sanctioned for using offensive terms in class. The free exchange of ideas is the lifeblood of democracy, but the desire to punish certain viewpoints and the people who espouse them through policies of speech or codes on campus threatens what the First Amendment is meant to protect.

At the personal level, whenever a student or professor censors their personal speech and mutes an idea, the chilling effect has taken another victim. U.S. students are now less likely to express themselves in a face-to-face context, and the Foundation for Individual Rights and Expression (FIRE) believes campus speech codes and how they are enforced are often to blame. FIRE awards universities symbols of red, green, and yellow lights to indicate their consonance with First Amendment freedom.

One way to defrost the social atmosphere of the chilling effect is by making ethical decisions to encourage freedom of expression and uninhibited debate without exchanging hostile communications. Any administration that stifles free expression to achieve supposed ideals of social justice can suffocate good-faith debate through compliance with authoritarian figures, and the lifeblood of democracy on campus loses the oxygen it needs to survive.

119. Foundation for Individual Rights in Education, "What Are Speech Codes?" June 27, 2013, *at* https://www.thefire.org/resources/spotlight/what-are-speech-codes/.

5

Libel

LEARNING OBJECTIVES

After reading this chapter, you should know

- whether defamation, slander, and libel are basically the same or legally different offenses
- the distinction between criminal and civil libel
- who is supposed to prove what to win a libel lawsuit
- why public figures have a harder time winning libel suits than private figures
- how it is media reporting someone else's libelous statement aren't immune from libel suits
- the good and bad news about "truth" as a defense in a libel suit
- the defenses for media sued for libel

On December 14, 2012, a gunman killed his mother then proceeded to Sandy Hook Elementary School, where he killed 20 children and six staff members in one of the most brutal school shootings in American history. In addition to the families affected, the whole community of Newtown, Connecticut, was devastated. Before the shooting, there hadn't been a single homicide for a decade in the town, located 60 miles from New York.

Alex Jones was a radio show host and conspiracy theorist who repeatedly asserted that there had been no shooting at Sandy Hook Elementary and that the whole thing had been staged by gun control advocates. The outrageous claim that the whole thing was a hoax might not seem at first to be libelous, but Jones claimed that the mourning parents were actors, and his followers harassed them and even sent death threats. Beginning in 2018, suits against Alex Jones were being filed in Texas (where he and his company were located) and Connecticut.

After *years* of legal wrangling, in 2022 first a Connecticut court and then a Texas court both found Jones liable for the claims of defamation and levied punitive damages totaling hundreds of millions of dollars. Parents were able to convince the courts that Jones damaged their reputations with false statements that caused measurable harm. A motion for retrial was rejected by the court, but Jones announced he would appeal. As of this writing, no payments have been made to any of the plaintiffs,[1] but the hoax Jones created about an actual mass

1. "Alex Jones Allowed to Liquidate Assets to Help Pay Debt in Sandy Hook Defamation Verdicts, Judge Rules," *NBC News*, June 14, 2024.

DOI: 10.4324/9781003462989-5

murder at the expense of family members' grief and suffering fit all the legal elements of defamation.

The Libel Suit That Changed Everything

On March 29, 1960, a full-page ad appeared in *The New York Times* requesting donations to the "Committee to Defend Martin Luther King and the Struggle for Freedom in the South." Written more like a news story than a traditional advertisement, the ad had a headline that read, "Heed Their Rising Voices." The ad claimed to describe the plight of African American students in the southern United States and the denial of rights suffered by black people. It appealed for donations to support the students, the right to vote, and Dr. King's legal defense in Montgomery, AL, on charges of perjury. The ad was then "signed" as a petition might be by 64 prominent citizens.[2]

Libel
Traditionally thought of as printed defamation, as opposed to spoken, which is slander, it describes statements that are untrue and cause harm to reputation.

At the time, L.B. Sullivan was one of three elected commissioners of the city of Montgomery, and part of his responsibility included supervision of the police department. He claimed that the advertisement libeled him. **Libel**, at that time in Alabama, was defined as making untrue statements about an individual that damaged their reputation. Although Sullivan was never named, he was able to provide witnesses who asserted that when they read the ad, they inferred from it that Sullivan was responsible for police misconduct. He claimed his reputation was damaged because portions of the advertisement read as follows:

> [A]fter students sang "My Country, 'Tis of Thee" on the State Capitol steps, their leaders were expelled from school, and truckloads of police armed with shotguns and tear-gas ringed the Alabama State College Campus. When the entire student body protested to state authorities by refusing to re-register, their dining hall was padlocked in an attempt to starve them into submission. . . . Again and again the Southern violators have answered Dr. King's peaceful protests with intimidation and violence. They have bombed his home almost killing his wife and child. They have assaulted his person. They have arrested him seven times – for "speeding," "loitering" and similar "offenses." And now they have charged him with "perjury" – a *felony* under which they could imprison him for *10 years*.[3]

Some of the statements made in the advertisement were incorrect. The students sang the national anthem rather than "My Country 'Tis of Thee." The student leaders were not expelled for their protest at the Capitol but instead because of a lunch counter demonstration on another day. Student protests did not include a refusal to register for a semester but a single day's boycott of classes. The dining hall was never padlocked, and the only students prohibited from eating there were those who lacked the requisite meal cards. Although the police had been dispatched to the campus, they had never "ringed" it. Dr. King had been arrested only four times rather than seven.

The Alabama courts awarded L.B. Sullivan a libel judgment against *The New York Times*. Under the applicable Alabama law at the time, Sullivan had been libeled because the *Times* published false information about him, which damaged his reputation. In 1960, that was the end of the argument. But the newspaper appealed the decision to the U.S. Supreme Court, and in 1964, the Court unanimously overturned the Alabama courts and found that the *Times* had *not* libeled Sullivan.[4]

2. While not part of the discussion of media law, the context of era needs to be noted. This was a case of a Northern metropolitan newspaper seen as sympathetic to the rights of minorities fighting a legal battle against a Southern government official at a time when the fight for civil rights was heated and undecided. Vitriol and violence were widespread. Some suggest that the case was about a lot more than just libel. For a detailed account, read Anthony Lewis's thorough examination, *Make No Law: The* Sullivan *Case and the First Amendment* (New York: Knopf Doubleday, 1992).
3. *New York Times Co. v. Sullivan*, 376 U.S. 254, 257–258 (1964) (emphasis in original).
4. *Id.*

The rationale of the ruling was that the Alabama law did not do enough to protect First Amendment rights (the Court called it "constitutionally deficient") if it allowed public officials to win libel suits against critics of their official conduct.[5] The case was ground-breaking for many reasons. It assailed the notion that speech appearing in an advertisement is not entitled to First Amendment protection (as discussed in Chapter 11).

Most importantly, the decision written by Justice William Brennan reaffirmed the notion that free expression must protect the ability of people to criticize their government and officials. "[D]ebate on public issues should be uninhibited, robust, and wide-open, and . . . it may well include vehement, caustic, and sometimes unpleasantly sharp attacks on government and public officials."[6] Brennan went on to assert erroneous statements were inevitable, but some errors had to be tolerated if free expression was to have the "breathing space" necessary:

> Allowance of the defense of truth, with the burden of proving it on the defendant, does not mean that only false speech will be deterred. Even courts accepting this defense as an adequate safeguard have recognized the difficulties of adducing legal proofs that the alleged libel was true in all its factual particulars. Under such a rule, would-be critics of official conduct may be deterred from voicing their criticism, even though it is believed to be true and even though it is in fact true, because of doubt whether it can be proved in court or fear of the expense of having to do so. They tend to make only statements which "steer far wider of the unlawful zone."[7]

Obviously, the Court did not want to rule any false, damaging statements made about public officials would be completely protected either. What was needed was some sort of compromise position to allow the kind of oxygen Brennan saw as essential to expression while still allowing libel suits in the most egregious situations.

Actual Malice
The requirement in cases of libel against public officials that the publisher acted with knowledge of falsity or a reckless disregard for the truth.

The solution was to create a new standard. In libel cases with public officials as plaintiffs, there would have to be **actual malice** for the plaintiff to win the suit. *Actual malice* was defined by the Court as the knowledge of falsity or a reckless disregard for the truth. In other words, inaccurate statements like those made about the unnamed commissioner, L.B. Sullivan, where the defendant did not know the statements to be false, nor *should* have known they were false, would not result in libel.[8]

This became a major principle in libel law, and *New York Times Co. v. Sullivan* has been the bedrock case for more than 60 years.[9] Over the decades, there have been other rulings that have modified the *Sullivan* decision (most notably expanding the actual malice standard to apply to public figures as well as public officials, discussed later in this chapter), but the impact remains. Libel torts became more than just a matter for state courts to decide because the Supreme Court's ruling in *Sullivan* served to federalize the key elements.

Bedrock Law
New York Times Co. v. Sullivan established the principle of **actual malice**, increasing the burden of proof necessary for public officials to win a libel suit. Media have a right to be wrong in those cases so long as there is no knowledge of falsity or reckless disregard for the truth.

Defining Libel

Libel is actually one form of **defamation**, which is defined as "holding up of a person to ridicule, scorn or contempt in a respectable and considerable part of the community."[10] Libel and **slander** are both forms of defamation. Traditionally, libel meant defamation that was printed, and slander meant defamation that was spoken.

5. *Id.* at 264.
6. *Id.* at 270.
7. *Id.* at 279 (citations omitted).
8. Concurring opinions written by Justices Black and Goldberg and joined by Douglas asserted that any criticism of government officials should be constitutionally protected without creating an actual malice standard. *Id.* at 293–305.
9. *Shepard's Citations* is an index (available electronically) that tracks court decisions. Searching for references to a particular case is referred to by the legal community as "Shepardizing." Shepardizing *New York Times Co. v. Sullivan* results in more than 8,000 citations.
10. *Black's Law Dictionary*, 417 6th ed. (1990).

Defamation
Holding up of a person to ridicule, scorn, or contempt to a respectable and considerable part of the community.

Slander
Traditionally, slander was thought of as spoken defamation, as opposed to libel, which is written defamation.

The intent was to have a tort that treated more severely widely distributed defamations in print than those spoken harms that were considered less damaging. But with the advent of broadcasting, spoken defamations could be just as widely distributed as written ones, so the distinction wasn't quite as clear. Some jurisdictions even went as far as to create a new category, "defamacast," to describe defamatory broadcasts as something that were ephemeral like speech but with a wider audience.[11]

The major distinction between these terms is the amount of damage caused and therefore the amount of recovery allowed in a successful suit. Slander was defamation that caused limited damage, while libel was defamation with more potential impact.[12] In either case the harm caused to reputation must involve a living individual who might reasonably suffer the pain of loss of status and social standing among peers and others.

Other torts protect individuals after they've died (such as the right of publicity or protections against misappropriation, discussed in Chapter 6), but not defamation. Common law has long established that one must be living to file a libel suit, even though seven states (Idaho, Kansas, Louisiana, Nevada, North Dakota, Oklahoma, and Utah) still have questionable provisions for protecting the reputations of the deceased on their books.

Aggrieved family members cannot file a claim for defamation to protect the reputation of their departed relatives. Precedent also has established that damaging the reputation of the deceased does not harm the reputation of surviving family members.[13] There is no "guilt by association," and one may not sue for libel on behalf of someone else. A legal entity such as a business or organization also can pursue a libel suit if its reputation has been damaged.

Product disparagement is a form of "trade libel," where instead of an individual, a product has had its good name tarnished. In a rather high-profile case a few years ago, Oprah Winfrey was unsuccessfully sued by cattle raisers in Texas who claimed that her nationally syndicated television talk show violated the Texas False Disparagement of Perishable Food Products Act by implying that consumption of Texas beef might lead to mad cow disease.[14] The law might have held Oprah responsible, but the Fifth Circuit Court of Appeals determined no knowingly false statements were made.

While businesses and organizations may sue for libel, government entities may not. A government official who is defamed has the right to sue as an individual whose reputation has been damaged, but a local, state, or federal governmental body may not sue for libel. The reputation of a public agency is open to all sorts of published attacks even though false since the freedom to level such criticisms and complaints will work to the public good.[15]

Criminal Libel
A crime in which a publisher could be charged with defamation by the government. In modern U.S. jurisprudence, trials for criminal libel are far fewer than trials for civil libel.

Civil Versus Criminal Libel

As discussed in Chapter 1, civil cases are those where one individual sues another, while criminal cases are those legal actions brought against individuals for the commission of crimes. Once upon a time, libel was seen as a crime and there were criminal prosecutions for it, but today most legal scholars view defamation as strictly a civil issue. Most states have eliminated their criminal libel laws, and such prosecutions are so rare they seem to be non-existent, but a few states still maintain criminal libel statutes, and law enforcement

11. The term *defamacast* first appeared in a court decision in Georgia, *American Broadcasting-Paramount Theatres v. Simpson*, 126 S.E.2d 873 (Ga. Ct. App 1962). For a thorough history, *see* L.L. Wood, "The Case of David v. Goliath: Jewell v. NBC and the Basics of Defamacast in Georgia," 7 *Fordham Intell. Prop. & Media Ent. L. J.* 673 (1997).
12. Law professor Eric E. Johnson poses a wonderful question: Is a message written in sand on a beach libel or slander? It's written but it's ephemeral. Conversely, words spoken but recorded are permanent but may only be heard by one person. Illinois, Louisiana, and Virginia do not even make a distinction between libel and slander.
13. *Rose et al. v. Daily Mirror*, 20 N.Y.S.2d 315 (N.Y. App. Div. 1940).
14. *Engler v. Winfrey*, 201 F.3d 680 (5th Cir. 2000).
15. *Rosenblatt v. Baer*, 383 U.S. 75 (1966).

officers use them to make arrests, according to the American Civil Liberties Union (ACLU).[16] Professor David Pritchard discovered 61 prosecutions for criminal libel from 1991 to 2007 in the state of Wisconsin alone.

In Louisiana, criminal libel charges against celebrated New Orleans district attorney Jim Garrison, after he publicly complained about parish judges, led to a Supreme Court decision in his favor.[17] Even though the high court ruled Louisiana's criminal libel law lacked the safeguards necessary for free speech, government authorities on occasion still use criminal libel charges as a tool against critics.[18] In 2023 the ACLU petitioned the U.S. Supreme Court to hear the case of a New Hampshire man arrested for comments he made about a retiring police officer. The Court had the opportunity to find criminal libel unconstitutional; instead, it declined to take the case.

Making a Case for Libel

The most practical way to approach defamation at this point is to discuss the six requirements a plaintiff must meet to have a legally sufficient case. As is the case in any civil lawsuit, the plaintiff has the burden of showing certain conditions have occurred to cause harm, while the defendant has a chance to refute any of the claims. Later we will examine possible defenses, but if the plaintiff cannot prove the six elements are present, the defendant needs no defense.

1 Identification

It's obvious that someone cannot win a libel suit unless that person has been identified, but – believe it or not – this condition was not always easily decided. In L.B. Sullivan's case, his name was never mentioned. Was he identified for the purposes of a libel suit? The Alabama courts said he was, and the U.S. Supreme Court chose to accept Sullivan's statement at trial he felt the ad was "associated with me," and six witnesses said after reading its description of Montgomery police activities it seemed to be referencing Sullivan.[19]

That's primarily because people can be identified in ways other than just by stating their name. A photograph might identify a person, although if it is blurred it may not. A description might also identify a person if enough characteristics are included. L.B. Sullivan was identified for the purposes of a libel suit by his job responsibilities. With Sullivan as with many other libel plaintiffs, courts will answer the **identification** question by having witnesses testify as to whether they believed that the defamatory statements were made about the plaintiff.

Identification
In libel law, plaintiffs must show that the defamatory publication was of and concerning them.

If there is enough context provided to identify a particular individual, then that's sufficient. Hollywood celebrity Johnny Depp sued his ex-wife Amber Heard for defamation after she wrote an op-ed article for the *Washington Post*. Although his famous name was never used in the article, the jury recognized Depp was defamed by several statements in her article where Heard indicated she had been victimized by sexual violence, domestic abuse, and speaking out against it. The element of identification was accomplished by public knowledge of her celebrity marriage and divorce.[20]

16. www.aclu.org/issues/free-speech/map-states-criminal-laws-against-defamation.
17. *Garrison v. Louisiana*, 379 U.S. 64 (1964).
18. E. Volokh, "Louisiana Sheriff (Jerry Larpenter) Illegally Uses Criminal Libel Law to Unmask a Critic," *The Washington Post*, August 30, 2016, *at* www.washingtonpost.com/news/volokh-conspiracy/wp/2016/08/30/louisiana-sheriff-jerry-larpenter-illegally-uses-criminal-libel-law-to-unmask-a-critic/.
19. *New York Times v. Sullivan*, supra note 3 at FN #28.
20. *Depp v. Heard*, No. CL-2019-2911 (Va. Cir. Ct. Jul. 25, 2019)

Victims of sexual assault often do everything than can to avoid attention, even choosing not to press charges rather than having to go public with their stories. What's more, victim advocates recognize "defamation lawsuits were being used to silence survivors of domestic violence."[21]

Such victims often lack the resources to fight a libel lawsuit for making an honest report, so they choose to remain silent rather than risk facing their predator again in court. Libel lawsuits against sexual assault accusers will "turn the system on its head" by giving additional power to the already-powerful to silence the truth-tellers.[22]

Later in this chapter we discuss how such ligation stifles the freedom of speech necessary to produce justice, and how that can be remedied by a special type of law that most of the states have adopted.

A libel suit against former attorney general Eliot Spitzer was dismissed because the plaintiff was not identified. In a column Spitzer wrote for *Slate*, he discussed his investigation of Marsh & McLennan (a professional services company) and "the many employees of Marsh who have been convicted and sentenced to jail terms."[23] Plaintiff William Gilman was an employee who had charges against him dropped, so a federal appeals court ruled Spitzer couldn't have been referring to him.

Individuals might be identified even if the speaker had not intended to identify them or was referring to someone else. This might happen either because the speaker misidentified someone, was not specific enough in the details of the identification or ended up identifying a real person while intending to create a fictional character. Misidentification is often just a case of a simple error.

Suppose for example, Mary Doe is arrested for driving under the influence, and the local newspaper reports Mary *Dow* was arrested. So has this second Mary Dow (not Doe) been identified for the purposes of a libel claim? Yes, she has. Still the other criteria for defamation outlined in this chapter determine whether she has a chance to win her case. Leaving out personal data also might result in more people being identified than intended.

When Mary Doe is arrested for driving under the influence, a newspaper printing that information might alarm *several* Mary Does if nothing more than her first and last name are published. That's why media usually print a middle initial, age, address, and/or a photo to make it clear. There might be more than one Mary Doe in town, but there's probably only one Mary E. Doe who lives at 123 Fourth Street.

Bedrock Law

In libel claims, names are not necessary to prove identification; context, circumstance, or association may be sufficient to identify the plaintiff.

Sometime the authors writing works of fiction come dangerously close to identifying real people. If a fictional character is recognized by a substantial number of viewers to be based on a real person, then that person may claim they were identified for purposes of a libel suit. In 1991, *Seventeen* magazine published a piece clearly described as fiction, containing a character named "Bryson" who in this story was called a "slut." The author had known someone with that surname who was successfully able to assert she was identified in this story. The fact it was a fictional tale did not change the potential damage to her reputation.[24]

If an individual is identified in defamatory statements made about their group, is there grounds for a lawsuit? The answer is that it usually depends on the size of the group. Defamation is a tort relating to the damage occurring to an *individual* reputation (or a corporate reputation, since the law sometimes treats corporations as individuals).

21. "The Depp Verdict Could Bring a Chilling Effect for Domestic Abuse Survivors," *NPR*, June 2, 2022.
22. Covert, "Years After #METOO, Defamation Cases Increasingly Target Victims Who Can't Afford to Speak Out," *The Intercept*, July 22, 2023.
23. *Gilman v. Spitzer*, 902 F. Supp. 2d 389 (S.D.N.Y. 2012).
24. *Bryson v. News America Publ'ns*, 174 Ill. 2d 77 (Ill. 1996).

If a newspaper published a story where members of a local club were engaged in illegal activity, then those individual members might be able to claim they were defamed if there were only ten members. But if the club consisted of 100 members, the court probably would hold no one person is identified. And even if the club had only ten members, *each plaintiff* would need to bring in witnesses to testify they believed the defamation was about them.

If 100 people comprise too large a group for any individual to claim identification, the next question becomes just how large the group can be for an individual to be identified. Unfortunately, there is no definite number; we can only look to common law and a relatively small number of cases. And because these rulings come from different states, they don't necessarily provide clear guidance, as the following cases illustrate.

In New York in 1952, a group of 25 Neiman-Marcus salesmen were able to claim they were identified when a book charged "most" of the menswear department staff were "fairies."[25] On the other hand, 21 police officers in Massachusetts were considered to be too large a group for any one person to be identified in 1977 when a newspaper column reported an officer had to call for help after locking himself in the back of a police cruiser with a female companion.[26] Of course, there are differences in the cases – the book claimed *most* of the salesmen were effeminate while the newspaper only claimed *one* of the officers was trapped in the vehicle.

Perhaps the largest group known to have been successful in asserting identification for the purposes of a libel suit was the University of Oklahoma football team, a group of about 60 young men. In 1962, *True* magazine asserted some team members used illegal drugs. One player sued for libel, and the Oklahoma Supreme Court upheld his claim on the premise he individually had been harmed.[27]

While not exactly a bedrock of law, we would place 60 members at the extreme end of acceptability. Yet because we have a case in which identification was successfully asserted with a group that size, we must acknowledge other groups of 60 *might* be able to claim identification. Would it be safe to say any group larger than that number is out of the question? We think so, and it is also safe to assert smaller groups – fewer than 20 people – should be able to claim any one member has been identified. Conflicting decisions have come about with groups between 20 and 60, so it's difficult to predict what a court might do in that middle range.

Defamatory Language
In libel law, the plaintiff must show that the libelous material was defamatory, meaning it harms a person's reputation in the eyes of a substantial and respectable minority of the community.

2 Defamatory Language

It might seem almost silly to say that defamation can only occur in situations in which **defamatory language** is used, but as with identification, this criterion is not always easy to meet. A prisoner once tried to prove that being labeled an FBI informant was defamatory.

Defamatory language must result in damage to one's reputation, by either lowering the person in the estimation of the community or by deterring third persons from associating or dealing with them. Certainly, among prisoners it would be harmful to be considered an informant (maybe even dangerous). Yet a Delaware court held the language was not defamatory because "it does not label one with unlawful or improper conduct."[28]

While recognizing that the label of informant certainly could damage the plaintiff's reputation in prison, the court explained that the public contempt or ridicule resulting from defamatory language must be in the minds of "right thinking persons." Some courts have gone so far as to label certain individuals as "libel-proof" because their reputations are so tarnished there is nothing left to protect. As one federal court put it, "An individual who

25. *Neiman-Marcus Co. v. Laitt*, 13 F.R.D. 311 (S.D. N.Y. 1952).
26. *Arcand v. Evening Call*, 567 F.2d 1163 (1st Cir. 1977).
27. *Fawcett Publ'ns v. Morris*, 377 P. 2d 42 (Okla. 1962).
28. *Saunders v. WHYY*, 382 A.2d 257 (Del. 1978).

engages in certain anti-social or criminal behavior and suffers a diminished reputation may be 'libel proof' as a matter of law, as it relates to that specific behavior."[29]

In 2020, a New York judge threw out a libel suit filed by former professional baseball player Lenny Dykstra against New York Mets announcer Ron Darling. Darling's autobiography claimed Dykstra made racist statements. In dismissing the case, Justice Robert Kalish of the New York Supreme Court noted "Dykstra was infamous for being, among other things, racist, misogynist, and anti-gay, as well as a sexual predator, a drug-abuser, a thief, and an embezzler" and as such could not expose him to further "evil opinion."[30]

Simple name-calling is not necessarily defamatory language. If the name you call someone is "murderer," that would be defamatory because it becomes a factual assertion about a person that is damaging to their reputation. On the other hand, calling someone "butthead" is hyperbole and not a factual assertion and therefore would not be considered defamatory. It might be embarrassing, and it could cause the person to feel bad, but the tort of defamation does not exist to protect feelings – it protects reputation.

For the same reason, most sketch comedy making fun of someone is probably not defamatory language because the people watching it know it is not a factual claim about the person being spoofed but simply humor intended as entertainment. Certainly, some humor has the potential to be libelous if it makes false factual claims about a person that are damaging to their reputation, but most comedy is not taken that seriously.

Bedrock Law
To be considered libelous, the expression is an assertion of fact and not mere opinion or humor.

In 2016, a California appeals court dismissed a lawsuit against the producers of the film *American Hustle*. The film contains a scene where Jennifer Lawrence's character asserts that microwaves take the nutrition out of food and says she read it in an article by Paul Brodeur, a former *New Yorker* writer. Brodeur asserted his reputation was damaged, but the court said viewers would recognize the screwball comedy was not to be taken seriously.[31]

As a rule, comments made on humorous news programs are seen as just comedy, not statements of fact. On shows such as *The Daily Show* and *Last Week Tonight with John Oliver*, we may see a plaintiff claim that a comedy routine is an assertion of fact, but they're unlikely to succeed. In one highly publicized case, a libel suit filed against comedian John Oliver in 2017 was thrown out by a West Virginia court after a coal company was lampooned by the program.[32] Reasonable viewers would not think his jokes were meant to be taken as facts.

Libel Per Se
Consists of those words which in and of themselves are so damaging as to be considered defamatory, meaning use of the words is ***prima facie*** evidence of defamatory language.

It is easy to see some language as defamatory. If you claim someone has broken the law as a crook, thief, or murderer, then those words might be deemed libelous. Language that casts aspersions on someone's sexual morality is defamatory, so terms such as *slut*, *whore*, *prostitute*, and *adulterer* must be used with extreme caution. It's also defamatory to call people incompetent in their profession. Stating that a doctor is a "quack" or a lawyer is an "ambulance chaser" would be defamatory.

While people who have diseases may not have engaged in unlawful or improper conduct, wrongfully stating that someone has a stigmatized ailment is defamatory. Venereal diseases easily fit into this category, as does AIDS. While that disease may be contracted in ways not involving sexual activity (such as a hypodermic needle puncture), the stigma surrounding AIDS warrants falsely labeling someone with the disease to be generally considered libelous.

In the past, much was made of the distinction between ***libel per se*** and ***libel per quod***. *Libel per se* (Latin for "through itself") consists of those words which in and of themselves

29. *Wynberg v. National Enquirer*, 564 F. Supp. 924, 928 (C.D. Cal. 1982).
30. *Dykstra v. St. Martin's Press*, *at* https://mlb.nbcsports.com/wp-content/uploads/sites/7/2020/06/153676_2019_LENNY_DYKSTRA_v_ST_MARTIN_S_PRESS_LLC_et_al_DECISION___ORDER_ON_74.pdf.
31. Appeals Court Burns Defamation Lawsuit Targeting, "American Hustle Microwave Scene," *The Hollywood Reporter*, June 6, 2016, *at* www.hollywoodreporter.com/thr-esq/appeals-court-burns-defamation-lawsuit-899957.
32. "John Oliver Victorious: Coal CEO's Defamation Suit Dismissed," *Variety*, March 1, 2021.

Libel Per Quod

Consists of words or phrases that require contextualization to identify the harm.

Bedrock Law

The context and construction of the offending words used must be examined to determine whether defamation has occurred.

Innocent Construction Rule

The legal principle courts use to interpret allegedly libelous statements that have multiple meanings according to the least harmful interpretation that is often favorable to the defendant.

Falsity

In defamation law, a defendant cannot be found liable for defamation unless their statement was false.

are so damaging as to be considered defamatory. Although no longer the case, if language was determined to be defamation per se, the plaintiff needed not to show proof of damages.[33]

Libel per quod (Latin for "by reason of which") encompasses the sort of defamatory phrases that require contextualization to identify harm. The surrounding language must be examined to determine its meaning. In years past, the distinction would be significant in the amount awarded to a successful plaintiff, but that is less the case today. The U.S. Supreme Court's 1974 decision in *Gertz v. Welch* minimized this distinction,[34] making it unnecessary because courts in a libel case will examine the entire context of the communication.[35]

Certainly, there are some words that are more likely to create defamatory impressions than others, but courts first must determine whether the language is defamatory or merely hyperbole. Calling someone *mentally retarded* or *schizophrenic* is likely to be defamatory because they are clinical terms used to indicate disease and disability. And if a speaker simply claims an individual is mentally incompetent, that language too would be defamatory.

Use of the word *crazy* though is not likely to be judged as such. Oftentimes speakers use the word *crazy* in a slang or vernacular sense, not to mean mental incompetence, but unconventional or divergent. If a sports commentator calls another prognosticator crazy for choosing a particular team to win the championship, it's highly unlikely that description would be deemed defamatory.

Determining whether language is defamatory usually requires more than just examining specific words; it requires evaluating the context in which the comments have been made. There have been lists created of "red flag" words[36] often considered defamatory, but such lists are still subject to contextualization. For example, libel scholar Bruce Sanford lists "addict" as one such word since the term might be used humorously suggesting someone who spends too much time watching TV or loves to go shopping.[37] Analysis of whether language is defamatory necessarily includes its context.

Some states recognize that words may have more than one meaning and are willing to give speakers the benefit of the doubt. **Innocent construction rules** are the means courts use to decide defamation cases in favor of defendants in those instances in which language can be interpreted in more than one way. Ohio has recognized this rule in the past.[38] Illinois continues to recognize innocent construction as an acceptable explanation for the defense.[39]

It is also important to note that what constitutes a defamatory statement can change over time. While precedent is helpful here, the meanings of some words change along with their effect on one's reputation. Examples include *fascist*, *divorced*, and *gay*.

3 Falsity

In most cases, the burden is on the plaintiff to prove that a defamatory statement is false. Only in some states is there an exception for plaintiffs who are private individuals, and the defamatory statement is not a matter of public concern. So, for example, if someone working as a social media influencer chose to complain on their website that they thought their next-door neighbor was stealing vegetables from their garden, the neighbor may not have to prove falsity, depending on their state libel law.

This situation would seemingly occur infrequently; however, influencers are in the business of generating likes with hot takes on items of public interest, but just the act of

33. See, e.g., *MacDonald v. Riggs* (Alaska Sup. Ct. 2007).
34. 418 U.S. 323 (1974).
35. At least six states have explicitly asserted that they do not distinguish between defamation per se and per quod: Arizona, Arkansas, Mississippi, Missouri, Oregon, and Tennessee.
36. See, for example, Bruce Sanford, *Libel and Privacy* 4.13 (2006).
37. In fairness to Mr. Sanford, he points out that the red flag words "often" are defamatory rather than "always"; the point remains that there is no definitive list.
38. *Yeager v. Teamsters Local 20*, 6 Ohio St. 3d 369 (1983).
39. *Tuite v. Corbitt*, 2006 Ill. Lexis 1668 (Ill. 2006).

publishing a defamatory statement does not suddenly make it a public matter. If an exception for proving falsity does relieve the plaintiff, then the defendant carries the burden of proving the social media statement is truthful as their defense.

A defendant cannot be found liable for defamation unless their statement is false. True statements damaging someone's reputation do not fit the legal definition of defamation. This was not the case centuries ago. Before the United States broke from England, making negative statements about the king or his designee was considered defamatory, whether the words were true or not. In fact, a true critical statement was considered more damaging to the crown's reputation since it represented a greater threat to royal authority. That view began to change, however, after the famous trial of John Peter Zenger in 1734 (as described in Chapter 3) in which his defense lawyer asserted that publishing the truth should not result in punishment. In the twenty-first century, this is now bedrock law: truth is not defamatory.

Without delving too deeply into philosophy, we ought to at least question what truth is and how we know it once we've found it. It's obvious if someone has been found guilty of murder, calling the person a murderer is truth. But what if we call a person a crook? If an adult stole a package of gum when they were 12 years old, would it be acceptable to call that person a crook? You might argue that technically someone who has stolen anything at any time is a crook, but that might not be how a jury would interpret the word.

Similarly, is someone who has had multiple sexual partners "promiscuous"? If those partners were simultaneous, many might say that would be promiscuity, but if a person engaged in serial monogamy (only one sexual partner at a time in a committed relationship), "promiscuous" might be considered a false statement of fact. Of course, all of this is subject to interpretation by a court.

Some people seem to operate under the misconception that you can say anything you want about a person if you qualify it with the word *alleged.* Calling a person an "alleged murderer" may be just as defamatory as to call the person a murderer if it is not true. If police have arrested and charged an individual with murder, that person is, in fact, alleged to have committed the crime, and it would be accurate to call the person an alleged murderer. But, if a person is suspected of murder and no charges have been filed, then calling that person an alleged murderer is defamatory.

To be defamatory, a statement must be false, but what about a statement of opinion that is not provably true or false? To call someone the "worst singer ever" or "the clumsiest dancer" is obviously a subjective judgment. The Minnesota Supreme Court held that an online review about a neurologist that referred to the doctor as "a real tool" was a protected statement of opinion.[40] No one would be able to prove whether such statements were true.

Opinions are not statements of fact. As with "alleged," though, it is not enough to qualify a statement of fact by simply prefacing it with "I think" or "I believe" attempting to make it sound like an opinion. For example, "I think the mayor is a crook" is a statement of fact even though it is framed as an opinion. Whether the mayor is or is not a crook can be proven true or false. It does not convert the statement of fact to an opinion simply by inserting "I think" in front of it. For a media defendant to claim a statement is not false because it is an opinion requires that the entire statement be taken as a subjective judgment that cannot be proven either true or false.

What's more, it is not enough to simply quote someone else's defamatory statement with attribution and claim that it is true. As is the case for the phrase "I think," the phrase "according to" will not necessarily protect a speaker from a libel suit either. For example, if John Smith calls the mayor a crook and the local newspaper reports, "The mayor is a crook, according to John Smith," it is not enough for the newspaper to defend itself by proving that John Smith did in fact make that claim, therefore it is true.

40. *McKee v. Laurion*, 825 N.W.2d 725 (Sup. Ct. Minn., 2013).

It has long been established that the republication of a libel is also libel.[41] It can, in fact, constitute even greater damage than the original defamatory statement. In the previous example, if John Smith makes his defamatory statement at a press conference where only a dozen people are present, and the newspaper read by thousands republishes the defamation, the republication is far more damaging than the original statement.

Bedrock Law

In libel claims, the person or entity quoting false words that harm a reputation can be held just as accountable for defamation as the person making the original statement.

There is precedent to suggest that some venues are more likely to present statements of opinion than others and consequently deserve more freedom of expression. The quintessential example is the editorial page of a newspaper. Editorials comprise opinions from people connected to the newspaper. Most newspaper readers distinguish between what they find on the front page (generally considered "hard news") versus what they find on the editorial page, which is opinion and interpretation.

A Wisconsin appeals court held that former Fox News commentator Megyn Kelly did not defame a Wisconsin firefighter with comments she made that were determined to be opinion and that her program was known to be a collection of opinions.[42] The fact that a statement is made in a venue recognized as a resource for opinions might help a defendant assert their statement was subjective rather than factual, but it does not in and of itself automatically make the offending words an opinion.

4 Publication

Publication

For the purposes of a libel claim, the term ***publication*** refers to any dissemination of a defamatory statement, not strictly in print. To damage someone's reputation, a defamatory remark must be communicated to a third party.

To damage someone's reputation, a defamatory remark must be made public. For purposes of a defamation claim, the term **publication** refers to any dissemination of a defamatory statement, not strictly in print. If someone makes a defamatory remark in a speech, it has been "published," whether it is ever printed anywhere or not. In fact, if you were to make a defamatory remark to just one other person, that conversation would be considered publication, although the level of damages might be small (we will discuss damages later).

What is *not* publication is when one person makes a damaging statement about a person *to* that person – and no third party has received the communication. If a professor accuses a student of cheating in a private meeting in the professor's office, the student may feel hurt but that would not be defamation. The professor has done nothing to damage the student's reputation to anyone else. If the student then leaves the office and tells a friend about the accusation, the professor has not defamed the student because the professor never published the remark to a third party – the student did.

Publication to a third party is usually intentional but can sometimes occur by accident. The student accused in the professor's office of cheating might be defamed because another student waiting outside the office overheard the conversation. The defamatory remarks were published to a third party, so would the professor be legally responsible or liable? That depends upon the circumstances. If the professor was speaking with the office door open, in a loud voice, the professor should have known that someone else could have heard. If, on the other hand, the door was closed and the professor is speaking softly, and then a nosy person presses an ear to the door to hear the conversation, the accidental publication cannot be blamed on the professor.

Recall that L.B. Sullivan filed his libel suit against *The New York Times* even though the newspaper did not create the advertisement that contained the defamatory content. Is a medium responsible for all the content appearing in its pages, website, or airwaves, whether it exercised any editorial control or not? If a book contains a defamatory passage, can the Barnes & Noble Bookstore chain be held responsible for republishing the libel? What about

41. Injury to a fair reputation by the repetition of a libel and the mention of the name of the earlier libeler is indefensible. *Palmer v. Mahin*, 120 F. 737 (8th Cir. 1903) citing *Times Pub. Co. v. Carlisle*, 94 Fed. 762 (8th Cir. 1899).
42. "Wisconsin Court Dismisses Defamation Suit Naming Megyn Kelly as Defendant," January 24, 2017, *at* http://legalnewsline.com/stories/511075821-wisconsin-court-dismisses-defamation-suit-naming-megyn-kelly-as-defendant.

an Internet service provider (ISP) that makes a webpage available for comments and one of its members posts a libelous remark?

The answers are all tied to the amount of content control exercised. *The New York Times* could be considered responsible for advertisements in its publication because, even though it did not *create* the content, it exercised *control* over the content. The *Times* sometimes rejects ads, which serves as evidence that advertisements appearing in the paper have met some minimum expectation.[43]

Bookstores and discussion websites do not reject content and as such are not responsible for the content they provide. They serve as passive conduits for the communication. This protection is not forfeited if, on occasion, a specific book or posting is rejected because it is found to be offensive. Prior to 1996, the common law from a few court cases gave guidance, but the Telecommunications Act of 1996 codified protection for ISPs, which merely make the conduit of communication available rather than being considered to be publishers of defamatory content.[44]

Sometimes the actual date of publication of the defamatory statement becomes important. Most states have a *statute of limitations* on a libel claim requiring the plaintiff to file suit within a certain length of time from the date of publication. Usually, the time limit is one[45] or two[46] years, with a handful of states extending liability up to three[47] years. The publication date for a newspaper is fairly easy to identify, but other publication dates are not always so clear. The date stamped on the front of a magazine is often later than the actual date of publication. Newsweeklies such as *Time* and *Newsweek* appear on the newsstand days before the date on their covers, and *Reader's Digest* appears weeks before the month dated on its cover. Courts generally operate under the assumption that publication occurs on the date when the defamatory content is available to most readers – by mail or on the newsstand.

Online defamation creates a new problem, however. Unlike a newspaper, a web posting is not as ephemeral. Archives of blogs and postings can be easily accessed. One might argue that a defamatory statement posted on January 1 might have been published on January 1 but is also republished every time someone accesses the archive, weeks or months later. Conceivably, this would extend the statute of limitations on such libels indefinitely.

A federal district court ruled that online libel should be treated the same as that in newspapers and the statute of limitations should expire one year after the date of the original publication.[48] If this were not the case, the print libel would no longer be actionable once the statute of limitations was passed, but online *the same words* would be actionable forever.

Judge David Godbey saw "no rational reason for distinguishing between the Internet and other forms of traditional mass media." The fact that the archives were accessible electronically was considered analogous to visiting the newspaper's print or microfilm archives at the local library. This case may not be binding precedent in other jurisdictions but certainly provides guidance in this emerging area of law.

It is generally accepted that re-accessing a once-published defamatory statement is not a republication. People read old copies of books, newspapers, and magazines in libraries, and that is not seen as republication of a libel. But then actually quoting a published libelous remark in a *new* publication, however, would start the statute of limitations clock ticking again at the date of republication.

For example, if a newspaper mistakenly reports that the mayor is a murderer, the statute of limitations would expire after a year or two in most states. But if a social media influencer

43. It is worth mentioning that in the *Sullivan* case, the *Times* was not held responsible in part because the paper had no reason to doubt the accuracy of the content in the ad.
44. 47 U.S.C. § 230.
45. California, Nebraska, and Louisiana, for example.
46. Florida and Indiana, for example.
47. This group includes New Hampshire and New Mexico.
48. Jonathan Rhein, "Federal Judge Rules Statutory One-Year Libel Limit Applies Online, Jurist," October 18, 2006, *at* https://www.jurist.org/news/2006/10/federal-judge-rules-statutory-one-year/.

took it from pages of the old newspaper and then shared the statement online, the opportunity for filing a lawsuit against the paper would have expired, but a new libel suit might take place against the influencer since the statute of limitations would then apply to the defamatory remark made online.

Global View: Hyperlinking in Australia

Whether a hyperlink on a webpage constitutes republication of that content has significant implications for libel law, but global opinion is not unanimous on how it ought to be handled. In the United States, several courts have found that simply providing a hyperlink to a libel found somewhere else on the Internet is ***not*** the republication of a libel.

A Connecticut court ruled such links are protected under Section 230 of the CDA.[49] A New York court ruled a hyperlink did not start a new clock for the statute of limitations in a libel suit.[50] In Australia, however, a defendant was found guilty of libel by linking to defamatory material on YouTube and Facebook merely because she "facilitated direct access to the defamatory material."[51]

In 2017, Katrina Bailey copied a link on her Facebook page that took readers to a YouTube video accusing David Bottrill of being a member of a pedophile group that kills and tortures victims. Bailey added nothing to the allegations: the only text that appeared on her page was that generated automatically when the link was posted.

The Supreme Court of the Australian Capital Territory asserted that some people who post defamatory links may not be liable if they engage in "innocent dissemination," where they lack knowledge that the material is defamatory. But in her case, "Bailey had engaged in a positive act of participation in the publication of the defamatory material."

The Australian high court made a point of the deliberate nature of Bailey's posting, as opposed to a link that appeared as the result of a Google search, where the search engine would not be held responsible. In 2019, her fine in U.S. dollars was about $13,000.

Blogging Perils

The temptation to openly express one's negative thoughts and feelings online has proven costly for more than one influencer, blogger, or podcaster in court, and there are dozens of cases in which those platforms and libel have intersected.

In Georgia, David Milum made the target of his online rage a former district attorney who had become a partner in a general practice law firm. The libelous words Milum used to blog against Rafe Banks III accused him of drug dealing and bribery. It took a jury about six hours to decide that Milum had libeled his former attorney to the tune of $50,000 in damages.

A Louisiana evacuee of Hurricane Katrina posted defamatory messages against the operator of a Florida website that helps parents screen boarding schools. The target of that posting, Sue Scheff, was awarded $11.3 million dollars in damages when the defendant failed to appear in court to contest her libel suit. The defendant, Carrie Bock, who had migrated to Texas, filed a motion to set aside the defamation judgment against her.

49. *Vazquez v. Buhl*, 2014 WL 1795574 (Conn. App. Ct. May 13, 2014).
50. *Haefner v. New York Media*, L.L.C. 2009 NY Slip Op 52765(U) [27 Misc 3d 1208(A)].
51. *Bailey v. Bottrill* (No 2) [2019] ACTSC 167, at 50.

In Texas, a San Antonio high school assistant principal took legal exception to two students for allegations about her sexual orientation posted on her MySpace.com page. Meanwhile in Miami, the host of DontDateHimGirl.com, faced a libel suit after some of her readers posted comments about a criminal defense lawyer's sexuality and personal health.

Professor Christine Corcos, editor of Media Law Prof Blog, warns her readers to know the difference between factual statements and opinions, especially if someone's reputation is involved. There is no question defaming someone online can produce damages for libel.[52]

5 Fault

Even if a defendant identifies a plaintiff, uses defamatory language, makes a statement of fact that is provably false, publishes that statement to a third party, and causes injury to the plaintiff, a court may not find the defendant liable for defamation. Since L.B. Sullivan's case went to the U.S. Supreme Court in 1964, courts have been required to consider one more element in determining that libel has occurred – whether the plaintiff's case has demonstrated the appropriate degree of fault.

One reason why Justice Brennan's majority opinion in *New York Times Co. v. Sullivan* is critical to our understanding is that it established that a public official who is a plaintiff in a libel suit must show that the defendant published with ***actual malice***, defined as knowledge of falsity or a reckless disregard for the truth. Prior to that time, Alabama (as many other states) operated on the principle of strict liability: a speaker was strictly responsible for damage caused by their expression. The U.S. Supreme Court changed all of that in 1964 by reasoning that free expression about public officials needs more "breathing space" than strict liability provides. Speakers need to be protected from lawsuits for honest mistakes; otherwise, a great deal of discussion will be stifled. In the interest of the marketplace of ideas, punishing speakers for error alone is never a good thing.

Malice and *actual malice* mean different things. When one generally speaks of malice, it suggests ill will or the desire to cause harm. In libel law, actual malice is not related to this. As stated previously, actual malice is knowledge of falsity or reckless disregard for truth. While someone who has malice might act with actual malice, do not be confused: there is no "ill will" test for defamation. In *Sullivan*, the Supreme Court considered the First and Fourteenth Amendments, stating its rationale regarding libel:

> The constitutional guarantees require, we think, a federal rule that prohibits a public official from recovering damages for a defamatory falsehood relating to his official conduct unless he proves that the statement was made with "actual malice" – that is, with knowledge that it was false or with reckless disregard of whether it was false or not.[53]

The Court then concluded that for Sullivan,

> the facts do not support a finding of actual malice. . . . [T]he evidence against the Times support, at most, a finding of negligence in failing to discover the misstatements, and

52. Robert D. Mitchell, "The Perils of Internet Defamation: $38.3 Million Jury Verdict," *at* https://www.mitchell-attorneys.com/internet-defamation.
53. *New York Times Co. v. Sullivan*, supra note 3 at 279–280. The Court held that "the Constitution delimits a State's power to award damages for libel in actions brought by public officials against critics of their official conduct." The Court had found Alabama's law confusing for jurors, where Alabama required proof of actual malice for an award of punitive damages but then "presumed" actual malice for an award for general damages. "Such a presumption is inconsistent with the federal rule." "Because of this uncertainty, the judgment must be reversed and the case remanded." At 283–284.

is constitutionally insufficient to show the recklessness that is required for a finding of actual malice.[54]

The 1964 decision was specifically couched in the context of L.B. Sullivan's public role as a commissioner with civic responsibility. Commentary about the job he was doing was certainly appropriate for the marketplace of ideas, and any minor errors or "misstatements" did not amount to proof of actual malice as required. The decision can be seen as a logical extension of the centuries-old tradition that the government ought not to be able to silence its critics by punishing them directly or indirectly for publishing criticism.

It's important to note that the actual malice standard of fault established in *New York Times Co. v. Sullivan* does not make it impossible for public officials to win libel suits, as the following case illustrates. Just a few years after the *New York Times* decision, the Supreme Court was afforded a rare opportunity to hold two cases side by side and demonstrate how one defendant had shown actual malice in a libel suit and another defendant had not.

In *Curtis Publishing v. Butts*,[55] an athletic director was defamed when the *Saturday Evening Post* magazine ran an article charging that he "fixed" a football game between his school, the University of Georgia, and the University of Alabama. Yet in *Associated Press v. Walker*,[56] the wire service was not guilty of actual malice when it ran a story alleging that a retired army official had led a mob of angry protesters over the desegregation of the University of Mississippi. Here are some of the relevant differences that help to demonstrate just what might be considered actual malice:

- *Consider the source:* In the *Associated Press* case, the source of information was one of the Associated Press's own reporters, who should certainly be considered trustworthy. In the *Curtis Publishing* case, the source of the story was a tip that came out of the blue from a man convicted of check forgery.
- *Deadline pressure:* The Associated Press is a news cooperative that provides news feeds to its thousands of affiliates. As such, someone is always on deadline. The *Saturday Evening Post* used to be a weekly publication, meaning that seven days would pass between deadlines. While having less time cannot be seen as an excuse for libel, the Court recognized it is understandable that the Associated Press had less time to check the story.
- *Believability:* In the early 1960s, it was certainly possible that General Edwin Walker had led a mob given his record of outspoken opposition to integration. Other news stories about the subject lent credence to the possibility that it happened as reported. No one at the Associated Press (AP) even questioned it. On the other hand, there were no allegations of wrongdoing made against Wally Butts, the University of Georgia athletic director. This one and only allegation came from a claim that the informant overheard a telephone conversation between Butts and the opposing coach, Paul "Bear" Bryant, when some phone wires got crossed. Despite the fact the *Saturday Evening Post* was told before publication that the story was untrue, it did not attempt to verify its substance.
- *Incentives:* By "breaking" a story, the Associated Press was unlikely to profit. New members join the cooperative to get world and national news. The General Walker story would not likely be reported to attract new members. On the other hand, the *Saturday Evening Post* "was anxious to change its image by instituting a policy of 'sophisticated muckraking.'"[57] A major exposé could easily lead to an increase in sales for that issue.

54. *Id.* at 288.
55. 388 U.S. 130 (1967).
56. *Id.*, noting the Supreme Court considered *Butts* and *Walker* together in the same case.
57. *Id.* at 158.

Negligence
Breach of a duty that results in reasonably foreseeable harm.

Categorizing Plaintiffs

Whether a plaintiff is determined to be a public or private figure can make the difference in who wins in a libel suit. Plaintiffs who are ruled to be public figures have a significantly higher bar of actual malice to hurdle: they must prove the defendant had knowledge of falsity or a reckless disregard for the truth.

Although the Supreme Court created the standard for public figures, it left to the states the determination of which standard to apply to private figure plaintiffs.[58] A private citizen in most jurisdictions must prove only that the defendant was negligent or behaved in an unprofessional way.[59] Legal **negligence** is generally defined as a failure to exercise reasonable care. "Reasonable care" is further defined as what an average member of that community would have done. Thus, a journalist who is negligent is one who does not exercise the amount of care (fact-checking, etc.) that the average professional would.

One other critically important point comes to us from the *Curtis Publishing* and *Associated Press* cases. In the earlier *New York Times* ruling, actual malice was applied to public officials. But it isn't just public officials who may invite critical commentary that needs "breathing space." Is a retired general a public official? What about an athletic director? It is somewhat limiting to restrict the discussion just to those publicly elected individuals or government employees who wield decision-making power. Other people might also belong to a certain class of citizens who are routinely subjected to public scrutiny and who also should have to show actual malice in a libel suit.

In the cases following this landmark decision, the Court expanded beyond the notion of "public officials" to a more inclusive category of "public figures." Public officials are a subset of public figures, but the question is who else should be included. A high-profile athlete or coach may not be a public official but would certainly be a public figure. The Court stated:

> a "public figure" who is not a public official may also recover damages for a defamatory falsehood whose substance makes substantial danger to reputation apparent, on a showing of highly unreasonable conduct constituting an extreme departure from the standards of investigation and reporting ordinarily adhered to by responsible publishers.[60]

The rationale for expanding the protection of speakers is easy to understand. The tort of defamation is intended to protect one's reputation, but the free expression rights of others cannot be ignored.

One argument is that certain issues are much more likely to be the subject of public discussion and thus need more "breathing space." Another position is recognition that a lawsuit is not the only way to restore one's reputation. In fact, if an individual can publicly refute a false claim, that statement may do more to restore their reputation than a lawsuit would. This explains the reasoning for requiring public figures to meet the fault requirement of showing actual malice.

A major motion picture star may not be a public official, but as a public figure that star would have instant access to mass media. When they are defamed, a simple phone call from a publicist would get that star an interview with major media outlets. If most "private figures" were to call a press conference, they would likely find themselves standing alone in a room with no one to hear their side of the story.

Public figures are those people who can command public attention instantly. There is not a standard list of public figures or a fail-safe test that can be applied, but generally speaking public figures are those who would be readily recognizable by a significant segment of the population. Such terms are open to interpretation: "readily recognizable" and "significant

58. *Gertz v. Welch*, supra note 34, at 333.
59. Some jurisdictions require the more difficult actual malice as the fault standard for all libel plaintiffs. In Indiana, even private figure plaintiffs must show actual malice in cases of public concern. *Journal-Gazette v. Bandidos*, 712 N.E.2d 446 (Ind. 1999).
60. *Curtis Publishing v. Butts*, supra note 55, at 155.

Limited Purpose Public Figure
In libel law, plaintiffs who are not otherwise public figures might be classified as such if they have gained notoriety by voluntarily injecting themselves into a matter of public controversy in an attempt to influence the outcome.

segment" are certainly subjective judgments – exactly the sort that a judge or jury would have to decide in a defamation suit.

One other category of public figure exists – the **limited purpose public figure**. These are the sorts of people who voluntarily inject themselves into a matter of public controversy in attempting to influence the outcome. Imagine someone who is not a public official or a public figure who speaks out at public rallies and demonstrations and maybe even petitions city hall about a new zoning proposal. Certainly, free speech principles tend to favor the same sort of breathing room if defamation occurs when commenting in this instance.

The limited purpose public figure is a concept that the Supreme Court arrived at through "trial and error" (pun intended). In a 1971 case, the Court expanded the actual malice standard so that it would apply anytime the case involved a matter of public interest or concern.[61] One of the problems with such an approach was that it made actual malice the applicable standard for nearly every case involving a media defendant. After all, if anything leading to a defamation suit had been in the newspaper or on television, wouldn't it then by definition become a matter of public interest or concern? Media coverage would instantly make it a matter of public interest, but three years later, the Supreme Court reversed itself.[62]

Instead of the general application of actual malice anytime there is a matter of public concern, the approach was narrowed to include only those people who *voluntarily* enter the "vortex" of a public controversy to try to influence it. Under the current scheme, it's hard to imagine anyone who becomes a public figure without knowing it. Through this litany of cases post-1964, the Supreme Court has determined the actual malice fault standard must be shown in defamation cases involving the following plaintiffs:

- Public officials – or those government officials responsible for exercising authority or discretion in the affairs of state. Obviously, any elected official qualifies here. As the Supreme Court has pointed out, anyone who decides to seek government office must expect close scrutiny by the public, and not just in the affairs of government. For that reason, candidates for public office, although not yet elected, still invite the same level of scrutiny as do public officials and can be considered equivalent. Their activities outside the duties of the elected office provide insight into the individual's character and as such are part of the public's interest in the fitness of that elected official.[63]
- Unelected government employees, depending on the duties involved. It's unlikely a court would find a state-paid janitor to be a public figure. On the other hand, police officers will likely be classified as public officials by virtue of the work they do. The more authority over the public, or greater discretion in public policy, the more likely a government employee will be classified as a public official. Those responsible for large sums of money or public health and safety always will be public officials for the purposes of a libel suit.
- All-purpose public figures – or the world-famous people of our society, the ones who are easily recognizable by almost everyone. Just imagine someone who would be the subject of a *People* magazine story or gossip piece, and you have *likely* categorized this person as a public figure, but you can't be sure. As one Supreme Court ruling held, an individual might be mentioned in a gossip column and still not be a public figure.

  A member of Palm Beach society who was involved in a divorce proceeding was mentioned in a *Time* magazine piece. Although the publication tried to argue that Mary Alice Firestone's status among the upper crust and her marriage to a member of the prominent Firestone family made her a public figure, the Court majority determined that she

61. *Rosenbloom v. Metromedia*, 403 U.S. 29 (1971).
62. *Gertz v. Welch*, supra note 34.
63. *Garrison v. Louisiana*, 379 U.S. 64 (1964).

did not have a role of "especial prominence in the affairs of society."[64] The fact that a national magazine chose to report on her divorce did not automatically transform her to an all-purpose public figure. Certainly, *Time*'s case might have been bolstered had dozens of national publications reported on Mrs. Firestone, but that had not been the case. In addition, while Mary Alice Firestone may have been a *local* all-purpose public figure, she was not a *national* one.

Some people might be celebrities in their own communities but not on a national scale, making them all-purpose public figures in a libel suit involving a local publication, but not public figures for a national publication. Consider a highly paid NFL lineman. Most do not get much publicity outside their own communities, yet their appearance at a local event can bring out hundreds of fans.

- Limited purpose public figures. According to the Supreme Court, this occurs when "an individual voluntarily injects himself or is drawn into a particular public controversy and thereby becomes a public figure for a limited range of issues."[65] This category consists of several qualifiers: first, there must be a *public controversy*. A person cannot become a public figure simply by walking down the street and being photographed by a newspaper.

  Even if the person walking down the street were photographed because of a newsworthy event (perhaps a car accident), there would be no public controversy, and the individual would not be a limited purpose public figure. The Supreme Court ruled that a person who engages in criminal activity is not automatically a public figure or even a limited purpose public figure without some voluntary action to gain publicity or influence a controversy.[66] Second, the individual must *voluntarily enter the controversy or be drawn into it.*

  Sometimes this occurs when an individual tries to sway public opinion as an advocate for a certain perspective. Sobriety coach Peter Dice was photographed with celebrity Lindsay Lohan. Despite *her* celebrity status, a California Court of Appeal ruled Dice was not a limited purpose public figure because he was not trying to influence public opinion on some controversy.[67]

  Someone arguing against the construction of a nuclear power plant would certainly become a limited purpose public figure because they spoke at public meetings, or held protest rallies, or got quoted in media coverage about the plant. That person had voluntarily entered the controversy.

  Voluntarily entering a controversy may not mean a conscious decision by the individual but is still purposeful. Some limited purpose public figures are drawn into a controversy by virtue of their actions or status. A court ruled that a female F-14 combat fighter pilot became a limited purpose public figure because of the controversy surrounding the status of women in combat positions.[68]

  An organization that deals with at-risk teenagers was ruled to be a limited purpose public figure.[69] A for-profit probation and counseling company was a limited purpose public figure.[70] In each of these cases, though, the third qualifier was also met: the defamation must be related to the public figure status of the individual. A limited purpose public figure is only a public figure for a *limited range of issues*.

64. *Time v. Firestone*, 424 U.S. 448, 453 (1976).
65. *Gertz v. Welch*, supra note 34, at 351.
66. *Wolston v. Reader's Digest*, 443 U.S. 157 (1979).
67. *Dice v. X17, Inc., at* www.loeb.com/articles-ipentertainmentcaselawupdates-20140127-dicev17x.
68. *Lohrenz v. Donnelly*, 350 F.3d 1272 (2003).
69. *Worldwide Association of Specialty Programs v. PURE*, 450 F.3d 1132 (10th Cir. 2006).
70. *West v. Media Gen.*, 120 Fed. Appx. 601 (6th Cir. 2005).

A female fighter pilot might be determined to be a limited purpose public figure in relation to the controversy of women in combat roles, but she would not be a public figure in a news story about women pilots – a much less controversial issue.

- Private figures. This is simply determined by a process of elimination. If a person is not a public official, not an all-purpose public figure, and not a limited purpose public figure, then that individual must be a private figure. As mentioned earlier, a plaintiff who is characterized as a private figure stands a much greater chance of winning a libel suit in most jurisdictions because the fault standard the plaintiff must prove is significantly lower. Regardless of the fault standard, in almost all cases involving media defendants, it is the plaintiff who bears the burden of proving the falsity of the allegedly defamatory remarks.

Questioning the Actual Malice Standard

Justice Clarence Thomas has asserted it is time to examine whether an actual malice standard ought to be applied in libel suits. In 2019 the Supreme Court denied certiorari requested by one of comedian Bill Cosby's accusers (she accused him of rape), who believed she was libeled when Cosby sent a letter to the news media attacking her credibility. In agreeing with the decision to deny cert., he anticipated a future case would give the Court an opportunity to reexamine the actual malice standard.

Justice Thomas believes the state courts are better suited for applying their own standards for libel cases rather than the national prescription provided by the Supreme Court. "The States are perfectly capable of striking an acceptable balance between encouraging robust public discourse and providing a meaningful remedy for reputational harm. We should reconsider our jurisprudence in this area."[71]

In 2021, Justice Thomas was joined by Justice Neil Gorsuch in voting to grant certiorari to a public figure who challenged the burden of actual malice necessary to win his case for defamation against a book author. Thomas felt it was time to reexamine that standard given the rapidly changing media environment, but the Supreme Court took a pass on this case.[72]

In 2022, Justice Thomas voted to grant cert. in a libel case where the Southern Poverty Law Center identified Coral Ridge Ministries Media, a religious group, as a "hate group" due to its anti-LGBTQ position. That designation cost revenue from a portion of Amazon sales based on customers selecting Coral Ridge as their charity. Coral Ridge sued for libel. Justice Thomas voted to grant cert. claiming the "case is one of many showing how *New York Times* and its progeny have allowed media organizations and interest groups 'to cast false aspersions on public figures with near impunity.' "[73]

In 2023, he agreed with the Court's denial of certiorari in another libel case yet took another opportunity to write a concurrence reminding the justices of his desire to revisit the actual malice requirement.[74] That established fault standard has stood for over 60 years, but Justice Thomas, the Court's senior justice, likely will continue calling for its reexamination.

71. *McKee v. Cosby*, 586 U.S. ____ (2019), *cert. denied.*
72. *Berisha v. Lawson*, 141 S.Ct. 2424 (2021), *cert. denied*, GORSUCH and THOMAS, JJ., dissenting.
73. *Coral Ridge Ministries Media v. Southern Poverty Law Center, 97 U.S. ____ (2022) cert. denied,* THOMAS, J., dissenting.
74. *Blakenship v. NBCUniversal*, 601 U.S. ____ (2023) *cert. denied,* THOMAS, J., concurring.

6 Damages

For a plaintiff to win a libel lawsuit, they must prove injury or harm to their reputation and also show the defamation was the cause of that injury. Sometimes damages can be demonstrated easily, but other times it can prove to be much more difficult.

If a media report falsely accuses someone of infidelity and that person's spouse leaves as a result, there is an obvious example of damage to reputation. If a contractor loses a bid because of a false media report of corruption by the contractor, it's easy to see the harm done. But what about instances in which someone's friends become elusive, or future business deals go unrealized? It's far more difficult to characterize the injury under those circumstances. There may be situations in which all other conditions of libel are met, but without a showing of reputational damage, the court will not find libel to have occurred. Prior to *New York Times Co. v. Sullivan*, damages were often presumed to have occurred if the other conditions for defamation were met.

Actual Damages
Also called compensatory damages, this is the monetary compensation designed to remedy the losses suffered by the plaintiff.

When a libel plaintiff wins, a court chooses between different types of damages: actual, special, presumed, punitive, and nominal. **Actual damages** or compensatory damages monetarily compensate the plaintiff for tangible and intangible losses, such as losing one's job or having one's value as an employee decrease, as supported by the evidence of witness testimony and other examples of lost contacts. The level of documentation required for **special damages** is more specific, often requiring precise figures for wages lost or business sacrificed and must not include projected or future losses.

Presumed damages are just as the name implies, thought to have occurred if the other criteria for defamation apply. In libel cases, presumed damages are generally not allowed unless actual malice is shown, although the First Amendment does not prevent states from allowing damages to be presumed where the plaintiff is a private individual and the defendant is a non-media person.

Punitive damages are also as the name implies: an attempt to punish the defendant for wrongdoing, perhaps deterring the defendant or anyone else from ever again committing such an act. Because punitive damage awards can be in the millions of dollars, courts will not award punitive damages to private figures in libel suits unless they can prove the higher fault standard of actual malice. In other words, some states may allow private figures to win libel suits by simply proving negligence, but the only amount they can recover is for actual damages.

Some states limit the level of punitive damages. Johnny Depp was awarded $5 million in punitive damages in his libel suit against his ex-wife Amber Heard, but that amount was reduced to $350,000 due to limits imposed by Virginia tort law.

Some states do not allow any punitive (or exemplary) damages in libel claims because the rewards are not directly linked to the ill effects of defamation and can inhibit truthful speech. In fact, a plurality of the Supreme Court reached that conclusion after ruling in *Dun & Bradstreet v. Greenmoss Building, Inc.*[75] In states where public officials or public figures are petitioning, and punitive damages are allowed, the court requires a showing of actual malice on the part of the plaintiff.[76]

It should be noted if a court finds a breach of duty occurred but no substantial harm to the plaintiff was shown, the judgment may award a small dollar amount known as **nominal damages**. In some libel cases, the plaintiff may prefer nominal damages just to restore their reputation without imposing a financial burden on the defendant.

75. 472 U.S. 749 (1985). See also C. Rothfield, "The Surprising Case against Punitive Damages in Libel Suits," 19 *Yale L Policy Rev*. 165 (2000).
76. The Supreme Court ruled, "The states, however, may not permit recovery of presumed or punitive damages when liability is not based on knowledge of falsity or reckless disregard of the truth, and the private defamation plaintiff . . . may recover compensation only for actual injury." *Gertz v. Robert Welch, Inc*. 418 U.S. 348–350 (1974).

From the Trenches: Using Experts in Determining Damages

By Eric W. Rose

One of the challenges faced in Internet defamation is determining the extent of damages that Internet defamation causes. For victims of Internet defamation, determining the extent of these future costs can be a difficult task.

Very few people who serve on juries have the knowledge, background, or understanding of how defamation works. They understand that it is alleged that one person/entity communicated something bad about another that was untrue, derogatory, or disparaging, thus harmful. However, they aren't trained communications professionals.

It's not enough for the plaintiff's attorney to say, "they did a person wrong" and we want "x" dollars in damages, without thoroughly educating the jury to multiple factors and applying them to the target's circumstances and case. Nor is it enough for the defendant's counsel to say "they have no case, and you need to acquit" without giving a rationale for why the allegations don't apply based on a thorough knowledge of the principles of defamation.

The expenses of cleaning up reputational damage on the Internet are often very high. Thus, many businesses and individuals often cannot afford them without forcing the defendant to pay for them through a lawsuit. Typical costs to clean up the damage are $50,000 to $125,000 per search term. In many instances, somewhere between 20 and 60 search terms – far beyond the name of the specific person or business – need to be restored.

Due to the ever-changing search engine algorithms, damaging information can unexpectedly resurface among top search results. Most cleanup efforts, therefore, require ongoing monitoring and ongoing maintenance – and, thus, potentially ongoing costs – to ensure that the harmed party's reputation is restored permanently. In fact, it is not uncommon to see total cleanup cost estimates of $500,000 to $5,000,000 or more.

A harmed party can typically have an expert establish cleanup expenses by looking at the damage and estimating the costs to bury the damaging content and conduct ongoing monitoring. Specifically, a harmed party should seek the following information from an expert:

1 How far the damaging material has spread across the Internet and social media

2 The required steps to clean up the damage

3 The estimated costs to perform this cleanup

4 What ongoing monitoring and corrective actions are needed going forward

The publication of defamatory or private information about businesses or individuals can have a ripple-like effect, with the posting and reposting of information allowing it to reach larger audiences. Similarly, a defamatory newspaper article or column can spread to other websites and publications and can remain online forever, even if the newspaper were to remove the original article. For victims, it often requires a very intense period of cleanup followed by a lifetime of additional, smaller tweaks. That is, many reputation cases are not a "fix it and done" type scenario.

With today's Internet and social media landscape, it is now easier than ever for a person's actions to harm another individual or a business online – and the impact is often larger. Thus, when remedying the situation becomes very costly, an attorney should make sure not to overlook the potential recovery of cleanup costs for the client.

Eric W. Rose is a partner in EKA, a strategic communications firm in Los Angeles.

Punitive Damages
This type of damage award is not intended to make the plaintiff whole but to act as an additional deterrent to the type of conduct the plaintiff engaged in.

One of the largest awards ever granted in a libel suit was a $222 million verdict in *MMAR Group v. Dow Jones*.[77] The *Wall Street Journal* was sued for libel by a Texas securities firm for statements made about the firm's dealings with a retirement account. MMAR subsequently went out of business. The judgment was for $22 million in compensatory damages and $200 million in punitive damages. Dow Jones appealed, and a federal appeals court remanded the case and ordered a new trial. The libeled plaintiff dropped the suit before it was retried. So a multimillion-dollar verdict at trial resulted in no payment by the defendant.

In another case, *Penthouse* magazine publisher Robert Guccione and *Hustler* magazine publisher Larry Flynt went to court and staged what one federal judge called a "grudge match." The two pornography publishers were known not to get along, but Guccione sued for libel when Flynt's publication accused Guccione of having a live-in girlfriend while still married. Guccione won at trial and was awarded $1 nominal damages[78] and $1.6 million in punitive damages. On appeal, the federal circuit court reversed because the statement was "substantially true," and the plaintiff was "libel-proof" as far as the claims of adultery were concerned.[79]

In the process of legal wrangling, sometimes cases are settled before they go to trial,[80] or they can be settled even after a jury issues a verdict. In 2021, Dominion Voting Systems sued Fox News for alleging Dominion had rigged its voting machines to keep Donald Trump from winning reelection.

Fox asserted its statements were opinion and as such were entitled to protection. Dominion produced evidence that Fox News presenters and executives were aware of the falsity of the statements, yet they were allowed to continue. At that point the judge ruled the statements to be true and ordered a trial to determine if it acted with actual malice. Within weeks, just before opening statements were made, Fox News agreed to pay $787.5 million, just under half of the amount specified in requested damages.[81]

A defendant who loses at the trial court often appeals and during the time between the trial and the appeal, the two litigants may settle out of court.[82] When they do, it is often a condition of the settlement that neither party reveals the exact terms of the agreement.

Lindsay Lohan sued E*Trade for a 2010 Super Bowl Commercial that she claimed defamed her. In the ad, a baby refers to a "milkaholic" named Lindsay. The parties settled the case out of court and though some speculated on the settlement, no terms were disclosed.[83]

In another case, Texas District Attorney Vic Feazell was the subject of an 11-part investigative series on WFAA-TV, where he was accused of being lax in prosecuting drug cases and perhaps taking bribes. A jury in his home of McLennan County found in favor of Feazell in 1991. He was awarded $17 million in compensatory damages and $41 million in punitive damages. The station's owners (Belo Corp.) planned to appeal but a settlement was reached prior to appeal.

77. 187 F.R.D. 282 (S.D. Tex. 1999).
78. Nominal damages are awarded in cases in which the court wants to recognize the "winner" of a lawsuit who has not sustained any actual damage. The district court had to award at least some nominal award to be able to assess punitive damages.
79. *Guccione v. Hustler*, 800 F.2d 298 (2d Cir. 1986), *cert. denied*, 479 U.S. 1091 (1987).
80. Singer Courtney Love paid $430,000 in a pretrial settlement with a fashion designer over derogatory tweets Love had posted. "Courtney Love Settles Twitter Rant Lawsuit," March 4, 2011, *at* www.cbsnews.com/news/courtney-love-settles-twitter-rant-lawsuit/.
81. "Fox Settles Dominion Lawsuit for $787.5 Million Over US Election Lies," *Reuters*, April 19, 2023.
82. Or, in some cases, between a trial and a retrial. Syracuse Basketball Coach Jim Boeheim was able to win a libel suit at the lower court, but a state appeals court overturned the ruling, sending it back for retrial. It was at that point that the parties reached a confidential settlement. "Syracuse, Jim Boeheim Settle Defamation Suit by Ex-Ballboys," August 6, 2015, *at* https://bangordailynews.com/2015/08/06/sports/syracuse-boeheim-settle-defamation-suit-by-ex-ballboys/.
83. "Lindsay Lohan Gets Paid in 'Milkaholic' Lawsuit," September 20, 2010, *at* www.tmz.com/2010/09/17/lindsay-lohan-etrade-milkaholic-lawsuit-settlement-money-drugs-alcohol-rehab/.

In what could be the longest-running dispute to settle out of court, a libel suit was filed in 2014 against singer Kesha by her producer, Dr. Luke. Kesha claimed the producer raped her. After nine years of legal preliminaries, the two parties settled out of court less than a month before the case was scheduled to go to trial in 2023.[84]

Other Defenses

We title this section "Other Defenses" because the first line of defense in a defamation suit is to disprove any of the six elements that must be shown by the plaintiff. If the truth of the offending statement is proven, the defendant may get the case dismissed before it gets to trial.

Summary Judgment
A final judgment for one party without trial when a court finds either no material fact is in dispute, or when the law alone clearly establishes one party's claim.

In most cases where the plaintiff files against a media defendant, the libel case never makes it to trial, sometimes because there is an out-of-court settlement but often because it is dismissed on **summary judgment**. Summary judgment is where a court summarily enters a judgment for one party because there is no genuine dispute as to any material fact and the law is settled. A judge dismisses a case on summary if it is obvious it has no chance for success.

Suppose a person wants to file a libel suit against a newspaper because an article correctly reports that person's arrest for driving under the influence. Should the newspaper have to spend thousands of dollars in legal fees defending itself, or should the state spend thousands of dollars conducting a meaningless trial? Remember that in the U.S. system of jurisprudence, anyone can file a legal claim against anyone else.

Privilege

Privilege
In libel law, privilege is an affirmative defense in which the defendant enjoys a certain entitlement or immunity for having defamed the plaintiff.

One defense against a claim of defamation is the assertion that the defendant has a particular entitlement or immunity for defaming the plaintiff. Certain people in certain conditions enjoy a **privilege**. For example, members of all three branches of government hold such a form of privilege, both at the state and federal levels. Members of Congress enjoy a privilege when carrying out the duties of their office.

The rationale for this right is easy to understand. Imagine that Congress is considering funding a major construction project. Imagine also that one of the contractors under consideration has a checkered past in fulfilling government deals. Should members of Congress have to worry about the potential for a libel suit if they debate the suitability of that contractor's past? To prevent situations like this one, the law protects legislators in their deliberations by providing them with an absolute privilege that their remarks will not be subject to libel suits.

The judicial branch provides a privilege for itself as well. Rather than facing the possibility that a witness should have to defend himself or herself in a subsequent lawsuit, individuals testifying in a court of law have an absolute privilege for the purposes of a defamation claim.[85]

The law has decided a privilege should exist for courtroom arguments and testimony to preempt subsequent suits for libel and protect the witnesses, litigants, and other trial participants, even though defenses exist that would preclude a lawsuit from succeeding (the opinion defense or the claim that the statements did not rise to the necessary level of fault).[86]

An interesting twist occurred in 2023 when Donald Trump was found guilty of defamation against E. Jean Carroll. In that year Carroll won a sexual abuse suit against Trump for an incident from the 1990s. In 2022, Trump stated that he didn't rape her, didn't know her, and she wasn't his type. While Trump's courtroom statements might be protected, making

84. Willman, "Kesha and Dr. Luke Settle Defamation Case Out of Court," *Variety*, June 23, 2023.
85. For example, Tennessee provides an absolute privilege. *Independent Life Ins. Co. v. Rodgers*, 55 S.W.2d 767 (Tenn. 1933).
86. V. Veeder, "Absolute Immunity in Defamation: Judicial Proceedings," 9 *Colum. L. Rev.* 463 (1909).

the statements outside of court were not protected. Saying she lied and it was a con, in light of factual evidence to the contrary, was libel.[87]

Executive branch privileges are the most obvious in law enforcement. Certainly, no one wants to hamper police officers with the fear that an arrest they make might result in a defamation suit. The administrative paperwork generated when police write up their reports is also absolutely protected.

It's important to understand that the privileges are limited. For the legislative, judicial, and executive branches, they are based on the need for each branch to do its job and do not attach to the people outside of the context of that governmental duty. A witness who has a privilege to speak freely in trial does not have the same freedom when speaking outside of the courtroom to journalists.

The police officer writing an arrest report is protected but not in a conversation later among friends. In 1979, the Supreme Court stated that a U.S. senator did not have an absolute privilege when he chose to make remarks about a researcher away from the floor of the Senate.

Sen. William Proxmire had an absolute privilege when conducting his business on the floor of the Senate, and he was protected when he implied that a college researcher was wasting government money with the sort of research he conducted. But when he stepped off the Senate floor, he did not enjoy the same protection in a press conference or a newsletter when he announced the awarding of his "Golden Fleece" Award to the researcher.[88]

Absolute Privilege
Absolute privilege means a privileged statement can never be the basis for a libel cause of action. An example is the absolute privilege given to legislators in their formal deliberations.

Qualified Privilege
In libel law, qualified privilege means a privileged statement may or may not be the basis for a cause of action, based on the specific facts. For example, it protects journalists who fairly and accurately report the contents of a police report, even if the report contains harmful untruths.

Engaging in legislative, executive, and judicial enterprises provides participants with an **absolute privilege**, but it also provides those reporting on that activity with a **qualified privilege**. A police officer has an absolute privilege in writing up an arrest report, and if any information happens to be false and damaging to someone's reputation, the officer is protected from a lawsuit. If a reporter writes a news story based on that arrest report, the journalist shares in that privilege as well, although the privilege is qualified: it only applies if the reporter's account of the privileged communication is accurate.

Some jurisdictions expand the qualification beyond just accurate to "fair and accurate." For example, a Louisiana statute asserted that a qualified privilege existed "where the publication or expression is a fair and true report of any judicial, legislative, or other public or official proceeding, or of any statement, speech, argument, or debate in the course of the same."[89]

Regardless of whether the rule is codified or not, it is safe to assume that reporting on any absolutely privileged communication by the legislative, executive, or judicial branches of state or federal government will be protected from a libel suit provided that the reporting is done professionally and responsibly.

There are also instances in which nongovernment officials can claim a privilege. One protected space is in job performance evaluations. A hair stylist on the CBS soap opera *The Bold and the Beautiful* had his lawsuit dismissed on summary judgment because the remarks he complained about were part of a job performance critique, privileged under California law.[90]

Fair Comment

Like protecting opinion because it is not a false statement of fact, the doctrine of fair comment protects media commentary about those sorts of things typically featured in newspapers and television reviews. Reviews of all sorts are protected in this way: critics review books, movies, plays, and restaurants, and their reviews are provided as guidance to the public.

87. "Trump Is Liable in the Second E. Jean Carroll Defamation Case, Judge Rules; January Trial Will Determine Damages," *CNN*, September 6, 2023.
88. *Hutchinson v. Proxmire*, 443 U.S. 111 (1979). Senator Proxmire awarded "golden fleece" awards monthly to what he characterized as wasteful government spending, that is, "fleecing" the public.
89. La. Rev. Stat., 1962 Cum. Supp., Tit. 14 § 49, as cited in *Garrison v. Louisiana*, 379 U.S. 64 (1964).
90. "CBS Defeats Defamation Lawsuit Brought by 'Bold and the Beautiful' Hairstylist," *The Hollywood Reporter*, August 15, 2012, *at* www.hollywoodreporter.com/thr-esq/cbs-defeats-defamation-lawsuit-bold-and-the-beautiful-hair-stylist-362806.

Make no mistake about it – a bad review can cost a publisher or restaurateur a lot of business. Still, in balancing the rights of the speaker and the rights of the performer, the law tilts in favor of the rights of speakers, *provided* the commentary is relevant to that subject matter that is deserving of comment.

In other words, statements about whether a performance was good or bad are protected under the fair comment privilege, but a false statement about the performer having a sexually transmitted disease would be defamatory. In a restaurant review, the doctrine of fair comment would protect criticism of the food, personality of the wait staff, décor, and anything else affecting the dining experience, but the privilege would not protect a speaker who made false statements about the owner's criminal record.

In one Ohio libel case, a sports columnist claimed a coach was lying about a brawl at a wrestling match, and the Supreme Court held his words to be a fact-based statement and not opinion as alleged by the writer. The decision held that fair comments include hyperbole, figures of speech, or statements that are not capable of being proven true or false.[91]

The very next year, the Supreme Court took up another libel case to distinguish between factual statements and opinion by suggesting four elements to try: **verifiability**, asking if the statement could be proven true or false; **accepted meaning** of the words used; the **message's context**; and the **social context** of the questionable statement.[92]

This became known as the Ollman test named for a Marxist professor in New York who sued two conservative columnists for libel. The fair comment defense protects speakers who provide commentary and criticism so long as the opinions are based in fact and related to topics appropriate for public comment.

Figure 5.1 Addie, Jessie, and Effie: The Cherry Sisters

91. *Milkovich v. Lorain Journal*, 497 U.S. 1 (1990).
92. *Ollman v. Evans*, 750 F.2d 970 (D.C. Cir. 1984).

Vaudeville Fair Comment

More than a century ago, a newspaper in an Iowa town wrote a review of a vaudeville act, the Cherry Sisters, shown in Figure 5.1. Although the language is somewhat different from current use, it's hard to imagine a more stinging commentary. The reviewer for the ***Odebolt Chronicle*** wrote:

> Effie is an old jade of 50 summers, Jessie a frisky filly of 40, and Addie, the flower of the family, a capering monstrosity of 35. Their long skinny arms, equipped with talons at the extremities, swung mechanically, and anon waved frantically at the suffering audience. The mouths of their rancid features opened like caverns, and sounds like the wailings of damned souls issued therefrom. They pranced around the stage with a motion that suggested a cross between the danse du ventre and fox trot – strange creatures with painted faces and hideous mien. Effie is spavined, Addie is stringhalt, and Jessie, the only one who showed her stockings, has legs with calves as classic in their outlines as the curves of a broom handle.[93]

The Cherry Sisters sued for libel, but the Iowa Supreme Court dismissed the case, stating that even a century ago, "it is well settled that the editor of a newspaper has the right to freely criticize any and every kind of public performance, provided that in doing so he is not actuated by malice."[94] Disparaging comments about the ages and appearance of the performers were protected because they are part of the entertainment.

Neutral Reportage
In some jurisdictions, neutral reportage is recognized as a defense to libel, which asserts if a speaker accurately recounts all sides of an argument, it acts as a neutral conveyance of information and should not be held responsible for defamation.

Neutral Reportage

Some jurisdictions recognize what is called the **neutral reportage** defense,[95] while others have not taken a position, and some have even gone as far as to outright reject it.[96] Simply stated, a neutral reportage defense asserts that so long as a journalist accurately recounts all sides of an argument, it acts as a neutral conveyance of information. If, in the course of this reporting, the journalist recounts defamatory remarks of one of the participants in the debate, the neutral reporting defense holds they should not be held responsible for the offending defamation.

While a possible defense in some jurisdictions, no media professional ought to count on this defense in a libel suit. It might become part of a defense strategy, but neutral reportage has not enjoyed enough judicial support to warrant complete confidence. In the only case to reach the U.S. Supreme Court containing the term *neutral reportage*, the Court did not affirm the defense, but one of the justices, Harry Blackmun, speculated in his concurrence, "Were this court to adopt the neutral reportage theory, the facts of this case arguably might fit within it."[97]

Journalists stand on firmer ground citing the privilege of *fair reportage* when reporting libelous content printed in official documents or spoken at public meetings such as legislative debates, courtroom trials, and school board meetings. The Second Restatement of Torts

93. *Cherry v. Des Moines Leader*, 114 Iowa 298 (Iowa 1901).
94. *Id.* at 301. It is important to note that the "malice" spoken of in this 1901 case is not the notion of "actual malice" as defined by Justice Brennan but the traditional definition of malice, which is to mean "ill will."
95. Including New York and Utah.
96. Including Pennsylvania.
97. *Harte-Hanks Communication v. Connaughton*, 491 U.S. 657, 695 (1989).

affirms the privilege of repeating defamatory expressions made in public by officials if the "report is accurate and complete or a fair abridgement of the occurrence reported."[98]

Anti-SLAPP Laws

Sometimes it can appear the legal system is being used by the rich and powerful to oppress those less privileged. Imagine you receive a terrible product from a retailer and when you try to deal with the company's customer service department, you are treated horribly. Your response might be to complain about that store through every form of social media you can use, telling everyone about your mistreatment and urging your followers to never shop there.

That retailer might file a lawsuit for defamation, even if everything you said is either true (protected) or opinion (also protected with some exceptions). Even though you have the law on your side, the case might cost you a lot of time and money to fight, and it might convince you to remove your negative comments rather than going to all that trouble. What that company did was engage in a strategic lawsuit against public participation (**SLAPP**).

About one-third of the states in the United States have enacted **anti-SLAPP** laws.[99] To prevent the more powerful from intimidating others, anti-SLAPP laws allow defendants to turn the tables and take a form of revenge against the plaintiff. Laws vary by jurisdiction, but generally speaking if it can be shown the suit has no likely chance of succeeding and/or was filed after the speaker was threatened to stop talking or asked to retract all public comments, then the lawsuit is a SLAPP.

Most states require the party that SLAPPs to pay the defamation defendant's legal fees. Anti-SLAPP laws are usually tied to matters of public concern, so anti-SLAPP lawsuits are unlikely to be useful in matters that are purely of private interest, but most states are lenient in interpreting what constitutes the public interest (except Utah, which only protects defendants if the subject of their original communication was related to executive or legislative branch decisions and decision-making).

Showing a plaintiff has no chance to win might be challenging, but in 2012 the website Gizmodo.com had a suit against it dismissed on anti-SLAPP grounds because the article in question was so extensively hyperlinked. A California court stated that Peep Telephony's lawsuit was unwarranted because the sources in the article were specified, and any reader who wanted to would be able to check their veracity.[100]

There is no national anti-SLAPP law,[101] and a federal appeals court has questioned whether state anti-SLAPP laws can ever prevail in federal courts. In 2019, MSNBC journalist Joy Reid retweeted a photo from a Simi Valley, California, City Council meeting that appeared to show an activist yelling at a boy, with text alleging she used racial epithets to threaten him. A federal district court determined the activist was a limited purpose public figure and was unable to show actual malice. As such she had no chance to win, so the court applied California's anti-SLAPP law to hold the plaintiff responsible for the legal fees.

On appeal, the Second Circuit Court of Appeals allowed the suit to proceed, asserting the anti-SLAPP law violated federal rules of procedure by lowering the standard of proof required.[102] With federal appellate courts divided on the question of whether state anti-

98. See American Law Institute, *Restatement of the Law, Second Torts 2d* (St. Paul, MN: American Law Institution Publishers, 1965). Sec. 611.
99. States without anti-SLAPP laws include Alabama, Alaska, Idaho, Iowa, Michigan, Minnesota, Mississippi, Montana, New Hampshire, North Carolina, North Dakota, Ohio, South Carolina, South Dakota, Wisconsin, and Wyoming, *at* https://www.rcfp.org/anti-slapp-legal-guide/.
100. *Redmond v. Gawker Media LLC*, 2012 WL 3243507 (Cal. App. Ct., 2012).
101. The SPEAK FREE Act of 2015 (H.R. 2304) died in committee. Efforts to reintroduce it have been unsuccessful.
102. "MSNBC Host Joy Reid Faces Revived Libel Claim Upon Big Appellate Decision," *Hollywood Reporter*, July 15, 2020.

SLAPP laws can be applied in federal courts, a Supreme Court decision may be required to settle it.

Among the states, the situation is constantly changing. Washington state, for example, had a strong anti-SLAPP statute, but its state Supreme Court struck down most of it as a violation of the state's constitutional right to a civil jury trial.[103] New York, considered to have weak anti-SLAPP protection, recently passed legislation to improve it.[104] In Ohio, a 2014 court decision encouraged the Ohio legislature to pass anti-SLAPP legislation. A 2017 bill never made it through committee, and the bill was reintroduced in 2019.[105] As of this writing Ohio has no anti-SLAPP measure, but around two-thirds of the states do have a law protecting freedom of speech, "slapping back" against lawsuits designed to silence public criticism.

Retractions

If an influencer, celebrity, or podcaster realizes they made a mistake criticizing someone and harming their reputation, and they attempt to correct it, will that response protect them from a libel suit? No, but it may impact the award the plaintiff receives.

The whole purpose of libel law is to protect the reputation of individuals. If a correction or retraction is published, it can be argued the damage was somewhat repaired. It can also be said that anyone willing to publish a retraction shows a sense of professional responsibility – something lacking in anyone who has a "reckless disregard for the truth." At the very least in some states, printing a retraction that fits predetermined criteria[106] will prevent a plaintiff from recovering punitive damages (often the most costly).[107]

On the other hand, some view making a retraction or correction as an admission of guilt. If the offender publishes a retraction, isn't it admitting that they were wrong? Legal advisors are cautious about blanket recommendations to publish retractions.

Rolling Stone's Retraction

The ***Rolling Stone's*** bold headline, "A Rape on Campus," grabbed readers in November 2014 with details about an alleged gang rape at a fraternity party at the University of Virginia – sensational news that even captured the nation's attention. The alleged victim identified only as "Jackie" claimed she had been taken to a bedroom at this one fraternity house and was sexually assaulted multiple times as part of an initiation ritual by its members.

A problem arose after authorities interviewed dozens of witnesses and followed every lead they could for several months. Charlottesville police simply could not verify the woman's account, and neither could other journalists who followed up on the *Rolling Stone* exclusive.

More telling was the fact the accused fraternity members were never contacted by the *Rolling Stone* reporter for their response. Even more damaging to the prestigious

103. "Washington Supreme Court Strikes Down Anti-SLAPP Statute as Violating the Right to Trial by Jury," *Washington Post*, May 28, 2015, *at* www.washingtonpost.com/news/volokh-conspiracy/wp/2015/05/28/washington-supreme-court-strikes-down-anti-slapp-statute-as-violating-the-right-to-trial-by-jury/.
104. "New York Legislature Passes Bill to Protect Free Speech from Frivolous Lawsuits," *Hollywood Reporter*, July 22, 2020.
105. "Ohio Bill Aims to Protect Critics from Being Silenced by Lawsuits," *Cleveland.com*, October 23, 2019, *at* www.cleveland.com/open/2019/10/ohio-bill-aims-to-protect-critics-from-being-silenced-by-lawsuits.html.
106. For example, Alabama's retraction statute states that a retraction must be demanded at least five days before a lawsuit is filed. The publisher then has five days to make a "full and fair retraction in a place as prominent and public as the original charge." Ala. Code § 6–5–186.
107. Alabama, Florida, Georgia, Kentucky, Mississippi, North Carolina, Oklahoma, and Tennessee all prohibit the awarding of punitive damages if a suitable retraction is published.

university was this poorly sourced story's portrayal of an insensitive administration unwilling to help rape victims at their time of need.

By the first week of December 2014, the *Rolling Stone* admitted there appeared to be "discrepancies" in its blockbuster story that failed to follow the basic norms of reporting, and eventually in April 2015 the magazine retracted its story in full.

So how did *Rolling Stone*'s retraction fare in the aftermath of this case?

The university's chief administrator for handling sexual assault issues filed a $7.5 million lawsuit claiming damage to her reputation and infliction of emotional distress, for which a jury decided she was owed $3 million in damages.

In 2017, *Rolling Stone* faced another lawsuit for the story filed by the fraternity mentioned that was settled for $1.65 million.[108] Virginia has no retraction statute that might have mitigated the magazine's damages in other states. Although the constitutionality of retraction statutes has been challenged in view of the plaintiff's right to recover damages.

One other factor that comes into play is libel insurance. Most news media carry some form of libel insurance as a standard cost of doing business. Typically, these policies grant the insurance company the right to insist on certain actions by the news medium if they are sued, and one of those actions would be to print a retraction to avoid punitive damages. Refusing to comply relieves the insurance company of having to pay any punitive damage award, thus coercing the medium to go along with the insurer's recommendation.

Politicians and Libel

A lot of mudslinging takes place during political campaigns in attack ads and at stump rallies, yet the number of libel suits filed by politicians is relatively low.

Why do you suppose that is?

Anyone involved in governing or running for office must prove actual malice (more difficult than negligence), and that means libel lawsuits can take years to run their course. So they draw more attention to the original defamatory remarks, and candidates simply elect to avoid that ordeal. Still, there are exceptions where politicians eagerly file defamation claims.

Before leaving office after his first term, President Donald Trump sued CNN, *The New York Times*, and *Washington Post* claiming they all libeled him. Courts dismissed all three cases. But he was not the first sitting president to unsuccessfully sue for libel. Teddy Roosevelt lost a case against *The New York World* in 1911 in a brief, two-page opinion from the Supreme Court.

Devin Nunes was a U.S. Congressman from 2003–2022. Between 2019 and 2023, Nunes filed 11 libel suits, one of which was filed against the creator of a Twitter parody account, "Devin Nunes' Cow" (the Nunes family owned a dairy farm). The suit drew even more attention to the parody account, which attracted new followers and exceeded Nunes' own number of followers.

As mentioned earlier in this chapter, libel is not a tort to protect hurt feelings, but lawsuits do generate publicity for the statement causing the offense. That is one reason among many why libel suits initiated by politicians are usually thought to be a fool's errand.[109]

108. S. Ember, "Rolling Stone to Pay $1.65 Million to Fraternity over Discredited Rape Story," *The New York Times*, June 13, 2017, *at* www.nytimes.com/2017/06/13/business/media/rape-uva-rolling-stone-frat.html.
109. For a scholarly view of the issue, see D. Hudson, "Anti-SLAPP Coverage and the First Amendment: Hurdles to Defamation Suits in Political Campaigns," 69 *Am. U. L. Rev.* 1541 (2020).

Intentional Infliction of Emotional Distress

Just to be clear, the tort of intentional infliction of emotional distress (IIED) is *not* defamation. It's a completely different tort, but we include this tort in the defamation chapter because it often is filed alongside actions for libel and slander. The name of the tort tells you three of its characteristics. Its purpose is to protect people from the following elements:

- intentional (or reckless)
- severe emotional distress
- caused by the defendant
- a fourth qualification that may not be obvious from the name of the tort concerns the defendant's behavior, which must be deemed extreme or outrageous

Earlier in this chapter, we explained the tort of defamation exists to save reputation, but it is not a salve to protect people's feelings. IIED can be construed as a tort for protecting feelings, but only in *extreme* cases. Just because you are insulted or embarrassed by some expressions, they do not necessarily rise to the level of severe emotional distress. A plaintiff in an IIED suit must show hard evidence ranging from a psychologist's report to a diagnosis of the onset of ulcers. The harm done must be a sustained infliction beyond an ephemeral upset. The other subjective criterion that is sometimes difficult to determine is whether the plaintiff's behavior is extreme or outrageous enough to warrant legal action. Behavior that exceeds "all possible bounds of decency"[110] would be considered outrageous.

There are thousands of court cases dealing with IIED, but only two have been heard by the U.S. Supreme Court, each providing important clarification to the tort. The first was a case involving the Rev. Jerry Falwell. In 1983, men's magazine *Hustler* published a parody ad (Figure 5.2) that featured the famous evangelist.

Campari liquor published a series of advertisements where people talked about "their first time," an intentional double entendre intended to make readers think of a sexual encounter but instead recounting the subject's first time taking a drink of Campari. In the parody ad reproduced in Figure 5.2, Falwell talks about his "first time" having been in an outhouse with his mother. It's difficult to imagine a statement more outrageous, especially given the fact that the statement was made about a famous evangelist who was always preaching morality. It truly exceeded "all possible bounds of decency."

A unanimous Supreme Court dismissed Falwell's intentional infliction of emotional distress lawsuit, creating a standard that makes it nearly impossible for public figures to win IIED suits. The Court ruled that public figures could not sue for IIED in cases in which the public realized there was no factual claim being made, as was the case for parody.

More to the point, to win a public figure would have to be able to show a false statement of fact that rose to the level of actual malice (as defined in the *Sullivan* case) *and* that the parody was describing actual facts rather than humorous, fictional content.[111] The Court did not say it was impossible for a public figure to win a suit for IIED, but the bar was set exceedingly high.

In 2011, the Supreme Court extended protection in IIED cases to issues of public interest, beyond just public figures. The father of a marine killed in the line of duty filed suit against a group of protesters outside the funeral holding signs that exceeded all possible bounds of decency with the statements "Thank God for Dead Soldiers," "Fags Doom Nations," "America is Doomed," "Priests Rape Boys," and "You're Going to Hell."

110. FindLaw, *at* http://injury.findlaw.com/torts-and-personal-injuries/intentional-inflictionof-emotional-distress.html.
111. *Hustler Magazine v. Jerry Falwell*, 485 U.S. 46 (1988).

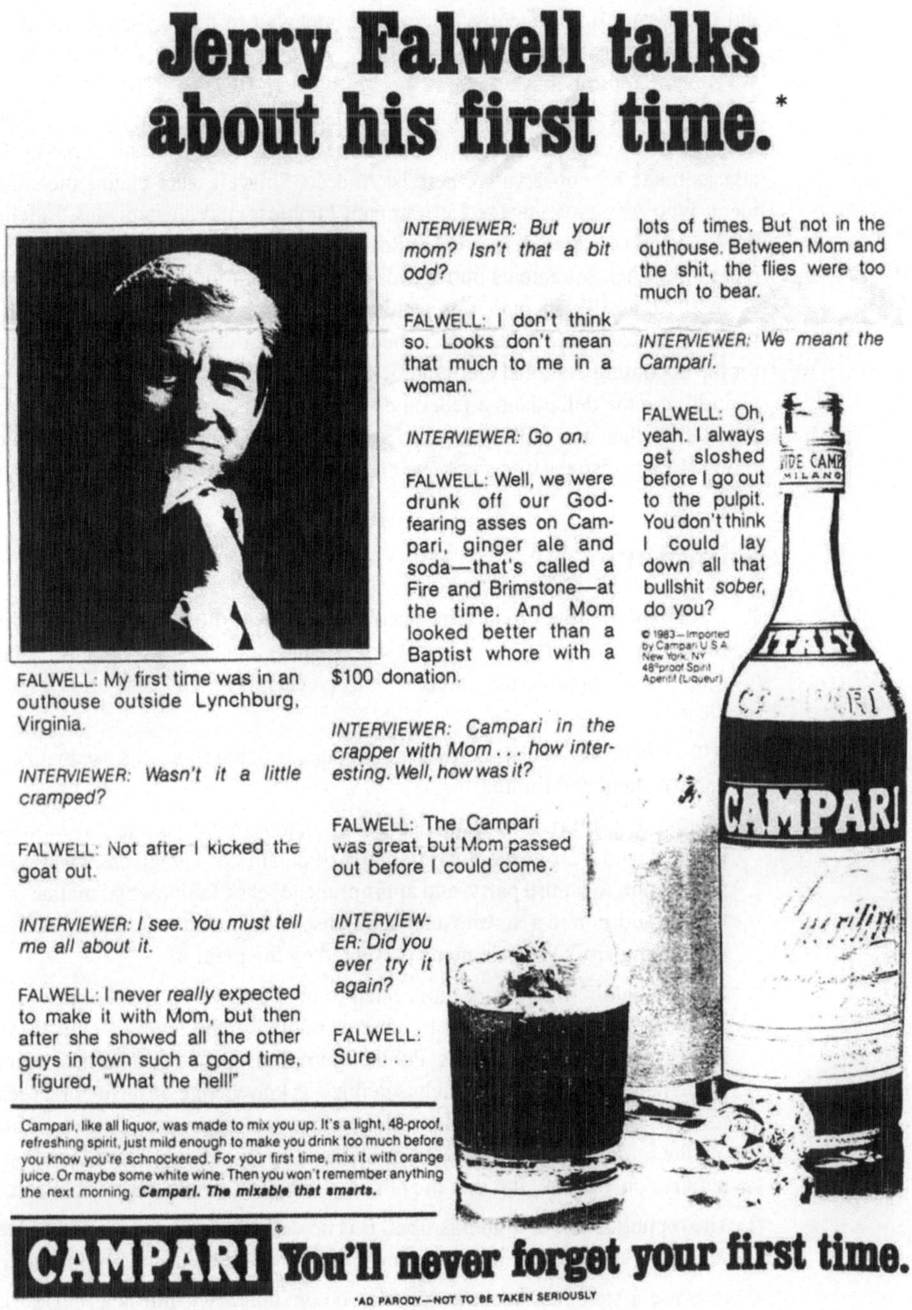

Figure 5.2 Parody ad as it appeared in *Hustler*

The Supreme Court ruled 8–1 that despite the disturbing nature of the messages, the peaceful protest in a defined public area required First Amendment protection. Though the funeral may have been private, the protesters were not disruptive, were on public land away from the church, and were addressing matters of public concern.[112] This decision, however,

112. *Snyder v. Phelps*, 562 U.S. 443 (2011).

did not mean all outrageous statements connected to public issues will be protected from IIED lawsuits. Chief Justice Roberts, who wrote the decision, called it a narrow ruling.[113]

You are not to believe a plaintiff never wins an IIED case. In 2015, an assistant attorney general for the state of Michigan was ordered to pay $3.5 million to a former University of Michigan student council president for IIED and other torts.[114] Among the many public attacks made by conservative activist Andrew Shirvell were claims the student body president, who was gay, engaged in rampant "homosexual shenanigans," including underage drinking and sex at churches and children's playgrounds.[115] The court said the jury was correct to find such statements outrageous and worthy of judgment for the plaintiff.

In 2020, an Illinois man won a suit for IIED, but the judge awarded him $0. The father was falsely accused of cheating on behalf of his children by acquiring the actual questions for the upcoming National Geographic Bee. In ruling on the decision challenged by both the plaintiff *and* the defendant, a federal district court ruled the jury acted reasonably. The court found the father was indeed shocked and humiliated, but he lacked the medical evidence to show why his distress was so severe "no reasonable man could be expected to endure it."[116]

Summary

- Defamation is the broad term encompassing both libel and slander. All are false statements about a person or company that cause damage to reputation. Slander generally refers to defamation that is ephemeral (such as spoken defamation), but the line is not clear.
- Although criminal libel is still on the books in some states, its use by law enforcement is controversial and limited.
- The burden of proof in a libel suit lies squarely with the plaintiff in most media cases. Plaintiffs must prove identification, use of defamatory language, falsity of the statement, publication to a third party, and appropriate level of fault (actual malice or negligence) to win. In addition to asserting a legal defense, a defendant can defeat a defamation lawsuit by refuting any of the elements presented by the plaintiff.
- Because public figures are more open to public scrutiny, and because of their ability to be heard when they respond to adverse publicity, the level of fault they must prove is higher than for private figures. Public figures must prove that the defamatory statement is made with actual malice, which is defined as knowledge of falsity or a reckless disregard for the truth. Some jurisdictions also hold private figures to the actual malice standard, but the Supreme Court has allowed states to apply the lower negligence standard, which requires only a showing that the defamer did not exercise reasonable care.
- The republication of a libel is libel. It is no defense to repeat someone else's defamatory statement and then claim no responsibility by pointing to the original source.
- Because a statement must be false to be defamatory, truth is a rock-solid defense in a defamation suit. Professional communicators are wise to make certain of the truth of any potentially damaging message, but sometimes proving truth is not as easy as it seems.

113. *Id.* at 460. *See also* Calvert, "Public Concern and Outrageous Speech: Testing the Inconstant Boundaries and the First Amendment Three Years after *Snyder v. Phelps*," 17 *U. Pa. J. Const. L.* 437 (2014–2015).
114. *Armstrong v. Shirvell*, 596 Fed. Appx. 433 (Sixth Cir. 2015). Armstrong's award also included claims of defamation and stalking.
115. *Id.* at 439.
116. E. Volokh, "Elementary School Geography Bee Cheating Scandal Leads to Litigation," *The Volokh Conspiracy*, July 15, 2010, *at* https://reason.com/2020/07/15/elementary-school-geography-bee-cheating-scandal-leads-to-litigation/.

- Defendants can defend themselves against libel suits by proving they had a protected privilege to libel (such as an accurate report of a government meeting) or were entitled to provide fair comment (such as in a review of a book or movie). Because opinion is not provably true or false, *pure* statements of opinion are protected, although statements of fact disguised as opinion (such as saying "I believe . . .") are not protected.
- Public figures will have an extremely difficult time winning lawsuits for intentional infliction of emotional distress, but private figures may be successful if they can show the defendant engaged in outrageous behavior that caused severe emotional distress.

Ethical Dilemmas: The Process of Protecting Reputation

An extensive national study of libel plaintiffs and media defendants was conducted in the 1980s by a group of University of Iowa professors.[117] Their interviews revealed many critical issues. They found that most libel plaintiffs' first reaction to the stories bothering them was to contact the source – the offending speaker – it was not to contact a lawyer. It was only after they were put off by unwavering claims of "we stand by our story" combined with an unresponsive attitude that they turned to seek a legal remedy.

Most often, a plaintiff will use an attorney whom they know and may have hired for other purposes – taxes, real estate transactions, and so on. These attorneys are not likely to spend much time litigating First Amendment issues and as such are less prepared than the media corporation's legal counsel, who is well versed in the principles and procedures.

Many libel cases never make it as far as a trial because a judge will dismiss the case on summary judgment, or the parties may choose to settle out of court. In those few cases that make it to trial, juries tend to be sympathetic to the plaintiff, the poor soul who appears to have been harmed by someone more powerful than them.

On the other hand, the defendant is often part of a deep-pocketed media conglomerate. The defense must try to argue against a judgment based on First Amendment principles and has no sad soul to parade before the jurors to claim the harm suffered. In a clash between personal harm and ephemeral First Amendment values, juries often side with the plaintiff.[118]

Then on appeal, the tables are turned. No longer is the decision left to untrained jurors but to appellate judges who are well schooled in the nuances of constitutional law.

Most libel judgments in favor of the plaintiff are reversed or reduced on appeal. Instead of being influenced by pity for the plaintiff, appellate jurists understand the importance of free expression and the history of providing "breathing space" so that expressive freedom prevails.

In 2014, former professional wrestler and governor Jesse Ventura was awarded $500,000 for defamation and $1.3 million for "unjust enrichment" in a suit over Chris Kyle's book *American Sniper*. On appeal, the Eighth Circuit threw out the defamation

117. *See* Bezanson, "The Libel Suit in Retrospect: What Plaintiffs Want and What Plaintiffs Get," 74 *Calif. L. Rev.* 789 (1986).
118. Siding with the plaintiff can also result in huge punitive damages awarded at trial. In 2016, a libel trial court awarded a plaintiff $1.5 million in compensatory damages and $7.5 million (five times as much) in punitive damages. Because North Carolina limits punitive awards in such cases, the total was reduced to $6 million. *See* "Wake Jury Awards $7.5 Million to Punish N&O in Libel Trial," October 19, 2016, *at* www.newsob-server.com/news/local/article109246927.html.

claim because of improper and prejudicial testimony, and it reversed the unjust enrichment award because it was unsupported by Minnesota law.[119]

So if most libel suits against media never go to trial, and the majority of those that do are eventually decided in favor of the defendants, why are major media outlets so concerned about libel? Isn't it much ado about nothing? Like so many other dangers, it's the mere *threat* of a libel suit that causes such concern.

Even suits that are unsuccessful against media outlets have real legal costs, not to mention the threat to credibility when news stories report on the initial filing of the suit. A terrorist attack on an airplane is a remote possibility, yet a great deal of time and effort is invested in preventing such attacks. Even though they are not analogous, both dangers are avoided by constant diligence.

Is there an alternative?

In 2011, a British report suggested doing away with libel suits and requiring mediation instead. The benefits could be realized in lower costs for all participants, the avoidance of juries awarding huge settlements eventually to be overturned or reduced, and finding solutions to maintain one's reputation, rather than looking to profit financially.[120]

In the United States, proposals have existed for decades to improve the structure of libel litigation. The Annenberg Project argued for a three-stage process.[121] First, before a suit is filed by someone who feels defamed, they would have to request a retraction or use their right to reply. If the potential defendant complies, there can be no lawsuit (after all, if maintaining one's reputation is the point, then why proceed to court if a party can effectively correct the record?).

If the first stage does not resolve the dispute, the next step is a hearing for a declaratory judgment. At this stage, the only argument is whether the offending material was true or not. In the hope of protecting one's reputation, often that's the only thing potential plaintiffs want proven – what was said about them was wrong.

If those two remedies are not enough, then a traditional trial is conducted, but only actual damages can be awarded.

The goal should be protecting the "breathing space" Justice Brennan so deeply regarded, while still protecting individual reputations. If there is some acceptable alternative to an expensive, lengthy court trial then why not take it?

119. Jesse Ventura's, "$1.8M Legal Win over 'American Sniper' Chris Kyle Overturned on Appeal," *The Hollywood Reporter*, June 13, 2016, *at* www.hollywoodreporter.com/thr-esq/jesse-venturas-18m-legal-win-902299.
120. The Alternative Libel Project, October 2011, *at* www.scribd.com/document/71553064/Alternative-Libel-Project-Preliminary-Report.
121. Rodney A. Smolla & Michael J. Gaertner, "The Annenberg Libel Reform Proposal: The Case for Enactment," 31 *Wm. & Mary L. Rev.* 25 (1989), *at* http://scholarship.law.wm.edu/wmlr/vol31/iss1/3.

6

Privacy

LEARNING OBJECTIVES

After reading this chapter, you should know

- where the Supreme Court has found a constitutional right of privacy
- how the terms of privacy protect a person's physical being, personal space, information, and emotional security
- how a reasonable expectation of privacy is used to determine protection
- the four types of privacy rights identified in court as causes of action
- what plaintiffs must prove when bringing different claims for invasion of privacy and what defenses are available
- how concepts of trespass, seclusion, secrecy, and access affect privacy rights in communication
- what types of information are considered private and subject to legal protection
- how privacy may be used to protect reputation when defamation claims do not apply
- what elements of privacy protect one's identity from being used for commercial gain

Private or Not?

Ruth Shulman didn't expect to appear on TV after a devastating car accident in 1990. The California mother and several family members were in a car that flew off Interstate 10, tumbled down a hill, and landed upside down in a drainage ditch. Ruth was pinned under the vehicle but was cut free by the "jaws of life" before a rescue helicopter flew her from the scene. She was seriously injured, spent months in the hospital, and left as a paraplegic.

At one point during her hospital stay she was told to turn on the TV, only to see her ordeal televised in a nine-minute segment of *On Scene: Emergency Response*. A camera operator employed by Group W Productions, Inc. and 4MN Productions had been at the accident scene, recording Ruth's extrication from the car including her saying, "Am I dreaming?" A flight nurse on the rescue helicopter had worn a wireless microphone recording Ruth saying things such as "I just want to die." Ruth was "shocked," saying she felt exploited, and her

DOI: 10.4324/9781003462989-6

privacy invaded. She had never consented to the recording or broadcast and felt "the whole scene was pretty private." She sued for invasion of privacy.[1]

This case illustrates the balance between privacy and press freedom, and in doing so, addresses two different privacy claims. Privacy is not a single cause of action; it covers different torts and statutes concerning very different interests. This "right to be let alone" can mean protection from unwanted intrusion by photography or from the public disclosure of personal details. It also can mean not having one's image appropriated for commercial gain or being portrayed in a "false light." Statutes requiring financial or medical records to be kept confidential are also part of privacy law, as well as federal and state statutes forbidding deceptive practices, wiretapping, and hidden cameras. There are exceptions and defenses of course, such as when First Amendment rights are at issue, which can serve to protect the media from liability given the public interest.

In Ruth Shulman's case, she won on her privacy claim of "intrusion" because the recording taken inside the private helicopter was without her consent. But she lost on her claim of "publication of private facts" because the coverage was found to be newsworthy. It is important for media practitioners to understand the different types of privacy actions, including what a plaintiff must prove to be successful and what defenses are available.

Constitutional Privacy

Right of Privacy
Covers a broad category of rights that extend from the right to be physically autonomous to the security of personal information. Although the Constitution never explicitly recognizes a right to privacy, the Supreme Court has found a general right to privacy in the "penumbras" created by the specific guarantees of several amendments in the Bill of Rights, including the First, Third, Fourth, Fifth, Ninth, Tenth, and Fourteenth Amendments.

There is no explicit mention of privacy in the U.S. Constitution, but a landmark ruling in the Supreme Court described the constitutional **penumbra** enlightening this right.[2] Essentially, the Bill of Rights and several amendments are combined to create a right of privacy, linked to historical antecedents, such as British philosopher John Locke's ideals about the government's duty to protect life, liberty, and property.

A right of privacy can be found in the First Amendment's right of association and the Fourth Amendment's protection against unreasonable search and seizure, which follow the British common-law tradition of protecting one's home as one's castle. There is a right found in the Third Amendment to preserve the sanctity of one's home against the quartering of soldiers. The Fifth Amendment guards against self-incrimination, which implies privacy protection for personal reasons.

The Ninth Amendment's overarching protection of all other rights to be retained by the people is also associated with privacy, and the Tenth Amendment grants to each state's governance and jurisprudence all powers not delegated to the U.S. Congress. The Fourteenth Amendment affords a broad right of privacy through its guarantee of due process prohibiting the government from intruding on someone's private life without a lawful reason.

At least ten state constitutions explicitly protect a right to privacy, including Alaska, Arizona, California, Florida, Hawaii, Illinois, Louisiana, Montana, New Hampshire, and Washington. For example, Florida's constitution states: "Right of privacy. Every natural person has a right to be let alone and free from governmental intrusion into the person's private life."[3]

In some states, such as Arkansas, Georgia, and Kentucky, the courts have recognized an implicit constitutional right to privacy. The Supreme Court of Arkansas, for example, held in 2002 that there is a "rich and compelling tradition of protecting privacy" and a "fundamental right to privacy guaranteed to the citizens of Arkansas."[4]

1. *Shulman v. Group W Publications, Inc.*, 18 Cal. 4th 200, 955 P. 2d 469, 74 Ca. Rptr.2d 843, 850 (1998).
2. In *Griswold v. Connecticut*, the U.S. Supreme Court ruled the "First Amendment has a penumbra where privacy is protected from governmental intrusion" 381 U.S. 479, 483 (1965). The traditional use of the term was the partial shadow during an eclipse. It is neither a full shadow (*umbra* in Latin) nor fully lit.
3. FLA. CONST. art. 1 §23 (2023).
4. *Jegley v. Picado*, 349 Ark. 600, 632 (2002). *See*, National Academies Press, "Chpt. IX, The Right To Privacy Under State Constitutions," (2017), *at* https://nap.nationalacademies.org/read/24730/chapter/12.

Statutory Privacy

Statutes also protect specific privacy interests. At the federal level, the Children's Online Privacy Protection Act (COPPA)[5] restricts how websites, advertisers, and others can collect data from kids under 13 over the Internet. The Privacy Act of 1974 governs the collection, use, and dissemination of information held by federal agencies about individuals, such as their Social Security numbers.[6]

Individual states also enact statutes and allow citizens to seek privacy protection by either civil suit or criminal prosecution.[7] Privacy laws vary from state to state. For example, three states have enacted "biometric privacy" laws, which prohibit unauthorized use of biometric identifiers such as fingerprints or retinal scans[8] and can limit how Facebook and advertisers use facial recognition to tag and identify users. In 2024, Facebook owner Meta agreed to pay $1.4 billion to the state of Texas for violating Texas law prohibiting the use of biometric data without consent.

"Ag-gag" laws in some states make it a crime for anyone – such as animal rights activists and news reporters – to intentionally record an image of an agricultural operation without consent.[9]

The most robust consumer-focused privacy laws are in California, which in 2020 expanded its California Consumer Privacy Act (CCPA), granting residents the right to know about, correct, and opt out of personal data collection used for behavioral advertising.[10] Since then, over a dozen states have adopted similar "data minimization" laws, and many more have bills under consideration.[11]

5. 15 U.S.C. §§6501–6506 (1998). The Federal Trade Commission announced revisions in late 2023 to update some of the provisions, such as limiting the ability of companies to monetize children's data without separate, opt-in parental consent. This effectively means behavioral advertising would need to be turned off by default. Companies would also not be allowed to nudge children to stay online (i.e., with push notifications), and they may retain kids' personal information only for as long as necessary to fulfill the purpose for which it was collected. *See* Lesley Fair, "FTC Proposes Enhanced Protections for Kids Online. Where Do You Stand?" *FTC*, Decembers 20, 2023, *at* https://www.ftc.gov/business-guidance/blog/2023/12/ftc-proposes-enhanced-protections-kids-online-where-do-you-stand. In 2023, Amazon agreed to pay $25 million for keeping recordings and data about children under 13 through its Alexa app. U.S. DOJ, https://www.justice.gov/opa/pr/amazon-agrees-injunctive-relief-and-25-million-civil-penalty-alleged-violations-childrens.
6. 5 U.S.C. § 552a.
7. "Peeping Tom" laws such as West Virginia's criminal invasion of privacy statute serve as an example (*see* W.Va. Code Ann.§61–8–28, 2008).
8. The states are Illinois, Texas, and Washington. In 2008, Illinois became the first state to restrict the use of biometric data for commercial purposes without consent. Other states are introducing similar bills, such as Colorado, Oklahoma, Minnesota, Missouri, Pennsylvania, New York New Jersey, and Massachusetts. *See*, "Tracking U.S. State Biometric Privacy Legislation," 2024 State Biometric Privacy Law Tracker, Husch Blackwell, 2024, *at* https://www.huschblackwell.com/2024-state-biometric-privacy-law-tracker.
9. States with ag-gag laws include Alabama, Arkansas, Missouri, Montana, and North Dakota. Legislation has failed to pass in some states, and the law has been found unconstitutional in such states as Kansas, Iowa, Idaho, North Carolina, Utah, and Wyoming. *See*, Ryann Glenn, Amanda Wall, and Daniel Zimmer, State Guide to Ag-Gag Legislation – October 2023, *JDSupra*, October 20, 2023, *at* https://www.jdsupra.com/legalnews/state-by-state-guide-to-ag-gag-6136263/. Aerial surveillance may also be specifically prohibited. Iowa prohibits the use of remotely piloted aircraft with surveillance equipment over a secure farmstead. *Id.* Texas bans the use of drone photography over concentrated animal feeding operations (CAFOs). HB 1643, Texas (2017).
10. The CCPA became effective in 2020. (Title 1.81.5 California Consumer Privacy Act of 2018, §§1798.100–1798.199.) California residents then voted on Proposition 24 to enact the California Privacy Rights Act (CPRA), which took effect January 1, 2023. The CPRA grants more rights to consumers, imposes greater penalties on businesses for violations, and adds protections for the personal information of children under the age of 16. For example, consumers will have the right to opt out of "cross-context behavioral advertising," data collection of their activities across different websites or devices for purposes of personalized and targeted advertising, and regardless of whether the advertising constituted a sale of that personal information.
11. *See* U.S. State Privacy Legislation Tracker *at* https://iapp.org/media/pdf/resource_center/State_Comp_Privacy_Law_Chart.pdf. For example, both Indiana and Kentucky passed a Consumer Data Protection Act to go into effect January 1, 2026.

A Common Law Right to Privacy

Until the twentieth century, no court recognized a right to privacy. In fact, references to privacy in the legal community did not appear until late in the nineteenth century. Perhaps the earliest mention of privacy appeared in an 1880 legal treatise on torts, in which Judge Thomas Cooley referred to the "right to be let alone," which he called a right to one's person and a right of personal immunity.[12]

The seeds for privacy protection were most famously planted in 1890 when a future Supreme Court Justice Louis Brandeis and his friend Samuel D. Warren II argued in the *Harvard Law Review* that government should uphold an interest in privacy by shielding citizens from gossip-hungry news reporters.[13]

The wealthy scion of a family with a paper mill fortune was frustrated by Boston's muckraking reporters covering his family's parties and social events to spice up their gossip columns. He was particularly upset about a society article written about a party he threw for his daughter's wedding. Warren and Brandeis expressed concern about advances in technology, such as "instantaneous photographs," as well as the mass production of newspapers having "invaded the sacred precincts of private and domestic life."[14]

In their influential law article, Warren and Brandeis argued that "political, social, and economic changes entail recognition of new rights" and the law should "protect the privacy of private life."[15] Eventually, some courts began to recognize a common law right to privacy. But it would be decades before various privacy rights would become enshrined in tort law.[16]

Privacy Defined

Bedrock Law
The right to privacy is recognized by statute in most states, by either case precedent or as a constitutional mandate, although legal definitions vary from state to state.

In legal terms, privacy is defined in one of several ways – the right to be personally autonomous in body and mind, independent without constraint; the right to be let alone; and the right to control over one's personal information.

This distinct rationale springs from the idea that individual solitude and personal well-being need protection like property rights, so long as it occurs where there is a reasonable expectation of privacy. As a result, communicators find themselves facing a legal predicament when an individual's seclusion is violated or when private affairs are publicized and some recovery of damages is required.[17]

The liability for violating privacy will depend on the state, while the ***Restatement (Second) of Torts*** defines four causes of action.[18] Professor William T. Prosser, then dean of the University of California, Berkeley College of Law, redefined the subject through his legal research in 1960.[19]

After reviewing hundreds of claims and cases, Prosser specified four torts of privacy defined generally as 1) **intrusion** upon personal solitude; 2) **public disclosure of embarrassing private facts**; 3) shining a **false light** on one's public identity; and 4) **appropriation**

12. Thomas M. Cooley, *Law of Torts* 29 (2d ed. 1888). *See*, Judith W. DeCew, *In Pursuit of Privacy: Law, Ethics, and the Rise of Technology* (Ithaca, NY: Cornell University Press, 1997).
13. Samuel D. Warren & Louis Brandeis, "The Right to Privacy," 4 *Harv. L. Rev.* 193 (1890).
14. *Id.* at 195. They also expressed concern over individual control over one's written work, thoughts, or likeness – what might be later known as a right to publicity.
15. *Id.* at 215.
16. After Warren's death, efforts were made to conceal what was ostensibly his suicide following a family dispute involving a trust fund Brandeis had managed for him.
17. *Restatement (Second) of Torts* § 652 (1977).
18. *Id.* The *Restatement (Second) of Torts* lists the four claims of privacy: 1) intrusion upon seclusion; 2) appropriation of another's name or likeness; 3) publicity to private facts; and 4) placing a person in a false light. § 652A(2).
19. William T. Prosser, "Privacy," 48 *Cal. L. Rev.* 383 (1960).

of one's name or image for commercial gain. Students of privacy law would be well served to think of these actions as four distinct torts. Conditions vary for each clause, as do the possible defenses, so it is good to clearly define the elements of each one.

1 Intrusion

The privacy tort of intrusion is what often comes to mind when people think of an act invading privacy because it involves intruding – physically or otherwise – on another person's private space, communications, or personal matters without permission. This act might include a physical intrusion into their home, apartment, hotel room, or some private space where they've secluded themselves. It might mean by one's senses – aided or unaided – where they view or overhear another person's private affairs by peeking into their bedroom window using binoculars or a drone, or by tapping into their phone conversation or computer communications. It might occur by prying into someone's personal email, ripping open their postal mail, rummaging through their purse or wallet, probing their private bank account, poring over their medical records, or gaining access to personal information online by phishing or some other means of misrepresentation.

For a claim of intrusion, a plaintiff generally must prove the defendant's action was

- intentional
- **intrusion**, physically or otherwise
- upon the **solitude**, **seclusion**, or **private affairs** of the plaintiff, and
- **highly offensive** to a reasonable person.

Intrusion

Privacy tort defined as an invasion of personal space and solitude. The offense, often associated with newsgathering, is viewed as the invasive act itself, so publication is not required.

The plaintiff also must possess a **reasonable expectation of privacy**.

Most states recognize the tort of intrusion, adopting its elements from the *Restatement (Second) of Torts*.[20] Definitions vary in some states, such as Massachusetts, which has not adopted a common law claim for intrusion but statutorily defines it as an "unreasonable, substantial or serious interference with privacy."[21] In other states, the definition for intrusion is quite a bit different. In Pennsylvania, the law cites persistent "hounding, harassment and unreasonable surveillance" as intrusion.[22] Florida includes stalking another person as one of its intrusion offenses.[23] Michigan requires an intrusion to be "objectionable" rather than offensive, while Illinois finds it can be either "offensive *or* objectionable."

Arizona previously but no longer requires an intentional infliction of emotional distress to prove intrusion.[24] There is the issue of privacy rights for corporations, where in New Jersey the law is clear – they have no such cause of action.

In some states, Virginia and New York, for example, intrusion claims are not recognized. What Virginia does uphold is an anti-stalking statute,[25] where it's also a crime to intentionally videotape, photograph, or film a nonconsenting person in a state of undress since a reasonable expectation of privacy over the exposure of one's body exists.[26] New York courts

20. The *Restatement (Second) of Torts* § 652B defines "Intrusion Upon Seclusion" as "One who intentionally intrudes, physically or otherwise, upon the solitude or seclusion of another or his private affairs or concerns, is subject to liability to the other for invasion of his privacy, if the intrusion would be highly offensive to a reasonable person."
21. M.G.L. c. 214, Section 1B.
22. *Wolfson v. Lewis*, 924 F. Supp. 1413 (E.D. Pa. 1996).
23. Florida Statute 784.048.
24. *Godbehere v. Phoenix Newspaper, Inc.*, 162 Ariz. 335 (1989).
25. Va. Code. Ann. 18–2–60.3.
26. Va. Code. Ann. 18.2–386.1. Other states such as Nebraska also make it a felony to secretly record an image of a person "in a state of undress" where there is a reasonable expectation of privacy. Neb. Rev. Stat. § 28–311.08.

do not recognize intrusion claims,[27] but they do recognize causes of action for trespass and other illegal acts committed in the course of newsgathering.

Trespass
Common law tort protecting people against interference with their person, land, and possessions. Often, the same set of facts for the intrusion claim can serve as a trespass charge.

Intrusion is often tied to related claims of **trespass**, nuisance, stalking, and voyeurism, and when committed by the government, a Fourth Amendment right is violated. Trespass is essentially a physical intrusion upon the property of another without permission from the person legally entitled to possession of that property.[28]

Nuisance is a close cousin to trespass but focuses more on the condition, activity, or situation interfering with the use or enjoyment of property by means such as loud noises, bright lights, or emitting foul odors. State and federal video voyeurism laws[29] as well as anti-stalking statutes[30] also address intrusion claims while focusing on specific safety concerns.

In matters involving agents of the government such as the police, a civil suit for intrusion is unlikely, but a complaint based on your constitutional right against unreasonable search or seizure of "persons, houses, papers, and effects" can be filed.[31]

Intrusion differs from the other privacy torts in several ways. Most significantly, the invasion of privacy occurs from the *conduct* or act of intruding itself. It does not depend on whether the intruder subsequently recorded or shared what was observed because publicity is not required. Instead, the invasive manner in which the information was obtained is the offense. For example, if someone secretly took a photo of gym patrons showering, the plaintiffs could rightfully claim an intrusion had occurred, regardless of whether the images were subsequently deleted.

The tort of intrusion does require the invasive act to be **intentional** because injury to the plaintiff is likely more serious if done on purpose. Lack of intent in intrusion cases is understandable if it was accidental. If someone walks into an unlocked bathroom or office, for example, or happens to see the contents of someone's papers left out on an open table, or if they inadvertently pick up a phone extension to overhear a private conversation, there would be no liability for intrusion so long as the invasion was brief and unintentional.

In other cases, a defendant may have truly believed they had consent or legal permission. In fact, **consent** is often the strongest defense to an intrusion claim. Consent can be explicit or implied, as with a written form to take photographs or when journalists clearly identify themselves as members of the media and no one objects to their presence or recording. Consent must come from someone who is legally able to give it though, such as the parent or guardian of a child or person with a mental disability.

Plaintiffs bringing an intrusion suit must show an unwanted invasion into their personal space or affairs. This tort is most often referred to as "intrusion upon seclusion," but it broadly encompasses intrusions into one's "solitude" and "private affairs or concerns."[32] While not significant legally, seclusion by definition suggests one's interest in isolating oneself, while solitude is more about being left alone or undisturbed while still engaging in society. In this sense, threats to solitude might include physical intrusions into one's personal space as well as interruptions from telemarketing robocalls and hovering drones.

The tort of intrusion also protects against acts of surveillance, where you may not even be aware your personal affairs are being remotely examined and information is collected

27. *Howell v. New York Post Co.*, 612 N.E. 2d 699, 703 (N.Y. 1993).
28. *Hoery v. United States*, 64 P. 3d 214, 217 (Colo. 2003).
29. *See, e.g*, Video Voyeurism Prevention Act of 2004, 18 U.S.C. §1801; Pub. L. No. 108–495 (2007). The law provides protection where a reasonable person would believe that a private area (such as genitals) would not be visible to the public, regardless of whether that person is in a public or private place.
30. *See, e.g.*, 18 U.S.C. §§ 2261, 2261A, 2262, 2265 (2006).
31. Const. Art. IV. The Fourth Amendment provides the following protection: "The right of the people to be secure in their persons, houses, papers, and effects against unreasonable searches and seizures, shall not be violated, and no Warrants shall issue, but upon probable cause, supported by Oath or affirmation, and particularly describing the place to be searched, and the persons or things to be searched."
32. *Restatement (Second) of Torts* § 652B.

without your consent. Hence, the tort more broadly protects the privacy one "has thrown about his person or affairs."[33] Although courts differ as to the precise definition and scope of the tort, at its most basic level a claim for intrusion upon seclusion alleges the defendant has unreasonably interfered with the plaintiff's legitimate interest in maintaining some degree of privacy in their personal affairs.[34] Even unsuccessful attempts at intrusion may make a defendant liable.[35]

Intrusion is also sometimes called the "newsgathering tort" because it often concerns the use of a hidden camera or microphones, and other techniques reporters use to uncover criminal or unethical conduct. Unlike other privacy torts, a showing of newsworthiness or legitimate public interest in the matter intruded upon is *not* a defense. It does not matter whether the information obtained is relevant, trivial, true, false, politically significant, or of great interest to an eager audience when it comes to liability because the law weighs the act of intrusion alone and not whether the ends of newsgathering justify its means. For this reason, journalists covering an important story but using invasive tactics will face an uphill fight against an intrusion lawsuit.

A plaintiff must also prove that the intrusion was **highly offensive to a reasonable person**. It is not sufficient that the plaintiffs show they were personally offended. The offensiveness must be great, beyond mere discomfort or embarrassment. While there may be some jurisdictional differences,[36] courts generally assess offensiveness by considering the degree, context, conduct, and circumstances surrounding the intrusion, including the setting.[37] For example, suppose a court found it "highly offensive" and awarded damages against a person who intruded upon a place where a woman was giving birth.[38] That actually happened when a Michigan doctor in 1881 invited someone to witness a baby's delivery without the mother's consent. A century later, a camera crew filmed a man's emergency medical treatment in his bedroom without even seeking consent from his wife. A California court found such an intrusion to be highly offensive, showing "a cavalier disregard for ordinary citizens' rights of privacy."[39] Courts are usually careful about guarding the privacy of patients who are undergoing personal health care.

Courts also consider the intruder's motives and objectives in determining offensiveness,[40] and here is where the news media find some relief. While the First Amendment does not immunize the press from liability for torts committed in an effort to gather news, a legitimate motive of gathering news and the societal interest in effective and complete reporting can mitigate damages.[41] Even so, the court in *Shulman* found the conduct of the TV producers who shot the emergency medical footage of the California mother inside the rescue helicopter to convey the feel of a tragic event to be highly offensive.[42]

Probably the most important legal element of an intrusion case is whether the plaintiff possesses a **"reasonable expectation of privacy."** This means that a reasonable person in the same situation as the plaintiff would have considered the place, conversation, or matter intruded upon to be a private one. Determining what constitutes an expectation of privacy depends on the exact nature of the conduct and the surrounding circumstances. Courts will make this determination, which is oftentimes left to the trial jury.

33. *Id.* at cmt c.
34. Eli A. Meltz, "No Harm, No Foul? 'Attempted' Invasion of Privacy and the Tort of Intrusion Upon Seclusion," 83 *Fordham L. Rev*. 3431 (2015).
35. *Id.*
36. For example, in Minnesota, some objectively based threshold degree of "repugnance" is required to sustain a claim of intrusion upon seclusion. *Fabio v. Credit Bureau of Hutchinson*, 210 F.R.D. 688, 692 (D. Minn. 2002).
37. *Miller v. National Broadcasting Co.*, 187 Cal. App. 3d 1463, 1483–1484 (1986).
38. *De May v. Roberts*, 46 Mich. 160, 9 N.W. 146 (1881).
39. 187 Cal. App. 3d at 1484.
40. *Id.*
41. *Shulman v. Group W Productions, Inc.*, supra note 1 at 867.
42. *Id.* at 868.

Reasonable Expectation of Privacy

What is a reasonable expectation of privacy? At the extremes, we have a high expectation of privacy when we are in our own homes and much less an expectation at a football stadium where thousands of people and television cameras are watching. It is those spaces in between the extremes where our privacy rights may not be as clear.

In the modern world, we voluntarily exchange private information for convenience or a free service. Every loyalty card from coffee shops, grocery stores, or airlines provides us with discounts in exchange for the ability to track our purchasing activity. Target was able to determine that one of its teenage shoppers was pregnant before the girl's parents even knew, based on her purchases.[43] Social media services are "free" for the users only because those platforms monetize all the data they collect from users. Smartphones need to track their location to provide so many of the services we use, which means phone companies know where we are.

If privacy laws are based on the principle of a reasonable expectation of privacy, what happens when we stop having any privacy expectations? If we come to believe that technological advances make privacy harder to expect, then privacy becomes less protected. The less privacy we expect, the less privacy we have.

Bedrock Law

Cause of action for privacy invasion exists in public places if the intrusion is found to be highly offensive and unreasonable.

Expectations of Privacy in Public Places

When it comes to intrusion, it can make a difference whether the matter occurs in public or private as it relates to one's "reasonable expectation of privacy," simply because a defendant usually is not liable if the plaintiff is in public view.[44] Dean Prosser explains how

> on the public street, or in any other public place, the plaintiff has no right to be alone . . . and it is no invasion of his privacy to do no more than follow him about. Neither is it such an invasion to take his photograph in such a place, since this amounts to nothing more than making a record.[45]

Courts have generally followed this reasoning when it comes to photographing people on a public sidewalk[46] or recording their vehicle license plates in a public parking lot.[47]

There is also no intrusion if the plaintiff is not physically in public but can still be easily observed by others from a public place. For example, someone undressing in front of an open picture window facing a public street would have no expectation of privacy if passersby on the public street got a glimpse of their nudity. A couple having a heated argument in their kitchen with their windows open similarly would have no valid privacy claim if their neighbors were to hear them and report what was said to the police.

Of course, there are exceptions to this general rule. Most courts agree an intrusion has occurred when "extraordinary means" are used to see or hear someone. If a photographer uses a large telephoto lens to shoot a sunbather who could not otherwise be seen from the sidewalk, then intrusion has occurred. Likewise, using a drone to fly over an enclosed backyard to capture photos of a private wedding party without permission would constitute intrusion.

A case from Seattle illustrates how courts might tell the difference. KING-TV was capturing video of a pharmacist outside his store window while he was on the phone. He sued for

43. "How Target Figured Out a Teen Girl Was Pregnant before Her Father Did," *Forbes*, February 16, 2012.
44. *Restatement (Second) of Torts* § 652B cmt c.
45. Prosser, supra note 18 at 391–392.
46. *Jackson v. Playboy Enterprises, Inc.*, 574 F. Supp. 10, 13 (S.D. Ohio 1983).
47. *International Union v. Garner*, 601 F. Supp. 187, 191–192 (M.D. 1985); *Tedeschi v. Reardon* v. 5 F. Supp. 2d 40, 46 (D. Mass. 1998).

invasion of privacy after the station aired a news story about suspicious practices at his place of work. The court held that for such videotaping to be intrusive, it must be of something the public would not normally be able to view. In this instance, there was nothing concealed, and no extraordinary effort taken to capture the footage. The pharmacist, despite his protests, was later convicted on criminal charges for issuing fraudulent drug prescriptions.[48]

Intrusions by Drones

Drones present one of the latest challenges to intrusion claims since their users are clearly using "extraordinary means" to record and transmit images from unique and ordinarily inaccessible vantage points. A drone may be capable of finding and tracking a specific person, use various sensors such as night vision and thermal imaging, and be small and relatively undetectable (Figure 6.1). Certainly, drones flying into private airspace such as a person's backyard could be liable for intrusion and trespass. But what about drones that can view private activity while flying hundreds of feet overhead or at a distance positioned high over nearby public spaces such as a park or street?

Case law shows no liability for intrusion when conventional airplanes pass overhead, as long as the aircraft is operating at an altitude defined in federal law as "navigable airspace."[49] For drones, however, the Federal Aviation Administration (FAA) requires nonrecreational users of unmanned aircraft systems (UAS) to fly at or below 400 feet and be certified before capturing images for commercial purposes such as film productions, advertisements, promotional videos, and even news.

The FAA has refrained from specifically addressing privacy concerns, other than to prohibit flying over groups of people without their permission and restricting their use over stadiums and sporting events, the National Parks, airports, and other airspace such as around Washington, DC. In the meantime, a patchwork of state and local laws provides legal remedies to citizens who have had their photograph taken by a drone

Figure 6.1 As drones become more common, their likelihood of intruding on privacy also increases

48. *Mark v. King Broadcasting Co.*, 618 P. 2d 512 (Wash. Ct. App. 1980).
49. *California v. Ciraolo*, 472 U.S. 207 (1986).

without permission or have been surveilled by a drone while on their own private property. For drone journalists in most states, caution is recommended because newsworthiness[50] and First Amendment claims are not defenses.[51]

While photographers and videographers are generally able to shoot subjects who are out in public without fear of being held liable for intrusion, their actions can be punished if they become harassing or threaten personal safety. Ron Galella, the godfather of American paparazzi, gained quite a reputation for his aggressive pursuit of the Kennedy family and Jacqueline Kennedy Onassis in particular. After President John F. Kennedy's assassination in 1963, his wife and young children became a frequent subject for this overly aggressive photographer. In a lawsuit against Galella, no contention was made the family was in a private place; instead, Galella's actions were alleged to be so disturbing as to frighten the children.

In one incident, he was said to have jumped out from behind the shrubs to snap a surprise photo of John, Jr. riding his bicycle in Central Park, causing Secret Service agents some alarm. A federal court required him to maintain a distance from the family members.[52] It also refused to allow Galella to use the First Amendment as a shield for what it considered to be harassment.[53] Because he violated a restraining order, the court barred him from taking pictures of Onassis and her family. The Galella case stands as an example of how aggressive acts of privacy intrusion can lead to court actions in equity to prevent encroachments.

State law may also restrict the actions of paparazzi who are filming celebrities – even in public places. California led the nation in enacting several anti-paparazzi acts beginning in 1999 following the tragic death of Princess Diana, who was killed in a limousine crash in Paris during a high-speed chase while eluding photographers on motorcycles. Basically, the law made it a crime to trespass on a celebrity's solitude to capture images or recordings where there is a reasonable expectation of privacy.[54] But it didn't go quite far enough for Gov. Arnold Schwarzenegger, who knew personally how celebrities felt when aggressively pursued by desperate photographers.[55] In 2005, he signed a "stalkerazzi" amendment to California's civil code allowing celebrities three times the damages from the paparazzi including profits from their photographs.

Bedrock Law

The right to privacy allows individuals to file intrusion claims when images are taken where there is a reasonable expectation of privacy, and the images are taken without consent.

California made it even tougher in 2009 by permitting lawsuits against media outlets that buy such photos from paparazzi. This action came after film and television star Jennifer Aniston was captured sunbathing topless in her back yard by photographer Peter Brandt. Aniston filed suit for intrusion based on the contention she was not visible to the public. Brandt asserted his photos were nothing more than what the neighbors might have seen. The disagreement turned on her expectation of privacy, but the case was settled out of court. Brandt said Aniston offered to drop the suit if he never published the pictures.[56] Aniston then led the fight for a new bill allowing suits against paparazzi with civil penalties of up to $50,000 against those who use celebrity images they know are obtained improperly.

50. North Carolina is an exception, creating a liability exemption for "newsgathering and newsworthy events, or events or places to which the general public is invited." N.C. Gen. Stat. § 15A-300.1. (b)(2).
51. The Fifth Circuit Court of Appeals found Texas drone laws did not violate the First Amendment rights of journalists, re-instating that state's surveillance prohibitions and "No-Fly" provisions over sensitive sites such as critical infrastructure facilities, prisons, and large sports venues. Miriam McNabb, "Controversial Texas Drone Law Re-Instated, in a Blow for Journalists," *dronelife*, October 25, 2023, *at* https://dronelife.com/2023/10/25/controversial-texas-drone-law-re-instated-in-a-blow-for-journalists/.
52. Originally set as 50 yards from Jacqueline Kennedy Onassis and 75 yards from the children, reduced to 25 feet and 30 feet, respectively, on appeal. *Galella v. Onassis*, 487 F.2d 986 (2d Cir. 1973).
53. *Id.*
54. *See* Cal. Civil Code § 1708.8.
55. Schwarzenegger was in an accident in 1998 blamed on paparazzi pursuing his vehicle to a preschool drop off.
56. "Names and Faces," *Washington Post*, September 4, 2006, C3.

Expectations of Privacy in Quasi-Public and Private Places

The tort of intrusion and one's expectation of privacy are not strictly defined by lines dividing public and private property. A state-supported university is "public property" in that it is publicly owned, but a student using a public restroom on campus still has a reasonable expectation of privacy. Yet people sitting on the front lawn of their homes, easily visible to passersby, are on private property but have yielded their reasonable expectation of privacy.

Writing for the *Journal of Intellectual Property Law*, Jim Coleman imagined a photographic stalker could pursue a ballet instructor in leotards, capture daily images and details of her life from public vantage points, and circulate the images with little regard for her personal privacy.[57] The stalker's actions could affect her feelings of safety, security, and personal dignity. Should this type of activity be free of legal constraint just because it took place on public property?

In some quasi-public places, such as restaurants, theaters, and other businesses open to the public, the expectation of privacy is less clear. A woman dining in a restaurant in Iowa sued after her requests not to be videotaped by a television reporter were ignored.[58] A trial court determined Theresa Stessman was not in "seclusion" while in a business building open to anyone who could walk in and see her eating there. But the Iowa Supreme Court could not decide whether Stessman was secluded or not. Although she was seated in a private dining room, the fact that she was seen by others did not necessarily mean she was not secluded.

The expectation of privacy among coworkers in an office not open to the public came into question in one California case. A reporter for ABC News took a job at a company called Psychic Marketing Group as part of a news investigation. Stacy Lescht secretly recorded workplace conversations of two "tele-psychics" who operated a call-in service for those seeking their fortunes over the phone. After the *PrimeTime Live* piece aired, the tele-psychics sued for intrusion even though coworkers could overhear the fortunes from the open cubicles. The case turned on whether they had a reasonable expectation of privacy in their workplace.[59]

The California Supreme Court agreed this intrusion had occurred because employees should enjoy a limited, but legitimate expectation of privacy in their office conversations, free from undercover reporters secretly video recording them. Advocates of a free press found the ruling troubling, however, since it seemed to establish a privacy zone rationale that would allow for differing expectations of privacy depending on the workplace.

A similar case in the workplace treated the investigative reporting by ABC News as trespass and addressed the deceptive act of "**posing**" to gain access. Two network producers obtained jobs at Food Lion supermarkets by submitting false résumés and references to investigate Food Lion's meat handling procedures. They secretly videotaped coworkers and supervisors and ultimately broadcast a report on *PrimeTime Live* alleging the meat department's practices were unsafe.

Food Lion unsuccessfully sued after the report aired for libel, fraud, and unfair trade practices and won on only two issues. The Fourth Circuit upheld their trespass and breach of duty of loyalty claims.[60] The court held the news producers had permission to act as Food Lion employees but not to secretly videotape others in the store's nonpublic areas. Moreover, they owed a duty of loyalty to their employer. Laws pertaining to employee loyalty and trespass are not exempt for journalists. Even though Food Lion was awarded nominal damages of only one dollar for each claim, the court made clear the First Amendment does not protect journalists who falsify their employment applications to gain access to private facilities and they still can be found guilty of trespass.

57. Jim Barr Coleman, "Digital Photography and the Internet, Rethinking Privacy Law," 13 *J. Intell. Prop. L.* 205 (2005).
58. *Stessman v. Am. Black Hawk Broadcasting*, 416 N.W. 2d 685 (1987).
59. *Sanders v. American Broadcasting Cos.*, 20 Cal. 4th 907, 85 Cal. Rptr. 2d 909, 978 P. 2d 67 (1999).
60. *Food Lion, Inc. v. Capital Cities/ABC, Inc.*, 194 F.3d 505 (1999).

The news media are especially susceptible to lawsuits for intrusion when they clearly occur on private property while concealing their true intent. A California plumber practiced medicine in his home but prevailed in his privacy lawsuit against a national magazine. *Life* magazine ran a story about his private practice based on the notes and recordings of an investigative reporter who posed as a patient in A.A. Dietemann's home.

The photographer and reporter used a ruse to gain access to his home for a physical examination by claiming to need the plumber's medicinal powers of herbs and minerals. The unlicensed amateur doctor diagnosed a lump in the reporter's breast and attributed it to eating rancid butter. While Dietemann was later convicted of fraud, he did manage to win his civil suit. The court agreed he deserved privacy in his home and noted how the *Life* reporters used false pretenses to intrude on his premises by posing as prospective patients.[61]

Even though there is no legal prohibition against posing (other than as a law enforcement official), such deception is not protected by the First Amendment. Coupled with the surrounding ethical issues, this case and others like it have discouraged news organizations from having reporters go undercover and masquerade as anything other than journalists.

What about the expectation of privacy in one's personal belongings, such as a car, backpack, cell phone, or trash? Courts will generally find an expectation of privacy when someone starts rummaging through another's purse, locker, laptop computer, or coat pockets without permission, finding such invasions to be "highly offensive." This finding, of course, depends on the answers to several questions. Was it an open backpack or laptop computer easily visible to everyone? Was the locker supplied and controlled by the school or employer with clearly stated policies limiting privacy? All work-related emails and phone calls on company property are subject to scrutiny by the employer, although case law suggests it can be intrusive once personal matters become involved.

When it comes to trash, once the discarded contents are placed outside at the public curb, the U.S. Supreme Court says there is no expectation of privacy and police do not need a warrant to conduct a search.[62] This finding should come as relief to some tabloid journalists like *The Enquirer's* Jay Gourley, who famously took five plastic bags of trash from outside the home of former Secretary of State Henry Kissinger. He found documents about Kissinger's Secret Service detail as well as a shopping list for three cases of whiskey.[63] Kissinger objected to the action as an invasion of privacy but never took his complaint to court.

Online Video Invasions of Privacy

In the digital age, it is easy to spread embarrassing images online where they may become viral sensations. If the videos are highly offensive and occur in locations where there is a reasonable expectation of privacy, both civil and criminal lawyers can cause substantial consequences for the defendants.

The celebrated wrestler Hulk Hogan (Terry Bollae) won a breathtaking $40 million lawsuit in 2017 against Gawker, a celebrity gossip website fascinated with his sexual escapades. Hogan's complaint came from Gawker posting a brief video of him engaging in a tryst with another man's wife. The high award of damages put Gawker out of business and into Chapter 11 bankruptcy.

At about the same time, network sportscaster and TV host Erin Andrews made her case of privacy invasion against a Nashville motel owner that gave a customer a room next to hers, which in effect allowed him a "peeping tom" opportunity to video record her in the nude. The jury, sympathetic to her humiliation, ordered a payment of

61. *Dietemann v. Time*, 449 F.2d 245 (9th Cir. 1971).
62. *California v. Greenwood*, 486 U.S. 35 (1988).
63. "Paper Says Kissinger's Garbage Had Secret Service Documents," *The New York Times*, July 21, 1975.

$55 million in damages on her behalf, although she eventually settled with the hotel chain outside of court.

The prosecution of a former Playboy playmate who posted a photo of an elderly woman undressing in a Los Angeles gym's locker room produced a criminal penalty. Dani Mathers added a caption to the Snapchat photo of the 71-year-old woman that read, "If I can't unsee this then you can't either." Her punishment was a sentence of three years' probation and 30 hours of community service removing graffiti.

These cases demonstrate how video intrusions in spaces where there is a reasonable expectation of privacy – a bedroom, hotel room, and locker room – are offenses addressed by both civil and criminal statutes.

What if the government grants the media access to a private place? It used to be customary for police and fire officials to let news reporters accompany them on to private property as they executed an arrest warrant or criminal investigation without fear of trespass or intrusion lawsuits. But in 1999, the U.S. Supreme Court ruled both the media and law enforcement may be liable if the police allow reporters on "**ride-alongs**" to enter a private home – even if the officers have a search warrant.

In *Wilson v. Layne*,[64] U.S. marshals invited a *Washington Post* reporter and photographer to join them as they entered the home of Charles and Geraldine Wilson in the early morning hours to arrest their fugitive son who no longer lived there. The reporters observed Charles Wilson coming out of his bedroom wearing only briefs, angrily demanding an explanation, and then being subdued by the armed officers who thought he was the son. In the meantime, Geraldine Wilson appeared, wearing only a nightgown.

Even though the *Washington Post* never published the photos taken of the scene, the Wilsons were outraged and sued the Marshals Service, contending their Fourth Amendment rights were violated by the news media's participation in the botched execution of the arrest warrant. The high court agreed, holding law enforcement officials liable for violating the Fourth Amendment and found the news media did not enjoy any qualified immunity in this case. The press should stay outside the confines of private property unless they have consent from the occupants.

From Wiretapping to Illegal Recordings

The history of electronic and digital surveillance law that shapes our understanding of intrusion and related Fourth Amendment rights begins with two wiretapping landmarks. In *Olmstead v. United States* (1928),[65] the Supreme Court ruled 5–4 that evidence was lawfully seized using a phone wiretap to convict fired police officer Roy Olmstead for bootlegging in Seattle. It was not considered an unconstitutional act under either the Fourth or Fifth Amendments to gain evidence that way because nothing tangible was seized, and no unlawful entry was made.

But four decades later in *Katz v. United States* (1967),[66] the high court reversed the conviction of a gambling bookmaker because the evidence seized against him came from an attached microphone and recording device outside a telephone booth. Defendant Katz had a "reasonable expectation of privacy," and for the first time, electronic intrusion into private communications was just as prohibited under the Fourth Amendment as an unwarranted physical intrusion. Justice Potter Stewart famously explained, "the Fourth Amendment protects people, not places."[67]

64. 526 U.S. 603 (1999).
65. 277 U.S. 438.
66. 389 U.S. 347.
67. *Id.* at 351.

Since *Katz*, the Supreme Court has further defined and expanded Fourth Amendment privacy protections in response to new technologies and the innovative opportunities they present for government surveillance and criminal investigations. These landmark cases cover the use of thermal imaging,[68] Global Positioning System (GPS) devices,[69] and personal cell phones,[70] including cell-site location information.[71]

There can be an exception to this protection, however, when information is shared with a third party. Invoking the **third-party doctrine**, the Supreme Court in *United States v. Miller* found no expectation of privacy and therefore no Fourth Amendment protection for bank documents, including checks and deposit slips shared with a third party, the bank.[72] Likewise in *Smith v. Maryland*,[73] the Court found no expectation of privacy in the phone numbers a person dials because a third party – the phone company – has this information. In *Smith*, police without a warrant were able to get the phone company to share phone numbers dialed by a suspected robber who was calling one of his victims at home. The Court reasoned Smith had voluntarily conveyed the dialed numbers to the phone company and as a result assumed the risk they could be disclosed.

More recently in *Carpenter v. United States* (2018),[74] the Supreme Court applied the expectation of privacy and third-party doctrine to the privacy of mobile phone *cell-site location information* (CSLI) and came to a different decision. In this case, the government obtained a week's worth of Timothy Carpenter's mobile phone location records from several wireless carriers without a warrant. As part of a criminal investigation, FBI agents used the phone records to create maps showing certain phones had been in the vicinity of a string of robberies. To obtain those location records, prosecutors relied on the Stored Communications Act, which in one provision affords police access without showing probable cause since a crime had been or was about to be committed.[75]

In reexamining Fourth Amendment jurisprudence, Chief Justice John Roberts observed how evolving technology such as CSLI does not "fit neatly under the existing precedents."[76] The *Carpenter* case determined the expectation of privacy in CSLI was reasonable because a cell phone is practically a "feature of human anatomy"[77] and its location data provide such a detailed and "intimate window into a person's life," revealing not only your movements but also associations.[78]

Chief Justice Roberts further distinguished CSLI from the precedents of *Miller* and *Smith* since it "is not truly 'shared'" information.[79] Instead, a cell-site record is generated without any affirmative act on the part of the user beyond powering up. The user does *not voluntarily*

68. *Kyllo v. United States*, 533 U.S. 27, 34 (2001). The Court held that the use of a thermal imager to detect heat radiating from the defendant's home constituted a search.
69. *United States v. Jones*, 565 U.S. 400 (2012). The Court held a warrant was required for the placement of a GPS device on a vehicle to monitor its movements. This was distinguished as being more sophisticated surveillance as compared to a simple beeper placed on a car to merely augment police tracking of movements in public. *United States v. Knotts*, 460 U.S. 276 (1983).
70. *Riley v. California*, 573 U.S. 373, 134 S. Ct. 2473 (2014). In recognizing the immense storage capability of modern cell phones, the Court held that police officers must generally obtain a warrant before searching the contents of a phone.
71. *Carpenter v. United States*, 585 U.S. 296; 138 S. Ct. 2206 (2018).
72. 425 U.S. 435 (1976).
73. 442 U.S. 735 (1979). A telephone pen register was used to capture the numbers dialed.
74. 585 U.S. 296; 138 S. Ct. 2206.
75. 18 U.S.C. §2703(d). The Stored Communications Act allows the government to compel the disclosure of telecommunications records when "specific and articulable facts show that there are reasonable grounds to believe" that such records "are relevant and material to an ongoing criminal investigation."
76. *Id.* at 7.
77. *Id.* at 9.
78. *Id.* at 12.
79. *Id.* at 17.

assume the risk of sharing the data because short of "disconnecting the phone from the network, there is no way to avoid leaving a trail of location data."[80]

The Court also would not extend the third-party doctrine to CSLI because of the enhanced collection capabilities of cell phone carriers. Even though the decision did not overrule *Miller* and *Smith*, Roberts made it clear "[t]here is a world of difference between the limited types of personal information addressed in *Smith* and *Miller* and the exhaustive chronicle of location information casually collected by wireless carriers today."[81] He pointed to the "seismic shifts in digital technology" that now make tracking such sensitive information so easy to do.[82]

When it comes to nongovernmental actors such as the media, accessing private user data is not a constitutional matter but one of federal statutory law. The Electronic Communications Privacy Act of 1986 (ECPA)[83] is the key federal law making it illegal for anyone to intentionally intercept "any wire, oral, or electronic communication."[84] Hence, wiretapping and related communication interceptions are a crime, and that includes procuring another person to do so or even making an attempt. Exceptions apply to communication service providers doing their "ordinary course of business," where user consent has been given.

What if the intrusion was committed by a third party who voluntarily, and without provocation, provides personally identifiable information to the police or the media? There would be no liability if a telecommunications company willingly shared with law enforcement their communication records of their customers, other than a breach of contract if it were part of their service agreement with the customer. But most telecommunication companies do not wish to violate their customers' privacy in that way, even when faced with a subpoena. Similarly, there would be no liability if a person inadvertently intercepts a neighbor's cordless telephone conversation and then shares what was heard with law enforcement if the neighbor was talking about criminal acts like drug dealing.[85] Most phone communications today are encrypted to minimize this possibility, however.[86]

Yet if a third party intercepts a communication *illegally* and then shares the communication, is the recipient of the recording liable for broadcasting, publishing, posting, or otherwise disseminating it? This was the case in *Bartnicki v. Vopper*[87] when a Pennsylvania radio station aired an intercepted cell phone recording delivered anonymously to a local taxpayer's group whose leader gave it to the station. The exchange broadcast a conversation between a local teachers union president and chief negotiator Gloria Bartnicki that took a dark turn. Union President Anthony Kane, Jr. was heard to say "If they're not going to move for three percent, we're gonna have to go to their, their homes. . . . To blow off their front porches, we'll have to do some work on some of those guys."[88]

Radio talk show host Fred W. Vopper (a.k.a. Fred Williams) had been critical of the union in the past, and aired the intercepted conversation during his public affairs talk show. Bartnicki and Kane claimed their right to privacy had been violated and ultimately sued WILK and WGBI, along with Vopper and others involved not knowing who actually intercepted

80. *Id.*
81. *Id.* at 15.
82. *Id.*
83. Pub. L. No. 99–508, 100 Stat. 1848 (1986) (codified at 18 U.S.C. §§ 2510–2521, 2701–2710, 3117, 3121–3126 (1988)).
84. *Id.* § 2511(1)(a).
85. *Tyler v. Berodt*, 877 F. 2d 705 (1989).
86. Although cordless phone transmissions may be unprotected because they are unencrypted and easily accessed, intercepting data from unencrypted Wi-Fi networks (Wi-Fi sniffing) can violate wiretap law. A Wi-Fi case concerned Google Street View vehicles that between 2008 and 2010 were recording unencrypted Wi-Fi communications. The Ninth Circuit ruled that while there is a broad exemption for intercepting radio communications that are generally accessible to the public, Wi-Fi is not a radio communication. *Joffe v. Google*, 729 F.3d 1262 (2013).
87. 532 U.S. 514 (2001).
88. *Id.* at 518–519.

and recorded the call. The key question was whether the wiretapping prohibition of the ECPA[89] gave Bartnicki and Kane the right to recover for this on-air exposure, or whether the First Amendment protected Vopper, his station, and the taxpayer's group.

Barnicki v. Vopper made it to the Supreme Court, which held the disclosures were indeed protected by the First Amendment. The Court recognized the broadcasters did not participate in intercepting the conversation, and "privacy concerns give way when balanced against the interest in publishing matters of public importance."[90] The 6–3 decision granted media the freedom to disseminate information illegally obtained by a third party so long as it is truthful and of public importance.

Bedrock Law

It is not an intrusion to make recordings of a person's voice, image, or other communications where there is no reasonable expectation of privacy.

Finally, secret recordings of a phone conversation when neither party is aware of the recording generally constitutes wiretapping, but federal law does permit it and in-person conversations when there is consent of at least one of the parties.[91] Thus, it is legal for people to secretly record their own conversations, whether they occur over the phone or face-to-face. But some state laws require the consent of *both* parties, and in these "two-party consent" states, such as California, Maryland, Pennsylvania, and Washington, it is an invasion of privacy to record a conversation unless both (or all) parties agree to it.[92] Journalists should check their state laws before recording calls and conversations. Broadcast stations are also required to get consent of callers and telephone interviewees before putting them on the air.[93] Notification is not necessary during a program that ordinarily broadcasts calls, though, when it can be presumed that the caller knows the conversation may be aired.

Global View: Data Privacy and Security

The European Union has the toughest privacy and security law in the world. Long committed to upholding individual privacy rights and protecting personal data, the EU's General Data Protection Regulation or *GDPR* went into effect in 2018. The GDPR governs how personal data of individuals in the EU can be collected, processed, and transferred, setting rules for data retention, storage limitation, and record keeping.

This comprehensive privacy law grants individuals such rights as to affirmatively consent and object to any data processing; access to rectify their personal data collected; gain clear information as to who is processing their data and why; be promptly notified if there's a data breach, and hold the "right to be forgotten," essentially erasing their personal data and preventing its further dissemination.[94]

Unlike the U.S., the EU views privacy as a basic human right, and individual rights come before business interests. This privacy law restricts all businesses and organizations within the 27-member EU[95] as well as entities outside the EU that monitor or offer goods or services to individuals in the EU.

89. *See* 18 U.S.C. § 2510.
90. 532 U.S. at 534.
91. *See*, 18 U.S.C. §2511(2)(d).
92. More than a dozen states require some form of two-party consent or have special provisions that require all-party consent in certain situations. These include California, Connecticut, Florida, Hawaii (when in private places only), Illinois, Maryland, Massachusetts, Michigan, Montana, Nevada (for telephone only), New Hampshire, Oregon (for in-person only), Pennsylvania, and Washington. *See* Reporters Committee for Freedom of the Press, *Reporters' Recording Guide*, *at* www.rcfp.org/reporters-recording-guide/.
93. Broadcast of telephone conversations, 47 C.F.R. §73.1206.
94. Rachel F. Fefer & Kristin Archick, "EU Data Protection Rules and U.S. Implications," *Cong. Research Service (CRS)*, July 17, 2020, *at* https://fas.org/sgp/crs/row/IF10896.pdf.
95. Although no longer an EU member, the United Kingdom (U.K.) incorporated the EU's GDPR provisions into U.K. data protection law which became effective in 2021. The UK GDPR essentially mirrors the EU GDPR with some differences. *See*, Erez Greenberg, "10 Differences Between UK GDPR and EU GDPR," *Papaya Global*, June 15, 2023, *at* https://www.papayaglobal.com/blog/10-differences-between-uk-gdpr-and-eu-gdpr/.

A company or organization that doesn't comply can be fined 20 million euros or more. Data Protection Authorities (DPAs) have imposed hundreds of GDPR fines against companies such as Amazon, TikTok, Google, and Meta (Facebook). Meta Platforms Ireland Limited was fined a record 1.2 billion euros in 2023 for unlawfully transferring personal data to the United States.[96] The Irish DPA also fined Meta Platforms Ireland Limited 390 million euros for violations regarding the processing of personal data for the purpose of personalized advertising.

The EU's stricter privacy protection poses challenges for U.S. companies that need to comply if they wish to engage in the European market.[97] Operating under separate privacy and data protection systems is difficult when communications and transactions span the globe and consumers travel between the U.S. and Europe. For example, U.S. rules would apply if a Georgia woman purchased an iPhone from a local retailer, but the GDPR would apply if she went on vacation to Spain and used a credit card to purchase a SIM card there to make calls.[98]

Adhering to the different data sharing and processing rules becomes complicated and potentially costly. Some U.S. businesses, including newspaper websites and digital advertising firms, simply opted out of the EU market rather than confront the complexities of the GDPR.[99]

The GDPR is nonetheless setting new global data privacy standards as firms and organizations worldwide strive for compliance. U.S. firms have made changes such as revising and clarifying user terms of agreement and asking for explicit consent.[100] Some states such as California have passed stricter consumer privacy laws with similarities to the GDPR. The EU's privacy law even prompted some consumer groups and policymakers in the U.S. to call for comprehensive legislation resembling the GDPR.

2 Public Disclosure of Private Facts

Public Disclosure of Private Facts
Protects people against the unwarranted dissemination of intimate personal information offensive to the public sense of decency.

The claim against a public disclosure of private facts comes to mind for many when they think of their "right" to privacy. And that does go to the heart of what Warren and Brandeis were concerned about when they wrote their famous article in 1890[101] – an overzealous press investigating and exposing details of the private affairs of citizens who wish "to be let alone."[102] This infringement occurs when something deeply personal and embarrassing is made publicly known. For example, someone suffering financial problems or an embarrassing medical condition, engaged in an extramarital affair, or seen partially naked in a locker room photo would be mortified to discover it circulating over social media or featured in a news story. What makes this different from libel is the information is *true* – a "fact." The truthfulness of the matter is not what is in dispute; rather, it's sharing something highly offensive and there's a good reason to keep it private.

This tort comes with the stipulation that the disclosed matter cannot be of legitimate concern to the public. In other words, the newsworthiness of the disclosure is an important

96. GDPR Enforcement Tracker, *at* https://www.enforcementtracker.com/.
97. For years, the EU-U.S. "Privacy Shield" program provided a voluntary compliance mechanism to enable U.S. companies to meet EU data protection requirements for transferring personal data. A July 2020 decision by the European Court of Justice invalidated the framework as inadequate. *See* www.privacyshield.gov/Program-Overview.
98. "Differences between European Privacy Laws and American Privacy Laws," *Compliance Junction*, February 23, 2018, *at* www.compliancejunction.com/differences-european-privacy-laws-american-privacy-laws/.
99. Fefer & Archick, supra note 94.
100. *Id.*
101. Warren & Brandeis, supra note 13.
102. *Id.* at 193.

consideration, which is often critical to the media's defense. This element serves to mitigate the vexing legal questions presented by this tort. On the one hand, the law seeks to protect an individual's right to control personal information about themselves. On the other hand, this is the one claim to privacy the U.S. Supreme Court has noted most directly confronts the First Amendment right of journalists to report the news truthfully and accurately.[103] Unlike other torts such as libel, damages can be awarded to a plaintiff, and the media can be punished for reporting truthful information.

The elements for a claim of publication of private facts that a plaintiff generally must prove are

- **publicity** given to a matter that
- concerns one's **private** life, that is
- **highly offensive** to a reasonable person, and is
- **not a legitimate public concern**.

Most states recognize an invasion of privacy action for public disclosure of private facts through their common law, and a few recognize it through statutory law.[104] Many states also have laws specifically restricting the public disclosure of information about minors, rape victims, HIV and AIDS status, abortion, Social Security numbers, and mental illness. A few states such as Nebraska, North Carolina, Virginia, and New York expressly reject an invasion of privacy action for public disclosure of private facts.[105] Note it does not apply to corporations, or to the deceased, although family members may sue if the offensive facts disclosed relate to them.

Because the first element requires publicity, the tort is sometimes referred to as "publicity to private facts." Unlike libel, where the element of publication requires only that a defamatory statement reach someone other than the plaintiff (see Chapter 5), here the publicity of a private fact requires wider dissemination. It is where "the matter is made public, by communicating it to the public at large, or to so many persons that the matter must be regarded as substantially certain to become one of public knowledge."[106] Exactly how large of an audience is not well defined by the case law, but the communication does not need to be through the mass media. It is probably fair to say social media, news releases, and even in-house company communications would satisfy the requirement for publicity.

Private Facts

"Private facts" refer to intimate details about a person's personal life that are not generally known to the public. These facts might include such information as one's sexual orientation, income, cosmetic surgery, diary entries, nudity, abortion, mental illness, religious practices, web browsing history, or personal correspondences. But the information cannot be something that is already publicly known; it must truly be private.

103. *Cox v. Cohn*, 420 U.S. 469 (1975). Some legal volumes refer to the tort as the publication of embarrassing private facts.
104. Most state definitions of the public disclosure privacy tort generally parallel the *Restatement (Second) of Torts*, § 652D, which states: One who gives publicity to a matter concerning the private life of another is subject to liability to the other for invasion of his privacy, if the matter publicized is of a kind that (a) would be highly offensive to a reasonable person, and (b) is not of legitimate concern to the public. § 652D.
105. Jonathan B. Mintz, "The Remains of Privacy's Disclosure Tort: An Exploration of the Private Domain," 55 *Md. L. Rev*. 425, 432 n. 37 (1996). Minnesota was included in this list but later adopted the tort in 1998. The Indiana Supreme Court expressed uncertainty as to whether a cause of action for publication of private facts existed in Indiana, although several appellate courts have subsequently held that it does. *See, e.g., Allstate Ins. Co. v. Dana Corp*., 759 N.E.2d 1049, 1057 (Ind. 2001) (citing *Doe v. Methodist Hosp*., 690 N.E.2d 681 (Ind. 1997).
106. *Restatement (Second) of Torts* § 652D cmt. a.

When Oliver Sipple heroically protected President Gerald Ford from a female assassin, he didn't expect to have his own private life put on display. Sipple, a former marine, was in the crowd watching President Ford approach the St. Francis Hotel in San Francisco in 1975 when he saw a woman point a pistol at Ford. Sipple grabbed her arm and deflected the bullet, saving Ford's life. But when Sipple was not publicly thanked by the White House for his heroism, a columnist for the *San Francisco Chronicle* investigated. Acting on a tip from Harvey Milk, a local and openly gay politician, the columnist speculated the sleight was because of Sipple's sexual orientation. Sipple, whose family in Detroit did not know he was gay, sued the *Chronicle* for publicizing this information about him.[107] But what Sipple claimed was a private fact was actually well-known in the San Francisco community where he frequented gay bars, marched in gay parades, and was the subject of a number of gay publications. The court ruled that his homosexuality was therefore not a private fact.

What happens when private facts are republished by others? A former congressional aide, Robert Steinbuch, sued another former congressional aide, Jessica Cutler, for discussing their otherwise private sexual relations on her blog, *Washingtonienne*. At the time, Cutler's blog had only a small number of readers, but she revealed embarrassing details (such as he "likes spanking"), and it caught the attention of *Wonkette*. Anna Marie Cox is *Wonkette*'s blogger who called widespread attention to Cutler's exposure, including excerpts and a hyperlink that spread widely in the blogosphere. While Steinbuch's case against Cutler could proceed, his case against Cox was dismissed.[108] Cox had only publicized a matter that was already now public, so Steinbuch had no publication of a private facts claim against her.

By the same token, if individuals publicly expose information about themselves, they have no private facts claim because the information is no longer private. For that reason, there is generally no liability for photographers and videographers to capture images and conversations of a person if that person is in a public or semi-public place in plain view and earshot of others. If the person can be readily observed in a public place, then facts about their communication, behavior, dress, and other observable characteristics are no longer considered private. For example, no liability for invasion of privacy by publication of private facts was found in a classic case in which a newspaper published a photo of a married couple in an affectionate embrace at a farmer's market in San Francisco.[109]

A football fan at a Cleveland Browns versus Pittsburgh Steelers game also learned this lesson when he acted up for a *Sports Illustrated* photographer. John Neff, along with a few others, was standing on a dugout prior to the game when they saw the photographer waiting to shoot photos of the Steelers players coming onto the field. When they learned he was with *Sports Illustrated*, they proceeded to jump up and down to get his attention, and the photographer took a series of photos. One photo ran in the magazine depicting Neff with his fly unzipped and appearing somewhat drunk, with the title of the article "A Strange Kind of Love." Neff sued for publication of private facts, but a federal district court dismissed his claim, saying the photo was taken in a public place and with Neff's knowledge and encouragement.[110]

Certainly, if a plaintiff gives consent, that can also be a defense against a private facts claim. If an adult capable of granting meaningful consent willingly shares information with a reporter, for example, then a claim cannot generally be made for a violation of privacy if that information is subsequently publicized. Voluntarily engaging in an interview or photo shoot will typically constitute implied consent, although it is good practice for journalists to get that consent with a written release form or in a recorded verbal statement. Violations, including agreements to keep the information "off the record," can then become a breach of contract.

107. *Sipple v. Chronicle Publishing Co.*, 154 Cal. App. 3d 1040 (1984).
108. *Steinbuch v. Cutler*, No. 1:05CV00970 (D.D.C. May 21, 2007). Note how this decision compares to republication of a defamatory statement, where all who republish a defamation may be sued for libel. *See* Chapter 5.
109. *Gill v. Hearst Pub. Co.*, 253 P. 2d 441 (Cal. 1953).
110. *Neff v. Time, Inc.*, 406 F. Supp. 858 (W.D. Pa. 1976).

Bedrock Law

The publication of a "private fact," if that fact has been made public already or is part of the public record, cannot be taken to be private.

If consent is given but later withdrawn and the material is publicized anyway, the media may be liable unless other defenses such as newsworthiness succeed. This was the case for surf enthusiast Mike Virgil, who agreed to an interview with *Sports Illustrated*. Virgil spoke about his crazy antics, such as eating insects, putting a cigarette out in his mouth, diving off stairs to impress women, and hurting himself to collect unemployment so he could go bodysurfing. But before the article went to press, Virgil had a change of heart and revoked his consent. The article was published anyway, and Virgil sued. The Ninth Circuit held Virgil's voluntary disclosure of private facts to the magazine writer was actionable since he withdrew his consent prior to publication.[111] *Sports Illustrated* later won the case, however, when a court determined the facts were not sufficiently offensive and the article was in fact newsworthy.[112]

Facts in Public Records

Facts contained within open public records are generally not considered private. In fact, most states recognize an absolute privilege for publishing information that is contained in public court records that are not otherwise sealed. This comes as a result of *Cox Broadcasting Corp. v. Cohn*, a 1975 case in which the Supreme Court ruled the First Amendment prohibits states from penalizing the media for publicizing accurate information obtained from public court records. In *Cox*, the Court had to determine if an Atlanta television station had run afoul of the law in its coverage of a 17-year-old girl's rape and murder when it identified her by name.[113] The victim's father sued the owners of WTSB-TV for invading his zone of privacy, and the Court had to draw the constitutional lines for such privacy lawsuits.

News media joined with Cox Communications and filed *amicus curiae* briefs asking the Court to ensure the principle that reporting truthfully facts obtained from open judicial records was protected since the television reporter encountered the woman's name in a court indictment open to public inspection. The high court was aware of a Georgia law preventing the naming of rape victims. But in writing for the Court, Justice White stated that the Court was "reluctant to embark on a course that would make public records generally available to the media but forbid their publication if offensive to the sensibilities of the supposed reasonable man."[114] The Court held such a rule would make it very difficult for the media to inform citizens about the public business and yet stay within the law. The rule would "invite timidity and self-censorship," possibly blocking future information from the public. "At the very least, the First and Fourteenth Amendments will not allow exposing the press to liability for truthfully publishing information released to the public in official court records."[115]

Many states have extended this privilege to all types of public records, although the Supreme Court has stopped short of saying that the media are always exempt from privacy lawsuits when disclosing sensitive information obtained from public records. Fourteen years after *Cox*, the Court again found the media defendant not liable. But this time, in *Florida Star v. B.J.F*,[116] the Court made clear its decision was limited. In *Florida Star*, a woman was raped and a newspaper reporter in training discovered her name in a county sheriff's report rather than an official court record. A Florida law prohibited the disclosure of a rape victim's name, but the newspaper mistakenly published the police report of the attack that included the victim's name. When B.J.F. began receiving threatening phone calls, she sued. The Court relied on its rationale in *Cox*, holding that the First Amendment was violated by imposing damages on the *Star* for publishing the name. Moreover, the information had been lawfully

111. *Virgil v. Time, Inc.*, 527 F.2d 1122 (9th Cir. 1975), cert. denied, 425 U.S. 998 (1976).
112. *Virgil v. Sports Illustrated*, 424 F. Supp. 1286 (S.D. Cal. 1976). (This was "round four" of the case, following the Supreme Court's denial of certiorari, where the district court was to reconsider Time Inc.'s motion for summary judgment applying the standard for newsworthiness.)
113. 420 U.S. 469 (1975).
114. *Id.* at 496.
115. *Id.*
116. 491 U.S. 524 (1989).

obtained from the government that had failed to safeguard it. The Court found that imposing liability on the *Star* did not satisfactorily serve to further a state interest. But the Court rejected a rule that truthful publications may never be punished.

> We do not hold that truthful publication is automatically constitutionally protected, or that there is no zone of personal privacy within which the State may protect the individual from intrusion by the press, or even that a State may never punish publication of the name of a victim of a sexual offense. We hold only that where a newspaper publishes truthful information which it has lawfully obtained, punishment may lawfully be imposed, if at all, only when narrowly tailored to a state interest of the highest order.[117]

What if the private facts obtained from public records occurred long ago? For years, some states such as California allowed an individual to sue for invasion of privacy by publication of private facts if their true but distant and embarrassing past was dredged up and publicized. In some cases, people had turned their lives around and paid their debt to society, only to have new friends, employers, and neighbors learn about their unflattering past. In 2004, California joined other states in recognizing the right to publicly disclose accurate information lawfully obtained from public records no matter how many years had passed.

In *Gates v. Discovery Communications*,[118] Steve Gates sued the Discovery Channel for invasion of privacy when it aired a documentary about a murder for hire in San Diego that took place 12 years earlier in which Gates had been convicted as an accessory after the fact. After Gates served his three-year sentence, he lived an obscure, lawful life, and became a respected member of the community. The state supreme court was nonetheless unwilling to impose sanctions "by the mere passage of time"[119] on the publication of truthful information obtained in public court records. Reiterating the need to further a state interest of the highest order, the court concluded that "any state interest in protecting for rehabilitative purposes the long-term anonymity of former convicts" falls short.[120]

Medical Records and HIPAA Restrictions

At some point while visiting your personal physician, you undoubtedly signed a document about keeping your medical information confidential. The Health Insurance Portability and Accountability Act (HIPAA)[121] creates a zone of privacy for "protected health information" (PHI). This confidential information includes health status and payment for health care and has been liberally interpreted to mean almost any part of a person's medical record. HIPAA requires certain healthcare providers to take steps to ensure the confidentiality of communications with patients.

What was not foreseen was the chilling effect this 2003 rule would have on breaking news coverage in cases in which emergency healthcare information was involved. Journalists found their ability to accurately report on fires, accidents, and disasters frustrated by HIPAA. For example, a Chicago porch collapse that harmed and killed local citizens received only sketchy coverage because the news media had no way of conveying the victims' names or those who had been injured in the collapse.[122]

The president of the Radio Television News Directors Association (RTNDA), Barbara Cochran, testified before the National Committee on Vital and Health Statistics that the

117. *Id.* at 541.
118. 34 Cal.4th 679; 21 Cal. Rptr.3d 663; 101 P. 3d 552 (2004).
119. *Id.* at 673.
120. *Id.* at 672–673.
121. HIPAA, Pub. L. No. 104–191 (1996) (amended 2003).
122. *See* Andrew M. Mar & Alison Page Howard, "HIPAA and Newsgathering," *The Freedom Forum Institute*, *at* https://www.freedomforuminstitute.org/first-amendment-center/topics/freedom-of-the-press/hipaa-newsgathering/.

privacy rule under HIPAA had impeded newsgathering efforts, "[p]articularly in times of emergency, disaster, and other events of high public interest."[123] The unintended consequence of this law, Cochran noted, was to have the government drop a "blanket of secrecy" over events of public interest, where victims of crime or disasters were being treated in the hospital while friends and family worried over their status or even their whereabouts. She noted misinterpretations of the privacy rule kept reporters from uncovering corruption and mismanagement at hospitals and other publicly funded healthcare facilities. The rule even has influenced sports coverage; some universities refuse to release injury information because of HIPAA's privacy provision.

Is Doxxing a Privacy Violation?

Doxxing is publicly revealing or publishing personal information about another person without their permission. While not a new phenomenon, this practice burst on the scene with the rise of social media making it incredibly easy for anyone – including Internet trolls – to research and share details about a person's home address, phone number, photo, place of work, family members, and so forth. Sharing such "dox" (short for documents) is generally done with the intent to shame, harass, intimidate, and even threaten.[124]

Roughly half of all doxxing incidents involve some philosophical or petty dispute over online posts that spark doxxers to seek revenge against those with whom they disagree.[125] Online gaming conflicts also give rise to many angry exchanges that boil over into acts of doxxing. Celebrities, journalists, activists, politicians, and government officials are also typical targets of doxxers. For example, a long-standing feud between two rappers allegedly led Nicki Minaj's fans to share the location of the gravesite of Megan Thee Stallion's mother.[126] Game developer Zoe Quinn became a high-profile target of doxxing and rape threats in what was known as "Gamergate" when her ex-boyfriend posted personal information after claiming she had cheated on him.[127]

Doxxing can have more serious consequences when it involves the personal identifying details of jurists and witnesses for a criminal trial. Yet even ordinary citizens can find themselves unwitting targets of doxxing, such as engineering professor Kyle Quinn who was mistakenly identified as having attended a White nationalist rally and had to flee his home after social media users posted his photo, home address, and employer's name.

In general, sharing publicly available information about a person – such as their address, phone number, and email address – is not a violation of privacy or a crime. There is no expectation of privacy in personally identifiable information contained in public records. Such details do not constitute "private facts" for purposes of a lawsuit.

123. *See* Proceedings of Department of Health and Human Services, "National Committee on Vital and Health Statistics," *Subcommittee on Privacy and Confidentiality*, July 14, 2004, *at* https://ncvhs.hhs.gov/transcripts-minutes/testimony-by-barbara-cochran-for-the-july-14-2004-ncvhs-subcommittee-on-privacy-and-confidentiality-hearing/. RTNDA is today RTDNA, the Radio Television Digital News Association.
124. Jonas Strandell, "What is Doxxing and How Do You Prevent it?" *Besedo*, May 27, 2024, *at* https://besedo.com/blog/what-is-doxxing/.
125. *Id.*
126. "Mom's Cemetery Amps Up Security," *TMZ*, January 30, 2024, *at* https://www.tmz.com/2024/01/30/megan-thee-stallion-mom-cemetery-doxxing-police-security-nicki-minaj-barbz/
127. Sen Nguyen, "What is Doxxing and What Can You Do If You are Doxxed?" *CNN*, February 7, 2023, *at* https://www.cnn.com/2023/02/07/world/what-is-doxxing-explainer-as-equals-intl-cmd/index.html.

Where doxxing could be considered a violation, however, is when the information disclosed is protected, such as personal healthcare and financial information and Social Security numbers. The act of doxxing can also be considered illegal when it involves other crimes, such as harassment, stalking, revenge porn, or cyberbullying.

There is otherwise no federal law against doxxing – at least for most citizens. There is only a law protecting certain people in the federal system, namely federal elected officials, employees, and members of the military, as well as those involved in the federal court system, such as jurors, witnesses, and people assisting federal criminal investigations. Federal law prohibits anyone from knowingly making "restricted personal information" publicly available about these "covered" persons or members of their immediate family.[128] The information that cannot be shared is their personal email, phone and fax numbers, home address, and Social Security number.

Efforts to make doxxing a federal crime if committed against anyone in the United States have not yet succeeded. Legislation introduced in 2016 stalled in committee.[129] In 2021, a bill was introduced to protect federal judges, prosecutors, and law enforcement officers from violence and doxxing by authorizing them to list a post office box instead of a home address.[130] In 2023, a Doxing Threat Assessment Act[131] was introduced to require the Department of Homeland Security to come up with a threat assessment regarding cyber harassment, including doxxing, by terrorists and foreign malicious actors.

In the meantime, doxxing may be addressed by states' laws. Some states such as Colorado are passing their own doxxing laws to make it a crime to dox certain classes of individuals in their respective state, such as healthcare and child protection workers, law enforcement officers, and public employees.[132] Other states, such as Illinois, allow for civil action where victims can sue doxxers for monetary damages if there is intent to harass or cause harm, including emotional distress or economic injury.[133]

Highly Offensive

To succeed on a claim of invasion of privacy by publication of private facts, the plaintiff must prove the publicized matter was highly offensive to a reasonable person. As with a claim of intrusion, this standard asks whether a hypothetical person who is reasonable and in the same position as the plaintiff would find the publication of the private facts to be highly offensive. This ensures that the standard is not based on the plaintiff's personal degree of sensitivity or embarrassment or set by those who are hypersensitive and easily offended. Here the *Restatement (Second) of Torts* says that no offense should be taken for disclosures about the "comings and goings" of ordinary daily activities and even for such "annoyances" as, for example, "a public disclosure of the fact that the plaintiff has clumsily fallen downstairs and broken his ankle."[134] Only when the publicity "is such that a reasonable person would feel

128. Protection of Individuals Performing Certain Official Duties, 18 U.S.C. § 119 (2021).
129. Interstate Doxxing Prevention Act, H.R. 6478, 114th Cong. (2016), at https://www.congress.gov/bill/114th-congress/house-bill/6478.
130. To Protect Federal Judges, "Federal Prosecutors, and Federal Law Enforcement Officers from Violence and Doxing, S.2247," 117th Cong. (2021), *at* https://www.congress.gov/bill/117th-congress/senate-bill/2247.
131. Doxing Threat Assessment Act, H.R. 3547, 118th Cong. (2023), *at* https://www.congress.gov/bill/118th-congress/house-bill/3547/text. Doxing can be spelled with either a single-x or double-x.
132. Kelly Jones, "Doxxing is a Federal Crime in Certain Cases," *VERIFY*, February 7, 2024, *at* https://www.verifythis.com/article/news/verify/national-verify/when-doxxing-is-federal-crime/536-6ed14017-b1fc-4227-b5fa-4a3cdfa635f0.
133. Civil Liability for Doxing Act, Ill HB2954, Public Act 103–0439, August 4, 2023.
134. *Restatement (Second) of Torts* § 652D(a) cmt. c.

justified in feeling seriously aggrieved by it" does this cause of action arise. Some states such as Oregon even require a high standard of outrageousness.

A classic example of highly offensive publicity occurred in 1964 when a woman was caught in an indiscreet pose while attending a carnival. Until this time, a claim of private facts was thought to only apply to private places, but that changed after the deeply embarrassing yet public moment was given publicity. In Alabama, a newspaper photographer had snapped Flora Bell Graham's photo just as she and her two boys exited a funhouse ride and jet blasts of air blew up her skirt. Graham was very upset to see her body exposed from the waist down in panties on the pages of *The Daily Times Democrat*. She sued and won for invasion of privacy.[135] In its ruling, the Alabama Supreme Court found the photo not only embarrassing but "offensive to modesty or decency."[136] The court created a rule taking into account how it's possible to be in a public place and still have your status involuntarily altered in such a way that it is "embarrassing to an ordinary person of reasonable sensitivity."[137] Needless to say, Graham's carnival predicament also had no legitimate news value.

Newsworthiness

Plaintiffs suing for invasion of privacy by publication of private facts must also show that the information is not a matter of public concern or newsworthy. This typically becomes the media defendant's best defense and is the reason why most cases brought on this privacy tort are ruled in favor of the media, at least on appeal. The First Amendment rights of the media will generally outweigh an invasion of privacy claim when the publicized private facts are deemed a legitimate public concern.

Defining what exactly is a legitimate public interest and proving newsworthiness can be challenging and even worrisome when judges and juries are determining news value. If a descriptive definition is applied that considers how many people are interested in consuming the information, then the act of publication by the media is the evidence the information is newsworthy. If a normative definition is used to consider whether the information merits public attention, then the courts become the editors or self-appointed guardians of public taste.[138] Neither approach is palatable by itself and thus requires a balancing of competing interests. Courts will consider such factors as the relevance of the facts disclosed to the issue or topic, and the social value of the published information.[139]

The *Restatement (Second) of Torts* finds a legitimate public interest does not include "a morbid and sensational prying into private lives for its own sake."[140] How intensely personal or intimate the revelation and the extent to which the plaintiff played an important role in the matter are also factors to weigh in determining legitimate public concern.[141] Still, a publication is newsworthy if some reasonable members of the community could entertain a legitimate interest in it. And newsworthiness is not limited to "news" in the narrow sense of reports of current events but extends to information for purposes such as education and amusement.[142]

A very early and often cited privacy example addressing a legitimate public concern came from a magazine series, "Where Are They Now?" including a biographical sketch about the disappointing accomplishments of a man who had been heralded as a child prodigy. William James Sidis was a mathematically talented teenager who graduated from Harvard University in 1916 before his peers even finished high school. His early prowess and lectures on mathematics became the subject of a whirlwind of publicity when he was only a teenager, but years

135. *Daily Times Democrat v. Graham*, 276 Ala. 380, 162 So. 2d 474 (1964).
136. *Id.* at 383.
137. *Id.* at 384.
138. *See*, *Shulman v. Group W Publications, Inc.*, supra note 1 at 855.
139. *Id.* at 857.
140. *Id.* at 859.
141. *Id.* at 858.
142. *Id.* at 859–860.

later his adult life failed to realize the anticipated fame and fortune. He lived in a "shabby" "hall bedroom," working merely as a clerk.[143]

When the *New Yorker* magazine decided to spotlight that sad fact under the subtitle "April Fool," Sidis sued for damages, saying the unwanted publicity robbed him of his right of privacy. The U.S. Court of Appeals did not consider the article offensive enough to award him damages and speculated Sidis's desire to live a private life was trumped by his previous media exposure. The court ruled that even though Sidis had cloaked himself in obscurity, the question of whether he had fulfilled his early promise was still a matter of public concern. There is public interest in the "misfortunes and frailties of neighbors," and "we think his uncommon achievements and personality would have made the attention permissible."[144] Besides, the magazine had not crossed any lines of truthfulness in reporting his story.

Another early privacy example considered newsworthiness, but this time found in favor of the plaintiff. The case began in 1939 when the story of the "Starving Glutton" appeared in *Time* magazine.[145] A wire service photographer captured without permission a hospital room photo of Mrs. Dorothy Barber, a Kansas City patient inflicted with a rare disease that caused her to eat constantly and still lose weight. This story made the woman appear to be an oddity, as the "insatiable-eater Barber" who "eats for ten."

Barber sued and won $3,000 in damages because her personality and image had become the focus of the news coverage and not the disease. "While plaintiff's ailment may have been a matter of some public interest because unusual, certainly the identity of the person who suffered this ailment was not," and her "picture conveyed no medical information."[146] Lawyers also entered into evidence Barber's vulnerable state in her hospital room, where she was subjected to a barrage of reporters and photographers and had protested having her photo taken.

The case of Hilda Bridges shows how a matter may be considered highly offensive yet still protected due to its newsworthiness. Her estranged husband took Bridges to their former apartment and made her disrobe to discourage any attempt to escape. Police were alerted and upon hearing a gunshot, stormed the apartment and rushed Bridges outside in public view to a police car while she clutched a dish towel to conceal her nudity.

A published photograph of Bridges captured her severe emotional distress and revealed little more than if she were wearing a bikini. She sued for invasion of privacy and won but lost on appeal.[147] The court acknowledged the photograph could be considered by some to be in bad taste, but "[j]ust because the story and the photograph may be embarrassing or distressful to the plaintiff does not mean the newspaper cannot publish what is otherwise newsworthy."[148]

> The right of privacy does not necessarily protect a person against the publication of his name or photograph in connection with the dissemination of legitimate news items or other matters of public interest. . . . At some point the public interest in obtaining information becomes dominant over the individual's right of privacy.[149]

A highly offensive video clip was also found protected when an Orlando, FL, television station ran video on its evening news of a police officer holding the skull of six-year-old Regina Mae Armstrong, who had been kidnapped and murdered. Station staff debated whether it should air, ultimately opting to run it during a story without screening it or warning viewers, even the family. The Armstrong family was devastated, and viewers were

143. *Sidis v. F-R Publishing Corp.*, 113 F. 2d 806, 807 (2d Cir. 1940).
144. *Id.* at 809.
145. *Barber v. Time, Inc.*, 348 Mo. 1199; 159 S.W. 2d 291 (1942).
146. *Id.* at 1207–1208.
147. *Cape Publications, Inc. v. Bridges*, 423 So. 2d 426 (Fla. Dist. Ct. App. 1982).
148. *Id.* at 428.
149. *Id.* at 427.

outraged. A Florida appellate court described the close-up image as "gruesome and macabre," "intended to create sensationalism for the report."[150] Even though the court ruled it may constitute a tort of outrage, the facts did not amount to an invasion of privacy. The abduction and the discovery of remains were considered legitimate matters of public interest.

False Light
Invasion of privacy claim based on distortion or misleading communication about an individual that is highly offensive to a reasonable person. This offense is not recognized in all jurisdictions since the same facts giving rise to a defamation lawsuit also can serve a false-light claim.

3 False-Light Invasion of Privacy

An area of privacy law that is closely tied to defamation is called false light. This tort addresses the privacy right of an individual to be free from publicity that places them in a false light. False-light invasion of privacy occurs when widespread media attention is given to someone portrayed in an inaccurate and oft-exaggerated light in a way considered "highly offensive to a reasonable person."

A false-light cause of action might occur if some embellishment of the truth, a photo or headline mix up, or when use of a stock photo, file footage, or photo caption gives a false and highly offensive impression about a person portrayed. When WJLA-TV in Washington, DC, ran a story about a new treatment for genital herpes on its 11 p.m. news, it showed general footage of pedestrians walking down a street. But just as the news anchor announced, "For the 20 million Americans who have herpes, it's not a cure," the camera zoomed in on one woman, Linda Duncan, as she turned toward the camera. Duncan, humiliated, sued and won for false light because the voice over narrative with her picture implied to viewers who would reasonably believe that she had a sexually transmitted disease when she did not.[151]

The elements for false light that a plaintiff generally must prove are

- **publicity** given to a matter that
- places a person in a **false light**, that is
- **highly offensive** to a reasonable person, and
- **fault**.

Most states, however, specifically require the fault standard of **actual malice**, requiring all plaintiffs to show defendants acted with knowledge of falsity or with reckless disregard for truthfulness.[152]

Not all states recognize the tort of false light. Approximately four out of five states allow their citizens to sue for false light by either common law or statute. Colorado rejected the tort in 2002 as did Florida in 2008. Yet in 2008, Missouri recognized false-light invasion of privacy claims, followed by Nevada in 2014.

False light is an intriguing and disputed area of privacy law because it closely resembles libel. In fact, some states such as Florida no longer recognize false light because of this similarity. It is also not uncommon for claims of false light and libel to be filed together in a lawsuit.[153] Yet in some cases, a false-light claim may prevail when a libel suit does not, and vice versa. The distinction between the two torts is that libel protects a person's interest in a good reputation, while false light protects a person's privacy interest in being let alone.

Unlike libel (see Chapter 5), false light does not require harm or injury to a person's *reputation*; instead, the plaintiff shows the publicized material was highly offensive to a

150. *Armstrong v. H&C Communications*, 575 So. 2d 280, 281 (1991).
151. *Duncan v. WJLA-TV*, 10 Med. L. Rptr. 1395 (D.D.C. 1984).
152. In fact, actual malice is one of the elements cited for false-light in the *Restatement (Second) of Torts* § 652(e), which provides that one who gives publicity to a matter concerning another that places the other before the public in a false light is subject to liability to the other for invasion of his privacy, if (a) the false light in which the other was placed would be highly offensive to a reasonable person, and (b) the actor had knowledge of or acted in reckless disregard as to the falsity of the publicized matter and the false light in which the other would be placed.
153. Although the *Restatement (Second) of Torts* § 652(e) says a case can proceed with both claims, the plaintiff can "have only one recovery of his damages upon one or all of the different grounds." cmt. d.

reasonable person. False light also requires wider dissemination or publicity of the matter than mere publication to a third party as required for libel. And while a plaintiff in both civil actions is concerned with proving the falsity of the defendant's statements or portrayal, some courts will allow the plaintiff in a false-light claim to show how the facts present only an overall false impression. For example, when *Baywatch* actor Jose Solano, Jr., agreed to be featured on the cover of *Playgirl* magazine, he objected to headlines on the cover saying, "12 Sizzling Centerfolds Ready to Score With You" and "TV Guys. Primetime's Sexy Young Stars Exposed." Solano won a false-light claim against the magazine because the court found the headlines put him in a false light by creating the wrong impression he would be seen posing nude inside the magazine.[154]

Still, proving false light may be more challenging for private individuals. While a few state courts accept a negligence standard for private individuals, more require the higher fault standard of actual malice for *both* private and public figure plaintiffs. This outcome was recently determined in Pennsylvania when an article about "The Case of the Fake Sherlock" prompted criminal profiler Richard Walter to file a false-light suit that was ultimately dismissed.[155] Walter argued a *New York Magazine* article characterizing him as a "fraud" was designed to "place him in a false light, and mislead readers." But the court determined Walter failed to prove the magazine published with actual malice as required in that state.

False and Highly Offensive

A false impression led to a false-light lawsuit filed by Jeannie Braun who worked at the Aquarena Springs amusement park in San Marcos, Texas. Braun's job included an act with "Ralph, the Diving Pig," which would dive into a pool to be bottle fed by Braun treading water. Braun signed a release authorizing the park to use photos of the act for advertising and publicity with the understanding that they would be used in good taste and without embarrassment.

Still the park permitted the photo to be used by an editor from *Chic* magazine who claimed his magazine was just a "fashion magazine" for men. When a stranger recognized Braun and showed her the depiction of her in a section called "*Chic* Thrills," she saw that *Chic* magazine was what a court would later describe as a "glossy, oversized, hard-core men's magazine" devoted exclusively to sexual exploitation and to disparagement of women.[156] Braun sued *Chic* and its publisher Larry Flynt for libel and false-light invasion of privacy, testifying that she "was very upset," suffered "embarrassment and humiliation," and "felt like crawling in a hole and never coming out."[157]

In *Braun v. Flynt*, the court was asked to accept the entire magazine as the context in which her photograph appeared, and that an ordinary reader automatically would form an unfavorable opinion about the character of a woman whose picture appeared in *Chic* magazine. The court agreed with the jury's findings that "a false impression as to Mrs. Braun's reputation, integrity or virtue" had been created and that was highly offensive to a reasonable person.[158]

No false light was found, however, in another case when videotaped sequences were taken out of context, sometimes to the embarrassment of extras appearing in a made-for-television movie. Volunteers for the Easter Seal Society of New Orleans agreed to stage a Mardi Gras-style

154. *Solano v. Playgirl, Inc.*, 292 F. 3d 1078 (9th Cir. 2002). The court found Solano's humiliation and embarrassment as sufficient for consideration on remand.
155. *Walter v. Herbert*, Civil Action 3:23-cv-2166 (M.D. Pa. May. 14, 2024). Also insufficient were Walter's allegations that the author violated a journalistic code of ethics or exhibited ill will toward him.
156. *Braun v. Flynt*, 726 F.2d 245, 247 (5th Cir. 1984), cert. denied, 469 U.S. 883, 105 S. Ct. 252, 83 L. Ed. 2d 189 (1984).
157. *Id.* at 248.
158. *Id.* at 249 and 252. The court added that even if an ordinary reader might not presume Braun to be unchaste or promiscuous, they might presume that she consented to appear in the magazine and approved of the opinions expressed therein.

parade and Dixieland celebration for the television cameras of the local PBS station. The goal was to help raise money, and a 17-minute videotape was produced and broadcast nationally as part of the Easter Seals Telethon. Afterward, WYES-TV kept the field tapes on file and used sequences to add color to programs such as a Dixieland Jazz series that the PBS station later broadcast.

Bedrock Law

False-light claims require a showing of distortion or embellishment of the truth that is not necessarily defamatory but highly offensive.

The trouble appeared when a Canadian filmmaker asked to repurpose the Mardi Gras parade footage for his project. WYES-TV's director of broadcasting agreed, unaware that the filmmaker planned to use some scenes as backdrop for a soft-core pornography film entitled *Candy, the Stripper*. The Playboy film focused on sex and drugs, causing no small embarrassment for the Easter Seal Society for Crippled Children and Adults. Because the staged parade scenes were used only as a backdrop and there was no embellishment or distortion involved, the court ruled there was no false-light portrayal.[159]

Actual Malice and the U.S. Supreme Court

Embellishment and distortion sometimes occur in fictionalizations such as novels, short stories, plays, and TV docudramas, where intentionally altering the truth is done for dramatic purposes. Supermarket tabloids and even some respectable publications – at least in the past – dabble with embellishing the truth to create a more compelling story. This was the case in the only two false-light cases that have ever been heard by the U.S. Supreme Court and where proof of actual malice was required.

In *Time, Inc. v. Hill*,[160] a sensationalized magazine article was at issue after three escaped convicts held the James J. Hill family hostage in their home for 19 hours and eventually released them physically unharmed. Two of the three criminals later died in a shootout. Novelist Joseph Hayes investigated the crime, writing a fictional book about the "Hilliard" family's ordeal, which also became a film and Broadway play. Before the play opened, however, *Life* magazine published a feature article stating that the play was based on the real-life nightmare of the Hill family.[161] Actors even appeared in Hill's former house in suburban Philadelphia, and a photographer captured them in poses suggestive of the Broadway play's fictionalized scenes. Hill sued *Life* magazine's publisher, *Time, Inc*., for invasion of privacy because the pictures were taken inside the Hill's real home and portrayed exaggerated and untrue scenes of beatings and verbal abuse by the convicts against the family.

The Supreme Court ruled against Hill's false-light claims, applying the fault standard of actual malice on the heels of its landmark libel ruling in *New York Times v. Sullivan* where it required public officials to prove actual malice (see Chapter 5). Even though Hill was not a public official, his family's hostage ordeal was newsworthy, and the Court reasoned that for false light, persons involved in a matter of public interest would need to show that the false story was published with knowledge of its falsity or with reckless disregard of the truth. The Court remanded the case, but the Hills chose to drop their suit instead.

The second false-light Supreme Court case also dealt with a journalistic embellishment or fictionalized portrayal. Indeed, whenever a journalist stretches the truth in a narrative so that it is enhanced to the extent that it brings about personal offense, the courts may find that a valid claim for false-light privacy exists. Such was the case in *Cantrell v. Forest City Publishing Co.*[162] when screenwriter Joe Eszterhas,[163] working earlier in his career as a reporter for the Cleveland *Plain Dealer*, was assigned to cover a story about the rush-hour collapse of the Silver Bridge on the Ohio River, which killed at least 44 people in 1967.

159. *Easter Seal Soc'y for Crippled Children & Adults of La., Inc. v. Playboy Enters*., 530 So. 2d 643 (La. Ct. App. 1988) *writ denied*, 532 So. 2d 1390 (1988).
160. *Time, Inc. v. Hill*, 385 U.S. 374 (1967).
161. The article was entitled, "True Crime Inspires Tense Play," with the subtitle, "The ordeal of a family trapped by convicts gives Broadway a new thriller, 'The Desperate Hours.'"
162. *Cantrell v. Forest City Publishing Co*., 419 U.S. 245 (1974).
163. Eszterhas later became famous for scripting the movies *Flashdance* and *Basic Instinct*.

Among those suffering from this accident was Mrs. Margaret Cantrell, who lost her husband when the weight of the cars caused the bridge to buckle and bend into the water. Eszterhas appeared at her home for an interview eight months after the tragedy to complete his follow-up on the story, but Mrs. Cantrell was away. Some of her children were present, though, so Eszterhas decided to use their descriptions along with his own contrived images of their mother, whom he described as a "proud woman," who "wears the same mask of non-expression she wore at the funeral."

After the story was published, Mrs. Cantrell was taken aback by the fictionalized portrayal. Her feeling of violation led her to file a lawsuit for false-light invasion of privacy, which made its way to the U.S. Supreme Court. In finding for Cantrell, the high court ruled Eszterhas knowingly included falsehoods in his article about the widow, including inaccuracies that Mrs. Cantrell had refused money from townspeople and that her family was living in dirty and dilapidated conditions.[164]

Unfortunately, the fault standard and its application to private individuals was not clarified in *Cantrell* when it was decided in 1974. That same year in *Gertz v. Welch*, the high court included public figures and distinguished the standard of negligence for private persons in libel cases (see Chapter 5). But in *Cantrell*, the Court simply found Eszterhas and the newspaper had showed actual malice with the "calculated falsehoods,"[165] leaving open whether the fault of negligence may ever apply to private persons in a privacy lawsuit.[166] As a result, some states explicitly require private persons to prove only negligence while most states require all plaintiffs to prove actual malice.

Other Celebrity Cases

While most false-light cases today tend to involve errors in judgment such as improper use of photos and video, fictionalizations and other journalistic embellishments or distortions are still a concern, especially for high-profile cases dealing with celebrities. In 2018, the acclaimed FX docudrama series *Feud: Bette and Joan* about the lives of film stars Bette Davis and Joan Crawford became the target of a false-light lawsuit by Olivia de Havilland.[167]

The 102-year-old actress, known for her roles in *Gone with the Wind* and *The Adventures of Robin Hood*, claimed Catherine Zeta-Jones's portrayal of her in the mini-series not only violated her right to publicity but depicted her in a false light. De Havilland claimed the series put false words in her mouth. She objected to being falsely depicted as a "hypocrite, selling gossip," who speaks "in crude and vulgar terms about others." She especially objected to her character calling her sister Joan Fontaine a "bitch." FX cited an interview with de Havilland calling Fontaine a "dragon lady."

The California appeals court did not find Zeta-Jones's portrayal of de Havilland to be highly offensive to a reasonable person, and de Havilland as a public figure was unable to prove actual malice by clear and convincing evidence. The Supreme Court declined to hear the case,[168] and de Havilland died in 2020.

Selectively omitting information rather than embellishing a story was the concern in another recent false-light case. E! Entertainment Television was sued for false light by former *American Idol* contestant Corey Clark, who appeared in season two and successfully

164. *Cantrell v. Forest City Publishing Co.*, *supra* note 160.
165. *Id.* at 253.
166. In fact, in writing for the Court, Justice Stewart stated "this case presents no occasion to consider whether a State may constitutionally apply a more relaxed standard of liability . . ., or whether the constitutional standard announced in *Time, Inc. v. Hill* applies to all false-light cases." *Id.* at 250–251.
167. *De Havilland v. FX Networks, LLC*, 21 Cal. App. 5th 845 (2018).
168. Eriq Gardner, "Supreme Court Denies Review of Olivia de Havilland's 'Feud' Lawsuit," *The Hollywood Reporter*, January 7, 2019, *at* www.hollywoodreporter.com/thr-esq/supreme-court-denies-review-olivia-de-havillands-feud-lawsuit-1174078.

made it to the top 10.[169] Even though Clark was then disqualified for failing to disclose that he had once been arrested, he claimed he had a romantic relationship with Paula Abdul, one of the show's judges. The alleged affair received a lot of attention across various media outlets and was even the subject of a sketch on NBC's *Saturday Night Live*.

Clark filed suit when stories mentioning his claim about the affair presented the information in such a way as to be false. He claimed E! Entertainment Television placed him in a false light by "selectively omitting" information and not presenting his side of the story, even though an *E! True Hollywood Story* program narrator reported Clark's allegation he had phone records documenting his calls with Abdul as well as a bottle of prescription cough syrup bearing her name. The court granted summary judgment for the defendant, finding Clark as a limited purpose public figure failed to prove the TV show purposefully avoided the truth or had reasons to doubt the veracity of its sources – so there was in fact no actual malice.

Appropriation
Privacy tort that discourages use of a person's name or likeness for commercial gain without consent. *See also* right of publicity.

4 Appropriation

The oldest form of invasion of privacy recognized as a legal tort is appropriation. Although sometimes broadly construed, in the eyes of the law, appropriation is taken to mean the use of another person's name or likeness without permission for one's own use or benefit, such as commercial gain. It is often described legally as **misappropriation**.

As a legal principle, this area of law can be traced to upstate New York and an incident involving a pretty face, a sack of flour, and brand advertising that took place at the turn of the twentieth century. In Albany, NY, young Abigail Roberson awoke one day to discover her face displayed on thousands of posters around the town advertising Franklin Mills Flour above the slogan "The Flour of the Family." Her parents said she suffered severe embarrassment and humiliation due to the unwanted publicity.

Ms. Roberson sued the flour company, asserting a common-law right of privacy. The New York court acknowledged the young woman indeed had suffered but that her case lacked legal standing in New York because the so-called right of privacy had "not yet found an abiding place in our jurisprudence."[170] Ms. Roberson's disappointment, however, had a salutary effect. The publicity emanating over her anguish from the advertising convinced state legislators that New York citizens had a right to privacy that should be coded into law.[171]

A few years later in 1905, the Georgia Supreme Court handed down the first judicial opinion protecting individuals from use of their pictures and testimonials for advertising purposes. A photograph of Paolo Pavesich appeared in a newspaper advertisement for New England Life Insurance, and the court ruled the insurance company was liable for damages.[172] Pavesich was not a customer of the insurance company nor had he consented to the use of his image, but his picture appeared in the *Atlanta Constitution* with a caption falsely indicating he was a customer next to an unhealthy individual who ostensibly did not buy insurance. The Georgia Supreme Court validated an individual's cause of action against this company using Pavesich's name and picture without permission to construct a false advertising testimonial.

Most states have since adopted the common law tort of appropriation or misappropriation, and a few jurisdictions such as New York and California have enacted statutory laws to recognize the cause of action.[173] As an invasion of privacy tort, this law essentially protects the "personal feelings against mental distress" caused by one's image being used for another's

169. *Corey D. Clark v. E! Entertainment Television, LLC*, No. 3:13-cv-00058 (M.D. Tenn. March 26, 2018).
170. *Roberson v. Rochester Folding Box Co.*, 171 N.Y. 538, 64 N.E. 442 (1902).
171. As a result of the *Roberson* case, New York drafted §§ 50 and 51 in its civil code to protect citizens from unauthorized use of their name or likeness for commercial advertising or profit.
172. *Pavesich v. New England Life Ins. Co.*, 50 S.E. 68 (Ga. 1905).
173. For a few jurisdictions, the law only applies to prominent persons.

benefit without permission.[174] Like other privacy rights, this protection is personal and does not get passed on to heirs when an individual dies. Yet because the interest protected is also the individual's exclusive use of their own identity, the right created is in the form of a property right. So in addition to protecting against a privacy infringement as an emotional harm, the rule recognizes that a plaintiff has an exclusive right to protect or license to others their identity as represented by their name or likeness.[175]

The elements of appropriation that a plaintiff generally must show are

- use of a person's **name** or **likeness**
- without consent
- by another for their own **benefit**.[176]

The use of a name or likeness of an individual is specific enough for an appropriation suit. The likeness of an individual is construed to mean photographs, film, and video of the actual person. This is a key distinction between the tort of appropriation and a right of publicity, discussed next, which more broadly defines one's image in the context of the economic interests of celebrities. For example, when *Wheel of Fortune* gameshow hostess Vanna White brought a lawsuit against Samsung for running an advertisement that depicted a robot turning letters, she was unable to succeed on a claim of appropriation because she, herself, was not portrayed in the ad.[177] Yet her claim of a right of publicity was another matter.

When it comes to one's name, the use of nicknames or other monikers may suffice, but a clear and reasonable connection to the plaintiff is necessary. When the TV sitcom *Seinfeld* assigned the name George Costanza to one of its main characters, a man named Michael Costanza sued Jerry Seinfeld and others for invasion of privacy by misappropriation. A New York court did not find Michael Costanza's lawsuit to be frivolous because he did appear briefly as an actor in an episode. But given the show never used the plaintiff's actual name and no photo or film of the plaintiff as himself appeared, the court did not find enough similarity to be "cognizable under the statute" of the state.[178]

A "benefit" is generally understood to mean commercial use, as in advertising or trade, but it can take various forms in this area of law. Appropriation of your identity for purposes of "image advertising" or a public relations promotion can run afoul of the law. When Jewel Food Stores ran an ad in *Sports Illustrated* congratulating basketball legend Michael Jordan on his induction into the Basketball Hall of Fame, Jordan filed suit claiming, in part, it was a misappropriation for the supermarket chain's commercial benefit. A district court sided with Jewel, which claimed it was noncommercial speech protected by the First Amendment. But the appellate court disagreed, finding the ad to be commercial speech in the form of image advertising designed to generate good will for the "Jewel-Osco" brand, creatively and conspicuously linked to Jordan in the text of its congratulatory message.[179]

Bedrock Law
Commercial appropriation protects a person's name and likeness for advertising purposes without permission.

A for-profit women's clinic faced an appropriation lawsuit when it produced and distributed a promotional calendar that included the name and photo of a notable physician. Choices Women's Medical Center produced 10,000 copies of a calendar titled "Women – Choosing to Make a Difference," which highlighted historical moments of the women's movement each month.

174. *Restatement (Second) of Torts* § 652C.
175. *Id.* at cmt. a.
176. The *Restatement (Second) of Torts* describes this as "One who appropriates to his own use or benefit the name or likeness of another is subject to liability to the other for invasion of his privacy." (§ 652C).
177. *White v. Samsung Electronics America, Inc.*, 971 F.2d 1395 (9th Cir. 1992).
178. *Costanza v. Seinfeld*, 719 N.Y.S. 2d 29; 279 A.D.2d 255 (2001). Moreover, the court held works of fiction fall beyond the narrow scope of statutory definitions of "advertising" or "trade."
179. *Jordan v. Jewel Food Stores, Inc. et al*, 743 F.3d 509 (7th Cir. 2014).

The month of June featured a Freedom Medal recipient and showed a second doctor above the caption reading "Here with Dr. Cordia Beverley." Dr. Beverley sued under New York's statute forbidding the use of the "name, portrait or picture of any living person" for "advertising purposes, or for the purposes of trade" without written consent. This court found in favor of Dr. Beverley's appropriation claim and held Choices Women's Medical Center could not override "privacy protection by wrapping its advertising message in the cloak of public interest, however commendable the educational and informational value."[180]

Newsworthiness can be a defense for the media's use of a person's identity under the First Amendment.[181] Courts will consider the public interest value and freedom of expression rights of the news media, even if the medium essentially benefits by attracting more readers or viewers and therefore profits from its use. Such coverage does not become a commercial use of the name or likeness even in articles blurring the line between news and entertainment.

For the TV program *Trauma: Life in the ER*,[182] plaintiffs consented to being videotaped as they were admitted to a hospital emergency room, only to complain later they were not competent to do so because of injuries and heavy medication. The court nonetheless ruled *The Learning Channel* program was newsworthy and the images were not aimed at a specific promotional or commercial purpose. Moreover, it was "irrelevant whether a videotape is broadcast in connection with a television story about important public events or a subject that provides only entertainment and amusement."[183]

Right of Publicity
Protects famous people and those who wish to protect their likeness, voice, or image from others exploiting it for commercial gain.

Right of Publicity

The **right of publicity** is a parallel claim to commercial (mis)appropriation. It gives famous people the right to control and profit from their likeness or name without fear that others will use it to their undeserved benefit. This tort recognizes valid claims from individuals who realize a loss of commercial value resulting from the unauthorized and usually promotional display of their image and/or name in public.

This tort is less about a right of privacy as celebrities generally embrace publicity, and more about an economic right, intended to compensate famous individuals who need to prevent economic harm to their public livelihood. For that reason, people who are not famous are generally unable to sue for a right of publicity. This civil action is comparable to intellectual property rights, particularly trademark (see Chapter 7), because of the interest in protecting one's "brand" from others trading on its value.

The concept of a right of publicity is usually traced to a lawsuit in the early 1950s between two baseball trading card companies. Topps Chewing Gum of Brooklyn, NY, and Haelan Laboratories were both competing to sign star Major League Baseball players to an exclusive contract for their images. A federal appellate judge coined the term *right of publicity* in this case, and the majority opinion recognized each player had a common-law right of property that could be transferred and legally protected from any unauthorized use.[184] Since that case, 24 states have enacted some form of right-of-publicity statute, with Alabama, Arkansas, Louisiana, and South Dakota among the most recent ones to pass legislation.[185] Thirty-eight states have some form of common law precedent.

180. *Cordia Beverley, M.D. v. Choices Women's Medical Center, Inc.*, 78 N.Y.2d 745, 587 N.E.2d 275, 579 N.Y.S.2d 637 (1991).
181. *See*, *Time, Inc. v. Hill*, *supra* note 158 where the U.S. Supreme Court found in favor of the media when balancing the public interest against a false-light invasion of privacy claim.
182. *Castro v. NYT Television*, 370 N.J. Super. 282, 851 A.2d 88 (2004).
183. *Id.* at 97.
184. *Haelan Laboratories v. Topps Chewing Gum*, 202 F.2d 866 (1953).
185. *See* rightofpublicity.com for an interactive map of state statutes as well as recent cases, articles, and history.

While varying from state to state, the most common elements of a right of publicity are

- use of a person's **name, image, or likeness**
- without consent
- to another's **commercial advantage**
- resulting in **injury**.[186]

Often filed as a companion claim to appropriation, the right of publicity extends its protections to celebrities, famous athletes, and others, but with certain distinctions. The benefit must be commercial in nature and the unlawful use produces some economic harm. The injury might be the loss of opportunity for the plaintiff to capitalize on their identity. Moreover, the right of publicity provides broader protection to the image of the famous.

Unlike appropriation, which is specific to one's name and likeness, the right of publicity protects *any distinctive*, readily recognizable aspect of identity. Not only might a photograph of a well-known person be protected, but also the voice, distinctive mannerisms, well-known catch phrase, unique attire or uniform, or even recognizable possessions such as a car. Your distinctive image also may be protected when recreated through drawings, paintings, and digital replicas, such as animation and animatronics, or lookalikes and impersonators.

A classic example of this distinction occurred when the Ford Motor Company's advertisers decided to use the song "Do You Want to Dance?" in its commercials for Ford's Mercury Sable car. The advertisers specifically wanted singer Bette Midler's very popular rendition of it, but her manager flatly refused the company's request, principally because she did not want to recreate it for advertising. Undaunted, the Young & Rubicam agency hired one of Midler's former backup singers to "sound as much as possible like the Bette Midler record."[187] A federal court found that the Midler's voice was distinctive enough that an imitation of it violated her right of publicity to the tune of $400,000 in damages.[188]

Longtime NBC *Tonight Show* host Johnny Carson was well-known for his sidekick's rousing introduction of "Heeeere's Johnny." The affable host was not amused when an outdoor toilet company named its product "Here's Johnny," reinforcing its reference to Carson with the tagline, "the world's foremost commodian." An appellate court held Carson's right of publicity had been violated by using what was a brand name for Carson.[189] Use of Carson's full name was not necessary for his successful right-of-publicity claim.

Years earlier, a race car with distinctive pinstriping and other markings was the subject of a lawsuit when its internationally known professional driver objected to a photo of it in an R.J. Reynolds cigarette commercial. The race car driver's face was not seen in the photo, and the company modified the photo by changing its number and adding a spoiler to the car with the product name attached. But a court found for the plaintiff because his identity was recognizably tied to the car.[190]

The case of *Muhammad Ali v. Playgirl* magazine involved nothing more than a silhouette drawing and a banner title, "The Greatest," accompanied by some verses about an unnamed boxer. Even though it was not Ali's true likeness, the court ruled it was close enough for a right-of-publicity suit.[191]

Turning a celebrity's image into an avatar will also draw their ire and prompt a suit. Selena Gomez filed suit against the makers of the "Clothes Forever – Styling Game" app,

186. The *Restatement (Third) of Unfair Competition* describes this harm as "one who appropriates the commercial value of one's identity by using without consent the person's name, likeness or other indicia of identity for purposes of trade." (46 cmts. [1995]).
187. *Midler v. Ford Motor Co.*, 849 F.2d 460, 461 (9th Cir. 1988).
188. *Id.*
189. *Carson v. Here's Johnny Portable Toilets, Inc.*, 698 F.2d 831 (1983).
190. *Motschenbacher v. R.J. Reynolds Tobacco*, 498 F.2d 821 (1974).
191. *Ali v. Playgirl*, 447 F. Supp. 723 (S.D. N.Y. 1978).

which lets players dress celebrity avatars. Gomez sued for $10 million, alleging the game harmed her right to market her own fashion-focused games.[192]

A well-known astronomer took issue when American Girl created its 2018 Girl of the Year, "Luciana Vega," a doll with a striking resemblance and described as "an aspiring astronaut ready to take the next giant leap to Mars." Lucianne Walkowicz sued American Girl and parent company Mattel for appropriating her image and identity without permission.[193] Aside from the similar first names, Walkowicz lectured on Mars exploration and was known on the TED Talks circuit for her research on the constellation Lyra whose center is the star Vega. And like Walkowicz, the doll featured a purple streak in its dark hair and wore similar looking boots and a cosmic-patterned dress. Walkowicz argued the unlawful use made it more difficult for her to profit from her image at a future date, if that's what she intended to do.

Use of a celebrity look-alike in an advertisement can also produce lawsuits. Singer and songwriter Ariana Grande filed a right-of-publicity claim against fashion retailer Forever 21 after it failed to secure an endorsement deal with her and subsequently ran a marketing campaign that included a look-alike model with Grande's signature hairstyle and clothes along with images that mimicked scenes from her "7 Rings" and "thank u, next" music videos.[194] The clothing company Old Navy also ran television commercials that featured a look-alike of Kim Kardashian who ultimately settled out of court.[195]

New Orleans chef Paul Prudhomme sued when Procter & Gamble, Inc., ran a series of commercials for Folger's coffee featuring an actor who bore a "striking resemblance" to Prudhomme.[196] The parties settled out of court, in part because Louisiana had yet to incorporate the right of publicity into its law. Most right-of-publicity cases are settled out of court.

While there is seemingly no limit to the range of distinctive attributes and means of appropriation that constitute a right of publicity, there is some confusion and dispute in the law because it is not always easy to define when someone's persona begins to clearly take shape and what attributes rightfully belong to a person. This is especially concerning today when AI-generated images borrow certain attributes of real people to create a "synthetic" performer.

The Ninth Circuit had some disagreement about this when game show hostess Vanna White sued Samsung and its ad agency David Deutsch Associates, Inc., in 1992.[197] In that case, a robot appeared in a series of Samsung ads wearing a gown, blonde wig, and jewelry while turning letters on a set that resembled the *Wheel of Fortune*. The ad was set in the future to suggest Samsung products such as its VCRs would still be in use at that time. There was text stating "Longest-running game show. 2012 A.D." Deutsch and Samsung even referred to it as the "Vanna White" ad. As noted, the TV host did not appear in the ad and so lost on the claim of misappropriation, but won on the common law right-of-publicity claim, with the court stating

> [i]f the celebrity's identity is commercially exploited, there has been an invasion of his right whether or not his "name or likeness" is used. It is not important how the defendant has appropriated the plaintiff's identity, but whether the defendant has done so.[198]

192. Jason Gordon & Erika Auger, "Fash-Shunned: Selena Gomez Sues Fashion App for $10 Million for Allegedly Using Her Name and Likeness without Permission," *Lexology*, April 27, 2020, *at* www.lexology.com.
193. Bruce Vielmetti, "American Girl Accused of Stealing Astronomer's Identity for its Girl of the Year Doll Luciana Vega," *Milwaukee Journal Sentinel*, May 11, 2020, *at* www.jsonline.com/story/news/local/wisconsin/2020/05/10/american-girls-luciana-doll-stole-astronomers-identity-lawsuit-says/3089985001/.
194. *Ariana Grande-Butera v. Forever 21, Inc.*, No. 2:19-cv-07600 (C.D. Cal. September 2, 2019). In the meantime, Forever 21, Inc., filed for bankruptcy.
195. "Kim Kardashian Settles Lawsuit over Look-Alike in Old Navy Ad," *Hollywood Reporter*, August 29, 2012.
196. *Prudhomme v. Procter & Gamble Mfg. Co.*, 800 F. Supp. 390, 394 (E.D. La. 1992).
197. *White v. Samsung Electronics America, Inc.*, supra note 175.
198. *Id.*

To this holding, the court cautioned against creating a laundry list of specific means of appropriating identity. Even so, Judge Alarcon disagreed, stating that in this case the identity attributes in question were of a *role* White played, not unique attributes of her personal identity. Therefore, representation of those attributes could not constitute a representation of Vanna White. Alarcon reasoned that such a position would allow any famous person to bring suit based on any advertisement that depicts a character or role performed by the plaintiff. Clint Eastwood would be able to sue anyone who plays a tall, soft-spoken cowboy; Sylvester Stallone could sue actors who play blue-collar boxers; Arnold Schwarzenegger could sue body builders paid to appear in public, and so forth. Judge Alarcon said advertiser Samsung's First Amendment defense was therefore given "short shrift."[199]

Artists' Right of Publicity and AI

The right of publicity is especially at risk now, given the ease with which images of others can be digitally manipulated and created using artificial intelligence. Artists such as musicians, actors, and other performers claim safeguards are urgently needed to protect their images, likenesses, and voices from the abuse of generative AI. Examples of this nonconsensual use include an audio publisher cloning an actor's voice for an audiobook narration; a video game company creating a digital replica of a sports broadcaster to announce a game; and an ad agency making a replica of a deceased performer for a commercial.[200]

Existing case law provides some remedy. Consider, for example, the parallels to Bette Midler's case when actor Scarlett Johansson declined OpenAI's request to use her voice for their new GPT-40 chatbot.[201] Johansson had earlier voiced an artificial intelligence chatbot in the 2013 movie "Her," and OpenAI CEO Sam Altman wanted to use her "comforting" voice. When she discovered their personal assistant "Sky" sounded just like her, OpenAI argued the recording was by an unnamed professional actor and not an "imitation" of Johansson's distinctive voice. But given the *Midler* precedent, it's not surprising that OpenAI ultimately decided to stop using the voice.

While no federal right of privacy statute has been adopted, Congress is giving it some consideration, given the concerns about AI. A bill was introduced in 2024 to recognize that "every individual has a property right in their own likeness and voice." The No AI FRAUD Act would prohibit making public a digital voice replica or digital depiction without permission.[202] It would also prohibit the nonconsensual use of a digital depiction or voice replica for a new performance in an advertisement or expressive work without proper consent. Violators would be subject to $50,000 per violation or actual damages plus any profits.

At the same time, contractual solutions have been crafted by the SAG-AFTRA union when it met in late 2023 to discuss the impact of generative AI on actors' livelihood.[203] SAG-AFTRA ratified a TV/Theatrical Agreement with the Alliance of Motion Picture and

199. *Id.*
200. "Digital Image Rights & Right of Publicity," *SAG-AFTRA*, 2024, *at* https://www.sagaftra.org/get-involved/government-affairs-public-policy/digital-image-rights-right-publicity.
201. Kat Tenbarge, "Scarlett Johansson Says She Was 'Shocked, Angered' When She Heard OpenAI's Voice That Sounded Like Her," *NBC News*, May 20, 2024, *at* https://www.nbcnews.com/tech/tech-news/scarlett-johansson-shocked-angered-openai-voice-rcna153180.
202. No Artificial Intelligence Fake Replicas and Unauthorized Duplications Act of 2024 (No AI FRAUD Act), H.R. 6943, 118th Cong. (2024), *at* https://www.congress.gov/bill/118th-congress/house-bill/6943/text?s=1&r=1&q=%7B%22search%22%3A%22NO+FAKES+ACT%22%7D.
203. "SAG-AFTRA Advocates for A.I. Protections on Capitol Hill," *SAG-AFTRA*, May 1, 2024, *at* https://www.sagaftra.org/sag-aftra-advocates-ai-protections-capitol-hill.

Television Producers, ensuring some protections against the use of "digital alteration," "digital replicas," and "synthetic performers" without permission.[204]

For example, if a digital replica of an actor – say, a younger version of them – is used in a scene, the actor must get paid. Actors must give explicit consent if certain body parts (such as eyes or mouth) are used to create an entirely AI-generated actor or "synthetic performer." Contracts with an actor's estate must be drawn before creating a digital replica of a performer who is deceased.

In the meantime, some state misappropriation and right-of-publicity laws were revised to handle the impact of AI, defining "digital replica"[205] and distinguishing the rights of performers. For example, Louisiana now makes it a crime to use a digital replica in a public performance if it "creates the clear impression that the professional performer is actually performing in the role of a fictional character."[206] Tennessee amended its "ELVIS" law to specifically protect celebrity voices and shield performers from nonconsensual uses based on AI extractions.[207]

Defenses and the First Amendment

Celebrities do not necessarily enjoy a complete privilege if their image is used. As with appropriation, there is an exception for the use of a famous name or image in a news context. This can prevent celebrities from claiming a right of publicity while trying to halt an unauthorized biography or docudrama that draws upon their fame in the public's eyes. Such noncommercial speech uses are constitutionally protected.

Actor Dustin Hoffman, who once appeared in the film "Tootsie," where he played a role dressed as a woman, learned this when he sued *Los Angeles Magazine* (LAM) for right of publicity. LAM had used an altered photo of him from the film to accompany a magazine article. The photo depicted Hoffman and a body double wearing the latest spring fashions, and text on the page identified the photo as being from the movie, stating "Dustin Hoffman isn't a drag in a butter-colored silk gown by Richard Tyler and Ralph Lauren heels."

A lower court found the photo to be an unprotected "exploitative commercial." But the appellate court determined that LAM was not using Hoffman's image in a traditional advertisement for the purpose of selling a particular product.[208] Rather, it was a complement to and part of the issue's focus on Hollywood past and present, "inextricably entwined" with expressive elements of humor and editorial comment.[209] The appellate court concluded that LAM was entitled to full First Amendment protection awarded noncommercial speech.[210]

Newsworthiness was also a successful defense in an Indiana case involving fantasy sports operators DraftKings and FanDuel, which used detailed information about real athletes in their games without consent. The Indiana Supreme Court ruled the plaintiffs – former college football players – were not entitled to compensation for material with "newsworthy value," an exception under that state's right-of-publicity statute. "Defendants' use of players'

204. Chris Frawley, "Unpacking SAG-AFTRA's New AI Regulations: What Actors Should Know," *Backstage*, January 18, 2024, *at* https://www.backstage.com/magazine/article/sag-aftra-ai-deal-explained-76821/.
205. For example, Louisiana defines "digital replica" as "a computer-generated or electronic reproduction of a professional performer's likeness or voice that is so realistic as to be indistinguishable from the actual likeness or voice of the professional performer." Allen Toussaint Legacy Act, SB No. 426 to enact Subpart K of Part VII of Chapter 1 of Title 51, Louisiana Revised Statutes (2022), at (4).
206. *Id.* at §470.4 (C).
207. Ensuring Likeness, Voice, and Image Security (ELVIS) Act of 2024, HB 2091 011887, amending Tennessee Code Annotated, Title 39, Chapter 14, Part 1 and Title 47 (2024).
208. *Hoffman v. Capital Cities/ABC, Inc.*, 255 F.3d 1180 (9th Cir. 2001).
209. *Id.* at 1185.
210. *Id.* at 1189.

Figure 6.2 Zacchini family cannon, on display at the Circus Museum in Florida

names, images, and statistics in conducting fantasy sports competitions bears resemblance to the publication of the same information in newspapers and websites across the nation." "[I]t would be strange law that a person would not have a First Amendment right to use information that is available to everyone."[211]

A claim of newsworthiness is not a complete defense, however. The only right-of-publicity case that has been heard to date by the U.S. Supreme Court is one that ruled in favor of a performer's right of publicity and rejected a broadcast station's First and Fourteenth Amendment defenses. In the landmark Ohio case of *Zacchini v. Scripps-Howard Broadcasting Co.*,[212] the high court ruled on whether a freelance photographer who filmed a human cannonball act for a local television station's newscast had encroached on the circus performer's right of publicity (Figure 6.2). The clip lasted only 15 seconds, but it showed the entire act. Hugo Zacchini felt his performance's marketability and consequent profits had been harmed by the nonconsensual publicity.

Zacchini specifically asked the TV crew *not* to record or broadcast his entire act. The visual news value of seeing a "Human Cannonball" flying through the air is easy to accept, but the Supreme Court could not let fly the station's First Amendment argument that it needed to show the entire performance without his consent.[213] The Supreme Court compared Zacchini's arguments in favor of controlling his personal publicity as consistent with the goals of patent and copyright laws that reward personal creativity for commercial gain.[214] Once viewers had a chance to see the human cannonball's act on television, there was less incentive for them to pay the price of admission to see him perform in person, which deprived him of a portion of his income. For that reason, the Court upheld his claim against the TV station's parent company, Scripps-Howard Broadcasting.

A newsworthiness defense may also come under scrutiny if the publicized matter bears no real relationship to the matter of public interest. After wrestler and model Nancy Benoit and

211. *Daniels v. FanDuel, Inc.*, 109 N.E. 3d 390, 396 (2018). Note the appeals court distinguished this decision from *Madden NFL* where consent was required, stating that case concerned "California's statute about strategic litigation rather than Indiana's right-of-publicity statute, and it was rendered by a federal court." *Daniels v. FanDuel, Inc.*, 884 F.3d 672, 674 (7th Cir. 2018).
212. 433 U.S. 562 (1977).
213. *Id.* at 584.
214. *Id.* at 573.

her son were murdered by wrestling superstar Chris Benoit, her husband, *Hustler* magazine ran a brief biography of her and reported the murder along with decades-old nude photos of her. The family sued and won when the Eleventh Circuit Court ruled the nude photos were "neither related in time nor concept to the current incident of public interest" and therefore "do not qualify for the newsworthiness exception to the right of publicity."[215]

Nonetheless, the court later vacated a jury's $19 million punitive judgment, stating the publishers had made "an innocent mistake," and mere negligence was not enough to be held liable for punitive damages.[216] They had "honestly and reasonably (albeit mistakenly) believed at the time that the photographs fit under the newsworthiness exception to the right of publicity."[217] This case highlights the difficulties faced by publishers in determining newsworthiness and the lines drawn between news, entertainment, and commercial speech.

Using a celebrity's image to promote a media outlet can also be an exception to a right-of-publicity claim if the use is tied to the medium's news or information content. This all stems from what is known as the *Booth rule*, named for the comic actor Shirley Booth, who became famous on a 1960s television situation comedy as the loveable maid "Hazel." Ms. Booth sued *Holiday* magazine after it repurposed photographs of her vacationing in Jamaica and used those images to promote their magazine's journalistic quality.

A New York appellate court ruled the images were constitutionally protected as an incidental use and because the media must be allowed to promote their content with materials they have collected.[218] As a result, newspapers, television stations, and the like have since been generally free to use images from their news stories and other content to advertise and promote their publications, newscasts, and websites without fear of violating a subject's publicity rights.

The Booth rule does not apply, however, if the advertisement suggests the celebrity is endorsing the medium. Such was the case for actress and singer Cher who agreed to an interview with a freelance writer for a certain publication but instead discovered the story had been sold to a Penthouse publication, *Forum*. *Forum* ran an ad proclaiming, "There are certain things Cher won't tell *People* and would never tell *Us*. She tells *Forum*. So take a tip from Cher and hundreds of thousands of other adventurous people and subscribe to *Forum*."[219] A California appeals court ruled in favor of the celebrity because the advertisement did not merely inform readers about the content but implied an endorsement.

Other right-of-publicity defenses are based on consent, incidental use, and parody. When it comes to consent, some states require the permission to be in writing. It is also important for the use of the individual's identity to not exceed the scope of the agreement, such as where, how, and for how long it may be used. In 2009, the rock band, No Doubt and singer Gwen Stefani filed suit against Activision for unauthorized use of their likenesses in the video game "Band Hero." The parties had a contract, but the musicians claimed the game company went beyond the contract. After three years, the parties settled out of court.[220]

An insignificant or fleeting use of a celebrity's name, image, or likeness in an advertisement may also escape legal consequence. Referred to as the "**incidental use doctrine**," this is an exception that applies to uses peripheral to the purpose of the advertisement. For example, use of Olympic athletes' names was considered incidental in the promotion of disposable drinking Dixie Cups because it was informational and did not imply the athletes used

215. *Toffoloni v. LFP Publishing Group, LLC*, 572 F.3d 1201, 1213 (11th Cir. 2009).
216. *Toffoloni v. LFP Publishing Group, LLC*, No. 11–12922, D.C. Docket No. 1:08-cv-00421-TWT (11th Cir., May 1, 2012).
217. *Id.* at 5.
218. *Booth v. Curtis Publishing Co.*, 223 N.Y.S.2d 737 (App. Div. 1962), aff'd, 182 N.E.2d 812 (N.Y. 1962).
219. *Cher v. Forum International*, 692 F.2d 634 (9th Cir. 1982), cert. denied, 462 U.S. 1120 (1983).
220. "No Doubt, Activision Settle Lawsuit Over Avatars in 'Band Hero'," *Hollywood Reporter*, October 3, 2012.

or promoted the product.[221] A four-second use of a plaintiff's photograph during a 29-minute infomercial promoting a Rolling Stones' rock music anthology was also considered incidental because it was "too fleeting and inconsequential" to violate a right of publicity.[222] The rationale for recognizing incidental use is that it has no commercial value, and allowing recovery to anyone briefly depicted would unduly burden expressive activity.

An expressive work using parody can be an exception when it comes to the right of publicity. While celebrity impersonators who perform tribute concerts would not be protected but obligated to pay licensing fees for profiting from a performer's image, those impressionists who make a living by mimicking such celebrities are generally protected. With impressionists, the audience is more engaged by the performer's talent, and such parodies are viewed as a form of commentary with "transformative value" protecting them from right-of-publicity claims.

Right-of-Publicity Tests

Depending on the jurisdiction, different tests have evolved to judge whether the use of a person's identity is protected by the First Amendment. Perhaps best known is the *transformative use* test, which derives from a case in California where not surprisingly many celebrity right-of-publicity cases originate. In *Comedy III*, artist Gary Saderup depicted The Three Stooges comedy trio in a charcoal drawing that he reproduced without permission on T-shirts and lithographs that he sold. Tasked with weighing whether the use infringed a right of publicity or had become an "expressive" work protected by the First Amendment, the California Supreme Court considered whether the likeness was "so transformed that it has become primarily the defendant's own expression rather than the celebrity's likeness."[223]

The transformative use test measures a work to see if it contains significant transformative elements or its value derives primarily from the celebrity's fame. Transformative elements such as parody or other original, creative factors will likely find First Amendment protection. However, if the work is simply a substitute for conventional depictions of the celebrity or celebrities, then the right-of-publicity claim is affirmed.[224] In *Comedy III*, the court determined Saderup's work was unprotected because the depiction was literal and conventional, and its value came only from the fame of the Stooges Larry, Moe, and Curly.

The California court clarified its transformative use test two years later in *Winter v. DC Comics*.[225] In that case, the court determined that a comic book series that depicted a pair of brothers as villainous "half-human, half-worm creatures" was clearly transformative and therefore protected. Musicians Johnny and Edgar Winter sued because the characters "Johnny and Edgar Autumn" had similar features, such as pale faces and long white hair, and one even sported a signature stovepipe hat that was worn during performances.

They argued the work was not a protected parody of them and that it traded on their likenesses and reputations to generate sales. But the court found "significant expressive content" in the distorted cartoon depictions from which the plaintiffs were "merely part of the raw materials."[226] Furthermore, "[w]hat matters is whether the work is transformative, not whether it is parody or satire or caricature or serious social commentary or any other specific form of expression."[227] The court also found how the work is marketed and its prof-

221. *Vinci v. American Can Co.*, 69 Ohio App.3d 727, 591 N.E.2d 793 (1990).
222. *Aligo v. Time-Life Books, Inc.*, No. C94-20707, 1994 U.S. Dist. LEXIS 21559, at *8 (N.D. Cal. December 19, 1994).
223. *Comedy III Prods., Inc. v. Gary Saderup, Inc.*, 25 Cal. 4th 387, 106 Cal. Rptr. 2d 126, 21 P. 3d 797 (2001).
224. *Id.* When an artist's work is "manifestly subordinated to the overall goal of creating a conventional portrait of a celebrity . . . then the artist's right of free expression is outweighed by the right of publicity."
225. 69 P. 3d 473 (Cal. 2003).
226. *Id.* at 641.
227. *Id.* at 642.

itability to be irrelevant. "[W]hen a work contains significant transformative elements, it is not only especially worthy of First Amendment protection, but it is also less likely to interfere with the economic interest protected by the right of publicity."[228] The court held parodies and other distortions are not good substitutes for conventional depictions of a celebrity and therefore do not generally violate what the right of publicity is designed to protect.

The transformative use standard was used for addressing the publicity rights of athletes whose likenesses as avatars appeared in video games such as *Madden NFL*, made by Electronic Arts (EA). In *Davis v. Electronic Arts*,[229] the Ninth Circuit found not only were the physical characteristics of the football players replicated in the game, but also their position, years in the NFL, and relative skill level in different aspects of the sport. The court ruled the unlicensed use of players' identities in video games was not transformative and therefore unprotected. It further rejected EA's "incidental use" defense, holding the use was indeed central to EA's main commercial purpose – to create a realistic virtual simulation of football games involving current and former NFL teams.[230]

NIL, College Athletes, and Video Games

College athletes could not enjoy a right of publicity to their name, image, and likeness or NIL, until recently.

The National Collegiate Athletic Association (NCAA) long considered college athletes "amateurs" since they are given no salary to speak of, despite some earning money for their colleges and universities, especially if they're lucky enough to be playing for NCAA teams showcased on national television. Their compensation amounted to a full scholarship with room, board, tuition, and fees, plus royal treatment in cafeterias and workout facilities on certain athletic campuses.

Graduation produced a different story, however. Most student athletes would not go on to profitable careers in professional sports, instead finding themselves in far less lucrative professions or even unemployed. Although the NCAA wouldn't stand in the way of former athletes licensing themselves, some found their old, uniformed college images being used without compensation to sell video games, depicting them in terms of their height, weight, build, and even the number on their jersey as well as their home state.

Electronic Arts is a multibillion-dollar video game enterprise that licenses its product to the NCAA, which in turn receives an undisclosed amount of money for licenses. A class action filed by attorneys for a former basketball star at UCLA, Ed O'Bannon, and 11 former college athletes demanded compensation for the use of their images and likenesses in video games, TV commercials, and sportswear. In 2010, a San Francisco judge opened the licensing contracts to the legal process known as discovery.

In 2013, former Nebraska quarterback Sam Keller sued EA Sports and the NCAA for allowing video game makers to continue the so-called identity theft. Hall of Famers Jim Brown and Herb Adderly signed on to Keller's cause of action. A separate and similar legal action was filed in the Third Circuit by former Rutgers University quarterback Ryan Hart.[231] In applying the transformative use test in these cases, the courts found the games did not sufficiently transform the players' likenesses and therefore held their use to be unprotected. As a result, EA stopped producing the series and agreed to multimillion-dollar settlements with the players. It seems in such cases the question boils down to whether video games are viewed as transformative expressions subject to First

228. *Id.* at 639.
229. 775 F.3d 1172 (9th Cir. 2015).
230. *Id.* at 1180–1181.
231. *Hart v. Electronic Arts*, 717 F.3d 141 (3rd Cir. 2013).

Amendment expression or not. Creative artists owe their subjects compensation under the right of publicity if all that is involved is the commercial promotion of their likeness.

In 2021, the NCAA began to change its rules so that current college student athletes could make money off their names, image, and likeness.[232] The new rules allow athletes to sign agents and endorse products, appear in commercials, promote their own commercial social media presence, and even launch businesses selling apparel. This rule change came after some state legislatures passed laws permitting athletes in their states to profit from their NIL, and the U.S. Supreme Court ruled in *NCAA v. Alston* that the NCAA could not limit any education-related payments to students.[233]

The effect is not uniform, however, with the NCAA deferring to the states, which have different state laws and school rules taking precedence. For example, some schools may permit an athlete to wear or otherwise use the school's logo and other trademarks in a commercial or other endorsement deal, while other schools forbid it. Nonetheless, NCAA rules still say that players cannot be compensated for their performance, and recruits cannot sign NIL deals contingent on going to a particular school.

To protect student athletes, the NCAA Division I Council created standards for NIL contracts to ensure some uniformity and transparency in the marketplace. The new rules also allow the NCAA and schools to educate and help players make informed decisions about NIL agreements.[234]

A different test from the U.S. Second Circuit is called the *relatedness test* or *Rogers test* because it involved a lawsuit filed by famed dancer Ginger Rogers. In *Rogers v. Grimaldi*,[235] Rogers claimed that the motion picture "Ginger and Fred" violated her Lanham Act trademark rights as well as her common law rights of publicity and privacy. The court adopted a test that looks at whether the use is "wholly unrelated" to the individual and is not used to promote or endorse a collateral commercial product.[236] The court stated the right of publicity does not bar the use of a celebrity's name in the title so long as it is for a literary work and not "simply a disguised commercial advertisement for the sale of goods or services."[237]

In finding for the defendant, the court found the title was "clearly related" to the content of the movie and not a disguised ad. The federal Sixth and Ninth Circuits have relied on the *Rogers test* particularly for Lanham Act cases (see Chapter 11), and media groups have advocated its use for both Lanham Act and misappropriation/right of publicity lawsuits because it weighs strongly in favor of protecting works of artistic expression.[238]

The Missouri Supreme Court articulated yet another standard referred to as the *predominant use* test. In *Doe v. TCI Cablevision*,[239] former National Hockey League player Tony Twist, a fan favorite notorious for his violent play, sued the creators of a graphic-novel series

232. *See, e.g.*, "NCAA Will Let College Athletes Earn Money Off of Name and Likeness," *National Public Radio (NPR)*, July 3, 2021, *at* https://www.npr.org/2021/07/03/1012832019/ncaa-will-let-college-athletes-earn-money-off-of-name-and-likeness#:~:-text=Weekend%20Edition%20Saturday –, NCAA%20Will%20Let%20College%20Athletes%20Earn%20Money%20Off%20Of%20Name,name%2C%20image%2C%20and%20likeness.
233. James Parks, "NIL in College Football: Here's What You Need to Know, and What's Next," *FanNation, Sports Illustrated*, January 17, 2024, *at* https://www.si.com/fannation/college/cfb-hq/ncaa-football/college-football-nil-rule-changes-what-you-need-to-know.
234. Meghan Durham Wright, "Division I Council Approves NIL Disclosure and Transparency Rules," *NCAA*, January 10, 2024, *at* https://www.ncaa.org/news/2024/1/10/media-center-division-i-council-approves-nil-disclosure-and-transparency-rules.aspx.
235. 875 F.2d 994 (2d Cir. 1989).
236. *Id.* at 1004.
237. *Id.*
238. Kelli L. Sager, "Summary of Right of Publicity Issues," MLRC Conference paper, September 2012, *at* https://law.ku.edu/sites/law.ku.edu/files/docs/media_law/Summary_of_Right_of_Publicity_Issues.pdf.
239. 110 S.W. 3d 363 (Mo. 2003).

called *Spawn* for violating his right of publicity. The series creator was an avid hockey fan who had introduced a character named Anthony "Tony Twist" Twistelli, who was a mafia don who committed murders, kidnapped children, and had sex with prostitutes. The graphic-novel character bore no physical resemblance to the real Tony Twist – they only shared the same name and personas as tough-guy "enforcers." But the court went beyond any assessment of similarities to weigh whether the predominant purpose of the use was expressive or commercial. The test posits

> [i]f a product is being sold that predominantly exploits the commercial value of an individual's identity, that product should be held to violate the right of publicity and not be protected by the First Amendment, even if there is some "expressive" content in it that might qualify as "speech" in other circumstances. If, on the other hand, the predominant purpose of the product is to make an expressive comment on or about a celebrity, the expressive values could be given greater weight.

In this case, the court concluded the use of Twist's name and identity were "predominantly a ploy to sell comic books and related articles" rather than an artistic or literary expression. The predominant use test has nonetheless been criticized for being subjective and calling upon judges to act as both impartial jurists and discerning art critics.[240] As a result, courts have generally declined to adopt this test for right-of-publicity cases.

The Hurt Locker

Hollywood's big night of star-studded glamour, the Academy Awards, is seldom lacking in controversy. The 82nd night at the Oscars proved to be a big one for *The Hurt Locker*. But it was also the subject of a lawsuit based on its portrayal of a master sergeant who dangerously defused bombs during the War in Iraq.

In the film, the soldier is named Sgt. Will James, but in the eyes of a Tennessee veteran, Sgt. Jeffrey S. Sarver, the story was actually his own. Journalist Marc Boal had interviewed Sarver in 2004 for a *Playboy* magazine article entitled, "The Man in the Bomb Suit." When Boal converted his magazine piece to a movie screenplay, he described it as a fictional work based on the lives of several soldiers. But Sarver saw it as *his* story, used without consent and without any profit. He sued on six counts, including invasion of privacy and right of publicity. He asked for a total of $450,000 in damages.

The legal question boiled down to Sarver's theory that he was owed a right of publicity for a work alleged to be a fictional composite. Hollywood screenwriters do seek releases for an individual's life story, but Boal made no such arrangement with Sarver to use any part of his story and other sources to produce the movie. The transformative nature of creating a feature screenplay is that it is essentially a work of fiction, drawing on more than a person's likeness for success. In 2016, the Ninth Circuit upheld the dismissal of Sarver's suit, concluding the film was protected by the First Amendment.

Right of Publicity After Death

Certain rights expire when a person dies – for example, privacy and defamation – but the right of publicity for dead celebrities is recognized by several courts, and more than half of the states have even codified the protection. In 1984, Tennessee adopted its Personal Rights Protection Act,[241] which became known in some quarters as the "Elvis Law," as it was designed to protect Elvis Presley's estate from commercial exploitation. His former manager

240. *See, e.g., Hart v. Electronic Arts*, supra note 231 at 154.
241. Tenn. Code Title 47, Chapter 25, Part 11 (1988).

Col. Tom Parker sold his interest in the estate, thereby prompting Elvis Presley Enterprises (EPE) to lobby for a state law ensuring that heirs have a right to deceased celebrities' images. This law was the protection afforded in Tennessee; similar laws vary from state to state.

New York more recently added protections for a "deceased performer" who had regularly engaged in acting, singing, dancing, or playing an instrument and for a "deceased personality" whose name, voice, signature, photograph, or likeness had commercial value at the time of death. The new law specifically prohibits the nonconsensual use of a deceased performer's "digital replica" in a scripted audiovisual work as a fictional character or for the live performance of a musical work.[242]

Among the first legal actions taken by the estate of a deceased celebrity for use of AI involved comedian George Carlin in 2024.[243] The estate of Carlin sued the creators of a video podcast comedy special for copyright and right of publicity for using Carlin's five decades of standup comedy to train an AI tool to produce the episode and incorporate his voice and likeness without consent or compensation. In the hourlong special titled *George Carlin: I'm Glad I'm Dead*, AI-generated narration mimicked Carlin's delivery style and cadence and addressed modern topics such as AI itself, even though Carlin died in 2008. Promotion of the special also featured the comedian "resurrected" with the use of AI tools. The video was described as a "first of its kind media experiment," but it was quickly taken down as the lawsuit was settled out of court.[244]

Summary

- The Supreme Court has found a constitutional basis for privacy in the Bill of Rights guarantees of association, due process, freedom from self-incrimination, unreasonable search or seizure, and peacetime prohibition of soldiers quartering in homes.
- Causes of action for privacy include intrusion upon seclusion, public disclosure of private facts, false light, and appropriation of one's name or likeness.
- Intrusion claims prevail where there is an expectation of privacy and the means of intrusion – such as the newsgathering technique – is highly offensive.
- The U.S. Supreme Court recognizes unauthorized wiretapping by a third party is an invasive and unlawful act. But communicators who had nothing to do with the actual wiretapping and only conveyed intercepted messages of public interest are not held liable.
- Ordinary people upset over the unnecessary exposure of their personal life in the media can recover for damages when the truthful facts conveyed about them are highly offensive and of no legitimate public concern.
- False-light claims are the least recognized of the privacy rights. Similar to libel, evidence of publicity and falsity is required, usually with actual malice. Instead of harm to reputation, it is highly offensive and often an embarrassing error.
- One's name and likeness are protected from others making a profit by selling or using them without consent.
- Celebrities' right of publicity is violated when their name, likeness, or image is used for commercial advantage, without any transformative value involved or legitimate public interest.

242. An Act to Amend the Civil Rights Law, in Relation to Establishing the Right of Publicity and to Providing a Private Right of Action for Unlawful Dissemination or Publication of a Sexually Explicit Depiction of an Individual, 5605-C, New York, February 14, 2019.
243. Winston Cho, "George Carlin Estate Sues Creators of AI-Generated Comedy Special in Key Lawsuit Over Stars' Likenesses," *Hollywood Reporter*, January 15, 2024.
244. Winston Cho, "George Carlin's Estate Settles Lawsuit Against Podcasters Over AI Special," *Hollywood Reporter*, April 2, 2024.

Ethical Dilemma: Politicians and Privacy

It's a given that individuals who run for and enter public office must give up some level of privacy that private individuals otherwise enjoy. In a democracy, voters need to know such things as the character, health, and financial well-being of those who would represent them. Citizens also want to know that their elected officials are trustworthy, practicing the virtue of truthfulness in both their private as well as public lives. After all, a politician who is cheating on their spouse or their taxes may not be trusted with tending to the public's business. Indeed, there can be a legitimate public interest in the personal lives and behavior of politicians.

But where should the media draw the line when investigating and disclosing deeply personal information about politicians? What are the ethical boundaries today?

Back when President Kennedy was having an affair with Marilyn Monroe, the press generally looked the other way. By the time President Clinton took office, however, the media found itself carefully describing some intimate details of the affair he had with an intern. Reporters subsequently investigated and reported on the private life of presidential hopeful John Edwards who had a lovechild with a mistress, as well as newly elected New Jersey Governor Jim McGreevey who admitted to hiring a man with whom he was having a sexual relationship. When President Trump's liaison with "Stormy" Daniels came to light, very intimate details were shared widely over social media and national television. Pressure has increased for journalists to uncover and expose the private lives of politicians, particularly when it is salacious and scandalous.

To be clear, various privacy laws as discussed in this chapter will make certain encroachments on the privacy of politicians unlawful. HIPAA, banking, and wiretap laws will restrict access to information about a politician's mental health, substance abuse, financial records, and backchannel communications, even though the politician's public performance could be greatly compromised.

Still, there are times when reporting on the private lives of politicians is legally protected. The media may disclose restricted information if it's leaked to them by a third party (see, e.g., *Bartnicki v. Vopper*), such as a healthcare provider, banking employee, or IT specialist. The media may also disclose embarrassing private facts of a politician if the matter is of public concern or newsworthy. As discussed earlier, it is the politician who needs to prove in a civil suit that the information was *not* a matter of public concern or newsworthy. The First Amendment rights of the media will generally outweigh this invasion of privacy claim.

So if you determine that divulging private information about a politician is most likely *permissible* under the law, the question of whether it *should be* divulged becomes a matter of ethics. Simply put, if you can report it, should you?

If we look to Aristotle and his virtue ethics, we can find some guidance in understanding the importance of virtuousness and how good citizenship became the highest virtue. To Aristotle, leaders should exhibit true virtue and even serve as moral exemplars. This provides some moral and ethical justification for the media's heightened scrutiny into the private life and character of a politician. Consider, for example, whether the politician is being disingenuous and duplicitous, grandstanding on "family values" while neglecting or mistreating their own family, or promising fiscal restraint while flirting with personal bankruptcy due to gambling debts.

For the same matter, Immanuel Kant would remind us to treat humanity as an end and never as a mere means only. So then is exposing the private life of a politician being done to promote democracy and accountability or to boost one's ratings and likes? This is where salacious stories become the siren song, tempting journalists to ignore best practices. Kant would contend that we consider whether invading a politician's privacy is for the right reason. The ends do not justify the means.

Finally, John Stuart Mill would have us consider the consequences of our actions. Here we might consider whether the politician's private behavior took place in the distant past, has a potential of reoccurring, or is still ongoing. Also consider whether the behavior poses a threat to the public. Is there a conflict of interest, such as nepotism or bribery, that would interfere with the duties of the office? Mill would also have us consider whether our actions produce the greatest good for the greatest number of people. Are constituents being served by exposing their representative's private behavior at the expense of harming that politician's political reputation and livelihood?

Consider a recent example of a politician whose private life was exposed. Apply the philosophies of Aristotle, Kant, and Mill to the media coverage. Did the media cross the line?

7

Intellectual Property

LEARNING OBJECTIVES

After reading this chapter, you should know

- how intellectual property rights are interpreted and enforced
- what infringing a trademark means and how it differs from copyright
- the legal basis for copyright protection and the "bundle of rights" covered
- how music authors license their music to collect royalty payments
- the tremendous value of derivative works
- what types of expression can and cannot be copyrighted
- the advantages of registering a copyright
- how long a copyright lasts
- the four elements of fair use and how they are applied
- what tools used to infringe copyright protection can be prohibited

When photographer Elliot McGucken posted to Instagram his photo of an ephemeral lake in Death Valley, he didn't expect it to appear in an online article by *Newsweek*. Apparently, someone at *Newsweek* tried to contact McGucken to request permission to upload his photo to its website. But when McGucken didn't respond, the magazine went ahead and embedded his Instagram image in an online article, "Huge Lake Appears in Death Valley, One of the Hottest, Driest Places on Earth."

Displeased with this use of his work, McGucken sued for copyright infringement. A preliminary ruling in 2022 found the news magazine's actions were not a "fair use."[1] But the court did set the matter for a jury to decide whether *Newsweek*'s use came under other categories: "transformative," commercial, in bad faith, too substantial (the entire photo), and had a negative effect upon the potential market or value of the copyrighted photo. The case never made it to trial; like most copyright disputes, the matter was settled out of court.[2]

1. *McGucken v. Newsweek LLC*, 19 Civ. 9617 (KPF), 2022 U.S. Dist. LEXIS 50231 (S.D.N.Y. Mar. 21, 2022).
2. Blake Brittain, "Newsweek Settles Copyright Fight Over Instagram Embedding," *Reuters*, April 14, 2022.

DOI: 10.4324/9781003462989-7

This copyright lawsuit was just one of several recent cases to reach U.S. courts over the issue of third-party websites embedding material from social media sites like Instagram. Every year, hundreds of copyright claims are filed[3] involving a wide range of audiovisual materials, literary works, and sound recordings. In addition, around 3,000 federal trademark cases are also filed each year.

It's important to understand how the elements of copyright and trademark law protect intellectual property rights, but it is even more important to recognize what constitutes the illegal taking of another's work. One of the common misapprehensions is to think because the copied content is easily available online or only a little bit is taken makes it at all permissible. Anyone – whether a college student, a small-town advertising executive, or a large media conglomerate –can get hauled into court for using someone else's "IP" without permission. Copyright and trademark lawsuits are expensive, and the damages can run into the millions of dollars.[4]

A Constitutional Right

Intellectual property law covers a lot of ground – patents, copyrights, trademarks or service marks, and trade secrets. It protects the authors and owners of creative works covering videos, music, photos, brand names, slogans, sensitive business information, and inventions. This book deals with communication law, and so rights protected by patents or trade secrets are beyond its scope; so are unfair competition laws invoked by states to settle trade disputes.

IP law protects different rights, and it applies different tests for evaluating violations. We think of the beverage Coca-Cola to differentiate trade secrets from trademarks. The cola recipe may be protected as a trade secret. The Coca-Cola® name with its distinctive script and red and white colors falls under trademark. And the advertisement for Coke with its arrangement of music, text, and images is protected by copyright. For inventors, the functional and original beverage dispenser design would qualify for patent protection. In fact, the contoured bottle unique to Coke was patented in 1917, and its distinctive shape as a product symbol was trademarked in 1977.

While the provisions vary, intellectual property rights can be traced to the same roots, the British Licensing Act of 1662, followed by the Statute of 8 Anne in 1710. Intellectual property became the province of our Congress in Art. I, Sec. 8 of the U.S. Constitution:

> To promote the Progress of Science and useful Arts, by securing for limited Times to Authors and Inventors the exclusive Right to their respective Writings and Discoveries.

The clause "to promote the Progress" is used to encourage Americans to create works for profit. Some authors, it's true, are motivated purely by a burning desire for self-expression, but many prefer to make a living doing it. Could best-selling authors make a living if their works were freely copied and distributed without permission or compensation?

Another part of this protection limits the rights for a specific time. With copyright, authors and owners eventually must allow others free access to their works. Authors have their successful compositions protected to promote creativity and profits, but at some point, they must surrender them to the public domain. Some artists and authors find this element of the law to be unfair. American author Mark Twain asked Congress to allow for copyright

3. More than 180 copyright claims were filed in 2022, although some years the number runs in the thousands. A record 5,042 infringement claims were filed in 2015.
4. The United States Sentencing Commission reports the median infringement amount for cases in 2021 was $229,302, and the average prison sentence for copyright and trademark criminal offenders was ten months. United States Sentencing Commission, "Quick Facts: Copyright and Trademark Offenses," *at* https://www.ussc.gov/sites/default/files/pdf/research-and-publications/quick-facts/Copyright_FY21.pdf.

Public Domain
Works in the public domain are no longer subject to private intellectual property claims, either because they were never copyrighted or because their term limit expired.

ownership in perpetuity for his publications, and though that never came to pass he did see the length of the copyright term extended.[5]

In the Public Domain?

A work enters the public domain for different reasons. It might fall under one of the exceptions like U.S. government publications; or the work was created before copyright laws originated, such as the Bible, Shakespeare's plays, and Beethoven's music; or copyright protection was never granted in the first place. Some creations are dedicated purposefully to the public domain and made available free of royalty fees.

Copyrights also expire. Certain works become available each year and pass into the public domain. Works created before 1978 are protected for 95 years (not the current term of the author's life plus 70 years). So, in 2021, copyrighted works from 1925 entered the U.S. public domain, including F. Scott Fitzgerald's *The Great Gatsby*, Virginia Woolf's *Mrs. Dalloway*, Ernest Hemingway's *In Our Time*, and Franz Kafka's *The Trial*. Also entering the public domain were silent films featuring Buster Keaton, and the musical works of Fats Waller, Duke Ellington, and Irving Berlin.

Some copyrights fall into the public domain after being challenged and forfeited. That was the case for the famous tune, "Happy Birthday to You," which was licensed so that performing it commercially would be violating its copyright. The song was the creation of sisters Patty Smith Hill and Mildred Hill in 1893, although it originally had different lyrics, "Good Morning to All."

The sisters assigned their rights to the melody and piano arrangement to the Clayton F. Summy Co., which registered it as "Happy Birthday to You" in 1935 and collected licensing fees for its use. Warner/Chappell Music later assumed the rights, but when it was challenged, a federal court determined Summy Co. never acquired the song lyrics and both companies should return the millions in licensing fees collected over the years.[6] "Happy Birthday to You" officially entered the public domain in 2016, giving everyone around the birthday cake something to sing aloud about.

What Is Copyright?

A simple way to think of copyright is to simply dissect the term – the right of copy. Controlling who may copy a work, including who can legally download the creative expression, is just one part of it. Most legal treatises refer to copyright as a bundle of rights. The creator of a book, play, poem, film, song, or any other copyrightable work has the exclusive rights to control four kinds of use:

- Reproduction – reproduction rights allow the owner to decide who may copy a work or what fee is to be paid for copying it, such as with music downloads.
- Performance – copyright holders also have a right to determine if their work can be performed, and the compensation when someone else performs their work. A songwriter, for example, is paid a royalty when a piece of sheet music is sold, but that songwriter also receives a royalty when someone else performs that song. A radio station that plays copyrighted music also needs to pay performance rights.

5. https//blogs.loc.gov/loc/2014/09/mark-twain-copyright/. The Copyright Act of 1909 established a term of 28 years that could be renewed for another 28 years. Twain died in 1910.
6. *Marya v. Warner/Chappell Music, Inc.*, 131 F. Supp. 3d 975 (2015).

Bedrock Law
The legal protection of copyright gives the owner exclusive rights to copy the material, derive other works from it, perform it, display it, and distribute it.

- Derivative Works – a copyright holder also controls the creation of any derivative works based on the copyrighted work. Someone who wants to make a movie based on a book needs the permission of the copyright holder, and someone who wants to make a new arrangement of a copyrighted piece of music needs the composer's permission.

Copyrightable Works

According to the U.S. Copyright Office, copyrightable works include the following:[7]

- literary works
- musical works, including accompanying lyrics and words
- dramatic works, including accompanying music
- pantomimes and choreographic works
- pictorial, graphic, and sculptural works
- motion pictures and other audiovisual works
- sound recordings
- architectural works.

What may be copyrighted within these categories vary in terms of original works. Maps, for example, may be protected as pictorial and graphic works, and even computer programs may be copyrighted as literary works.

For a work to be copyrighted, it must be an original work and be recorded in a fixed medium. The 1976 Copyright Act states,

> Copyright protection subsists . . . in original works of authorship fixed in any tangible medium of expression, now known or later developed, from which they can be perceived, reproduced, or otherwise communicated, either directly or with the aid of a machine or device.

Copyright is therefore determined by fixation and originality. Fixation is defined broadly, and protection exists from the moment a work is "fixed" in a tangible medium. Certainly, a story published in a magazine is fixed in a tangible medium of expression, but so is a posted blog because it resides on some computer storage device somewhere in the world, even if seemingly in the "cloud." Even a live broadcast or streamed content, such as a sporting event or morning radio talk show, is usually considered fixed because it likely involved some script (fixed) and was simultaneously recorded to a computer hard drive or other medium.

Do not be fooled by the word tangible; digital files that can be easily erased are still considered a tangible medium. Likewise, pantomimes and choreographic works are covered because even though a live dance performance is not fixed, if it is written or recorded, the choreography could be copyrighted.

Even tattoos are considered fixed in a tangible medium and can be copyrighted, as Warner Brothers discovered after releasing *Hangover 2* (2011) featuring the replica of boxer Mike Tyson's tattoo on an actor's face. That film image prompted the tattoo artist, who owned the copyright, to sue Warner Brothers, which quickly settled out of court for its use.[8]

Originality is also required for a work to be protected. It is "the bedrock principle of copyright" and "the very premise of copyright law."[9] This does not mean a work must be

7. U.S. Copyright Office, "Copyright Basics," *at* www.copyright.gov/circs/circ01.pdf.
8. "Warner Bros: Settles 'Hangover II' Tattoo Lawsuit," *Hollywood Reporter*, June 20, 2011.
9. *Feist Publications, Inc. v. Rural Telephone Service Co., Inc.*, 499 U.S. 340, 347 (1991).

highly creative or entirely novel though. The work must be "independently created by the author" and possess "at least some minimal degree of creativity."[10] The law does not specify how much creativity is required, but the Supreme Court has defined what an original work is.

Originality is explained in *Feist Publications, Inc. v. Rural Telephone Service Co.*[11] Feist had copied Rural's "white-page" phone book, but it did not violate copyright because Rural's work was not original. It was merely a compilation of facts not original in selection (subscribers to the phone service) or arrangement (alphabetically). The *Feist* case made clear a work is not considered original just because it required a lot of work. "[O]riginality, not 'sweat of the brow,' is the touchstone of copyright protection in directories and other fact-based works."[12]

What Is Not Copyrightable

Facts cannot be copyrighted. The *Feist* case underscores one fundamental concept: A fact does not owe its origin to the author. What copyright does protect, however, is the way in which facts are expressed. Thus, a history book can describe and present facts about the United States, and those expressions can be copyrighted. Likewise, a sports reporter's choice of words and phrases to describe play-by-play action in a basketball game can be copyrighted.

These principles are essential to commercial media, which rely on creative professionals to engage audiences. A radio station would be infringing copyright if it simply broadcast reports straight from the local newspaper, but it could report the same facts – even "exclusive" stories – without violating copyright.

In 2013, the Associated Press won a lawsuit against a company electronically aggregating AP stories and selling them to customers. A federal district court observed those facts contained in the stories were not copyrightable, but AP's original compilation of those stories was protected.[13]

Bedrock Law

Some works cannot be copyrighted due to their nature like lists of names or facts. Only original expressions fixed in tangible form are subject to copyright protection.

It is the expression of an idea, fixed in tangible form, that is copyrightable, but not the idea itself. Fledgling scriptwriters quickly learn that sharing casually in conversation an original, creative idea for a movie or TV series is a foolish thing to do since it must be transcribed to be protected by copyright.

Common story themes or "scènes à faire" are not copyrightable. *Scène à faire* is a French term referring to the "scene to be made" or "scene that must be done." It refers to elements that are customary to a particular genre, such as a gunfight in a western or a love-making scene in a romance novel and not subject to copyright protection.

This doctrine first evolved in a copyright dispute where both the plaintiff's book and the defendant's movie portrayed a couple taking shelter from a storm in a church.[14] The judge considered the story idea to be an old and inevitable part of the storytelling, not original enough for copyright protection.

Short phrases and names generally cannot be copyrighted, although they might be subject to trademark law. It's possible to protect some words, but only if they demonstrate originality in their composition and use. A lawsuit against Taylor Swift claimed the lyrics in "Shake It Off" (2014) violated the copyright of "Playas Gon' Play" (2001) by 3LW. If you listen to 3LW's lyrics you hear "Playas, they gonna play/And haters, they gonna hate." Swift sings "players gonna play, play, play, play, play and the haters gonna hate, hate, hate, hate, hate." The judge found the contested lyrics to be too brief, unoriginal, and uncreative to warrant copyright protection. Suit dismissed.[15]

10. *Id.* at 345.
11. *Id.*
12. *Id.* at 359–360.
13. *Associated Press v. Meltwater*, 931 F. Supp. 2d 537 (2013).
14. *Cain v. Universal Pictures, Co.*, 47 F. Supp. 1013 (1942).
15. To compare songs, *see* Anne M. Lum, "Taylor Swift Shakes Off 'Playas' Infringement Claim," *The Biederman Blog*, February 22, 2018, *at* www.biedermanblog.com/

According to the U.S. Copyright Office, other works unprotected by copyright include[16]

- Procedures, methods, systems, processes, concepts, principles, or discoveries. But written descriptions and illustrations of a discovery or process may be copyrighted, while certain processes are instead patentable.
- Familiar symbols or designs. This would include currency symbols, navigational symbols such as arrows, musical notes, religious crosses, and emoticons. General layouts and formats of a website or poster, nor would blank forms be copyrightable.
- Mere variations of typographic ornamentation, lettering, or coloring. Copyright law does not protect a typeface, for example.
- Mere listings of ingredients or contents. This would include such things as recipes, but the corresponding text describing how to assemble and prepare a dish may otherwise be copyrighted.
- Mere copies. A scanned, photocopied, dubbed, digitized, or otherwise reproduced work is not copyrightable.
- *De minimis* authorship. Works that contain no expression or a very small amount cannot be copyrighted. This would include editing a work that merely consists of spelling and grammatical corrections, touching up or restoring an old photograph, and producing a musical phrase of only several notes.

Images and works are not copyrightable if created by a mechanical or natural process instead of a person. A photogenic crested black macaque monkey in Indonesia caused a flurry of attention by grabbing wildlife photographer David Slater's camera and proceeding to take amazingly good selfies (Figure 7.1). Wikimedia, a nonprofit entity behind Wikipedia, posted the photos and refused to remove them at Slater's request because technically the macaque and not Slater created the photos. As a result, a Compendium of U.S. Copyright Office Practices (3rd ed.) redefined "authorship," as a work created by a human being or at least with human creative input or intervention.[17]

The Copyright Office also will not register works created by supernatural forces, robots, or mechanical processes. For this reason, the Copyright Office has declared works generated by artificial intelligence to not be copyrightable. In 2023, the Copyright Office released its policy on Works Containing Material Generated by Artificial Intelligence.[18] Based on current generative AI technologies, it reported most "users do not exercise ultimate creative control over how such systems interpret prompts and generate material."

The policy came on the heels of a case involving *Zarya of the Dawn*, a graphic novel that featured AI-generated images. The Copyright Office held registration would be limited to only the human-authored text of the novel. The "selection, coordination, and arrangement of the Work's written and visual elements are protectable under copyright law" but not the AI-generated images themselves.[19]

In 2023, the Copyright Office Review Board affirmed the decision to refuse registration to a generative AI painting app. Artist and lawyer Ankit Sahni submitted his application to register a photograph of a sunset. He also listed a software application as the author of

---

taylor-swift-shakes-off-playas-infringement-claim-federal-judges-harsh-finding-unoriginal-uncreative-banal-lyrics/.

16. U.S. Copyright Office, *supra* note 9; *Compendium of U.S. Copyright Office Practices (3rd ed.)*, infra note 19.
17. §§ 306, 313.2, December 22, 2014, *at* www.copyright.gov/comp3/docs/compendium-12-22-14.pdf.
18. 37 CFR Part 202, *at* https://public-inspection.federalregister.gov/2023-05321.pdf.
19. *Id. See also* Eileen McDermott, "Copyright Office Makes AI Authorship Policy Official," *IPWatchdog*, March 15, 2023, *at* https://ipwatchdog.com/2023/03/15/copyright-office-makes-ai-authorship-policy-official/id=157831/.

Whose Selfie?

Figure 7.1 Macaca nigra female self-portrait

Source: Commons.Wikimedia.org.; photo taken in 2008

a digital piece of artwork titled, SURYAST, in the style of Vincent van Gogh's *The Starry Night*. The Copyright Office questioned the artist/lawyer's use of the app, refusing to register his work because of the lack of human authorship, saying the human element could not be distinguished from "the final work produced by the computer program." If the AI-generated content "is more than *de minimis*," then it must be considered in the public domain.[20]

The Copyright Office examined the level of control Sahni exercised over the app, which he claimed was only an "assistive software tool." The application's interpretation of the photo was a function of its digital processing and was not based on the instructions received from Sahni.[21] In addition, while Sahni was the copyright holder of the underlying work and has a right to the creation of derivative works, he could not claim this digitally manipulated output from AI was a protected derivative.

20. The Copyright Office emphasized the importance of applying the *de minimis* standard, taken from the Supreme Court's decision in *Feist v. Rural Telephone*.
21. Franklin Graves, "Copyright Office Affirms its Fourth Refusal to Register Generative AI Work," *IPWatchdog*, December 12, 2023, *at* https://ipwatchdog.com/2023/12/12/copyright-office-affirms-fourth-refusal-register-generative-ai-work/id=170564/#:~:text=On%20December%2011%2C%20the%20Review,artificial%20intelligence%20(AI)%20software.

Copyright Policy on AI-Generated Works

Faced with a growing number of copyright applications and challenges for works using artificial intelligence and even naming AI technologies as authors, the Copyright Office released in 2023 its policy on Works Containing Material Generated by Artificial Intelligence.[22]

The policy reiterates the Office's long-standing rule that only the product of human creativity can be protected by copyright. This means determining the following:

> whether the "work" is basically one of human authorship, with the computer [or other device] merely being an assisting instrument, or whether the traditional elements of authorship in the work (literary, artistic, or musical expression or elements of selection, arrangement etc.) were actually conceived and executed not by man but by a machine.[23]

Thus, works containing AI-generated material will be evaluated as to "whether the AI contributions are the result of 'mechanical reproduction' or instead of an author's 'own original mental conception, to which [the author] gave visible form.'" If the "AI technology determines the expressive elements of its output, the generated material is not the product of human authorship."[24]

Works from apps requiring just a single prompt from a human would not qualify for copyright. That would include AI tools like ChatGPT and Midjourney, which generate complex written, visual, and musical works at the push of a button.

So far, the Copyright Office considers most of today's generative AI technologies to operate without sufficient creative control by users for copyright registration.[25]

It is possible certain AI-generated works may contain enough human authorship to qualify for copyright registration. This would include works where a person selected or arranged AI-generated material "in a sufficiently creative way that the resulting work as a whole constitutes an original work of authorship." It also would include works where "an artist may modify material originally generated by AI technology to such a degree that the modifications meet the standard for copyright protection"[26]

To be clear, grants of copyright will only protect the human-authored aspects of the work, "which are 'independent of' and do 'not affect' the copyright status of the AI-generated material itself." This was the case with one of the first applications for a work containing both human-authored elements combined with AI-generated images. The Office determined that the graphic novel *Zarya of the Dawn* constituted a copyrightable work but the AI-generated individual images in the novel were not protected.

What about works using tools such as Adobe Photoshop for editing images? The U.S. policy explains that copyright protection will continue to be granted to works created with sophisticated tools as part of the creative process. After all, copyright has long been awarded to photographs despite the use of a camera. The key is the "extent to which the human had creative control over the work's expression and 'actually formed' the traditional elements of authorship."[27]

22. 37 CFR Part 202, supra note 18.
23. *Id.* at 6.
24. *Id.* at 7. For example, the policy explains that if a user instructs a text generating technology to "write a poem about copyright law in the style of William Shakespeare," she can expect the system to generate text that is recognizable as a poem, mentions copyright, and resembles Shakespeare's style. But the technology – not the user – will decide the rhyming pattern, the words in each line, and the structure of the text.
25. *Id.*
26. *Id.* at 8.
27. *Id.*

The Copyright Office cautions applicants they have a duty to disclose AI-generated content and provide an explanation of their human-authored contributions in the "Author Created" field of the application. AI-generated content that is more than *de minimis* should be explicitly excluded from an application. In addition, applicants must never list the AI technology or the company that provided it as author or co-author.

Works produced by the U.S. government fall in a narrow class not subject to copyright. The U.S. government in 1895 placed its materials outside of copyright protection so they can be used, reproduced, and performed without payment or even permission. The President's Commission on Obscenity and Pornography may not have liked it in 1970 when publisher Earl Kemp decided to illustrate its report with erotic content, but there was no "bundle of rights" for the government to assert. Kemp did go to jail for distributing the material, however.[28]

Bedrock Law
Documents and other works created by the U.S. government are placed in the public domain unless produced by a third party working for the government.

This copyright restriction applies only to the federal government, not the states,[29] and it only applies to works produced by the government and not those purchased by it. For example, the Federal Communications Commission might produce a research paper on smartphone use, and it would not be copyrighted. If the FCC paid an independent researcher to produce such a paper, then it could be subject to copyright.

Copyright Registration

Copyright exists from the moment a creative work is fixed in a tangible medium, such as a poem when it is first written or when a song is recorded. It does not need commercial publication to be copyrighted. Even displaying a copyright notice on the work is no longer required since the United States joined the Berne Convention in 1988.

Formal registration with the U.S. Copyright Office in the Library of Congress is important if the owner plans to sue for infringement. And affixing the copyright notice lets people know the author is claiming ownership, which makes it harder for takers to argue their use was unintentional and innocent.

Copyright Notice
Under older laws, prominently displayed notices were required including the copyright symbol ©, year, and the owner's name. While these notices are still a good idea, notification rules are no longer in effect.

A proper copyright notice should prominently display the word "Copyright" (or abbreviation "Copr.") and/or the copyright symbol © with the year of first publication and the copyright owner's name – e.g., Copyright © 2025 Olivia Brown. Using both the word "Copyright" and the symbol is useful for international copyright agreements.

Officially registering the work with the U.S. Copyright Office also provides important benefits. First, it provides *prima facie* evidence of the copyright's validity by creating a public record of the authorship and ownership. Second, it makes clear the date of creation for determining the term length. Third, it provides useful information to prospective licensees. Finally, registration makes it possible for agents to seize foreign pirated copies. Perhaps most importantly, it's a prerequisite to filing a lawsuit for infringement. Both the original work and certificate must be on file with the Copyright Office before its owner can sue for actual damages; show losses in revenue, and claim the profits taken by the infringer.[30]

28. Kemp was not found guilty for copyright infringement but was convicted on other charges. *See* John Semonche, *Censoring Sex: A Historical Journey through American Media* (Lanham, MD: Rowman & Littlefield, 2007).
29. Although in 2020, the U.S. Supreme Court ruled that Georgia does not have a copyright over its annotated legal code. They said that official works of the Georgia legislature could not be copyrighted as that would deny citizens of knowledge of those laws. The "government edicts doctrine" does not extend to works such as the annotations in the Official Code of Georgia Annotated. *Georgia v. Public.Resource.Org, Inc.*, No. 18–1150, 590 U.S. (2020).
30. "In establishing the infringer's profits, the copyright owner is required to present proof only of the infringer's gross revenue, and the infringer is required to prove his or her deductible expenses and the elements of profit attributable to factors other than the copyrighted work." 17 U.S.C. § 504(b).

Bedrock Law
An original fixed expression has copyright protection from the moment of its creation, but to recover damages for infringement, the work must be registered with the Copyright Office in the Library of Congress.

The Copyright Act allows the owner to recover attorney's fees and statutory damages – ranging from $750 to $30,000 at the low end; but that figure can shoot up to $150,000 for willful and repeated infringements.[31] Opting for statutory damages is advantageous, but the work must be registered before the infringement began or within three months after its first publication. For that reason, it is wise to register within 90 days of publication.

Most copyrights can be registered online by uploading the work and paying a $45 fee.[32] The "old fashioned" forms are more expensive[33] because the paper processing requires more time and expense. Those filing electronically receive certification sooner than paper submitters. Courts consider the copyright term to begin the date the Copyright Office receives the request.

Copyright Duration

Copyright protection lasts the life of the author plus 70 years, depending on when the work was created and other factors.[34] Congress has periodically chosen to extend the length of time for copyright. In 1976, Congress made U.S. copyright protection conform to international standards by making the length of a copyright equal to the life of the author plus 50 years. This approach made it more difficult to know exactly when a copyright expired because it also required knowing when the author's life had expired.

The most recent change in the length of copyright came in 1998 when Congress passed the Sonny Bono Copyright Term Extension Act, which added 20 years to the copyright's duration, making it the life of the author plus 70 years. The law was named for a deceased congressman and former singer-songwriter, half of the Sonny and Cher pop music duo. Bono was supported in this legislation by the Disney corporation that sought to extend its protection for the cartoon copyright, *Steamboat Willie* (Mickey Mouse).

Opponents of the extension argued Congress was protecting large corporate interests. In 2001, a group filed suit claiming this extension violated the Constitution's provision to secure exclusive rights for "limited times." The Supreme Court ruled 7–2 it was constitutional, and Congress was within its authority to extend the term to the author's life plus 70 years.[35]

Works for Hire
Copyrightable material owned by a firm or business and made as a condition of employment.

Copyright law also distinguishes the duration of works created on a "work for hire" basis as 95 years after publication.[36] In this case, authorship and therefore the copyright, goes to the business or organization that employed the author. For example, a reporter's work belongs to the newspaper or station that employs them; public relations and advertising agencies typically own the copyright of the promotional campaigns created by their employees.

A work for hire exists when a work is created as part of the employee's regular duties or when the written agreement states their work is made for hire.[37] There is some ambiguity over works created by freelance writers and photographers. Ownership of those materials generally go to the author unless otherwise stipulated in a freelance work for hire agreement.

31. *Id.* § 504(b). Yet if "the court finds that such infringer was not aware and had no reason to believe that his or her acts constituted an infringement of copyright, the court in its discretion may reduce the award of statutory damages to a sum of not less than $200."
32. $45 applies to a single work, single author, online application. All other electronic filings are $65. For the full schedule of fees, *see* www.copyright.gov/about/fees.html.
33. $125 at this time. *Id.*
34. For example, the copyright for works created prior to January 1, 1978, is 95 years. Works created by more than one person (joint authors) are based on the life of the last living author plus 70 years. Anonymous and pseudonymous works as well as "works for hire" enjoy copyright protection for 95 years from the year of first publication.
35. *Eldred v. Ashcroft*, 537 U.S. 186 (2003).
36. Or 120 years after creation, whichever is shorter. 17 U.S.C. § 302(c). This term is also true for anonymous or pseudonymous works, for which there are no identifiable authors and therefore no ability to calculate the duration of the term based on their death.
37. U.S. Copyright Office, supra note 7 *at* 3.

Bedrock Law

Works for hire become the intellectual property of the employer when produced in the scope of the employee's duties or forged in an express, written agreement.

Works for Hire According to the Copyright Act of 1976

A "work made for hire" is

1 a work prepared by an employee within the scope of their employment; or

2 a work specially ordered or commissioned for use as a contribution to a collective work, as a part of a motion picture or other audiovisual work, as a translation, as a supplementary work, as a compilation, as an instructional text, as a test, as answer material for a test, or as an atlas, if the parties expressly agree in a written instrument signed by them that the work shall be considered a work made for hire.[38]

Works for hire are generally those copyrightable works that are made as a condition of employment. This means that the author of the work is a salaried employee who produces the work while on company time using company resources.

The Supreme Court ruled in 1989 on whether a sculptor commissioned to create a Nativity scene depicting the Holy Family as modern-day homeless people was entitled to the copyright of his work. The not-for-profit group commissioning the work claimed it was a work for hire and therefore belonged to the group. The Court unanimously decided the case by examining the Copyright Act to show Congress enumerated nine types of works for hire, none of which could be interpreted to include that sculpture.[39]

Magazines often purchase articles and photos from freelancers. Who holds the copyright on these works? Unless a contract clause holds differently, the author of a freelance work owns the copyright and merely sells the one-time publication rights to the periodical. Increasingly though, publications are writing contracts to require their authors provide more than just a one-time publication before they will consent to publish their works. The issue became acute in the digital age, when a photograph or article published in a magazine could be accessed later in an electronic database.

In the early 1990s, six freelance writers sold articles to *The New York Times*, *Newsday*, and *Time*. The publications unquestionably had the right to publish their articles in print, but their work also was made available through electronic databases like Lexis/Nexis. The freelancers, led by Jonathan Tasini, were frustrated that the publications continued to profit from the databases offering their works for purchase while freelancers received no additional compensation. The U.S. Supreme Court sided with the freelancers holding their copyright was violated by the online publications.[40] Publishers paying freelance writers were only entitled to the original use unless a contract stipulated otherwise.

The decision in the *Tasini* case produced an uptick in contracts granting publishers the right to use freelancers' work in databases without additional compensation. Of course, freelancers still have the right to decline such terms, but then they risk losing work to others willing to agree to such terms.

The effect of one small but significant change in the 1976 law was keenly felt by recording artists. Congress added a Copyright Termination Right provision to allow copyright holders to revoke any previous agreements they had made to transfer their copyrights after 35 years.[41] For example, if a singer-songwriter signed with a record label for a small amount of revenue and then had a huge hit, the artist would love to gain more earnings from the song's popularity, but the existing contract would not require the record label to oblige – at least not until 35 years passed.

38. 17 U.S.C.§ 101.
39. *Community for Creative Non-Violence v. Reid*, 490 U.S.730 (1989).
40. *New York Times v. Tasini*, 533 U.S.483 (2001).
41. 17 U.S.C. § 203.

This "second bite of the apple" idea was intended to allow artists who lacked negotiating power in their early careers a chance to renegotiate or void a contract once they become more established, and likely more bankable. This idea, however, flew in the face of another principle. A contract is written in perpetuity, but the copyright holder is allowed to terminate it because a statute – the Copyright Act – says so. In the hierarchy of law, statutes supersede contracts, so this Copyright Act provision logically would prevail.

Because the Act went into effect in 1978, those holding a copyright for 35 years or more would begin to invoke this right starting in 2013. This calculation made record labels nervous thinking their copyrights would be terminated,[42] and some feared lawsuits "could change the music industry."[43]

It is a complicated rule. On the one hand, rights may be terminated only within a five-year window of time once the 35-year clock has run out of time, and only after the author has given proper notice.[44] In addition, a work for hire cannot use the provision, and joint works require most of the authors to join in the termination. The legal record is mixed.

The heirs of J. Fred Coots successfully terminated the copyright agreement with EMI for the song "Santa Claus is Coming to Town."[45] Copyright termination action also was part of a lawsuit filed by actor-writer Harry Shearer over the film *This is Spinal Tap*.[46] Smokey Robinson terminated contracts to his music including "My Girl,"[47] and Sir Paul McCartney sued Sony to regain control of the works he cocreated with John Lennon.[48]

Licensing Performance Rights

A composer who writes a piece of music owns the entire bundle of rights including performance rights, but the collection of fees from restaurants, music halls, or radio stations playing those songs poses a problem that licensing the music was meant to solve. For that reason, a group of musicians created an organization to protect their rights, the American Society of Composers, Authors and Publishers (ASCAP) in 1914.

Licensing the use of music in restaurants, malls, grocery stores, and even universities is required for "performance" in public spaces. The addition of radio performance rights sent music revenues skyrocketing for ASCAP in 1923. Radio execs became frustrated with ASCAP's terms since they had no alternative to broadcast copyrighted music, but that all changed in 1939.

American radio broadcasters founded Broadcast Music Incorporated (BMI) to upend the ASCAP monopoly. A third licensor, the Society of European Stage Authors and Composers (SESAC) started to license European authors in 1930, and its library of U.S. composers has

42. Eriq Gardner, "Copyright Battle Comes Home," *Law.com*, October 8, 2009, citing prominent intellectual property attorney Ross Charap.
43. Eriq Gardner, "How the Legal Fight over 'Y.M.C.A.' Could Change the Music Industry (Analysis)," *Hollywood Reporter*, August 17, 2011.
44. *See, e.g.*, R.B. Jefferson, "The Music Professionals Guide to Copyright Termination Rights," *Lawyers Rock*, October 1, 2017, *at* www.lawyersrock.com/copyright-termination-rights/; Brittany L. Kaplan-Peterson, "Copyright Termination: A Primer," *Cowan, DeBaets, Abrahams & Sheppard, LLP (CDAS)*, January 18, 2017, *at* https://cdas.com/copyright-termination-prime/.
45. The song would have entered public domain decades ago were it not for a series of copyright extensions. Eriq Gardner, "Appeals Court Rules EMI's 'Santa Claus Is Coming to Town' Rights Terminate Next Year," *Hollywood Reporter*, October 8, 2015.
46. Eriq Gardner, "Harry Shearer Files $125M 'Spinal Tap' Fraud Suit, Copyright Termination," *Hollywood Reporter*, October 18, 2016.
47. Eriq Gardner, "Smokey Robinson Settling with Ex-Wife over Terminated Song Rights," *Hollywood Reporter*, December 12, 2014.
48. Ray Kelly, "Paul McCartney Sues Sony to Regain Rights to Beatles Songs," *Hollywood Reporter*, January 18, 2017. McCartney and Sony reached an out-of-court settlement. "Paul McCartney Settles with Sony/ATV to Reclaim Beatles' Song Copyright," *Fortune*, June 30, 2017.

grown in recent years. Today, almost all U.S. songwriters license their music performance rights through either ASCAP, BMI, or SESAC.

When a songwriter signs with a licensor, that agency takes responsibility for collecting fees and distributing them to its members based on some established formula. The vast majority are for blanket usage of music.

A blanket license allows users to pay a flat fee for an entire year's worth of music regardless of how much they use. Users pay based on their revenues and what portion of their business depends on the use of licensed music. Typically, licensors ask the establishments they license, radio and TV stations, bars, and restaurants, to keep track of all the music they use during a sample week. Those fees help to fairly distribute royalties to copyright holders.

The licensing agencies collect the fees, but they also work to expand the list of establishments paying fees. They travel the country in search of bars, restaurants, and stores – even local theater – looking for places that are "profiting" from copyrighted music without paying for it.[49]

Violations can cost hundreds of thousands of dollars to businesses in terms of fines, legal fees, and penalties, causing some businesses to have to close. When venues are unaware of their obligation, licensing agencies may "educate" them by offering contracts for blanket licenses rather than taking them to court for infringement.

Congress passed the Fairness in Music Licensing Act in 1998 to balance the rights of music authors and the needs of small businesses. It sets an arbitrary size limit on restaurants, bars, and grills. Any such establishment smaller than 3,750 square feet does not need a license to play radio or TV music. Retail establishments smaller than 2,000 square feet also qualify for an exemption to play broadcast music.[50] Otherwise, any non-broadcast recorded music or live performance must be licensed, even if the business is small.

It is important to note what licensing agencies do not do. They do not handle rights other than performance. There is some misunderstanding among media industries about this circumstance. A radio station paying a blanket license to ASCAP, BMI, and SESAC has permission to perform (play) all the music in their libraries, but it would be a violation for that station to reproduce digital copies of the music and give it away to listeners (reproduction) or to use a portion for the music bed of a commercial (derivative work).

It's also important to view this factor from the songwriter's perspective. Imagine you wrote a song about a topic you feel strongly about. You want it to get as much airplay as possible, not only because your licensing agency will pay you more but because you want the world to hear what you have to say and feel in this music. Suppose someone takes your song and uses it for some unrelated purpose, like a dog food commercial. Imagine an offensively inane video – animated dogs singing or dancing to your melody and lyrics. As the songwriter, shouldn't you have the right to say, "No way!"?

Well, you do.

Putting music to video is known as synchronization, which is a derivative work – part of the author's bundle of rights. Authors have the right to allow their music to be performed while at the same time preventing other uses.

There are tales of artists who refused to allow their works to be used in commercials at any price, and then others who "sold out" for huge payments. Whether these stories are true or fantasy is beside the point. It is the copyright holder who has final say over the work's use.

49. *See, e.g.*, Gordon Firemark, "ASCAP Sues Restaurants Over Music Use . . . Are Theatres Next?" *Law Office of Gordon P. Firemark*, August 23, 2007, *at* https://firemark.com/2007/08/23/ascap-sues-restaurants-over-music-use-are-theatres-next/; Sergio Bichao, "BMI Song Lawsuits Make Rounds in Jersey Bars," *USA Today*, June 10, 2015.
50. 17 U.S.C. § 110 (5)(B). Larger establishments of any kind may play radio or TV music if the audio is limited to no more than six loudspeakers (and no more than four in one room), and any visual display is limited to no more than four audiovisual devices – one per room – and no greater than 55 inches in screen size.

Synchronization

A synchronization (or sync) license allows the licensee to combine copyrighted music with visual elements. Synchronization is a type of derivative work.

Political Candidates' Use of Music

Political campaigns have long been energized by the unique power of music to inspire and motivate voters. George Washington effectively used the song "God Save Great Washington" (a parody of "God Save the King"), Franklin Roosevelt lifted spirits with "Happy Days are Here Again,"[51] and John F. Kennedy roused his supporters with Frank Sinatra's "High Hopes."[52] Presidential candidate Kamala Harris inspired her campaign launch with Beyoncé's "Freedom."

Yet an unauthorized use of music in presidential campaigns has also produced a long litany of disputes between musicians and politicians: Bruce Springsteen versus Ronald Reagan ("Born in the USA"), Sting versus George W. Bush ("Brand New Day"), Sam & Dave versus Barack Obama ("Hold On I'm Coming"), Van Halen versus John McCain ("Right Now"), and R.E.M. versus Donald Trump ("It's the End of the World as We Know It").[53]

Whenever the campaign or the venue (e.g., stadium, arena) purchases a blanket license from ASCAP and does nothing more than play the song at rallies, the musician can object and share their aversion toward the candidate, but the candidate's use is lawfully protected.

In 2015, singer-songwriter Neil Young complained when Donald Trump used "Rockin' in the Free World" at his candidacy announcement. The Trump campaign quickly responded, promising to stop using it but noting how it paid ASCAP for a blanket license and was on solid legal ground to use it.[54] Yet at Trump's inaugural in 2017, Queen's "We Are the Champions" was played despite claims this political use wasn't authorized. Elton John requested the campaign not play his music at rallies. In 2018, Rihanna sent the Trump campaign a cease-and-desist letter after they played her song "Don't Stop the Music." And again in 2020, Tom Petty's estate sent the president a cease-and-desist letter after his supporters played Petty's song "I Won't Back Down" at a campaign rally.[55]

It's quite another matter when a candidate uses music in an advertisement. Because ASCAP does not license synchronization, a candidate cannot claim to have their permission to use music in commercials. In 2016, presidential candidate Mike Huckabee ran a political ad with Adele's song "Hello" while changing the words and showing shots of the former Arkansas governor on the campaign trail. The campaign immediately deleted the video when the singer-songwriter complained, even though it was only a web video shot on smartphones.[56] Whether a video is played on television or online, there are copyright implications.[57]

51. ASCAP, "Using Music in Political Campaigns: What You Should Know," *Guidelines*, *at* www.ascap.com/~/media/files/pdf/advocacy-legislation/political_campaign.pdf.
52. Charles Stockdale & John Harrington, "35 Musicians Who Famously Told Politicians: Don't Use My Song," *USA Today*, July 16, 2018.
53. *Id.*
54. Katie Atkinson, "Donald Trump Won't Use Neil Young's 'Rockin' in the Free World' Again," *Hollywood Reporter*, June 17, 2015.
55. Isabel Togoh, "Tom Petty's Family Send Trump Cease and Desist over His Use of 'I Won't Back Down' at Tulsa Rally," *Forbes*, June 21, 2020.
56. Andrew Flanagan, "Adele: Donald Trump Does Not Have Permission to Use My Music in His Campaign," *Hollywood Reporter*, February 1, 2016.
57. Meredith Filak, "Campaigns, Copyrights, and Compositions: A Politician's Guide to Music on the Campaign Trail," *Public Knowledge*, July 6, 2011, *at* www.publicknowledge.org/blog/campaigns-copyrights-and-compositions-a-politicians-guide-to-music-on-the-campaign-trail/; *See also*, ASCAP's guidelines for using music in political campaigns, *supra* note 57.

Relying on cover bands is one solution, as it was for the Republican National Committee at its 2024 convention.[58] By having a cover band on stage perform the songs, the RNC avoided the copyright issues from using the original sound recordings. They only needed a PRO (performing rights organization) license for the venue. The idea is musicians who don't support a politician are less offended when their own voice and performance aren't featured.[59]

Production Music

Like any other production, low-budget video productions need music. Some corporate and industrial videos lack the robust budgets needed to pay rights fees for popular music as feature film studios routinely do. Low-budget videos usually turn to production music libraries that provide everything from a few seconds of music to hours of downloadable tracks. As with performance rights, synchronization rights can be purchased on a per-use or "needledrop pricing" basis. There is also a way to pay a blanket-licensing fee covering unlimited use of any music in the production library.

Some libraries provide buyout licenses. Unlike blanket licenses requiring the payment of annual fees, buyout libraries own production music purchased in perpetuity. A quick Internet search for "production music" yields dozens of companies that provide stock music. This option may be cheaper, but the music quickly ages in the long run.

Buyout License
Unlike blanket licenses requiring the payment of annual fees, buyout libraries purchase music in perpetuity.

Derivative Works

Derivative works can result in more money for an author than any royalties resulting from performance rights. Every band that records someone else's music – a "cover" song – creates a derivative. The band is creating a new work based on the author's original, "deriving" new material and thus owing the original author some form of compensation.[60]

A movie based on a book is a derivative work and can bring in more revenues than the original work, especially in a worldwide market. Not only are movies defined as derivative works if based on books, but the characters in those books and movies can spawn other creative works required to pay for use of the intellectual property.

It is well-known among television writers that it can be profitable to introduce a character. If that character recurs in future episodes, the writer responsible for the character's creation continues to collect royalties.

The Star Trek franchise demonstrated the value of derivative works. Gene Roddenberry created the original series in the 1960s, and the show ran for only three years on the NBC television network. After it was canceled in 1969, it ran in syndication and continues to this day. Gene Roddenberry died in 1991, but because copyright continues beyond the death of the author, his estate continues to receive royalty payments from his creation. But the story does not end there. Movies based on the TV show were produced beginning in 1979. Other TV series based on the Star Trek concept, but without the original characters, were created, starting with *Star Trek: The Next Generation* in 1987.

After Roddenberry's death, Star Trek movies and TV shows were produced, obviously without his input, but based on the original, so his estate received remuneration. Klingons,

58. Cody Mello-Klein, "Can Donald Trump or Joe Biden Play Whatever Music They Want at a Rally or Convention? Legal Expert Says It's More Complicated," *Northeastern Global News*, July 17, 2024, *at* https://news.northeastern.edu/2024/07/17/music-at-political-rallies-trump/.
59. *Id.*
60. Licensing is rather easy via Harry Fox Agency, www.songfile.com/.

Vulcans, and Star Fleet, as well as their specific attributes, are protected intellectual property, and so their use requires a contract and some form of compensation.

It's not just TV shows and movies, but also derivative products based on the original that require licensing. If a new Star Trek movie is released, the licensing of toys, costumes, and even plastic drink cups based on its characters yield royalty payments for the copyright holder. Star Trek merchandise easily rivals the royalties paid for performance or reproduction rights.

An Exception to Distribution Rights

Doctrine of First Sale
After a particular copy of a work is sold, the author no longer controls that copy. The author still owns the intellectual property, but the copy of it belongs to the purchaser.

Just like reproduction and derivative works, copyright owners are empowered to exercise control over the distribution of their works. A book author could give exclusive distribution rights to one bookstore, for example. Authors usually don't do this because there is no financial incentive for them to exclude others, but there are times when an exclusive release of intellectual property to a particular distributor is part of a marketing strategy.

Congress did create one exception to distribution rights, which is known as the **doctrine of first sale**. Once a copy of a work is sold, the buyer controls use of that copy, even though the copyright owner holds the rights to determine what is done with the original, use of the copy that is sold is out of their hands.

The doctrine of first sale strikes a balance between the copyright holder's rights and the purchaser's rights. The basic premise is that the author was compensated in the original sale, and subsequent redistribution of it does not entitle the author to further payment. It is important to note this principle does not apply to making copies; it applies only to the resale of a work.

In 1984, Congress passed a statute that prohibited redistributing records (the old vinyl sort). And a 1990 amendment restricted the redistribution of computer software. In both cases, the essence of the rule was to discourage violation of copyright by making illegal copies rather than just using the content and returning it to the owner.

In recent years, there has been a good deal of disagreement over computer software. With the ability to easily duplicate the digital files, software creators recognize the potential loss of millions of dollars in sales. To bolster their claims for protection, software companies have used shrink-wrap licenses, meaning as soon as customers remove the software's wrapping, they are bound by the terms and conditions on the box.

EULA
End User License Agreement indicating terms and conditions of software use.

Given the downloading mode of software applications, shrink-wrap is known in that context as a click-wrap license. In either case, the End User License Agreement (EULA) implies an agreement exists between the software buyer and the licensor once software is unwrapped or downloaded. Opinions vary as to the enforceability of EULA "contracts" because the terms are usually not available for review before the software purchase is made.

Is Digital Music "Licensed" or "Sold"?

Distribution services like Amazon and iTunes might appear to be selling digital files, but if that were the case then they wouldn't be able to delete them from users' devices, which they have been able to do. Despite the fact many users download these services believing they own the products they pay for the licensing agreements dictate otherwise.[61]

In fact, the Federal Trade Commission advises consumers to always check the fine print when clicking to "buy" a digital item, whether that's a song, video game, e-book, or movie. It's often merely a license to access the content. You may have access to it

61. "When You Buy Digital Content on Amazon or iTunes, You Don't Exactly Own It," *Los Angeles Times*, May 13, 2016.

only while you have an active account with the platform or website that sold it, or only for as long as that platform or website stays in business.

Digital Rights Management (DRM) software, which is attached to many digital items, is the thing that makes it impossible to play a video game on a different console brand.[62] The FTC also warns "if the seller itself has licensing issues with the content you bought, then your own license to use the digital item can become worthless."

Copyright Royalty Board

When a global artist as popular as Taylor Swift rejects a popular channel to reach her fans, then something is definitely up. In 2014, the popular songstress announced in an op-ed piece for the *Wall Street Journal* she was pulling her albums from the music streaming service Spotify.[63] Swift explained how her album sales had been hurt by what she saw as the enemies of musical artists and composers: "piracy, file sharing and streaming."

This battle between streaming webcasters and musical performers dates to 2007, when a legal authority known as the Copyright Royalty Board (CRB) set new rates for webcasting that were lower than what the musicians desired. Basically, commercial webcasters and streaming tech companies like Pandora and Spotify agreed to pay a rate based on the number of unique listeners and the number of record plays. The problem for musicians was the royalty received through this means was far less than the money made from fans downloading their albums or songs.

The CRB is a tribunal of three judges that decides the terms and rates for copyright statutory licenses. It was created by the Library of Congress to resolve such disputes. Songwriters and performers like Swift want to be sure that the CRB does not favor tech companies that use their popular tunes to sell Amazon Echos or Google Home devices.

It's challenging to find the correct rate that compensates artists without gouging their audience. Setting the streaming rates for a webcast is a contentious business that can put some webcasters out of business if the rates are set too high. Despite the pleas of artists to raise those rates, there is a delicate balance in determining the correct figure.

What happened in 1998 added to the royalty controversy when the U.S. Congress passed the Digital Millennium Copyright Act (DMCA) that slapped an additional fee for satellite and Internet radio, and that separated digital streams from radio broadcasters.

Rates are reviewed every five years. In 2018, the CRB ruled on-demand subscription streaming services (such as Spotify and Apple Music) had to increase their percentage of revenue paid to songwriters and publishers by almost 5%, the largest rate increase in the history of the CRB. Some streaming services appealed, but the decision was affirmed in 2023.[64]

Copyright Infringement

Bringing a copyright lawsuit against an infringer requires a few steps and elements to prove in court. As noted, the copyright must be registered with the Copyright Office and registered prior to the infringement occurring (or within 90 days of first publication) to recover

62. Amy Herbert, "Consumer Alert: Do You Really Own the Digital Items You Paid For?" *Federal Trade Commission*, April 17, 2024.
63. "For Taylor Swift, the Future of Music Is a Love Story," *Wall Street Journal*, July 7, 2014.
64. Murray Stassen, "Copyright Royalty Board Confirms Streaming Royalty Rate for Songwriters for 2018–2022," *Music Business Worldwide*, May 26, 2023, *at* https://www.musicbusinessworldwide.com/copyright-royalty-board-confirms-streaming-royalty-rate-for-songwriters-for-2018-2022/.

statutory damages. The lawsuit should be brought within three years because copyrights have a statute of limitations.

What about infringements that are ongoing? Under the separate-accrual rule that attends the copyright statute of limitations, when a defendant has committed successive violations, each infringing act starts a new limitations period. So each time an infringing work – such as a film or book – is reproduced or distributed, the infringer commits a new wrong, and each wrong gives rise to a discrete claim that is actionable for three years.[65]

In general, plaintiffs discovering an infringement should not wait years to file a lawsuit because the "doctrine of laches" may apply – a concept in equity that means a claim must not be enforced if there has been a long delay that harms the defendant.[66]

Pursuing a lawsuit against an infringer can be costly and time-consuming, so it is important to assess one's actual damages as well as prospects for winning when deciding if litigation is the best course of action. Most cases are settled outside of court for an agreed-upon lump sum in exchange for releasing all legal claims. Other remedies such as eliminating the infringing works or stopping further infringements may achieve a solution. A mediator is useful in settling the dispute at this stage. Otherwise, an attorney who ideally specializes in intellectual property law is needed for the matter to proceed as a lawsuit filing.

Proving Infringement

To establish copyright infringement, the holder of the copyright (plaintiff) must prove the following elements:

- ownership of a valid copyright, and
- copying of the constituent elements of the work that are original, as shown by
  - access to the work by the defendant, and
  - direct or circumstantial evidence of copying, such as substantial similarity.

Showing the court that one is indeed the owner of a valid copyright should be easy with the certificate obtained from the U.S. Copyright Office as *prima facie* evidence. But having registered the copyright doesn't necessarily mean the government determined it is an original work that could be legitimately copyrighted. When the U.S. Copyright Office registers a work, it does not go back searching through the hundreds of millions of copyrighted works to find if there is one of substantial similarity.

It must then be proven the infringer copied the original work without permission. Two things are required here. First, the plaintiff needs to show how the defendant had access to the work to be able to copy it. Some reasonable opportunity to copy the work must exist; otherwise, similarity in the defendant's work might simply be a coincidence.

Failing to show the defendant had access can end a lawsuit. A band complained that Dua Lipa's "Levitating" song borrowed its core hook from one of their songs, but they dropped their lawsuit in 2023 after the judge said there was no indication that Dua Lipa or anyone involved in creating "Levitating" had access to the challenger's lesser-known tune, "Live Your Life."[67]

65. This does not mean that the previous harms are continuing. For separately accruing harm, each new act must cause harm to the plaintiff over and above the harm that any earlier acts caused. *See Petrella v. Metro-Goldwyn-Mayer, Inc.*, 572 U.S. 663, 668 (2014).
66. The doctrine of laches is based upon the maxim that "equity aids the vigilant and not those who slumber on their rights." Knowledge, unreasonable delay, and change of positions are essential elements. Laches requires an element of estoppel or neglect that prejudices the defendant. *Black's Law Dictionary*.
67. Bill Donahue, "Dua Lipa's Copyright Accusers Drop 'Levitating' Infringement Lawsuit," *Billboard*, June 7, 2023.

Sometimes a plaintiff can prove access by presenting a chain of events theory, showing how the work was passed through various people to the defendant. Another approach is to point to a "striking" similarity between the works as apparent proof that access to the work surely must have occurred.[68]

Of course, if the plaintiff's work had been published and was therefore available, then defendant's access to it may simply be presumed. The plaintiff would not have to prove the infringer read the novel, viewed the advertisement designs on the web, or listened to the podcast series. If the work was unpublished, such as a draft of a manuscript, musical composition, recording, photo, or sketch, then the plaintiff must explain how the defendant was able to read, hear, or see the copyrighted work.

A plaintiff is likely to enjoy more success in proving the defendant had access to their work when the work is not only published but is well-known. This was a hard lesson for musician George Harrison, former member of The Beatles, who fought for years in court to prove he did not copy the former No. 1 song "He's so Fine" recorded by the Chiffons when he recorded his hit song "My Sweet Lord" in 1970.[69]

Harrison explained how he got the idea for "My Sweet Lord" after a concert when he slipped away and started to play some guitar chords around the words "Hallelujah" and "Hare Krishna." Over the following week, he worked with others to polish the song.

In its ruling, the court determined while the lyrics differed, the harmonies of both songs were identical, and several repetitions of short musical phrases or motifs in "My Sweet Lord" were just the same as in "He's So Fine."[70] The judge agreed Harrison did not deliberately or consciously copy "He's so Fine." But given the popularity of "He's So Fine" and Harrison's awareness of the song, the court concluded he had "subconsciously" plagiarized the work and infringed its copyright. The matter was put to rest and damages reduced to less than $600,000 when Harrison's former manager attained the ownership rights to "He's so Fine."

In addition to proving access, the plaintiff must show direct or circumstantial evidence that copying occurred. Direct evidence consists of testimony from others or documentation clearly showing the work had been copied. The uncovering of such evidence or witness to copying are less likely at this stage. More often, the plaintiff provides indirect or circumstantial evidence, such as showing a "substantial similarity" exists between the works.

Substantial Similarity

Proving substantial similarity ends up at the crux of many copyright lawsuits. Cases where someone makes an exact copy of a copyrighted work are complicated enough, but the matter becomes even more difficult when a contested work is similar, but not the same as a copyrighted work.

The vague measure used by the law is substantial similarity. The plain meaning suggests a court must make a subjective judgment about whether a challenged work is "too much" like the original. But how much is too much is not clearly defined. There certainly must be more than minor similarities between the two works, rising above a *de minimis* threshold. Simply sharing the same song title is not enough. For example, Nickelback prevailed in a 2024 case brought by a challenger with a song of the same title – "Rockstar."

Courts and legal scholars have tried to devise tests over the years to clarify a standard for substantial similarity. Circuit Judge Learned Hand believed a "test for infringement of

68. *See, e.g., Arnstein v. Porter*, 154 F.2d 464, 468 (2d Cir. 1946) where the court considered "striking" similarity. "If evidence of access is absent, the similarities must be so striking as to preclude the possibility that plaintiff and defendant independently arrived at the same result." Here, a plaintiff shows that "the similarity is of a type which will preclude any explanation other than that of copying." *Selle v. Gibb*, 741 F.2d 896, 905 (7th Cir. 1984).
69. *Bright Tunes Music Corp. v. Harrisongs Music, Ltd.*, 420 F. Supp. 177 (1976).
70. *Id.* at 178.

a copyright is of necessity vague"[71] and offered one of the more famous definitions over 60 years ago. He observed a substantial similarity between two works exists where "the ordinary observer, unless he set out to detect the disparities, would be disposed to overlook them, and regard their aesthetic appeal as the same."[72]

The Second Circuit adopted an "ordinary observer test," which seeks to discover "whether an average lay observer would recognize the alleged copy as having been appropriated from the copyrighted work."[73]

In addition, the court will apply a "total concept and feel test" to the two works. Depending on the nature of the work, the court will scrutinize for similarities by going beyond just a comparison of expressions in isolation and the overall use of both its protectable and non-protectable elements. That way an infringer could not skirt copyright liability by copying available non-protected elements while carefully taking only a minimum of the original's protectable elements.[74] And for fiction works, the court will examine them for similarities to see how they express abstract concepts, such as structure, mood, details, and characterization.[75]

The federal appeals court in California hears a lot of copyright infringement cases and has devised a similar two-part approach for assessing substantial similarity. The Ninth Circuit applies an extrinsic test, which is an objective measure that considers expert testimony and breaks down the work to its constituent elements. It compares the similarities of the expressive elements for both works, such as "plot, themes, dialogue, mood, setting, pace, characters, and sequence of events."[76] Once the extrinsic test is done, a more subjective intrinsic test considers whether an "ordinary, reasonable audience" would find the two works substantially similar in "total concept and feel" based on the testimony and evidence presented.[77]

Regardless of a federal court's jurisdiction, there are some common approaches in use. While expert testimony is certainly admissible, courts principally ask if the average lay observer would regard the suspect work as a copy of the original. Those similarities must be found in the creative expression and not elements such as ideas, facts, and scènes à faire – except for their expressive qualities. Not every detail must be copied to be substantially similar; some differences are to be expected, and the dissimilarities do not automatically relieve an infringer of liability.

Dan Brown's best-selling novel *The Da Vinci Code* offers a good example of how a federal court might judge substantial similarity when it comes to literary works. Novelist Lewis Perdue took Brown to court,[78] claiming *The Da Vinci Code* infringed his 2000 book, *Daughter of God*.[79] The issue came down to whether the novels were substantially similar.

The court scrutinized in detail the two works for similarities in their thematic expression, plot, characters, sequence, pace, setting, total concept, and feel. While both novels are

71. *Peter Pan Fabrics, Inc. v. Martin Weiner Corp.*, 274 F.2d 487, 489 (2d Cir. 1960).
72. *Id.*
73. *Warner Bros. Inc. v. American Broadcasting Companies, Inc.*, 654 F.2d 204, 208 (2d Cir. 1981). If there are both protectable and non-protectable elements in the work, then the Second Circuit may apply a "discerning ordinary observer test" where the court considers only whether the protectable elements – standing alone – are substantially similar. *Hogan v. DC Comics*, 48 F. Supp. 2d 298, 309 (S.D.N.Y. 1999); *Knitwaves, Inc. v. Lollytogs Ltd.*, 71 F.3d 996, 1002 (2d Cir. 1995).
74. Aaron Lichter, "Clarifying the Liability Threshold in Copyright Infringement Claims," *N.Y.U. Proceedings*, *at* https://proceedings.nyumootcourt.org/2016/10/clarifying-the-liability-threshold-in-copyright-infringement-claims/.
75. *Id.*
76. *Kouf v. Walt Disney Pictures & Television*, 16 F.3d 1042, 1045 (9th Cir. 1994). Here the court examined for substantial similarity the works *Honey, I Shrunk the Kids* and *The Formula*, finding the two works to be dissimilar in plot, themes, sequence of events, characters, dialogue, mood, setting, and pace.
77. *Id.*
78. *Brown v. Perdue*, 2005 U.S. Dist. LEXIS 15995 (S.D.N.Y., August 4, 2005).
79. Perdue also claimed Brown infringed on his earlier novel from 1983, *The Da Vinci Legacy*, but Perdue offered no evidence or argument for this, and the judge dismissed that claim. *Id.*

mystery thrillers, *Daughter of God* is more action-packed with gunfights, violent deaths, and sex scenes that are not present in *The Da Vinci Code*, which was portrayed as more of an intellectual treasure hunt. Perdue produced emails from "lay observers" who felt Brown had plagiarized his work, and a forensic linguist supported the claims.[80] But the court concluded a reasonable average lay observer would not find *The Da Vinci Code* was substantially similar to *Daughter of God*.[81]

The factors used to determine whether two works are substantially similar will vary for other works, such as music, photos, and graphic illustrations. Careful attention to the "total concept and feel" affords some guidance, but the decision-making process is often unclear, ad hoc, and subject to the unpredictable conclusions of juries and judges.

Substantial similarity came under scrutiny in a highly publicized music case, raising concern about its chilling effect on creators and performers of popular music. In 2015, a federal court found "Blurred Lines" songwriters Robin Thicke and Pharrell Williams guilty of infringing a Marvin Gaye song.[82] The Gaye family accused Thicke and Williams of copying the "feel and sound" of "Got to Give It Up." The original verdict was a whopping $7.3 million, although the judge reduced it to $5.3 million while giving Gaye's estate a portion of its future profits.[83] The Ninth Circuit upheld the decision in 2018.[84]

The "Blurred Lines" case prompted over 200 musicians and 10 musicologists to raise a red flag in amicus briefs over the chilling effect such an untoward judgment might have.[85] On the one hand, the case was criticized for punishing songwriters for creating something that is merely inspired by prior works. At trial, both sides brought expert testimony showing both similarity and a lack of similarity between the two songs.[86] The jury applied the intrinsic test – comparing the two works from the ordinary observer's perspective. But critics complained the jury wrongly concluded the overall "feel" or "groove" of the songs was similar.[87] They also pointed out all music is inspired by prior works, and even Marvin Gaye was influenced by the works of Nat "King" Cole and Frank Sinatra, among others.

The decision was also criticized for its initial reliance on the "inverse ratio rule," which dates back to the 1930s.[88] It functioned like a "sliding scale" where the greater the access to the original work, the lesser the need to show substantial similarity.[89] Since Thicke indicated publicly "Got to Give It Up" was an influence for "Blurred Lines," and both he and Williams admitted at trial to a "high degree" of access, the burden of proving substantial

80. *Brown v. Perdue*, 177 Fed. Appx. 121, 2006 U.S. App. LEXIS 13877 (2d Cir. N.Y., April 18, 2006).
81. Michelle Pauli, "US Supreme Court Throws Out Da Vinci Suit," *The Guardian*, November 14, 2006.
82. Kory Grow, "Robin Thicke, Pharrell Lose Multi-Million Dollar 'Blurred Lines' Lawsuit," *Rolling Stone*, March 10, 2015; *Williams v. Bridgeport Music, Inc.*, Case No. LA CV13-06004 JAK (C.D. Cal. 2015).
83. Daniel Kreps, "'Blurred Lines' Ruling Sliced to $5.3 Million, With a Catch," *Rolling Stone*, July 15, 2015.
84. *Williams v. Gaye*, 895 F.3d 1106 (9th Cir. 2018).
85. Eriq Gardner, "'Blurred Lines' Appeal Gets Support from More Than 200 Musicians," *Hollywood Reporter*, August 30, 2016.
86. The similarities identified were in the "signature phrase, hooks, hooks with backup vocals, 'Theme X,' backup hooks, bass melodies, keyboard parts, and unusual percussion choices." 895 F.3d at 1117. Similarity was also limited to the copyrighted sheet music, given that Gaye's work was released in 1977, prior to when the 1976 Copyright Act went into effect (January 1, 1978), covering sound recordings. Critics argued that the jury should not have heard even a stripped-down version of the song. *Id.*
87. *Id.*
88. Alyssa Chavers, "Note: *Williams v. Gaye*: Further Blurring the Lines between Inspiration and Infringement," 50(1) *Golden Gate U. L. Rev*. Art. 6 (2020).
89. *Id.* "[W]here there is access, there is a high degree of probability that the similarity results from copying and not from independent thought and imagination. Indeed, it might well be said that where access is proved or admitted, there is a presumption that the similarity is not accidental." *Shipman v. R.K.O. Radio Pictures*, 100 F.2d 533, 538 (2d Cir. 1938). The approach became known as a "rule" in a case in 1954. *Morse v. Fields*, 127 F. Supp. 63, 66 (S.D.N.Y. 1954).

similarity was lowered. A modified court opinion later omitted this inverse ratio analysis, though, which makes sense given the easy access and high availability of music through streaming services.[90]

Indeed, the inverse ratio rule was rejected altogether in another famous case rocking the music world. In *Skidmore v. Led Zeppelin*,[91] the appeals court reinstated a 2016 jury verdict, holding the famous guitar riff beginning Led Zeppelin's "Stairway to Heaven" did not infringe on the 1967 instrumental album cut "Taurus" by the band Spirit. The decision was hailed as a win for the music industry that had feared that a ruling against Led Zeppelin would usher in harmful overprotection of copyrights.[92]

At trial, the objective extrinsic test was applied, comparing the protected elements, and a jury determined "Stairway to Heaven" and "Taurus" were not substantially similar. In rejecting the inverse ratio test and overruling its own precedent, the Ninth Circuit concluded all plaintiffs must satisfy the same standard of proof in showing the allegedly infringing work is substantially similar. Proving access alone "in no way can prove substantial similarity."[93]

The *Skidmore* (Led Zeppelin) decision marked a major shift in how substantial similarity would be evaluated between two musical works. For some, it meant the tide had turned while others saw it as a return to the status quo for copyright, before the disruptive "Blurred Lines" decision. At any rate, cases that followed ended in favorable settlements or jury findings for the accused infringers. Katy Perry, for example, was one of the first to benefit, winning her appeal in a copyright infringement case over her song "Dark Horse." Sam Smith was later granted summary judgment in a case brought against his "Dancing with a Stranger" song where the court relied on *Skidmore* (Zeppelin), applying both the extrinsic and intrinsic (jury) tests and saying it would not "deem substantially similar two vastly dissimilar musical compositions . . . for sharing some of the same notes [or] words."[94]

Most notably, in 2023 a unanimous jury found Ed Sheeran's 2014 hit "Thinking Out Loud" did not violate the copyright to Edward Townsend's words and Marvin Gaye's 1973 classic "Let's Get it On." Sheeran acknowledged that the chords in the two songs are similar. But he persuasively explained they are simply "common building blocks" "used by songwriters every day, all over the world" and "long before 'Let's Get It On' was written."[95]

Who Else Is Liable? Contributory Infringers

Copyright violators are responsible for their own actions, but should anyone else assume a degree of culpability for copyright violations? Since photocopiers are so often used as instruments for violating copyright, should their manufacturers also have to accept some share of the responsibility? What about those who provide the technology and the sites that allow for digital sharing of copyrighted works?

90. Chavers, "Note: *Williams v. Gaye*," supra note 88 *at* 5. The first opinion was published on March 21, 2018, applying the inverse ratio rule. But four months later on July 11, 2018, the court unexpectedly published a modified opinion. *Williams v. Gaye*, 885 F.3d 1163 (9th Cir. 2018), *amended by* 895 F.3d 1106 (9th Cir. 2018).
91. 952 F.3d 1051 (9th Cir. 2020), *cert. denied* (No. 20–142, October 5, 2020); *reh'g denied* (No. 20–142, December 7, 2020).
92. Sarah Bro, "Ninth Circuit Shows Led Zeppelin a Whole Lotta Love in 'Stairway' Copyright Win," *The National Law Review*, March 25, 2020, *at* https://natlawreview.com/article/ninth-circuit-shows-led-zeppelin-whole-lotta-love-stairway-copyright-win.
93. *Id.* at 1083.
94. *Sound and Color, LLC v. Samuel Smith*, No. 2:22-cv-01508-WLH-AS (C.D. Cal. 2023), citing *Skidmore*, 952 F.3d at 1075–76.
95. Ben Sisario, "Ed Sheeran Wins Copyright Case Over Marvin Gaye's 'Let's Get It On,'" *NYTimes*, May 4, 2023. Sheeran performed his song in person to a jury, which then compared the lyrics, melodies, and chords of both tracks by examining paper notations because the earlier song's copyright registration was limited to sheet music at that time.

Device Manufacturers

When it comes to the equipment involved, the U.S. Supreme Court gave its landmark opinion in 1984. In *Sony v. Universal*,[96] Universal Studios wanted to hold Sony responsible for copyright infringements because their Betamax videotape recorders could be used to violate copyright by recording copyrighted movies and television programs. In a 5–4 decision, the Court ruled the simple purpose of "time shifting," recording a program for later viewing was a fair use that did not harm the market for the copyright holder. Besides, Sony was not somehow "vicariously liable" for the actions of those who purchased the recorders.

The legal doctrine of "contributory infringement" had been previously used to show a relationship between an infringer and someone who had provided the means for infringement. In those cases, however, there was a continuous relationship between the infringer and the "contributor."[97] Sony's relationship ended as soon as the recorder was purchased and as such it did not "contribute" to any possible copyright infringement.

The *Sony* decision came as a great relief to a variety of recording and copying equipment manufacturers. Photocopier manufacturers had a vested interest in not being held responsible for the copyright infringements committed by the users of their machines. Audio cassette recorders also had the ability to record and copy tapes. The industry adjusted by adding encryption to its recordings and broadcast signals. But the ruling paved the wave for future capabilities, such as digital video recorders (DVRs) and mobile phones.

Sharing Services

Sharing copyrighted works with others can constitute contributory infringement. Shawn Fanning learned this when he started college at Northeastern University in Boston and developed Napster, a peer-to-peer (P2P) file-sharing service. Napster was not the first P2P service, but it quickly became popular in 1999 because it focused on MP3 music files and had an easy-to-navigate interface. It was simple for anyone with an Internet connection to share copyrighted music with other music lovers around the globe. In less than two years, more than two billion files (mostly songs) were being traded each month.

Napster soon became the lightning rod for the music industry's concern over file sharing. The Recording Industry Association of America (RIAA) filed the first of several lawsuits against Napster in 1999. Heavy metal band Metallica was outraged when one of its songs was shared on Napster before the band had even publicly released the music. In 2000, the band filed suit against the P2P service, which was followed by rapper Dr. Dre's suit. Then another suit was filed by a collection of recording companies.

A federal district court presided over the case and essentially put Napster out of business[98] by ruling that even though Napster itself was not violating copyrights, it was liable for "contributory" and "vicarious" copyright infringement, a ruling upheld by the Ninth Circuit.[99]

Although the defendants attempted to argue that Napster was just like Sony and the service should not be penalized for the illegal uses some people might engage in, the Ninth Circuit rejected the premise. The court noted how Napster still had control over the use people

96. 464 U.S. 417 (1984).
97. In the *Sony* case, the Court cited "dance hall cases" as examples of an ongoing relationship between a business and a copyright violator. Violations were facilitated by a racetrack, a cocktail lounge, and a dance hall. In those cases, there was a continuous relationship between the copyright infringer and the "facilitator." *Id.* at 437–438.
98. The Napster name still exists as a legal paid music streaming service but bears no resemblance to the P2P service as it was founded. Over the years, it was sold to Best Buy, Rhapsody, and then MelodyVR. In 2022, Napster was sold to blockchain company Algorand and crypto-focused investment firm Hivemind, releasing a new and rebranded version of its music streaming app.
99. *A&M Records v. Napster*, 239 F.3d 1004 (9th Cir. 2001).

made of the service, unlike those who purchase a video deck and then never interact again with the manufacturer. Napster's involvement with copyright infringers was continuous.

The court also noted how Napster's index system was used by file traders to search for songs they wanted to obtain, but it also allowed Napster to search its files for copyrighted material and remove it from the system – a capability Sony lacked. Sony had no way to police its equipment owners for infringing acts. Napster had that ability and opted not to use it.

The story didn't end there, though. Other file-sharing networks rolled out, including Gnutella in 2000 followed by Kazaa, Morpheus, BitTorrent, and Grokster in 2001. While the *Napster* case never made its way to the Supreme Court, the high court did rule in 2005 against Grokster and Morpheus, a service of StreamCast.[100] The P2P services were sued by a group of movie studios, songwriters, music recording companies, and publishers. The Court found Grokster and StreamCast had promoted themselves as free services for users to download copyrighted works,[101] made concerted efforts to attract Napster users, and made no effort to prevent copyright infringement – even appearing to thwart efforts by anyone to monitor whether or how much infringement was occurring. The Court held that "one who distributes a device with the object of promoting its use to infringe copyright, as shown by clear expression or other affirmative steps taken to foster infringement, is liable for the resulting acts of infringement by third parties."[102]

The *Sony* precedent would not be interpreted to protect any product (or service) simply because it is capable of substantial lawful use. Yet the Supreme Court declined to clarify the *Sony* formula, preferring instead to "leave further consideration of the *Sony* rule for a day when that may be required."[103]

Grokster was shut down in 2005 as a result of the ruling, but torrent sites located outside the United States can make federal prosecutions more difficult, although not impossible. Others like Kickass Torrents and The Pirate Bay soon sprang up, attracting millions of visitors searching for free content – often pirated – such as movies, music, video games, and software. Kickass Torrent was eventually taken down by U.S. law enforcement.[104] But The Pirate Bay, founded in Sweden, continues as a torrent giant,[105] flying frequently to distant shores, while avoiding threatened consequences of jail sentences,[106] lawsuits, and blocked access in other countries.[107]

Sharing Platforms

Platforms that carry shared copyrighted works may be subject to lawsuits and court-ordered injunctions. This was the case for video sharing platform YouTube. Founded in 2005 and purchased by Google the following year, it wasn't long before it was sued for copyright infringement.

100. *MGM v. Grokster*, 545 U.S. 913 (2005).
101. *Id.* at 923–924.
102. *Id.* at 919.
103. *Id.* at 934.
104. The shutdown was the result of a law enforcement operation lead by Homeland Security Investigations and the Internal Revenue Service, "Kickass Torrents Alternatives: The Best Websites," *VPN Overview*, January 2, 2021, *at* https://vpnoverview.com/privacy/downloading/kickass-torrents-alternatives/.
105. *Id.* Other well-known torrent sites include 1337x, YTS, EZTV, and Limetorrents. *See, e.g.*, James Everard, "12 Best Torrent Sites that are Safe and Work in 2024," *vpnMentor*, May 31, 2024, *at* https://www.vpnmentor.com/blog/10-best-torrent-websites/.
106. "Last Remaining Pirate Bay Founder Freed from Jail," *The Guardian*, June 2, 2015; "US and Kickass Torrents Go Head to Head in Court," February 2, 2017. A copy of the criminal complaint can be found at www.techworm.net/2017/02/5-fast-facts-need-know-kickasstorrents-owner-artem-vaulin.html.
107. "Bypass the Pirate Bay Restrictions," *VPN Overview*, October 20, 2020, *at* https://vpnoverview.com/privacy/downloading/the-pirate-bay/. Where blocked, users will use a virtual private network (VPN) to effectively change location to a country where The Pirate Bay is permitted, such as Switzerland.

In March 2007, media giant Viacom filed suit against YouTube and its parent company for $1 billion, claiming YouTube encouraged unlawful uses. YouTube acknowledged it may have had some infringing content on its site but defended itself by asserting it was not encouraging it. In fact, YouTube maintained it responded immediately to any request it received to act against suspect recordings posted.

YouTube's actions were found to be in compliance with the 1998 Digital Millennium Copyright Act (DMCA), which includes protection for online services that might be used for copyright violation, provided those services quickly comply with any take-down requests.[108] The so-called Safe Harbor provision of the DMCA protects good-faith efforts by those who don't violate the copyrights but whose websites provide opportunity for others to infringe copyright. Website operators such as YouTube are not responsible for infringements if they quickly respond. Indeed, YouTube's policy has been to remove material when requested to do so and then later reinstate it if it is determined the copyrighted material may still be used.

Some providers are being sued for turning a blind eye to the copyright infringements on their platforms. A class action suit was brought by content creators claiming YouTube does not always issue copyright strikes under its two-tiered enforcement regime that disproportionately protects major studios and record labels with their large user volume and ad revenue over smaller creators.[109] They argued YouTube has turned into a "hotbed of copyright infringement."[110]

In 2022, Comcast, Verizon, and AT&T settled several lawsuits from production companies behind such films as *Dallas Buyers Club* after the ISPs allegedly refused to expel customers who repeatedly pirated their movies.[111] In 2023, major record companies Universal, Sony, Warner, and others sued Twitter (X) for $250 million for refusing to secure music licensing rights, claiming the platform "consistently and knowingly hosts and streams infringing copies of music compositions" to "fuel its business."[112]

The same music conglomerates filed a whopping $2.6 billion lawsuit in 2024 against Verizon. Plaintiffs claimed their complaints were ignored despite sending hundreds of thousands of copyright infringement notices to the ISP, identifying individual subscribers accused of stealing their recordings.[113]

From the *Sony* case to the present, the message appears to be that creating a means for violating copyright is not a problem if there are also non-infringing uses. Promoting something as a means of violating copyright, however, will not escape scrutiny. And platforms that fail to affect a remedy within their ability may be culpable.

108. 17 U.S.C. § 512.
109. In fact, the U.S. Copyright Office has been reconsidering the § 512 safe harbor provision of the DMCA after conducting a study that showed rights holders were concerned that infringements were not being meaningfully addressed by the big tech online service providers, including the "whack-a-mole" approach to taking down content that would reappear. Eriq Gardner, "Copyright Office Says Landmark Piracy Law Needs Fine-Tuning," *Hollywood Reporter*, May 21, 2020. A 2022 white paper by the International Center for Law and Economics (ICLE) suggested solutions for overhauling the provision, such as raising the lay person standard of knowledge for online service providers, requiring users be identified as a deterrent, and bolstering the use of filtering technologies on the platforms. Alec Pronk, "White Paper Proposes Solutions for Overhaul of Section 512," *IPWatchdog*, October 15, 2022, *at* https://ipwatchdog.com/2022/10/15/white-paper-proposes-solutions-overhaul-section-512/id=152162/.
110. Corrado Rizzi, "YouTube Hit with Class Action Over 'Rampant' Copyright Infringement, Lack of Protections for 'Ordinary' Content Creators," *ClassAction*, July 6, 2020, *at* www.classaction.org/blog/youtube-hit-with-class-action-over-rampant-copyright-infringement-lack-of-protections-for-ordinary-content-creators.
111. Winston Cho, "Comcast, Verizon, AT&T Settle Piracy Suits," *Hollywood Reporter*, September 19, 2022.
112. Winston Cho, "Twitter Hit With $250M Lawsuit From Music Publishers Over 'Massive Copyright Infringement' Claim," *Hollywood Reporter*, June 14, 2023.
113. Winston Cho, "Verizon Hit With $2.6B Anti-Piracy Lawsuit From Major Record Labels," *Hollywood Reporter*, July 15, 2024.

Generative AI Products and Services

There may also be consequences for companies that offer generative AI products and services that draw from copyrighted source work. Powerful artificial intelligence systems continue to be developed that use enormous amounts of text, images, and videos pulled from the Internet to train their models. Generative AI companies argue that their systems trained on copyrighted works do not violate copyright law because the models are not copying the training data but rather learning associations between elements like words and pixels.[114]

Lawsuits have been filed when AI tools are alleged to have produced derivatives infringing on copyrighted works. Sony, Universal, and Warner sued AI startups Suno and Udio for copying the labels' music to train their music-generating AI models. The record companies complained their music was copied to teach the AI systems to create music that would "directly compete with, cheapen, and ultimately drown out" their human artists' work.[115]

Another issue is the extent to which copyright liability rests with the end users. Most generative AI tools that output images, text, or video do not provide any warnings to unwitting users about potential infringement.[116] Observers have asked then are AI companies liable for contributory infringement, and what legal responsibility do the AI customers bear. The proper licensing of copyright content is a solution. Indeed, some businesses have signed lucrative deals with AI companies, such as academic publisher Taylor & Francis, which agreed to sell access to its authors' research as part of an artificial intelligence partnership with Microsoft for roughly $10 million in its first year.

Another solution to the copyright problem is for AI companies to build guardrails for their applications. This might be to create a method for making generative AI models "unlearn" copyrighted data or reduce the similarity between the outputs of generative AI and copyrighted material.[117] Regulation may also be needed to minimize AI copyright infringements.

What Can I Use? The Doctrine of Fair Use

Copyright holders have a bundle of rights, but how do others use their copyrighted works? The rights of the copyright holder must be balanced with the free expression rights of others who would like to use copyrighted works, regardless of the owner's wishes.

Fair Use
Section 107 of the Copyright Act allows copyrighted material to be used for fair use, which is determined by considering 1) the purpose of the use, 2) the nature of the copyrighted work, 3) the amount of the work used, and 4) the effect on the market for the work.

If use of a copyrighted work is considered a fair use, the holders have no right to prevent its use, nor are they entitled to any compensation for its use. The Copyright Act lists some examples of things that may be considered fair use, such as news reporting, criticism, comment, teaching, scholarship, and research. But no use is presumed to be a fair use.

Section 107 of the Copyright Act clearly spells out four factors to be considered in determining whether a specific use is fair. All must be considered in determining whether a use is fair. Most cases typically split across the four factors, with the decision resting on the strength of the arguments and evidence presented. We will examine each of them in turn.

1 Purpose and Character of the Use

The first consideration in determining whether someone's taking of the material is fair use is to define the purpose and character of the new use. Nonprofit educational uses have an

114. "Generative AI Could Leave Users Holding the Bag for Copyright Violations," *The Conversation*, March 22, 2024, *at* https://theconversation.com/generative-ai-could-leave-users-holding-the-bag-for-copyright-violations-225760#:~:text=Builders%20of%20generative%20AI%20tools,closely%20resemble%20copyright%2Dprotected%20content.
115. "Sony, Universal, Warner Sue AI Startups, Claiming Copyright Infringement in Training Models," *NY Post*, June 24, 2024.
116. "Generative AI," supra note 114.
117. *Id.*

almost mystical appeal. Educators everywhere often justify any copying they may do for class as fair use because it is for educational purposes, and certainly educational use is the sort of purpose Congress was trying to protect in the statute.

Congress specifically mentioned nonprofit educational purposes in its description of an appropriate fair use, but it is not the only acceptable purpose. Review and criticism are also acceptable purposes. Certainly, a critic commenting on a book, play, or movie ought to be able to include excerpts of the copyrighted work as examples for the audience. Research, scholarship, and news reporting are also acceptable fair use purposes.

It is because news reporting is an acceptable fair use that there aren't many lawsuits for broadcast outlets routinely showing video recordings they find online. One person who tried to sue for just such a use objected to ABC's *Good Morning America* program showing a portion of his Facebook Live stream of his wife giving birth.[118] The complaint was tossed by the judge.

Transformative Use

U.S. Supreme Court definition: "adds something new, with a further purpose or different character, altering the first with new expression, meaning or message."

The transformative nature of the new use is also considered. Courts will weigh whether the second work was transformed in such a way as to change the meaning for its audience. For example, artist Tom Forsythe used Barbie® dolls in a series called "food chain Barbie" to offer his social commentary. A federal appellate court called the work transformative and found his art did not infringe Mattel's copyright or trademark.[119]

There is no fair use, however, when the use is for the same purpose as the original and it is commercial in nature. The U.S. Supreme Court made this clear in a 2023 case involving the work of renowned artist Andy Warhol.[120]

It all began when photographer Lynn Goldsmith granted a limited license to one of her photos of Prince to *Vanity Fair* magazine for a "one time" use as an artist reference. *Vanity Fair* then hired Warhol to create an illustration, and Warhol used Goldsmith's photo to create a series of silkscreen prints known as the "Prince Series."

After Prince died in 2016, the Warhol foundation licensed one of the Prince Series portraits ("Orange Prince") to Condé Nast to appear on the cover of a commemorative edition magazine about Prince. (Figure 7.2) When Goldsmith recognized her photography on the magazine cover, she complained to AWF that this was an infringing use. AWF sued to get a declaratory judgment in its favor. While a use may be transformative, the Court found AWF's use of the Prince Series weighed against a finding of first fair use because it shared the same purpose as the original and declared its use was commercial in nature.[121]

Warhol's famous depiction of Campbell's Soup cans was judged to be different though. "The purpose of Campbell's logo is to advertise soup. Warhol's canvases do not share that purpose. Rather, the Soup Cans series uses Campbell's copyrighted work for an artistic commentary on consumerism."[122]

Parody is an acceptable purpose for the fair use of copyrighted material, as ruled by the Supreme Court in 1994. In this case, the rap group 2 Live Crew had written and recorded "Pretty Woman," which by the group's own admission was a parody take on the 1964 Roy Orbison hit "Oh, Pretty Woman." Acuff-Rose Music controlled the rights to the Orbison song and did not want 2 Live Crew to make fun of it. But contrary to Acuff-Rose's wishes, 2 Live Crew released the song and shortly after found itself embroiled in a copyright suit.

118. "Dad Who Live-Streamed His Son's Birth on Facebook Loses in Court," *Ars Technica*, February 16, 2017.
119. *Mattel v. Walking Mountain Productions*, 353 F.3d 792 (Ct. App. Ninth Circ. 2003).
120. *Andy Warhol Foundation for Visual Arts, Inc. v. Goldsmith*, 598 U.S. ____ (2023); No. 21–869, slip op. (U.S. May 18, 2023).
121. *Id.* at 33.
122. *Id.* at 26–27.

No Fair Use for Warhol's Orange Prince

Figure 7.2 Goldsmith photo, Andy Warhol prints, and Orange Prince cover

Source: Andy Warhol Foundation for Visual Arts, Inc. v. Goldsmith, 598 U.S. ____ (2023); No. 21–869, slip op. (U.S. May 18, 2023)

Figure 7.2 (Continued)

As the case made its way to the U.S. Supreme Court, it attracted a good deal of attention. Amicus briefs are often filed by third parties interested in the outcome, and in this case the National Music Publishers' Association, the Nashville Songwriters' Association International, and the National Academy of Songwriters along with well-known songwriters Michael Jackson, Dolly Parton, and the estate of George Gershwin lined up to support Acuff-Rose Music to protect its works from parody use. Conversely, well-known parodists supported 2 Live Crew, including *The Harvard Lampoon*, *MAD Magazine*, and the Capitol Steps, a popular Washington, DC, comedy troupe specializing in musical parody of politics.

In a unanimous decision, the Court ruled 2 Live Crew's use was not a copyright infringement but a legitimate fair use. The Court removed any doubt as to whether parody was an acceptable defense when it held that "parody, like other comment or criticism, may claim fair use under §107."[123]

123. *Campbell v. Acuff-Rose Music*, 510 U.S. 569, 579 (1994). In this case, the parody also met the other fair use factors by copying only enough of the original work to be able to "conjure up" the object of its critical wit and being unlikely to serve as a market substitute for the original. At 588.

Parody Mash-Up? No Fair Use

Figure 7.3 Comparison of the Seuss original – *Oh, the Places You'll Go!* – to the ComicMix primer *Oh, the Places You'll Boldly Go!*

Source: Dr. Seuss Enterprises v. ComicMix LLC, D.C. No. 3:16-cv-02779-JLS-BGS (9th Cir. 2020)

Parody
Not merely comedic or sarcastic but a spoof, send-up, caricature, or comment on another work.

To be clear, however, a parody is of the original work. Simply creating a work that is comedic or sarcastic does not mean that copyrighted music, images, or other elements can then be used with impunity. Unless the work comments at least in part on the original author's work, it is not a parody subject to this fair use factor.

This unlawful use was the case when ComicMix created and sold a funny primer that used Dr. Seuss's works in a mash-up of Star Trek and Dr. Seuss[124] (Figure 7.3). The Ninth Circuit explained that a "parody is a spoof, send-up, caricature, or comment on another work."[125] Situating the "sophisticated adult entertainment of Star Trek in the context of [Dr. Seuss] to create a 'funny' book" is not a parody. A protected parody is one that critiques or comments on the original work, not using the work "to get attention" or "avoid the drudgery in working up something fresh."[126] ComicMix could not use parody as a fair use defense because the court found it only wanted to "evoke" rather than "ridicule" the Seuss works.

2 Nature of the Copyrighted Work

This second criterion is the least debated of the four. At issue is whether the author of the copyrighted work created something that should be open to fair use by others. Here, the nature of that original work is considered.

For example, was the copyrighted work unpublished? Someone might produce poetry with no intention to ever publish it. The poems were certainly copyrighted as soon as they were fixed in a tangible medium, but the author might choose to keep them forever in a desk drawer, or only share them with the lover who is the subject of the poems. Publishing excerpts of those poems for the purpose of comment or criticism might constitute a fair use, but the unpublished nature of the copyrighted work would be considered as such the use would not be fair.

Another consideration is whether the copyrighted work was fiction or nonfiction. Fair use generally is easier to claim for nonfiction works and for good reasons. Facts cannot be copyrighted, and the public benefits from the dissemination of information, so it is easier to claim the nature of a nonfiction copyrighted work is suited to fair use. For example,

124. *Dr. Seuss Enterprises v. ComicMix LLC*, D.C. No. 3:16-cv-02779-JLS-BGS (9th Cir. 2020).
125. *Id.* at 14.
126. *Id.* at 13.

scientific articles are more suited to fair use than "creative" content such as a science fiction novel.

Finally, "consumable" works are considered less suited to fair use than other sorts of intellectual property. Workbooks are created with the intent to be used one time. Unlike books that can be read and passed along to another reader, a workbook depends on each use to "consume" the content. Photocopying a portion of a workbook is much less likely to be seen as an acceptable fair use than photocopying a similar portion of a textbook.

3 Amount and Substantiality of the Use

Most people can easily understand the fair use of a copyrighted work requires using only a limited amount. It's easy to see how photocopying an entire textbook and making enough copies for an entire school district is not a fair use. What's not so easy to see is just how much of a work can be used while still qualifying as fair use, and Congress provides no formula to help with the guesswork.

The operative phrase is "amount and substantiality," which is both a qualitative and quantitative evaluation of copied content. With no quantitative guidelines, the use is generally weighed in proportion to the original. A few paragraphs taken from a 400-page book might not be a large amount, but it may constitute "the heart of" the original copyrighted work. In 1979, *The Nation* magazine rushed to press with a 2,250-word article containing excerpts from the soon-to-be-released memoir of former President Gerald Ford. *Time* magazine already had an exclusive contract with publisher Harper & Row for prepublication excerpts from the book.

After the article appeared in print, *Time* canceled its contract with the publisher and refused to pay the second half of an agreed-upon amount for the rights: $12,500. In 1985, the Supreme Court ruled 6–3 that *The Nation* infringed on Harper & Row's copyright, and the article was not an acceptable fair use. In addition, the Court noted that the copied material was used before it had been published, emphasizing the nature of the copyrighted work as one of the criteria as well as how the market value was affected.[127]

4 Effect on the Market

Copyright infringers who gain no profit from their use of copyrighted material wrongly assume the taking falls under fair use. But copyright infringement is not about illegally profiting from it. It's about denying copyright holders the fruits of their intellectual property.

A loss of potential profits from future derivative works is also considered. For example, it is not a fair use for a band to create a new arrangement of an old song or do a "cover" of it without permission. The copyright holder has a right to create and profit from any derivative works. In the *ComicMix* case discussed earlier, the court recognized "ComicMix's non-transformative and commercial use of Dr. Seuss's works" likely led to "cognizable market harm to the original."[128] ComicMix had planned to release its comic book primer to the same target market (school graduates), and the court concluded that could curtail Seuss's potential market for derivative works.

127. *Harper & Row Publishers v. Nation Enters*, 471 U.S. 539 (1985).
128. D.C. No. 3:16-cv-02779-JLS-BGS, at 25.

A Compromise: Creative Commons and Royalty-Free Sites

In 2001, Creative Commons was founded as a not-for-profit organization hoping to change the culture and dynamics around copyright. It creates a middle ground where copyright holders retain the copyright to their work while giving permission to others to use it under certain conditions. Owners can waive or accept certain uses of their copyrighted work, ranging from full freedom to allowing no modifications (derivative works) or no commercial use. It essentially shifts content from "all rights reserved" to "some rights reserved."

Creative Commons (CC) makes it easy for creators to share their work. Many media platforms like Flickr, YouTube, and SoundCloud have built-in Creative Commons capabilities that let owners mark their material with a CC license for users searching for CC-licensed material.

The ability to share and access copyright-free content has been a boon to the media professions. Photographers, for example, use CC licenses to gain new audiences for their work on photo-sharing platforms such as Flickr. Flickr contains over 200 million CC-licensed photos, establishing it as the web's single largest source of CC-licensed content.

Journalists also benefit from Creative Commons licensing. With the rights to copy, distribute, or adapt pre-cleared content, news can be distributed more rapidly and widely. This allows for innovative business models that must rely on free and legal content sharing and reuse. Al Jazeera was the first major news source to use Creative Commons, building and making available to news organizations a CC video repository of the war in Gaza. ProPublica also encourages other news sites to reproduce their stories so long as they are credited and linked.

Aside from Creative Commons, sites such as NASA, the Smithsonian, and the National Park Service offer open access to millions of their images and media files. There are certainly many other databases such as Pixabay, Canva, and AudioJungle offering royalty-free stock photos, videos, illustrations, templates, music, sound effects, and more for free or at a modest price. Of course, there are also commercial services that will help those wanting to pay for uses that do not qualify as fair use.

Those trying to do the right thing when it comes to copyright and fair use should consult the various fair use codes and best practices for the visual arts, media literacy, journalism, video, and documentary filmmaking from the Center for Media & Social Impact at American University.[129]

Trademarks

Another form of intellectual property is a trademark. The simplest way to think of a trademark is as a means for customers to identify a product by its brand name or logo. A person out driving who gets hungry and spots what looks like the classic green and yellow sign of a Subway® might be fooled into buying a sandwich from a place called "Subsway." Likewise, someone purchasing a pair of Nike brand shoes would be unhappy to discover despite the iconic swoosh they were actually a poorly made knock-off. Trademarks are a way of distinguishing one product brand from another, and they are protected by federal law under the Lanham Act.[130]

129. The guides can be accessed through the Center for Media & Social Impact's website, https://cmsimpact.org/program/fair-use/.
130. Pub L No 79–489,60 Stat. 427 (1946), *codified at* 15 U.S.C. § 1051 *et seq* (2006). The Lanham Act prohibits trademark infringement, trademark dilution as well as false advertising (see Chapter 11).

A trademark is a word, name, symbol, device, or any combination of those used to identify and distinguish goods in commerce and inspire consumer trust. Trademarks include names such as Hilton Hotels, Louis Vuitton, and Baskin Robbins, as well as words or catchphrases such as "Bam!" (Chef Emeril Lagasse) and "What's in your wallet?" (Capital One).[131] There are also protected images and animation, such as the symbolic golden arches of McDonalds, the Starbuck's mermaid, and the talking Geico gecko.

If it's not inherent to the functioning of the product, there also are device marks, such as the layout design of an iPhone home screen and the red dripping wax seal on a bottle of Maker's Mark bourbon, as well as three-dimensional marks such as the distinctive shape of a Toblerone (long chocolate bar with triangular peaks). The same is true for color marks, such as the pink Fiberglass insulation sold by Owens-Corning, as well as sound marks, such as the "da dummmm" title screen sound viewers hear when Netflix launches.[132]

If it's not the function of the product itself (i.e., perfume), the courts have held a scent can be trademarked, such as Hasbro's "sweet, slightly musky, vanilla fragrance, with slight overtones of cherry" Play-Doh. Unusual motions, like that of the vehicle doors of a Lamborghini are trademarked. The overall appearance of a business known as "trade dress" also can be a mark, such as a Fuddruckers restaurant (its décor, menu, and dining layout as a whole).

The purpose of a trademark is to clearly associate the product or service with its owner and prevent customer confusion as to which product or service they are buying. A trademark also serves to represent the goodwill and quality of a company's goods and services. It is therefore important to register and protect so that competing businesses do not infringe on the mark and unfairly capitalize on that goodwill and quality reputation. Companies will spend millions of dollars protecting their marks from infringement.

Trademark Registration

After a mark is used in commerce, it may receive trademark protection under state laws, but it is best to officially register one's mark through the U.S. Patent and Trademark Office (USPTO). Unlike copyrights, trademarks are registered after they have been in use, although an intent to use the mark within a limited time can be filed. The claim for trademark by a company is that a word, phrase, or logo has come to be associated with a product, and that usually takes some time to establish.

Registration has its advantages. It gives the holder exclusive use of the trademark and prevents others from being able to register the mark. Like copyright, it is also *prima facie* evidence of a valid mark in an infringement lawsuit. If infringement is found, the owner of the mark may be entitled to damages, costs, and the infringer's profits.

Registration can be done online[133] and requires the payment of fees for each class of goods on which the mark will be used.[134] Before applying, you should search their database of registered trademarks and prior pending applications to see if there's already a trademark,

131. In what could be the oddest attribute disputed, two entertainers had a trademark dispute over their distinctive uses of the catch phrase "Yuuup"; they settled out of court. "'Storage Wars' Star and Rapper End Legal Battle Over 'YUUUP!' Catchphrase," *Hollywood Reporter*, June 25, 2012. Other catchphrases that have been trademarked include "Who Dat," "Let's get ready to rumble," and "That's hot," as well as "You're Fired!," "This sick beat" (Taylor Swift), and "three-peat."
132. "Netflix Files Trademark Application for Title Screen Sound," *Tantalizing Trademarks.com*, April 5, 2016, *at* www.tantalizingtrademarks.com/2016/04/netflix-files-trademark-application-for.html#:~:text=Co.%2C%20199%20USPQ%20560%2C,arbitrary%2C%20unique%2C%20or%20distinctive.&text=If%20this%20application%20matures%20to,listed%20in%20its%20trademark%20application.
133. United States Patent and Trademark Office (USPTO), Trademarks, Apply Online *at* www.uspto.gov/trademarks-application-process/filing-online.
134. Fees might run several hundreds of dollars. Trademark (and patent) fees are available *at* www.uspto.gov/learning-and-resources/fees-and-payment/uspto-fee-schedule#Trademark%20Fees.

which would create a likelihood of confusion and prevent registration.[135] The duration of a trademark is quite different from a copyright. A trademark registration is valid for only ten years but can be renewed an indefinite number of times. Coca-Cola was first registered as a trademark in 1893 and has been continually renewed.

Once registered, the symbol ® should be prominently displayed next to the mark to give notice to others that the mark is protected. The symbol should not be used, however, until the USPTO has registered the trademark. Instead, the symbol ™ may be used. It has no legal meaning, but it lets others know that the owner means to protect the mark.

Registering a trademark also makes it easier to license use to other franchisees, and they can be sold or transferred. A company may go out of business and no longer need the name, so it is sold along with other assets. Brands USA Holdings is a company that acquires trademarks and then resells them. It has held auctions where brand names like Handi-Wrap went for $30,000; Meister Brau, a former beer, was sold for $32,500; and Shearson, a former financial company, was auctioned at $45,000.

Classes of Trademarks

Being able to acquire and protect a registered trademark depends on how the mark is classified. Some words, phrases, symbols, and images will be awarded trademark protection quickly based on the strength of their distinctiveness, while others will need to show they have acquired a "secondary meaning" in the marketplace. Still others will not be successfully trademarked because they're simply too common or generic.

The strongest class of marks consists of fanciful marks. Unique names of companies existing nowhere else have a strong claim as fanciful trademarks. Company brands such as Kodak, Verizon, Lexus, Oreo, and Exxon are considered fanciful because they're not English-language words.[136] As such, these distinctive trademarks can enforce their brand name across industries. Even though Kodak is not involved in oil exploration and refining, for example, it could prevent another firm from registering as the Kodak Oil Company. Similarly, Exxon could prevent another company from branding an Exxon digital camera.

Comparing Apples to Apples

Apple Computer provides an example of how seemingly different businesses might become interrelated and thus create trademark confusion. In 1978, Apple Corps Ltd., the company that owned The Beatles' record label, was concerned the California computer business, Apple Inc. would infringe the record label's trademark. The situation was exacerbated by the fact that both international companies headquartered in different nations – the record label in the United Kingdom and the computer company in the United States were subject to different trademark laws.

For nearly 30 years, the two Apples negotiated their differences. Apple Inc. paid Apple Corps, Ltd., and both companies agreed to stay out of each other's core business. In 1978, the similarity in brands was not much of an issue because of the different

135. USPTO, Trademark Electronic Search System (TESS), *at* www.uspto.gov/trademarks-application-process/search-trademark-database.

136. The creation of the Exxon name has become a legend in trademark circles. In 1911, the Supreme Court broke Standard Oil into 34 companies, one of which was Standard Oil of New Jersey, which used the name "Esso" (a vocalization of the abbreviation S.O.). Because of the other Standard Oils in existence, Standard Oil of New Jersey could only use Esso in parts of the United States. In the early 1970s, the company changed its name to Exxon. The name was an attempt to resemble Esso while creating a name distinctive enough to withstand trademark challenges worldwide. The double-X does not naturally occur in any major language.

products involved, but in the twenty-first century, Apple Computer became a major player in the music industry with its iTunes service and suddenly things had changed.

Apple Inc. successfully defended itself in 2006 against a trademark infringement claim brought by Apple Corps Ltd. in a British court, and a new agreement was signed between the two companies in 2007. They eventually "settled" in the United States, but the ensuing decades proved the intellectual property issues between Apple Corps Limited and Apple Computers Incorporated were anything but settled.

Arbitrary marks are the next strongest type of trademark. They use an existing word that is entirely unrelated to the good or service, such as Domino's (pizza), Pledge (furniture polish), Adobe (software), Indeed (employment), Camel (cigarettes), and Shell (gasoline). They may also use dictionary words in an odd combination or mash-up that makes them unique for that industry, such as 7–11, Starbucks, and Pinterest.

What does an apple have to do with a computer? Absolutely nothing of course – but combining the words makes Apple Computer a strong and enforceable trademark. Arbitrary marks are only protected, however, within the confines of that specific industry. Apple Computer could not win a claim of copyright infringement against Big Apple Grocery in San Francisco, Apple Tree Daycare in Connecticut, or Apple Bail Bonds in New Jersey. Consumers are not likely to be confused into believing that the same company that makes the computers operates the grocery store, daycare, or bail bonds service.

Suggestive trademarks indicate some feature of the product without saying it outright. Consider labels such as PayPal, Netflix, Chicken of the Sea (tuna fish), Coppertone (suntan oil), Roach Motel (insect trap), and Tide (laundry detergent). Suggestive trademarks are useful from both advertising and marketing perspectives because consumers more easily connect a new product or service with the mark. However, they are somewhat weaker because they can be misconstrued as being more descriptive than suggestive. This distinction makes it more difficult to obtain a registered trademark and win an infringement claim.

Descriptive marks simply describe something about the attributes of the goods or services without requiring much thought or imagination. Think of brands like Pizzazz (pizza), Bed & Bath (store), After Tan (after sunning lotion), Wheaties (cereal), Lyft (transportation), Park 'N Fly (airport parking), and Tender Vittles (cat food). Descriptive labels might not receive or retain trademark protection. Raisins and oat bran flakes, for example, form a cereal familiar to Americans, and multiple cereal companies sold their own versions, but none of them could trademark raisin bran. Only by adding the distinctive brand name "Kellogg" did Kellogg's Raisin Bran secure its registered trademark.

Companies can get a trademark for a descriptive mark if it takes on a secondary meaning or acquires distinctiveness. American Airlines is not especially fanciful or arbitrary, but consumers understand *the* American Airlines to be a specific company. Taken together and used in commerce over time, those two terms have taken on a secondary meaning in the minds of consumers.

Trademark questions revolve around consumers and whether they are likely to recognize the brand as an indication of a specific company's product. For descriptive marks, however, this may take years of advertising and marketing before a company's mark can be registered and therefore protected.[137] Trademark attorneys naturally recommend companies avoid descriptive brands and try to create marks more distinctive and fanciful, if possible.

137. Five years is what the USPTO generally accepts as prima facie evidence for acquired distinctiveness, although distinctiveness may be acquired at any time.

The Battle Over "Model E" – Too Similar to the Model T?

Is the name "Model E" for an automobile too similar to Ford's iconic "Model T?"

As electric vehicles were being introduced, Ford Motor Company applied to register Model E as a trademark for its EV division of electric-powered boats, cars, scooters, SUVs, trucks, buses, vans, and more. Ford didn't have a car named Model E, but the trademark was registered in October 2003.

Tesla founder and CEO Elon Musk soon wanted to use the trademark for his electric vehicles and engaged in a trademark fight with Ford. Ford threatened lawsuits to keep companies like Tesla from using the term Model E because they argued it sounded too much like Model T, the first affordable car for the masses built by Henry Ford in 1908. In 2010, the two companies came to an agreement that Tesla would not use the letter "E" for its car models.

Musk nonetheless tried to register the term but was blocked in 2014 with Ford citing their earlier agreement and intent to use the mark. Musk responded with "OK, fine we won't use Model E." He had hoped to include the name with a lineup of cars that would include Models S, E, and X (humorously spelling "sex"). Musk went with "Model 3" instead, although styling the figure 3 so it might appear as a backward uppercase letter E.[138]

Yet to Musk's chagrin, the coveted mark did finally appear – sort of. In 2022 Ford named its electric vehicle unit "Model e."

Generic labels fall in a category unacceptable for trademark registration because they simply describe entire categories or classes of goods and services. Trademarks would be denied to businesses trying to register brands like Movie Theatre, Shoe Store, or Barbeque. The courts have even ruled "Texas Toast" and "Duck Tours" too generic to be trademarked. A registered mark that becomes generic over time can also be canceled.

In 2016, a federal court upheld the Trademark Trial and Appeal Board's refusal to register "Churrascos" for a restaurant chain known for its grilled steak. Churrascos was considered generic because it is a common term for grilled meat and a type of restaurant.[139] It was understood by the general public to be referencing a broader group of restaurants.[140] Stylizing a graphic mark also was shown not to have created a separate impression on purchasers or acquired distinctiveness (secondary meaning).

What about the online branding of "dot-com companies"? The U.S. Supreme Court provided more leeway to "generic.com" marks in its decision for Booking.com.[141] Booking.com was repeatedly rejected for trademark protection on the grounds that "booking" was a generic term and that adding ".com" could never turn a generic mark into a non-generic mark, any more than simply adding the word "Company" or "Inc." But in 2020, the Court determined that Booking.com is not generic because it does not signify to consumers a genus of goods or services; instead, it is descriptive of services involving booking. For example, consumers would not understand Travelocity to be a "Booking.com." Moreover, while such marks are weak, "Booking.com" had acquired a secondary meaning, acting as a source identifier for a specific provider of hotel reservation services.

138. Dan Mihalascu, "Ford Calls EV Unit Model e, A Name Tesla Wanted for Model 3," *InsideEVs*, March 3, 2022, *at* https://insideevs.com/news/571138/ford-model-e-name-tesla-wanted/.
139. *In re Cordua Restaurants, Inc.*, 823 F.3d 594 (Fed. Cir. 2016).
140. A two-part test was applied to 1) determine "the genus of goods or services at issue" and 2) whether "the term sought to be registered or retained on the register [is] understood by the relevant public primarily to refer to that genus of goods or services." This test was established in *H. Marvin Ginn Corp. v. International Ass'n of Fire Chiefs, Inc.*, 782 F.2d 987 (Fed. Cir. 1986).
141. *United States Patent and Trademark Office v. Booking.Com B.V.*, No. 19–46 (U.S. June 30, 2020).

The Court therefore held a "generic.com" mark is protectable when the mark as a whole signifies a specific brand to consumers as opposed to an entire class of goods or services, essentially making it a descriptive mark instead, subject to secondary meaning. This means similar "generic.com" brands may be eligible for trademark protection and not invalid per se.

Classes of Trademarks

- Fanciful – most protected; exist nowhere else in language, for example, Kodak, Oreo
- Arbitrary – common terms unrelated to the product or service or in an odd combination, for example, Adobe, Apple Computers, Fox Broadcasting
- Suggestive – suggests features about the product or service, for example, Citi-bank, Greyhound bus
- Descriptive – describes the product or service but must create a secondary meaning, for example, American Airlines, Bed & Bath
- Generic – describes a broad category of goods or services and cannot be trademarked, for example, Hair Salon, Movie Theater

Celebrity names create special issues in trademark law. Julia Roberts is a famous movie star who has performed in dozens of motion pictures, appeared on television, and is a favorite subject of the tabloids. Certainly, her persona is associated with her name, and when most people hear "Julia Roberts," they think of her. So should Julia Roberts be able to trademark her name, and, if so, does it mean all the other Julia Roberts are not entitled to use their name?

Famous people do have the right to trademark their names once consumers are likely to associate it with their commercial persona. Even though there may be dozens of Jennifer Lopezes in the world, the singer/actor/entrepreneur claims the right to use that name and to prevent others from commercially using it even if it happens to be their name. Trademark laws attempt to prevent consumer confusion, so buyers will know a song or piece of clothing with the name "Jennifer Lopez" on it came from *the* Jennifer Lopez, and no one else. Trademark use by others must then be denied.

Celebrities want to protect the exclusive use of their names on all sorts of products and on the Internet as well. Julia Roberts won a legal battle to prevent a cybersquatter from using the URL "juliaroberts.com." In 1999, Congress passed the Anticybersquatting Consumer Protection Act (ACPA) specifically in response to complaints about exploitive registrants who tried to extract large payments from individuals and companies after acquiring the URL resembling their names. Despite the fact Roberts's name was not trademarked at that time, she was able to demonstrate her name had acquired a "secondary meaning" and as such she had common-law trademark rights.

A California court ruled trademarks are also protected against infringement claims even though they might not be seen. Meta tags are terms attached to websites that may not be seen by website visitors but help search engines find the site. In 1997, a court ruled that a porn website infringed Playboy Enterprises' trademark by including "playboy" in the meta tag data, attempting to attract anyone searching for the company to find the porn site, thereby "profiting" from the use of Playboy's trademark.[142] But in another case involving Playboy, a former playmate was allowed to use the trademarked name in the meta tags of her website. Because she had, in fact, been featured in *Playboy*, and her website contained a disclaimer, the court considered it to be factual information rather than infringement.[143]

142. *Playboy Enters. v. Calvin Designer Label*, 985 F. Supp. 1220 (Calif. N.D. 1997).
143. *Playboy Enterprises, Inc. v. Welles*, 7 F. Supp. 2d 1098 (Cal. S.D. 1998).

Losing Trademark Protection

Companies invest in protecting their trademarks for several reasons, but chief among them is the fear that failure to aggressively protect a trademark will cost them exclusive use of their brand name. While a trademark can be renewed indefinitely, trademark protection can be lost if it is not protected. Failing to use the trademark in commerce for as much as three years constitutes abandonment. Allowing it to be used in a generic sense can also prevent renewal and even cancel the trademark registration.[144] That is why owners prominently note the ® symbol, capitalize their brand names, and clearly promote their registered mark to warn consumers of the protection and avoid any generic uses.

There is a remarkable history of trademarks that were lost over time because companies did little to protect them. Aspirin was developed in the 1890s and was once the exclusive trademark of the international drug company Bayer, but the term became so commonly associated with any company's version of acetylsalicylic acid, the scientific name of the chemical compound, Bayer could no longer claim the exclusive right to use the name.[145]

A similar fate has befallen the trademarks for air fryer, dry ice, escalator, cellophane, heroin, hovercraft, kerosene, linoleum, trampoline, thermos, dumpster, yo-yo, zipper, and teleprompter. Videotape was originally trademarked by Ampex Corporation, and flip phone was trademarked by Motorola. All were once exclusive brands that have since become generic terms.

Other trademarks facing genericization and fighting to preserve their trademark registrations include Chap Stick, Taser, Bubble Wrap, Realtor, Frisbee, Popsicle, Jumbotron, Jacuzzi, Photoshop, Jeep, Ping Pong, Crock-Pot, Jet Ski, Coke, Q-tips, and Post-It Notes (including its trademarked canary yellow color). Companies like Kimberly-Clark and Johnson & Johnson collectively cringe when consumers use the terms "Kleenex" and "Band-Aid" as generic names for tissues and adhesive bandages. Each year, Xerox places advertisements touting its trademark and discouraging its use as a verb (you can photocopy a document; you cannot "Xerox" it). Companies also notify media whenever they see their trademarks being misused to protect their trademarks. If a TV reporter happens to mention needing a "Kleenex," a Kimberly-Clark attorney may contact the television station advising them not to use their trademark as a generic term for a tissue. It provides evidence that the companies have aggressively protected their trademarks, which is a consideration used in determining whether the trademark deserves renewal.

Some brands ultimately choose to abandon their trademarks. This was the case for the term "Taco Tuesday," which Taco John's owned as a registered trademark for more than three decades. The regional restaurant chain didn't want to continue paying the hefty legal fees needed to defend its mark after its larger rival Taco Bell filed a petition to cancel it, claiming the commonly used phrase "should be freely available to all who make, sell, eat and celebrate tacos."[146]

144. The Lanham Act allows for cancellation of a registered trademark if it is primarily understood as a "generic name for the goods or services, or a portion thereof, for which it is registered." 15 U.S.C. § 1064(3).
145. While "aspirin" is considered a generic term in the United States, it is still a registered trademark in dozens of countries, including Bayer's international headquarters of Germany. Some trademarks are valid in some countries but not others. "Zorro" is a valid trademark in the United States but not in the European Union. *See* "'Zorro' Trademark Declared Invalid in Europe," *Hollywood Reporter*, July 6, 2015.
146. Jordan Valinsky, "The Battle for the 'Taco Tuesday' Trademark is Over," *CNN*, July 18, 2023. As a regional company, Taco John's trademark did not extend to one state – New Jersey – where Gregory's Restaurant and Bar in Somers Point owned the term "Taco Tuesday" for more than four decades. The phrase became freely available in all states in late 2023, however, when like Taco John's, the smaller restaurant chose not to shoulder the legal fees and forfeited its trademark registration. Jordan Valinsky, "Taco Bell's Battle to Free the 'Taco Tuesday' Trademark is Officially Over," *CNN*, October 24, 2023.

What Cannot Be Trademarked

Some things cannot be registered as a trademark. For example, federal law forbids any trademark that "[c]onsists of or comprises the flag or coat of arms or other insignia of the United States, or any State or municipality, or any foreign nation."[147] Some flag designs may be registered, however, if they are stylized versions that use different colors or shapes or change a significant feature to become distinctive of the applicant's goods in commerce. So using the stars and stripes to outline a shape, for example, may get registered.

Unless written consent has been given, the law prevents trademark registration of any mark that "[c]onsists of or comprises a name, portrait, or signature identifying a particular living individual."[148] In fact, the law prevents someone from trademarking any living person's name – even their own – by itself. This doesn't mean, however, that a trademark cannot contain someone's own name as part of the mark. But they cannot use the mark containing their name to the exclusion of another person with the same name.

Given that this rule covers living individuals, it seems to leave open the possibility of trademarking features of deceased individuals. But it does specifically prohibit trademarking the "name, signature, or portrait of a deceased President of the United States during the life of his widow" unless the widow has given written consent.[149]

As noted earlier, registration will be denied to a merely descriptive mark (without a secondary meaning), such as a surname or a matter that, as a whole, is functional.[150] A feature that is a function of the product cannot be trademarked, such as the color brown for the tinted glass used for beer bottles to protect the contents from harmful light. But UPS has registered the shade of brown it uses for its trucks because the color is not a function of the service, and trademarking it does not interfere with the ability of other delivery companies to operate.

The law also specifically prohibits registering a mark that is only geographically descriptive of the goods, except as an indication of regional origin. In particular, the law frowns upon deceptively misdescriptive marks and expressly forbids it when used as primarily a geographical mark. Examples of rejected geographic brands include New York Ways Gallery luggage and handbags, which are not made in or connected to New York,[151] and Colagnac liqueur, which does not come from Cognac, France.[152]

If a mark "resembles" an existing trademark and is likely to "cause confusion, or to cause mistake, or to deceive," it will be refused registration.[153] This likelihood of confusion would include marks that have a different spelling but otherwise sound alike (phonetic equivalent). Likewise, stylizing the font or adding other stylistic elements might still create the same commercial impression.

It's also a problem if a mark conveys a similar general meaning to produce the same reaction (i.e., "Guy," instead of "Man"), or substitutes a foreign translated word ("Agua" instead of "Water"). It is likely to cause consumer confusion and would be rejected unless a court permits concurrent registrations with the U.S. Patent and Trademark Office prescribing conditions and limitations as to how and where each of the marks may be used.

A likelihood of confusion primarily only exists when the goods or services are related, however. This doesn't mean they have to be identical but that consumers are likely to mistakenly assume they come from the same source. The concern is whether there is a likelihood

147. 15 U.S. Code § 1052(b).
148. *Id.* § 1052(c).
149. *Id.*
150. *Id.* § 1052(e).
151. *In Re Hiromichi Wada*, 194 F. 3d 1297 (Fed. Cir. 1999).
152. Kevin R. Casey, "'Problem' Trademarks of the Descriptive-Misdescriptive-Deceptive Types," *Intellectual Property Law Newsletter*, Summer 2002, *at* www.stradley.com/-/media/files/resourceslanding/publications/2002/06/problem-trademarks-of-the-descriptive-misdescrip__/files/krc-problem/fileattachment/krc-problem.pdf.
153. 15 U.S. Code § 1052(d).

of confusion as to the source of the goods or services, not simply between the two goods or services. For example, a trademark application for "Golden Knights" by a Las Vegas NHL franchise was denied because The College of Saint Rose already held that trademark for use in "entertainment services, namely, professional ice hockey exhibitions"[154] and asserted there would be a likelihood of confusion. On the other hand, Twentieth Century Fox Television was allowed to continue using *Empire* for its television drama despite a claim of confusion by the record label Empire Distribution.[155]

Disparagement

For decades, federal law (Lanham Act) stipulated trademarks could not be granted for names that disparage people or groups.[156] In *Matal v. Tam*,[157] the Supreme Court unanimously struck down this restriction as an infringement on free speech. An Asian-American rock band "The Slants" was denied a trademark based on the 1946 regulation against disparagement. Consulting dictionaries, the Patent and Trademark Office examiner had determined the name to be disparaging to a substantial composite of Asian Americans. But the band contended that as Asian Americans themselves, they should be allowed to "reclaim" and "take ownership" of the derogatory term used against their own people of Asian ethnicity.

The government argued registered trademarks are benefits indicating government speech, not private speech, but the Supreme Court was unpersuaded and found troubling the overly broad "disparagement clause discriminates on the bases of 'viewpoint.'"[158] Writing for the Court, Justice Alito stated, "Speech may not be banned on the ground that it expresses ideas that offend."[159]

This case held implications for other controversial trademarks, most notably the Washington Redskins, which was trademarked in 1967 but faced repeated challenges to its mascot as a disparaging racial slur against Indigenous Americans. The team had its federal trademark registrations canceled, but an appeals court vacated the decision after the Supreme Court's decision in *Tam*. The team nonetheless retired the name and ultimately adopted its new name, the "Washington Commanders," which was officially trademarked in 2023.

Another part of the same provision of the Lanham Act restricted the registration of "immoral" or "scandalous" matter, and it met a similar fate.[160] In this case, artist and entrepreneur Erik Brunetti wanted to trademark his clothing line called "FUCT." Although pronounced as four letters in sequence, F-U-C-T, the mark might be read differently as the past participle of a well-known profanity.

The PTO Board rejected his application, concluding that "[w]hether one considers [the mark] as a sexual term, or finds that [Brunetti] has used [the mark] in the context of extreme misogyny, nihilism or violence, we have no question but that [the term is] extremely

154. USPTO, "Letter about Trademark Application," *at* http://tsdr.uspto.gov/documentviewer?caseId=sn87147239&docId=OOA20161207114432#docIndex=0&page=1.
155. "Fox Gets to Keep 'Empire' Series Title after Beating Hip-Hop Record Label in Court," *Hollywood Reporter*, February 3, 2016.
156. § 1052(a) stated, in part, that registration would be refused to any marks that "disparage or falsely suggest a connection" with persons (living or dead), institutions, beliefs, or national symbols, or "bring them into contempt, or disrepute."
157. 582 U.S. ___ (2017); No. 15–1293, slip op. (U.S. June 19, 2017).
158. *Id.* slip op. at 22. In saying that the disparagement clause is too broad by applying to *any person, group, or institution*, the Court explained that it could conceivably apply to trademarks like "Down with racists," "Down with sexists," "James Buchanan was a disastrous president," or "Slavery is an evil institution," at 25–26. Only "positive" marks about a person were allowed. This was the essence of viewpoint discrimination.
159. *Id.* at 1.
160. 15 U.S. Code § 1052(a) stated, in part, that registration would be refused to a mark that "[c]onsists of or comprises immoral, deceptive, or scandalous matter." The Supreme Court did not address the "deceptive" part of the provision in this case.

offensive."[161] But as in *Tam*, the Supreme Court found the "immoral or scandalous" criterion to be "substantially overbroad"[162] and not viewpoint-neutral, but viewpoint-based.

The Court explained that marks that championed conventional moral standards were approved but not marks that denigrate the concepts. For example, registration was refused to marks that communicated "immoral" or "scandalous" views about such things as drug use, religion, and terrorism, such as You Can't Spell Healthcare Without THC, but registration was approved for "more accepted views on the same topics" such as D.A.R.E. To Resist Drugs and Violence.[163]

Proving Elements of Trademark Infringement

What happens when one's trademark is used or misused by a competitor, the media, or others?

The most common remedy for trademark infringement is injunctive relief, where a court orders the infringer to immediately cease its unlawful use of the mark. Proof of irreparable harm is necessary for an injunction to be granted, however. A court may also require the infringer to produce corrective advertising or publish a disclaimer to dispel confusion.

Out of court resolutions are also common. Otherwise, registration provides an automatic right to sue in federal court where a wronged party can enforce its rights against an infringer in court and seek monetary relief, including actual damages (such as lost income due to the infringement and up to three times the amount), the infringer's profits[164] (proven by the plaintiff), and court costs (plus attorneys' fees in exceptional cases).[165]

Statutory damages may be chosen instead, ranging from $1,000 to $200,000 per counterfeit mark, and up to $2 million for willful use.[166] Plaintiffs bringing an infringement complaint must demonstrate that 1) they have a valid and legally protectable mark,[167] 2) own the mark, and 3) the defendant

- used a reproduction, counterfeit, copy, or imitation of the mark
- without consent
- in commerce
- in the connection with the sale of goods
- and is likely to cause confusion.

Use of a trademark must be proven so that its holders don't assert a generalized right to control language. The use must also be in commerce and in connection with the sale of goods since federal trademark law stems from congressional power to regulate interstate commerce. This evidence not only shows the movement of goods but the advertising in media with interstate distribution.

The central focus of most cases, however, is whether the defendant's use of a similar mark caused or was likely to cause consumer confusion. If consumers viewing the allegedly infringing mark would likely assume the product or service it represents is associated with the source of the plaintiff's trademarked product or service, it would be infringement.

161. *Iancu v. Brunetti*, 588 U.S. ___ (2019); No. 18–302, slip op. at 3 (U.S. June 24, 2019).
162. *Id.* at 11.
163. *Id.* at 6–7.
164. Willful infringement is no longer required for trademark owners to recover infringers' profits. *Romag Fasteners v. Fossil Group, Inc.*, 590 U.S. ___ (2020).
165. 15 U.S.C. § 1117(a) and (b).
166. *Id.* at (c).
167. One way to show a mark's validity is by being registered for at least five years, becoming "incontestable" under 15 U.S.C. § 1065.

If the goods or services directly compete and the two marks are sufficiently similar, courts rarely need to look beyond the mark itself for evidence of confusion. But if the goods or services are unrelated, courts must look beyond the trademark to the nature of the products themselves and the context in which they are marketed and sold.

For this, courts have developed a multifactored test to determine the likelihood of confusion.[168] This considers and weighs eight qualities of trademark registration:

1 strength of the plaintiff's mark
2 relatedness of the goods
3 similarity of the marks
4 evidence of actual confusion
5 marketing channels used
6 likely degree of care exercised by the purchaser
7 defendant's intent in selecting the mark, and
8 likelihood of expansion of the product lines.

Evidence of actual confusion may come from surveys and testimony, and the degree of purchaser care relates to the scrutiny given to making the purchase (e.g., a candy bar at a convenience store checkout versus a luxury automobile). Courts also consider whether the same marketing and advertising channels are used to reach the same consumers.

The likelihood of expansion into other product lines is relevant to consider since the trademark holder may otherwise be precluded from someday entering the accused infringer's market. Courts need not accept or reject all of these factors to rule in either party's favor. They will determine which party has the stronger case by balancing the factors.

This was the case in a trademark dispute over a decorative seal used on a bourbon producer's bottle.[169] Maker's Mark Distillery, Inc., had a registered trademark since 1958 on its distinctive, red dripping wax seal. Then in 2001, Jose Cuervo began selling its premium tequila in the United States with a red dripping wax seal. In the ensuing dispute, Cuervo sought to cancel Maker's Mark's trademark, saying the seal was merely functional, but the court determined Maker's Mark had a valid trademark in its aesthetically functional wax seal that wasn't otherwise necessary for sealing a bottle.

The court then applied the test for likelihood of consumer confusion. The ruling gave weight to the similarities of the marks as well as the strength of the plaintiff's mark, which it found to be "extremely strong" as highly distinctive both conceptually and commercially, acquiring "secondary meaning through fifty years of use, extensive advertising and consumer recognition."[170]

The goods were also somewhat related, and the marketing channels were more or less similar. On the other hand, neither party produced evidence of actual confusion or expansion plans, and the court found Cuervo did not intend to infringe. In addition, the likely degree of purchaser care favored Cuervo because of the difference in liquor and high purchase price involved, although the court noted that consumers may still assume the seller is affiliated with the other party. In balancing the likelihood of confusion factors, the court found the majority – strength, relatedness of goods, similarity, and marketing channels – favored Maker's Mark.[171]

168. *See, e.g.*, *Scott Paper Co. v. Scott's Liquid Gold, Inc.*, 589 F.2d 1225 (3d Cir. 1978); *Toho Co., Ltd. v. Sears, Roebuck & Co.*, 645 F.2d 788, 790 (9th Cir. 1981); *Frisch's Rests., Inc. v. Elby's Big Boy, Inc.*, 670 F.2d 642, 648 (6th Cir. 1982).
169. *Maker's Mark Distillery, Inc. v. Diageo North America, Inc.*, 679 F.3d 410 (2012).
170. *Id.* at 420.
171. *Id.* at 424.

Dilution of Trademark

Disputes over trademark infringement are sometimes more about the negative impact the infringer's use has on a well-established brand. In 1972, Coca-Cola filed a legal action against a company making posters proclaiming, "Enjoy Cocaine" using the same script of the "Enjoy Coca-Cola" slogan. Gemini Rising attempted to defend its poster by asserting Coca-Cola had not shown any loss of income due to their posters, and no consumers were misled into thinking the posters were a product of the Coca-Cola Company.

A federal district court in New York found in favor of Coca-Cola and ordered a halt to the posters for three reasons: 1) associating cocaine with Coca-Cola disparages the product; 2) consumers might be confused into believing Coca-Cola was somehow involved in the poster (the trademark claim); and 3) the poster is likely to damage Coca-Cola's business reputation.[172]

In the years since this case, Congress added legislation making it easier for companies to protect their trademarks from dilution, the legal term to describe how such a similar image or script diminishes the value or distinctiveness of the mark, regardless of whether it is competing or causes a loss of revenue. The Federal Trademark Dilution Act of 1995[173] allows lawsuits for dilution that can lead to an injunction prohibiting the defendant from using the mark and diminishing the famous mark's value.

The Lanham Act recognizes two types of dilution – dilution by blurring and dilution by tarnishment. Dilution by blurring is the more common claim. It occurs when a junior mark is so similar to a more famous senior trademark that it impairs the distinctiveness of the famous mark in the minds of the consumer. Examples include Dupont shoes, Buick aspirin, and Kodak pianos.[174] Dilution only applies to famous marks, which may need to prove their fame with evidence of sales volume, geographic reach, and extensive advertising and publicity. To establish blurring, the marks do not need to be identical or nearly identical. In 2006, Congress passed the Trademark Dilution Revision Act,[175] lowering such standards. Instead, courts will consider such factors as the degree of similarity between the marks, the distinctiveness of the famous mark and its degree of recognition, the extent to which the famous mark makes exclusive use of it, the actual association between the marks, and the defendant's intent.

Dilution by tarnishment occurs when a similar mark harms the reputation of a famous mark. This is usually where the junior mark is being used in an unsavory or unwholesome context (e.g., pornography) or to sell shoddy or inferior goods. One case that made it to the U.S. Supreme Court involved a sex toy and apparel shop operated by Victor Moseley in Kentucky that went by the name "Victor's Little Secret."[176] Lingerie shop Victoria's Secret sued for trademark dilution by tarnishment. In 2003, the Court said that Victoria's Secret needed to prove actual dilution of their mark, not merely a likelihood of dilution. But after Congress amended the law in 2006, Victoria's Secret was able to win an injunction against Moseley.[177]

The Supreme Court erupted in laughter when the decision was announced in a dilution by tarnishment case in 2023 pitting Jack Daniel's Whiskey against a dog toy maker. While reading the decision, Justice Elena Kagan held up a "Bad Spaniels" squeaky, chewable dog toy, which resembled a Jack Daniel's bottle.[178] The toy featured a drawing of a spaniel, and

172. *Coca-Cola v. Gemini Rising*, 346 F. Supp. 1183 (E.D. N.Y. 1972).
173. 15 U.S.C. § 1125(c) (1995). This is codified at section 43(c) of the Lanham Act.
174. Kathleen B. McCabe, "Dilution-by-Blurring: A Theory Caught in the Shadow of Trademark Infringement," 68 *Fordham L. Rev.* 1827 (2000).
175. 15 U.S.C. § 1125(c) (1995), *amended by* Pub. L. No. 109–312, 120 STAT. 1730 (2006).
176. *Moseley v. V Secret Catalogue, Inc.*, 537 U.S. 418 (2003).
177. *V Secret Catalogue, Inc. v. Moseley*, 2010 WL 1979429 (6th Cir. 2010).
178. Nina Totenberg, "Supreme Court Sides with Jack Daniel's in Trademark Dispute with Dog Toy Maker," *NPR*, June 8, 2023.

instead of the words "40% alc. by vol.," it substituted "43% poo by vol." and "100% smelly" (Figure 7.4).

In its brief to the Court, Jack Daniel's Properties said it "appreciates a good joke as much as anyone," but it didn't want its customers to be confused or "associating its fine whiskey with dog poop," diluting by tarnishment their mark.[179] The high court agreed.[180] The parody exception to the Lanham Act would also not shield the toy maker, who admitted to using the mark "as a designation of source" for its own goods.[181]

Bad Dog – Don't Tarnish Jack Daniel's

Jack Daniel's Old No. 7 Tennessee Sour Mash Whiskey bottle. "Jack Daniel's" is a registered trademark, as is "Old No. 7," as well as the product's arched logo, the stylized label with filigree (twirling white lines), and the distinctive square bottle.

Bad Spaniels dog toy. The faux bottle has a black label with stylized white text and white filigreed border. The name is in a like font and arch, although a spaniel is added. "The Old No. 2 On Your Tennessee Carpet" replaces "Old No. 7 Tennessee Sour Mash Whiskey" in similar graphic form. The small print at the bottom substitutes "43% poo by vol." and "100% smelly" for "40% alc. by vol. (80 proof)."

Figure 7.4 Jack Daniel's versus Bad Spaniels Trademark Dilution by Tarnishment

Source: *Jack Daniel's Properties, Inc. v. VIP Products LLC*, 599 U.S. ____ (2023); No. 22–148, slip op. (U.S. June 8, 2023).

When Can a Trademark Be Used? "Fair Use" Defenses

There are times when using another's trademark might make sense or seem fair, so trademark law provides some exceptions and defenses. For example, protection from liability is

179. *Id.*
180. *Jack Daniel's Properties, Inc. v. VIP Products LLC*, 599 U.S. ____ (2023); No. 22–148, slip op. (U.S. June 8, 2023).
181. *Id.* at 19, citing 15 U.S.C. §1125(c)(3)(A).

available to anyone who uses a descriptive term, "fairly and in good faith" and "otherwise than as a mark" merely to describe their own goods.[182] Congress also expressly exempted "fair use" of a trademark from a dilution claim since dilution could infringe on protected uses of a mark. Sometimes referred to as "trademark fair use," the dilution defenses are more limited than the more familiar doctrine of copyright fair use.

There are some parallels though. The Federal Dilution Act specifically excludes as actionable any fair use of a famous mark in connection with comparative advertising, criticism, comment, or parody, as well as all forms of news reporting and news commentary and any noncommercial use of a mark.[183]

Use of a trademark in a comparison ad or promotion will not be considered trademark dilution. When Pepsi runs commercials showing someone preferring the taste of Pepsi over that of Coke with a trademark bottle or logo of Coke clearly visible, there is no trademark dilution.[184]

The purpose of this type of fair use is to allow consumers to compare goods or services. It is not, however, to permit the use of another's mark for any other advertising or promotional purpose. For example, advertisers are careful to avoid using the trademarked words "Super Bowl" unless they have paid the NFL for the right to do so. That is why in advertisements in the weeks preceding the Super Bowl, grocery stores invite you to stock up for "the big game," department stores hold a "super Sunday sale," and restaurants promote "super weekend" specials.

Criticism and comment are also protected under the dilution law when focused "upon the famous mark owner or the goods or services of the famous mark owner."[185] This means well-known brands may be reviewed and critiqued in the media without invoking trademark dilution liability. It should be noted though that this law and the Anticybersquatting (ACPA) law will not prevent others from using a trademarked name in a URL when criticizing that person or company.

Parody of a famous mark is also protected as a fair use under trademark dilution. A favorite target of parody is one of the best-known logos around the world – the Nike swoosh. Commercial artist Michael Standard decided to parody the famous symbol by producing T-shirts and sweatshirts with a swoosh and the name "Mike," just one letter off from the athletic company's name. Standard then marketed the clothes to people named Mike, admitting that the whole intent was for people to see the similarity to the famous Nike logo.

A federal district court issued a summary judgment and enjoined Standard from marketing his parody logo, but on appeal the Seventh Circuit found that the evidence was not as clear as the district court implied. Standard had provided a list of customers who knew they were not purchasing Nike clothing, and Nike provided no evidence of consumer confusion.[186] Nike could not claim the product had been somehow disparaged or the brand damaged by the parody, and the appellate court was unwilling to enjoin the use of the logo without evidence of consumer confusion.

The federal dilution statute exempts all news reporting and commentary from a dilution claim, and the 2006 amendment expressly covers the defense of noncommercial use. The news media refer to all sorts of trademarks in their reporting without fear of transgression. Major sporting events such as the Super Bowl, March Madness, and Olympics are all trademarked terms. Unlike advertisers, newscasters can talk about the Super Bowl all they want without infringing trademark, even when the game is being played on another network.

182. 15 U.S.C. § 1115(b)(4).
183. 15 U.S.C. § 1125(c)(3). The 2006 amendments added an express defense for noncommercial use.
184. Of course, the advertisement must be accurate; otherwise, it could be misleading – a topic covered in Chapter 11.
185. 15 U.S.C. § 1125(c)(3)(A)(ii).
186. *Nike v. "Just Did It" Enters.*, 6 F. 3d 1225 (7th Cir. 1993).

There is little case law on the defense of this measure, although a California court did extend this fair use beyond traditional news media to a blogger who reported critically on a company reselling goods on eBay.[187] The article titled "Special Report: You Gotta Be Beserk to Use an eBay Listing Company! The Whole Story," depicted BidZirk's trademark and related the author's experience using an eBay listing company such as BidZirk. The court determined that it qualified for a news defense under the Federal Dilution Act.

Global View: International Pirating

When it comes to the global theft of intellectual property, the United States went from being a notorious outlier to one of the most targeted and vocal critics of counterfeiting and pirating. How so?

When other countries signed on in 1886 to the Berne Convention for the Protection of Literary and Artistic Works, the United States declined. At the time, Americans led the world in copyright pirating, primarily republishing European works without paying royalties. Joining the Berne Convention meant moving to change some of the U.S. copyright laws.

The growing need for international copyright protection eventually led this nation to join the Universal Copyright Convention (UCC) and participate in its less restrictive, reciprocal agreements with individual nations. Publishers became creative in finding ways to protect their works across borders by publishing in the member countries of the Berne Convention. Throughout the twentieth century, U.S. copyright holders in the growing film, music, and software industries demanded greater global protection against piracy. Finally in 1989, the United States joined the Berne Convention, expanding its reach of copyright protection. U.S. authors and creators could gain copyright protection in foreign nations by applying the baseline standards of the Berne Convention to avoid domestic legal formalities.

Of course, the reverse is also true. While U.S. registered copyright holders may sue international infringers for actual damages, so too can foreign rights holders sue American infringers for actual damages. Based on the Berne Convention standards, they do not need to follow U.S. law by registering their copyrights with the Copyright Office in the U.S. Library of Congress.

To comply with the requirements of the Berne Convention, U.S. law was amended in several ways. The copyright notice requirement was eliminated, but even more controversial was the Berne requirement recognizing moral rights. This change granted the creators of a copyrighted work the right to say what happens to it after their work is sold. This provision was part of the reason the United States was reluctant to join the Berne Convention. Its enforcement has been controversial though because copyrighted works are often sold and transferred to media companies, including publishing houses and motion picture firms that have edited, reformatted, and even colorized images without seeking the original author's permission.

Most of the world's countries now belong to the Berne Convention. China joined in 1992, and the Russian Federation followed suit in 1995. While it is the most significant international copyright treaty, there are many other treaties and agreements signed by various countries. One international agreement that further expanded protection to include trademark is the General Agreement on Tariffs and Trade (GATT),

187. Brooke Erdos Singer & Maxine Sharavsky, "Using Third Parties' Trademarks: Unpacking Commerciality, Competition, and Confusion," 26(1) *NYSBA Bright Ideas* (Spring 2017), *at* www.dglaw.com/images_user/newsalerts/2342_Using_Third_Parties.pdf, citing *Bid-Zirk, LLC v. Smith*, No. 6:06 709-HMH, 2007 U.S. Dist. LEXIS 78481 (D.S.C. October 22, 2007). In that case, the court stated that the content and not the format should be considered when determining whether the material constitutes journalism subject to fair use.

administered by the World Trade Organization through WIPO (World Intellectual Property Organization).

The need to protect trademarks in foreign markets has also grown. In 2003, the United States joined the Madrid Protocol for streamlining international registration of trademarks. U.S. registered trademark holders apply for an international registration (IR) through the U.S. Patent and Trade Office (USPTO), which sends it to WIPO for protection in over 100 countries, including China, Japan, and the European Union. An IR is valid for ten years and is renewable. The Madrid Protocol does require the use of a mark in another country to be governed by that country's local use laws.[188]

Despite the many treaties, the problem of pirating and counterfeiting goods persists and has intensified to staggering levels in recent years.[189] In 2023 alone, nearly 23 million counterfeit goods were seized by U.S. Customs and Border Protection agents.[190] If the seized goods had been genuine, their estimated value would have been over $2.75 billion.

Wearing apparel and accessories account for the most seized items, with watches and jewelry topping the list in terms of value, followed by handbags and wallets. The People's Republic of China remains the primary source for seized counterfeit and pirated goods.[191] Louis Vuitton, for example, discovered a massive counterfeiting operation in China selling fake bags. Companies insert programmable Near-Field Communication (NFC) sensors inside their trademarked goods to track and protect authenticity, but apparently even NFC tags can be hacked.[192]

Unfortunately, the only other remedy for enforcement is through the courts. International copyright claims are handled with a lawsuit in the courts of the country where the infringement occurred. A lawsuit can be brought in the United States if the copies were made in the Unted States and exported without consent, or if the infringing copies were created in another country and then imported to the United States.

International trademarks disputes are limited to the infringement rules of the country, making it less clear as to how trademark cases may be litigated and in what court system. Under U.S. law, goods marked or labeled as violating trademark cannot be imported into the United States.[193]

Summary

- Intellectual property is given by the U.S. Constitution to the protection of Congress to secure the ownership of patents, trademarks, and copyrights.
- Copyright is defined by law as a bundle of different rights, including copying (reproduction) rights and rights to control performance of the work, derivative works, distribution, and public display of the work.

188. For more on the Madrid Protocol, *see* "Protocol Relating to the Madrid Agreement Concerning the International Registration of Marks, World Intellectual Property Organization, *at* www.wipo.int/treaties/en/registration/madrid_protocol/. The United States is *not* a party to the *Madrid Agreement*, which is a separate treaty.
189. Federal seizures of infringing goods increased tenfold between 2000 and 2018, according to a report by the Organization for Economic Co-operation and Development (OECD) submitted to and available in the U.S Department of Homeland Security (DHS), "Combating Trafficking in Counterfeit and Pirated Goods," January 24, 2020, *at* www.dhs.gov/sites/default/files/publications/20_0124_plcy_counterfeit-pirated-goods-report_01.pdf.
190. "Intellectual Property Rights," U.S. Customs and Border Protection, *at* https://www.cbp.gov/trade/priority-issues/ipr.
191. *Id.*
192. Laura Batzella, "China: The War of Louis Vuitton against Fake Bags," *Mondaq*, November 13, 2020, *at* www.mondaq.com/china/trademark/1005630/the-war-of-louis-vuitton-against-fake-bags.
193. 15 U.S.C. § 1125(b).

- Original creative work in a fixed medium can be copyrighted, but ideas and facts cannot.
- The author owns a copyright whether or not the work is registered. However, registering it affords the author important advantages.
- For single-authored works in the United States today, copyright lasts for the life of the author plus 70 years. The U.S. Congress has repeatedly expanded the copyright's length of term, most recently in 1998.
- Music authors usually collect royalties for the performance of their works via one of three major licensing agencies: ASCAP, BMI, or SESAC, all of which can act as licensing agents for the authors and collect fees from those using their music, such as broadcasters, retail stores, or other commercial outlets.
- A copyright holder cannot prevent fair use by others of their work. There is no finite list of acceptable and unacceptable fair uses – only four criteria to be considered: the purpose and character of the use; the nature of the copyrighted work; the amount and substantiality used; and the impact on the market.
- Creating hardware and software suitable for use as a tool of copyright infringement (like a video recorder) is not legally actionable, but creating or promoting devices as the means to violate copyright ownership is considered to be unlawful.
- Trademarks are words, short phrases like slogans, logos, or images that identify a product as belonging to a particular vendor. Trademark law is based on the premise of preventing a likelihood of confusion over product brands in the marketplace to protect consumers.

Ethical Dilemmas: Fan Fiction – Harmless Hobby or Copyright Infringement?

Fan fiction is a popular pastime for fans who love to write about characters and expand on story lines using their favorite TV shows, movies, or books.[194] Generally, the owners of the intellectual property inspiring the fan fiction offer no rights to do so. Some copyright holders are quite comfortable with fan fiction, believing it keeps online readers engaged with their characters and might even attract new fans to the original work. But other copyright holders are vehemently opposed to it fearing how amateur prose can denigrate, diminish, or detract from original characters and story lines.

Novelist J.K. Rowling does not categorically oppose fan fiction based on her Harry Potter character, but her lawyers sent a cease-and-desist order to one fan fiction website in 2002, where characters were depicted in sexually explicit activities.[195] There is also concern the author of a derivative piece of fan fiction might attempt to claim the original copyright holder "stole" their work and incorporated it in a later book or film.

Some authors of fan fiction assert their work is simply fair use. Examining the four requirements of a fair use defense, however, does invite inquiring how the derivative work affects the market for the original, and whether the amount and substantiality used is excessive. Certain websites seem to be "profiting" from the intellectual property of others by posting fan fiction stories for free with a minimal amount of advertising.

Perhaps the best-known lawsuit concerning fan fiction involved a parody of the Civil War novel, *Gone with the Wind*. The estate of author Margaret Mitchell filed suit against the creator of "The Wind Done Gone." Despite a lower court victory for the estate, on appeal the court found the parody nature of the work protected it.[196] That ruling does not imply, however, that all fan fiction is parody and thereby entitled to the same protection.

194. Fan fiction can also be based on comic books, plays, video games, or any other narrative form. For a comprehensive list, visit www.fanfiction.net.
195. "Harry Potter and the Copyright Lawyer," *Washington Post*, June 18, 2003.
196. *Suntrust v. Houghton Mifflin*, 268 F.3d 1257 (Ct. App. Eleventh Circ. 2001).

Paramount Pictures posted Fan Film Guidelines on the Star Trek website[197] and went to court in 2016 over a crowd-funded fan film based on its franchise.[198] A judge initially ruled the short YouTube video "Axanar" was not a fair use. The case was ultimately settled out of court, with the fan-made work subject to substantial changes in compliance with the studio's guidelines.

Undoubtedly, derivative works are included in the bundle of rights held by copyright owners, and yet there are so many questions to be answered in this area. Is it worth the time and expense for copyright owners to seek out others creating derivative works based on their originals? Do fiction authors need a licensing agency like music authors have ASCAP, BMI, and SESAC to enforce their copyrights?

Licensing agencies survive by extracting a portion of the licensing fees. Should fan fiction authors who write for no money pay licensing fees? Assuming there is no profit to be made from licensing fan fiction, should authors be allowed to control the uses of their intellectual property? Assuming for a moment that the transformative nature of fan fiction makes it a fair use, is there no limit? Should fan fiction be allowed to do anything with characters taken from others' work, including involving them in content offensive to the original author? These are questions of ethics while awaiting answers that perhaps only a court may provide when resolving future disputes between intellectual property attorneys.

In the meantime, fan fiction writers who want to continue creating their work without repercussion might want to look to fan fiction authors who successfully avoided copyright infringement lawsuits.[199] The popular trilogy Fifty Shades of Grey by E.L. James is a good example, as it was originally a fan fiction of the popular book series Twilight by Stephenie Meyer. It's possible that Fifty Shades of Grey has never been confronted with a lawsuit because the work is easily defended as a fair use.[200] For example, Fifty Shades does not appeal to the science fiction fans of Twilight, posing little effect on the potential market or value of the original work. Thus, in the absence of more explicit legal protection, fan fiction writers might strive to emulate how other fan fiction authors have managed to carefully create their work as protected by fair use.

197. www.startrek.com/fan-films.
198. Eriq Gardner, "CBS, Paramount Settle Lawsuit Over 'Star Trek' Fan Film," *Hollywood Reporter*, January 20, 2017.
199. Gabriella Fernandez, "A Brief Overview of the Fair Use Analysis in the Fanfiction Context," *Cardozo Arts & Ent. L.J.*, October 31, 2023, *at* https://larc.cardozo.yu.edu/cgi/viewcontent.cgi?article=1365&context=aelj-blog.
200. *Id.*

8

Broadcasting and Telecommunications

LEARNING OBJECTIVES

After reading this chapter, you should know

- how the FCC defines the public interest, convenience, or necessity
- procedures established for licensing radio and television stations
- how rules are drawn to guide cable and satellite television's development
- how multichannel video program distributors (MVPDs) are defined and regulated
- how the introduction of online video delivery (OVD) affected federal regulation
- what key legal terms (e.g., common carrier) mean in terms of U.S. media law

Instead of discussing recent cases that are significant or precedent-setting, this chapter begins with a few rather mundane, minor actions taken by the Federal Communications Commission (FCC). Over one month's time in late 2023, here are *some* of the Commission's actions – the first four of which tend to be procedural in nature while the last one reflects a larger issue:

- The West Central Minnesota Educational TV Corporation was fined $3,000 for failing to comply with issues and program list rules. The FCC requires radio and television stations to make public a list of issues the stations believe need attention in their communities, and a list of programming content provided for the community to address those issues. The lists need to be made public every three months, and the Appleton, MN, station was late posting its lists multiple times.
- Sunflower Community Action in Kansas was fined $2,500 for erecting a 13-meter antenna in Wichita when it was supposed to be 24 meters high. The low-power FM station signed a consent decree acknowledging its error and asked to modify its application, allowing for the lower height.
- Boulder Creek Recreation & Park District avoided a fine, signing a consent decree admitting it violated rules regarding its online public file and implementing corrective measures. The California FM station failed to "timely place records" online.

DOI: 10.4324/9781003462989-8

- Elmira College (NY) was fined $500 for filing a late license renewal application.
- The FCC issued Notices of Illegal Pirate Broadcasting to two New York City property owners. The FCC identified unlicensed FM transmissions originating from their properties and threatened them with fines up to $2 million each if the broadcasts continued.[1]

The pages that follow illustrate how and why the federal government targets its regulation and policies for electronic media.

Roots of Telecommunications Regulation

From the wireless era of ship-to-shore communications to the digital age, broadcast regulation has shaped electronic media invention, competition, and content. Along the way, the U.S. government guided "communication by wire and radio so as to make available, so far as possible, to all the people of the United States a rapid, efficient, nation-wide, and worldwide wire and radio communications service with adequate facilities at reasonable charges."[2] When a temporary U.S. agency for radio control sprang to life in 1927, Washington, DC, lawmakers did not anticipate permanent government oversight and were nervous about regulating wireless communications at all.

Wireless Ship Act of 1910

The Wireless Ship Act of 1910
U.S. law requiring large U.S. ships to carry long-range radio transmitters and receivers.

Before radio broadcasting emerged as the national medium known today, Guglielmo Marconi promoted the wireless telegraph transmitter designed to tap the steady pulse of Morse code from ship to shore. The **Wireless Ship Act of 1910** placed a radio transmitter and wireless operator aboard oceangoing vessels traveling more than 200 miles from their port, but this 1910 law missed an important detail: the need for 24-hour radio operations, which if addressed might have alleviated history's worst ocean liner disaster.

When an iceberg floating near Nova Scotia gashed the R.M.S. *Titanic*, the famously "unsinkable" ocean liner transmitted wireless signals of distress after midnight. A radio operator on a nearby ship had retired for the evening, while amateur operators reported random noise interfering with the *Titanic*'s wireless signals. The urgent signal went largely unheeded. News of the drowning of 1,500 passengers in the icy waters of the North Atlantic prompted Congress to amend the wireless law to correct this tragic oversight.

Radio Act of 1912

The Radio Act of 1912
Federal law requiring ships to maintain radio reception around the clock with licensed operators.

The Radio Act of 1912 required wireless radio operators for oceangoing vessels to stay on duty around the clock. More to the point, it authorized the U.S. Department of Commerce and Labor to *grant licenses* so each station would have its own frequency "for the prevention of interference."[3]

When World War I erupted, the issuance of radio licenses to ordinary citizens was called to a halt. The U.S. Signal Corps, however, began training soldiers in the use of wireless radio. Once they returned home after the war, army veterans started building radio transmitters and receivers as a home hobby. Their on-air experiments gave rise to announcements of news and musical recordings, but it was all upset by noise – signal interference – a *cacophony* of on-air clashes frustrating the desire to listen to radio at all.

1. The FCC provides public notice of its actions online at https://www.fcc.gov/news-events (Accessed December 15, 2023).
2. Communications Act of 1934, 47 U.S.C. § 151 (1976).
3. Radio channels were measured in meters rather than the frequency of cycles in this early era.

Forcing Hoover's Hand

U.S. Secretary of Commerce and Labor Herbert Hoover assigned wireless licenses to companies and individuals in 1920 while the medium found its voice in programming. Hoover was authorized to grant only two frequencies for transmissions, which was insufficient for the booming traffic on U.S. airwaves. Two additional channels were dedicated in 1923, but unauthorized amateurs still created sonic chaos.

Secretary Hoover summoned industry leaders to Washington, DC, with the hope of organizing some system of self-regulation.[4] No effective agreement was forged in those conferences to guard the new wireless medium against renegade operators threatening radio's development. Two cases further sealed the fate of any private sector solution.

In *Hoover v. Intercity Radio Co.* (1923), a federal appellate court ordered Hoover to find a frequency for the company with the "least possible interference" to use although he could find none.[5] And when he tried to stop the Zenith Corp. from interfering with a radio broadcaster in Canada, a district judge held Hoover had no "express grant of power in the [Radio Act of 1912]" to prevent Zenith's broadcasts.[6] Taken together, both rulings reached the same end – the U.S. commerce secretary lacked the authority to control the nation's airwaves.

Federal Radio Commission (1927)

The Federal Radio Commission
The Radio Act of 1927 created the Federal Radio Commission (FRC) with eight members, each one representing a region of the country.

Congress proposed a new administrative agency to overcome such legal hurdles, the **Federal Radio Commission**. At first, there were eight members appointed to the commission representing different regions of the nation. The FRC began granting licenses to radio stations for three-year terms with the warning their renewal applications could be refused if they were not serving the public interest, convenience, or necessity – later known as the PICON standard.

Rationale for Regulation

What exactly gave the U.S. government the right to control broadcast radio by licensing? The **commerce clause** (U.S. Const. Art. I, §8) provides for oversight of interstate commerce.[7] The rationale supporting broadcast station licensing was based on two legal premises: the *scarcity doctrine* and *public ownership* of the airwaves. That is, electromagnetic energy emanating from station towers in the United States belongs not to any corporate owner but to the American people. Broadcast licensing then functions as a "lease" for broadcasters; it grants a temporary period in which radio and TV station owners are licensed to serve as public trustees.

Spectrum Management

The electromagnetic spectrum refers to all electronic waves, not only those used for broadcasting but also microwaves, light, X-rays, and gamma rays. Only a portion of the

4. Andrew F. Inglis, *Behind the Tube: A History of Broadcasting Technology and Business* 84 (Burlington, MA: Focal Press, 1990).
5. *Hoover v. Intercity Radio Co.*, 286 F. 1003 (D.C. Cir. 1923).
6. *United States v. Zenith Radio Corp.*, 12 F. 2d 614 (N.D. Ill. 1926).
7. Congress drew upon the commerce clause (U.S. Const. art. 1, §8) for the power "to regulate Commerce with foreign nations, and among the several States" for its rationale to regulate broadcasting. Even if a signal does not migrate across a state's boundary, that station still falls under federal supervision.

spectrum is used for broadcasting. The portion of the spectrum designated as "radio waves" includes all sorts of human transmissions, not just broadcasting.

Frequencies within the radio spectrum are **allocated** for different uses. Allocations must be coordinated for the same reason that licenses must be issued – to prevent interference problems. Garage door openers, for example, are small transmitters. Thousands of them can operate on the same frequency without any problem but imagine if a powerful radio station operated on the same frequency. It could cause havoc with garage doors all over town. For this reason, FCC approval is required for equipment using radio waves. That doesn't mean your microwave needs an FCC *license*, although all sorts of devices from medical equipment to microwave ovens receive FCC authorization. They may emit a signal, but they are not broadcasters.

Land regulation provides a useful analogy for spectrum regulation. While it might be physically possible to build a factory in a residential neighborhood, zoning laws prevent that from happening. If the spectrum space a television station wants to use is on the same "land" as a garage door opener, then the FCC would apply the rule to prevent it. Just as land zoned for certain purposes has restrictions, so, too, does the broadcast spectrum. There is, of course, no public service obligation imposed on garage door openers as there is on broadcasters.

Zoning will allow for some "mixed use" spaces, and spectrum allocations allow some frequencies to be shared for non-interfering purposes. Just as not all land in the United States is zoned (usually remote rural areas), not all spectrum is licensed by the FCC because certain areas, referred to as "white spaces," are set aside and left open for experimentation.

Bedrock Law
The U.S. government's authority over broadcasting is based on the commerce clause (Art. I, §8, U.S. Constitution). Its power to license stations is derived from the scarcity doctrine defining electromagnetic spectrum as a limited public resource.

The Supreme Court spelled out this doctrine in 1969 when it declared "broadcast frequencies constituted a scarce resource whose use could be regulated and rationalized only by the government . . . where there are substantially more individuals who want to broadcast than there are frequencies to allocate."[8] The broadcast license entitles individual stations to use this scarce resource locally for a community or designated market area. Yet the FCC does not license commercial broadcast networks; nor does it regulate noncommercial organizations such as PBS and NPR that exist to offer programming to public stations that are licensed.

Both the FRC and its successor, the Federal Communications Commission (FCC), license broadcast stations to serve the public interest. Part of the problem is defining "public interest, convenience or necessity," which one legal scholar summed up in two apt metaphors: "delivering the mail" and seeking the "Holy Grail."[9]

Just as the U.S. Postal Service is responsible for the mail delivery, the FCC ensures the delivery of broadcast content to households. Krasnow's reference to the "Holy Grail" implies loftier goals, such as ensuring ownership opportunities for women and minorities or meeting children's educational needs. The PICON standard is more specifically defined in terms of *competition, diversity, and localism*. How the government defines those terms is covered later in detail.

The Federal Communications Commission

Congress felt that once everything was ironed out with station licenses, the FRC would no longer be needed, and it could be closed for business. The Secretary of Commerce would

8. *Red Lion Broadcasting Co. v. Federal Communications Commission*, 395 U.S. 367 (1969).
9. Erwin G. Krasnow & Jack N. Goodman, "The 'Public Interest' Standard: The Search for the Holy Grail," 50(3) *Federal Communications Law Journal* 5 (1998).

issue an "occasional" radio license. While the FRC was scheduled to "sunset" and cease operations by the end of 1933, the U.S. Congress made ready for its replacement agency.

Federal Communications Commission (FCC)
U.S. government agency established by the Communications Act of 1934 to oversee interstate and global communications by radio, television, wire, satellite, and cable.

The Federal Communications Commission (FCC) was formed from the Communications Act of 1934 combining regulations of broadcasting with telephone and wired telegraphy. When the FCC was created, many of the same rules were carried over from the 1927 law and recodified in the 1934 act. The agency also formulated its own rules and followed the laws passed by Congress delegated to its seven bureaus and eleven offices.

The Commissioners

FCC Commissioners
Five individuals appointed by the president and confirmed by the U.S. Senate for five-year terms. They adopt rules and set policy for wired and wireless media.

Five men and women are appointed by the president and confirmed by the Senate to serve five-year terms as commissioners, although some commissioners leave without completing their five-year terms. The president nominates up to three commissioners from his own party and designates one commissioner to preside as chair.[10]

They adopt and modify rules, establish telecommunications policy, and rule on license renewals and infractions.[11] When any commissioner's term expires, the president has the responsibility of naming a replacement. If there are only two commissioners from the president's party, then the replacement may come from the president's political party and the FCC will switch from a 3–2 Republican majority to a 3–2 Democratic majority just like that.

The FCC's administrative duties are carried on through 11 offices such as the *general counsel*, *administrative law judges*, *economics and analytics*, *inspector general*, and *legislative affairs*. There also are seven operating bureaus: *Public Safety & Homeland Security*, *Wireless Telecommunications*, *Wireline Competition*, *Consumer and Governmental Affairs*, *International*, *Media*, and *Enforcement*. So far as broadcasters are concerned, Media and Enforcement are the two most important bureaus since they oversee radio and TV along with satellite and cable regulations.

Rulemaking Process

Federal agencies generally cannot impose new rules or revise old ones without first proposing regulations publicly and inviting public comment. The FCC is no exception. It begins by calling attention to a legal issue by a *Notice of Inquiry* (NOI). The NOI alerts media owners, consumers, and interested groups to the stated problem and invites comments. The NOI process is open to all, and the *Daily Digest* publishes the feedback and posts it on the website.

When a rule change is imminent, the FCC sends another announcement, a *Notice of Proposed Rulemaking* (NPRM) to give media owners and those interested another chance to comment on the issue and recommended resolution. After the agency reaches its decision, a Report and Order (R&O) is drafted and approved so that the U.S. Government Publishing Office can disseminate it.[12] The R&O explains how the rule will be enforced and the rationale for its adoption.

10. 47 CFR 1 (a).
11. The FCC's broadcast rules are contained in Title 47 of the Code of Federal Regulations (CFR), Parts 73 and 74 (broadcast) (auxiliary broadcast), including low-power TV and translator stations.
12. *The Federal Register* is also found online at https://www.federalregister.gov/.

From The Trenches: Trade Association Advocacy and Old McDonald: E, I, E, I, and O

By Barry D. Umansky, J.D.

Trade associations play a central role in the shaping of legislation, regulation, and overall government policy at federal, state, and local levels. A trade association typically represents the interests of companies, in a particular industry, which are "members" of the association.

In terms of issue advocacy, trade associations serve their members through:

E – Educating Policymakers on Often Complex Issues of Regulation and Legislation

Not all persons elected or appointed to high offices in government are "rocket scientists" with full knowledge of the range of issues confronting them on the job, particularly those issues that are complex. So one role of trade associations is to educate government officials as to the background and key elements of particular issues being decided, but with a "spin" to emphasize the trade associations' preferred way for the government official to decide it. Financial contributions to legislators' political campaigns – through trade associations' "political action committees" – often are used to supplement the association lobbying efforts to influence favorable legislative actions.

I – Instituting Agency Inquiry and Rulemaking Proceedings

Trade associations file "petitions for rule making or inquiry," thereby urging the government to start proceedings leading to rule changes benefiting the associations' members. Once a proceeding begins, trade associations traditionally file the most comprehensive and compelling sets of "comments" and "reply comments" in agency proceedings. These filings can be the work product of the associations' attorneys and, depending on the nature of the proceeding, of staff engineers, technologists, and/or economists in making the case. Sometimes associations contract with "outside" organizations to produce economic, technical, and other "studies" to support the associations' filings. Trade associations also play a lead role in opposing regulatory agency actions antithetical to the interests of association members.

E – Encouraging Association Members' Advocacy and Relationships with Policymakers

Trade associations encourage and guide their members in submitting their own comments in agency proceedings, as well as invite them to join association leaders and staff in lobbying visits with agency officials or legislators (federal and state). Trade association members also are encouraged to maintain year-round good relationships with federal and state senators and representatives and to be available, at a moment's notice, to contact those officials personally and ask them to introduce and/or support legislation important to the members' businesses and to the association that represents them.

I – Instituting Industry Self-Regulation

There are strategic reasons why trade associations may choose to "self-regulate." For example, the government may be prevented from imposing media "content regulations" that would violate First Amendment speech protections. However, industry trade associations (which aren't "the government") can establish their own "codes of conduct" or take other self-regulatory actions to achieve the same result. This often is done to "curry favor" with the government; but it also serves to discourage government regulation in the same or different areas. Additionally, industry self-regulation helps improve the public image of the industry, thus gaining the public support often needed to fend off unwanted government regulation. However, trade associations must take care not to adopt self-regulatory provisions violating antitrust or other laws aimed at preserving competition.

O – Organizing Members and Allies in Agency Proceedings, Legislative Lobbying, and Court Battles

Trade associations form coalitions of industry groups to help "make the case" before agencies and legislatures. These coalitions sometimes include "strange bed-fellows" – parties that often are adversaries but on certain issues may participate in "joint" petitions and comments in agency proceedings and/or coordinate their agency and legislative lobbying to achieve common goals.

Trade associations typically orchestrate and present federal and state testimony in government "hearings" conducted to consider regulatory and/or legislative action. Associations frequently coordinate the filing of court appeals of government actions and spearhead efforts among like-minded parties in submitting "friend of the court" filings in judicial proceedings.

Barry D. Umansky, Professor Emeritus at Ball State University, is the former Deputy General Counsel of the National Association of Broadcasters in Washington, DC. He is a former broadcaster who served as an attorney at the FCC and also in the private practice of communications law.

Bedrock Law
The FCC is authorized to draft and enforce rules for commercial and noncommercial media in the United States after it invites and receives public comment on a regulatory issue.

The FCC administers its tasks under the agency's procedures for rulemaking and policy enforcement. That way it is to oversee "all the channels of radio transmission; and to provide for the use of such channels, but not the ownership thereof, by persons for limited periods of time under licenses granted by federal authority."[13] Simply put, the FCC handles broadcast licenses and maintains a record of each station's service.

Regulatory Response to Technological Change

Historically we've seen how the government responded to communication technology changes, and how some responses were more welcome than others. In the 1940s, AM was well-established for radio while FM transmissions were just getting started. FM was assigned to 42–50 megahertz, certainly adequate for the handful of stations wanting to broadcast in FM during World War II. When the war ended in 1945, demand increased for radio and television stations. The FCC accepted a proposal to increase the size of the FM band, and moved it to 88–108 megahertz, making every existing FM receiver obsolete.

In 1948 the FCC struggled with another spectrum dilemma, this time involving television. The first TV stations licensed were assigned to the VHF (Very High Frequency) band, which would not be enough to accommodate the increased demand for TV stations. The FCC would begin licensing TV stations in the UHF (Ultra High Frequency) band which, using existing technology, could not propagate as far as VHF.

The Commission had to decide whether to make some markets all VHF stations while others were all UHF (and if so, which ones), or to "intermix" VHF and UHF in every market. It was not an easy decision. If some markets were UHF only, areas further from the

13. 47 U.S.C. §301.

transmitter (depending on terrain, maybe as little as 20 miles) might not get reception. On the other hand, intermixing the two would result in a definite market advantage for the VHF stations. In the end (meaning 1952), the FCC decided on intermixture.

For decades VHF stations were more profitable than their UHF counterparts in the same market. Not only were UHF signals less effective but many U.S. TV sets had no UHF tuners and were only able to pick up VHF stations. Congress enacted the All-Channel Receiver Act, authorizing the FCC to make rules requiring any new televisions sold in the United States after 1963 to be able to receive both UHF and VHF stations, which provided a major boost to struggling UHF TV stations.

The most complex transformation of spectrum use arrived when television stations converted from analog to digital broadcasting. Americans became interested in HDTV – High Definition television – when Japan began demonstrating its spectacular images in the 1980s. Very early in the process, the United States decided a shift to HDTV also would mean a shift from analog to digital television broadcasts.[14]

Lots of issues first had to be resolved,[15] including where the FCC would find enough spectrum for HDTV stations. A strategic decision was made to bring vested interests together through the "Grand Alliance," a consortium overseen by former FCC Chair Richard Wiley, well-respected for his knowledge of the issues. Competing interests agreed to collaborate[16] to come up with a way to transition from analog standard definition to digital HDTV without viewers ever losing a signal, whether they purchased a new digital TV or used a converter to allow their old TV to receive the new system.

The cost of the converters was subsidized by a coupon system so consumers wouldn't be forced to pay out-of-pocket for the devices to continue watching TV. They were even able to devise a system that not only did not require massive amounts of new spectrum but would result in large swaths of spectrum being cleared for the new Internet access people were starting to demand on their cell phones.

Licensing Requirements

The FCC typically receives more applications for broadcast licenses than there are available channels, which explains why once a frequency becomes open, the agency staff is careful to see the following criteria are met:

- **Good financial standing** is required, which means the applicant has sufficient capital to program a station for 90 days without commercial sponsorship.
- **Ownership concentrations** limit the number of license applicants per medium (radio, television, cable, newspaper) as well as by individual market.
- **Good-character criteria** require the applicant to have no felony convictions under the U.S. Criminal Code and offer no misrepresentations on licensing forms.
- **Technical criteria** cover audio and video standards to be maintained according to broadcast coverage maps drawn to prevent interference with other media.

14. To be literal High Definition means only improved resolution. Japan was experimenting with analog HDTV. The fact that HDTV is digital was a U.S. policy choice.
15. Some of the issues to be resolved were the number of lines of resolution and whether screens would use interlace scanning (like analog TV) or progressive scanning (like computer monitors). For those who want a deep dive, the FCC has archived decades of reports. https://www.fcc.gov/general/digital-television.
16. At one point in the process, four different – and incompatible – system proposals were under consideration. The collaboration that resulted in a single system was nothing short of miraculous and a tribute to Wiley's leadership.

The broadcast license is free, but the government assesses an annual fee varying by market and medium. It could be thousands of dollars a year for a major market station, or quite a bit less – perhaps only a few hundred dollars a year – for a small-market station.[17]

Public Inspection File

Once a license has been obtained from the government, broadcasters no longer are bound to maintain paper records for people to inspect at the station. The inspection file is available to view online, including the license application, station reports to the FCC, digital contour maps of the coverage area, and emails along with other documents. What is not required in the public inspection file are the station's financial records, including profit and earnings statements, payroll accounts, and tax forms that if disclosed to the public would put the licensee at a disadvantage with its media competition.

Broadcasting and the First Amendment

The First Amendment rights of broadcasters prohibit government censorship, which simply means the station licensee – not the government – is responsible for selecting the material to be aired. Congress prohibited the FRC from censoring the nation's radio stations in §29 of its original charter, but it also prohibits "obscene, indecent, or profane language."[18]

Section 326 forbids censorship by the FCC and protects broadcast content that may be viewed by some as objectionable because "the public interest is best served by permitting free expression of views"; however, the FCC has punished broadcasters after the indecent broadcast, which would not be considered censorship, which is also referred to as *prior restraint*.

Bedrock Law

The FCC does not censor broadcast stations, but it does serve notices of apparent liability (NALs), letters of reprimand, forfeitures (fines), and can even revoke a license for prolonged violations of its rules.

Infractions

The government can and does fine a station for the broadcast of hoaxes as well as indecent material. It also forbids soliciting money under false pretenses and advertising or promoting illegal lotteries. The FCC moves against violators with fines, or "forfeitures," levied after a **Notice of Apparent Liability** (NAL) is sent to the station. The agency rarely exacts monetary fines for a station's first offense and even more rarely commands stiffer penalties, but it can.

The commission renews broadcast licenses for eight-year terms about 98% of the time. The rare license revocation that does occur is usually made in response to a pattern of infractions such as sending in false reports,[19] sometimes referred to as a "lack of candor," or a poor record of public service. Beyond forfeitures and revocations, penalties include short-term license renewals, letters of reprimand, or cease-and-desist orders to halt offensive practices.

17. For example, in 2023 the lowest fee for a commercial broadcast station was $370/year for AM Class C stations in markets with populations below 10,000. The most expensive AM fee was $16,920 for a Class A station in a market with a population of 6 million or more. FM regulatory fees ranged from $650 in smaller markets to $21,190 for the powerful, large market stations. Full power TV stations pay based on population. A station in a city population one million would pay $7,799.
18. Section 29 reads as follows: "Nothing in this Act shall be understood or construed to give the licensing authority the power of censorship over the radio communications or signals transmitted by any radio station, and no regulation or condition shall be promulgated or fixed by the licensing authority which shall interfere with the right of free speech by means of radio communications."
19. It would be impossible for FCC staff to monitor thousands of broadcast stations 24/7, so they must rely on stations to self-report. Because so much monitoring depends on this self-reporting, the FCC is especially hard on false reporting.

The Telecommunications Act

Electronic media are dynamic in terms of their changing technology and popularity; therefore, it is necessary to ensure federal rules keep pace and encourage the growth of new media. In 1996, Congress approved a major overhaul of the Communications Act of 1934. The **Telecommunications Act of 1996** re-established the foundation of media policy for new competition and Internet expansion.

It was billed as a competition-friendly law to speed up the deployment of new consumer services for Internet and telephony. Some rules from the 1934 act stayed on the books, while others were revised. Undergirding the public interest standard were as noted, the principles of localism, competition, and diversity.

The **principle of diversity** had been interpreted to mean, in broadcast terms, the "widest possible dissemination of information from diverse and antagonistic sources is essential to the welfare of the public."[20] Now, the new policy deregulated ownership limits based on how many stations a single owner could control. The agency, however, was ordered to provide a review every four years to see if it had a reasonable basis for its ownership rules, which led to a series of challenges involving the U.S. government's oversight of ownership.[21]

Ownership Diversity

The theory behind station ownership control is the necessity of diversity in the variety of broadcast voices in the local marketplace of ideas, which affords a check on distant corporate powers controlling radio and TV stations. The emphasis is on community because "promoting localism is a key goal of the Commission's media ownership rules."[22] When the FCC came up with new policies regarding the amount and type of local content to be aired and reported, it created a conflict between broadcasters and special interest groups.

Minority Ownership

Before 1978, the FCC granted less than 1% of all broadcast licenses to women and minority owners – only 40 stations out of more than 8,500. The agency adopted a tax certificate program designed to encourage the sale of cable systems and radio and television stations to women and minorities. This plan created a tax benefit by relieving the stations of having to pay on profits from the sale – a capital gains tax – to the U.S. government.

There was another move toward diversity in ownership. The FCC encouraged distress sales of broadcast and cable properties to minority and women licensees by allowing the seller to recover some of the market value of their intangible assets. In 1995, however, a Supreme Court ruling spelled the end of such programs. In *Adarand Constructors, Inc. v. Peña*, it ruled against government programs applying racial criteria unless they were meant to remedy specific acts of discrimination rather than creating a general solution for the ills of prejudice.[23]

20. *Associated Press v. United States*, 326 U.S. 1, 20 (1945), cited in Philip M. Napoli, "Deconstructing the Diversity Principle," 49 *J. Comm.* 7 (1999).
21. The Telecommunications Act of 1996 mandates a review by the FCC of its media ownership rules to determine "whether any of such rules are necessary in the public interest as a result of competition." See https://docs.fcc.gov/public/attachments?DOC-226188A1.pdf
22. *See* FCC Localism Hearing to be Held in Washington, DC, October 31, *at* http://fjallfoss.fcc.gov/edocs_public/attachmatch/DOC-277560A1.pdf.
23. *Adarand Constructors, Inc. v. Peña*, 515 U.S. 200 (1995).

To improve the situation, the FCC adopted a Diversity Order to reform measures in broadcast transactions, including a ban on discrimination in all such station sales, adoption of a zero-tolerance standard for ownership fraud, and nondiscrimination clauses in advertising sales contracts to eliminate "no urban/no Spanish" requirements. The order also banned the practice of advertisers urging their agencies to avoid minority media because of "undesirable" demographics. The FCC further sought to make capital more accessible to minority groups by creating new distress sale rules for eligible broadcast stations.

Minority Employment

The FCC's equal employment opportunities (EEO) rules were on the books for years and are credited with increasing the minority media workforce from 9.1% to 20.2%. Women fared well among the employee ranks, gaining more than 40% of the available jobs, but only 15% were promoted to station general managers.

The next step taken to increase diversity of station ownership was the FCC's incubator program. It was based on the notion new entrants in the radio broadcasting business could move toward owning and operating a full-service radio station with larger, experienced broadcasters helping them.

First, incubating parent stations would pair up with small new entrants or existing struggling stations for a three-year incubation period. Second, incubating parent stations would offer mentoring, financial, engineering and/or technical assistance, and operational support. The program temporarily came to a halt due to a court decision by the U.S. Court of Appeals for the Third Circuit in *Prometheus Radio Project v. FCC*.[24]

Prometheus Radio Project

The FCC upholds diversity as it applies to ownership and content. The widest possible dissemination of information from diverse sources of content is affirmed, while ownership is dispersed by market and medium. The FCC's enforcement of this rule was challenged by the Prometheus Radio Project – a group of low-power FM stations, formerly pirate radio stations that banded together in Philadelphia.

Prometheus filed its first suit in this matter in 2003. It challenged the FCC for what it called its "analytical shortcomings," pointing to the government's diversity index. It argued some of the FCC's moves to deregulate were illegally taken without vetting the impact on broadcast ownership by minorities and women and therefore were arbitrary and capricious.

The commission's proposed incubator program where successful broadcasters would help struggling stations owned or operated by women and minorities was challenged. After the U.S. Court of Appeals for the Third Circuit ruled in favor of Prometheus Radio Projects and against the FCC (2019), the agency not only halted the incubator program but also reinstated regulations such as its newspaper/broadcast cross-ownership rule, the local television and local radio ownership rules, and the television joint sales agreement attribution rule among others.

One key point in the *Prometheus* case challenged how section 202(h) of the Telecommunications Act of 1996 should be viewed in terms of the quadrennial review. The ruling held part of the law did not contain a "deregulatory presumption," and the burden remains on those seeking to modify or eliminate standing rules. The FCC appealed this decision to the U.S. Supreme Court.[25]

24. 939 F.3d 567 (3d Cir. 2019).
25. *Id.*

The Supreme Court had the final say when it came to deregulating ownership rules for broadcast stations. Its 2021 ruling affirming the FCC's deregulation ended a four-part legal drama (2004, 2006, 2011, 2016) featuring disputes dating back to 2002. The unanimous opinion handed down by newly appointed Associate Justice Brett Kavanaugh, who had been with the U.S. Court of Appeals for the D.C. Circuit that handled most of the FCC cases, essentially eliminated the cross-ownership restrictions from 1975 and addressed minority ownership by allowing larger companies to help minority-owned media outlets through the incubator program.[26]

Localism
Broadcast ownership and program decision-making at the community level ensure the programming offered by each radio and television station serves the community of license.

FCC Analysis of Competition

To make its ownership standards clear and maintain a competitive environment, the FCC began with the premise larger media markets must be distinguished from smaller ones. In the top 20 U.S. markets, defined by A.C. Nielsen as Designated Market Areas (DMAs), media ownership patterns covering newspaper, radio stations, and TV stations were measured by different standards than those in smaller markets.

The FCC had maintained limits on broadcast station ownership by one person or company since the beginning. What changed in the digital age was Congress began requiring it to review media ownership rules every four years, known as the quadrennial review, to judge if the agency should repeal or modify any FCC rules to better serve the public interest. These regulations do limit network ownership, national television station ownership, local station ownership, and media cross-ownership.

Station Ownership Limits

Suppose one billionaire media mogul decides it is time to fight the rise of streaming TV that is viewed as siphoning off viewers from broadcast stations. This hypothetical mogul's strategy is to buy and merge two or three of the four major U.S. networks: ABC, CBS, FOX, and NBC, and put the streaming services out of business. There is a problem, however. The FCC rules would stop a merger between any two of the four broadcast television networks, and it would take a judicial review to reverse that FCC rule and allow a merger of any two major networks.

Competition
Competing broadcasters have equitable opportunities to influence their market because FCC policy promotes rather than limits competition to meet the supply-and-demand curve.

Suppose this media owner moves on to Plan B. They try to buy up as many TV stations nationwide as possible so that one station group collectively reaches 59% of all TV households. Again, the FCC would shake its head and point to the National Television Ownership rule setting a cap of 39% of the national audience gaining access to one owner's TV stations. In this case, UHF (Ultra High Frequency) stations would count only half as much as VHF (Very High Frequency) channels, which is what is called the UHF Discount.[27]

So that means Plan C is the next option. The media mogul's dreams would require owning an unlimited number of radio stations in every market. Limitations on the number of radio stations owned nationally have been lifted, but at the market level, a check is placed on a sliding scale changing the ownership limit according to the size of the market.

26. *Federal Communications Commission, et al., v. Prometheus Radio Project, et al.* 592 U.S. ___ (2021).
27. VHF (Very High Frequency) television occupy channels 2 to 13, transmitting between 54 and 216 MHz. UHF (Ultra High Frequency) channels are numbered 14 to 51, and broadcast between 470 and 890 MHz. According to the Congressional Research Service in 2021, TV stations owned by Nexstar reached 62% of U.S. households, thanks to the UHF discount. "Federal Communications Commission (FCC) Media Ownership Rules," *at* https://sgp.fas.org/crs/misc/R45338.pdf.

So there is one limit in cities with 45 or more stations (eight maximum, no more than five AM or FM). Another limit for markets of between 30 and 44 radio stations (seven maximum, no more than four AM or FM). And the sliding scale continues down to 15 and 29 radio stations (six maximum, no more than three AM or FM). And for a market with 14 or fewer radio stations (five maximum, no more than three AM or FM), so long as they do not equal 50% or more of all radio stations in the market.

Rethinking Cross-Ownership

One rule that remained in place until 2017 was the prohibition of ownership of full-service broadcast stations (radio or television) by any newspaper operating in the same market. That rule originally went into place in 1975, when metropolitan newspapers were much more influential in their communities. Forty-two years later the cross-ownership prohibition was among the rules challenged by the Prometheus Radio Project and lifted by the Court ruling.

The original cross-ownership rule forbidding partnerships between newspapers and broadcasters came before the rise of cable and satellite television, which was followed by Internet sites making the issue of protecting diversity and competition even more relevant. Although more channels were available for consumers, only a few large corporations had the financial stability necessary to compete in small, medium, and large markets.

Newspaper firms were allowed to control broadcast stations in cities where they owned the only daily newspaper. The same media groups also gained approval to buy TV stations in markets where they owned cable systems, radio stations, or other media outlets. In 2017, the FCC disposed of the radio-television cross-ownership rule, which held in check the conglomerates seeking to control both radio and TV stations in one market. Both cross-ownership rules (newspaper + broadcast stations; radio + TV stations) were eliminated due to the online success of news and entertainment competition.

Content Regulation
The FCC has rules regarding programming content, although the FCC is forbidden from censorship by §326 of the Communications Act.

Hello to "KidVid"

Rules for children's television have long been of concern to parents and politicians. Action for Children's Television (ACT) was formed in 1968 in response to cartoons with host characters touting brand cereals and action heroes teaching youngsters aggressive and even violent resolutions to social conflicts.

In 1974, ACT urged broadcasters to devote educational time to young people and to be wary of how advertisers approached young viewers. ACT began its battle in 1983 to regulate children's television programs, and seven years later, Congress drew up the Children's Television Act, which took effect in 1990. TV stations had to locate three hours in their weekly line up for educational and informational content. Licensees failing to comply were invited to explain why they had missed the mark or risk forfeitures.

Core Programming for "KidVid"

After the enactment of the Children's Educational Act of 1990, the FCC began seriously promoting the broadcast of educational and informational programs for children. This type of "core programming" is defined as "programming that furthers the positive development of children 16 years of age and under in any respect, including the child's intellectual/cognitive or social/emotional needs." The original rules called for programming to meet three criteria:

- program at least 30 minutes in length
- air between the hours of 7 a.m. and 10 p.m.
- show at least one regularly scheduled weekly program

The new rules adopted in 2019 extended the time frame for core children's programming to start one hour earlier from 6 a.m. to 10 p.m. It still required regularly scheduled weekly programs of at least 30 minutes but opened the door to shorter-form programs by allowing 52 of the 156 hours of core programming to be aired on a multicast channel rather than its broadcast channel.

Deregulators especially welcomed the use of a broadcaster's multicast channel for what is called "Kidvid use," but some disagreed with the idea a multicast frequency would be as beneficial to children as the principal channel previously required. Core programming must be identified on-screen with an E/I "bug" for Educational/Informational to indicate it met the FCC's standards for children.

Political Content

The federal pendulum on political controls for broadcasting content tends to swing between the extremes of regulation and deregulation. For example, the old fairness doctrine requiring balance in news coverage was developed from a rule against broadcast editorials in 1949 and concerned broadcasters for years because it required coverage of controversial issues of public importance from contrasting viewpoints. In 1987, it was deemed unenforceable and rescinded. There are, however, regulations on political content the FCC continues to enforce at times.

Equal Opportunities

One rule known by the misnomer, "equal time," was established for the purpose of assessing equal opportunities for politicians, but there is no legal obligation for broadcasters to provide equal *time* to candidates seeking public office. Now if a candidate buys time on a station and an opponent wants to buy just as much time, the station is obligated to provide the same opportunity to both candidates to purchase commercial minutes at the same rates.

Who Is a Legally Qualified Candidate?

The reasonable access requirement applies only to federal candidates, but the equal opportunities rule applies to all elected offices. A candidate is qualified if they

- publicly announce their candidacy
- meet the qualifications for office
- qualify for a place on the ballot or is eligible for write-in methods
- are duly nominated by a political party that is commonly known or makes a substantial election showing.

Reasonable Access

The bill creating the Federal Radio Commission in 1927 had political candidates in mind when it advised broadcasters to afford them equal opportunities. The law further stipulated stations "shall have no power of censorship over the material broadcast."[28]

Under §312 (a), the Candidate Access Rule held no broadcaster should be allowed to sell airtime to promote a particular candidate while blocking other candidates running for the same office from gaining access to its airwaves. In theory, there is no rule requiring that

28. 47 U.S.C. §315(b)(1)(A).

broadcasters provide access to candidates for local or state office, but they still must act in the public interest, which is why most broadcasters provide commercial time anyway.

Broadcasters can provide political candidates with free airtime or charge them a fee for that time slot, but the opportunities must be equal for all campaigns. These fees are provided under §312, which specifies the lowest unit charge for advertising prices and discount offers to the political candidates. This rule takes effect 45 days prior to the date of a runoff or primary election and 60 days prior to the date of a general or special election.

Exemptions

There are exceptions to prove the rule, such as what happens when a candidate makes an inadvertent appearance in entertainment programs. If they log an appearance in a situation comedy or a televised motion picture, it could open a station to competing claims for airtime from opponents.

The law requires equal opportunities for each "use" by a candidate but excludes certain types of appearances. This "use" does not trigger §315 obligations if the candidate only appears in one of the following exempt programming categories:

1 bona fide newscast
2 bona fide news interview
3 bona fide news documentary (if the appearance of the candidate is incidental to the presentation of the subject covered by the news documentary)
4 on-the-spot coverage of bona fide news events (including but not limited to political conventions and other campaign activities, such as debates).

FCC and Political Advertising

The term *use* refers to the candidate's voice or image, and the FCC rule forbids any type of broadcast censorship or editorial control over the political advertisement. In other words, the broadcaster has immunity from liability for any false or defamatory content that candidates place in their ads.

The FCC has held that the no-censorship provision holds regardless of threats from the candidate's opponent.[29] In fact, broadcast stations are even forbidden from requiring a recording or script of the political advertisement in advance to edit the copy. The only thing a station can do is to add a disclaimer but one that cannot be construed as an editorial comment. Here are the five exemptions:

Newscasts. "Bona fide" newscasts are usually easy to identify; they are those regularly scheduled programs that cover current events.

News Interviews. Similarly, a "bona fide" news interview is a regular scheduled program that routinely deals with news issues.

News Documentaries. The exemption for bona fide news documentaries recognizes that a candidate's appearance in a documentary might have nothing to do with the election.

Spot News Coverage. The on-the-spot news event exemption was first created to allow full coverage of the Republican and Democratic national conventions.

Debates. The spot news coverage exemption was expanded to include candidate debates.

29. Note that this protection only applies if the candidate "appears" (i.e., is seen or heard) in the ad. Broadcasters can be liable for content in political ads where a candidate does not appear.

Public Broadcasting

The Public Broadcasting Act of 1967[30] established the Corporation for Public Broadcasting and gave the necessary support to form two networks: the Public Broadcasting Service (PBS) and National Public Radio (NPR). It divided radio and television stations into two categories: commercial broadcasters and noncommercial educational broadcasters. The FCC licenses noncommercial educational (NCE) broadcasters to meet their operating expenses through the support of listeners and viewers in addition to government funding.

The law also allowed noncommercial broadcasters to acknowledge personal and corporate contributions in terms of underwriting donations through on-air announcements, but NCE stations are prohibited from broadcasting commercial or other promotions on behalf of for-profit supporters.

Public Television's Heroine

When the FCC issued its *Sixth Report and Order* in 1952, the allocation plan included 242 channel assignments for noncommercial educational (NCE) stations. This was due in large part to the work of the first woman commissioner on the FCC, Freida C. Hennock, who encouraged universities and communities to apply for noncommercial educational licenses and advised NCEs of the best ways to gain the support of community leaders and organizations. She enlisted the cooperation of businesses and corporations by affording grants and helping early NCE stations find their needed facilities and equipment.

The historic battle to set aside spectrum was not easily won once commercial broadcasters fought to prevent federal support of broadcast licensees through tax-based revenues. Hennock felt differently. She was a Polish immigrant and President Truman's appointment to the FCC, who recognized the problem was one of stability.

When the FCC began reorganizing TV channels in 1951, the agency included dial positions for educational broadcasting, but there was no assurance they would be permanent. Commercial broadcasters were set to win that "television real estate" (VHF channels 2 and 13), but Hennock felt the public needed to be notified first. Her message began to filter down to the American people, who responded in support of noncommercial educational broadcasting.

In June 1953, the first educational TV station took to the air, and Hennock was invited to Houston to speak at KUHT-TV's inaugural program. By mid-1955, 12 educational stations were broadcasting and more than 50 applications for noncommercial licenses had been filed with the FCC.

This woman's belief in educational broadcasting was realized, thanks largely to her strong will and tenacity. She recognized what was at stake in 1952 when it came time to allocate television channels and to afford commercial-based broadcasting all the VHF bandwidth. More than any other individual, Hennock was responsible for securing the assignment of noncommercial TV channels and eventual creation of public broadcasting.

The 1967 law gave support to educational radio and television stations by providing funds for their facilities and declaring when noncommercial broadcasters produce programs, they should be encouraged to take "creative risks" and meet the needs of underserved audiences, including children and minorities in service to the public interest.

Public television and radio stations, like commercial broadcasters, are required to address local problems through their outreach programs. From time to time, commercial broadcasters

30. 47 U.S.C. §396.

have sought legislation to curtail any government funding for noncommercial educational broadcasting, but this is a perennial feud in Congress typically resolved in support of public broadcasting.

The 1996 law gave the FCC authority to preempt any local or state ordinance that would obstruct the entry by telecommunications firms seeking to supply local customers with services for television, telephone, or the Internet. Incumbent services would allow media competition to interconnect with wired networks to reach U.S. households.

At first, new modes of technology placed telephone and television services in competition, supplying the same service through different channels. Americans could access long-distance service on the Internet, for example, by using Skype or Zoom competing against phone networks. This intermodal competition amounted to selling the same services of television, telephone, and audio through different modes of technology. Eventually, the competition shifted to broadband with mobile delivery relying on established players like AT&T and Verizon, which needed more bandwidth.

Spectrum Auctions

Applicants for broadcast licenses bid in auctions to win the right to a new local channel by pledging the most money to the government for the channel frequency. To raise funds for the federal government, spectrum auctions were established in Washington, DC, after two previous methods for granting licenses – comparative hearings and lotteries – were tried and abandoned.

The shift away from lotteries or the public interest comparison of license applicants to a financial competition was one of several steps the FCC took to further its deregulatory policy. A federal court ruled in 1993 against comparative hearings, and Congress did an about-face by giving the green light to competitive bidding. Spectrum auctions threw open the door to virtually any participant who would submit an advance payment for a broadcast station license.

After the U.S. Congress decided to shore up its revenue stream by granting an auction system for radio and television licenses, it devised an online system of bidding.

Applicants for a broadcast frequency were invited to participate online in a series of rounds in which eventually one bidder was granted the station's license. The FCC first certified the bidders were qualified license holders (good character, etc.) and then ruled on the deal based primarily on the worth of the applicant's bid. While critics at the time considered the new licensing process mercenary, no one could argue it wasn't easier and met far fewer legal challenges. When licenses were assigned before by assessing competitive applications, it could take years before all the legal appeals of a decision were exhausted.

A New Kind of Spectrum Auction

The FCC in 2010 issued a National Broadband Plan (NBP) designed to "connect America" with the needed spectrum for mobile broadband services. The NBP ambitiously set a goal of 500 MHz of additional spectrum for wireless services to be made available by 2020.

This plan included 120 megahertz of broadcast television spectrum to be reallocated through an "incentive auction" so that certain TV stations would give up all or part of channel bandwidth for other uses. The stated goal was to "open up new business opportunities for current holders of spectrum licenses while helping to meet the demand for spectrum by new services."[31] The aim was to relieve congestion on wireless

31. www.fcc.gov/topic/incentive-auctions.

networks and make way for the introduction of 5G (fifth generation), the next phase of wireless growth.

Eventually, the FCC announced it would repurpose 84 megahertz of spectrum and begin the reassignment of TV stations to new channels. Under the Spectrum Act, the FCC conducted a "reverse auction" and set the amount of compensation each broadcast television licensee would receive in return for giving up all or part of its channel frequency.

The FCC made 5G the vision of the future and for marketing purposes used the acronym FAST (**F**acilitating **A**merica's **S**uperior **T**echnology). The rollout proposal included multiple auctions for spectrum bands, deployment of wireless infrastructure, and modernizing of FCC regulations.

One point added to this plan was the U.S. government's Secured and Trusted Network Communications Act that took aim at "ripping and replacing" Chinese manufacturers Huawei and ZTE's facilities based on the notion that U.S. technology was needed to secure the infrastructure of U.S. 4G and 5G networks.

Global View: Making Broadcast Ownership Global

A dispute over what rates would be charged to a music streaming service led to a rather significant relaxation in FCC rules. Once a patriotic standard, the FCC required majority ownership of broadcast stations by American citizens, usually 75%. This ownership rule became an issue in 2013 when Pandora's streaming service applied for a Rapid City, SD, station license, KXMZ, in view of the lower rates it would pay for streaming music.

The FCC responded to this request for entry into U.S. broadcasting by seeking assurances it was at least 75% American owned. Pandora countered by questioning if such a requirement is realistic in an age when the digital trading of stock shares puts media ownership on a global basis. Pandora doubted any publicly traded media corporation with a large shareholder base could meet such an ownership standard. Eventually, the commission loosened its rules regarding foreign ownership and issued a Declaratory Ruling inviting increased foreign ownership of U.S. broadcast stations.[32]

Community Antenna Television

The government appeared at first to be reluctant to draft regulation for community antenna television. The FCC's position for most of the 1950s was CATV simply fell beyond its jurisdiction, but that stance failed to satisfy U.S. broadcasters, who saw the wired TV service as a threat to their business and felt federal oversight was necessary.

The use of microwave towers for CATV by the Carter Mountain Transmission Co. created a test case in Wyoming. Relaying broadcast signals along microwave towers to import TV programs from Denver alarmed KWRB-TV's owners in Riverton, WY. They did not appreciate the new competition and asked the FCC to find those CATV relays to be unlawful, which the commission felt obliged to do.[33]

Community antenna television clearly posed a problem in Washington, DC, when it came to arriving at a simple definition in law. Was it a broadcast medium or a **common carrier**?[34] The term *common carrier* evolved from public transportation services like trains and buses

32. The foreign ownership limit of 25% is still on the books – Section 310(b) of the Communications Act (47 USC) – but is not given to enforcement.
33. *Carter Mountain Transmission Co. v. Federal Communications Commission*, 321 F.2d 359 (D.C. Cir. 1963).
34. *Frontier Broadcasting Co. v. Collier*, 24 F.C.C. 251 (1958).

available to all. In media terms, it was defined as a communication system offering its information transmission services to the public without interfering with the content.

Common Carrier
Transmitting communications via wire or airwaves based on nondiscrimination of sources or messages.

Common carriers have been under the watchful eye of federal regulators for years, but cable television seemed different – more like a small set of TV channels for rent than something akin to a telephone service. Rather than confuse the issue, the FCC simply avoided taking jurisdiction over the growing cable television platform.

FCC Jurisdiction

The arrival in San Diego of high-powered TV channels via cable lines from Los Angeles threatened smaller TV stations in southern California, and that dispute forced the government's hand. In 1968, the Court ruled in *U.S. v. Southwestern Cable* the FCC should exercise its congressionally mandated authority over wired communications and draft needed regulations. The FCC's "regulatory authority over CATV is imperative" to ensure local broadcast television is preserved and equitably distributed around the country.[35]

The legal jurisdiction for CATV was placed in the commission's hands so long as its rules were "reasonably ancillary" to broadcasting. The federal authority over cable was needed to protect local TV stations, and as a result the agency adopted more expansive rules. The FCC asked cable firms to register for a certificate of compliance and establish their franchise agreements, along with technical elements, signal carriage standards, and syndication terms.[36] Some of these policies were later revised or deleted altogether, but not before legal precedents were established directly impacting cable's regulatory landscape.

Early Competitors

MVPD
Multichannel video program distributor – commercial providers of TV channel choices, such as cable systems, satellite dish providers, and online streaming services.

One question was raised over the lack of competition among cable systems when competing companies at first encountered a government challenge.[37] They were called *overbuilders* because they were *building over* a system in a market already served by one multichannel video program distributor or **MVPD**.

Under the Telecommunications Act of 1996, an MVPD could be either an individual cable operator or a video delivery system serving customers multiple channels of video. It also could be a television receive-only satellite or direct broadcast satellite service offering to viewers multiple channels of video programming.

Just how broadly does the FCC define its term MVPD? It became almost encompassing when "channel" was defined as part of the "frequency spectrum used in a cable system and which is capable of delivering a television channel." MVPDs are, in the commission's terms, "based on the similarity of the video services offered," including "but not limited to a cable operator, a multichannel multipoint distribution service, a direct broadcast satellite service, or a television receive-only satellite program distributor, who makes available for purchase, by subscribers or customers, multiple channels of video programming."[38]

So this naturally raises the question of where to place the newer online video distributor (OVD) platforms. Streaming services like Netflix, Amazon Prime, YouTube, and Hulu are major OVD distributors, but other companies also offer video programming by means of Internet Protocol (IP).

OVDs are not viewed in legal terms the same as MVPDs because they compete with other channels offering programming online, while cable and satellite television rules were

35. 392 U.S. 157 (1968).
36. *See 1972 Cable Television Report & Order*, 36 F.C.C. 2d 143 (1972).
37. *See Community Communications Company, Inc., v. City of Boulder, Colorado et al.*, 630 F.2d 704 (10th Cir. 1980), where an incumbent cable system was discussed as a natural monopoly.
38. *See* 47 U.S.C. § 522(13) and § 602(13).

designed to prevent anticompetitive behavior involving their system subscribers. What OVDs have in common is the principle of competition, which is complicated because MVPDs offer online video services that do not require a subscription but are enhancing the competition by launching their own streaming services, such as Hulu (Disney), CBS All Access, HBO NOW, Showtime, and Starz.

Natural Monopoly

At the economic level, cable television systems were originally viewed as a **natural monopoly**. By looking at their public utility features, the term seemed to fit. Cable systems used an electronic wired infrastructure requiring right-of-way easements; accommodating just one cable system posed challenges, technically and economically.

The so-called natural monopoly characteristics were associated with economies of scale, which encouraged all the various cable systems to merge in consolidation with the larger media corporation or conglomerate. As a result, Multiple System Operators (MSOs) began to concentrate on acquiring more cable systems and providing more services in larger groups.[39]

LFA Agreements

Because cable systems, including MSOs, had to install wires across city streets, use utility poles and/or underground easements to reach viewers' homes, a franchise agreement with the local or state government was necessary. This system contract was not unlike the agreement cities sign with utility firms, such as water, electricity, and natural gas companies, but it was also different in terms of federal law.

The FCC referred to the Local Franchising Authority (LFA) as the public agency that should address matters of cable television service, customer complaints, signal quality, and use of public, educational, and government (PEG) channels. Competition eventually shattered the natural monopoly perspective, but not before mergers and acquisitions catapulted MSOs into huge media conglomerates and put out of business the original "mom & pop" systems selling cable television to neighbors, families, and friends.

Congress finally disposed of the natural monopoly era through the Telecommunications Act in 1996. By that time, MVPD competition had evolved into what some would consider an *oligopoly*, with a few major corporate players dominating the phone, television, and Internet markets. Economist Eli Noam observed "we may have to get used to the idea of living with oligopoly in telecom rather than the hoped-for competition."[40]

No town or city can unreasonably refuse to allow competition and prevent an additional telecom franchise from doing business alongside the cable system. If a city refuses to grant a rival company its franchise, it must demonstrate its reasoning, while the aspiring MVPD competitor can appeal that decision.[41]

Pendulum of Cable Regulation

For years, regulators engaged in a tug of war with cable systems over a variety of issues; it was not just between the FCC and telecommunications carriers. The Internal Revenue Service (IRS) in 1951 decided to levy an excise tax of 8% on CATV systems. The nascent

39. Eli M. Noam, "Is Cable Television a Natural Monopoly?" 9 *Comm. Int'l J. Comm. Res.* 241 (1983–84).
40. Eli M. Noam, "The Emerging Cyclicality of the Telecom Industry," in *Global Economy and Digital Society*, eds. E. Bohlin, S. Levin, N. Sung, & C.H. Yoon (Somerville, MA: Emerald Pub., 2004).
41. 47 U.S.C. § 555.

Bedrock Law
Cable television evolved from a natural monopoly to many competitors in the market of multichannel video program distributors (MVPDs).

industry responded by gathering at a hotel in Pottsville, PA, and forming the National Community Television Council.

A district court of appeals subsequently threw out that excise tax, but that legal battle did create a voice for the industry. The trade association, NCTA – The Internet & Television Association, is a direct descendant of the Pottsville delegates organizing as cable system operators and agreeing to join their media properties to address a host of public issues.

Copyright Issues

Broadcast television station owners were under the impression their licensing agreements with networks, syndicators, and show producers would entitle them to receive copyright payments from cable systems. That was not the case.

In 1976, the Copyright Act gave cable operators the freedom to retransmit TV shows so long as their systems bought the compulsory licenses. A copyright royalty panel was established to collect money based on a share of each cable system's receipts. Those cable revenues were deposited with the Copyright Royalty Tribunal (CRT), which converted it into royalty payments for the TV program owners.

In 1993, Congress replaced the CRT with federal arbitration panels appointed by the Librarian of Congress to address copyright issues for program owners. Twice a year, cable systems file a statement of account regarding their revenues with the licensing division of the Copyright Office in the Library of Congress. The cable firms are then assessed a fee based on gross receipts of local and distant TV channels. TV copyright holders receive royalties for the cable programs based on these fees.

Is It Cable TV If There Are No Cables?

In 2012, a new technology company called Aereo marketed over-the-air television on Internet-enabled devices via dime-sized remote antennas. This Internet-enabled TV service would make it possible to time shift the programs Aereo was transmitting because it would provide its customers with connections to both the antennas and remote space on digital video recorders. Broadcasters took Aereo to court once it started collecting subscription fees without purchasing a license for the copyrighted content.

In 2014, broadcasters got the outcome they had hoped for when the Supreme Court voted 6–3 to reverse the lower court decision and remand the case.[42] Justice Stephen Breyer (writing for the Court) saw Aereo as equivalent to cable television and wrote that any "differences concern not the nature of the service that Aereo provides so much as the technological manner in which it provides the service."[43] Less than five months after the Supreme Court decision, Aereo filed for Chapter 11 bankruptcy.

Syndicated Exclusivity

The conflict over syndicated programming between broadcast and cable television has produced additional twists and turns in the legal road map. Syndicated programs such as *Jeopardy* and *Friends* are offered to local TV stations and aired as either second-run network productions or original syndication, often licensed for exclusive showing to a local broadcaster.

42. *American Broadcasting Company et al. v. Aereo*, 134 S. Ct. 2498 (2014).
43. *Id.* at 2511.

Figure 8.1 A taping of the game show *Jeopardy*

Syndicated Exclusivity (Syndex)
An FCC regulation allowing local television stations to enter into exclusive contracts for syndicated content that required MVPDs to honor those contracts.

Ratings Dilution
Diminished measurement of a TV station's audience when cable channels air programs also broadcast by the local station. A negative effect syndicated exclusivity was intended to prevent.

Once a TV station buys a license to air a syndicated program, it might lose both ratings and advertising revenue if the same show is on a competing channel. The FCC's rule of **syndicated exclusivity** or "syndex" called for the deletion of competing cable programs to protect local TV broadcasters from viewer migration to cable channels.

This syndex rule was abolished in 1980 to encourage cable's development, but that policy was reversed once it became clear that local broadcasters were harmed by its absence. Nielsen confirmed that audience ratings suffered for local TV channels when superstations like WGN-TV in Chicago and WTBS-TV in Atlanta duplicated syndicated fare. This negative impact became known as **ratings dilution**, which translated into depressed rates for local commercials on syndicated programs.

In 1988, the FCC reinstated its syndex rule, an action that was upheld by a federal appeals court one year later.[44] This rule affords some assurance to broadcasters who pay a premium for the exclusive contract to televise a syndicated program so the force of law will support their contracts. Not all syndicated shows have exclusive contracts though; it's cheaper for a local TV station to obtain a nonexclusive program.

A lot of older shows are sold nonexclusively so that syndicators can sell to both local stations and cable networks, but many first-run game shows (like *Jeopardy* or *Family Feud*) (Figure 8.1) are only available by exclusive agreement. The rule allows for cable systems to choose *not* to delete syndicated programs, including ones on a "significantly viewed" channel. Given the business model of broadcasting, most TV stations try to reach as many households for their advertisers as possible, which means a guaranteed spot on the cable dial.

44. *United Video v. Federal Communications Commission*, 890 F.2d 1173 (D.C. Cir. 1989).

Must-Carry Rule
FCC requirement for cable companies to carry various local and public television stations within their system's service area.[46]

Bedrock Law
The must-carry rule was judged to be content-neutral and therefore remains on the books as a means of protecting the local TV channels' reception by pay TV viewers.

Must-Carry Regulation

The original **must-carry rule** was adopted in 1965,[45] and it required a cable system to retransmit all local TV stations within a certain radius of its service area. Generally, a cable system with 12 or more channels must carry local TV stations on up to a third of its programming tiers. When cable channels became popular, and system operators began to sell advertising time to local businesses, it put cable companies in competition with broadcasters.

That created a problem when cable operators were forced to carry local TV channels because they felt it entitled broadcasters to rob them of valuable space, thus preventing more lucrative programming for their channel slots. Cable operators were able to persuade the courts in the 1980s their position had some merit.

In the *Quincy* and *Century Communications* cases, the must-carry rule was twice rejected because it was considered a form of forced speech for cable systems.[47] Congress settled the question by giving broadcasters the choice of either seeking compensation from the cable company or demanding must-carry rights. As a result, popular local TV channels were able to forge retransmission consent agreements.

Early retransmission deals were usually for carriage of a second channel rather than in exchange of money from cable systems to retransmit their primary channel.[48] It was inevitable that cable systems would wage a legal fight against this additional expense. Cable television entrepreneur Ted Turner, acting on behalf of his media empire including CNN and Turner Broadcasting, chose to fight the must-carry rule by taking the FCC to court – twice.

Turner I & II

In *Turner* I, by a 5–4 vote the Court upheld the new must-carry rule giving broadcast stations the right to demand a channel on their community cable system dial.[49] The majority recognized the interest in keeping weaker TV stations on the air and entitled them to reach the cable audience over local system channels. In *Turner* II, the high court ruled the FCC's interest "in preserving a multiplicity of broadcasters" did not violate cable's freedom of speech.[50]

Cable Act of 1984

The **1984 Cable Franchise Policy and Communications Act** freed cable systems from some of the more extravagant demands imposed by local franchising authorities through their legally binding agreements.[51] Its economic protections relieved escalating franchise fees that were capped at 5% of gross revenues.

In general, the 1984 cable law determined how much authority the FCC could exercise over cable system operators. Cable franchising had to be handled by either state or local governments, so that operators would serve communities on the basis of the franchise agreement. Cable systems would be protected from overly ambitious agreements, and franchise authorities were prevented from terminating a contract without identifying a just cause.[52]

This congressional intervention in 1984 came as a breath of fresh air to the cable industry, which seized the opportunity to expand systems' channel capacity, increase the number of

45. *First Report & Order* in Docket Nos. 14895 & 15233, 38 F.C.C. 683 (1965).
46. *See Turner Broadcasting Sys. v. Federal Communications Commission*, 512 U.S. 622 (1994).
47. *Quincy Cable TV, Inc. v. Federal Communications Commission*, 768 F. 2d 1434 (D.C. Cir. 1985); *Century Communications Corp. v. Federal Communications Commission*, 835 F.2d 292 (D.C. Cir. 1987).
48. Cable Television Consumer Protection and Competition Act of 1992, Pub. L. No. 102–385.
49. *Turner Broadcasting Sys. v. Federal Communications Commission*, 512 U.S. 622 (1994).
50. *Turner Broadcasting Sys., Inc. v. Federal Communications Commission*, 520 U.S. 180, (1997).
51. Pub. L. No. 98–549, 47 U.S.C. § 521.
52. *See* Cable Communications Policy Act of 1984, 47 U.S.C. § 546.

households served, and raise the charges it billed to local subscribers. Seven years later, it appeared cable system operators had exploited their customers who complained about their bills rising three times faster than the inflation rate. It was not long before Congress was back at the legislative table drawing up a new cable bill not nearly as generous as the 1984 law.

Cable Consumer Act of 1992

Cable Consumer Act of 1992 Congressional law to ensure local television on cable by requiring that systems carry the local TV stations without charging for them. Superseded by the 1996 Telecommunications Act.

The **Cable Television Consumer Protection and Competition Act of 1992** established a variety of subscriber-friendly measures. Its provisions kept cable rates in check and upheld new standards of competition. Under this 1992 act, the FCC adopted a plan giving franchising authorities the responsibility for regulating basic rates and equipment. This law stipulated that no cable operator should establish an exclusive franchise without a signed agreement. Most importantly, the 1992 law secured cable access for local TV stations. It also rekindled a debate about the proper relationship between broadcasting and cable systems.

The 1992 Cable Act required television production companies supplying affiliated cable systems with programming via satellite to offer the same programming to cable competitors, such as the satellite systems DirecTV and Dish. This law also prevented cable systems and programmers from signing exclusive contracts or conspiring to restrict market access to its choice programming and compete unfairly.

The ban on exclusive agreements between cable programmers and operators was set to expire in 2002, but it was extended until 2012. Some MSOs own part of regional sports or news channels distributed by microwave or fiber-optic lines, and so they do not have to share these networks with their competitors.

In 1992, Congress authorized the FCC through §613 of the 1992 act to "prescribe rules and regulations establishing reasonable limits on the number of cable subscribers a person is authorized to reach," and the commission's response was a 30% limit on audience reach. The FCC took additional action to discourage vertical integration by limiting the number of cable networks owned by large system operators, especially the ones carried on its systems. No more than 40% of the first 75 channels could be used for programming affiliated with the cable system's owner, and the remaining 60% had to be made available to broadcast or other channels in which the system's owner owned no more than a 5% share. The two largest cable MSOs at the time, Time Warner and AT&T, challenged the rules and the D.C. Circuit Court of Appeals found the limit reasonable at first. But in 2001, it overturned the rules for the government's failure to adequately justify either horizontal or vertical limits.[53]

Telecommunications Act of 1996 Law that rewrote provisions of the Communications Act of 1934 increasing competition in media, promoting cross-market communications, prohibiting transmission of obscene or indecent content to minors, and increasing congressional oversight in media policymaking.

The Telecommunications Act of 1996

The **Telecommunications Act of 1996** was the first major overhaul of U.S. media law in more than six decades. It was enacted in an era when policymakers envisioned an "information superhighway" and spoke excitedly about providing access to all thoroughfares. The new law added Internet and online media to the FCC's oversight of radio and TV broadcasting, cable television, and telephone services. And it allowed any media company to compete by offering customers subscription-based telephone, television, and Internet services.

The advantage to consumers would be greater choice in subscription media services. The telephone companies had a special advantage by owning the well-established infrastructure of wires and pole attachments to offer delivery of television and broadband services to the home. Traditionally, telephone companies were subject to common carrier regulation, and the "telcos" resisted attempts to reregulate their services.

53. *Time Warner Entm't Co. v. FCC*, 240 F.3d 1126 (2001).

Some state governments became involved and joined in the franchising process as telephone companies expressed their preference for a regional rather than a local agreement for their media services. State lawmakers, however, found this embrace a difficult one to manage, since municipalities relied on existing revenues from local franchise agreements (LFAs).

Incumbent cable operators argued that it would be unfair competition for them to face new rivals following different rules set by the state rather than municipal government. Twenty-three states have taken over the role of franchising authority since 2000,[54] reducing the number of contracts one cable company would have to sign.[55] The franchising authority dictates terms like franchise fees and access channels, which Congress *allows* (not requires) in the Cable Act.

Effective Competition

The FCC approved an unprecedented merger of broadband and MVPD services when DirecTV was given the green light to merge with AT&T in 2015. Five years later, AT&T was looking to sell that satellite service. The pay subscriptions for satellite and cable began to shrink as cord cutters in the United States found ways to avoid that large monthly bill.

The pay TV numbers continued shrinking by about 1%–2% over several years to the point where over one-third of American households in 2020 no longer subscribed to a traditional pay TV service. Instead, broadband options offered by cable and satellite services were growing in number.

Viewers were looking for OVD options through services such as Netflix, Amazon Prime, Hulu, and Apple TV, which began delivering content in diverse and smaller packages. Before jumping to the conclusion that this erosion in pay television subscribers was doing irreparable harm to the industry, consider the one thing Americans still love to do, which is watch TV, as programs, videos, online, on the go, or even at home. The broadband delivery players compete now with all platforms of television – legacy and contemporary are in the race.

Public, Educational, and Government Channels (PEG)
Public access channels, as a local cable franchising authority's asset, are disappearing, although available to some citizens seeking an opportunity to produce TV for the local cable community.

Public Access Obligations

At one time, the government mandated cable television systems to serve communities with local programming by building studios for public access television to offer **public, educational, and government** (PEG) programs. The words found in the 1984 Cable Act give franchising authorities the right to "require as part of a cable operator's proposal for a franchise renewal . . . that channel capacity be designated for public, educational, or governmental use."[56]

Public access channels were envisioned as an ideal forum for democracy allowing viewers a chance to voice opinions or showcase their talents on a first-come, first-served basis. In some locations, they became amateur hours for unconventional personalities.

These channels not only served the public by televising local city council meetings but also allowed video artists, politicos, and musicians to appear on local cable systems. That venue began to diminish after the FCC chose to allow cable companies to deduct from the franchise fees "in-kind contributions" specified by their agreements. Cable systems sought to reduce both the expense and controversy surrounding PEG channels and began curtailing those services.

54. "What Do Local Leaders Need to Know about the FCC Cable Order?" *National League of Cities*, *at* https://www.nlc.org/article/2019/08/08/what-do-local-leaders-need-to-know-about-the-fcc-cable-order/ (Accessed December 15, 2023).
55. For example, Comcast might have had to apply to 100 different jurisdictions in Indiana for authorization to operate cable systems. Since 2006, it needs only a single state authorization to operate those same systems.
56. *See* Cable Communication Act of 1984, 47 USC § 531 (a).

Midwest Video Cases

The FCC's oversight role for cable television's obligations was questioned before the Supreme Court in 1972.[57] The ruling in *United States v. Midwest Video Corp.* upheld FCC rules requiring that cable systems create their own programming. The FCC required **leased-access channels** to be offered to the public for a fee. In this regard, they function like a common carrier such as the telephone. Cable systems were asked to dedicate at least 10% of their channels for leased access if they had 35 or more channels on their systems.[58]

Leased-Access Channels Channels provided at reduced rates to independent programmers and producers for television time on a local cable system.

In the second *Midwest Video* case, the U.S. Supreme Court held the FCC had overplayed its hand with this rule requiring cable systems with 20 or more channels to allocate four access channels for inexpensive use by the community, including public, educational, and governmental (PEG) studios. The 1979 ruling in *FCC v. Midwest Video* prevented the government from regarding cable systems as common carriers like the telephone company.

Congress stepped in five years later, however, and passed the 1984 Cable Franchise Policy and Communications Act giving local governments the right to require PEG channels and preventing system operators from exercising any editorial control over the content while absolving them of liability for whatever content was televised over their access channels. As the law stands, franchise authorities (whether statewide or local) *may* require cable companies to provide one or more access channels but are no longer required to do so now.

Satellite Television Regulation

Cable's power to retransmit TV channels and offer new programming options, such as premium channels and pay-per-view, has produced serious competition for local TV stations. The FCC encountered political pressure during the 1970s to stop cable systems from competing against broadcasters, especially through their purchase of movies for cable distribution. That was when Home Box Office (HBO) came along and began offering movies without commercial interruption, which seemed to be just what TV viewers wanted. However, HBO was stymied by FCC rules restricting the quality and age of films available for cable viewing.

In 1977, the U.S. Supreme Court sided with cable and against regulation in *HBO v. FCC*.[59] The Court found the FCC had gone too far in its efforts to protect broadcasters with rules that would prevent the showing of movies on cable for at least three years after commercial release to theaters.

Consequently, the ruling gave HBO and other cable channels the freedom to televise satellite-transmitted movies. So-called **anti-siphoning rules** also prevented cable channels from purchasing sports programming "traditionally" provided by free over-the-air broadcasters. If such rules were still in place today, ESPN would not be carrying college football or NFL games today.

Open Sky Policy FCC action in 1972 to permit the use of communication satellites by private industry for broadcasting television programs.

Open Sky Policy

In the 1970s, communication satellites were launched into space to begin bouncing broadcast signals back down across the global terrain. The FCC encouraged cable networks to draw upon satellite signals by adopting an **Open Sky policy** in 1972. This action gave the green light for cable companies to enter the domestic satellite business so long as they had

57. *See United States v. Midwest Video Corp.*, 406 U.S. 649 (1972). In addition, this decision also preserved syndication agreements that prevented cable systems from airing a syndicated program from a distant channel if the local TV station had already secured the rights to it.
58. *Federal Communications Commission v. Midwest Video Corp.*, 440 U.S. 689 (1979).
59. 567 F.2d (D.C. Cir. 1977), *cert. denied*, 434 U.S. 829 (1977).

the essential know-how and financial backing to do so. Competing satellite firms began auctioning off transponders – satellite circuits – leasing them to carry programming from earth to space and back again.

In 1975, satellites began feeding HBO shows to cable viewers, which created a new system of television networking. The Showtime network challenged HBO for cable viewers in 1978 with its lineup of new motion pictures and original programming. Cable channels multiplied quickly as subscribing viewers eagerly signed up for premium tiers. Pay cable enabled subscribers to buy programs by charging them more than the basic monthly fee.

Cable's new business model based on tiers afforded a menu of programming options by subscription plans. Cable television systems principally rely on two sources of revenue – subscriptions and advertising. Some channels like TNT and CNN would carry commercials, while others, like American Movie Classics and HBO, relied solely on subscriber fees.

Direct to Home Satellites

Satellite television does not transmit directly to the public over the airwaves, nor does it use spectrum reserved for radio and television stations, and so the law treats it as a subscription service rather than as a broadcaster. The 1992 Cable Act gave the FCC authority to regulate satellite television by drafting must-carry provisions.[60] In 1999, the FCC also adopted an access rule requiring satellite television services to set aside 4% of their channel capacity for noncommercial education and information programming.

In the same year, Congress passed the Satellite Home Viewer Improvement Act (SHVIA) permitting satellite television systems to provide local broadcast TV channels to all subscribers in a designated market area (DMA). SHVIA 1999 revised the 1988 Satellite Home Viewer Act and allowed satellite television to offer local broadcast channels to all subscribers within the local market area. It also permitted satellite companies to provide distant network broadcast stations to its subscribers. There were about ten million households in the United States taking satellite television, but that number would double in ten years.

SHVIA had the effect of placing satellite television on a level playing field with cable in terms of broadcast channel selection. By 2002, the FCC required satellite television companies like DirecTV to carry all local TV channels in markets where they carried any at all, which became known as the "carry one, carry all" rule. That same year, the government dealt with the picture quality standard, which it called its "good quality signal" rule and essentially held that satellite carriers were entitled to the same quality signal from local broadcasters as competing cable systems had sold to their customers.

Digital Delivery Options

A different rulebook applies to telecommunication carriers based on the channels involved. Whether the television supplier is a cable company located in smaller communities of residences, linked to growing networks through the Internet, or part of the expansion of phone services, regulatory features vary according to technology and jurisdiction. When electronic media began converging on the Internet, the Telecommunications Act of 1996 allowed new players to compete with broadcasting television, cable, and satellite services such as telephony.

60. Cable Television Consumer Protection and Competition Act of 1992, supra note 48.

Telephone Competition

Congress in 1996 gave telephone companies the right to compete with traditional video services by means of wired or wireless delivery systems. Different portions of the law governed telephone companies, broadcast stations, and cable systems, but the law changed the basic understanding of telephone services and their regulatory oversight. Under the 1934 Communications Act, Congress defined telephone companies as common carriers that were to provide nondiscriminatory services at similar rates to anyone wishing to send and receive messages by voice.

During the early years of the cable industry, telephone companies became involved in cable system ownership, and cable systems reported difficulty gaining access to telephone poles needed for their wires to reach home subscribers. Cable operators complained that the phone companies were refusing to rent them space at a reasonable rate on their poles.

The passage of the Telecommunications Act of 1996 simply codified what the courts had already seen fit to do and set the stage for competition in new media services. It eliminated the telephone-cable cross-ownership ban, and it allowed local phone companies to provide video programming as a common carrier or as a wireless cable provider with its own programming channels.

The legal term for this hybrid enterprise is called an *open video system* or OVS. If a telephone company chooses to enter the television subscription business and compete against cable or satellite television, it still faces the prospect of franchising.

Deregulation over the past 30 years has not made the telephone landscape a "Wild West" without rules. Most of those rules are detailed, regulating rates, service obligations, and interconnections far exceeding the detail possible in this text. One major piece of legislation that affects communication industries is the Telephone Consumer Protection Act (TCPA), passed by Congress in 1991 and amended several times.

These rules govern telemarketing calls and the use of autodialing equipment. The law requires companies that engage in telemarketing to maintain and respect "do not call" lists. The Federal Trade Commission maintains a national do not call registry, while most states have their own.

The TCPA applies to text messages as well as phone calls, and violators can be fined up to $1,500 *per incident*. Violations of this law can result in action by the FCC *or* civil suits from those who receive the calls. Law firms specializing in this area have filed class actions against perpetrators, sometimes resulting in multimillion-dollar settlements.[61]

Wireline Competition

Major phone firms like Verizon, T-Mobile, AT&T, and Sprint turned their corporate vision to capitalizing on the media channels that were the province of satellite and cable systems. In *Verizon Communications v. Federal Communications Commission* (2002), the U.S. Supreme Court held smaller competitors should have access to cable programming channels at reasonable rates.[62] Common carriers offering video services were regulated as cable systems unless they fell under the open video systems provision of the 1996 Telecommunications Act.

The regulatory term for the local telephone company is Local Exchange Carrier, and an LEC can provide video services without granting access to others. To spur competition

61. For example, Bank of America ($32 million), Navient ($20 million), and Discover Home Loans ($5 million) all agreed to class action settlements. Many more can be found online by searching "TCPA class action settlement." According to the U.S. Chamber Institute for Legal Reform, there were only 354 TCPA litigants in 2010. By 2015, the number had increased tenfold, to 3,710. *See* "TCPA Litigation Continues to Skyrocket; 1,272 Percent Increase Since 2010," *at* www.instituteforlegalreform.com/resource/tcpa-litigation-continues-to-skyrocket-1272-percent-increase-since-2010.
62. 535 U.S. 467 (2002).

between cable operators and LECs, the local phone company is classified as a common carrier, which in the eyes of the law makes it an *information* service. If, on the other hand, an LEC is reclassified as a *telecommunications* service, it can deliver video programming in competition with MVPDs based on approval of its open video application.[63]

Telecommunications firms rivaled cable for subscribers through transmission by direct broadcast satellite (DBS), the telephone company, and the Internet. The telephone company's retreat from marketing of video products illustrates the fierce competition for subscription television marketed by an online video distributor or OVD.

Competitors emphasized how they should be able to access Internet content, run software applications and services, while also connecting to safe, legal devices. Most significantly, American consumers were entitled to benefit from the Internet competition among networks, applications, and service providers.

IPTV, Virtual MVPD, and Regulation

The world markets continue migrating to online video, and rather than flipping through conventional broadcast and cable channels, IPTV (Internet Protocol Television) engages the viewer through both mobile and stationary media. IPTV was first defined as multiple program transport streams (MPTS), but that term still did not resolve the regulatory issues.

The FCC moved to apply regulations to telecommunication services with unequal legal burdens. For example, suppose emergency alert messages were required of OVD – as they are of broadcasting and cable systems – but how would viewers be served with emergency alert messages and how would streaming services get the urgent words to the right customers?

In 2014, the FCC classified OTT television, video, audio, and programming delivered over the Internet as an online video distributor but not as a multichannel video programming distributor. The difference being whether the provider offered local television and cable programming and, more importantly, would it be subject to the same rules and fees as MVPDs.

The FCC made this allowance for online video to make it more competitive with local cable and satellite providers. To say that goal was achieved is something of an understatement. Streaming TV is how most people get their television today. By way of an Internet service provider, millions of Americans turn to streaming platforms like YouTube, Hulu, Disney, Netflix and Amazon Prime Video on their Apple and Android mobile smart TVs, laptops, etc.

There was still controversy though as local TV stations see the revenue shift to virtual MVPD platforms. The National Association of Broadcasters asked the FCC to re-classify them and force streaming TV to submit to the same rules and obligations broadcast and cable systems are required to comply with, but to no avail. Adding to the incentive to re-classify streaming TV is the increasing conflict between broadcast affiliates and their network partners that are reaping profits through NBC Peacock, CBS Paramount, and ABC Disney. At this writing, however, there is only talk of regulating virtual MVPDs but no FCC action forcing streamers to pay the same fees and obey the same rules as broadcasting, cable, and satellite operators.

Future Vision: Universal Service

One of the tenets of basic telephone service in the twentieth century was the concept of **universal service**. The idea promoted by AT&T in the 1920s was that telephone service increased in value as more people had telephones, so it ought to be a matter of

63. *See Implementation of the Telecommunications Act of 1996: Telecommunications Carriers' Use of Customer Proprietary Network Information and Other Customer Information*, CC Docket No. 96–114, Report and Order and Further Notice of Proposed Rulemaking, 22 F.C.C.R. 6927 § 54 (2007).

policy to increase the number of households with phones. Under a monopoly system, it was relatively simple for AT&T to redistribute its income to cross-subsidize higher-cost services.

Today, there is no doubt broadband is a major component, if not the essential item, of media vitality for twenty-first-century communities. Broadband deployment is not just about the ability to download movies at high speeds; it's about economic development. Businesses are less likely to locate in areas where broadband is lacking, and local communities are aware of that.

It is more costly to provide broadband services to rural areas primarily because of the density of homes. Extending a fiber-optic line, for example, for one-mile costs about the same whether there are two homes (i.e., potential subscribers) along that mile or 50. Pricing for rural broadband is prohibitive in many locations. Either the cost is high due to the low density of households, or there must be some form of subsidy to bolster subscriptions.

One solution is to create more government incentives for rural broadband networks in the same way early telephone carriers received funding for rural service. Instead of asserting that the network is more valuable as a justification for the subsidy, rural broadband proponents can certainly claim health care, education, and commerce all rely on broadband connections.

The Telecommunications Act of 1996 made it possible for Universal Service Funds to help subsidize these expenses. USF fees are collected from phone customers and companies and allocated via multiple programs to rural and low-income users, rural health care, schools, and libraries.

Summary

- The Federal Communications Commission was created to oversee both structural and content issues. Its regulations cover both the technology and programming content of radio and television stations. In terms of structure, rules oversee the technology, channel assignments, tower lighting, and the ownership of broadcasting stations. In terms of content, the rules engage areas of political broadcasting, children's television, indecency, and commercial sponsorship.
- The FCC derives its authority from the interstate commerce clause of the U.S. Constitution. Based on the rationale that the American public owns the airwaves, the FCC exercises its legal authority by allocating the use of spectrum and licensing stations in their interest. Further, the bandwidth is too limited to grant licenses to all applicants, so broadcasters are given only a temporary license to use them as public trustees.
- The FCC can revoke licenses or invoke fines for failing to heed government regulations created to protect the public's interest. The agency reviews its rules regularly and decides whether to revise any regulations found to be no longer useful or practical.
- Telecommunications policy is crafted by five commissioners assigned a regulatory role. They are appointed by the president to serve five-year terms and represent both political parties. They not only oversee broadcasting but also regulate other electronic media, including cable and satellite channels, telephone, and Internet networks.
- In terms of infractions and penalties broadcasters might receive from the U.S. government, the FCC enforces its rules by first issuing notices of apparent liability. It also can move against violators with fines or "forfeitures" in addition to a letter of reprimand. If there is a pattern of abuse in violation of the public interest, convenience, or necessity, the government can revoke a license, but seldom does.
- The FCC does enforce political rules designed to afford federal candidates an equal opportunity to reach local voters through broadcast and cable channels. Equal opportunities

mean broadcast stations must not favor one candidate over another in terms of selling or offering commercial time in the weeks before an election. The FCC also requires campaigns be charged the lowest unit rate for their on-air spots during this period.

- Promoting localism, competition, and diversity is central to the FCC's mission. One way it accomplishes that objective is by placing limits on how many stations one group can own. A sliding scale of media channel ownership is based on the size of the market.
- Congress and the FCC have also acted on behalf of children's educational and informational needs by requiring TV stations broadcast programs to improve adolescent cognitive skills and meet their emotional needs. The "core programming" must reach adolescents 16 years and younger and air at least weekly between 6 a.m. and 10 p.m.
- Cable television in the United States began as community antenna television (CATV), a means by which people could gain reception of over-the-air broadcast signals from distant cities.
- In the early days of CATV, most communities had just one multichannel video program distributor, the cable company. With the entry of other multichannel video program distributors (MVPD), such as satellite and video over telephone, local competition for subscribers became the rule.
- Cable companies must carry local television stations by including their channels in the cable system's basic tier of offerings.
- The cable industry had little regulation at first and was protected in law by a congressional act in 1984, but the pendulum swung toward more regulation in 1992.

Ethical Dilemmas: Fairness

Journalists inevitably pursue stories that spark controversy, and broadcast journalists consequently face an editorial dilemma when it comes to deciding how to balance issues with facts and opinions from all sides. At one point, the answer was a matter of law.

The fairness doctrine was used by the FCC beginning in 1949 to affirm news coverage by broadcasters of all valid sides of a controversial issue. At first an informal policy, the FCC made it a regulation in 1967, and the Supreme Court affirmed it twice in 1969 (*Red Lion Broadcasting v. FCC*) and 1984 (*FCC v. League of Women Voters of California*).

Without judicial or legislative intervention, the FCC chose to rescind the policy in 1987, finding it to be unenforceable on an equitable basis. As a lesson in ethical newsgathering, the fairness doctrine does reflect a cardinal principle of professionalism. Ethicists believe journalists need to practice balance and fairness in reporting; nonetheless, and broadcast newsroom's policies should affirm fairness as a professional norm rather than the law.

The Radio-Television Digital News Association (RTDNA), for example, warns reporters to resist "false dichotomies . . . and consider a range of alternatives between the extremes" because journalists must challenge assumptions, reject stereotypes, and illuminate ignorance. Their role is not to force a particular narrative to chill the expressions of minority voices but give voice to the silent who have something important and relevant to say.

9

Online Media

LEARNING OBJECTIVES

After reading this chapter, you should know

- the legal grounds of regulation for *posting* content versus *hosting* content online
- how different approaches to Internet regulation are taken by U.S. government agencies
- how cybercrimes like cyberbullying or cyberstalking legally relate to cybersecurity
- what responsibilities businesses have in terms of their legal obligations for data privacy
- what obligations carry over to law enforcement searches of digital devices for information
- what rules make social media content unlawful to viewers
- key concerns for social media use, and how lawsuits affect big technology firms
- how global regulations compare to U.S. oversight of Internet communications

When Congress adopted the Communications Decency Act (CDA) in 1996 it could not foresee the multibillion-dollar growth of adult entertainment websites in the twenty-first century, nor could it predict the predators of children accessing sexual imagery on their smartphone. What it did realize was a court challenge by the American Civil Liberties Union claiming the CDA was unconstitutional since it conceived of the Internet as a medium like broadcasting. In *Reno v. American Civil Liberties Union,* Justice John Paul Stevens responded to the lawsuit by noting the Internet's characteristics as a *unique medium* that stood in contrast to broadcasting where indecency regulation had been affirmed. The Court held "any person or organization with a computer connected to the Internet can 'publish' information," and as such should be given broader First Amendment rights.[1] While the ruling in *Reno* struck down restrictions on sharing digital content due to indecent characteristics it did save one important provision of the Communications Decency Act. The section of the law surviving by the means of judicial severability was Title 47 U.S.C. §230 (c) (1) stating,

> No provider or user of an interactive computer service shall be treated as the publisher or speaker of any information provided by another information content provider.[2]

1. *Reno v. ACLU,* 521 U.S. 853 (1997).
2. 47 U.S. Code §(c)(1) 230.

DOI: 10.4324/9781003462989-9

These 26 words created a safeguard for Internet service providers to advance a business model where viewers could freely share their user-generated content without the host platform fearing liability. This shield against litigation was in force whenever the platform chose to edit or censor the controversial expressions of its viewers or chose not to do so.

What gave rise to this federal shield was a decision by the New York Supreme Court in *Stratton Oakmont, Inc. v. Prodigy Services Co.* (1995).[3] The petitioners asked Prodigy to pay damages after a defamatory comment appeared on its *Money Talk* page alleging the financial firm perpetrated a crime through its initial public offering. Rather than accepting the publisher's liability for this defamation, Prodigy claimed it was only an intermediary channel for user-generated content. The court rejected Prodigy's defense. It had exercised editorial control through its Bulletin Board software and therefore acted as co-publisher of that content. This ruling prompted Congress to consider the possible litigation facing online media.

Section 230 of the Communications Decency Act
Immunizes third-party platforms that serve as the conduit for others' communication online.

The safe harbor for Internet platforms was written into the CDA to give technology companies the power to control offensive content from third parties without suffering liability. When the indecency provisions of the CDA were struck down in *Reno v. ACLU* (1997), the Court severed part of Sec. 230 affording digital platforms a safe harbor for all the user-generated content that became the Internet's stock in trade.

Section 230 secures from litigation a wide variety of online activities. It protects Internet service providers from customers claiming material received via the ISP was damaging to their interests. Websites could allow injurious comments without having to defend themselves against defamation claims or privacy invasions. It protects websites like YouTube from copyright infringement so long as they take down contested content in a timely manner. It considers platforms like Facebook to be safe from offensive third-party postings. There are other legal hurdles it serves to avoid.

When scrolling down pages of X, Facebook, or other social media platforms, the viewer might see them as free and open to public comment, but digital platforms are different. The authority to take down content based on a platform's terms and conditions is one of the special features of the lawful supervision Section 230 provides its corporate owners. One example involved an Ohio teacher who tried to protect her reputation from malicious disinformation.

She tried to protect her reputation from online defamation by suing TheDirty.com. It was a gossip platform given to displaying anonymous postings including an attack against her as both a Cincinnati Bengals cheerleader and a schoolteacher. The online slurs began charging her with sleeping "with every other Bengal Football player." The secret poster attributed to her sexually transmitted diseases, adding that she was having sex on school grounds where she worked. The aggrieved woman filed a lawsuit against the site for defamation and intentional infliction of emotional distress. After two jury trials – the first resulting in a mistrial – a federal district court awarded $338,000 in damages. The platform filed several motions to have it dismissed using the Sec. 230 shield, but those motions were denied. On appeal, a federal court overturned the lower court ruling and concluded the federally approved safe harbor for TheDirty.com should be protected.[4]

Would the outcome have been different had the court discovered the platform owner or its employees were the ones posting the injurious content? The answer is *yes*. Section 230 (c)(1) of the CDA affords immunity from liability when information comes from a third party, but *not* when the website or its employees posts the content.

A federal district court in an Arizona case refused to grant immunity to a website "responsible . . . for the creation or development of information."[5] If a news outlet posts a defamatory

3. *Stratton Oakmont, Inc. v. Prodigy Services Co.*, 23 Media Law Reporter 1794, N.Y. Sup. Ct. 1995.
4. *Jones v. Dirty World Entertainment*, 755 F.3d 398 (Ct. App. Sixth Cir. 2014).
5. *Hy Cite Corporation v. badbusinessbureau.com*, 418 F. Supp. 2d 1142 (Ariz. D. 2005).

story on its website, then §230(c)(1) will be without effect. If the same website posts a non-libelous but controversial item, and then viewers respond by posting defamatory words, those plaintiffs will likely find it is shielded by the CDA's provisions.

Models of Regulation

It is a natural tendency for government to regulate new technology based on old models. In the twentieth century, the common carrier concept was imposed on telephone regulation based on a previously existing transportation scheme. So while trying to decide how (or whether) to regulate the Internet, the FCC and courts debated whether the Internet was more like newspaper, broadcasting, or cable television and turned to thinking of pre-existing regulatory schemes.

In decades past, wires that carried phone calls did only that and the telephone service was simply regulated as a common carrier. In the 1970s, such a classification was too simplistic, so a two-tiered system of regulation was created. Title I was the category for "information services" rather than "communication services." When an ATM communicates with a bank's computer, for example, financial data are transferred between two machines. That is a **Title I service** as regulated under Title I of the Communications Act of 1934. Traditional telephone, which was seen as a *means of communicating between people*, is a **Title II service**. Title II services, telecommunications, are more heavily regulated than Title I services. The proponents of a policy called *network neutrality* advocated for the regulation of broadband equivalent to the Title II regulation of basic phone services.

Network Neutrality

Network Neutrality
Refers to the general principle of equal access to Internet resources and content, as opposed to a tiered structure, which prefers certain users, technology, and content over others.

Who owns or directly controls the wire that provides the information and entertainment channels, along with how and whether to regulate it, became part of the legal calculus. Those were the challenges of **network neutrality** in 2015 when the FCC embraced the policy of net neutrality with an Open Internet Order.

The idea was to make sure Internet providers distribute online services to homes and offices fairly and to grant access without degrading content by download speeds or bandwidth limitations. That order was challenged in court, but the D.C. Circuit Court of Appeals affirmed the FCC's rule despite corporate challenges.[6]

Once the administration changed hands, the perspective at the FCC on net neutrality changed as well. Describing the Open Internet Order as "1930s-era utility-style regulation," the agency's website decried it for "threatening the very open Internet it purported to preserve." Such a policy would mean Internet service providers would have to "divert resources to comply with unnecessary and broad new regulatory requirements" that threaten to take away corporate investments from what consumers want and need.

Posting under the heading, "Restoring Freedom on the Internet," the FCC in 2018 promised a light touch toward online regulations, and in that context proposed to reinstate the Internet's classification as a Title I information service. But sometimes partisan politics gets in the way; one issue in particular generated controversy.[7] The FCC's net neutrality rules are a classic example of a politicized media policy. Republican administrations curtailed the rules, and then Democratic administrations reinstated them. At this writing in 2024, the FCC has chosen to enforce net neutrality rules.[8] State policies vary widely, and in some cases,

6. *United States Telecom Assoc. v. FCC*, 359 F. 3d 554 (2015).
7. *See* https://www.fcc.gov/document/fcc-releases-restoring-internet-freedom-order.
8. Wikipedia provides an excellent timeline of events, *at* https://en.wikipedia.org/wiki/Net_neutrality_in_the_United_States.

states chose to implement their own regulatory policy. In 2018 California was the first state to pass its own net neutrality legislation.[9] Other states followed with a wide variety of legislation, executive orders, and utility commission action.[10]

Regulation of Social Media

The Supreme Court gave protection to online media (*Reno v. ACLU*, 1997),[11] but commercial services and social networks did not necessarily protect freedom of expression in the same way. As noted in the previous chapter, the platform now known as X, for example, banned President Trump for violating its terms and conditions based on Twitter's "Glorification of Violence" policy following the U.S. Capitol riot of January 6, 2021.

Two tweets were deemed offensive after the destructive and lethal rioting at the Capitol following the president's speech on January 6, 2021. Trump tweeted, "The 75,000,000 great American Patriots who voted for me, AMERICA FIRST, and MAKE AMERICA GREAT AGAIN, will have a GIANT VOICE long into the future. They will not be disrespected or treated unfairly in any way, shape or form!!!" The president followed that comment with a tweet promising he would forgo any appearance at President Biden's inauguration.

Twitter took the tweets together to mean the president was refusing to accept the election results and was encouraging followers to act with violence to prevent the certification of an election he had convinced them was fraudulent and did not reflect the will of the people. The president responded to Twitter's ban through his White House account @POTUS, and followers retweeted from their Twitter accounts. The president accused the platform of conspiring against him with his opponents "to silence me – and YOU, the 75,000,000 great patriots who voted for me."[12] Twitter deleted his followers' retweets.

This incident made social media users wonder just how far giant corporate owners of Facebook, Instagram, X (formerly Twitter), TikTok, and others would go in muting or amplifying user-generated content. Republican governors in two states, Florida and Texas, felt the corporate owners had gone too far and violated users' rights by regulating their content. Both states adopted laws to keep social media companies from discriminating against viewpoints and removing posts or blocking users because of their speech. Two appellate courts differed on whether the online laws enacted by Texas and Florida legislatures were constitutional. The Supreme Court entered the picture to resolve the matter.

The Court consolidated two cases under *Moody v. NetChoice, NetChoice v. Paxton.*[13] The Florida law would among other things punish social media platforms for blocking a political official for over 60 days. The Texas law would stop social media platforms from removing or hiding posts based on their content. The Court vacated both lower court rulings – affirming Texas and opposing Florida – remanding the cases for rehearing to determine whether the two states would be violating First Amendment rights of the companies based on their content-moderation rules. It boils down to a simple question with vast implications: Should tech giants be granted the continued freedom to moderate social media content without being

9. California Internet Consumer Protection and Net Neutrality Act of 2018. California was not the first state to act, however. Montana has that distinction with an executive order by the governor months before California's legislation. "Montana Governor Signs Order to Force Net Neutrality," *NY Times*, January 22, 2018.
10. S. Klein, "State Responses to Net Neutrality," *NRRI* (2022), *at* https://pubs.naruc.org/pub/45ACE3A2-AAEA-417D-2416-B6862C9D4435.
11. 532 U.S. 844 (1997).
12. Twitter, Inc., "Permanent Suspension of @realDonaldTrump," January 8, 2021, *at* https://blog.twitter.com/en_us/topics/company/2020/suspension.html.
13. *Moody v. NetChoice, LLC* and *NetChoice, LLC v. Paxton*, 603 U.S. ___ (2024).

treated as publishers facing liability challenges? Supreme Court justices opposed to granting this much power to technology giants sum up their position this way:

> In the platforms' world, they are fully responsible for their websites when it results in constitutional protections, but the moment that responsibility could lead to liability, they can disclaim any obligations and enjoy greater protections from suit than nearly any other industry. The Court should consider if this state of affairs is what §230 demands.[14]

What happens when it is not the social media platform blocking viewers and banning content but an individual subscriber – does that pose any issues? When a public official is dealing with the government's business online and using a social media channel to respond to constituents it could be a problem. After a Michigan city manager in Port Huron, James Freed, deleted posts of Kevin Lindke's critical comments, Lindke felt his rights to speak in such a public forum were violated. In *Lindke v. Freed*,[15] the Supreme Court addressed this challenge where elected officials used social media for their campaigns and continue to do so after their election using the platform for public business. In a unanimous decision, the Court held that a private social media account does not necessarily constitute a public forum for government speech – unless the account becomes a type of public forum for the politician to speak on behalf of the government office.

The dangers to mental health posed by social media have been the subject of a lot of conversation. In 2023, the surgeon general issued an advisory about the effects on young people, calling on parents and tech companies to act, but also on policymakers to limit children's access and strengthen safety standards.[16] That same year Texas passed a law under consideration by several states to require parental consent for minors to use social media.[17]

AI Bill of Rights

Years ago the media world contemplated the promise of global peace through innovation when Facebook announced a joint digital project with Stanford University "to bring together opposing sides in some of the most bitterly divided areas of the planet, encouraging online friendships between Jews and Muslims, US liberals and conservatives, and Turks and Greeks."[18] Founded in 2009 as *peace.facebook.com,* B.J. Fogg, director of the Persuasive Technology Lab at Stanford, declared it would serve to resolve global conflict through digital innovation. "Lots of it. There's no single answer, no single solution. Together we must innovate to create more empathy, understanding, tolerance, and so on."[19]

The promise of digital innovation took a darker turn in 2022 when artificial intelligence was defined in part as algorithmic curation. The U.S. government published a "Blueprint for an AI Bill of Rights," where proposals for peace and understanding gave way to warnings against "the use of technology, data, and automated ways that

14. See *Doe v. Snap, Inc.*, No. 23–961. 595 U.S., at ___–___ (statement of Thomas, J.) (slip op., at 1–2).
15. *Lindke v. Freed,* 601 U.S. 187 (2024).
16. "Surgeon General Issues New Advisory About Effects Social Media Use Has on Youth Mental Health," *US Dept. of HHS*, May 23, 2023, *at* https://www.hhs.gov/about/news/2023/05/23/surgeon-general-issues-new-advisory-about-effects-social-media-use-has-youth-mental-health.html.
17. At the time of this writing the Texas law has been challenged. "Georgia Joins Four Other States in Restricting Social Media Use by Children," March 29, 2024, *at* https://stratnewsglobal.com/north-america/georgia-joins-four-other-states-in-restricting-social-media-use-by-children/.
18. "Facebook Project Gives World Peace a Chance," *The Guardian*, October 28, 2009, *at* https://www.theguardian.com/technology/2009/oct/28/facebook-world-peace-online-project.
19. *Id.*

threaten the rights of the American public."[20] High on the list of AI perils: "algorithmic discrimination" where "automated systems contribute to unjustified different treatment or impacts disfavoring people" focusing on identity variables like "race, color, ethnicity, gender identity, religion, age, national origin, disability, veteran status . . . or any other classification projected by law."[21] The innovations of AI were viewed as more likely to create conflict than resolve it. Not just politicians, but AI employees also warned of the dangers. In an open letter, current and former AI workers expressed concern for an AI environment that lacks oversight.[22]

Algorithmic Terrorism

The idea of algorithmic curation aiding terrorist violence caught the attention of Supreme Court justices in two cases where technology companies were accused of *aiding and abetting* terrorist attacks in Europe. Following an ISIS onslaught in Istanbul, Türkiye, that left 39 people dead at a nightclub, one victim's family sued Facebook, Twitter, and YouTube's owner Google for algorithmically pushing videos to terrorists.[23] The Court also heard a case against social media platforms from family members of a U.S. college student, Nohemi Gonzales, 23, killed in France during the 2015 terrorist attacks.[24] ISIS terrorists killed the student while she sat with friends at a Paris Bistro.

In both cases, the digital content spread by algorithms contained violent imagery to attract suicidal followers who were willing to embrace deadly solutions. The Supreme Court held the social media's curation and dissemination of violent content did not fulfill the legal definition of *aiding and abetting* as required by law.[25] The Antiterrorism and Effective Death Penalty Act of 1996 would not define algorithmic sharing that way. The larger question turned to focus on what content should be considered safe from such challenges, and then how would the anonymity of algorithms impact the legal process.

TikTok's Impact

Protecting the mental health of young people is a priority in the United States given the alarming rise in statistics showing unprecedented levels of adolescent depression and suicide. Social media is seen as one of the key factors leading to the ills of addiction based on the success of attracting and holding juveniles glued to their platforms. TikTok is at the forefront of this discussion; collecting demographic data on juveniles is one of the tools in the process.

The Federal Trade Commission and the Department of Justice joined to sue TikTok and its parent company ByteDance for illegally collecting data from adolescents in violation of the Children's Online Privacy Protection Act or COPPA. The U.S. government in its filing claimed TikTok collected data from children it knew were under 13 and used their data to send commercial messages to their screens without seeking their consent or giving parental notification as required by law.

20. White House Office of Science and Technology Policy, "Blueprint for an AI Bill of Rights – Making Automated Systems Work for The American People," (October 2022), *at* https://www.whitehouse.gov/ostp/ai-bill-of-rights.
21. *Id.* at p. 10.
22. "Current and Former OpenAI Employees Warn of AI's 'Serious Risks' and Lack of Oversight," *CNBC*, June 4, 2024, https://www.cnbc.com/2024/06/04/openai-open-ai-risks-lack-of-oversight.html.
23. *Twitter, Inc. v. Taamneh*, 598 U.S. 471 (2023).
24. *Gonzalez v. Google LLC*, 598 U.S. 617 (2023).
25. See *Antiterrorism and Effective Death Penalty Act of 1996* (AEDPA), Tooltip Public Law (U.S.) 104–132.

It is not the first time TikTok had come under scrutiny by state and federal governments in the United States. Nor is it the first time TikTok was sued for its data collection techniques. A class action lawsuit in 2019 alleged TikTok violated privacy law by transferring personally identifiable information of Americans to Chinese computer servers. A college student alleged she downloaded a TikTok app but never created an account. TikTok created one for her using biometric data. It transferred her information to Baidu, another Chinese tech firm.

Lawsuits were filed against TikTok not only for violating privacy law for children, but for making inappropriate content available to juveniles. Claims were made in court that children died in 2021 from a "Blackout Challenge" that popped up on smartphone screens. In 2024, Nebraska alleged TikTok was damaging the mental health of young people due to an algorithmic design for cultivating compulsive behavior.

Anonymity Online

When it comes to online provocations, if a news website is not legally responsible – does that mean individuals harmed are left without legal recourse by postings made anonymously? For example, how can a plaintiff sue someone without knowing the identity of the speaker? The Supreme Court clarified the right of speakers to remain anonymous in *Talley v. California* (1960).[26] Justice Black traced the historical importance of anonymity to the actual founding of the country, and how framers concealed their identities for constructive purposes so the readers would focus on the message and not on personal retaliation.[27] In this context, victims must know the communicator's identity to pursue a remedy for their injuries.

One case in which a court provided a test for determining whether an anonymous poster's identity would be revealed arose from online attacks in New Jersey. A publicly traded company, Dendrite International, Inc., served the pharmaceutical and consumer package goods industry and noticed a Yahoo message board was aflame with attacks on its financial policies. The company asked the court to force the disclosure of its online detractors, and the result was a legal method for balancing the competing interests of responsibility and anonymity.[28]

The Delaware Supreme Court proposed a process for unmasking,[29] which became known as the ***Dendrite* test**. Under its terms, those seeking to identify an online speaker accused of defamation should take the following steps:

1 Attempt to contact the speaker and allow a reasonable time for response.
2 Identify the precise comments triggering the claim.
3 Present sufficient evidence to avoid any summary judgment.
4 Provide adequate evidence on each element of the offense except actual malice (without knowing the offender's identity, knowledge of falsity would be impossible to prove).

In view of these requirements, it seems First Amendment protections for anonymous speech are substantial. It is not that courts *never* require posters to be unmasked, nor do they *always* require disclosure; they simply ask for sufficient evidence prior to reaching any disclosure decision. The *Dendrite* test eliminates the possibility of artful lawsuits with little substance or merit filed simply to embarrass or intimidate online speakers.

26. *Talley v. California*, 362 U.S. 60 (1960).
27. "Even the Federalist Papers, written in favor of the adoption of our Constitution, were published under fictitious names. It is plain that anonymity has sometimes been assumed for the most constructive purposes." *Id.* at 65.
28. *Dendrite Int'l v. Doe*, 342 N.J. Super. 134 (2001).
29. *Doe v. Cahill*, 884 A.2d 451 (Del. 2005).

A case in point was the dispute where Maryland's highest court struck down a lower court order to disclose three persons' identities who posted offensive comments about a doughnut shop owner.[30] No unmasking occurred because the court found the doughnut baker failed to sustain a valid claim for defamation, and under the *Dendrite* test that item must precede any disclosure requirement.

In one more case of anonymity affirmed, the Trump administration in 2017 turned to Twitter seeking information to reveal the identities of online speakers purporting to be employees of the U.S. Citizenship and Immigration Services. One or more critics were tweeting highly negative comments about President Trump's immigration and border policy.[31] In its refusal to reveal the president's online critics, Twitter filed suit against the Customs Border and Patrol unit claiming it failed to cite any criminal or civil offense necessary to require a disclosure. Before the account holders' identities would be revealed the government needed to show unmasking was the least constitutionally violative solution.[32] CBP withdrew the request.

Glassdoor Case

Anonymous speech is essential to third-party platforms like "Glassdoor," where employees share candid comments about their working conditions and even salaries. Glassdoor launched its company ratings website in 2008, and within seven years had 30 million users worldwide. A dilemma confronted the site after U.S. prosecutors began digging up evidence against a contractor accused of fraud, waste, and abuse. Investigators needed the names of eight employees who posted online since they might have eye-opening evidence about any suspected crimes at the workplace.

The online platform took exception to the investigators' request and instead chose to keep Glassdoor commenters anonymous. Briefs were filed by the Center for Democracy & Technology and the Electronic Frontier Foundation to maintain the secrecy of the Glassdoor users. They argued the protected right of confidentiality must be safeguarded. The Ninth Circuit Court of Appeals disagreed because the eight users were lawfully summoned for an ongoing grand jury investigation, and Glassdoor's appeal was denied.[33] Such a ruling might discourage others from sharing offensive opinions online about their employers knowing that a grand jury subpoena or criminal investigation could produce a disclosure of secret identities.

Anonymous speech online is protected, but an anonymous speaker's identity can be revealed by a court order for a legal complaint or by subpoena.

One narrow area in which anonymity online is prohibited involves stock market dealings, where affirmative disclosure is required by U.S. statute. Publicly traded companies, for example, are restricted in what they can and cannot say that might affect stock prices. They cannot use anonymity to shield tactical moves to manipulate the market or engage in insider trading by posing as a company or securities research firm.

In the political arena, state campaign laws sometimes require disclosure for advocates of messages supporting a candidate. A federal court in Maine punished one resident, a journalist, for creating an anonymous blog criticizing a candidate who was hoping to become Maine's governor. The law in that state required disclosure when expenditures for or against a candidate exceed $100. The plaintiff tried to claim he fit under an exemption for journalists,

30. *Independent Newspapers v. Brodie*, 407 Md. 415 (2009).
31. "Twitter Sues U.S. Government over Attempt to Unmask Anti-Trump Tweeters," *Hollywood Reporter*, April 6, 2017.
32. "The U.S. Government Has Withdrawn Its Request Ordering Twitter to Identify a Trump Critic," *Washington Post*, April 7, 2017.
33. *In re* Grand Jury Subpoena, 875 F.3d 1179 (9th Cir. 2017).

but the court rejected that argument because his website was not a periodical publication.[34] His fine for blogging anonymously about a political candidate was upheld.

What is legally required to disclose an online communicator's identity varies from country to country. In France, for example, Twitter (now X) had to reveal the identities of anonymous speakers who transmitted anti-Semitic tweets. Europe often enforces laws against hateful expressions while the United States allows ethnic aspersions. Twitter did provide the identifying data so those who posted the tweets could be prosecuted.[35]

Age Disclosure and Pornography

The detrimental effects of pornography and its easy access by minors prompted lawmakers in nine states to pass laws requiring age verification with a health warning to viewers in Arkansas, Indiana, Kansas, Louisiana, Mississippi, Montana, Oklahoma, Utah and Virginia. Porn sites in those states were required by similar laws to ask for age verification from users and publish warnings stating their content was addictive and that it could impair cognate development and increase the level of crimes of prostitution and child sexual abuse.

Targeting the age verification law in Texas, a trade association for the sexual entertainment industry and the Free Speech Coalition filed a request to stop the law from taking effect. They sought an emergency appeal from the U.S. Supreme Court claiming it should not be immediately enforced since it trespassed on sacred First Amendment ground. Lawyers for the state of Texas responded by saying they had a right to impose "commercially reasonable steps to ensure that those who access the material are adults," especially since mobile devices like smartphones created an "explosion of access to hardcore pornography by kids," causing a public health crisis. The Supreme Court allowed the Texas law to stay on the books until it could review a federal appeals court ruling on the subject.[36]

One final note about using "age gates" – verifying users are old enough. It requires websites to store personal information, which means a tradeoff between protecting minors and increased risk of privacy invasions.

Cyber Predators[37]

Sometimes a Supreme Court decision defending freedom of expression appears to afford nefarious actors more breathing space than they deserve. Consider the case of *Elonis v. United States* (2015), where the Supreme Court reversed the conviction of Anthony Douglas Elonis, who was found guilty under a federal law prohibiting explicit threats of violence: "communication containing any threat to kidnap any person or any threat to injure the person of another" (18 U.S.C. Sec. 875(c) [1994]).

Elonis's Facebook postings showcased fantasies of cruelty and violent murder directed at his estranged wife. "I'm not going to rest until your body is a mess, soaked in blood and dying from all the little cuts," he posted.[38] Elonis defended his social media threats by claiming to be an aspiring rap artist, who was just posting rap lyrics – a defense challenged by his wife's testimony who saw little interest or inclination toward rap music from her unhappy

34. *Bailey v. Maine Commission. On Govt. Ethics*, 900 F. Supp. 2d 75 (F.D. Maine 2012).
35. "Twitter Gives France Identities of Users Who Posted Anti-Semitic Tweets," *Hollywood Reporter*, June 12, 2013.
36. A. Howe, "Court Allows Texas to Enforce Age Verification for Online Porn Sites," *SCOTUSblog*, April 30, 2024, *at* https://www.scotusblog.com/2024/04/court-allows-texas-to-enforce-age-verification-for-online-porn-sites/.
37. This title is taken from an issue of the Department of Justice's U.S. Attorneys' Bulletin, May 2016, *at* www.justice.gov/usao/file/851856/download.
38. J. Russomanno, "Facebook Threats: The Missed Opportunities of Elonis v. United States," 21 *Communication Law & Policy* 1–37 (2016).

husband. The Court searched for evidence of his subjective intent to threaten his wife. Lacking the *mens rea* (guilty mind) requirement, the Court reversed and remanded the case to the federal Third Circuit. The comments of dissenting Justice Samuel Alito are telling:

> Well, this sounds like a roadmap for threatening a spouse and getting away with it. So you put it in rhyme and you put some stuff about the Internet on it and say, I'm an aspiring rap artist. And so then you are free from prosecution.[39]

It would be a mistake to conclude the *Elonis* ruling gave online license to all violent musings in disregard of victims' safety. Still, some viewed it as a missed opportunity to explore the seriousness of cyber threats since "proscribing true threats does not compromise free speech values; it enhances them," observed Russomanno.[40] Elonis did serve time for his social media postings held to be true threats by the Third Circuit Court of Appeals.

As noted in Chapter 3, the Supreme Court redefined a digital true threat in 2023 when it took up the case of a man diagnosed as mentally ill who was convicted of stalking. Billy Counterman was enamored with a female musician. He posted thousands of messages to and about her; some were regarded as a true threat by the musical artist. The Supreme Court vacated Counterman's conviction, however, due to Colorado law's lack of subjective intent. The state should prove the pursuer was aware his reckless words were threatening to the victim. The Court held the law must require he "consciously disregarded a substantial risk that his communications would be viewed as threatening violence."[41]

Cyberbullying
"(Willful) and repeated harm inflicted through the use of computers, cell phones and other electronic devices" (according to the Cyberbullying Research Center).[44]

Cyberbullying

While bullying has been around for as long as there have been despicable characters trying to intimidate and dominate others, cyberbullying has grown to become a national concern. The physical and psychological damage resulting from cyberbullying is well documented.[42] As with other forms of speech, the law weighs the speakers' First Amendment rights, and the safety and security of others hang in the balance. Childish teasing may be protected, but once it rises to the level of harassment, preventive measures must be taken, although state laws vary on how it must be done. Forty-eight states have some legal prohibition against cyberbullying or harassment; 44 states provide criminal punishment. Jurisdictions distinguish between teasing and torment, but that distinction is not always clear in a courtroom.[43]

Despite the widespread existence of laws, criminal convictions for cyberbullying are rare. The tragic case of a Missouri mother who created a fake Myspace profile posing as a 16-year-old boy who was flirting online with one of her daughter's classmates is one example. The 13-year-old victim, Megan, believed her new online boyfriend was real. The mother thought Megan was spreading false information about her daughter, and she created this fake suitor as her revenge. After weeks of phony romantic allusions, the fictitious liaison, "Josh" became increasingly mean to Megan, finally telling her that "the world would be a better place without her in it." Later that day, Megan hanged herself in her closet.[45] State prosecutors understood they lacked evidence to press charges in connection with the suicide.

39. See transcript of Oral Argument at 59, *Elonis v. United States,* 135 S. Ct. 2001 (2015) (No. 13–983).
40. Russomanno, "Facebook Threats," supra note 38.
41. *Counterman v. Colorado*, 600 U.S. 66 (2023).
42. See National Bullying Prevention Center at https://www.pacer.org/bullying/info/cyberbullying/.
43. A state-by-state listing can be found at http://cyberbullying.org/bullying-laws.
44. See Cyberbullying Research Center at https://cyberbullying.org/ and S. Hinduja & J.W. Patchin, *Bullying Beyond the Schoolyard: Preventing and Responding to Cyberbullying*, 3rd ed. (Thousand Oaks, CA: Corwin Pub, A Sage Company, 2023).
45. www.meganmeierfoundation.org/megans-story.html.

A federal prosecutor in California, however, filed charges against the mother for a violation of the Computer Fraud and Abuse Act since she had created a fraudulent profile in violation of the Myspace user agreement. A federal district court acquitted her on the grounds that such a user agreement does not carry the force of law.[46]

Government attempts to regulate online media to stop cyber-aggression often meet with mixed results. A state appellate court in New York took a closer look at an Albany ordinance criminalizing cyberbullying because it was overbroad and violated constitutional rights of freedom of expression.[47] And the North Carolina Supreme Court struck down that state's cyberbullying law in 2016 because it was "not narrowly tailored to the State's asserted interest in protecting children from the harms of online bullying."[48]

Even though court decisions punishing cyberbullying are infrequent, actions taken by school districts against students are more common. In *J.S. v. Bethlehem Area School District* (2002), a state court in Pennsylvania chose to expel a student (J.S.) who created a webpage to denigrate an algebra teacher and school principal. The online attack listed reasons for killing the teacher and administrator depicted in deadly animation; it was all created off campus. After the Supreme Court heard the case, the majority concluded the website disrupted the learning environment and that of the entire school community, so the student's expulsion was upheld.[49]

The National Crime Prevention Council's data show 43% of U.S. high school students have either been bullied personally or have seen it happen to others online. Some states have required local school boards to adopt policies prohibiting harassment, intimidation, and bullying by students who turn to aggressive behavior online.

Cyberstalking

Cyberstalking
The repeated use of digital media to harass or frighten someone.

Like cyberbullying, the offense of cyberstalking is another menace crossing over from the physical world to cause digital alarm. In terms of definition, the crime of cyberstalking requires the repeated, undesired personal contact through digital messaging written to harass or frighten the recipient. It too requires *personal* attacks. Someone making repeated sexist or racist comments on a website would not be viewed as stalking anyone; but aggressive and hostile comments texted to someone would meet the defining elements of this offense.

Unlike cyberbullying, there are federal statutes to deal with cyberstalking and threatening communications. One statute specifically deals with the "intent to abuse, threaten, or harass another person . . . by means of a telecommunications device."[50] This statute covers harassment when the victim does not know the identity of the perpetrator. Location of the perpetrator does make a difference; threatening interstate or foreign communications would be covered under a different statute.[51]

The federal stalking statute has been amended to include "any interactive computer service or electronic communication service or electronic communication system of interstate commerce."[52] The number of suits filed, and the defendants found guilty of cyberstalking is greater than for cyberbullying.[53] Some states passed cyberstalking legislation and included it in their laws against cyberbullying. Cyberstalking and cyber harassment are defined in statutes like the one in Louisiana (La. R.S. Sec. 14:40.3) carrying the penalty of a fine and up to a year in prison. The reach of the Internet is virtually global, so laws bound by state

46. *U.S. v. Drew*, 259 F.R.D. 449 (C.D. Calif. 2009).
47. *People v. Marquan M.*, 2014 WL 2931482 (Ct. App. NY July 1, 2014).
48. *North Carolina v. Bishop*, 368 N.C. 869, 870 (N.C. Sup. Ct. 2016).
49. *J.S. v. Bethlehem Area School District*, 757 A.2d 412 (Pa. 2002).
50. 47 U.S.C. § 223.
51. 18 U.S.C. § 875.
52. 18 U.S.C. § 2261A.
53. U.S. Attorneys' Bulletin, supra note 37, at 10–11.

jurisdictions lead some perpetrators to mistakenly believe they can harass their victims after crossing state lines.

What comes to mind is the case of a Maine woman who broke off a relationship with a dating partner; he then stalked and harassed her through online media. The jilted ex, Shawn Sayer, posted pictures of his former girlfriend dressed in lingerie and offering favors. She obtained a protective order against him but that did little to dissuade the strangers showing up at her home at all hours looking for "a good time" as advertised. After eight months of this harassment, the victim changed her name and moved to Louisiana, where she fell prey to fake social media profiles attached to online porn sites. Sayer was eventually convicted for cyberstalking, but he appealed on First Amendment grounds, thinking such a law should be struck for vagueness. It was affirmed by the First Circuit in Maine that upheld his conviction.[54]

Encouraging others to commit acts of violence can be classified as incitement, but such low-valued speech is denied First Amendment protection. The standard of proof for prosecution of incitement produces few convictions; that's often because the government must first demonstrate the defendant intended to provoke others to violence and that imminent harm would be likely to occur.

Cybersecurity

Today, security breach reports seem almost commonplace when so many major retailers and employers have been hacked by digital intruders. Every year spectacular hackers manage to steal data from the giant cash registers of online retail outlets. Digital burglars stole 60 million credit card numbers over a five-month period in 2014 from Home Depot. And hackers stole personal information from Target computers concerning almost 100 million customers.[55] These cybersecurity crimes can summon a response from the Federal Trade Commission with the authority to act against companies that fail to properly secure their customers' private data.

> The Federal Trade Commission acts against companies if they fail to protect their customers' private data as required by law or their terms and conditions.

When customer data stores were hacked from one giant hotel firm, the FTC alleged there was an unnecessary exposure of customers' personal data, due to lack of encryption, easily guessed passwords, and failure to use security measures such as firewalls.[56] Other episodes of cyberbreaches include an unauthorized hack of celebrity images posted online first to an image board, and then to other popular websites like Imgur and Reddit.com. The images were hacked from iCloud accounts. Reddit originally allowed the posts but stopped them after one of the celebrities involved claimed she was under 18 when her photo was taken. Reddit's immediate response was to remove her photos and warn viewers that reposting would result in child pornography charges. Eventually, Reddit banned any sub-Reddit[57] associated with the photo hack, claiming copyright law made such posts a violation.[58] After an FBI investigation of the hack, two individuals pleaded guilty in 2016 facing separate legal actions.[59]

54. *U.S. v. Sayer*, 748 F.3d 425 (Ct. App. First Cir. 2014).
55. "5 Huge Cybersecurity Breaches at Companies You Know," *Fortune*, October 3, 2014.
56. *FTC v. Wyndham Worldwide*, 799 F.3d 236 (Ct. App. Third Circ. 2015).
57. Reddit is an aggregation site where users upload content. Sub-reddits are content areas into which posts are divided, and users can create new categories as needed.
58. "Reddit Gives Mixed Messages after Pulling Leaked Celebrity Photos," *Forbes*, September 8, 2014.
59. "Chicagoan Gets Prison for 'Celebgate' Nude-Photo Hacking That Judge Calls 'Abhorrent'," *Chicago Tribune*, January 24, 2017.

For websites making the hacked photos available, famed Hollywood attorney Martin Singer threatened Google with a $100 million lawsuit claiming it failed to act quickly enough to remove the photos. Google noted it had removed "tens of thousands" of images and closed hundreds of accounts.[60]

The law is continuing to see an evolving trend in this area of digital privacy. Cybersecurity is no longer a novel concern, but legislation tends to fall behind the technology curve of innovation. Most of the states in the United States have introduced multiple bills with cybersecurity in mind. The measures deal with diverse issues of training, awareness, and penalties for computer crimes.[61] Federal law also requires special data protection for health[62] and banking information.[63] The rules specified a "reasonable" amount of security, which some claimed weakened cybersecurity enforcement due to the vagueness of the law.

Internet security is a global concern, but there are few worldwide agreements, and in the U.S. some question the federal law's effectiveness against skilled hackers. A class action was filed in 2016 against a law firm claiming its cybersecurity measures were inadequate to protect clients.[64] Target's retail customers filed suit together after its breach. A survey of corporate board members three years later showed 60% expected an increase in lawsuits over cybersecurity by shareholders whose companies had been hacked.[65] Such a metric leads to the expectation of more cybersecurity acts by states, federal agencies, and international commissions along with more penalties to recover personal damages from ripped-off consumers.[66]

Deepfakes

Deepfakes are videos that have been altered to appear to be someone different, or to make it appear someone has said something that they haven't. At the time of this writing, there is no comprehensive federal legislation that bans or regulates deepfakes, but the U.S. Senate passed a bill that would give victims a path to a civil suit.[67] Several states have created legislation to regulate deepfakes, falling into two categories. Indiana, New Mexico, Oregon, and Texas regulate deepfakes as they might be used to influence an election. Florida, Louisiana, South Dakota, and Washington have laws dealing with deepfakes of a sexual nature.[68]

Computer Fraud and Abuse Act (CFAA)

Congress created the Computer Fraud and Abuse Act in 1986, which was amended on several occasions. In its original form, the statute protected mainly government computers, but over the years, its scope was expanded to cover nearly any networked computer, including smartphones. The law makes it a crime to intentionally access a protected computer without proper authorization to obtain information.[69] The unguarded use of someone else's login information under such conditions could invite prosecution.

David Nosal was an employee of Korn/Ferry International, a management consulting company headquartered in Los Angeles. He and a few of his associates decided to leave the firm and initiate a competing business in 2005. When he left Korn/Ferry, his access to its computers was terminated, but he was still able to access them via an accomplice's credentials, allowing him to download some company data. When prosecuted, Nosal asserted he was only guilty of password sharing, which he believed was not a crime. The Ninth Circuit Court of

60. "Google Threatened with $100-Million Lawsuit over Celebrity Nude Photos," *Los Angeles Times*, October 2, 2014.
61. Cybersecurity Legislation, "National Conference of State Legislatures," September 13, 2020, *at* www.ncsl.org/research/telecommunications-and-information-technology/cybersecurity-legislation-2020.aspx.
62. Health Insurance Portability and Accountability Act of 1996, Pub.L. 104–191.
63. Financial Services Modernization Act of 1999, Pub.L. 106–102.
64. "Chicago's Johnson & Bell First US Firm Publicly Named in Data Security Class Action," *The American Lawyer*, December 9, 2016.
65. "Shareholder Cybersecurity Lawsuits Expected to Increase in 2016," *at* https://edepoze.com/cybersecurity-lawsuits/.
66. "You've Been Hacked, and Now You're Being Sued: The Developing World of Cybersecurity Litigation," 90 *Florida Bar Journal* 30 (July 2016).
67. "Anti-Deepfake Legislation Just Took a Major Step Toward Becoming Law," July 25, 2024, https://mashable.com/article/deepfake-defiance-act-passes-senate-vote
68. "Deepfakes: Federal and State Regulation Aims to Curb a Growing Threat," https://www.thomsonreuters.com/en-us/posts/government/deepfakes-federal-state-regulation/.
69. 18 U.S.C. § 1030.

Figure 9.1 Internet hacktivist Aaron Swartz protesting proposed legislation in 2012

The Computer Fraud and Abuse Act makes accessing a computer without permission to obtain information (hacking) a crime.

Appeals held his access "without authorization" was unambiguous and ruled Nosal violated the CFAA.[70] Dissenters insisted this case was only about password sharing[71] and offered in comparison the common sharing of Netflix passwords.[72] But the majority opinion bluntly stated that was not the case. Nosal served a federal prison term for this mistaken belief.

The CFAA and Intellectual Property

The Consumer Fraud and Abuse Act came under severe criticism following an unfortunate set of circumstances surrounding the death of a popular Internet activist.[73] Aaron Swartz was involved with certain websites, including the not-for-profit Creative Commons, Watchdog.net, and the news aggregator Reddit. He supported the open access movement, sincerely believing online research ought to be shared freely by all.

In 2008, Swartz downloaded over two million federal court documents from the U.S. courts' PACER system, an electronic record system (Figure 9.1). He made the documents available to Public.Resource.Org, a not-for-profit that shares government documents. The group's founder complained about the exorbitant costs of court data, which Swartz contended should be available for free.[74] The FBI investigated, but no charges were filed. Then in 2010, Swartz used his MIT access for downloading millions of academic articles from JSTOR, a subscription service for journals that libraries pay to access.

After this downloading was discovered, federal authorities decided to press charges against him. By 2012, U.S. attorneys had filed 13 different charges against Swartz – 11 of them were CFAA violations, which might have amounted to a million dollars in fines and

70. *U.S. v. Nosal*, 844 F.3d 1024 (Ct. App. Ninth Circ. 2016).
71. *See, e.g.*, "Appeals Court Rules That Sharing Password Can Be a Federal Crime," *Fortune*, July 10, 2016.
72. "Sharing Netflix and HBO Passwords Is Now a Federal Crime, But Here's Why Not to Worry," *Market Watch*, July 13, 2016.
73. "Fixing the Worst Law in Technology," *New Yorker*, March 18, 2013.
74. "FBI Investigated Coder for Liberating Paywalled Court Records," *Wired*, October 5, 2009.

50 years in prison. Swartz rejected a plea bargain though that would have reduced his sentence to only six months in a minimum-security prison.

Swartz instead committed suicide on January 11, 2013. This death sparked a series of critiques over the government's decision to prosecute and raised other questions about MIT's support for one of its fellows, and the exercise of power over the Internet. "Aaron's Law" was drafted in 2013 as an effort to modify the CFAA.[75] Two criticisms concerned the relative length of prison terms under the law and harsh criminalizations for violation of user agreements.[76]

Computer Fraud and Abuse Act

18 U.S. Code § 1030

The relevant portion of the Act used by federal officials against Aaron Swartz covered the following elements:

a Whoever –

1 intentionally accesses a computer without authorization or exceeds authorized access, and thereby obtains – information from any protected computer;

2 knowingly and with intent to defraud, accesses a protected computer without authorization, or exceeds authorized access, and by means of such conduct furthers the intended fraud and obtains anything of value, unless the object of the fraud and the thing obtained consists only of the use of the computer and the value of such use is not more than $5,000 in any 1-year period;

b (c) The punishment for an offense under subsection (a) or (b) of this section is –

(1)(A) a fine under this title or imprisonment for not more than ten years, or both, in the case of an offense under subsection (a)(1) of this section which does not occur after a conviction for another offense under this section, or an attempt to commit an offense punishable under this subparagraph

Cell Phone Searches

As noted earlier in the privacy chapter, police searching words and images on a suspect's mobile phone might be treading on constitutional rights. Two cases were joined by the Supreme Court to determine the right of police to conduct warrantless searches to find evidence. San Diego officers pulled over a driver with expired license tags in 2009 and that eventually led to the arrest of a murder suspect on weapons charges with two loaded firearms in his vehicle.

One police officer took David Riley's mobile phone from his pants pocket and began examining it. He noticed a text term associated with gang activity appeared repeatedly. Riley and his phone were taken to the police station, where another detective specializing in gang-related crimes also examined it. He came across messages, videos, and photographs connecting Riley to a shooting weeks earlier. Was that cell phone search by police unconstitutional?

In the companion case, police were on the lookout for crack cocaine deals in South Boston when they arrested Brima Wurie after they saw him involved in what looked like a street

75. "Computer Fraud and Abuse Act Reform," *Electronic Frontier Foundation, at* www.eff.org/issues/cfaa.
76. "It's Time to Reform the Computer Fraud and Abuse Act," *Scientific American, at* www.scientificamerican.com/article/its-times-reform-computer-fraud-abuse-act/#.

drug sale. After the arrest, police searched his cell phone's call log and traced one number they suspected to be Wurie's apartment and would yield evidence; there they later found drugs and firearms, resulting in criminal charges against him.

Both Riley and Wurie were arrested at different places and times, but the police method of searching their property raised a key question: Should law enforcement officials be able to seize and search cell phones without a warrant? Both men filed motions to suppress the evidence obtained from their phones without a search warrant, but two different trial courts denied those motions. They appealed their cases to the U.S. Supreme Court, which decided to hear the appeals together.

A unanimous opinion held that police exceeded their authority in both searches and should not have examined the phones without a warrant.[77] Law enforcement officials attempted to explain how the suspect can be searched, and information examined in the suspect's phone is not significantly different from looking through the contents of their pockets or purse.

Writing for the majority, Chief Justice Roberts commented ironically, "That is like saying a ride on horseback is materially indistinguishable from a flight to the moon. Both are ways of getting from point A to point B, but little else justifies lumping them together."[78] He noted cell phones are really minicomputers with multiple functions and vast storage capacity, and that searching them is nothing like searching a suspect's pockets. Before cell phones, people did not walk around with "a cache of sensitive personal information."[79] The chief justice acknowledged it would make combating crime more difficult, but it was not prohibiting cell phone searches, only requiring that police affirm the Fourth Amendment with a search warrant.

Bedrock Law

Law enforcement must obtain a warrant before searching through a suspect's cell phone.

Encryption Technologies

Encryption is a technique by which data are kept from unintended audiences. Lots of messages are encrypted, not just highly sensitive government secrets. Smartphones encrypt data on the device when the user sets a passcode.[80] When violent acts are planned on a mobile handset, police naturally want to find out more from the device as one mass shooting in San Bernardino, CA, made clear after it was brought to the public's attention.

It was reported as the deadliest terrorist attack on American soil since 9/11, only this time a married couple of Pakistani origin turned violent extremists after viewing jihadist propaganda on the Internet. At a party in a not-for-profit corporation office, Rizwan Farook and Tashfeen Malik murdered 14 people and wounded 22 others three days before Christmas. Police chased them for hours, and the couple was killed in a shootout. But the investigation of their terrorist network had just begun.

As part of the follow-up, FBI officials desired access to the data on an iPhone 5C used by Farook and owned by San Bernardino County.[81] The U.S. National Security Agency could not unlock the phone at first, and so the FBI turned to Apple to obtain a software app allowing them to enter the phone. But Apple refused to comply, arguing there was no assurance such a program would be used for legitimate purposes – a controversial response. A court hearing was scheduled to hear Apple's challenge to the federal probe, but before the proceedings began, investigators had unlocked the phone by other means, and so the case was withdrawn.

77. *Riley v. California* and *U.S. v. Wurie*, 134 S. Ct. 2473 (2014).
78. *Id.* at 2488.
79. *Id.* at 2490.
80. *See* this link about encryption for helpful information: www.cnet.com/news/iphone-android-encryption-fbi/.
81. Ten incorrect attempts to enter a password would wipe the phone clean.

Since the Apple–FBI showdown, Apple products have added more security features that are harder to crack, but the access debate continues. Members of Congress took up encryption legislation, and Americans who were previously unaware of government access to phones began using encryption tools. Prosecutors sought legislation requiring technology companies to provide "back doors" to access encrypted devices needed for effective law enforcement. Still privacy advocates saw as paramount the right to be free from unreasonable search and seizure.

Tracking Cell Phones

Law enforcement agencies have been tracking criminals' locations via mobile phone transmissions for more than a decade. A device known as a stingray[82] works by simulating a cell tower so that phones will connect to it, enabling law enforcement's capture of phone data. The ACLU identified 27 states where law enforcement agencies have used stingrays.[83] Originally authorized to track suspected terrorists, it is also used for ordinary police activities such as investigating thefts.[84] Maryland police used one to track down a suspect who allegedly stole 15 chicken wings and three sandwiches from an eatery.[85]

While new technology to catch criminals is attractive to law enforcement, the constitutional issues that police use of stingrays raise deserves examination.[86] To surveil one suspect's phone, hundreds of other phones also are tracked. Those people are suspected of no crime, but their data are collected too. A civil rights group petitioned the FCC to investigate the use of stingrays by law enforcement agencies.[87] Congress considered legislation regulating this technology, including an obligation to require a warrant for their use.[88] The states of Utah, Virginia, and Washington passed bills requiring law enforcement agencies to get a warrant before using a stingray and to immediately delete any data collected on non-suspects.[89]

In some cases, stingray manufacturers require nondisclosure agreements with law enforcement agencies.[90] The FBI encourages such secrecy, even to the extent of drafting nondisclosure agreements with local police departments.[91] Concerns have been raised about police departments refusing to acknowledge whether they own such equipment and then denying public records requests.[92] Nondisclosure agreements require law enforcement agents to avoid discussing a stingray's use even in a criminal proceeding,[93] which raises more concern.

82. Stingray has become the generic term for these surveillance devices. StingRay (with capitalization) is a brand name device.
83. An interactive map is available at https://www.aclu.org/issues/privacy-technology/surveillance-technologies/stingray-tracking-devices-whos-got-them.
84. "Police Secretly Track Cellphones to Solve Routine Crimes," *USA Today*, August 23, 2015.
85. "Cops Deploy StingRay Anti-Terror Tech against $50 Chicken-Wing Thief," *The Register*, May 4, 2016.
86. J. Norman, "Taking the Sting Out of the Stingray: The Dangers of Cell-Site Simulator Use and the Role of the Federal Communications Commission in Protecting Privacy & Security," 68 *Fed. Comm'n L. J.* 139 (2016).
87. Petition for an Enforcement Advisory on Use of Cell Site Simulators by State and Local Government Agencies, August 16, 2016, *at* http://s3.documentcloud.org/documents/3015561/CS-Simulators-Complaint.pdf.
88. "Stingray Surveillance Sparks Privacy Concerns in Congress," *USA Today*, August 3, 2015.
89. *Id.*
90. "A Police Gadget Tracks Phones? Shhh! It's Secret," *New York Times*, March 15, 2015.
91. "The FBI Agreement with the Milwaukee P.D.," *at* https://assets.documentcloud.org/documents/2190206/milwaukee-pd-fbi-nda-13aug2013.pdf.
92. "Police Contract with Spy Tool Maker Prohibits Talking about Device's Use," *Wired*, March 4, 2014.
93. "EFF and ACLU Expose Government's Secret Stingray Use in Wisconsin Case," April 22, 2016, *at* www.eff.org/deeplinks/2016/04/eff-and-aclu-expose-governments-secret-stingray-use-wisconsin-case.

Accessibility Online

In 1990, Congress passed the Americans with Disabilities Act (ADA). This sweeping bill was designed to ensure people with disabilities were granted equal opportunities to participate in activities, programs, and services.[94] Title III of the Act specified "public accommodations" (e.g., businesses, schools, offices) constructed or modified after 1990 be made accessible to people with disabilities. The law was enacted before Amazon, Facebook, and YouTube were fully formed, although over the years that followed, accessibility advocates advanced the law's application to online social networks and public accommodations.

For the most part, the U.S. government has been at the forefront of making websites accessible by asking federal agencies to make their electronic and information technology available to people with disabilities.[95] Additionally, more than a dozen states enforce accessibility laws specifying online requirements for state websites.[96]

In 1999, the National Federation of the Blind (NFB) filed suit against America Online (AOL), claiming that platform was not making its software accessible fast enough to the blind.[97] The suit was withdrawn though when the parties signed an agreement promising AOL would cooperate to update its accessibility and continue to do so in the future.

The NFB filed another lawsuit in 2008 over accessibility, this time against a major U.S. retailer, Target discount stores. A class action was filed on behalf of its customers, claiming Target's website was inaccessible using the screen-reading technology they were using on other sites, enabling them to hear a website's contents or transferring the contents to Braille. Target countered that only physical locations and not websites were covered by the ADA, but the federal district court rejected this argument.[98] Target stores closed the case by paying $6 million to a settlement fund with their promise to update their website for those needing help.

One example of how much diversity of opinion exists on how online "places" should be accessible to the impaired is illustrated by two legal claims against Netflix. The rulings of federal district judges came to exactly opposite conclusions one year. In 2012, a California federal district court rejected a claim that Netflix was obligated to make its films accessible to the blind and deaf, concluding a website is not a place of public accommodation and holding the ADA applies only to physical spaces.[99] On the other hand, a federal district court in Massachusetts found the ADA did apply to Netflix because Congress intended for this law to keep pace with technology.[100]

Twenty-First Century Communications and Video Accessibility Act

In 2010, Congress added the Twenty-First Century Communications and Video Accessibility Act (CVAA) to the statutes, ensuring access for people with disabilities. Under the CVAA, smartphones and web browsers were required to offer accessibility to anyone with hearing or visual impairments. It also required closed captioning on all video playback devices displayed on television.

The devices must not only be capable of showing the closed captions on the screen, but the programmers who produced the content had to take steps to provide the text for captioning. CVAA requires closed captioning for content aired on both broadcast television and online. At first, the requirements applied only to whole programs online, but between 2014

94. 42 U.S.C. § 12101.
95. Rehabilitation Act of 1973, as amended. 29 U.S.C. § 794 (d).
96. An interactive map is available at www.3playmedia.com/resources/accessibility-laws/.
97. "AOL Sued by Federation of the Blind," *Washington Post*, November 5, 1999.
98. *National Federation of the Blind v. Target*, 2007 U.S. Dist. LEXIS 73547 (D.C. N.D. Cal. 2007).
99. *Cullen v. Netflix*, 880 F. Supp. 2d 1017 (D.C. N.D. Calif. 2012).
100. *National Association of the Deaf v. Netflix*, 869 F. Supp. 2d 196 (D.C. Mass. 2012).

and 2017, the rules were expanded to cover single video clips, then montages, and eventually live and near-live clips.[101] CVAA does not require user-generated content to include captions.

CVAA captioning rules apply only to content aired on broadcast television, so websites streaming video not classified as broadcast television are unaffected. Yet other video regulations might require captioning under the Americans with Disabilities Act. This law is central to the debate over whether online streams such as Netflix should be treated the same as physical public accommodations. Conventional wisdom holds websites posting straight-to-web videos are free of the obligation to caption them in advance, but if a "public accommodation," say a hotel or restaurant posts a video and receives a request for captions, it would have to comply.

CVAA also requires video description[102] for the visually impaired for some programming. Not quite as strict as the closed-captioning requirement, the FCC requires each of the four major broadcast networks – ABC, CBS, Fox, and NBC – and the top five non-broadcast networks to provide 50 hours of video-described content every three months, about four hours per week. Technically, video descriptions are required for cable or satellite systems reaching more than 50,000 subscribers.[103] As a practical matter, most TV subscription services provide them to consumers. In addition, Netflix, which is not bound by CFAA but possibly obligated by ADA, entered into an agreement with the American Council of the Blind to include more video-described titles, as well as making screen-reading technology available.[104]

Global View

In an online world, it isn't just U.S. laws that affect American business and citizens. Because the Internet is international, laws in other countries affect online behavior as well. Early in 2021, Australia took aim at two giant platforms, Google and Facebook, requiring them to pay for news content – a move that was contested vigorously by both U.S. based tech giants. Canada followed with a similar law in 2023.

> Video description (also referred to as audio description) provides audio-narrated descriptions of a television program's key visual elements.

Titled the "News Media Bargaining Code," it required Facebook and Google to negotiate payment deals with content creators in Australia or, if necessary, to produce satisfactory agreements. To that end an independent arbitrator would set the price Google and Facebook had to pay domestic media. With some understatement, the Australian Competition and Consumer Commission (ACCC) observed that Australian content creators – including news media – were at a disadvantage without this law, given the power big tech monopolies wield in the world. The government estimated that for every AU$100 spent by Australian advertisers, AU$49 went to Google and AU$24 to Facebook.

Then comes the question of censorship. Legal communications originating in one country may be accessed in another, where the message is prohibited. Few are surprised, for example, to find China and North Korea block websites from access in their countries, but democratic countries such as South Korea also block websites. In Germany, Holocaust denial is a violation of the law, and Google also censors such sites from its German search engine. Facebook attempts to block or remove hate speech posts in Europe.[105]

101. www.3playmedia.com/2015/02/17/legal-requirements-closed-captioning-online-video-us-ada-section-508-cvaa-fcc/.
102. The FCC uses the term "video description," but the American Council of the Blind prefers "audio description." Ironically, the terms describe the same process: additional audio to explain the visuals for visually impaired audience members.
103. *See* Video Description, *at* www.fcc.gov/consumers/guides/video-description.
104. "Netflix to Expand Audio Descriptions for Blind Subscribers," *Variety*, April 14, 2016.
105. "Facebook, YouTube, Twitter and Microsoft Reach EU Agreement to Block Hate Speech," *Newsweek*, June 1, 2016.

The U.S. government does not block websites, but U.S. companies doing business overseas can be thwarted. Over the objections of an American delegation, 89 International Telecommunication Union countries signed a treaty allowing countries to decide for themselves how the Internet will be controlled within their own borders.[106] Facebook and other social networking sites are not accessible in China, for example.[107]

Skype's video communication systems have been blocked in dozens of countries.[108] Even YouTube was blocked by some governments. The political argument officials make is they are attempting to protect their populations (especially children) from offensive content. Some bluntly argue that without the oversight of their national monitors, outside platforms would harm the peace of their nation.

The Right to Be Forgotten

In the United States, it is an accepted principle once information has been made public, it cannot later be claimed to be private.[109] In Europe, that principle is subject to different limits. The European Union passed legislation in 1995 regulating what it classifies as "personal data," which include the sort of information Americans would regard as a matter of public record, such as a person's address or criminal record. The Data Protection Directive regulates the use of personal data in a wide variety of contexts. Agencies collecting personal data can be asked to delete them once they are no longer necessary. The law was created before the Internet became as common as it is today, and even before Google was established.

In 2010, the rule was put to the test in a major legal decision. A Spanish citizen complained to the Spanish Agency of Data Protection that Google continued to link to information in a Spanish newspaper about the auction of his repossessed home, which had occurred more than a decade earlier. The agency found the newspaper was not wrong for having the data, but it agreed allowing the information to be found in search results violated privacy.

Google appealed the decision, arguing that the part of the company located in Spain was not responsible for the search engine that provided the results; the parent company was located outside European jurisdiction. It also asserted no personal data were processed.[110] In 2014, the European Court of Justice affirmed the agency's decision and required Google to remove the links.[111] The court held that search engines accessible from Europe would have to comply with requests to remove personal information that was "inaccurate, inadequate, irrelevant, or excessive."[112] Would the right to be forgotten then be considered absolute, or would each request have to be balanced against other rights? Because such questions of when information is irrelevant or excessive are subjective, the court adopted a case-by-case approach to determine whether removing certain links would achieve justice.

The Internet and legal communities exploded with comments reacting to that ruling. One major concern was the burden it would place on search engines to respond to all the requests to delete links. In the year following the decision, Google received more than 700,000 requests to remove links and rejected just over half of them.[113] When links were removed,

106. "The UN Approved a Treaty Said to Let Governments Censor the Internet," *Business Insider*, December 14, 2012.
107. A list can be found at www.indexoncensorship.org/2014/02/10-countries-facebook-banned/.
108. A list can be found at https://nordvpn.com/blog/why-is-skype-blocked-in-certain-countries/.
109. *Sidis v. FR Pub. Corporation*, 113 F.2d 806 (2d Cir. 1940); *Cox Broadcasting Corp. v. Cohn*, 420 U.S. 469 (1975).
110. "The Solace of Oblivion," *New Yorker*, September 29, 2014.
111. Judgment of the Court (Grand Chamber) of May 13, 2014. Google Spain SL and Google Inc. v. Agencia Española de Protección de Datos (AEPD) and Mario Costeja González, *at* http://curia.europa.eu/juris/liste.jsf?num=C-131/12.
112. *Id.*, paragraph 93.
113. "Google Rejecting 59 Percent of Right-to-Be-Forgotten Removal Requests," *Ars Technica*, May 13, 2015.

they were not visible within European Union countries, whether searched on the local country's version, such as Spain's Google.es or on the more global Google.com.

In 2016, a French court asserted the right to be forgotten protects European citizens no matter where the data may be housed, and Google should be required to delete links anywhere in the world.[114] The fear of free expression advocates was that if the French court's opinion prevailed, other countries wanting links removed for dubious reasons might be allowed to do so. This line of reasoning would allow China to censor information about the Tiananmen Square massacre, which it does inside its borders, to outside its national boundaries. It would mean Türkiye could remove all online references to the Armenian genocide.[115]

EU-US Privacy Shield

Some Americans believe the federal government diligently avoids violating their constitutional rights by tracking personal communications online without probable cause of criminal activity. That mistaken belief was put to rest in 2013 by a computer security agent doing contract work for the U.S. National Security Agency. Edward Snowden shared his findings of illegal government surveillance with the news media as a wakeup call to all Americans. One of the consequences of his massive release of surveillance data was an increased scrutiny of U.S. agency policies for online surveillance of personal information. Prior to 2015, more than 4,000 companies in the European Union and the United States operated under the Safe Harbor Framework, an agreement regulating the transfer of personal data between the European Union and the United States.

After the Snowden revelations (discussed in previous chapters), a new Privacy Shield Framework was adopted. No business in the United States is obligated to abide by the agreement, but it may be in its own business interests to do so since European countries are less likely to engage in commercial activity with U.S. companies that are not signatories to the agreement. Once agreed to, however, a U.S. business will be legally required to adhere to those terms as defined by the U.S. Department of Commerce.[116]

Stipulations of the framework include requirements that individuals be allowed to opt out from sharing their data with third parties or be given an affirmative *opt-in* choice for any data sharing deals covering "sensitive" details, such as personal medical or health conditions, racial or ethnic origin, political opinions, religious or philosophical beliefs, trade union membership, or details of an individual's sex life. Nearly 2,000 U.S. companies signed onto the Privacy Shield Framework, now Data Privacy Framework, including Facebook, Google, Microsoft, and other technology-based companies.

European Cookie Law

Cookies are bits of data stored on a computer and used by a website to identify a visitor. This technique of data logging can be done to improve the web visitor's experience by learning an individual's preferences and targeting information of greatest interest. Cookies work to the website's advantage through the collection of data that can be harvested and used to push more products or even sell the online logs to third parties.

A 2009 amendment to the European Union Data Protection Directive that resulted in the "right to be forgotten" also spawned the EU's "Cookie Law." Simply put, the European Union requires all websites to ask for consent from visitors before using cookies. At first,

114. "Google Takes Right to Be Forgotten Battle to France's Highest Court," *The Guardian*, May 19, 2016.
115. "A French Court Case against Google Could Threaten Global Speech Rights," *Washington Post*, December 22, 2016.
116. "Data Privacy Framework," *at* https://www.dataprivacyframework.gov/.

some websites chose to satisfy this requirement by using a banner at the head or foot of a website to say something like, "We are using cookies. You can find out more or switch them off if you prefer. However, by continuing to use the site without changing settings, you are agreeing to our use of cookies." Then, of course, the website would provide the opportunity for visitors to turn off cookies. But once visitors turned off cookies, some of the platform's functionality could be lost.

The purpose of the rule was to obtain informed consent, not to prohibit the use of cookies. Supporters of the law say it added to the privacy protection available to web users. Critics of the regulation argue it failed to reward consumers with any benefits and only raised website costs and added one more step to click-through before reaching the desired content.[117]

Online Gambling

Online gambling in the United States has had a checkered history dating back to one major law's passage prior to the Internet. In 1961, Attorney General Robert F. Kennedy pushed for a law to go to the heart of organized crime's interstate racketeering via wired wagering. That law's application to the Internet became controversial due to the lack of a U.S. Supreme Court precedent. Until 2011, the Justice Department asserted the federal Wire Act of 1961 prohibited all forms of online gambling, and it became involved in several suits. In 2000, Jay Cohen was prosecuted and sent to jail for operating an online gambling site.[118] The Fifth Circuit Court of Appeals ruled the Wire Act prohibited online betting, but other games like poker were legal.[119]

Major legislation was signed in 2006 with the passage of the Unlawful Internet Gambling Enforcement Act (UIGEA).[120] Technically speaking, the law did not ban online gambling but instead restricted its financial transactions. This law was controversial because it could eliminate all games of chance online but contained a provision that the Treasury Department would create the specific regulations. The Treasury issued a call for comments, and after hundreds of organizations and businesses lobbied for their causes, final rules were enacted late in 2009. Penalties allowed for imprisonment of up to five years.

After passage of UIGEA, other countries criticized the United States for what they thought was some sort of restraint of trade, in violation of World Trade Organization agreements. They claimed the United States had no right to restrict the activities of non-Americans. Antigua, Japan, and the European Union filed requests for multibillion-dollar trade sanctions to be imposed, and Antigua also moved to ignore U.S. patent and trademark laws.[121]

There was a good deal of confusion regarding what was acceptable.[122] In 2011, a U.S. attorney in New York indicted 11 people and initiated a $3 billion lawsuit against major online poker websites, claiming they were in violation of UIGEA.[123] Those indicted were accused of attempting to disguise gambling payments as other online transactions, such as selling merchandise. In 2014, a federal appeals court affirmed a three-year prison sentence.[124] Online gambling site PokerStars agreed to a $700 million settlement.[125] The website still allowed people to play for fun but prohibited gambling. After several years of inactivity in the United States, PokerStars.com in 2016 gained approval to invite gamers in New

117. "Cookie Law Reform in 2016?" *at* www.cookielaw.org/blog/2015/2/10/cookie-law-reform-in-2016/.
118. *U.S. v. Cohen*, 260 F.3d 68 (2nd Cir. 2001).
119. *In re MasterCard International*, 313 F.3d 257 (5th Cir. 2002).
120. 31 U.S.C. 5361–5366.
121. "Antigua Disputes US Gaming Bill's Depiction of WTO Row," *Law 360*, October 25, 2012.
122. "Online Gambling Toes a Confusing Line," *CNN Money*, June 10, 2013.
123. "Department of Justice Flip-Flops on Internet Gambling," *Forbes*, December 23, 2011.
124. *U.S. v. Rubin et al*, 743 F.3d 31 (Second Cir. 2014).
125. "PokerStars Will Pay $731 Million to Settle U.S. Government Charges and Buy Full Tilt Poker," *Forbes*, July 31, 2012.

Jersey to play for money. New Jersey was among only a handful of states to legalize online gambling.[126]

For people wanting to operate or participate in online gaming today in the United States, the status quo is rather fractured. The Justice Department has limited its enforcement of UIGEA to sports gambling, while states retain the authority to regulate gambling. Companies profiting from gaming are quick to point out no federal law penalizes anyone for gambling online; penalties are focused on website operators or those who handle the financial transactions of gambling.

Antitrust Issues

The world's digital economy became more concentrated in the twenty-first century, so much so that U.S. congressional leaders called for legal remedies to address the dominance of Meta, Apple, Google, and Amazon and their business practices. Lawmakers described their activities as exploitive and anticompetitive. One 450-page report from the House Judiciary Committee proposed that the digital economy should be repaired by reestablishing enforcement of antitrust laws. Congress also charged Meta through its acquisition of competitors like WhatsApp and Instagram created a social network monopoly.

During the committee's investigation, news media publishers raised concerns about the effect of such concentrated market power on independent journalism since they were economically beholden to technology giants. This concentration of online power by popular influencers and their platforms undermined the availability of high-quality journalism, according to the congressional report. Among the nine key recommendations were proposals to prohibit online platforms from offering services incompatible with competing networks, keeping corporations from making strategic acquisitions to reduce competition in their businesses, and seeing to it online platforms provide due process before taking any action against their customers or users.[127]

Late in 2024, a federal judge found that Google was not only a monopoly, but that its parent company, Alphabet, violated antitrust law as it grew to dominate online searches around the world. For example, Google pays smartphone manufacturers billions of dollars to make sure Safari is the default option for searches. U.S. antitrust lawyers have also moved against other big tech companies with lawsuits claiming they illegally maintain monopolies.

Labor

Businesses have been using social media for years, most obviously to promote themselves, but in other ways, too. Many employers have used social media to keep track of their employees' behavior or even to investigate the background of potential employees before hiring them. Are such actions legal? Like similar inquiries, the answer is quite equivocal, "it all depends."

U.S. companies draw up social media policies to prohibit employees from doing things online that might disparage the company. These rules, however, should be carefully drawn so they don't violate the National Labor Relations Act.[128] Certainly, an employer can discipline or fire an employee if that employee publicly complains about customers, harasses a coworker, or calls in sick and then posts pictures attending a sporting event the same day. The NLRA, however, protects an employee's right to criticize management policy, complain about salary,

126. "New Jersey Now Allows Gambling via Internet," *New York Times*, November 26, 2013.
127. *Investigation of Competition in Digital Markets: Majority Staff Report and Recommendations*. Subcommittee on Antitrust, Commercial and Administrative Law of the Committee on the Judiciary. U.S. House of Representatives (2020).
128. National Labor Relations Act, 29 U.S.C. §§ 151–169.

or discuss other conditions of employment online. If an employer fires an employee for a social media post complaining about salary, it would be a direct violation of the NLRA.

In 2016, the National Labor Relations Board challenged Chipotle Mexican Grill when the Board found Chipotle had fired an employee over some tweets. The board stated the company's media policy could not punish workers for posting information that was "merely false or misleading." Further, employees could not be prohibited from using the company name.[129] Chipotle did not violate the law by asking the employee to delete offensive tweets, but the company's social media policy went too far.[130] According to the National Labor Relations Board (NLRB),

> You have the right to address work-related issues and share information about pay, benefits, and working conditions with coworkers on Facebook, YouTube, and other social media. But just individually griping about some aspect of work is not "concerted activity": what you say must have some relation to group action, or seek to initiate, induce, or prepare for group action, or bring a group complaint to the attention of management.[131]

In 2012, the NLRB announced its approval of the firing of a BMW employee over Facebook posts concerning an embarrassing accident at the Land Rover dealership. The employee felt the social media posts were protected but the NLRB disagreed; they were not a concerted activity.[132] On another occasion, the board ruled against a not-for-profit group that fired five employees over Facebook postings when they complained to management about their work performance. Those posts were protected since the communication was a concerted activity.[133] Although courts have yet to test its criteria, the NLRB has drawn up a list of *nine* factors to be applied to employees' use of off-site social media, including ones about evidence of antiunion activity, the content's location, and whether the employer had a specific rule in place that had been violated.[134]

When it comes to comments on the company's own digital platforms, employers have more authority. The NLRA may protect an employee's right to criticize management policy, but that would not prohibit employers from punishing workers for making such criticisms on the company's own website, as opposed to social media platforms like Facebook or X (unless those platform pages were linked to the employer's business). Just as a McDonald's employee might be allowed to wear a button in public saying, "Eat at Burger King," but not at work, an employee's speech can be restricted on the company's media but not elsewhere.

While employers often search social media records before hiring a candidate, labor lawyers advise against such actions.[135] An employer who views a Facebook profile might find out about marital status, race, sexual orientation, or other information that should not be used in hiring. If a candidate is not selected for a position and then asserts the employer used discriminatory information in the decision-making process, the employer cannot assert lack of knowledge of the candidate's sexual orientation, religious preference, or other such details.

Some employers have even been known to ask employees for their social media usernames and passwords. Twenty-one states have explicit legislation prohibiting this practice.[136] While it may not be ethical, it appears to be legal in the remaining 29 states.

129. "Chipotle Under Fire for Illegal Workplace Policies," *CNN Money*, August 24, 2016.
130. "Chipotle's Social Media Policy Violated Law, Says NLRB," *Media Post*, August 23, 2016.
131. "Social Media, NLRB Website," *at* www.nlrb.gov/rights-we-protect/whats-law/employees/i-am-not-represented-union/social-media/.
132. Knauz BMW and Robert Becker. Case 13-CA-046452, NLRB, 2012.
133. Hispanics United of Buffalo, Inc. and Carlos Ortiz. Case 03-CA-027872, NLRB, 2012.
134. "'Tantrums' Aside, the Law Leans toward the Employee in Issues of Social Media and Free Speech," June 8, 2017, *at* www.socialgameslaw.com/2017/06/social-media-employee-free-speech.html.
135. "5 Ways Social Media Can Land Employers in Court," *at* www.law360.com/articles/761008/5-ways-social-media-can-land-employers-in-court.
136. Bruce H. Raymond, "Keeping Your Online Accounts Private: Can Employers Request Access to Your Facebook?" *Nat'l L. Rev.*, June 22, 2015, *at* https://natlawreview.com/article/keeping-your-online-accounts-private-can-employers-request-access-to-your-facebook.

Employers may restrict certain employee speech online, but not if it is protected speech under the National Labor Relations Act.

Survey research has confirmed that about one of three employees turn to access social media sites from work for relief in their routine schedule.[137] Employers may legally monitor their employees' activity on workplace electronic devices and networks. This means that employer-provided laptops, computers, and even smartphones may be monitored. Even when employees use their own smartphones, but do so over the employer's network, their activity may be legally monitored. Connecticut and Delaware require employers to notify employees if their email is monitored.

Those who offer digital services understand how a certain sense of freedom felt with smartphones and laptops might overwhelm a user's sense of civility and decency, so much so that some speech posted online can cause dire consequences offline. After President Obama was re-elected, an employee of Cold Stone Creamery posted on her Facebook page "another 4 years of the (n —). Maybe he will get assassinated this term!!" She was fired.[138]

It is a misconception to believe an imaginary constitutional protection exists for employees to keep them safe from punishment in the workplace after posting comments that reflect poorly on the employer. In most states, employees generally may be terminated for a controversial tweet or an offensive Facebook posting. There are some exceptions, of course. Let's say a public relations employee is tweeting about working conditions for the benefit of their coworkers. The National Labor Relations Board (NLRB) declared that when it comes to social media, the employer rules should not be so severe as to silence feelings protected by law, such as conversations about wages or working conditions. But "if they are mere gripes *not* made in relation to group activity among employees," then protection is absent under law.[139]

The NLRB ordered an employer to hire back workers let go for criticizing their employer online (*Hispanics United of Buffalo*, 2012;[140] *New York Party Shuttle*, 2013)[141] and protected communications about the job "for mutual aid or protection" (29 U.S.C. Sec. 157, 2012). However, when the NLRB ordered Bettie Page Clothing to reinstate three employees who had been fired, it was because their Facebook exchange showed they felt that their boss was abusive (*Design Technology Group, LLC d/b/a Bettie Page Clothing*, 2013).[142]

It is a different story if an employee chooses to tweet bad jokes. One reporter was fired by the *Arizona Daily Star* for tweeting "What?!?!?! No overnight homicide. . . . You're slacking, Tucson," followed by, "You stay homicidal, Tucson."[143] One high school coach posted critical comments about her fellow teachers but lost her case when the court upheld the administration's right to transfer her. The coach's speech touched on a matter of public concern, but the administration had more important concerns than the employee's First Amendment rights (*Richerson v. Beckon*).[144] By publicly criticizing her colleagues, she lost trust and directly undermined her ability to continue coaching.

A Virginia sheriff, on the other hand, who refused to renew the contracts of two employees who "liked" and favorably commented on an opponent's Facebook page during an election

137. "Monitoring Employee Social Media Activity at Work," *at* www.thehartford.com/business-playbook/in-depth/employee-social-media-monitoring.
138. Associated Press. "Obama Threat Gets Turlock Woman Fired, Reports Secret Service," *San Jose Mercury News*, *at* www.mercurynews.com/top-stories/ci_21969395/obamathreatgets-turlock-woman-fired-reported-secret.
139. The NLRB and Social Media, *at* www.nlrb.gov/about-nlrb/rights-we-protect/your-rights/the-nlrb-and-social-media.
140. 359 NLRB 037 (2012).
141. *New York Party Shuttle, LLC*, 359 NLRB No. 112 (2013).
142. Design Technology Group, *LLC d/b/a Bettie Page Clothing*, 359 NLRB No. 96 (2013).
143. S. Greenhouse, "Even If It Enrages Your Boss, Social Net Speech Is Protected," *The New York Times*, January 21, 2013, *at* www.nytimes.com.
144. *Richerson v. Beckon*, 2008 WL 833076 (W.D. Wash. March 27, 2008).

Figure 9.2 Social media icons

campaign, lost his case in *Bland v. Roberts* (2013). The Fourth Circuit held the employees were speaking as private citizens on matters of public interest, and their right to express support for the opposing candidate "outweighed the Sheriff's interest in providing effective and efficient services to the public."

The appellate court also settled the question of whether pressing the "like" button constituted speech that merits constitutional protection. It does because such an action clearly indicates that someone likes something and "is itself a substantive statement" (*Bland v. Roberts*, 2013).[145]

Social Media and Free Speech

It is important to remember TikTok, Facebook, X, Instagram, and other social networks are private venues owned by corporations. If the online administrators remove someone's post, there is *no* violation of the First Amendment involving government interference. Users agree to terms when they sign up for a service, and those terms usually include an acknowledgment the service can censor their posts. "We can remove or restrict access to content that is in violation of these provisions," states Facebook.[146] Instagram puts it a little differently.

> We can remove any content or information you share on the Service if we believe that it violates these Terms of Use, our policies (including our Instagram Community Guidelines), or we are permitted or required to do so by law.[147]

145. *Bland v. Roberts*, No. 12–1671 (4th Cir. 2013).
146. Facebook Statement of Rights and Responsibilities, *at* www.facebook.com/terms, accessed August 16, 2024.
147. "Instagram Term of Use," *at* https://help.instagram.com/581066165581870/?locale=en_US (Accessed August 16, 2024).

As noted earlier, user agreements do not have the force of law, so a user who violates the terms of service is not guilty of a crime just for breaking the agreement. But all other laws are applicable in cyberspace, so a violation of terms might also be a crime; for example, posting a nude picture of a minor on Instagram might be a violation of the terms of service, *and* it could be felony child pornography.

Neither is a social media platform guilty of any crime if it chooses to discontinue someone's account or even to block the use of a service. In 2010, a Facebook user who had been blocked tried to file suit, but a federal court dismissed the suit, and the Ninth Circuit upheld the dismissal.[148] In 2015, a not-for-profit tried to sue Facebook for blocking access to their page in India, claiming a civil rights violation and a breach of contract. Indian officials had requested that the page be blocked in their country, and Facebook complied. The court absolved Facebook, mostly by relying on Section 230's immunity clause: "No provider or user of an interactive computer service shall be treated as the publisher or speaker of any information provided by another information content provider."[149]

In 2017, the Supreme Court unanimously ruled that North Carolina violated the First Amendment by enacting a law barring convicted sex offenders from popular websites children might use.[150] Lester Packingham, Jr. was convicted of taking "indecent liberties" with a minor in 2002. Eight years later, authorities saw him post on Facebook and arrested him for violating the state statute. The Court asserted that there were other ways to protect children that did not infringe on Packingham's First Amendment freedoms. In striking down the law, the Court solidified social media's place as "the modern public square."

Sharing Copyrighted Material on Social Media

In 1998, Congress created the Digital Millennium Copyright Act, which criminalized actions to circumvent the digital rights management connected to a copyrighted work, including making hardware or software to do so.[151] It also created a mechanism for people who believe their copyrights have been violated online to request removal of that material until the claim can be either substantiated, in which case removal would be permanent, or invalidated and the material put back online.

Some defend online use of another source's content by claiming either ignorance or accident. A devastating earthquake killed more than 250,000 people in Haiti in 2010. Haitian photographer Daniel Morel took several photos and posted several of them to his Twitter account. Agence France-Presse and Getty Images distributed those images without permission, which were used by media outlets.

> Copyright laws apply online, as do laws punishing defamation and invasion of privacy.

Getty images attempted to argue in court that it was an innocent mistake, the result of a Twitter user who posted Morel's photos without attribution. The judge was unpersuaded.[152]

Agence France-Presse attempted to claim Twitter's terms of service (TOS) permitted republication of the photo, but the court pointed out that Twitter's terms of service allowed users to retweet images, but it did not permit them to be used commercially. The court awarded over $1.5 million in damages for violating the DMCA. "Construing the Twitter TOS to provide an unrestrained, third-party license to remove content from Twitter and commercially license that content would be a gross expansion of the terms of the Twitter TOS."[153]

148. *Young v. Facebook*, 621 Fed. Appx. 488 (Ct. App. 9th Cir. 2015).
149. *Sikhs for Justice v. Facebook*, 144 F. Supp. 3d 1088 (N.D. Cal. 2015).
150. *Packingham v. North Carolina*, 582 U.S. 98 (2017).
151. 17 U.S.C. § 101.
152. *Agence France Presse v. Morel*, 934 F. Supp. 2d 547 (S.D. N.Y. 2013).
153. *Id.* at 562.

The Curious Case of Memes

Memes are extremely popular on social media. Originally, the term was created to connote a unit of cultural transmission, but its far more common meaning today is to describe something humorous that spreads quickly via the Internet. Memes can be text, pictures, or videos, but they often involve an image with text superimposed.[154] Not all memes are created equal. Noncommercial memes using images of public figures in a political statement have a much higher level of protection than memes produced to sell a product or that use a private figure, and that raises other issues.

Couldn't the subjects of certain memes file lawsuits for defamation, invasion of privacy, or even copyright infringement? Guiding precedents are few, but in at least one instance, a subject was successful in a lawsuit. In 2015, a Tennessee federal court awarded $150,000 to a man with Down syndrome, whose picture had been taken and added to a photo-sharing website with the label "Retarded Handicap Generator."[155]

Sometimes copyright holders will attempt to be compensated for the use or to have offending memes removed, with varying results. The image behind a once popular meme titled, "Socially Awkward Penguin" was owned by National Geographic, and Getty Images, which licensed National Geographic's images, pursued action against multiple parties for its unauthorized use. Several parties settled with Getty and agreed not to disclose the terms.[156]

More often, those who attempt lawsuits are frustrated that so little can be done. Most people who create memes could defend themselves in suits for libel or copyright if a court would find the meme to be a parody. Even in cases in which this defense would be unsuccessful, the nature of Internet distribution is such that just stopping one person's use of a photo or video would still not solve the problem of hundreds – or thousands – of other versions appearing.

A 2004 film *Downfall* contained a scene with an actor playing Adolf Hitler that became a meme, superimposing different English subtitles over the actor's German. Constantin Films, which owned the copyright, filed a claim with YouTube to stop the memes, but as soon as some were removed, more would be posted on YouTube or on other websites.[157] There is something of a "whack-a-mole" challenge in taking down infringing videos[158] when some are protected for parody,[159] and others hope to monetize multiple versions.[160]

Social Media and Commercial Activity

Social media may be a great place for connecting with friends, but it's also a place where people try to connect with celebrities they have never met. Soccer star Cristiano Ronaldo has more than 100 million likes on Facebook, actress-singer Selena Gomez attracted more than 100 million Instagram followers, and singer Katy Perry counted over 96 million followers on X.

Celebrities who attempt to cash in on their large number of followers must be sure to abide by laws that affect commercial activity. In 2015, Kim Kardashian posted praise for a

154. "These Are the Most Popular Memes of All Time," March 27, 2016, *at* www.digitaltrends.com/social-media/most-popular-memes/.
155. "Nashville Jury Awards Man in Altered Pics $150K," *The Tennessean*, November 5, 2015.
156. "How Copyright Is Killing Your Favorite Memes," *Washington Post*, September 8, 2015.
157. "Hitler 'Downfall' Parodies Removed from YouTube," *CBS News*, April 21, 2010, *at* www.cbsnews.com/news/hitler-downfall-parodies-removed-from-youtube/.
158. Whack-a-mole is an arcade game in which players attempt to hit rodents as they appear and disappear from holes. As some go away, others appear.
159. Parody as a protected fair use is discussed in Chapter 7.
160. Owners of copyrighted works uploaded to YouTube can get paid via advertising insertions.

Bedrock Law

People who are compensated for saying positive things online about a business or product must disclose the sponsorship.

morning sickness medicine she was taking to Instagram and Twitter. There would have been no issue had the posts simply been from a satisfied customer, but the celebrity was a paid spokesperson for the company, so her posts were under the Food and Drug Administration's jurisdiction. The FDA ordered the posts taken down because they lacked the necessary warnings required for all prescription medication ads.[161]

Google v. Oracle – Creativity in Computing

Computer code is one of those items most of us take for granted in digital communications. We seldom think much about it much unless it becomes our computer issue or an important news item. One tech company in Austin, Texas, thought a lot about its code especially after noticing 11,500 lines had been taken from its Java platform for use in Google's Android operating system to create one of the most popular smartphones in the world. Oracle sued Google for copyright infringement, and the litigation between the two U.S. companies bounced back and forth in the courts for years before the Supreme Court granted certiorari to put the whole matter to rest.

By that time, there were powerful players lining up on both sides of the case awaiting the outcome of this copyright dispute. Book publishers and movie and record companies agreed with the copyright protections sought by Oracle to preserve its intellectual property rights and protect the genius necessary to create computer code. Major companies like Microsoft and IBM, on the other hand, were hoping the high court would see the merits of Google's case since 11,500 lines of code was a small part of a programming recipe using millions of lines of computer code.

The Supreme Court in 2021 ruled in Google's favor by 6–2 holding the Java code used was transformative. Android added something new and significant to it, and thus the lines of Java code copied constituted a fair use.[162] As a result, software developers could breathe a sigh of relief, showing less concern over the possibility that that part of the code they were using might trigger an expensive copyright case.

The following year, the Kardashian-Jenner family was notified by a consumer watchdog group that more than 100 Instagram posts had been identified as paid product endorsements without being labeled as such, in violation of Federal Trade Commission rules. The group threatened legal action if the posts were not deleted.[163] Paid product endorsements need to be labeled as such.[164] In clear language, the FTC states,

> If you endorse a product through social media, your endorsement message should make it obvious when you have a relationship ("material connection") with the brand. A "material connection" to the brand includes a personal, family, or employment relationship or a financial relationship – such as the brand paying you or giving you free or discounted products or services.[165]

The FTC rules on endorsements apply across media regardless of whether a person is a celebrity. Even individuals who post on a blog that may only have a few hundred views *must* disclose any business association – even if it's just free products the individuals have

161. "The FDA Just Recalled Kim Kardashian's Instagram Post," *Washington Post*, August 11, 2015.
162. *Google LLC v. Oracle America, Inc.*, 593 U.S. ______ (2021).
163. "Kardashians in Trouble Over Paid Product Endorsements on Instagram," *Variety*, August 22, 2016.
164. "When It Comes Influencer Marketing, Better Safe Than Sorry," *Forbes*, March 30, 2017.
165. Disclosures 101 for Social Media Influencers, "FTC," *at* https://www.ftc.gov/business-guidance/resources/disclosures-101-social-media-influencers.

received.[166] Receiving free products alone does not require disclosure, but if the speaker is acting on behalf of the product, it must be disclosed. In 2015, the FTC acted against video game company Machinima. The company was paying influencers to post videos to YouTube endorsing several games.[167] The company explicitly told the posters what to say and paid them up to $30,000 to say it. The FTC had a bit of a problem with the company telling their influencers what they wanted them to post online, thus fooling viewers into believing they were actual consumer feelings rather than a promotional message.

Lord & Taylor also settled with the FTC over-paying 50 fashion "influencers" to post Instagram pictures of themselves wearing a dress from Lord & Taylor's collection.[168] In 2016, public interest groups wrote to the FTC claiming that their research identified influencers who endorsed a product without disclosure and were disguising their advertising on social media.[169]

Even contests can run afoul of the FTC's endorsement requirements. In 2014, Cole Haan sponsored a contest asking people to post to Pinterest five pictures of their favorite Cole Haan shoes and places to wear them, and to tag them with #WanderingSole. Winners would receive $1,000. The FTC found the hashtag to be inadequate disclosure of the fact that people were pinning the photos for a financial incentive stating, "entry into a contest to receive a significant prize in exchange for endorsing a product through social media constitutes a material connection that would not reasonably be expected by viewers of the endorsement."[170]

Emojis

Emoticons, which use punctuation to depict, for example a smiley face :), and emojis (using pictures rather than punctuation) are phenomena driven largely by our twenty-first-century communications media. While most people consider emojis to be fun ways to liven up the text in a message or social media post, a surprising number of court cases have included the use of emoticons and emojis as part of the evidence. Santa Clara University Law Professor Eric Goldman has been tracking this phenomenon for years, finding the first incident in a Virginia case from 2004 involving use of a smiley emoticon in an email in a trade secret case.[171] From that single case, there was a steady and precipitous rise of emojis appearing in court trials including First Amendment and defamation cases.

In one of the more dramatic cases, a teen possibly avoided jail because of emojis. The teen and her mother had been arguing, so the teen vented by texting a friend, including some texts that could be interpreted as threatening. The trial court found the texts were true threats, but the appeals court overturned the conviction in part because "laugh out loud" and "rolling on the floor laughing" emojis indicate the conversation was not to be taken seriously.[172]

E-Personation

E-personation occurs when someone uses the Internet to pretend to be someone else. This can occur to harass a person, obtain a benefit, or commit fraud. In 2009, Texas became the first

166. "The FTC's Endorsement Guides: What People Are Asking," *at* www.ftc.gov/tips-advice/business-center/guidance/ftcs-endorsement-guides-what-people-are-asking.
167. "In the Matter of Machinima," *at* www.ftc.gov/system/files/documents/cases/160317machinimado.pdf.
168. "In the Matter of Lord & Taylor," *at* www.ftc.gov/system/files/documents/cases/160315lordandtaylororder.pdf.
169. Letter to FTC from Center for Digital Democracy, September 7, 2016, *at* https://www.citizen.org/wp-content/uploads/letter-to-ftc-instagram-endorsements.pdf.
170. Letter from FTC to law firm representing Cole Hahn, Inc., March 20, 2014, *at* https://www.ftc.gov/system/files/documents/closing_letters/cole-haan-inc./140320colehaanclosingletter.pdf.
171. *MicroStrategy, Inc. v. Business Objects*, S.A., 331 F. Supp. 2d 396 (E.D. Va. 2004).
172. *State v. D.R.C.*, 2020 Wash. App. LEXIS 1992 (Wash. App. Ct. July 14, 2020).

state to make e-personation a crime.[173] While only a handful of states have specifically made online impersonation a crime,[174] most other states could still prosecute false online identities under statutes addressing other crimes, including fraud or cyberstalking.

New Jersey indicted a woman for allegedly creating a false Facebook page portraying her ex-boyfriend in a very unfavorable way. Though the state has no statute addressing e-personation, she was charged with identity theft and could have spent 18 months in jail.[175] The state agreed to dismiss charges after she participated in the state's pretrial intervention program.

Not all e-personations are actionable. In 2013, a group of Oregon middle school students created fake social media accounts using their assistant principal's name and photo. The administrator filed suit against the students and their parents for defamation, negligent supervision, and violation of the CFAA, but the court dismissed the case prior to trial, finding the students were creating a parody that did not amount to fraud.[176]

Legal scholars are not unanimous in support of e-personation laws. The Electronic Frontier Foundation has said temporarily impersonating a company or public official "has become an important and powerful form of political activism, especially online."[177] They further contend laws against fraud and defamation already protect against truly harmful e-personation and that expanding the law to cover other less harmful speech infringes free expression.

Most social media have policies against creating accounts impersonating others, unless the accounts are clearly labeled as parody or otherwise make it clear that they do not belong to the person identified. Facebook has a policy against pretending to be someone else.[178] X allows parody, commentary, and fan accounts that are clearly labeled.[179] In a strange case, the mayor of Peoria, IL, became outraged about @peoriamayor, a parody account established in 2014 by Jon Daniel, using the mayor's photo and making rather outlandish statements, such as implying drug use. Peoria's police raided Daniel's home and seized computers, phones, gaming systems, and a tablet, claiming state law prohibited impersonating a public figure. Daniel sued the city, which settled the suit by paying Daniel $125,000.[180] Twitter suspended the @peoriamayor account; despite the settlement, the account was not restored.

On the other hand, Section 230 protects social media from any culpability in cases in which fake accounts have been created that impersonate others. In 2016, Franco Caraccioli tried to sue Facebook because the company did not remove a fake account when he first reported it. Facebook does not allow parody accounts but didn't recognize the account as e-personation at first. After further examination, Facebook deleted the account. Caraccioli's suit was dismissed by a federal district court in California based on the grounds Section 230 had made Facebook immune.[181]

173. Texas Penal Code § 33.07.
174. California, Hawaii, Mississippi, New York, and Texas.
175. "Vindictive Ex-Girlfriend Could Face 18 Months in Prison for Facebook E-Personation," *at* www.lexology.com/library/detail.aspx?g=65048aa6-3eb7-4ab0-9cf0-f1590b0c2a1c.
176. "Creating Parody Social Media Accounts Doesn't Violate Computer Fraud & Abuse Act," *at* http://blog.ericgoldman.org/archives/2013/09/creating_parody.htm.
177. "'E-personation' Bill Could Be Used to Punish Online Critics, Undermine First Amendment Protections for Parody," *at* www.eff.org/deeplinks/2010/08/e-personation-bill-could-be-used-punish-online/.
178. "What Names Are Allowed on Facebook?" *at* www.facebook.com/help/112146705538576?helpref=faq_content. Facebook makes exceptions to its fake names policy for individuals who can claim special circumstances, such as abuse victims, on a case-by-case basis.
179. Misleading and Deceptive Identities Policy, *at* https://help.x.com/en/rules-and-policies/x-impersonation-and-deceptive-identities-policy.
180. "Police Raid over Fake Twitter Account Costs Peoria $125,000," *Chicago Tribune*, September 3, 2015.
181. *Caraccioli v. Facebook*, 167 F. Supp. 3d 1056 (N.D. Calif. 2016).

Summary

Online communication has key characteristics demanding legal attention; its capacity for rapid and widespread distribution of content algorithmically curated, stored, manipulated, and easily redistributed creates the potential for harms unimaginable on earlier media platforms. Digital networks instantly reach worldwide audiences with images, sounds, and texts that are virtually limitless. Messages once confined to small, familiar communities fly across international jurisdictions. Online media is used to perpetrate fraud, invade privacy, distribute obscenity, steal intellectual property, and defame reputations, among other abuses. When online viewers share their feelings without real-world filters, interpersonal conflicts result. These principles of digital media and the rules of social media include the following items:

- Websites are immune from suits for content posted to their site, as opposed to content they create themselves.
- Network neutrality rules were a measure from the FCC designed to prohibit Internet service providers from favoring or disfavoring the load speeds of any source or type of download, treating all bits equally.
- People can speak anonymously online, but their identity might be exposed if a court orders disclosure.
- States vary significantly regarding statutes for cyber misbehavior, such as cyberbullying, cyberstalking, or revenge porn. Cyberstalking has federal statutes, but the other types rely on state laws for action.
- Cybersecurity is a growing concern, and increasingly companies are being held responsible when personal data are compromised that should have been secure.
- Intentionally accessing a computer without authorization is a violation of federal law.
- Data on cell phones is private. Law enforcement needs a search warrant to look through a phone.
- Federal law requires online content to be accessible to people with handicaps.
- The Internet does not stop at borders, and other countries' laws differ from those of the United States. This can sometimes affect Americans doing business in other countries.
- Behavior on social media is subject to the same regulations as activities in the physical world. Social media platforms may enforce terms in a user agreement, but they do not have the force of law.
- Adopting a false identity online may or may not be legally actionable, depending on the reason for adopting the identity.

Ethical Dilemmas: Social Media Registration

Given today's social media circumstances, lawmakers confront a dilemma when examining the streams of widely circulated content crossing cultures and countries easily and often. Politically subversive groups have weaponized social media, and this is a concern since democracy is declining and a principal cause is the global dissemination of social media technology, contends the V-Dem Annual Democracy Report.

The Mueller report found extensive interference in the 2016 U.S. presidential election due to Russian hackers, and the Computational Propaganda Research Project found authoritarian states such as Iran, Venezuela, Pakistan, China, and Iran were using "computational propaganda for foreign influence operations."

David Sloss, professor at the Santa Clara University School of Law, believes Congress should act to require platforms to register social media users based on the nature of their state's governance. Citizens of democracies like the United States would be allowed to engage in unrestricted free speech on social media. But agents of authoritarian regimes should be blocked from American social media channels. Ordinary residents of authoritarian states would be allowed to register on Facebook and Twitter, for example, but their content would come with a warning: "This message is transmitted by a citizen or national of an authoritarian state." Sloss admits his proposed registration system might raise objections based on issues of privacy, anonymity, and the chilling effect on free speech, but he believes it is better than doing nothing against authoritarian states that use "social media platforms to suppress democratic dissent at home and to interfere with democratic elections abroad."[182]

182. D.L. Sloss, "Weaponization of Social Media by Authoritarian States," *Markkula Center for Applied Ethics*, December 5, 2019, *at* www.scu.edu/ethics-spotlight/social-media-and-democracy/weaponization-of-social-media-by-authoritarian-states/.

10

Obscenity and Indecency

LEARNING OBJECTIVES

After reading this chapter, you should know

- the definition of obscenity by both its historic and modern terms
- how to apply the three-pronged test the Supreme Court uses to determine what is obscene or what is just offensive
- the lawfulness of selling, advertising, and possession of obscenity
- how to judge various standards for obscenity based on the content
- the law's treatment of child pornography as unprotected speech
- how to define the restriction on access to pornography in public libraries
- where public conduct like erotic dancing is constitutionally protected
- the difference between indecency and obscenity based on channel and content
- what safeguards exist for sexual and violent content in video games
- the law's treatment of sexually explicit content over phones

It was a typical TV weather forecast during a Sunday evening newscast in Spokane, Washington, when viewers were suddenly shocked to see a pornographic video playing in the background. Meteorologist Michelle Boss was entirely oblivious to the pornography that appeared over her shoulder on a monitor in the background of her weather set while she talked with the weekend anchor and then gave an otherwise pleasant weather forecast. The video was on-screen for about 13 seconds and primarily showed a naked woman's backside and buttocks. Callers to station KREM-TV immediately complained, and the Spokane Police Department Special Victims Unit responded to conduct the investigation. Even though no employee culpability was found, and the station issued an apology on its 11 p.m. newscast, the explicit broadcast raised criminal concerns. Moreover, the station could face a very large fine from the Federal Communications Commission.[1]

1. Yaron Steinbuch, "Washington State Local News Airs 13-Second Porn Clip During Weather Forecast," *New York Post*, October 20, 2021, *at* https://nypost.com/2021/10/20/washington-state-local-news-airs-porn-clip-during-forecast/; Emma Nolan, "Local Weather Report Accidentally Broadcasts Porn Instead," *Newsweek*, October 19, 2021, *at* https://www.newsweek.com/local-weather-report-accidentally-broadcasts-porn-spokane-krem-1640302.

DOI: 10.4324/9781003462989-10

Indeed, it was just six years earlier in 2015 when the FCC fined Roanoke, Virginia, TV station WDBJ $325,000 for an image that appeared in its evening newscast for about three seconds. It was during a human-interest story about a woman working for a local volunteer rescue squad who had previously been an adult movie star. To illustrate the point, the story showed her on the website of the adult movie company where she had worked. Unfortunately for WDBJ, viewers spotted an image of an erect penis at the extreme margin of the screen.[2]

Are these broadcasts considered "obscene" and a crime under state or federal obscenity laws? Are they "indecent" and subject to federal administrative law? Yet why is similar content found in a book or online considered neither obscene nor indecent? In fact, why do neither obscenity nor indecency laws apply to ESPN when it briefly showed a female reveler baring a breast on the streets of New Orleans during its coverage of the 2024 Sugar Bowl?

While most media practitioners do not set out to produce and disseminate pornographic content, it's important to understand what may be considered obscene or indecent and how that content is treated under the law. Context, intent, audience, and type of media platform can make a difference.

For example, a brief description of a passionate sexual encounter in a fictional book about World War II would not likely render the book obscene. But a similar passage in a coming-of-age book for young teenagers might be viewed differently. For the same matter, songs with vulgar language may be heard by anyone over online services such as Spotify but could be considered indecent if broadcast by a radio station, subjecting the station to penalties. A local broadcast news anchor – but not a cable TV news anchor – might need to rethink airing such swear words spoken by an interviewee. Yet there may be an exception if the swear words were uttered by a political candidate in a political ad or during a bona fide debate. Even so, there seems to be little exception for an accidental "wardrobe malfunction" on a televised live awards show revealing a naked body part. Should it matter what words were spoken or whether it was buttocks, breasts, or genitalia exposed?

Lawmakers have long struggled with how to treat sexually explicit content. Such content may be considered harmful to children and society as a whole. Yet there may also be positive social value in content that is literary, artistic, political, or scientific. Few would argue that a seventeenth-century painting with nude subjects or a modern medical text on anatomy are obscene. Yet most would agree that sexualized images of children or "child porn" is prohibited obscenity. In general, the work as a whole must be considered, and the harms and the merits of offensive content must be weighed.

Contemporary community standards must be taken into account since what might have been viewed as pornographic many years ago may no longer be offensive to reasonable persons today. Likewise, the norms and values of the local community are an important consideration since tastes and sensitivities vary across the country. Yet what cannot vary in the United States is one's constitutional right of free speech under the First Amendment. Any response by the government – such as removal, ban, fine, or imprisonment – must not infringe on First Amendment rights.

One significant challenge for lawmakers, the courts, as well as content producers and media practitioners is determining exactly what type or level of sexual content may be subject to government restriction. If a state law, for example, prohibits obscenity, then what exactly makes a work obscene? If indecency over the public's airwaves may be restricted, what constitutes an indecent broadcast? And who decides the matter? A judge, jury, or some regulatory body?

2. FCC, "FCC Plans Maximum Fine Against WDBJ for Broadcasting Indecent Programming Material During Evening Newscast," March 23, 2015, *at* https://www.fcc.gov/document/fcc-plans-max-fine-against-wdbj-indecent-material-evening-news-0; Jonathan Peters, "The Huge FCC Fine Against a Virginia Station is a Sign We Need to Rethink Broadcast Indecency Rules," *Columbia Journalism Review*, March 26, 2015, *at* https://www.cjr.org/united_states_project/fcc_fine_wdbj_virginia.php.

Obscenity

Bedrock Law
Obscenity is viewed as a crime against public morality that was prosecuted for both possession and the commerce of pornographic content.

"I know it when I see it," is how Supreme Court Justice Potter Stewart famously addressed the issue of obscenity in 1964. In determining whether an imported French film, *Les Amants* (The Lovers), violated local standards for obscenity, Justice Stewart opined that "trying to define what may be indefinable" was difficult. "But I know it when I see it, and the motion picture involved in this case is not that."[3]

Obscenity is a term that holds different meanings depending on where you are standing – outside the courtroom or before a judge. In conversation, obscenity may define something that is disgusting and deplorable.[4] But to lawmakers, it means a crime has taken place. Most states outlaw some form of pornography, specifically prohibiting obscenity. And content found to be obscene has no First Amendment protection.

Early Controls

What constitutes obscenity and why and how it should be treated have evolved in both society and before the courts. During colonial times, for example, it was something that threatened public morality, decency, and good manners the British monarchy and its subjects justified outlawing. The original legal theory was based on the premise that such content tended to "corrupt" minds and create a "loss of affection for decency and morality."[5] In the United States, sexually explicit publications and artwork were met at American docksides where a federal agent was assigned to stop them from entering.

This led to laws such as the **Tariff Act of 1842**, which banned the "importation of all indecent and obscene prints, paintings, lithographs, engravings and transparencies" and gave the government the authority to dispose of pornographic cargo from France or other foreign ports.[6] Once ashore, local authorities kept citizens safe from such influences by enforcing obscenity ordinances against possession.

***Hicklin* Rule**
An early legal test for obscenity enforcing its prosecution based on any part of an explicit work's influence on the most susceptible mind.

British influence continued into the late 1800s when the question of how to legally define obscenity came before British magistrate Benjamin Hicklin. Hicklin was appointed in 1868 to judge a defendant's pamphlet, *The Confessional Unmasked*, about the practice of confessing sins to a Catholic priest. Despite a lack of intention, the author's recounting of sins was thought to stir impure thoughts in readers.

The obscenity conviction created what became known as the ***Hicklin* rule**, an early test for obscenity that held that material was obscene if it tended "to deprave and corrupt those whose minds are open to such immoral influences."[7] The *Hicklin* rule took root in the United States where entire books were judged obscene if any passage tended to arouse libidinous feelings in a susceptible mind.

Applying *Hicklin*

An early appeal to the U.S. Supreme Court for an obscenity conviction that used a *Hicklin*-style definition came from a Chicago newspaperman, Joseph R. Dunlop, who in

3. *Jacobellis v. Ohio*, 378 U.S. 184, 197 (1964). This film was a celebration of extramarital affairs minus graphic nudity and sex scenes. The justices struggled in *Jacobellis* with the idea of a local standard for obscenity in terms of the law's specificity.
4. The Latin root of the word is derived from a theater term indicating action happening off scene in classical drama because it is too offensive to show the audience.
5. Francis Ludlow Holt, "Of Libels against Morality and the Law of Nature," in *The Law of Libel* (J. Butterworth & Son, 1816).
6. Donna I. Dennis, "Obscenity Law and Its Consequences in Mid-Nineteenth Century America," 16 *Colum. J. Gender & L.* 43 (2007).
7. *Regina v. Hicklin*, LR 3 QB 360 (1868), in English Common Law.

1895 was fined $2,000 and sentenced to two years of hard labor in the penitentiary for mailing a newspaper, the *Dispatch*, from Chicago to St. Louis displaying advertisements on page 11 under the headings of "Personal" and "Baths."

Many of the classified ads were from women announcing their desire to meet gentlemen. While none of the ads said anything about sex, many invited men to visit addresses in Chicago's red-light districts.[8] It is hard to say what words the Court considered to be "obscene, lewd, lascivious, and . . . of too indecent character" because it declined to quote any passages of the advertisements. What was quoted were instructions to jurors to follow their "conscience and your own opinion" to determine if the ads were "calculated with the ordinary reader to deprave him, deprave his morals, or lead to impure purposes."[9]

Dunlop contested the jury instructions based on the doctrine requiring clarity over what represents guilty behavior rather than relying on jurors' personal opinions. This vagueness doctrine stems from a constitutional requirement of due process under the Fourteenth Amendment that informs Americans in advance of what is or is not a criminal act.

If the law fails to adequately define illegal behavior, then it may be struck for vagueness. In Dunlop's case, the Supreme Court found no error in having the Chicago jurors rely on their conscience and opinion about what words are to be judged as lewd, lascivious, or lead to impure purposes, and so Dunlop's conviction was upheld.

"Comstockery" was soon added to the *Hicklin* rule to characterize the American treatment of pornography into the early twentieth century. Comstockery described the passionate efforts of a famous postal clerk, Anthony Comstock, who advocated Victorian morality and led in the burning of books, pushed for the prosecution of pornography, and successfully fought to get a law passed to have authorities seize all erotic imports from French postcards to nude paintings and explicit novels.

Comstockery
Named for a zealous advocate of Victorian morality, Anthony Comstock, whose advocacy of censorship on the basis of sexual morality was notorious.

It was James Joyce's *Ulysses* that began to move the law toward a more comprehensive analysis of literature and away from moral assessments based on isolated passages that might provoke the least sophisticated reader.[10] Even though passengers disembarking from Ireland with a copy of the novel drew little attention in the 1930s from U.S. customs agents, publisher Random House wanted the book to be seized as a test case in obscenity to ensure its sales in the United States without fear of embargo. While the court found *Ulysses* contained passages "obscene under any fair definition,"[11] it found the book was not obscene when read in its entirety.

An emphasis on the social value of a work helped to further define obscenity when the U.S. Supreme Court adopted its *Roth-Memoirs* approach starting in the late 1950s. The high court made clear that no First Amendment protection would be given to content deemed obscene,[12] but not all material dealing with sex should be classified as obscene.[13] Rejecting the *Hicklin* rule,[14] the *Roth* Court defined a test for obscenity and stated that material could

8. Robert Loerzel, "On Joseph R. Dunlop's Chicago Dispatch," *Chicago Magazine*, February 18, 2010.
9. *Dunlop v. United States*, 165 U.S. 486 (1897).
10. *United States v. One Book Called "Ulysses,"* 5 F. Supp. 182 (S.D. N.Y. 1933), aff'd, 72 F.2d 705 (2d Cir. 1934).
11. *Id.* at 72 F.2d at 706–07.
12. *Roth v. United States*, 354 U.S. 476, 485 (1957). This case joined together appeals from federal and state courts; one prohibiting the mailing of books like *American Aphrodite*, for which Samuel Roth was convicted, and one prohibiting the possession of other books like *American Aphrodite*, for which David Alberts in his mail-order business in Los Angeles was convicted.
13. *Id.* at 489. The Court explained that sex and obscenity are not synonymous. "Obscene material is material which deals with sex in a manner appealing to prurient interest. The portrayal of sex, *e.g.*, in art, literature and scientific works, is not itself sufficient reason to deny material the constitutional protection of freedom of speech and press." At 487.
14. *Id.* at 489.

only be criminalized if it was "utterly without redeeming social importance" and thus undeserving of the First Amendment's safeguards.[15]

In its 1966 *Memoirs* decision, the Court emphasized that such material must be "utterly without redeeming social value."[16] Here the Court determined a book (*Memoirs of a Woman of Pleasure*, first published in 1748) had redeeming social value in the hands of those who publish or distribute it on the basis that it had "a modicum of literary and historical value."[17] The social value criterion became widely accepted by lower courts until the high court replaced it just a few years later with its current three-part test for obscenity.

Banning *Fanny Hill*

One of the most prosecuted and banned books in history is *Memoirs of a Woman of Pleasure* (Figure 10.1), more popularly known as *Fanny Hill*, an erotic novel first published in London in 1748. The British novel describes the adventures of a fictional orphaned girl named Fanny Hill who is tricked into becoming a prostitute in London and recounts through letters her encounters with homosexuality, flagellation, orgies, and other erotic affairs. At the end, Fanny Hill abandons that life, comes into riches, and marries her first lover.

Publishing Fanny Hill's erotic journey soon earned a criminal prosecution for its author, English novelist John Cleland, and for his publisher and printer – all of whom chose to renounce the book rather than risk prison for "corrupting the King's subjects." Pirated editions nonetheless appeared, and *Fanny Hill* eventually found its way to the United States where in 1821 a Massachusetts court outlawed it. A publisher of the book was convicted of printing a "lewd and obscene" novel, and the Massachusetts Supreme Court called him "scandalous and evil" for trying to raise and create in the minds of citizens "inordinate and lustful desires."

In the context of the 1960s sexual revolution, however, Putnam Books published a new edition of the book in the United States. An unusually large number of orders were placed by universities and libraries, and even the Library of Congress requested the right to translate the book into Braille. An anti-obscenity campaign led to the arrest of a bookstore owner in New York City, but the conviction was overturned, and a ban on *Fanny Hill* was lifted in New York.

Still, in Massachusetts, the book was banned and judged to be obscene. This led to the landmark reversal in 1966 by the Supreme Court in what became known as the *Memoirs* decision. The prevailing opinion relied on language from the state court which candidly admitted that *Fanny Hill* has at least "some minimal literary value."[18] The Supreme Court was persuaded by considerable expert testimony of the work's literary, historical, and social importance, while hearing virtually no proof[19] of the book being "utterly without redeeming social value" – a requisite standard (at that time) for the work to be found obscene.[20]

15. *Id.* at 484–485. The Court in *Roth* defined obscenity as "whether, to the average person, applying contemporary community standards, the dominant theme of the material, taken as a whole, appeals to prurient interest." At 489. While it was emphasized in *Roth* that obscene works lack any "redeeming social importance," it was not clear whether the absence or presence of social importance was part of the test for obscenity.
16. *A Book Named "John Cleland's Memoirs of a Woman of Pleasure" v. Massachusetts*, 383 U.S. 413, 418 (1966). The *Memoirs* Court acknowledged but said it did not need to apply other criteria from its definition of obscenity, namely whether "the dominant theme of the material taken as a whole appeals to a prurient interest," and also whether the material was "patently offensive because it affronts contemporary community standards." *Id.*
17. *Id.* at 421.
18. 383 U.S. 426 (Douglas, J., concurring).
19. *Id.*
20. 383 U.S. 419-420.

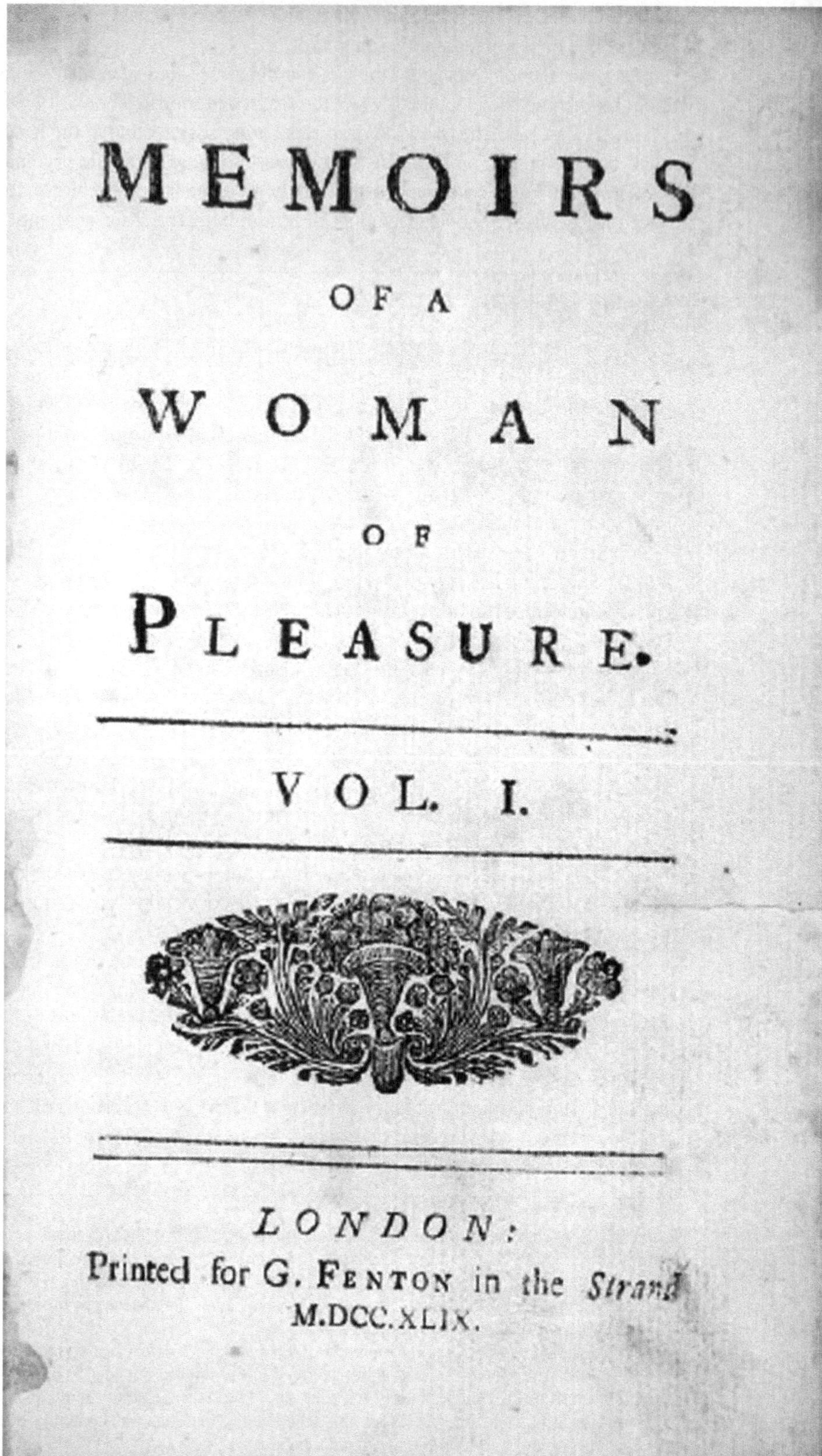

MEMOIRS
OF A
WOMAN
OF
PLEASURE.

VOL. I.

LONDON:
Printed for G. FENTON in the *Strand*
M.DCC.XLIX.

Figure 10.1 The 1749 book that led to a 1966 case protecting works that have literary value

Miller v. California

The landmark *Miller v. California* decision in 1973 is what guides jurisprudence in the area of obscenity today. The case was about the marketing by mail of sexually oriented literature. Unaware of the contents, an unidentified restaurant owner in Long Beach, CA, opened a mail item in the presence of his mother – mail that contained pornographic pictures advertising books with titles such as *Man-Woman, Intercourse, An Illustrated History of Pornography* and *Sex Orgies Illustrated*, all bulk-mailed by Marvin Miller. Miller was convicted of a misdemeanor under a California law prohibiting the distribution through the mail of knowingly obscene materials. His conviction was upheld in California, but he appealed to the U.S. Supreme Court.

In a 5-to-4 decision, the Supreme Court upheld the prosecution of Miller for the distribution of obscene materials under California's obscenity law, holding that obscene materials do not enjoy First Amendment protection. Chief Justice Warren Burger wrote the majority opinion and called Marvin Miller's marketing strategy an "aggressive sales action." California was within its constitutional rights to convict anyone who dealt in public with materials containing a "prurient, patently offensive depiction or description of sexual conduct" absent "serious literary, artistic, political or scientific value" to merit constitutional protection.[21] In finding the materials obscene, the Court modified its test for obscenity established in *Roth-Memoirs*, creating what is known as the *Miller* test.

Miller Test
The standard under which material is classified as obscene if the average person applying contemporary community standards would find the dominant theme of the work taken as a whole: 1) appeals to the prurient interest, 2) depicts patently offensive sexual conduct, and 3) lacks serious literary, artistic, political, or scientific value in the view of a reasonable person. See *Miller v. California*, 413 U.S. 15 (1973).

The *Miller* Test

The *Miller* test established the current three-prong test for obscenity based on questions concerning the values of the content, the community, and the consumer.

1 Would the average person applying contemporary community standards find that the work, taken as a whole, appeals to **prurient interest**?
2 Does it depict or describe in a **patently offensive** way sexual conduct as defined by applicable state law?
3 Does the work, taken as a whole, lack **serious literary, artistic, political, or scientific value**?

This test for obscenity essentially replaced the social value prong of the *Roth-Memoirs* test with the **"SLAPS"** test, which meant lacking in serious literary, artistic, political, or scientific value. It relieved prosecutors of having to prove the all-encompassing negative proposition of judging content to be "utterly without redeeming social value." Instead, it evaluates the literary, artistic, political, or scientific merit of the published work.

The *Miller* standard also moved back to the state's purview the task of defining **contemporary community standards**. The First Amendment allows states great latitude in how they define contemporary community standards, and it's the jury and not the judge who gauges those factors. As a result, most obscenity cases are decided at the state court level. Of course, if a conservative jury reflects community standards, then a minimum standard for obscene content may be little more than mere nudity for an otherwise serious artistic or literary work. Instead, local juries must apply all parts of the *Miller* test, including the "patently offensive" criterion.

Contemporary Community Standards
Jurors apply this rule to determine what is obscene. It localizes the definition of obscenity by time and place that was adopted by the U.S. Supreme Court in *Roth v. United States* (1957).

Dominant Theme
A work is only obscene if its most important subject matter taken *as a whole,* appeals to prurient interest. For example, a specific sexual scene in a movie can't be taken alone without considering the rest of the film.

21. *Miller v. California*, 413 U.S. 15, 23–24 (1973).

Prurient Interest
Shameful or morbid interest in nudity, sex, or excretion. See *Roth v. United States*, 354 U.S. 476 (1957).

Patently Offensive
Obscene material must be clearly offensive based on contemporary community standards.

Bedrock Law
Contemporary community standards are determined by average persons from the local community (such as would be found on a jury), but serious literary, artistic, political, or scientific value is determined by a more objective source.

Bedrock Law
If material is determined to be obscene, laws can prohibit its creation, sale, performance, importation, or mailing – even by consenting adults – but not its possession.

Applying Contemporary Community Standards

Even though the *Miller* decision left to the states the task of applying contemporary community standards, this did not mean states had unlimited latitude in determining what is patently offensive. In *Jenkins v. Georgia*,[22] the Supreme Court found the trial court's application of contemporary community standards missed the mark when a cinema manager in Albany, GA, was convicted for showing a film with some nudity but less than explicit "ultimate sexual acts."

The Supreme Court felt a person of average sexual sensitivities in that community should be unlikely to find the acclaimed Mike Nichols film *Carnal Knowledge* starring Jack Nicholson, Candice Bergen, and Ann-Margret patently offensive. The film lacked the sort of graphic depiction that constitutes hard-core pornography, and Justice William Rehnquist noted, "nudity alone is not enough to make material legally obscene under the *Miller* standards."[23]

Affirming all three questions meant a purveyor could be tried on obscenity charges without offending the U.S. Constitution. *Miller* showed how "hard-core pornography" fit the description of obscenity, and no protection for it would be granted because to do so "demeans the grand conception of the First Amendment and its high purposes in the historic struggle for freedom."[24]

Public Exhibition Versus Private Ownership

On the same day *Miller* was decided, the Supreme Court handed down a companion ruling in *Paris Adult Theatre I v. Slaton*[25] considering whether adult movie theaters deserved constitutional protection. After all, it was argued consenting adults should enjoy a certain right of viewing cinema fare seen as explicit in sexual content. Yet the Court affirmed a Georgia law against public obscenity when it found two films, *Magic Mirror* and *It All Comes Out in the End*, appearing at the Paris Adult Theatre I, contained the type of obscene content Georgia had a right to prosecute as "hard-core pornography." The law in this respect protected the community's valid interest in the quality of life for its families, social decency, public safety, and the "social interest in order and morality."[26]

Ownership of pornography in the privacy of one's home is a different matter. In an earlier case, *Stanley v. Georgia* (1969),[27] the Supreme Court ruled Robert Eli Stanley's pornography stash was of no valid legal interest to police officers in Georgia. The discovery of super 8-mm reels of pornographic film police seized in the midst of a search for gambling evidence produced a conviction that would be overturned. Even though Stanley's pornography was neither covered nor anticipated in the search warrant for illegal gambling evidence, the majority held the privacy of one's home is simply not the same as a commercial exhibition of movies and ownership was legal.

Child Pornography

There is one area of law in which the *Miller* test for obscenity does not apply – child pornography. The landmark case in this area is *New York v. Ferber* (1982),[28] which involved

22. *Jenkins v. Georgia*, 418 U.S. 153 (1974).
23. *Id.* at 161.
24. *Id.* at 34.
25. 413 U.S. 49 (1973).
26. *Id.* at 61.
27. 394 U.S. 557.
28. 458 U.S. 747.

Manhattan bookstore owners Paul Ferber and Tim Quinn, who sold to undercover police films of adolescent boys masturbating.

Child Pornography Material depicting sexually explicit acts involving a minor. On its face, this class of material has no constitutional protection.

In this instance, the U.S. Supreme Court gave a variety of reasons why child pornography represented so great an evil to society that no judge need weigh the explicit material's danger or worth as *Miller* would have directed in obscenity trials. The physical and psychological harm of sexually exploiting children, the lasting record of the crime scarring them, the economic incentives, the negligible artistic value, and the Court's record against it were enough for the justices unanimously to favor censorship for child pornography in Ferber's case. The Supreme Court created a category of speech, **child pornography**, without any constitutional protection.

Bedrock Law Child pornography is considered illegal, without requiring any application of the *Miller* test.

Ferber dealt only with the merchandising of child pornography, but the Court later moved to uphold a ban on even the *possession* of it in *Osborne v. Ohio* (1990).[29] In Columbus, OH, Clyde Osborne received certain mail-order pictures he had requested of 14-year-old boys in sexually explicit poses that caught the attention of a U.S. postal inspector, who in turn notified local police. Officers searched Osborne's home, seized the children's pictures, and charged him under an Ohio law prohibiting the possession of nude adolescent pictures that are not of one's own children and without any consent from their parents. In light of the *Ferber* decision that effectively outlawed child pornography without proving it as obscenity, the Ohio law charged and the Court affirmed as criminal the mere possession of child pornography.

Child Pornography Laws

For decades, Congress has worked to ban child pornography at the national level.[30] Various federal statutory laws forbid the manufacture, distribution, and possession of child pornography to protect minors from exploitation.[31] For example, it is illegal to persuade, induce, entice, or coerce a minor to engage in sexually explicit conduct for purposes of producing visual depictions of that conduct.[32] Penalties for such crimes are harsh. Producing child pornography can result in a sentence of 15 to 30 years in federal prison for first-time offenders. Possession of child pornography on one's computer can also mean prison time. And those convicted of child pornography must register as a sex offender.

But what happens if no actual children are involved in the production of the sexually explicit content? In 1996, Congress passed an ill-fated law to ban computer-generated images of minors engaged in sexual conduct. Because child pornography fell outside the *Miller* test for obscenity, the Child Pornography Prevention Act (CPPA)[33] conceivably would prohibit all visual images of pre-adult teenagers engaged in sexual activity without considering the possible literary and artistic merits of this content. This deduction created the astounding scenario in which the law could conceivably ban digital transmission of *Romeo and Juliet* given the lack of a SLAPS test. Since nowhere did it call for judging offensive works in their entirety, a "single explicit scene" was only necessary to produce criminal consequences. In *Ashcroft v. Free Speech Coalition* (2002),[34] the Supreme Court struck down the CPPA as violating the First Amendment for being overbroad, saying the government would first have to show how the CPPA would protect real children from exploitation.

Congress nonetheless found success in its legislative agenda to protect children from sexual exploitation in 2003 when it adopted the Prosecutorial Remedies and Other Tools

29. 95 U.S. 103.
30. Many organizations including law enforcement that work to end child pornography prefer to use the term "child sexual abuse material" or CSAM instead of child pornography.
31. 18 U.S.C. § 2251; 18 U.S.C. § 2252; 18 U.S.C. § 2260.
32. 18 U.S.C. § 2251.
33. 18 U.S.C. § 2256 (8).
34. 535 U.S. 234 (2002).

to end the Exploitation of Children Today (PROTECT Act).[35] This law reworded the ban on digitally produced child pornography by prohibiting a "computer-generated image that is, or appears virtually indistinguishable from that of a minor engaging in sexually explicit conduct."[36] It also prohibited such material if it qualified as obscene under the *Miller* test. In other words, virtual child pornography would be constitutionally protected speech unless it meets the criteria of obscenity. This law was challenged in *United States v. Williams*,[37] but the Supreme Court held the PROTECT law was not unconstitutionally overbroad.

The first convictions in 2008 under the PROTECT law involved a comic book collector from Iowa and a state government employee in Virginia, both of whom had a taste for anime and manga – Japanese cartoon books – featuring art that U.S. prosecutors said depicted sex acts with children and animals.[38] The PROTECT Act is viewed as a potential tool for combating AI-generated and manipulated sexualized images of children in animation.

Protests and Public Libraries

Public librarians in the United States have met with fierce criticism over the past few years from parents and politicians who claim they are making obscene materials too easily available to adolescents. They demand librarians do more to protect children from sexually graphic literature. A "Protecting Innocence" report from the Louisiana state attorney general (now governor) asked public librarians to enforce stricter policies limiting minors' access to such content especially LGBTQ materials.[39] In some states, parents even went to court.

Two public library books that faced obscenity charges in Virginia were *Gender Queer* and *A Court of Mist and Fury*. A case of obscenity was filed by a school board member against both books that were eventually removed from the Virginia Beach public school libraries. The circuit court judge ruling in that case, however, found the petition against both books lacking the legal requirements of obscenity, and she noted the little-used statute in Virginia was in effect unconstitutional.[40]

Generally, public libraries house materials with adult readings shelved in adult sections. How then should librarians restrict access to sexually explicit literature that some parents find to be harmful? The American Library Association answers this way. "The fact that a work has topics addressing sex, or contains sexual content, does not make the material 'harmful to minors.' Whether materials are considered 'harmful to minors' is determined by a court using the same three-part test for obscenity" (as the Supreme Court did in *Miller v. California*, 1973).[41]

Curtailing *access* by minors *to* pornography became a growing concern once it began to proliferate on the Internet. Early on the Communications Decency Act (CDA) sought to punish those who reached out to minors online with materials featuring "sexual or excretory

35. Pub. L. 108–121, 117 Stat. 650 (2003).
36. Amended by 1466A of 18 U.S.C. § 2256(8)(B).
37. 553 U.S. 285 (2008).
38. *United States v. Handley*, 564 F. Supp. 2d 996 (S.D. Iowa 2008); *United States v. Whorley*, 386 F. Supp. 2d 693 (E.D. Va. 2005).
39. *See* "Attorney General Jeff Landry Releases Protecting Innocence Report," *at* https://www.youtube.com/watch?v=jXXd4Bvhbew.
40. ACLU, "Virginia Obscenity Proceedings against Two Books," June 22, 2022, *at* https://www.aclu.org/cases/virginia-obscenity-proceedings-against-two-books.
41. American Library Association, Intellectual Freedom and Censorship Q & A, *at* https://www.ala.org/advocacy/intfreedom/censorship/faq.

activities or organs" that would be deemed "patently offensive as measured by contemporary community standards."[42]

The 1996 law was short lived, however, with the landmark case of *Reno v. American Civil Liberties Union*.[43] The Supreme Court found the CDA was overly vague and too blunt an instrument to achieve the goal of denying minors access to "potentially harmful speech" since it would suppress a wide swath of online content adults were entitled to share.[44] Two CDA sections banning such content were deemed unconstitutional because Internet communications deserved as much protection as print and more than broadcasting, according to the high court.

In 1998, Congress tried again to make the Internet safe for minors by passing the Child Online Protection Act (COPA).[45] It blocked online commercial websites from allowing children access to sexually explicit materials. But COPA was also found unconstitutional for limiting the First Amendment rights of adults in order to protect minors. The Supreme Court reaffirmed this decision in 2004 in *Ashcroft v. American Civil Liberties Union*.[46]

One federal law surviving a legal challenge is the Children's Internet Protection Act (CIPA).[47] Enacted in 2000, CIPA requires public libraries and school districts receiving federal technology funds to purchase and employ protection measures on all computers connected to the Internet to block or filter content that is "harmful" to minors, including child pornography and obscenity. Schools and libraries subject to CIPA had to adopt a policy ensuring the online safety of minors. Even though CIPA initially was ruled unconstitutional, the Supreme Court in 2003 took up the case of *United States v. America Library Association*[48] and ruled the law should be reinstated because libraries still had the freedom to offer unfiltered access to the Internet by simply refusing to accept federal funding.

Most states also have child pornography laws that generally track the federal laws, and child pornography crimes can be prosecuted under both state and federal laws. One difference, however, is that age of consent may be lower in some states, making an action criminal under federal law but not state law.[49]

Some states also proscribe certain actions, such as Massachusetts forbidding the posing or exhibiting of a child in a "state of nudity or sexual conduct."[50] Other states such as Georgia prohibit anyone from making "obscene telephone contact with a child"[51] (i.e., "sexting" – addressed later in this chapter).

States have also rolled out laws requiring age verification for accessing adult websites. Louisiana was the first state in 2022, followed by Utah, Mississippi, Virginia, Arkansas, Texas, Montana, North Carolina, and others, to pass laws requiring online sites like Pornhub to require visitors to prove they are at least 18 years old, such as by presenting digital ID or undergoing background checks to establish age. Companies failing to comply face harsh civil penalties and have complained and even blocked consumers in those states from their sites altogether.[52] These laws have been challenged as unconstitutional.[53]

42. Pub. L. 104–104, § 502, 110 Stat. 133, 47 U.S. C. § 223.
43. 521 U.S. 844 (1997).
44. *Id.* at 874. The Court held the CDA unconstitutional because it was not narrowly tailored to serve a compelling governmental interest and because less-restrictive alternatives were available.
45. 112 Stat. 2681–736, codified at 47 U.S. C. § 231 (2003).
46. 542 U.S. 656 (2004).
47. Pub. L. 106–554, (2000).
48. 539 U.S. 134 (2003).
49. For example, in Maryland for a person to be convicted of possessing child pornography, the image must be of a minor under the age of 16, whereas federal law specifies the age of 18.
50. MGL c.272, § 29A.
51. GA Code § 16–12-100.3 (2022).
52. Ashley Belanger, "Texas Law Requiring Age Verification on Porn Sites Ruled Unconstitutional," *Ars Technica*, August 31, 2023, *at* https://arstechnica.com/tech-policy/2023/08/pornhub-wins-injunction-that-blocks-texas-age-verification-law/?mc_cid=51ff85d9fc&mc_eid=b7740047d1.
53. *Id.* A law was upheld in Utah in 2023, but then a federal judge struck down a similar law in Texas.

Politics of Pornography

The federal laws against obscenity specify a variety of crimes covering everything from its transmission to merchandising it. Several laws ban the shipping of obscenity by postal carrier (18 U.S.C. 1461); by express company or common carrier (18 U.S.C. 1462); by interstate commerce for retail sales (18 U.S.C. 1465, 18 U.S.C. 1466); or by telephone, cable, or satellite television (47 U.S.C. 223, 18 U.S.C. 1468). U.S. postal inspectors, attorneys, and customs officers carry out the legal enforcement against hard-core porn, but federal prosecutions vary depending on who occupies the White House.

When President Bush took office in 2001, he began a crackdown on hard-core pornography that culminated in the appointment of an Obscenity Prosecution Task Force. The OPTF worked out of the Department of Justice with aid from three Sections of the Criminal Division: Organized Crime and Racketeering, Asset Forfeiture and Money Laundering, and Computer Crime and Intellectual Property.

That aforementioned last office focused on Internet methods of spreading porn. Among more than 40 cases prosecuted by federal agents were cases against "Girls Gone Wild" filmmaker Joseph R. Francis, shock artist Ira Isaacs, and a filmmaker who used the name Max Hardcore (Paul F. Little). The most publicized case was *United States v. Extreme Associates, Inc.,*[54] where Robert Zicari and Janet Romano pleaded guilty to charges of transmitting obscenity by mail and the Internet, including graphic depictions of rape and murder.

After President Obama took office in 2008, the legal focus shifted toward prosecuting hard-core pornography that threatened children but avoiding the noxious content produced by and for adults. Attorney General Eric Holder dissolved the OPTF in 2011 and began leaving federal prosecutions of pornographers to the Child Exploitation and Obscenity Section (CEOS) of the Department of Justice.[55]

When President Trump took office in 2017, Attorney General Jeff Sessions was asked for his views on obscenity and was surprised to learn the OPTF was shuttered, albeit absorbed by the CEOS. Sessions vowed to renew enforcement of U.S. obscenity laws, but the president who appeared in *Playboy* did not make criminal obscenity enforcement one of his priorities. An executive order was passed, however, at the very end of Trump's administration to combat online child exploitation and human trafficking.

During the Biden administration, special units of the CEOS and other agencies would continue their work in combating child pornography. These include the CEOS High Technology Investigative Unit (HTIU), responsible for conducting computer forensics and analysis of Internet technologies commonly used to disseminate child pornography.

There is also the FBI's Violent Crimes Against Children (VCAC) program, which conducts child pornography research and supports law enforcement efforts across the country, as well as the USA Ministry of Internal Security: Operation Predator, which combats all forms of child abuse and pornography. Many states have also stepped up enforcement, with some even declaring pornography a public health crisis.

Broadcast Indecency

For over-the-air broadcast stations, a different legal standard – **indecency** – applies. Just as with other forms of expression, obscenity on the airwaves is always against the law, and

54. *United States v. Extreme Associates*, 431 F.3d 150 (3rd Cir. 2005).
55. *See*, U.S. Department of Justice, Child Exploitation and Obscenity Section (CEOS), *at* www.justice.gov/criminal-ceos.

the three-pronged test refined in *Miller v. California* applies. In fact, federal statutory law explicitly prohibits obscenity over the public's airwaves[56] as well as over cable and satellite services.[57] But the Supreme Court has also given its support to federal regulation of profane and *indecent* programming when delivered over the air, namely, broadcast radio and television (but *not* over subscription media such as cable or satellite radio or TV).

Indecent content is defined as patently offensive language or material as measured by contemporary community standards regarding sexual or excretory activities or organs. Profane content includes "grossly offensive" language that is considered a public nuisance. Indecency and profanity do not rise (or sink) to the level of obscenity. So given its First Amendment protection and federal law that forbids broadcast censorship,[58] indecency and profanity cannot be swept off the air completely. But the Court agreed the law can restrict airing such content to times when children presumably are asleep and away from broadcast channels.[59] The FCC defined this **safe harbor** as the hours between 10 at night and 6 in the morning.[60] Thus broadcast stations may carry profane or indecent content at night, but not during the day.

Seven Dirty Words and *Pacifica*

When George Carlin was posthumously awarded the 11th Annual Mark Twain Prize for American Humor at the Kennedy Center for the Performing Arts in Washington, DC, humorist Bill Maher introduced the event saying, "Well, what can you say about George Carlin that hasn't already been argued before the Supreme Court?" Indeed, the once buttoned-down, family-friendly comedian whose act was a popular staple of 1960s television variety and talk shows reinvented himself as an iconoclastic, self-described class clown whose satirical witticisms cast searing and profane commentary to expose societal foibles and human failings.

It was a track from a 1973 comedy album after his iconic transformation that led to a landmark Supreme Court case. Rife with profane language, the 12-minute track, an expansion of Carlin's earlier bit titled "Seven Words You Can Never Say on Television," was broadcast on New York radio station WBAI-FM at 2 o'clock in the afternoon. A father, driving a car with his teenage son, complained to the Federal Communications Commission about the explosive profanity, and in response, the federal agency sent the station's owner a letter of reprimand, alleging WBAI-FM violated FCC prohibitions against transmitting indecent material.

Pacifica Foundation appealed to the U.S. Court of Appeals for the District of Columbia, which agreed the FCC's order constituted censorship and reversed the order against the station. But the FCC then appealed to the Supreme Court, which ruled

56. Under 18 U.S.C. § 1464, "[w]hoever utters any obscene, indecent, or profane language by means of radio communication shall be fined under this title or imprisoned not more than two years, or both."
57. 18 U.S.C. § 1468(a) states "[w]hoever knowingly utters any obscene language or distributes any obscene matter by means of cable television or subscription services on television, shall be punished by imprisonment for not more than 2 years or by a fine in accordance with this title, or both." Likewise, under 47 U.S.C. § 559, "[w]hoever transmits over any cable system any matter which is obscene or otherwise unprotected by the Constitution of the United States shall be fined under Title 18 or imprisoned not more than 2 years, or both."
58. 47 U.S. Code § 326. This states that "Nothing in this chapter shall be understood or construed to give the Commission the power of censorship over the radio communications or signals transmitted by any radio station, and no regulation or condition shall be promulgated or fixed by the Commission which shall interfere with the right of free speech by means of radio communication."
59. *Federal Communications Commission v. Pacifica Foundation*, 438 U.S. 726 (1978).
60. *See* www.fcc.gov/consumers/guides/obscene-indecent-and-profane-broadcasts.

5–4 that Carlin's seven-words routine was "indecent" and gave broad authority to the commission to ban broadcasts during times when children might be in the audience.[61]

The case cemented the government's role in regulating broadcast speech; the justices distinguished radio and television from print media, citing the sometimes-inescapable omnipresence of broadcast media, and as a result, it was clear broadcasting would receive less constitutional protection than print media. The same language that may be acceptable in print might be considered offensive if heard or seen broadcast because of the ubiquity of radio and the lack of control over its consumption in a public space, the justices said.

This tension between what is the right time, place, and manner to display or perform such material – and to what audience – ironically played out on stage during the 2008 Mark Twain Prize tribute to George Carlin at the Kennedy Center, which was later broadcast nationwide on Public Broadcasting System television stations. During the tribute show, producers showed a video clip of a 1978 HBO cable television network presentation of Carlin's now-infamous "Seven Words You Can Never Say on Television" bit. The routine builds up layers of word play delineating all the descriptive words and phrases people use to politely describe the language in question. At the punch line when Carlin ticks off each of the words in rapid succession, producers of the TV show ironically censored each one of Carlin's shocking words with bleeps.

Documented complaints from the public are what spur the FCC to action when it comes to sanctioning profane, indecent, or obscene material on the air. The staff in Washington, DC, is assigned to review the complaints of broadcast programming, and a detailed context of the offensive expression is used in determining if a violation has occurred. That is why the station call letters, location, date, and time of the broadcast are essential, and a recording or transcript of the offense is considered helpful to resolve the question.

When the FCC reviews a claim of a violation that has generated enough attention to warrant an official response, its staff begin the inquiry with a letter to the broadcast station. The agency can also send a letter of dismissal to the complaining party explaining why the material is either legal or why evidence of the offense is insufficient to determine if a violation has occurred.

The complaining party has a right of appeal if the FCC denies the complaint, but the complainant has the option of filing a petition for reconsideration or can appeal to the full commission. A Notice of Apparent Liability (NAL) is what the FCC issues the station when it determines a patently offensive broadcast involving profanity or indecency has occurred in violation of the law. This preliminary finding of the NAL can be reduced, rescinded, or affirmed before the terms of punishment for the station are levied.

Critics say the agency is too backlogged to even begin to fulfill that legal mandate. The Parents Television and Media Council (formerly the Parents Television Council) has delivered thousands of broadcast indecency complaints to the FCC, sometimes over just a single TV show, such as the Fox comedy *Family Guy*[62] or *The Mick*.[63] This group found more than a million complaints awaiting FCC review, and some over five years old were simply discarded.

61. 438 U.S. 726.
62. James Hibberd, "Parent Group Files FCC Complaint Against 'Family Guy,' *Hollywood Reporter*, March 11, 2009, *at* https://www.hollywoodreporter.com/tv/tv-news/parent-group-files-fcc-complaint-51352/. The complaint was for a particular episode they said included "bestiality, orgies and babies eating sperm."
63. Parents Television Council, "PTC Delivers Thousands of Broadcast Indecency Complaints to the FCC," July 20, 2017, *at* www.parentstv.org/blog/ptc-delivers-thousands-of-broadcast-indecency-complaints-to-the-fcc. Fox canceled the series after two seasons.

One complaint that did gain FCC attention occurred in 2012. As mentioned at the beginning of this chapter, it was against the Roanoke, VA, CBS affiliate, WDBJ-TV, for broadcasting a news story about a former adult film star containing footage of an erect penis at the margin of the TV screen taken from an adult website. The indecent content that was plainly visible to the audience during the 6:00 evening newscast occurred outside the FCC's safe harbor period for indecent material. The agency also claimed it could have been prevented if station personnel were more attentive. The FCC imposed the maximum fine of $325,000 – the largest levied against a television station for a one-time instance of indecent content.

Industry Guidance on Indecency

To clarify for broadcasters what constitutes indecency and how policies would be enforced, the FCC issued its "Industry Guidance" on broadcast indecency in 2001.[64] While no factor is decisive and each case is unique, the FCC states for a broadcast to be found indecent, the material must first fall within the scope of its indecency definition – that is, the material must describe or depict sexual or excretory organs or activities. The presentation must also be patently offensive by contemporary community standards, which are not local standards but based on the average broadcast viewer or listener. Offensiveness is also determined in the full context of the broadcast.

One factor the FCC considers is the explicitness or graphic nature of the material. It also judges whether the broadcaster appears to be pandering, using the material to titillate, or presenting it for shock value. Finally, the FCC considers whether a description or depiction "dwells on" or repeats the offensive terms or images at length. In fact, the guide provides several examples where the FCC refused to hold a fleeting use of profanity to be indecent. This latter position would soon change, however.

Fleeting Exposures and Expletives

Some called it the Golden Globes rule, which followed by almost three decades the *Pacifica* decision against George Carlin's filthy words monologue. The controversy sparked afresh during the 2003 Golden Globes Award ceremony on NBC network television stations when jubilant rock singer Bono exulted with profanity for winning the best original song award for "The Hands That Build America," featured in the film *Gangs of New York*. "This is really, really, fucking brilliant," exclaimed the Irish singer on live television. The FCC recognized even though Bono's use of the f-word was not expressive of sexual or excretory activity, it did inherently have a sexual connotation, although no fine was levied against NBC in this case.

What the case did accomplish was a policy shift that held **fleeting expletives** could be legally penalized. Fox Television was the first network to feel the sting of the stricter enforcement of unguarded profanity on the air. When pop singer Cher and actor Nicole Richie used "f and s bombs" from the podium at two consecutive annual broadcasts of *Billboard*'s Music Awards in 2002 and 2003, the explosive profanity on Fox's airwaves surprised viewers.

Sometimes a prior notice warning viewers of explicit content is not an option, especially when television is covering live events. But the first-blow theory the FCC uses to justify its strict measures against indecency is based on the notion that without warning, an ugly word or indecent comment can enter the home and strike a child's eyes or ears to the detriment of the family's welfare.

64. Federal Communications Commission, *Industry Guidance on the Commission's Case Law Interpreting 18 U.S.C. §1464 and Enforcement Policies Regarding Broadcast Indecency*, File No. EB-00-IH-0089, April 6, 2001, *at* https://www.fcc.gov/document/industry-guidance-commissions-case-law-interpreting-18-usc.

In *Fox v. FCC* (2009), the U.S. Supreme Court ruled so-called fleeting expletives taking place in the context of awards shows or on reality television can be sanctioned with fines. This was the first time since *Federal Communications Commission v. Pacifica* in 1978 the high court found the whole issue of indecency worthy of its attention. A lower court thought the new approach was an arbitrary and capricious departure from the agency's long-standing policy and refused to affirm it. But by a 5–4 majority, the Supreme Court agreed it was acceptable for the FCC to penalize the broadcasters, although six justices felt compelled to write individual opinions indicating just how divisive policing profanity and punishing use of the "f-bomb" and "s-word" ("shit") on the air had become.

Justice Antonin Scalia, writing for the majority, concluded that although the FCC policy shifted under President George W. Bush's administration to take a tougher stance with regard to profanity, the agency was still acting within its congressional mandate to guard the airwaves from indiscreet use of profane terms as expletives and not just as literal descriptors of sexual or excretory functions.[65] In other words, the argument that the FCC was "arbitrary" or "capricious" in changing its policy proved unconvincing to the majority, but the dissenting justices felt that isolated and fleeting expletives should not be penalized out of context.

U.S. broadcasters felt this ruling against fleeting expletives chilled their free speech and threatened the future programming of live television in general. But the Supreme Court decided to affirm the FCC's policy on procedural grounds and returned the case to the New York-based Second Circuit Court of Appeals to consider the constitutional arguments involved.

In 2010, Judge Rosemary Pooler wrote for a three-judge panel, holding that the FCC had acted unconstitutionally to punish broadcasters for fleeting profanities, which celebrities blurt out during live programming. Her opinion held the commission's policy was chilling to free speech because broadcasters had no way of knowing when references to sexual and excretory actions and the like crossed the line into indecency. The indecency regulation promoted self-censorship, and so it was struck, but the court said an alternative rule on indecency could be drafted by the FCC. What the decision did was encourage the FCC to avoid promoting "wide self-censorship" among broadcasters by prohibiting all patently offensive references to sexual content.

The case bounced back up in 2012 to the Supreme Court where the matter came to an end. In a unanimous opinion, the Court simply invalidated all fines issued against the broadcasters for fleeting expletives in this specific case. The Court determined that the regulations had not adequately covered the issue prior to enforcement, and as a result the broadcasters had a right to expect due process under the Fifth Amendment.[66]

Nipplegate

Most American football fans can hardly remember last year's Super Bowl, much less what happened in years previous. But what happened during the Super Bowl of 2004 appears indelibly etched in the national consciousness. Justin Timberlake and Janet Jackson were performing during the halftime show when a "wardrobe malfunction" exposed for a fraction of a second Jackson's right breast. It was a fleeting exposure, but it excited enough Americans to complain en masse to the Federal Communications Commission, which in turn levied a fine to each CBS-affiliated station for violating the indecency rule by carrying the network broadcast.

65. *FCC v. Fox Television Stations*, 556 U.S. 1, 129 S. Ct. 1800 (2009).
66. *FCC v. Fox Television Stations, Inc.*, 132 S. CT. 2307 (June 21, 2012). This decision consolidated with the Fox appeals one from ABC subject to an indecency action for an "NYPD Blue" episode that included a scene in which a woman's nude buttocks were seen for less than ten seconds and the side of her breast for about one second. This ruling relieved 45 ABC affiliates of $27,500 fines for airing this brief nudity.

For years after the fleeting glimpse of the singer's breast, lawyers fought over the FCC's extraordinary fine until a three-judge panel of the Third Circuit Court of Appeals ruled in favor of CBS in 2008. The FCC had not given enough prior notice that it would strictly enforce its policy against fleeting nudity during the daytime hours of television. The federal panel also took issue with the idea that local TV stations were to blame for this wardrobe malfunction. (Timberlake was the one who sang the lyric, "Gonna have you have naked by the end of this song" and pulled at Jackson's breastplate to cause the exposure, yet he escaped much of the criticism afterward.)

The FCC argued this fleeting image of a breast was not to be held exempt from its prohibition against indecency. There was in fact no departure from standing policy at the FCC to fine CBS Viacom on behalf of its television stations broadcasting the event. The U.S. Supreme Court set aside the Third Circuit Court of Appeals ruling in 2009 and asked that the lower court reexamine its jurisprudence, leaving open the possibility that the appellate court could rule in favor of CBS.[67] However, the Third Circuit Court ruled again that the $550,000 fine ($27,500 per station) for showing Jackson's nipple for less than a second to a broadcast audience was "arbitrary and capricious," and the FCC's fine would not be levied. The Supreme Court decided to let that decision stand.

Broadcast Indecency Act

Following the infamous wardrobe malfunction, which heightened public concern with broadcast decency, the FCC began to step up its enforcement of these infractions. President Bush took one step further and signed into law the Broadcast Decency Enforcement Act, which was sponsored by a former broadcaster, Sen. Sam Brownback (R-Kan.).[68] This law established a sizable increase in the fine for such violations, giving the commission the authority to require $325,000 per station for each violation of the rules, a more than tenfold increase of the original maximum forfeiture for indecency on the air.

Cable Television

Although cable and satellite are not subject to the same FCC indecency regulations as over-the-air broadcast licensees, these subscription media have not escaped scrutiny. Parental concern with cable television pornography spurred congressional action after a Florida mother was stunned to find her seven- and eight-year-old children watching sex scenes on the Spice Channel one afternoon. As a result, one part of the Communications Decency Act required cable operators selling adult channels to install necessary filters to scramble or block erotic programming from reaching non-subscribing households or limit adult-oriented programming to overnight hours.

That provision of the CDA covering scrambling filters for sexually explicit content, §505, was held to be in violation of the First Amendment because it was not the least restrictive means of achieving the government's goal.[69] Cable operators already were bound to completely block any channel without charge once a customer made the request. The trial judge said giving customers adequate notice of that alternative would be a less-restrictive rule than barring all adult-oriented content during the day. Parents would simply have to call the cable company and have them block the channel or buy digital devices to do it.

67. *CBS v. FCC*, 663 F. 3d 122 (3d Cir. 2011).
68. Pub. L. No. 109–235 (2005).
69. *United States v. Playboy Entertainment Group*, 529 U.S. 803 (2000). Section 505 is found in Title V of the Communications Decency Act of 1996 (CDA).

Cinema Censorship

For the film industry, the regulation of sexually explicit movies has taken a different approach, relying more on self-regulation with the creation of what is now called the Motion Picture Association (MPA) ratings system. This was not always the case, though. For years, movies were subject to various state and local censorship boards exercising prior review. Early in the twentieth century, the U.S. Supreme Court held that censorship boards did not violate the First Amendment because "the exhibition of moving pictures is a business," "not to be regarded as part of the press," and lacking in a "worthy purpose" because it could appeal to "prurient interest" and "may be used for evil."[70]

By 1952, however, the Supreme Court recognized the power of motion pictures to convey important ideas when it ruled in favor of a film distributor of the movie *The Miracle*, which New York had banned. *The Miracle* had been called "sacrilegious and blasphemous mockery" by the Roman Catholic Legion of Decency which sought to have it declared obscene for its biblical portrayal of Christ's virgin birth, depicting a bearded stranger portrayed by Federico Fellini seducing a deluded peasant girl, who (not knowing the consequences of sexual relations) mistakenly believes a miraculous child of divine origin has been given to her.

The Court declared motion pictures "may affect public attitudes and behavior in a variety of ways, ranging from direct espousal of a political or social doctrine to the subtle shaping of thought which characterizes all artistic expression."[71] The landmark *Miracle* decision meant filmmakers could join newspapers in enjoying full freedom of expression with the assurance that offending blasphemies would not lose constitutional protection.

Yet despite the *Miracle* decision, unfazed censorship boards continued to restrict access to movies, requiring distributors to submit their film stock reels for prior review. In *Times Film Corp. v. City of Chicago*, the Supreme Court in 1961 by the slimmest of margins upheld Chicago's authority to exercise prior review over the film *Don Juan* without offending the First and Fourteenth Amendment protections.[72] Apparently the film corporation's mistake had been to rush past the city's censorship standards, leveling a "broadside attack" against a city's right to preview films prior to their release.

Views about the cinema were changing, though. In New York, an American film importing company, Kingsley-International Pictures, had brought to the United States a French film, *L'Amant de lady Chatterley* (*Lady Chatterley's Lover*), which had been banned (Figure 10.2). Licenses were required to show movies in the state, but this one was denied for the "immoral, perverse, or lewd sexual acts" depicted in the film. The license denial was upheld by the New York Court of Appeals because of how *L'Amant de lady Chatterley* "alluringly portrays adultery as proper behavior." The U.S. Supreme Court found otherwise in 1965.[73] This time, in citing the *Miracle* case, the Court held that the state law violated "the freedom to advocate ideas which is guaranteed by the First Amendment."

Film censorship controversies were largely put to rest in the 1960s with the high court's *Freedman* rules, after Baltimore theater manager Ronald Freedman challenged censorship practices against films in his state. Maryland's law required both a license fee and a board of censors' approval prior to a movie's commercial release. Freedman refused to submit for review his film about the Irish Revolution, *Revenge at Daybreak*. He was convicted of violating Maryland's statute and he appealed. The U.S. Supreme Court ruled the government must prove a need for censorship, give prompt judicial review, and do it soon enough so an

70. *Mutual Film Corp. v. Industrial Comm'n of Ohio*, 236 U.S. 230, 242 (1915).
71. *Joseph Burstyn, Inc. v. Wilson*, 343 U.S. 495 (1952).
72. *Times Film Corp. v. City of Chicago*, 365 U.S. 43 (1961).
73. *Kingsley Int'l Pictures Corp. v. Regents of the University of the State of New York*, 380 U.S. 51 (1965).

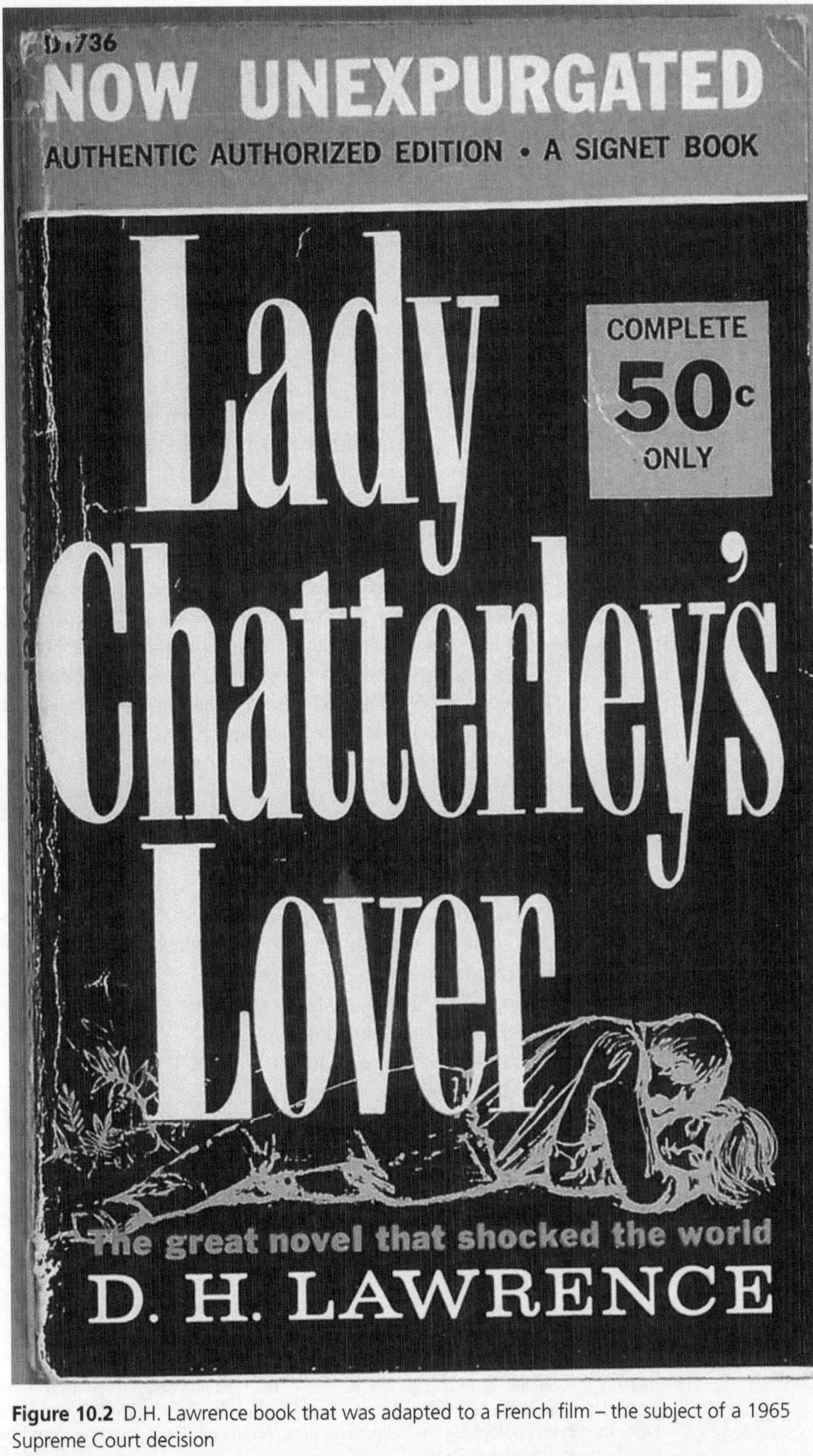

Figure 10.2 D.H. Lawrence book that was adapted to a French film – the subject of a 1965 Supreme Court decision

exhibitor could safely advertise a film's opening.[74] Justice William Brennan's opinion effectively discouraged state and city governments from practicing movie censorship.

The Rise of the Ratings System

Voluntary Self-Regulation Industry drafting of rules for itself without government oversight or enforcement.

Public demands for censorship nonetheless continued, prompting the film industry to adopt acts of **voluntary self-regulation** to stave off congressional oversight. These efforts began during the 1920s when movie makers faced an intense public outcry over the reckless behavior of Hollywood celebrities.[75] The film industry determined it needed to preempt Congress from acting against it by forming a self-governing association called the Motion Pictures Producers and Distributors Association (MPPDA), later known as the Motion Picture Association of America (MPAA), and then simply the Motion Picture Association (MPA).

The association initially adopted a strict moral code, which was eventually administered as a Production Code. But there was pushback from filmmakers and the Hollywood studios for requiring all films to obtain a certificate of approval and agree to script changes.[76] It was said, for example, that cartoon character Betty Boop had to change her dress from that of a flapper to a housewife's modest skirt.

By the mid-1960s, pressure to retreat from its rigorous stance against nudity signaled the end of the Production Code. Then president of the MPAA Jack Valenti decided not to edit words like "screw" and "hump" from the script of *Who's Afraid of Virginia Woolf*. He decided instead to classify the movie "SMA," which indicated that it was "Suggested for Mature Audiences" for its release. Thus began the association's move away from censorship and toward a voluntary ratings classification system in 1968 based on the age of suitable audience members (G, M, R, X). This led to today's MPA rating system with its classifications of G, PG-13, R, and NC-17 as a way to advise families of the nature of a film's violent and sexual content without changing or censoring its content.

What the Ratings Mean

The movie rating system offers parents three factors for judging a film's content. One of five ratings is chosen by the MPA film review board to suggest the level of caution a parent should use in determining whether it is appropriate for their children. Take, for example, a G-rated movie. The first element is a rating to indicate the motion picture is suitable for *general* audiences. The second element is the definition, indicating "all ages admitted." The third element, the descriptor, explains that a G-rated film has nothing in the way of "theme, language, nudity, sex, violence, or other matters" deemed unsuitable for children.

The MPA cautions that a G rating does not indicate either a certificate of approval or that it is a children's motion picture.

The other four ratings are

- *PG, Parental Guidance Suggested, Some Material May Not Be Suitable for Children*: "There may be some profanity and some depictions of violence or brief nudity.

74. *Freedman v. Maryland*, 380 U.S. 51, 61 (1965).
75. In 1921, Americans were enraged by reports of the rape and death of an aspiring actress involving a popular silent film comedian, Roscoe "Fatty" Arbuckle. He was tried several times and acquitted. One court even apologized for his prosecution. Yet the public was outraged and demanded Hollywood reform the film industry.
76. The code's standards banned references to sexual hygiene and venereal diseases and forbade any obscenity by "word, gesture, reference, song, joke, or by suggestion (even when likely to be understood only by part of the audience)."

But these elements are not deemed so intense as to require that parents may be strongly cautioned . . . there is not drug use content in a PG-rated motion picture."

- *PG-13, Parents Strongly Cautioned, Some Material May Be Inappropriate for Children Under 13*: "A PG-13 motion picture may go beyond the PG rating in theme, violence, nudity, sensuality, language, adult activities or other elements, but does not reach the restricted R category," according to the MPAA.
- *R, Restricted, Under 17 Requires Accompanying Parent or Adult Guardian*: "An R-rated motion picture, in the view of the Rating Board, contains some adult material . . . adult themes, adult activity, hard language, intense or persistent violence, sexually-oriented nudity, drug abuse, or other elements, so that parents are counseled to take this rating very seriously."
- *NC-17, No One 17 and Under Admitted*: An NC-17 rating means "most parents would consider patently too adult for their children 17 and under . . . (it) can be based on violence, sex, aberrational behavior, drug abuse or any other element that most parents would consider too strong and therefore off-limits for viewing by their children."

See www.filmratings.com

It bears repeating that motion picture ratings are *voluntary self-regulation*. Filmmakers are not obligated to submit their films for rating, nor are theater owners obligated to deny admission because a patron is too young based on the movie's rating.

The Classification and Ratings Administration (CARA) of the MPA handles the task of evaluating the content of 800–900 motion pictures each year for language, violence, nudity, and sexual situations unsuited for children. The ratings board is composed of between 8 and 13 parents who have no prior film industry experience and typically remain anonymous to avoid outside pressure from filmmakers. The MPA also evaluates movie advertising, including thousands of billboards, print and Internet advertisements, and radio and television spots.

Erotic Performances

Bedrock Law
Erotic dancing is deemed a form of expression entitled to some First Amendment protection.

Adult entertainment in the form of live public performances also enjoys some First Amendment protection. This includes nude dancing performed at strip clubs and sexually oriented businesses, long condemned as promoting harmful sexist culture and lowering neighborhood property values and morals. Communities across the United States have grappled with how to ban or regulate such establishments.

Of course, erotic dancing has been a provocative art form since ancient Egypt, when undulating and alluring movements exposing a dancer's navel fascinated pharaohs. The question of whether more revealing variations rose to the level of First Amendment protection was addressed in 1972. California's ABC (Alcohol Beverage Control) board was concerned that nightclubs serving drinks and featuring topless and bottomless dancers would lead to secondary effects, such as prostitution and drug use. The U.S. Supreme Court upheld California's right to prohibit such sexual acts where alcohol was served, noting the Twenty-First Amendment gave the state broad authority to control such establishments. Nude dancing did fall within the "limits of the constitutional protection of freedom of expression."[77]

77. *California v. LaRue*, 409 U.S. 109 (1972). Dissenting Justice Thurgood Marshall cast doubt on the state's secondary effects argument, claiming nude dancing must be properly identified as obscene before it loses First Amendment protection.

The subject came up again in upstate New York when city fathers of North Hempstead decided to prohibit local dancers, waitresses, and barmaids from exposing their breasts. The Supreme Court held the government had gone too far in its righteous zeal.[78] The reason was because the anti-nudity ordinance went beyond the regulation of alcohol-serving establishments to basically prohibit nudity in any and all public places. It conceivably could interfere with dance ballets or other artistic performances.

These two decisions persistently raised questions in subsequent cases in New Jersey, Indiana, Ohio, Washington, and Pennsylvania. For example, the city of Mt. Ephraim, NJ, chose to restrict the practice of coin-operated nude dancing in adult bookstores by placing this nonliterary expression beyond the city limits through zoning restrictions. Mt. Ephraim argued it was simply concerned with the attendant problems of sanitation, parking, and police protection, yet it had not imposed the same restrictions on other live-entertainment venues. Since its regulation was a ban on all nude dancing, the Court held it to be unconstitutional.[79] Nude dancing could be zoned out of neighborhoods, but not zoned out of existence.

Bedrock Law
Communities can regulate adult businesses using zoning regulations. These rules can be used to limit their location (for example, not within 1,000 feet of a church or school).

In 1991, the Supreme Court had to consider whether the First Amendment was violated by an Indiana law requiring thongs and pasties for the dancers in establishments serving alcoholic beverages. The case of *Barnes v. Glen Theater* (2000) challenged the state law on public decency that prohibited nudity in public places, including bars and other drinking establishments, but what about requiring dancers to wear g-strings and pasties? The Supreme Court found the requirement to be a minimal restriction since it did "not deprive the dance of whatever erotic message it conveys; it simply makes the message slightly less graphic."[80] A similar result was reached in *Erie v. Pap's A.M.* (2000), where even though nude dancing falls in the outer perimeter of First Amendment protection, erotic dancers could be required to wear pasties and a g-string rather than dance completely nude.[81]

The Show Me Less State

Ever since the turn of the twentieth century, Missouri's motto has been the "Show Me State," after Congressman Willard D. Vandiver declared that "frothy eloquence neither convinces nor satisfies me. I am from Missouri. You have got to show me." The legislature of Missouri, however, informed its adult entertainment industry in 2010 that it would prefer that dancers show customers *less*, at least in nightclubs.[82]

What made its law remarkable was its breadth and depth. Not only did it ban total nudity, but it prohibited females from showing breasts uncovered along a horizontal swath from the top of the areola to the lower portion of the breast and also prohibited the exposure of either anal cleft or cleavage. It further prevented dancers from coming closer than six feet to patrons, touching them or touching their clothing, along with lap or booth dances.[83]

Besides making it a crime for either male or female dancers to go beyond semi-nudity in their artistic expression, it outlawed alcoholic consumption and forced the strip clubs to close at midnight. Missouri further elected to ban strip clubs from locating within 1,000 feet of churches, schools, parks, or residential areas. Adult entertainment proponents argued the government was using a moral club to clobber a healthy part of its economy, the adult entertainment industry.

78. *Doran v. New Salem*, 422 U.S. 922 (1975).
79. *Schad v. Mt. Ephraim*, 452 U.S. 61 (1981).
80. *Barnes v. Glen Theater*, 501 U.S. 560, 571 (1991).
81. 529 U.S. 277 (2000).
82. Chris Blank, "Missouri Governor Bans Nudity, Alcohol at Strip Clubs," *Associated Press*, August 10, 2010, *at* www.columbiamissourian.com/news/missouri-governor-bans-nudity-alcohol-at-strip-clubs/article_a148aba0-48c3-5254-9edb-b2aee62a7c79.html.
83. MO Rev Stat §§ 573.528 (8), 573.528 (12), and 573.531.4.

A similar law was struck down in Missouri in 2005. But despite challenges by adult business owners and others, the Missouri Supreme Court in 2011 upheld the strip club restrictions, considered among the most comprehensive in the nation.[84]

Phone Sex Crimes

Telephones have long provided an opportunity to share and engage in pornographic and indecent content. The first phone sex line, for example, was reportedly launched in 1977 by adult entertainer Gloria Leonard, who as publisher of the erotic magazine *High Society*, wanted to promote the magazine to her readers.[85] She started by recording her own voice teasing the magazine's content to anyone willing to make a seven-cent call to a "dial-it" number. Revenues took off, and an unregulated industry was born. Complaints and concerns soon erupted and demands for regulation quickly intensified.

By 1988, Congress acted to ban indecent and obscene commercial phone messages by amending the Communications Act of 1934. This "**Dial-a Porn Law**" effectively put out of business operators who would sexually titillate callers with their conversation, which was the stock in trade of Sable Communications of California. A district court judge upheld the ban on obscene messages but not on *indecent* conversations. The U.S. Supreme Court followed suit and held in 1989 that so long as the conversations were merely indecent rather than obscene, the First Amendment protected such commercial communications.[86]

Sexting

The mobile phone introduced new ways of conveying young people's attraction for each other. In what might be called an extreme form of flirtation, the sharing of sexually explicit images and words between mobile phone users gave way to laws concerning *sexting*. This form of communication first became popular among teens around 2005, raising a legal problem for countries where child pornography laws forbid explicit sexual images of minors. Charges of child pornography – both the distribution and possession of it – were soon filed against adults and minors in possession of mobile phones containing sexually explicit words and images.

In the United States, sexting is not illegal when it involves consenting adults, but federal and state child pornography laws are invoked when the exchange involves a minor. This is true even if the sexting is initiated by the minor. In many states, sexting with a minor is considered a *strict liability*, meaning a person is liable regardless of their intent or mental state when sexting, including believing the minor was an adult at the time.[87] Merely receiving a sexually explicit message is not a violation, however. Sexting laws only prohibit the "receiving and keeping" of sexts, meaning the recipient is only liable for child porn possession if they subsequently retain or save the inappropriate image to their mobile phone or digital device.

Minors sexting other minors is also illegal but subject to different state laws. For example, Connecticut punishes teens between the ages of 13 and 15 for sending inappropriate

84. "Mo. Supreme Court Upholds Strip Club Restrictions," *Associated Press*, November 15, 2011, *at* www.joplinglobe.com/news/local_news/mo-supreme-court-upholds-strip-club-restrictions/article_31f714fa-276c-58b9-a49b-da7e5bff5faa.html.
85. Stephanie Buck, "This Feminist Single Mom Invented the Phone Sex Business in the 1970s," *Timeline*, February 7, 2017, *at* https://timeline.com/gloria-leonard-phone-sex-39846a484d51.
86. *Sable Communications v. FCC*, 492 U.S. 115, 126 (1989).
87. Suren, "Is Sexting Illegal?" *Mobicip*, February 17, 2021, *at* www.mobicip.com/blog/sexting-laws.

images of themselves, and those in the age group of 13 to 17 for receiving and not reporting the images.[88] Texas prohibits minors sexting unless they are dating and their difference in age is no more than two years. Penalties for juveniles engaged in sexting also vary by state, with some imposing a warning, fine, detention, probation, community service, or counseling.

The American Civil Liberties Union in 2009 filed a lawsuit in Pennsylvania against a district attorney who threatened to proceed with the prosecution of several teenage girls on child pornography charges if they did not enter a counseling program to cure their habits. The girls shared by mobile phone their personal seminude photos in bras and bath towels. High school officials in Tunkhannock, PA, confiscated the pictures from student mobile phones, and 14 girls entered a counseling program while three others refused. Prosecutor George Skumanick threatened the holdouts but was enjoined from proceeding with child pornography charges against them by the Third Circuit Court of Appeals.[89]

Still, the question of whether such legal actions constituted a correct application of the law remained. Writing for the American Bar Association, Hannah Geyer recommended a *Romeo and Juliet* exception should be enacted. Juveniles of about the same age who sext each other should not fear criminal prosecution, particularly for child pornography, she reasoned.[90]

Revenge Porn

Revenge porn is a more recent legal concern where, as the name suggests, a pornographic image or video of someone is intentionally shared without their consent in an act of retaliation or extortion. This might occur in anger over a bad breakup, as a means to extort money, or even to blackmail the victim into supplying more sexually explicit images. The intent is to humiliate and intimidate the victim whose reputation is threatened.

Not all revenge porn is motivated by revenge or any personal feelings toward the victim, however. In some cases, the motive may be notoriety, profit, or perverse entertainment. For this reason, other terms, such as "nonconsensual pornography" (NCP), are suggested to better define the distribution of sexually graphic images of an individual without consent.[91] Yet often the motive is to annoy or harass an unsuspecting victim. In that case, revenge porn is thought of as a form of cyber sexual harassment, or even "cyberbullying."

Revenge porn incidents have gained considerable attention, affecting celebrities such as Jennifer Lawrence and Taylor Swift who now must endure pornographic AI-generated images of them. An increasing number of civil lawsuits have been filed, including one that resulted in one of the largest judgments to date – $1.2 billion, awarded to a Texas woman in a case against her former boyfriend in 2023.[92] When the couple had officially ended their relationship, the woman identified only as D.L. told her ex-boyfriend Marques Jamal Jackson she no longer wanted him to have access to "visual intimate material" of her. He retaliated by sending intimate images of her to her family, friends, and coworkers from fake online accounts over several social media platforms and websites, including a porn site. Jackson also identified D.L. and even tagged accounts for her personal gym and her employer. D.L. sued, claiming the revenge porn had psychologically and sexually abused her. Much of the jury award – $1 billion – was for punitive damages.

88. *Id.* This gives a state-by-state list of links to sexting-related rules as provided by the Cyberbullying Research Center.
89. *Miller v. Skumanick*, 605 F. Supp. 2d 634, 637 (M.D. Pa. 2009).
90. Hannah Geyer, "Sexting: The Ineffectiveness of Child Pornography Laws," *Juvenile Justice e-Newsletter*, June 2009, *at* www.abanet.org/crimjust/juvjust/newsletterjune09/june09/sexting.htm.
91. "48 States + DC + One Territory Now Have Revenge Porn Laws," *Cyber Civil Rights Initiative*, *at* www.cybercivilrights.org/revenge-porn-laws/.
92. Amanda Holpuch, "Woman is Awarded $1.2 Billion in 'Revenge Porn' Lawsuit," *New York Times*, August 15, 2023, *at* https://www.nytimes.com/2023/08/15/us/houston-texas-revenge-porn.html.

In the wake of increasing incidents and lawsuits, nearly all states have passed legislation[93] outlawing the practice.[94] These laws may be specific to revenge porn or amendments to existing digital laws governing child pornography, harassment, and the like. They vary in their particulars with some states like North Carolina classifying it as a felony, while others such as Maryland define it as a misdemeanor. Utah considers the first offense a misdemeanor and repeat offenses to be felonies.

In general, such laws require the publishing or distributing of an image that is sexual in nature, revealing an intimate body part or engagement in a sexual act. The image must have been shared by one of the parties without consent of the other, violating an understanding between the parties regarding the privacy of the image. Intent to cause harm is often required, and in some states, the victim must also have suffered serious emotional distress that the distributor of the image intended to cause.[95]

There is no specific federal law against revenge porn; a 2016 effort at federal legislation was unsuccessful. But in 2022, Congress created a federal civil cause of action for revenge porn victims. Compensatory and punitive damages as well as attorney fees may be sought.[96]

Revenge Porn
Posting sexually explicit or revealing pictures online without the consent of the subject, usually as revenge after a breakup. Often referred to as nonconsensual pornography.[99]

Free speech advocates objected to revenge porn laws on First Amendment grounds. The U.S. Supreme Court has not directly ruled on those constitutional challenges, but five states – Illinois, Indiana, Minnesota, Texas and Vermont – have adjudicated their states' revenge porn laws.[97] Concluding their laws prohibit more than just obscenity, courts in all five states ultimately rejected the First Amendment claims and found the laws passed strict scrutiny by serving compelling government interests in protecting privacy and preventing the psychological and reputational harms from public disclosure of intimate images. The state courts also found the laws were narrowly tailored and used the least restrictive means for achieving those ends.

With the proliferation of artificial intelligence (AI) software, deep fakes provide another variant of revenge porn. Faces, usually of celebrities, are digitally stitched onto pornographic pictures or videos. As of 2024, 10 states made deepfake pornography illegal.[98]

Video Game Ratings

Ever since the Columbine school massacre of 1999, when teenagers Eric Harris and Dylan Klebold, who were obsessed with the video game "Doom," killed 12 students and one teacher in Colorado, there has been public concern over video game violence. From Europe to Asia, from the United States to the United Kingdom, dozens of violent and lethal acts have been linked to the inspiration of video games with names like "Grand Theft Auto," "Mortal Kombat," "Warcraft," "Manhunt," and "Halo," just to name a few. Whenever a spectacular act of violence occurs and authorities suggest a link to someone's obsession with violent video games, it provokes public dismay and renewed pressure for law enforcement.

93. Massachusetts and South Carolina do not have statutes specifically addressing revenge porn although persons in those states may still be prosecuted under other statutes. *See*, "State Revenge Porn Laws," *FindLaw*, October 23, 2023, *at* www.findlaw.com/criminal/criminal-charges/revenge-porn-laws-by-state.html.
94. *Id.* This site provides links to individual state revenge porn laws.
95. *Id.*
96. *Id.*
97. "Federal Civil Action for Disclosure of Intimate Images: Free Speech Considerations," *Congressional Research Service*, April 1, 2022, *at* https://crsreports.congress.gov/product/pdf/LSB/LSB10723.
98. "Can Taylor Swift Sue Over Deepfake Porn Images? US Laws Make Justice Elusive for Victims," *USA Today*, January 26, 2024. The states are California, Florida, Georgia, Hawaii, Illinois, Minnesota, New York, Texas, South Dakota, and Virginia.
99. The Cyber Civil Rights Initiative advocates for the term "nonconsensual pornography," as not all perpetrators are motivated by revenge. See www.cybercivilrights.org/. While their argument is valid, we use the term revenge porn because of its more pervasive use in legal circles.

The U.S. Congress first called hearings on the issue in 1992–1993 to discuss possible solutions to the violent influence of gaming. The entertainment software industry was encouraged to devise some sort of rating system to restrict the sale of violent video games to minors. Video game manufacturers such as Sega Inc. and 3-DO formed their own rating groups in response to the congressional hearings, but they were eventually phased out and replaced by the Entertainment Software Rating Board (ESRB) that was approved by Congress in 1994.

The ESRB initially established five levels of game suitability based on levels of maturity beginning with "Early Childhood," "Kids-to-Adults" (replaced with "Everyone" in 1998), "Teen," "Mature," and "Adults Only." Later, precise ages were added to the labels, including "10+" for "Everyone." Critics have charged the ESRB has not been sensitive enough in certain game ratings and too quick to award the M rating for Mature, when the video game violence deserved an "Adults Only" (AO) label.

Some games have gone back into production to temper their content and achieve an M rather than an AO rating. For example, one game titled "Mass Effect" contained two sexual scenes but was awarded an M rating that created some controversy among conservative critics. The ESRB points out that video game producers do not qualify as video game raters, who instead come from various sectors of society, including educators, parents, and professionals but not the interactive entertainment industry.

In 2005, the California legislature decided to put some teeth into its video gaming ratings by enacting a law to punish retailers who rent and sell video games without checking the purchaser's age to see if they meet the restriction of an M or AO rating. The law was quickly challenged by the video game industry, which succeeded in having it overturned, although Gov. Schwarzenegger appealed to the federal Ninth Circuit district court and lost there as well.

California defended its legislative restriction on First Amendment grounds, arguing violent games are comparable to sexually indecent materials that the Court has held can be legally restricted from sale to minors. At least a half-dozen other states passed similar laws, although they too were struck down on First Amendment grounds.

The U.S. Supreme Court agreed to hear the case of *Schwarzenegger v. Entertainment Merchants Association* in 2010. The action movie star-turned-governor cited studies that showed a link between playing ultra-violent video games and violent behavior. "We have a responsibility to our kids and our communities to protect against the effects of games that depict ultra-violent actions."[100] Yet a large contingent of psychologists and medical researchers disputed the claim of a causal link between video game violence and adolescent aggression. The California law used a three-prong test similar to the obscenity construction in *Miller* to define the type of offensive violence it would limit to adult purchase of video games.

The Supreme Court ruled 7–2 to strike down laws seeking to ban any video game sales to teenagers or younger. The 2011 case was now known as *Brown, et al. v. Entertainment Merchants Assn. et al.*, after Jerry Brown was elected governor and therefore defender of California statutes. Writing for the majority, Justice Antonin Scalia digressed into references to Grimm's Fairy Tales and Hansel and Gretel in his defense of video games like "Mortal Kombat." Two dissenting justices, Clarence Thomas and Stephen Breyer, who favored the California law that imposed a fine of $1,000 for selling violent video games to anyone under 18, believed protecting minors from interactive, hands-on video violence was within the First Amendment's reach as shown in the Ginsberg case establishing variable obscenity. The

100. Jesse J. Holland, "Top Court to Rule on State Video Game Regulation," *NBC News.com/ Associated Press*, April 26, 2010, *at* www.nbcnews.com/id/36779537/ns/technology_and_science-games/t/top-court-rule-state-video-game-regulation/#.WVEEgBPyvjA.

Entertainment Merchants Association representing a multibillion-dollar industry strongly disagreed and won a decisive victory.[101]

Crush Videos

The video games decision in *Brown* followed another victory related to obscenity law based on the landmark *Ferber* decision against fetishes viewed as perversion.[102] In this case, the high court struck down a federal law directed at commercial trafficking of so-called crush videos, which appeal to the fetish of watching the cruel death of animals. The Supreme Court was concerned with the law's wording that included terms like "wounding" and "killed" that could possibly criminalize hunting videos and other types of protected speech.[103]

After this ruling, the statute's author, Rep. Elton Gallegly (R-Calif.), introduced a more carefully crafted law, the Animal Crush Video Prohibition Act of 2010, which President Obama signed into law.[104] In 2014, the federal Fifth Circuit affirmed its constitutionality in *United States v. Richard, et al.*, which upheld the conviction of Ashley Nicole Richards, who was videotaped binding small animals (kitten, puppy, and rooster), then sticking her shoe heels into them, chopping off their limbs and ripping off their heads. The circuit court upheld the constitutionality of the new law.[105]

Global View: Pornography Around the World

Different countries view and treat the publication and distribution of pornography differently as a legal issue. Some censor it on the Internet, for example, while others consider pornographic material to be a form of free speech that deserves some level of protection that also varies. Even the treatment of obscenity and child pornography differs, with some countries levying the highest level of censorship and others not prohibiting it. These differences have global consequences, as pornography finds a safe haven in low-censorship countries but then crosses international borders via the Internet.

Not surprisingly, the level of censorship corresponds with a country's overall human and press freedom rankings.[106] North Korea has the highest censorship of any country, where everything flowing in and out of the country is censored by the government, and pornography is not allowed.[107] China and Iran also prohibit and censor pornography, even when delivered over virtual private networks (VPN). Yet other Muslim-majority countries, such as Türkiye, Pakistan, Oman, Eritrea, and the United Arab Emirates, will block access to pornography to protect Islamic values, but apparently not when accessed over VPNs.[108] Russia presents an interesting case in which VPNs and some pornographic websites are blocked, but in general, while producing pornography is illegal, viewing it is not.

101. *Brown, et al. v. Entertainment Merchants Assn. et al.*, 564 U.S. 786 (2011).
102. *New York v. Ferber*.
103. *See* 559 U.S. 460 (2010) and 18 U.S.C. § 48.
104. Congress revised the law to make it a crime to knowingly create, sell, market, advertise, exchange, or distribute an animal crush video that 1) depicts actual conduct in which one or more nonhuman animals is intentionally crushed, burned, drowned, suffocated, impaled, or otherwise subjected to serious bodily injury and 2) is obscene. 18 U.S.C. § 48 (2010).
105. *United States v. Richard*, Justice, No. 15–10895 (5th Cir. 2016).
106. *See, e.g.*, "2021 World Press Freedom Index: Data of Press Freedom Ranking 2021," *Reporters without Borders*, *at* https://rsf.org/en/ranking_table; Ian Vásquez & Fred McMahon, "Human Freedom Index," *CATO Institute*, *at* www.cato.org/human-freedom-index/2020.
107. "Countries Where Porn Is Illegal 2021," *World Population Review*, *at* https://worldpopulationreview.com/country-rankings/countries-where-porn-is-illegal.
108. *Id.*

Countries with greater freedoms will also constrain the distribution of and access to pornography, although to a lesser extent. Australia and the United Kingdom, for example, permit the use of VPNs while otherwise restricting access to pornography in order to protect the safety of children.[109] The United Kingdom, in fact, passed but has yet to enforce a "porn block" system, which requires every porn website to direct visitors from a UK IP address to a landing page that verifies the visitor is at least 18 years old, or face a hefty fine.[110]

Yet while the protection of children is often a justification for the regulation of pornography, a study of Interpol member countries has found that more than half have no laws addressing child pornography at all.[111] The study found that in 138 countries, possession of child pornography is not a crime. And in 122 countries, there is no law that specifically addresses the distribution of child pornography over the Internet.

Only 22 countries have laws in compliance with standards set by the International Centre for Missing & Exploited Children (ICMEC). They include Hong Kong, Germany, France, Peru, Romania, and the United Kingdom. Just five have laws considered comprehensive enough to significantly affect crime: Australia, Belgium, France, South Africa, and the United States.

Still, countries such as the United States, which recognize rights of free speech and view porn regulation as a violation of individual freedoms, are among those hosting most of the world's Internet pornography. In fact, the United States hosts a whopping 60% of it.[112] The world's most visited adult website is Canada's *Pornhub* followed by France's popular *Xvideos* and *Xnxx*. Operating out of Cyprus is fourth-ranked *Xhamster*, with the UK's *OnlyFans* coming in fifth.[113]

Low-censorship rules are also the reason controversial sites such as *8chan* (or *8kun*) intentionally choose to operate from a less-restrictive United States when otherwise prohibited in countries such as Japan and the Philippines.[114] The image board website *8chan* permits anonymous users to post anything, no matter how violent or obscene. Some countries such as Australia and New Zealand block access to the site.

Summary

- The British common law considered sexually provocative literature worthy of punishment. An English magistrate's ruling in 1868 was adopted as the *Hicklin* rule in the United States. It defined material tending to "deprave and corrupt those whose minds are open to such influences" as obscene, and Americans came to judge as criminal creative works that were in whole or in part a sexual lure for the most susceptible people.
- The U.S. Supreme Court began to look anew at the crime of obscenity, including marketing and owning it, not just by scrutinizing offensive passages but by judging the work

109. *Id.*
110. Matt Burgess, "The UK Porn Block, Explained," *Wired*, October 16, 2019, *at* www.wired.co.uk/article/porn-block-uk-wired-explains.
111. "New Study Reveals Child Pornography Not a Crime in Most Countries," *International Centre for Missing & Exploited Children*, *at* www.icmec.org/press/new-study-reveals-child-pornography-not-a-crime-in-most-countries/.
112. Jessie Merriam, "Regulate Pornography: See Centuries of State Obscenity Laws," *National Review*, December 23, 2019, *at* www.nationalreview.com/2019/12/pornography-regulation-state-obscenity-laws/.
113. For a listing of all adult industry websites worldwide, *see* Open Trends, "Explore the World's Most Visited Websites," *Semrush.com*, December 2023, *at* https://www.semrush.com/trending-websites/global/adult.
114. Bhaskar Sunkara, "Fredrick Brennan Is the Founder of 8chan: Now He Wants to Take It Offline," *Jacobin*, April 20, 2021, *at* www.jacobinmag.com/2021/04/fredrick-brennan-8chan-internet-4chan-qanon.

in its entirety. In the landmark case of *Miller v. California* following the predecessors of *Roth* and *Memoirs*, the high court crafted a test that required suspect material to appeal to the prurient interest and to be, by contemporary community standards, patently offensive to an average person, not a person of extreme sexual interests or aversions. The material further had to be shown to be without serious literary, artistic, political, or scientific value.

- The laws against obscenity cover not only owning sexually offensive material but also advertising and marketing it, which is known as pandering. Landmark cases involving the mail-order sale of pornography have shaped both the U.S. law's definition and approach to obscenity, which was further challenged by the Internet's wide distribution of pornography.
- Under the principle of variable obscenity, government can punish the sale or distribution to minors – young people under 18 years old – of pornography that has not been declared as obscene under the *Miller* test.
- Child pornography is considered to be of such significant harm to minors that Congress and the courts have criminalized its possession and sale without requiring that it be judged by the standards of the *Miller* test.
- Congress has passed several laws to restrict the access to Internet pornography, some of which have been struck down as unconstitutional if they encroach upon the free expression of adults who wish to exchange ideas about sexual activities online. In 2003, the Supreme Court upheld the Children's Internet Protection Act, which requires public libraries to block access to online pornography that would be harmful viewing for children or offensive to other patrons. The Court held that a public forum analysis did not apply in this instance, and libraries that felt filters for pornography infringed on free expression could simply refuse federal funds to overcome the law's effect.
- Nude dancing in local bars and night clubs is given some First Amendment breathing room, but the mixed set of rulings in this area also upholds the government's right to deal differently with drinking establishments and address the secondary effects of crime, prostitution, and drug abuse in its ordinances.
- U.S. law recognizes different standards based on the different media channels used. Cinema was subjected to censorship boards, but that gave way to a self-regulated classification system.
- Broadcast stations are forbidden from airing profane or indecent content at certain hours of the day, outside a "safe harbor." This is defined as "language or material that, in context, depicts or describes, in terms patently offensive as measured by contemporary community standards for the broadcast medium, sexual or excretory organs or activities."
- Several states have recognized the potential harm of selling sexual and violent content in video games to young people and enacted laws to prevent it, but several statutes have been overturned as unconstitutional.
- Laws restricting sexually explicit content over phones have been found unconstitutional, although sexting that involves a minor violates child pornography laws. Revenge porn laws are now in nearly all states but may be challenged as unconstitutional.

Ethical Dilemmas: Violating Expected Norms

Justice Scalia used his best Latin in *Pope v. Illinois* to remind his brethren that in matters of taste, there can be no disputes: *De gustibus non est disputandum*. Yet disputes of moral values are inevitable when reasonable people judge profanity, negative depictions of family life or mocking matters of religious faith, all of which were unacceptable at one time on the U.S. broadcast airwaves.

The Code of Practices for Television Broadcasters, known as the Television Code, prohibited such programming along with other offenses such as negative portrayals of police, scenes of illicit sex, intoxication, or use of horror for the sake of scaring viewers. Abiding by these limits on programming won broadcasters a "Seal of Good Practice," but a Justice Department settlement in 1983 put an end to ethical restrictions, and those seals are gone now.

In the early days of television, the least objectionable programming was the network rule of thumb, but in a blizzard of channel choices, that "lop" strategy was turned on its head. Conservative watchdog groups who track indecent references in primetime television argue that moral ethics have been replaced by the drive to "push the envelope" and give the audience as much sensational content as possible to cut through the clutter.

Communication scholar Judee Burgoon studied how violating expected norms in communication tends to arouse attention and make the source of the violation memorable. So does it normalize indecent and aggressive behavior by casting it as edgy and innovative on TV?

Reality television has used cruel insults and acts of aggression as part of its programming recipe since its early days, relying on conflict, shock, and outrage. And conservative groups waging a cultural war believe the nation has suffered as a result. In 2016, the American people elected their first reality television star as president, making the question of normalizing aggressive and insulting behavior a fair one for ethicists and media practitioners. Does any responsibility rest in part with the audience? How should writers, producers, distributors, promoters, and advertisers of such content respond?

Consider the philosophy of communitarianism, which asserts protecting political, social, and community interests supersedes individual interests, albeit without trampling on individual rights.[115] The outcome of this ethical decision-making is analyzed in light of how a certain choice affects society. Communitarian reasoning allows media practitioners to understand their institutional role and evaluate their performance against shared societal values. What are these shared societal values? What do you think should be the role of the media?

115. *See, e.g.*, Philip Patterson, Lee Wilkins & Chad Painter, *Media Ethics: Issues and Cases* (New York: Rowman & Littlefield, 2019).

11

Advertising Law

LEARNING OBJECTIVES

After reading this chapter, you should know

- how advertising's legal protections evolved to their present constitutional status
- what Supreme Court decisions established the commercial speech doctrine
- what the Central Hudson test means – what it is and how its four parts are applied
- what the Federal Trade Commission's regulations do to limit advertising expression
- how to determine if an advertisement is illegally deceptive
- how advertising claims must be substantiated
- what rules apply to testimonials and endorsements
- how other federal agencies are involved in advertising regulation
- what enforcement actions may be taken to address issues in advertising

The influencer marketing industry is booming, with more people than ever working or aspiring to work as social media influencers for brands in fashion, beauty, online gaming, and more. While some influencers are well-known celebrities, many others are lesser-known individuals – including students – with relatable content and engagement that generates a social media following. Few are getting rich, but it's seen as a great way to launch a career and supplement one's income, telling or showing followers how they like and use a particular brand.

So is the work of an influencer considered advertising, subject to any regulations? The short answer is yes, although it's not widely known. Both influencers and advertisers can face penalties if there's a lack of transparency. For example, influencers must truly like and use the product they're endorsing and make clear that they're getting paid, otherwise they're engaging in a misleading or deceptive practice. And it might also be found deceptive if they use readily available AI-powered image enhancements to retouch or augment what they're endorsing.

This chapter explores the laws pertaining to commercial speech and how they're used in advertising and public relations. Federal Trade Commission rules for misleading and deceptive advertising are also covered, including guidelines for testimonials and endorsements, including influencer marketing.

DOI: 10.4324/9781003462989-11

Regulating Commercial Speech

Advertising for any product or service imaginable appears just about everywhere these days. Advertising, after all, is considered **commercial speech**, which means it is a protected form of expression. But this was not always the case. It was quite different decades ago when the Supreme Court took two advertising cases both involving health and medical services.

Prior to the 1973 Supreme Court decision[1] guaranteeing women a right to an abortion, each state enforced its own laws against abortions. While some states had no regulation, others simply made the procedure illegal. In the Commonwealth of Virginia, not only was the procedure of abortion illegal but publishing information "encouraging" an abortion was also against the law. On February 8, 1971, the *Virginia Weekly* ran an advertisement for a New York center assisting women who sought an abortion where such services were legal. The newspaper was sold to students at the University of Virginia.

The managing editor of the newspaper, Jeffrey Bigelow, was charged with violating an 1878 statute making it a crime to encourage abortions through advertisements or other means. Bigelow was found guilty, and his conviction was affirmed as an acceptable use of the state's power by the Virginia Supreme Court "to ensure that pregnant women in Virginia who decided to have abortions come to their decisions without the commercial advertising pressure usually incidental to the sale of a box of soap powder."[2]

The U.S. Supreme Court, however, overturned the Virginia court's ruling in 1975. In *Bigelow v. Virginia*, the Court found the state's interest in shielding pregnant women from abortion advertising was outweighed by the First Amendment.[3] For the first time, the Court affirmed that at least some commercial advertising should receive constitutional protection, even though it was "commercial" speech.

Historically, the courts held commercial speech was entitled to less protection from regulation than other forms of expression – most notably, political speech found at the core of the First Amendment. But this ruling made it clear that less protection is not the same as no protection. In declaring advertising worthy of safeguarding, the Court referenced *New York Times v. Sullivan*, where a political ad's purpose may have been commercial, but it still "conveyed information of potential interest and value to a diverse audience."[4] Because advertising is rarely if ever exclusively about a commercial transaction, its implications for the marketplace of ideas must be considered. "The relationship of speech to the marketplace of products or of services does not make it valueless in the marketplace of ideas."[5]

A second Virginia case then went a step further the next year, taking up the issue of advertising prices in *Virginia State Board of Pharmacy v. Virginia Citizens Consumer Council*.[6] The concern was a Virginia law passed in 1968 prohibiting the listing of prescription drug prices. The Virginia Board of Pharmacy considered it unprofessional conduct if a pharmacist "publishes, advertises or promotes, directly or indirectly, in any manner whatsoever, any amount, price, fee, premium, discount, rebate or credit terms . . . for any drugs which may be dispensed only by prescription."[7] Virginia's law was challenged in 1974 when the Virginia Citizens Consumer Council, the Virginia AFL-CIO, and a patient who took daily prescription medication sued the pharmacist organization in federal district court.

Despite the fact similar laws had been repealed in other states,[8] the Commonwealth of Virginia argued advertising of this sort should be under its control. As a licensed profession, the pharmacist's work is subject to review by a state board with duties that include

1. *Roe v. Wade*, 410 U.S. 113 (1973).
2. *Bigelow v. Commonwealth*, 213 Va. 191, 196 (1972).
3. 421 U.S. 809 (1975).
4. *Id.* at 822.
5. *Id.* at 826.
6. 425 U.S. 748 (1976).
7. *Id.* at 750.
8. Florida in 1968, Pennsylvania in 1971, and Maryland in 1973.

"maintaining the integrity" of pharmaceutical services. After all, the law already sustained one challenge by a drug company in 1969.[9]

What was different this time was the interest of the plaintiff. When the drug company challenged the constitutionality of the Virginia regulation, the Court abided by earlier rulings that gave limited protection to commercial speech, balancing it against the state's interests. Drug companies wanting to advertise their prices were prevented due to the professional concerns of pharmacists. But when it came to the *consumer's* right to learn the comparative pricing of prescription medication, the equation changed. The Court recognized the health-care interest that was at stake. The federal district court ruled in favor of the drug consumers, and the Supreme Court affirmed the decision.

The Court explained how the distinctions and differences in prescription pricing from one pharmacy to another merited public access to such information. As such, consumers had a vested interest in obtaining prices to compare costs and make their decision. The Court made it clear such speech was not unprotected simply because it was commercial in nature, even if the speaker's interest was "purely economic," with no value to a marketplace of ideas. Oftentimes this type of information is of greater interest to citizens. The Court wrote,

> Advertising, however tasteless and excessive it sometimes may seem, is nonetheless dissemination of information as to who is producing and ***selling what product, for what purpose, and at what price*** (emphasis added). So long as we preserve a predominantly free enterprise economy, the allocation of our resources in large measure will be made through numerous private economic decisions. It is a matter of public interest that those decisions, in the aggregate, be intelligent and well informed. To this end, the free flow of commercial information is indispensable.[10]

The *Virginia Board of Pharmacy* landmark case provides a framework for understanding how commercial speech is protected speech because it provides information consumers want, even if the information is simply the price. Governments (city, state, or federal) cannot restrict advertising with some vague assertion their doing so is in the public's best interest. Even so, this does not mean there can be no restrictions on advertising content. Subsequent decisions explain how commercial speech may or may not be regulated.

Roots of Advertising Regulation

Although never explicitly overruled, but certainly revised, constitutional scholars find the Supreme Court's ruling in *Valentine v. Chrestensen*[11] to be a good starting point for examining the commercial speech doctrine's legacy. *Valentine* was the first case in which the Court explicitly addressed commercial speech. In that case, the Court upheld a New York City ordinance prohibiting the distribution of advertising handbills along the city's port side to reduce littering in the port. F.J. Chrestensen wanted to promote the fact that his U.S. Navy submarine, a "Fighting Monster!", was in the port available for tours for 25 cents per person.

To evade the rule, Chrestensen reprinted his handbills with his advertisement on one side and a protest of the antilittering rule on the reverse. He maintained his submarine handbill was not purely commercial speech because he published a political statement and consequently should be entitled to First Amendment protection. The U.S. Supreme Court thought otherwise, concluding his "political speech" was simply a form of subterfuge for what in effect was advertising and thus not entitled to protection. "We are equally clear that the

9. *Patterson Drug Co. v. Kingery*, 305 F. Supp. 821 (W.D. Va. 1969).
10. 425 U.S. at 765.
11. 316 U.S. 52 (1942).

Constitution imposes no such restraint on government as respects purely commercial advertising,"[12] declared Justice Owen Roberts, placing commercial speech beyond First Amendment protection.

In subsequent cases, the Supreme Court revisited the *Valentine* rationale and limited its precedent-setting influence. In 1964, for example, advertising was given constitutional protection in *New York Times v. Sullivan*. Recall that an Alabama police commissioner filed suit against the *Times* for an advertisement he considered libelous. L.B. Sullivan won damages for defamation at the state level and held to the belief that this advertisement was lacking First Amendment protection, citing *Valentine* as precedent, but the unanimous Supreme Court disagreed. "That the *Times* was paid for publishing the advertisement is as immaterial in this connection as is the fact that newspapers and books are sold."[13] Thus, the Court began to rewrite the broad shorthand of *Valentine* and added breathing room for commercial speech.

No Discriminatory Ads

As the courts were defining the First Amendment's position with respect to commercial speech, the issue of discriminatory advertising arose. In 1969, the National Organization for Women (NOW) filed a suit against the Pittsburgh Commission on Human Relations. The city of Pittsburgh had an ordinance that prohibited discrimination in hiring by gender, yet the *Pittsburgh Press* continued to segregate classified ads under "Help Wanted Male" and "Help Wanted Female" categories. NOW demanded the commission closely examine such advertising, and the agency ruled the words were in violation of the city's ordinance. The *Pittsburgh Press* asked the Supreme Court to strike down the rule on First Amendment grounds but came away disappointed.

In a 5–4 ruling, the Court held the newspaper could be censored from using discriminatory designations in its advertisements.[14] In weighing the newspaper's First Amendment rights against the public's interest in curbing gender-based discrimination, the Court narrowly sided with the latter.

Commercial Speech Redefined

Although the Supreme Court designated commercial speech a "subordinate position in a scale of First Amendment values," it has not always applied the same definition to what constitutes commercial speech. In *Bates v. Arizona State Bar* (1977),[15] the Supreme Court ruled that a state rule against lawyer advertising was outdated and served only to create entry barriers for new lawyers seeking to challenge the dominance of established law firms. Yet one year later in *Ohralik v. Ohio State Bar Association*,[16] the Supreme Court held a lawyer's solicitation is not the same as "truthful advertising about the availability and terms of routine legal services." The Court later used a three-part formula in *Bolger v. Youngs Drug Products*[17] to identify commercial messages based on their *advertising format*, reference to a *specific product*, and *economic motivation*. Another case in 1985 defined commercial speech as communication that does "no more than propose a commercial transaction" or is "solely motivated by the desire for profit."[18]

12. *Id.* at 54.
13. 376 U.S. at 266.
14. *Pittsburgh Press Co. v. Pittsburgh Commission on Human Relations*, 413 U.S. 376 (1973).
15. 433 U.S. 350.
16. 436 U.S. 447 (1978).
17. 463 U.S. 60 (1983).
18. *Dun & Bradstreet v. Greenmoss Builders, Inc.*, 472 U.S. 749, 762 (1985).

The Supreme Court added a twist to the commercial speech doctrine in 2011 in the data mining and marketing case of *Sorrell v. IMS Health Inc.*[19] when it ruled unconstitutional a Vermont Prescription Confidentiality law restricting the sale, disclosure, and use of data for marketing purposes taken from a prescriber's history without the doctor's permission. The pharmaceutical marketers and data mining companies felt the law violated their First Amendment rights, and the Supreme Court agreed. It held that this law was not an effective means for Vermont to protect the medical privacy of its citizens and improve public health care. Because this law restricted speech based on both the content and the identity of the speaker, it was a different sort of commercial speech that had to be put to the test of strict scrutiny. Intermediate scrutiny was insufficient. This heightened standard has been described as an intermediate scrutiny test with modifications.

Central Hudson Test
Four-part analysis used to determine the constitutionality of any law designed to restrict advertising: 1) commercial speech must not be misleading and must concern lawful activity; 2) asserted state interest promoted by the restriction must be substantial; 3) restriction must directly advance the asserted state interest; and 4) the regulation does not restrict speech any more than necessary.

The *Central Hudson* Test

In 1973, the United States was facing an energy crisis, and many communities even faced fuel shortages. In December, the New York State Public Service Commission ordered all its state's electric utility companies to curtail any advertising promoting use of electricity. Three years later, fuel shortages were no longer a problem, but the commission opted to continue this ban in the interest of energy conservation. Central Hudson Gas & Electric Corp. opposed the ban on First Amendment grounds. New York courts upheld the ban, but the U.S. Supreme Court reversed.[20] In doing so, the Court provided its landmark four-part test.

It's important at the outset to understand precisely what the *Central Hudson* test actually asks about a commercial speech rule. It establishes a sequence of probes to assess if any governmental entity (city, state, or federal; legislature; university; or commission) has unconstitutionally restricted advertising. It is not a test to judge if the advertisement is legal because it is the government's regulation that is being tested, not the advertising communication. Consider carefully each of the four parts of the test.

Part 1: Is the Commercial Speech Entitled to Protection?

Simply put, two forms of commercial speech are not protected:

- advertisements for illegal products or services
- false or misleading advertising

Regulations that restrict either of these kinds of advertisements do not create constitutional issues because the government is well within its rights to criminalize the advertising of illegal drugs, the promotion of prostitution (outside Nevada), or a host of other criminal activities. In fact, one Supreme Court decision even allowed a community to regulate advertising that was for products "marketed for use with" illegal drugs. Hoffman Estates, IL, required such shops to obtain a license, which was challenged by The Flipside, a Hoffman Estates store that sold novelty devices, including drug-related paraphernalia. The Supreme Court ruled the Village of Hoffman Estates was within its rights to require the licensing, even though the products were legal. The Court noted the drug-related items were sold alongside publications advocating the illegal use of drugs, and commercial speech for illegal products could be regulated.[21]

The examples of government regulation of false and misleading advertising are extensive and will be discussed in a later section. For now, it's important to know that the Federal

19. 564 U.S. 552 (2011).
20. *Central Hudson Gas & Electric Corp. v. Public Service Commission*, 447 U.S. 557 (1980).
21. *Village of Hoffman Estates v. Flipside*, 455 U.S. 489 (1982).

Trade Commission assigns an entire division to determine whether advertisements are misleading. If a commercial ad is not false, misleading, or promoting an illegal product or service, the second part of the test is applied.[22]

Part 2: Does the Government Have a Substantial Interest in Regulating?

Government regulations are subject to different levels of scrutiny. When discussing political speech, for example, we refer to how strict scrutiny is applied by the Supreme Court to see if the law stands. Courts expect regulators to be able to show a compelling interest in regulating political speech. As discussed, commercial speech requires a less stringent level of protection, so the intensity of the scrutiny applied to this regulation is relaxed as well. The government can show it has a substantial or legitimate interest without much trouble. Usually, governments have a substantial interest anytime they try to protect the public. Protecting the morals of the public can be a legitimate substantial interest, for instance, as is public health and safety.

In a narrow 5–4 vote, the Supreme Court ruled Puerto Rico could prevent casino gambling advertising directed toward its citizens as a means of combating crime. The Court held in *Posadas de Puerto Rico Associates v. Tourism Co.* that "the Puerto Rico Legislature's interest in the health, safety, and welfare of its citizens constitutes a 'substantial' governmental interest."[23] This regulation was a curiosity because it allowed advertising for casinos aimed at foreign tourists and also allowed local residents to see commercial messages for hotels with casinos, but it banned casino advertising aimed at Puerto Rican residents. The decision was criticized later because it failed to show the link between the law and the health, welfare, and safety of residents when gambling for horse racing and cockfighting was promoted.[24]

If it is so easy to satisfy the second prong of the *Central Hudson* test, then why is it even necessary? Some say it is not needed; the threshold of this standard is so low that almost any substantial interest conveyed by the government would be accepted, but it is important that the law addresses a *public* concern and not merely a private interest. The third prong is tied to the second, though, and that is not so easily met.

Part 3: Does the Rule Actually Advance the Government Interest Asserted in Part 2 of the Test?

It is one thing to claim that the government has a substantial interest in protecting our health, safety, or even the aesthetic beauty of a community. It is quite another thing to prove how a regulation directly advances the stated interest. For example, if the government shows an interest in discouraging excessive alcohol consumption, it might try banning price advertising for such beverages. Rhode Island did just that with a law it passed in 1956, which was challenged on two fronts: a Rhode Island liquor store wanted to advertise in a Massachusetts newspaper (the store was in a border town), and a Rhode Island newspaper wanted to accept the Massachusetts liquor store advertisements.

22. Some law texts consider *Central Hudson* a three-part test, removing this part and focusing on the other three. There is some logic to this since this prong of the test doesn't really test the government's behavior but rather the nature of the communication. We use all four questions since the Court refers to it as a four-step analysis in *Central Hudson*. Whether the test is seen as three or four parts, the result is the same: governments are permitted to regulate false or misleading advertising as well as advertising for illegal products and services.
23. *Posadas de Puerto Rico Associates v. Tourism Co.*, 478 U.S. 328, 341 (1986).
24. Ronald D. Rotunda, "The Constitutional Future of the Bill of Rights: A Closer Look at Commercial Speech and State Aid to Religiously Affiliated Schools," 65(5) *North Carolina L. Rev*. 917–934 (1987).

When the case of *Liquormart, Inc. v. Rhode Island*[25] reached the U.S. Supreme Court in 1996, the law was struck down in part because it failed the third prong of the *Central Hudson* test, which calls for evidence the law can achieve its desired ends. The Court found a "lack of unanimity among researchers" as to whether liquor advertising affects the amount of consumption.[26] It further held that the government carries the burden of proving the regulation advances the State's interest "to a material degree."[27]

At this point, the Court departed from the earlier thinking of the *Posadas* question, where the government was given unlimited discretion in asserting a government interest.[28] When Puerto Rico asserted casino ads targeting its residents would cause an increase in gambling and harm poorer residents, the Supreme Court accepted the assertion with little or no evidence. In this sense, the Court clarified the *Central Hudson* test and would challenge claims that a regulation advanced the government's interest without concrete evidence for support.

Part 4: Is the Restriction on Expression Narrowly Drawn?

This part of the test requires the rule in question to confine its restrictions to only what is necessary, curbing no more communication than necessary to achieve the substantial goal. In the *Central Hudson* case itself, the Court determined the ban on advertising encouraging energy consumption was unconstitutional by failing to meet this standard. The State of New York had a substantial interest in energy conservation (Part 2 of the test), and the Court accepted the claim of an "immediate connection between advertising and demand for electricity" (Part 3).[29] However, the New York regulation was found to be unconstitutional because it went too far. The power company showed how this advertising rule prevented it from encouraging efficient uses of energy, such as purchasing a heat pump to improve efficiency. This would mean the regulation prohibited too much expression. What's more, the Court concluded an alternative law might permit the ads if they contained certain energy efficiency information, much as tobacco advertisements require statements about smoking's impact on health.[30]

More recent Court decisions have made it clear that a regulation does not have to be a "perfect fit" with the substantial interest but rather "narrowly drawn" to achieve the goal. It would impose quite a burden on the state to prove that every advertising regulation was the least restrictive means possible. If any petitioner could claim a scheme that would be less restrictive, the law would have to be ruled unconstitutional. The Court did not go that far.

In 1982, a representative of American Future Systems, which sold housewares to college students, was invited by a resident to hold a Tupperware party in a dormitory on the SUNY Cortland campus. But the State University of New York had a rule restricting commercial enterprises on campus. The AFS representative was asked to leave by campus police but refused and was arrested on a charge of trespassing. The representative's challenge went all the way to the U.S. Supreme Court, which applied the *Central Hudson* test. The Supreme Court refuted the district court's claim that the rule had to be the "least restrictive" measure possible to pass the *Central Hudson* test's fourth prong. Instead, only a "reasonable fit" was necessary between the "legislature's ends and the means chosen to accomplish those ends . . . not necessarily perfect, but reasonable."[31]

25. 517 U.S. 484.
26. *Id.* at 493.
27. *Id.* at 505.
28. *Id.* at 509. The Court stated, "on reflection, we are now persuaded that *Posadas* erroneously performed the First Amendment analysis."
29. 447 U.S. at 569. About the only "evidence" provided was the assertion "*Central Hudson* would not contest the advertising ban unless it believed that promotion would increase its sales. Thus, we find a direct link between the state interest in conservation and the Commission's order."
30. *Id.* at 571.
31. *Board of Trustees of the State Univ. of N.Y. v. Fox*, 492 U.S. 469, 480 (1989) (quoting *Posadas*).

Summary

Commercial speech doctrine has evolved in the twentieth and twenty-first centuries, and it is not too daring to speculate that it will continue to be defined as more cases are tried. We have moved far from the no-protection thinking of *Valentine* on commercial speech to a First Amendment position, where advertising that does no more than list prices is entitled to breathing room. The *Central Hudson* test was an attempt to strike a balance between zero protection and full protection, and its refinement in subsequent decisions continues to evolve.

The Federal Trade Commission

FTC (Federal Trade Commission) Created in 1914 to prevent monopolies and unfair methods of competition in commerce, the FTC is charged with protecting consumers and regulating advertisements. The FTC requires all advertisements be truthful, nondeceptive, and fair. It also checks for advertising evidence to back up advertisers' claims.

Public attitudes toward advertising content a century ago might be best summed up in a familiar Latin phrase: *caveat emptor*, "let the buyer beware." There was no government agency charged with protecting consumers, but in 1914 Congress approved the Federal Trade Commission Act, creating the five-member **Federal Trade Commission** (FTC).[32] Figure 11.1 shows the Commission's seal. Although today the agency enforces all sorts of

Figure 11.1 Seal of the Federal Trade Commission

32. *See* Federal Trade Commission Act, Chapter 311 of the 63rd Cong., 38 Stat. 717 (1914).

regulations on advertising to protect consumers, that wasn't the reason Congress created the FTC. The major thrust for the commission's creation was to prevent anticompetitive business practices. Monopolies and monopolistic practices were a major concern for President Woodrow Wilson early in the twentieth century.

At the outset, the FTC regulated deceptive advertising on the premise that it represented unfair competition.[33] In 1922, the agency was challenged on this belief after it ordered an underwear manufacturer to stop labeling underwear as natural wool that actually contained only 10% wool. The Supreme Court ruled that any advertising attempting to deceive consumers was in fact a form of unfair competition.[34]

It was not until 1938 that the Federal Trade Act was amended to authorize the FTC to protect consumers. The Wheeler-Lea Act decreed "unfair or deceptive acts or practices in commerce are hereby declared unlawful."[35]

Years later, Congress expanded the scope of the FTC's powers with the 1975 Magnuson-Moss Consumer Product Warranty Act.[36] This made unlawful "unfair methods of competition in or affecting commerce or unfair or deceptive acts or practices in or affecting commerce." By adding "in or affecting," Congress gave the FTC industry-wide jurisdiction over all local businesses that otherwise affect interstate commerce.

Some authority of the FTC was later reined in, however, with amendments to the FTC Act, most notably in 1980[37] and 1994.[38] The FTC became limited in its regulatory authority over certain industries, such as children's advertising, insurance, agricultural cooperatives, and the funeral industry. In particular, the commission would only be able to declare a practice unfair if it was likely to cause consumers a substantial injury they could not reasonably avoid. The FTC would also have to find outlawing an unfair practice outweighed its benefits.

The Federal Trade Commission's five members are appointed by the president and confirmed by the Senate. Members serve rotating seven-year terms[39] (so no more than one commissioner's term expires in any given year), although many leave office before completing their terms. No more than three members can come from any one political party. Generally, three commissioners come from the president's party. The president appoints the commission chair. While commissioners are the most visible part of the agency, staff members serving in divisions and bureaus of the FTC perform the day-to-day tasks of the agency. Generally, commissioners are not involved in enforcing deceptive advertising rules but leave such tasks to the commission's Bureau of Consumer Protection.

Even with a staff of about 900 employees, it is impossible for the FTC to monitor the millions of American advertisements in print, on the air, or online. The FTC relies on complaints from consumers and businesses (about competitors) to inform it of possible legal infractions.[40] Like other administrative agencies, it must also be responsive to the wishes of Congress, both explicit and implicit. Congress can pass legislation that requires action by the FTC or modifies the law, which the FTC is bound to enforce. Sometimes Congress may simply investigate without passing any legislation, but the signal is heard loud and clear at the FTC. It's important to remember that Congress controls the agency's appropriations and can vote to increase or decrease funding as it sees fit.

33. Federal Trade Commission Act, Sec. 5 [15 U.S.C. 45], prohibits unfair or deceptive practices in commerce.
34. *Federal Trade Commission v. Winsted Hosiery*, 258 U.S. 483 (1922).
35. 15 U.S.C. § 45(a)(1).
36. 15 U.S.C. § 2301 et seq.
37. Federal Trade Commission Improvement Act of 1980, Pub. L. 96–252, §23, May 28, 1980, 94 Stat. 397.
38. Federal Trade Commission Act Amendments of 1994, Pub. L. 103–312, §15, August 26, 1994, 108 Stat. 1697.
39. Agencies vary by size and length of term. The FTC's board was reduced from seven to five members as part of the Reagan administration's effort to reduce the size and scope of federal government.
40. The FTC provides a sample complaint letter at https://consumer.ftc.gov/articles/sample-customer-complaint-letter.

The commission sometimes provides industries with guidance by means of its industry "Guides" that outline what is and is not acceptable for advertising within a certain industry. Such publications offer advice and recommendations to industries and, although not the same as law, are referred to if complaints are registered against an advertiser. These include "Guides Against Bait Advertising," "Guide Concerning Fuel Economy Advertising for New Automobiles," and "Green Guides" (for substantiating environmental marketing claims).[41]

The commission goes beyond Guides when it enacts administrative law in the form of FTC rules. Unlike Guides, the rules are law and advertisers who are not in compliance can be fined. A well-known FTC rule is the 1964 decision to require cigarette companies to include health warnings in advertisements and on the packages. A 2003 FTC rule created the National Do Not Call Registry, limiting the ability of telemarketers to contact those wanting to avoid such calls.

The FTC is a quasi-judicial agency in that it not only enforces law but also has a branch responsible for hearing legal appeals to its decisions. If a company wants to contest a finding by the commission, an administrative law judge (ALJ) likely will hear the case. The ALJ's ruling could be accepted, appealed, or referred to the full commission. A ruling also can be appealed to a U.S. court of appeals.

Deceptive Advertising

Deceptive Advertising
According to the FTC's Deception Policy Statement, an ad is deceptive if it contains a statement – or omits information – that is 1) likely to mislead consumers acting reasonably under the circumstances and 2) is "material" – that is, important to a consumer's decision to buy or use the product.

One of the major tasks faced by the FTC is to act against **unfair and deceptive advertising**. Section 5 of the FTC Act declares unfair or deceptive acts or practices to be unlawful, and Section 12 specifically prohibits false ads likely to induce the purchase of food, drugs, devices, or cosmetics. Liability for deceptive advertising could be leveled against the product or service, against the advertising agency that created the disputed message or even against the media outlet carrying the message. Even though there is an explicit definition, deception still carries a degree of subjectivity.

The FTC considers a deceptive advertisement to be a **representation, omission, or practice that is likely to mislead a reasonable consumer and is material to a decision to purchase a product or service.**[42]

Be sure to notice that nowhere in this definition is there specific mention of the truth or falsity of a claim. A statement that is 100% true may be considered deceptive, while one that is false may be not deceptive. For example, in 1972, the FTC found that Ocean Spray Cranberry Juice was being deceptive when it claimed that cranberry juice contains more "food energy" than orange juice.[43] Ocean Spray never mentioned in the ad that it was defining food energy as calories, which, after all, is the source of the human body's energy. As defined, the advertisement was true, but the FTC found it to be deceptive because information was omitted that made it likely to mislead a reasonable consumer.

Conversely, an advertiser may be able to make an obviously false statement that would not be considered deceptive. For years, Red Bull Energy Drink used the slogan "Red Bull gives you wings." The TV commercials showed animated characters sprouting wings after drinking the product. This claim was demonstrably false; no one grows wings after drinking Red Bull. And yet the spot was not deceptive because no reasonable consumer would accept

41. FTC rules can be searched at https://www.ftc.gov/legal-library/browse/rules. Occasionally, the FTC will rescind its industry Guides when they outlive their usefulness, as it did in 2002 with the guides for the household furniture industry.
42. *See* FTC Policy Statement on Deception, appended to Cliffdale Associates, Inc., 103 F.T.C. 110, 174 (1984), *at* www.ftc.gov/system/files/documents/public_statements/410531/831014 deceptionstmt.pdf. Though over 40 years old, this document provides an excellent review of what constitutes deceptive practices.
43. *Ocean Spray Cranberries, et al.*, 80 F.T.C. 975 (1972).

Puffery
Hyperbole or exaggerated statements of opinion that cannot be understood as assertions of fact. They are a lawful way of promoting a product or service where no reasonable person would take the advertising claims literally or seriously.

such an outlandish claim.[44] This is what the law accepts as ***puffery***, an obviously inflated claim made in advertising but never intended to be taken seriously.

In *Pizza Hut v. Papa John's*,[45] Pizza Hut filed suit against Papa John's commercials, claiming Papa John's slogan, "Better ingredients. Better pizza" was deceptive. Pizza Hut claimed the ads were deceptive by showing Pizza Hut workers using canned sauce but did not show Papa John's using canned sauce, which they do. Pizza Hut asserted that the claim "better" in this context was deceptive, and the trial court agreed. On appeal, however, the appellate court ruled that the slogan was an example of puffery. Without a showing by Pizza Hut the ads were likely to deceive, the court decided in favor of Papa John's.

Note also that nowhere in the definition of deceptive advertising is there any mention of the intent of the advertiser. It really doesn't matter whether an advertiser purposely or accidentally deceives consumers. The FTC has gone so far as to state that advertisers must correct misleading advertising, whether intended or not.[46]

There are three criteria for defining deceptive advertising.

1 Likely to Mislead

How is it possible to know whether an advertisement is "likely to mislead"? Certainly, false advertising that would be believed by consumers (unlike puffery) is likely to mislead. Truthful advertising might also mislead, however, as evidenced by the Ocean Spray example mentioned earlier. Advertising can be likely to mislead because of information that is included or excluded. The fact that the cranberry juice ad omitted important information made it deceptive. Information might be included but in such a way as to be incomprehensible, which is also likely to mislead.

The use of technical language that might not be understood by consumers is likely to mislead, as would be disclaimers in advertisements too small to be read. Ads that have dual meanings could be considered misleading if either of the meanings is likely to mislead. Examples of practices the FTC has ruled likely to mislead include price claims (such as misleading retail, list, and former price comparisons), the inadequate disclosure of harms associated with hazardous products, the use of **bait and switch** techniques, and failure to meet the express obligations in a warranty.

Bait and Switch
A term for illegally advertising a low-priced product to entice a customer into a store only to be out of the advertised item, at which time the staff tries to pressure the customer to buy a more expensive version. The FTC prohibits "an alluring but insincere offer to sell a product or service which the advertiser in truth does not intend or want to sell."[47] To avoid such accusations, stores advertise "quantities limited" or offer rain checks.

A representation can mislead even when an advertisement's words do not. Tropicana Orange Juice once advertised that it was "pure pasteurized juice as it comes from the orange." Tropicana was in fact pure, and it was pasteurized. The problem was the television commercial showed an Olympic champion squeezing an orange and pouring the juice into a Tropicana container. The deception was the misleading visual. The juice was pasteurized, which meant that after it was extracted from the orange it was heated, but the visual showed the juice going straight from the orange to the carton. The FTC considered it a misleading representation.[48]

The FTC can "presume" a practice is likely to deceive, but in some cases, it requires evidence that an advertisement or practice is *likely* to mislead, not just a claim that it might. The commission dismissed a claim that selling unmarked products in Alaska misled consumers into believing that the products were handmade by natives. The FTC said elaborate proof was unnecessary but at least "some extrinsic testimony evidence" was needed from the

44. The FTC did act against Red Bull in 2014, but it was not for the "gives you wings" claim but rather for exaggerating the effects. Red Bull settled the claim. *See* www.truthinadvertising.org/wings-red-bull-cash/.
45. 227 F.3d 489 (5th Cir. 2000), *cert. denied*, 532 U.S. 920 (2001).
46. In addition to action by the FTC, a company can file a suit against a competitor for deceptive advertising by claiming that the deceptive advertising damages their business. Remember the FTC not only protects consumers but also prevents unfair business practices.
47. 16 C.F.R. § 238 (2008).
48. *Coca-Cola v. Tropicana*, 690 F.2d 312 (2d Cir. 1982).

complainants.[49] In determining if an advertisement is likely to mislead, the FTC often relies on expert testimony or consumer surveys.

2 Reasonable Consumer

While evidence of someone actually deceived by an advertisement helps make the case that an ad is deceptive, it might not be conclusive. If a million people see an advertisement and only one person is misled, that ad will not be considered deceptive. If a consumer is not "acting reasonably" in the circumstances, the FTC will not hold the advertiser liable for any misunderstanding. More than 50 years ago, the FTC stated,

> An advertiser cannot be charged with liability with respect to every conceivable misconception, however outlandish, to which his representations might be subject among the foolish or feeble-minded. Some people, because of ignorance or incomprehension, may be misled by even a scrupulously honest claim. Perhaps a few misguided souls believe, for example, all "Danish pastry" is made in Denmark. Is it therefore an actionable deception to advertise "Danish pastry" when it is made in this country? The answer is obviously no. A representation does not become "false and deceptive" simply because it will be unreasonably misunderstood by an insignificant and unrepresentative segment of the class of persons to whom the representation is addressed.[50]

It is possible, however, that advertising that targets a specific population might be considered deceptive to that population, in which case the commission will find it deceptive. When children's discernment skills are not as well developed as those of adults, the TV spots targeting them might be ruled deceptive even though they would not be seen as deceptive for adults. The U.S. Supreme Court has explained this doctrine. "The determination whether an advertisement is misleading requires consideration of the legal sophistication of its audience."[51] For this reason, a toy company agreed to stop showing commercials where a ballerina doll pirouetted on one toe unassisted when in fact the doll could not do so.[52]

Children are not the only unique audience. The FTC has pointed out that terminally ill patients "might be particularly susceptible to exaggerated cure claims."[53] Even weight-loss claims might be judged in part by the target audience who would be considered more susceptible to exaggerated claims. "To these corpulent consumers the promises of weight loss without dieting are the Siren's call, and advertising that heralds unrestrained consumption while muting the inevitable need for temperance, if not abstinence, simply does not pass muster," stated the commission.[54]

It also matters how a reasonable consumer interprets the entire message, not just selected words or images. Disclaimers can be effective means for fending off a claim of deception as long as those disclaimers are clearly presented and understood. Yet that can be a difficult and subjective judgment. For example, the FTC found one instance in which fine print in an advertisement was an adequate disclosure and another where it was inadequate.

Litton Industries advertised its microwave ovens in newspapers and magazines with a headline stating, "76 percent of the independent microwave oven service technicians surveyed preferred Litton." The FTC held the fine print that explained only Litton-authorized service technicians were surveyed was not enough to inform the public. On the other hand, the fine print describing "independent technicians" as those who worked on Litton and at

49. Leonard F. Porter, et al., 88 F.T.C. 546, 626 n. 5 (1976).
50. Heinz W. Kirchner, 63 F.T.C. 1282, 1290 (1963).
51. *Bates v. Arizona*, 433 U.S. 350, 383 n. 37 (1977).
52. Lewis Galoob Toys, Inc., 114 F.T.C. 187 (1991) (Consent Order).
53. FTC Policy Statement on Deception, at 174, supra note 42.
54. Porter & Dietsch, 90 F.T.C. 770, 864–865 (1977), *aff'd*, 605 F.2d 294 (7th Cir. 1979), *cert. denied*, 445 U.S. 950 (1980).

least one other brand was considered adequate notice.[55] The FTC measures its enforcement based on the hypothetical reasonable consumers to judge if they would be attentive to a particular disclaimer in terms of relative size and technical format and presumably would read it.

Native Advertising

In 2015, the FTC began to react to an innovative trend in digital advertising referred to as "native advertising." A native ad consists of content that "bears a similarity to the news, feature articles, product reviews, entertainment, and other material that surrounds it online."[56] For example, an ad for a snow blower might be presented as part of an online news story or embedded in a video about how best to remove snow. But since the ad doesn't readily appear to be an ad, are consumers being fooled? Are consumers able to differentiate the advertising from the other content?

The commission issued an Enforcement Policy Statement on Deceptively Formatted Advertisements[57] and released its "Native Advertising: A Guide for Businesses"[58] as a supplement to help businesses apply the policy. In general, the FTC will consider misleadingly formatted ads to be deceptive, even if the underlying product claims conveyed to consumers are truthful. Since an ad is deceptive if it materially misleads consumers about its commercial nature, a native ad could be deceptive if it suggests to consumers that it's from a source other than the sponsoring advertiser and materially affects those consumers who might give it weight and credibility.

The Enforcement Policy boils down to three considerations:

1 From the FTC's perspective, the watchword is transparency. An advertisement or promotional message shouldn't suggest or imply to consumers that it's anything other than an ad.
2 Some native ads may be so clearly commercial in nature they would be unlikely to mislead consumers even without a specific disclosure. In other instances, a disclosure is necessary to ensure that consumers understand what they're viewing is advertising.
3 If a disclosure is necessary to prevent deception, the disclosure must be clear and prominent.[59]

The commission is monitoring native advertising and taking action against deceptive infringers. For example, in 2020 the FTC settled a case for $22 million that involved, in part, the defendants' use of native advertising. Physician's Technology and Willow Labs sold a device called Willow Curve for the treatment of pain relief and other health benefits. The defendants hired a marketing company to write articles such as the online magazine story, "Understanding the Gender Gap in Sports Injuries and Treatments," to resemble the non-advertising content of the magazines and newspapers in which they ran. But the FTC found the articles were actually advertising for Willow Curve without being identified as advertisements, including when consumers posted or shared them on social media or in email.[60]

55. Litton Indus., 97 F.T.C. 1 (1981), *aff'd as modified*, 676 F.2d 364 (9th Cir. 1982).
56. FTC, "Native Advertising: A Guide for Businesses," December 2015, *at* www.ftc.gov/tips-advice/business-center/guidance/native-advertising-guide-businesses.
57. FTC, "Enforcement Policy Statement on Deceptively Formatted Advertisements," 2015, *at* www.ftc.gov/system/files/documents/public_statements/896923/151222deceptiveenforcement.pdf.
58. FTC, "Native Advertising," supra note 56.
59. *Id.*
60. Lesley Fair, "Lights Out on Unsubstantiated Pain Relief Claims and Deceptive Native Advertising," *FTC*, June 25, 2020, *at* https://www.ftc.gov/business-guidance/blog/2020/06/lights-out-unsubstantiated-pain-relief-claims-and-deceptive-native-advertising.

3 Material to Purchasing Decision

Deception becomes "material" if the act or practice is likely to sway the conduct or decision of consumers regarding a product or service. Individuals who buy a good or service based on deceptive advertising are also likely to suffer what is described as an *injury*. While injury may take many forms, the commission considers it an injury if consumers would have chosen a different product or service if not for the deception.

It's easy to see how most ad claims would be considered material. After all, if advertisers are trying to persuade people to purchase products, most of what they state (or omit) in their ads will be material to making a purchase decision. Express claims are presumptively material, as well as claims where the seller knew or should have known that an ordinary consumer would need omitted information to evaluate the product or service.

For example, in 1980, the FTC ruled a New York City publishing company and its Chicago subsidiary were deceptive in their advertising of correspondence courses.[61] The violations included not only omissions of information about admissions and misrepresenting the job market for graduates but also inadequate information about the costs a student would incur. The price of a product or service can be material to the purchasing decision.

Even messages that are only implied may be considered material. The FTC ruled it was deceptive for a mattress manufacturer to use a picture of a man in a white jacket next to the word *orthopedic*. This implied that the mattress had somehow been endorsed by medical professionals or in some other way had been designed for medical use.[62] Materiality will be inferred if there is evidence that a seller intended to make an implied claim.

Yet to date, no successful claims have been made against advertisers for the sort of implied messages most advertising relies on to sell products. Sex appeal has long been used to sell everything from automobiles to toothpaste, yet no ad has been found deceptive for suggesting a particular brand of beer will make a man more popular with women.[63] An unsuccessful suit was filed in California claiming minors were being deceived by tobacco ads that glamorized smoking, but the California Supreme Court rejected the claim.[64]

Of course, deception is not material if it's the sort of misinformation making little or no impact on the purchase decision. If a magazine advertisement happened to make a printing mistake and showed a perfume bottle as a different color, the ad might mislead a reasonable consumer to believe the perfume was orange when in fact it was yellow. Such a false impression would not reasonably affect a consumer's decision, so it is immaterial and therefore not deceptive.

Ads can pose a material deception in cases in which the average consumer doesn't know any better. The FTC ruled Carnation was deceptive when it claimed that its instant breakfast product contained as much "mineral nourishment as two strips of bacon."[65] The ad was deceptive because bacon provides protein, but not much in the way of minerals. A Baggies commercial was ruled deceptive because it showed that a sandwich dunked underwater and swirled in a baggie stayed dry while water seeped into a competitor's bag. The FTC held the demonstration would deceive viewers into believing the baggie was keeping food fresher, while ignoring temperature, moisture, air, and a "myriad" of other factors that affect food freshness.[66]

Mock-Up
A substitution or simulation of a product being advertised. It is generally deceptive to use an undisclosed mock-up of a product in an ad. Demonstrations must show the performance that consumers can typically expect to achieve.

Sometimes the demands of creating an advertisement require simulations or **mock-ups** to be used in advertisements. For example, if an amusement park wants to produce a television commercial, it might want to include a scene with a family eating an ice cream cone as they

61. MacMillan, Inc., 96 F.T.C. 208 (1980).
62. *In re* 2361 State Corp., 65 F.T.C. 310 (1964).
63. In 1997, the National Council on Drug Dependence and Mothers Against Drunk Driving filed an unsuccessful petition with the FCC requesting that counter-advertisements be required for alcohol advertising on television in part because of the deceptiveness toward minors of the sex appeal of the advertising.
64. *In re Tobacco Cases II*, 41 Cal. 4th 1257 (2007), *cert. denied sub nom. Daniels v. Philip Morris*, 2007 WL 4231074 (2007), *cert. denied*, 552 U.S. 1257 (2008).
65. *In re Carnation Co.*, 77 F.T.C. 1547 (1970).
66. *In re Colgate-Palmolive*, 77 F.T.C. 150 (1970).

walk through the park. If the TV spot has to be shot on a hot day, it might be difficult to get a shot without having ice cream dripping everywhere. So the production company might elect to substitute something that looks like ice cream but would not melt as fast, such as mashed potatoes. Clearly, the mock-up of an ice cream cone in an ad for the amusement park would not be material or deceptive. Consumers would not be moved to purchase tickets to the park because of the ice cream being consumed in the ad. It would be a different matter, however, if the advertisement was actually for a brand of ice cream or an ice cream shop and the substitution was not disclosed to viewers.

When a mock-up is material and deceptive, the FTC can act. An iconic illustration of a deceptive mock-up was broadcast in 1959–1960. In a TV commercial, Colgate-Palmolive's Rapid Shave shaving cream "demonstrated" how it moistened whiskers so well you could shave a piece of sandpaper clean with it. The material deception in the spot was that the televised demonstration used Plexiglas covered with sand instead of actual sandpaper. Sandpaper would have to be soaked in shaving cream for over an hour to achieve the same effect. Rapid Shave claimed it was simply using production techniques to dramatically portray to a TV audience truthful claims of how the product worked. The FTC disagreed and ruled it deceptive, and the U.S. Supreme Court affirmed the judgment.[67] The Court found the commercial purported to offer proof of a product claim that did not actually prove it.

Another type of mock-up involved the classic case of Campbell's Chicken & Stars soup. An ad featured the soup being properly prepared according to label instructions and poured into bowls. But because the noodles, vegetables, and chicken sank and mostly broth was visible from the tops of the bowls, the ad agency BBDO placed clear glass marbles at the bottom of the bowls to raise to the surface the soup contents. The FTC found this to be a deceptive mock-up because the ad misrepresented the quantity of the solid ingredients in a can of Campbell's Chicken & Stars soup.[68] The case made clear that an ad cannot visually suggest a product has a quality that it does not in fact possess.

Substantiation

One of the most common complaints brought against advertisers and their agencies is the demand that they substantiate their product claims. It is reasonable to expect if an advertisement claims a product can do something, the product must in fact be able to do what is claimed. Relatively speaking, this is easy to discern. If an advertiser claims a product "kills germs," it is scientifically simple to apply the product to a surface and measure whether the germs have been killed. If the advertising says, "9 out of 10 dentists surveyed . . ." the claim should be supported by a survey, conducted legitimately, in which 90% of the dentists responded as reported.

Factual Advertising Claims

FTC guidelines require any claims advertisers assert as factual must have a reasonable basis in proof.

The FTC will find an ad deceptive when the advertiser lacks a reasonable basis for substantiating its express and implied claims. If an advertiser makes a claim that the FTC questions, the agency may ask for proof. It is very important that advertisers have this substantiation before they disseminate their advertisements, not after.[69] While the FTC may

67. *Federal Trade Commission v. Colgate-Palmolive*, 380 U.S. 374 (1965).
68. Although it was standard practice for food stylists and prop masters to dress foods for ads in 1968, the FTC was prompted to investigate after reportedly receiving complaints from a competitor, H.J. Heinz company, and/or a consumer group formed by law students at The George Washington University that called themselves Students Opposing Unfair Practices (SOUP). After filing a consent decree, the FTC ultimately accepted the Campbell Soup Company's promise to remove the marbles from its soup advertisements in 1970.
69. FTC Policy Statement Regarding Advertising Substantiation, appended to Thompson Med. Co., 104 F.T.C. 648, 839 (1984), *aff'd*, 791 F.2d 189 (D.C. Cir. 1986), *cert. denied*, 479 U.S. 1086 (1987).

consider additional post-claim evidence under some circumstances, advertisers lacking prior substantiation violate Section 5 of the FTC Act and may be subject to adjudication.[70]

The use of certain terms in advertising can constitute a factual claim subject to substantiation. Calling a piece of furniture "antique" is a factual claim, and so is calling an automobile tire "safe." The Federal Trade Commission ruled Firestone misled customers when it claimed to be "The Safe Tire." When the FTC asked Firestone to prove its claim, the company simply asserted the tires had passed all the company's inspections, and that meant they were safe. The commission thought otherwise and ruled it as deceptive.[71]

The requirement to substantiate factual claims with valid evidence, however, does not force an advertiser to disclose all contrary data. For years Pepsi conducted "The Pepsi Challenge," in which people coming out of grocery stores were asked to blind taste Pepsi and Coke before selecting their favorite drink. The commercial only showed those who preferred Pepsi, and it did not say or imply everyone chose Pepsi.[72]

Legitimate Evidence

An advertiser cannot ask ten of their best friends if they like a product and then announce, "9 out of 10 people surveyed prefer our product." It obviously would not be a valid sampling of opinion. Making a claim people prefer a product in a "blind taste test" also requires such a test be conducted fairly. The preferred soft drink can't be served in a crystal glass while the competitor is served in a small paper cup. Conscientious advertisers usually hire research firms to conduct the independent testing of their claims.

There are acceptable ways, however, to allow advertisers to get the results they want. A lot can be done with a question's phrasing, order of items, and overall approach to solicit the "right" answers. Consider for a moment the phrase "Nine out of ten dentists surveyed recommend sugarless gum for their patients that chew gum." The phrase may seem to imply dentists recommend sugarless gum, but that's not quite right. The clause "for their patients who chew gum" qualifies it. Ninety percent of the dentists are actually agreeing with the statement "If your patient is going to chew gum no matter what, would you prefer that patient chewed sugared gum or sugarless gum?" That's quite a bit different from asking whether dentists want their patients to chew any gum. If an advertisement says, "surveys show" or "tests prove," then legitimate evidence would require results from at least two surveys or tests.

Clinically Proven?

The billions of dollars Americans spend on cosmetics may be motivated in part by commercial spots such as the familiar tagline for L'Oréal: "Because I'm worth it!" Such a claim defies legal scrutiny since its subjective nature is beyond factual verification. But when an advertisement adds the credibility of science to its claims through terms like "clinically proven," the government can get involved.

The Federal Trade Commission moved against L'Oréal USA when it felt the science was lacking in its promotion of L'Oréal Paris Youth Code. The ads spoke of a "new era of skincare: gene science" and said that consumers could "crack the code to younger acting skin." The ads labeled a bar graph "CLINICAL STUDY" to show how specific genes make skin act younger and respond to "aggressors." The issue was whether

70. *Id.*
71. Firestone, 81 F.T.C 398 (1972), *aff'd*, 481 F.2d 246 (6th Cir.), *cert. denied*, 414 U.S. 1112 (1973).
72. No deceptive advertising claim has been lodged against "the Pepsi Challenge," and Pepsi has always maintained its beverage was chosen by more people, but not necessarily all people.

L'Oréal Paris Youth Code products or their ingredients actually were scientifically tested to substantiate those claims with "competent and reliable scientific evidence."

The FTC specifies three important legal obligations advertisers must accept:

- **Data must support the claim:** "When the substantiation claim is express (e.g., **tests prove**, **doctors recommend**, and **studies show**), the Commission expects the firm to have at least the advertised level of substantiation."
- **Do not overstate the science:** The FTC advises advertisers, "Make sure your ad claims fit the data."
- **Advertising representations require proof:** Once companies make fact-based claims, the FTC will apply substantiation principles.

Opinion Advertising Claims
Cases based on subjective claims (taste, appearance, smell) are generally not actionable. Claims based on opinions are actionable, however, if they misrepresent the speaker's qualifications, the basis of the opinion, or if they are reasonably interpreted as implied statements of fact.

What About Statements of Opinion?

Is it deceptive to claim a food or beverage "tastes great"? What valid evidence can an advertiser show to support a quality claim based on an individual's personal preference? If a statement is purely a statement of opinion, no evidence or substantiation is required. Claiming some product tastes great or smells fantastic is a subjective impression and therefore would not be judged to be deceptive. But if an advertisement boasts, "most people say it tastes great," it would imply a survey or test determined what most people believe, putting the advertising claim on a factual basis.

The FTC also holds presenting the opinion of an expert will be generally considered as a statement of fact and not opinion. A commercial showing a physician saying it is her "opinion" that a topical ointment is safe leaves consumers believing a scientific statement of fact.

It's not always easy to say whether a statement is purely opinion. The FTC ruled against an advertiser that claimed its television antenna was an "electronic miracle" and that its product was superior to others.[73] The advertiser in this case claimed the term *miracle* was puffery and should not be actionable, but the commission disagreed, holding "in the context of . . . grossly exaggerated claims" reasonable consumers could be deceived.

Testimonials and Endorsements

Testimonials and endorsements are special sorts of statements with a formal set of FTC guidelines, recently updated to include social media influencers and AI-generated images.[74] The FTC says an endorsement or testimonial is any advertising message that consumers are likely to accept as the opinions, beliefs, findings, or experiences of a party other than the sponsoring advertiser. Endorsers in an ad may be an individual, such as a celebrity, or a group or institution. Endorsements may also be conveyed in a variety of ways, such as through verbal statements, demonstrations, or depictions of the name, signature, seal, likeness, or other identifying characteristics of the endorser. The FTC does not require that the endorsement be explicit; just depicting a well-known athlete using the product in the ad, for example, will constitute an endorsement by the athlete even if the athlete never speaks about the product.

To be clear, testimonial and endorsement ads are distinct from those that feature actors performing in a role and announcers voicing a spot, even when the public recognizes the actors and voices. In that case, the FTC reasons such ads are not deceptive because the public

73. Jay Norris, 91 F.T.C. 751, *aff'd*, 598 F.2d 1244 (2d. Circ.), *cert. denied*, 444 U.S. 980 (1979).
74. FTC, Guides Concerning the Use of Endorsements and Testimonials in Advertisements, 16 CFR pt. 255 (2023).

understands the performances of those actors actually represent the views and words of the advertiser.

In general, "[e]ndorsements must always reflect the honest opinions, findings, beliefs, or experience of the endorser."[75] If someone claims in an ad, for example, that a brand of shower cleaner removed mold and mildew in their own bathroom, the FTC expects their claim to be true.[76] In addition, an endorser must not convey any message that would be considered deceptive if conveyed directly by the advertiser.

FTC rules also require anyone claiming to use a product to actually use it in their everyday life at the time the endorsement is given. And advertisers may only continue to run the ad so long as they have good reason to believe that the endorser remains a bona fide user of the product.[77] This provision is pertinent to celebrity endorsements where fans of a celebrity are especially influenced to make a purchase based on that endorsement. If consumers suppose Beyoncé prefers a specific line of leisure wear shown in an ad, they presumably would purchase it assuming someone they admire like "Queen Bey" certainly knows what type of fashion to wear. The question for regulators would be whether she actually wears and continues to wear that brand throughout the ad campaign.

In an earlier era, pop singer Pat Boone endorsed an acne medication claiming his daughters used the cream. The FTC responded in part on the belief the Boone children did not in fact use the product and notified the medication company and the singer.[78] Not only was the advertiser found liable, so was Boone, who made history in 1978 as the first celebrity to be held accountable for giving a false and misleading endorsement. He eventually signed a consent order, agreeing to stop appearing in the ads and to pay up to $5,000 in restitution into a fund to compensate misled customers. The FTC action shocked the celebrity world, prompting many personalities to demand *indemnification clauses* in their endorsement contracts, making the advertiser responsible for any penalties the celebrity may incur.[79]

When it comes to endorsements made by consumers, the FTC has some specific rules.[80] In the first place, endorsements that relate the experience of a consumer will be considered as representative of what consumers should generally achieve with the product or service. Therefore, the advertiser must have adequate substantiation for the representation. If the consumer endorser's experience is not typical or substantiated as typical, then the ad must clearly state this. So if in a testimonial ad, a consumer claims he got excellent results from using a particular hair product, the testimonial might be deceptive even with substantiation if viewers cannot expect the same result. Testimonial advertisements will therefore often include such disclaimers as "Actual results may vary," although the commission says disclaimers do not necessarily exonerate an advertiser unless strongly conveyed and substantiated.[81]

In addition, where an ad appears to use "actual consumers," the people in the advertisement must be actual consumers, not actors.[82] Otherwise, the ad must clearly and conspicuously disclose the truth – the actors are not actual consumers. For example, a "taste-test" ad that portrays a woman expressing amazement her dog is enjoying a brand of dog food gives the net impression that she is an actual consumer. If she is an actor or even a participant approached in advance to stage a testimonial, then that arrangement must be disclosed.

75. *Id.* at §255.1 (a).
76. *Id.* at §255.1 (b).
77. *Id.* at §255.1 (c).
78. Cooga Mooga, Inc., 92 F.T.C. 310, 312 (1978).
79. Nicholas A. Persky, "Rules of Endorsement," *Los Angeles Lawyer*, May 2012, *at* www.admedialaw.com/uploads/File/LA%20Lawyer%20Article%20%20May%202012.pdf.
80. FTC, Guides, supra note 74 at §255.2.
81. *Id.* at ft.n. 1.
82. *Id.* at §255.2 (c).

Endorsements by organizations and experts are also subject to specific FTC rules. Organizational endorsements must be based on a fair, collective judgment of the organization and not just some members.[83] When an expert is featured, the ad must ensure the endorser's qualifications represent actual expertise in the field being represented.[84] An expert's endorsement must also be supported by an actual exercise of the endorser's expertise.

Astronaut Gordon Cooper attracted the FTC's attention when he endorsed G.R. Valve, a gadget promising to increase the fuel efficiency of automobiles.[85] Cooper had an engineering degree that might cause the misimpression he had expertise in car fuel efficiency (his degree was in aerospace, not automotive, engineering). The FTC contended Cooper implied expertise in fuel efficiency when he had none.

The FTC would stand to be more accepting of an ad campaign where actress Mayim Bialik, who played a neuroscientist on the TV show *Big Bang Theory*, promoted a dietary supplement called Neuriva that promised to aid brain performance. She explained in the commercial how she is an actual neuroscientist, which is true, having studied neuroscience for 12 years and earning a PhD in neuroscience from UCLA.[86]

If there is any connection between an endorser and the seller of an advertised product that might materially affect the credibility of the endorsement, then that connection must be fully disclosed.[87] Certainly, consumers will assume that most people in testimonials are compensated for their appearance. An advertisement where a celebrity endorses a product does not require a disclaimer stating that the celebrity was paid for the appearance. The same is true of actors appearing in commercials.

The situation is different, however, if someone in a blind taste test commercial selects one soft drink over another, or if diners in a restaurant being observed by hidden camera are surprised that they were served a brand of instant rice. Audiences will assume those persons were not compensated for their endorsements, and if they were compensated, even if only free food or vouchers, the sponsors have an obligation to provide that information in the ad.

In 2009, the FTC added to its Guides on endorsements, making clear that its guidelines also apply to online advertising. The FTC was grappling with an increasing number of complaints about the undisclosed use of paid endorsers who were promoting products through their blogs, Facebook pages, X accounts, and other social media. As a result, bloggers and other social media influencers who receive cash or in-kind payments to review or promote a product or service must disclose the material connection they share with the seller.

The FTC has gone after violators with warning letters and more. In 2020, they settled with a marketer of teas and skincare products on charges Teami, LLC, promoted its products using deceptive healthcare claims and endorsements from celebrity influencers like Cardi B without adequately disclosing that they were paid to promote their products. Consumers could only see the disclosures on Instagram if they clicked a "more" link. The FTC ordered the advertiser to return one million dollars to consumers who were harmed.[88]

83. *Id.* at §255.4.
84. *Id.* at §255.3.
85. Leroy Gordon Cooper, Jr. a/k/a Gordon Cooper, *Consent Order*, 94 F.T.C. 674 (1979).
86. Beth Snyder Bulik, "Newly Rebranded Reckitt Casts 'Big Bang' Actress: And Real-Life Neuroscientist-Mayim Bialik in New Neuriva Campaign," *Fierce Pharma*, March 24, 2021, *at* www.fiercepharma.com/marketing/newly-rebranded-reckitt-casts-big-bang-actress-mayim-bialik-campaign-for-otc-brand.
87. FTC, Guides, supra note 74 at §255.5.
88. FTC, "Tea Marketer Misled Consumers, Didn't Adequately Disclose Payments to Well-Known Influencers, FTC Alleges," March 6, 2020, *at* www.ftc.gov/news-events/press-releases/2020/03/tea-marketer-misled-consumers-didnt-adequately-disclose-payments. The order imposed a $15.2 million judgment – the total sales of the challenged products – which would be suspended upon payment of $1 million, depending on the defendants' ability to pay.

From the Trenches: The Case of Paid Endorsers in Public Relations

By Michael C. Lasky

The relationship between the Federal Trade Commission (FTC) and the public relations (PR) industry is one characterized by greater scrutiny and quite possibly, on the side of the FTC, mistrust. The tension between FTC and the PR industry has produced closer scrutiny for disclosures of relationships in nontraditional media, such as online and social media. The FTC periodically revises its Guides on the Use of Endorsements and Testimonials (Guides) to make clear that material connections that consumers would not normally expect between an endorser and a marketer must be disclosed in new media forms, such as in blogs, social media posts, and on talk shows.

After revising its Guides in 2009, the FTC resolved its first action for unfair and deceptive practices arising from noncompliance with the Guides. The action was against Reverb Communications, Inc., a PR agency in the video game industry, and its sole owner, Tracie Snitker. The settlement resolved claims that Reverb and Snitker engaged in deceptive marketing by having employees pose as ordinary consumers and post reviews on iTunes of a game application they were hired to promote. According to the FTC, Reverb's and Snitker's postings did not disclose that employees posting were hired to promote the products or that Reverb's fee often included a percentage of its client's sales of the game applications. This action has shown that the FTC is intent on enforcing the revised Guides' disclosure requirements, not only with respect to the companies whose products are marketed but also with respect to the public relations agencies that market those products.

The FTC's settlement with Reverb Communications should be viewed as a warning message to the PR industry that it is now more important than ever to adopt the ethical disclosure practices set forth in the revised Guides and to err on the side of more disclosure to consumers regarding the relationships between public relations agencies, their hired spokespeople, and the marketers they represent.

Michael C. Lasky is a senior partner, public relations law,
and cochair of the Litigation Practice Group at
Davis & Gilbert LLP Attorneys at Law.

The FTC provided more detail in its 2023 update to the Guides.[89] For example, voluntary reviews and tags in social media posts may be considered endorsements. The FTC also makes clear that it's a deceptive practice to purchase or create indicators of social media influence when used to misrepresent such influence for a commercial purpose. An advertiser cannot deceptively procure a fake positive consumer review for their own product and have it published on a third-party review website; in this case both the advertiser and review site operator will be liable for misleading consumers. In addition, intermediaries such as advertising agencies and public relations firms will be liable for their roles in creating ads with endorsements that they know or should have known are deceptive.[90]

Social media influencers are more specifically addressed. Like all endorsers, influencers are liable for their actions, such as falsely representing that they personally used a product or experienced a service.[91] They must also be sure to disclose to their followers their material connections to the brand they are promoting. This includes all financial connections, such as receiving pay, free or reduced-price products, or anything of value including incentives to win prizes or appear in media promotions. If there's any connection to the advertiser through

89. FTC, Guides, supra note 74. *See also* 88 Fed. Reg. 48,092 (July 26, 2023), codified at 16 C.F.R. pt. 255.
90. *Id.* at § 255.1.(f).
91. *Id.* at § 255.1.(e).

employment or personal and family relationships, that must be disclosed, too. These disclosure obligations fall not only on the advertisers but on the influencers themselves, who can be subject to civil penalties of up to roughly $50 thousand dollars per violation. Advertisers are expected to monitor the compliance of their endorsers.

The updated guidelines also touch on the use of generative AI-powered virtual personalities. Virtual influencers and other fabricated endorsers will be held to the same standards as their real counterparts. But liability for failing to follow disclosure and other rules will fall to the brands that sponsor the posts. Advertisers must also not misuse images of endorsers. The FTC says that the use of an endorsement with the image or likeness of a person *other than the actual endorser* is deceptive if it misrepresents an attribute of the endorser that would be material to consumers.[92]

Enforcement Actions

The FTC has a variety of tools in its arsenal when dealing with deceptive advertising. As with any enforcement agency, whether to politely ask a company to stop doing something or take harsh legal action with penalties attached is completely up to the commission. Here are the various enforcement mechanisms.

Staff Advisory Letter

The FTC staff can inform an advertiser of their opinion as to whether a particular ad or practice is deceptive. Such an advisory letter does not have the force of law.

Consent Agreement

When the FTC believes that an advertiser has engaged in unfair or deceptive advertising, the advertiser might actually accept the claim by the commission and willingly enter into a settlement. A consent agreement is a judgment agreed to by both the FTC and the advertiser that settles the matter. The agreement may be a simple wrist slap or may involve a much harsher penalty.

The advertiser, however, does not have to admit to any wrongdoing. In 2000, the FTC and Bayer Aspirin entered into an agreement that Bayer would spend $1 million in an educational campaign to inform the public that not everyone ought to take aspirin to reduce the risk of heart attack or stroke and that a physician ought to be consulted before anyone begins taking aspirin regularly. Bayer also consented to refrain from making claims about the benefits of a daily aspirin regimen without mentioning potential risks (simply saying "Just ask your doctor" was not considered good enough).[93]

Cease-and-Desist Order

It has been the FTC's tradition to try to come to agreement with advertisers, so often cease and desist is actually part of a consent agreement that an advertiser willingly accepts. In 2003, the FTC filed actions against the makers of weight-loss supplements containing ephedra. The commission asserted that the advertisements made claims that the product was safe and would result in rapid, substantial, and permanent weight loss without diet or exercise. Health Laboratories of North America signed off on a consent agreement to cease and desist in addition to paying a $370,000 settlement.

On the other hand, cease-and-desist orders can be unilateral; they do not need the advertiser's agreement but can be an order to immediately stop doing what the FTC considers to be deceptive. This was the case in 1996 when the FTC issued a cease-and-desist order to the

92. *Id.* at § 255.1.(g).
93. www.ftc.gov/sites/default/files/documents/cases/2000/01/sterlingdecree.htm.

Home Shopping Network for making unsubstantiated claims about vitamins it was showing and stop-smoking sprays.[94]

Consent Decree

The FTC may choose to issue a consent decree with the negotiated agreement entered as a court order. Unlike consent agreements, consent decrees are enforceable by a court, and violations can result in civil penalties. Since a consent decree is a mutual agreement, it is binding on both parties and cannot be appealed unless it can be proven it was based on fraud by one of the parties or a mutual mistake.

An advertisement for Copa, a popular hair-straightening product targeted primarily to African American women, was challenged by the FTC for claiming it had a unique hair-strengthening property that the agency held could even weaken hair. The ad showed "before and after" pictures that implied that consumers would experience the hair straightening with just one use, while the FTC charged that multiple applications may be necessary to achieve the depicted results. The company, GoodTimes Entertainment Limited, agreed to settle the charges, and the FTC voted to file the complaint and consent decree in district court for a judge's approval. The consent decree prohibited the company from, among other things, making unsubstantiated claims about Copa's strengthening properties and required it to affirmatively disclose the number of applications needed to produce the depicted results.[95]

Corrective Advertisement

The FTC may order an advertiser to do more than cease and desist its deceptive advertising. It can ask it to refrain from future advertising for a period of time unless it corrects the misleading impression it created.

Corrective Advertising

One of the more creative ways the FTC tries to correct the false impression made by deceptive advertising is to require the advertiser to correct the misimpression. This remedy is not used too frequently, but when it is imposed it often attracts a fair amount of media attention. The FTC says corrective advertising is appropriate when challenged ads substantially create or reinforce a misbelief that is likely to continue if not corrected.

The FTC first ordered corrective advertising in 1971. Profile Bread had been advertising it contained fewer calories than other bread. When compared slice-to-slice, the claim was true, but this was because Profile was sliced thinner than its competitors. Ounce per ounce, there was no significant difference in calories. The FTC ordered that the company devote 25% of one year's advertising budget to correcting the misimpression it had made.[96]

In 1999, the FTC ordered Doan's Pills to correct an unsubstantiated claim that the product was more effective at treating back pain than other over-the-counter medications. The commission said the product was an effective pain reliever, but implying it was superior to others was deceptive.[97] The commission required the parent company to spend $8 million on advertising to correct the unsubstantiated claims. It based the amount on what was spent annually to advertise Doan's Pills over the eight years of the campaign.

The FTC can order corrective advertising, but it cannot order language that is punitive to the advertiser. For years, Listerine mouthwash claimed it helped to prevent colds. The FTC took Listerine to task because it could not substantiate its claim and ordered parent company Warner-Lambert to spend $10 million in advertising that included the message that "contrary to prior advertising," there was no evidence that Listerine prevented colds. Warner-Lambert appealed the FTC decision, and the D.C. Circuit Court of Appeals upheld the $10 million

94. Home Shopping Network, Inc., 122 F.T.C. 227 (1996).
95. *United States v. Goodtimes Entertainment, Ltd.*, No. 03 CV 6037 (S.D.N.Y. 2003). *See*, FTC, "Marketers of Copa Hair System Agree to Settle FTC Charges," August 18, 2003, *at* www.ftc.gov/news-events/press-releases/2003/08/marketers-copa-hair-system-agree-settle-ftc-charges.
96. ITT Continental Baking Co., 79 F.T.C. 248 (1971).
97. *Novartis Corp. v. F.T.C.*, 1999 F.T.C. Lexis 90 (1999), *aff'd*, 223 F.3d 783 (2000).

corrective advertising order, but it struck the requirement that the ads contain the phrase "contrary to prior advertising."[98]

The FTC can also order an advertiser to disclose certain facts to prevent from being deceptive. Aspercreme is a topical medicine for arthritis pain. The name itself almost implies the product contains aspirin, but the company went further in one commercial by asserting, "When you suffer from arthritis, imagine putting the strong relief of aspirin right where you hurt. Aspercreme is an odorless rub which concentrates the relief of aspirin." The D.C. Circuit Court of Appeals upheld an FTC ruling forcing the company to disclose its product contains no aspirin.[99]

A Final Note About FTC Action

Cynics complain that most of what the FTC does with regard to deceptive advertising is too little, too late. An advertiser can create a false impression with impunity for weeks or even months before the commission is notified, goes through a lengthy investigation process, and then acts, which of course can be appealed. Most often, when the commission does act, it is by consent decree. In more than 90% of cases, only an agreement to stop the deceptive practice is required. A preponderance of advertising campaigns do not extend beyond a few months, so advertisers usually don't suffer much by an order to stop a particular ad's run. In those few instances where a deceptive advertisement results in a fine from the FTC, even that is often seen as just the cost of doing business.

In one historic case, however, the commission acted against the makers of Geritol, a vitamin supplement marketed primarily to older Americans. Geritol was a bottled medicine advertised as a way of dealing with tiredness. The FTC believed the ads were deceptive because fatigue is only occasionally the result of vitamin or mineral deficiencies, a fact the advertiser did not make clear. In 1964, the commission issued a cease-and-desist order, but Geritol continued to advertise using the same message. In 1966, the FTC called on the U.S. Justice Department to intervene. Geritol's parent company was eventually fined $800,000, but in 1974, a new trial was ordered, and Geritol was ordered to pay a reduced sum of $280,000. For 14 years, Geritol was able to engage in what the FTC considered a deceptive practice and did so at a cost of $20,000 per year. Given the size of national advertising budgets, such a sum would be small enough to dismiss as the cost of doing business.

Other Agencies and Advertising

In addition to the FTC, other federal agencies have become involved in advertising regulation and enforcement. The Food and Drug Administration is contacted when commercial advertisements relate to food, drug, or cosmetic products, and the FDA is especially active in product labeling.[100] The FDA plays an important role in the regulation of prescription drug advertising, having issued guidelines in 1997 that permit drug makers to advertise directly to consumers. Congress gave the FDA the responsibility to regulate tobacco products in 2009, and the agency assumed authority over e-cigarettes in 2016. The FDA issued a marketing ban on Juul Labs vaping products in 2022, although rescinding the order in 2024.[101]

Advertisements for stocks and bonds come under the purview of the Securities and Exchange Commission, and a deceptive advertisement in this arena can be judged by the

98. *Warner-Lambert v. FTC*, 562 F.2d 749 (D.C. Cir. 1977).
99. *Thompson Med. Co. v. FTC*, 253 U.S. App. D.C. 18 (1986), *cert. denied*, 479 U.S. 1086 (1987).
100. *See* Food Labeling Guide, *at* www.fda.gov/Food/GuidanceRegulation/GuidanceDocuments RegulatoryInformation/LabelingNutrition/ucm2006828.htm.
101. Carma Hassan and Jen Christensen, "FDA Rescinds Marketing Ban on Juul Vaping Products," *CNN*, June 6, 2024.

SEC as a securities fraud, which also gives rise to both civil and criminal penalties. Stock advertising and other communications a publicly traded company employs to encourage investment are subject to legal action if they're based on false information. If a corporation's annual report purposely ignores a liability or is unduly optimistic about revenue, the SEC might view such material as a fraudulent attempt to move the market. Endorsers may also be liable. Celebrity influencer Kim Kardashian was fined by the Securities and Exchange Commission for failing to disclose an Instagram endorsement was paid for by a crypto company. She paid one million dollars to settle the case in 2022.

While the Federal Election Commission does not directly monitor advertising, it does regulate campaign financing for elected federal offices. The candidates and political groups actively promoting their candidacy for office are regulated as well. Political action committees are groups formed, as their name implies, to engage in political activities supporting both issues and candidates. The FEC monitors their activity and limits individual donations to PACs to one $5,000 contribution per candidate per election. PACs may spend as much as they like independent of the candidate to support or oppose federal candidates. Let's say hypothetically a PAC contributes $5,000 directly to Ms. Polly Tician's campaign for U.S. Senate. Now it also may spend a million dollars or more airing commercials supporting her candidacy for Senate so long as there is no coordination between the PAC and Ms. Polly's campaign. That's the reason for the required disclosures during the PAC's commercials. PACs must register with the FEC and provide a public accounting of all expenditures on behalf of candidates. Disclosure of who paid for an ad is required of candidate ads, whether directly by a candidate, a political party, or a PAC.

The Federal Communications Commission gets involved in advertising through its broadcast regulations. The best-known rule of the FCC is the ban on cigarette advertising, not imposed directly by the commission but by federal statute. In 1967, however, the FCC responded to public criticism of cigarette advertising by instituting a rule requiring radio and television stations to carry free antismoking public service announcements if they accepted paid advertising that promoted smoking. In the 1960s, the fairness doctrine was still enforced (discussed in Chapter 8), and cigarette smoking was deemed to be a controversial issue requiring fair treatment by broadcasters, hence the mandate for public service announcements to "balance" cigarette commercials. The FCC agreed the rule need not exact a one-to-one quota but instead accepted one PSA for every two paid commercials. After years of wrangling between the FCC, tobacco industry, and public interest groups, the government considered a total ban on cigarette advertising. Congress acted on that idea, passing the Public Health Cigarette Smoking Act[102] that took cigarette commercials off the air of U.S. radio and television stations in 1971. In 1986, the law was expanded to prohibit smokeless (i.e., "chewing") tobacco ads as well.

States can also get involved in legal action against advertisers. Multiple states, municipalities, and even school districts filed suit against JUUL for marketing and advertising its e-cigarettes to youth, resulting in several multimillion-dollar settlements as recent as 2023 that require, in part, for JUUL to restrict its advertising with no product placements in media and no individuals under the age of 35 appearing in ads. New York's attorney general's office is among the more proactive jurisdictions settling deceptive advertising suits, such as one in 2015 against a distributor of Snuggie blankets and one in 2017 against DeVry Education Group. In 2020, the Southern District of Florida found Burger King's promise of a nonmeat patty in its plant-based "Impossible Burger" did not amount to a promise that the burger would be prepared separately from their meat items.[103] The District Court of Vermont dismissed a false advertising lawsuit by a consumer allegedly disappointed

102. Public Law 91–222, 84 Stat. 87.
103. *Williams v. Burger King*, No. 19–24755 (S.D. Fla. July 20, 2020).

that Ben & Jerry's ice cream is not, in fact, made exclusively from milk sourced from "happy cows."[104]

Self-Regulation

One way for advertising businesses to fend off regulatory intervention by the government is to enact self-regulation in the form of codes, guidelines, and standards. This solution is accomplished through the cooperation of trade associations and interest groups where advertising is a major element of their business enterprise.

Several organizations oversee advertising abuses, but a leading one is the National Advertising Division, an extension of the Council of Better Business Bureaus. The NAD investigates deceptive advertising claims much the same way as the FTC, but it lacks any judicial authority to impose sanctions. The NAD can ask an advertiser to "cease and desist" a dishonest promotion, but it has no power to enforce such a ruling. It relies in large part on the publicity that its decisions attract to influence advertisers in the court of public opinion.

The NAD, for example, responded to a complaint in 2009 about advertising and labeling for Hunt's Tomato Sauce. The NAD accepted that Hunt's sauce is made from "all-natural vine-ripened tomatoes," although it objected to the label's claim, "packed full of Hunt's 100% natural vine-ripened tomatoes." The NAD reasoned Hunt's sauce was "made from" or "prepared from" vine-ripened tomatoes, but since the sauce was made from a puree (concentrate) and water, the phrase, *packed full of 100% natural vine-ripened tomatoes* was deceptive. Parent company ConAgra respectfully disagreed, but they agreed to cease labelling it in those terms.[105]

Such a voluntary solution is more attractive than government intervention for certain reasons. First, the costs associated with self-regulation are significantly less. NAD judgments also avoid government disclosure rules that the courts and the FTC must follow. It also can keep its data confidential, releasing only the decision and the participants' positions. Finally, its decisions are reached sooner than court or agency action since the NAD's policy is to offer a written decision within 60 business days. NAD handles about 150 cases each year.

Dispelling Some Myths About Advertising Regulation

There is a lot of misinformation about advertising regulation. What has been industry self-regulation has been believed by many people to be a legal requirement. Here are four of the most frequently stated myths.

1 **Drinking in TV commercials**. There has never been a prohibition on showing anyone drinking beer, wine, or hard liquor. The National Association of Broadcasters used to have a recommendation in its Television Code about advertisements not showing the consumption of alcoholic beverages, but in 1982 the Code was abandoned by the NAB as a result of an antitrust suit based on its limitation of commercial minutes per hour broadcast stations could air. Rather than simply amend portions of the Code violating antitrust rules, the NAB decided just to discontinue it.

104. "A Legen-dairy Victory: Ben & Jerry's Wins 'Happy Cows' False Advertising Lawsuit," *National Law Review*, July 23, 2020, *at* www.natlawreview.com/article/legen-dairy-victory-ben-jerry-s-wins-happy-cows-false-advertising-lawsuit.
105. National Advertising Division Press Release, "NAD Examines Advertising for Conagra's Hunt's Tomato Sauce," January 15, 2009, *at* https://bbbprograms.org/archive/nad-examines-advertising-for-conagra-s-hunt-s-tomato-sauce.

2 **Commercials for hard liquor**. After nearly four decades of voluntary restrictions on alcohol advertising in radio and TV commercials, the American liquor industry agreed in 1996 to end what was only a voluntary ban on advertising whiskey, vodka, gin, and other spirits on radio and television. Despite some public criticism and a request from then President Clinton and his FCC Chairman Reed Hundt to continue the voluntary ban, radio and television stations have accepted more and more liquor ads. The first advertisement on a licensed station for hard liquor was for Seagram's Crown Royal. By 2017, the National Football League announced it would start advertising hard liquor spots during its marquee matchups each week on television. Today, White Claw, Smirnoff, and Twisted Tea are among the dominant alcohol advertisers on TV.

3 **The number of commercial minutes allowed per hour**. This myth is once again a vestige of the National Association of Broadcasters' codes. Both the Radio and Television Codes prescribed maximum numbers of commercial limits, and the rules were purely self-regulation, not law. In fact, an entire hour of content can be commercials (precisely what an "infomercial" is).

There is one area, however, in which the law does restrict the number of commercial minutes: children's television. Within the three hours of children's core programming required of every television station (including over-the-air, cable, and satellite providers), stations may not exceed 10.5 minutes of advertising per hour on weekends or 12 minutes per hour on weekdays (children's television rules are discussed in Chapter 8).

4 **Using the names of competitors in ads**. Some believe that advertisers must say "Brand X" or use some other alias in ads when comparing their product to a competitor rather than using the actual name of the competitor. In fact, quite the opposite is the case. In its policy statement on **comparative advertising**, the FTC states that it "encourages the naming of, or reference to competitors" in comparative advertising but cautions that such ads must be clear and not deceptive.[106] The commission's policy statement on comparative advertising points out that it has been industry self-regulation that has often discouraged comparative ads because of their tendency to "disparage" a competitor's product, but that the FTC does not prohibit disparagement as long as it is truthful and not deceptive.

Global View: International Advertising Laws

Understanding and complying with a myriad of international advertising laws and regulations can be incredibly challenging. This task is even more daunting as more businesses are actively involved in or looking to enter international markets with the advertising and marketing of their products and services. Advertising agencies also operate globally, servicing clients from offices located in cities around the world.

While globalization has integrated national markets, there is little formal international advertising law to turn to, other than what the European Union has adopted among its member states. Most advertising law exists at the local or national level, while self-regulation has historically defined the international realm. The European Advertising Standards Alliance (EASA) is the coordination point for national advertising self-regulatory organizations throughout Europe.[107] The International Chamber of Commerce is also well-known for providing guidance on self-regulation and advertising

106. 16 C.F.R. § 14.15.
107. For links to the EASA and different national organizations, see "International Advertising Law-Self-Regulation Links: Advertising Self-Regulatory Organizations," *at* www.lawpublish.com/international-links.html.

issues. Self-regulatory systems with rules based on the ICC's Code of Advertising and Marketing Communication Practice operate in over 35 countries, across six continents. The ICC codes are touted as the gold standard for self-regulation, adaptable to local laws and culture while regularly updated.[108]

It's not surprising to find that the local advertising laws of different nations vary significantly, given the different regulatory structures and cultural influences. Countries have their own special rules, such as for agricultural products, financial products and services, gambling, cannabis, and alcohol as well as different policies on such things as price comparisons in advertising and what constitutes misleading and deceptive advertising. Unlike the United States and Australia, some countries, for example, have strong restrictions against comparative advertising, such as Argentina, China, El Salvador, Greece, Japan, Italy, and South Africa. The regulatory treatment of online behavioral advertising also varies considerably, with stronger protections for consumers in the EU with its General Data Protection Regulation (GDPR).

Many countries have laws intended to protect children from advertising messages, but Sweden has prohibited all advertising aimed at children since 1991.[109] Advertising junk food to children is limited in Germany, Chile, Norway, Taiwan, Ireland, and the United Kingdom. In 1980, Canada became one of the first countries to have a law restricting junk food marketing in general.[110]

Alcohol advertising is regulated in many countries while banned outright in others, especially Muslim countries. Even in countries that accept alcohol, such as France with its famous wine industry, the hazards of alcohol have prompted regulation. French law requires ads to carry messages about the dangers of alcohol abuse to one's health, and ads for alcohol are prohibited on TV and in movie theaters.[111] In Ireland, spirits cannot be advertised on radio and TV.

When Brazilians learned in 2015 that they consumed 40% more alcohol than other developed countries, they passed a host of regulations controlling the advertising of alcoholic beverages. Such ads can only be broadcast after 9 p.m. in Brazil, and print ads must contain visible warnings to "Drink moderately." Ads also cannot associate drinking with driving, healthy activities, professional success, or sexual performance.[112]

Other national advertising laws include Germany's restriction of no more than 12 advertising minutes per hour on television. China and the EU ban tobacco advertising across all media. And in China, celebrity endorsers must be at least ten years old, and celebrities can be held responsible for false advertising claims.[113]

Some regulatory approaches are relatively universal, however, such as strict laws governing the advertising of pharmaceuticals. False advertising is also widely banned, from India and the United Kingdom to China and elsewhere. Most countries, including the United States, even require "advertorials" – native ads presented as editorial content, to be clearly marked as advertisements.[114]

108. International Chamber of Commerce, "Marketing and Advertising," *at* https://iccwbo.org/global-insights/.
109. Olivia Wakeman, "What Is Considered Illegal Marketing in Other Countries?" *Chron*, *at* https://smallbusiness.chron.com/considered-illegal-marketing-other-countries-73863.html.
110. "Societal Norms and Advertising Changes: Advertising Restrictions by Time and Country," *GradSchools.com*, *at* www.gradschools.com/degree-guide/advertising-norms-by-era-and-country.
111. Wakeman, "What Is Considered Illegal Marketing in Other Countries?" supra note 109.
112. "Societal Norms," supra note 110.
113. *Id.*
114. Wakeman, "What Is Considered Illegal Marketing in Other Countries?" supra note 109.

Summary

- For most of the nation's history, the Latin phrase *caveat emptor* ("let the buyer beware") was the operative term for advertising oversight, but that changed at the dawn of the twentieth century when muckrakers discovered the harms perpetrated by false and misleading claims. The U.S. government did not, for the most part, engage in the regulation of advertising. Consumers were expected to be wary of advertising claims.
- In 1942, the U.S. Supreme Court ruled that "purely commercial speech" was not entitled to First Amendment protection. Since then the Court has acknowledged that a great deal of information is conveyed through advertising and that while it may not be on the same plane as political speech, commercial speech still deserves some degree of protection.
- To establish a line between permissible government regulation and rules that would be unconstitutional, the Court created the *Central Hudson* test. The four-part test first asks whether the advertising in question is protected (e.g., a nondeceptive ad for a legal product) and then examines whether the government has a substantial interest in the regulation, whether the regulation advances that interest, and if it is done in a narrowly defined way.
- Originally created to protect businesses from one another's anticompetitive behavior, the Federal Trade Commission's role was expanded to include consumer protection. This included prohibiting unfair or deceptive acts in commerce, extending regulatory authority over advertising.
- For content to be determined to be deceptive, an advertisement must be 1) likely to mislead 2) a reasonable consumer 3) and be material to a purchasing decision.
- Advertisers who make factual claims about products can be made to substantiate those claims. Opinion enjoys more protection, but sometimes lines between factual statements and opinion can be blurred.
- Testimonials and endorsements must reflect the honest opinion and experience of the endorser who must use the product or service. Any material connections to the seller such as payment must be disclosed. Consumer endorsers must be actual consumers, and experts must be true experts in the field unless otherwise disclosed in the ad.
- The FTC has various enforcement tools in its arsenal, ranging from simple warnings in a Staff Advisory Letter up to fines and the requirement that the advertiser run corrective advertising to fix any public misperceptions.
- Advertising can also fall under the jurisdiction of other agencies, including, but not limited to, the Food and Drug Administration, the Securities and Exchange Commission, and the Federal Communications Commission.
- Advertisers have created self-regulatory remedies to preempt government regulation. The National Advertising Division of the Better Business Bureau investigates misleading advertising claims without involving government action. Advertising restrictions that the public believes to be laws are instead self-regulated restrictions.

Ethical Dilemmas: Online Influencers

Corporations have learned the power of online influencers, and some have used them in ethically dubious ways. Consider how national retailer Lord & Taylor chose to settle with the Federal Trade Commission in 2016 following allegations it paid for what seemed to be impartial journalism covering fashion in the online publication, *Nylon*. The FTC charged the retailer paid 50 online influencers who showed up on Instagram wearing the same colorful dress from the Lord & Taylor collection without disclosing the payment for their endorsement or the free dress each one was given to wear.[115]

The FTC since updated its Guides for endorsers, including social media influencers. One example the FTC provides is about a developer of a new video game who pays a college student influencer to play and live stream their new game. The student plays the game and appears to enjoy it as seen in a post the game developer then promotes and advertises. Yet the college student does not expressly recommend the game.

Is the influencer's apparent enjoyment an implicit recommendation that constitutes an endorsement? If so, does the student need to be sure to disclose getting paid by the game developer? The FTC would say yes and may hold the influencer liable along with the game developer if the endorsement guidelines are not followed.

What if the student just goes along and "pretends" to enjoy the game in deference to the advertiser paying the student? Influencers need to know that this, too, will constitute deceptive or misleading advertising.

All of this is also a matter of ethics. The American Advertising Federation provides the *Principles and Practices for Advertising Ethics*.[116] The AAF's Fourth Principle of ethics specifically requires advertisers to clearly disclose all payments or free product gifts before using any endorsement regardless of the forum, on social or traditional media channels. In addition, the First Principle says that advertising, public relations, marketing communications, news, and editorial all share a common objective of truth and high ethical standards in serving the public. Dishonesty in endorsing a product or service is clearly contrary to this principle.

What about a production company or division that produces such a deceptive ad? The FTC explicitly states that production companies that merely provide production services are not considered liable.[117] But is doing this work for an advertiser, knowing it violates these principles, unethical?

115. "Lord & Taylor Settles FTC Charges It Deceived Consumers Through Paid Article in an Online Fashion Magazine and Paid Instagram Posts by 50 'Fashion Influencers,'" *FTC*, March 15, 2016, *at* www.ftc.gov/news-events/press-releases/2016/03/lord-taylor-settles-ftc-charges-it-deceived-consumers-through. This case was also the first brought by the FTC for deceptive native advertising.
116. *Principles and Practices for Advertising Ethics*, American Advertising Federation, *at* https://www.iaethics.org/principles-and-practices.
117. FTC, Guides, supra note 74 at § 255.1.(f).

12

Media Business Law

LEARNING OBJECTIVES

After reading this chapter, you should know

- what a contract is and the elements that make up a legally binding contract
- how release forms serve as a sort of contract
- why clauses in contracts (like morals clauses) matter, and how each clause is exercised
- how media companies are subject to the same antitrust laws as other corporations; the First Amendment is not a shield against the regulation of commerce
- the obligations of media organizations in dealing with employment laws
- whether corporations have rights of free expression
- what restrictions exist on the speech of people with "insider information" about publicly traded corporations

While most of the aspiring actors and writers drawn to Hollywood probably think mainly about the *art* of television and film, they would be wise to remember that entertainment is also a *business*. Cynical as it may seem, studios don't produce content for benevolent reasons; they exist to (and their shareholders insist they) make a profit. One of the ways they do this is by reducing costs when and where they can.

The year 2023 was a difficult one for labor relations in the entertainment industry. In May, the Writers Guild of America, representing more than 11,000 screenwriters, went on strike. With more movies and shows carried by streaming services, writers claimed they were earning less money. They were also concerned for the future of their jobs as new AI software could make it possible for studios to hire fewer writers.

Then in July, SAG-AFTRA,[1] the union representing more than 150,000 performers, walked off the job over similar issues. Streaming was resulting in lower pay for members, and new technology could allow studios to hire fewer actors, using digitally created people instead (sometimes mimicking real actors, either living or deceased).

Both strikes were resolved by November, and the industry returned to work, but not without consequences. It was the first time Hollywood had been hit with simultaneous actors and

1. Abbreviation for Screen Actos Guild-American Federation of Television and Radio Artists

DOI: 10.4324/9781003462989-12

writers strikes in more than 60 years, and the effect was devastating. *Deadline Hollywood* reported the southern California economy lost more than $6 billion and 45,000 jobs.[2]

It may be hard for the public to sympathize with the plight of actors because they hear so much about the salaries of celebrity performers who earn millions, but SAG-AFTRA reported in 2021 the median salary for its members was below $50,000, and only 2% of its members earn enough to make a living just by acting.[3]

Labor Unions

The misery of the Great Depression led to the organization of labor unions to protect members from abuses at the hands of their employers. These groups represent media professionals in contract disputes and other negotiations. The National Labor Relations Act (§7) gave American employees "the right to form, join or assist labor organizations, to bargain collectively through representatives of their own choosing, and to engage in other concerted activities for the purpose of collective bargaining or other mutual aid or protection."[4]

Three labor unions organize most of the employees in the entertainment media: the National Association of Broadcast Employees and Technicians (NABET), which joined with the Communications Workers of America (CWA) in 1994; SAG-AFTRA, a merger in 2012 of the Screen Actors Guild and the American Federation of Television and Radio Artists; and the International Alliance of Theatrical Stage Employees (IATSE).

Right-to-Work Laws
Laws enacted in states that prohibit unions from requiring workers in unionized workplaces to join a union or pay for representation.

The unions tend to be more active in states where **right-to-work** legislation has not been adopted, including 28 states located predominantly in the South and Midwest with more conservative voting patterns. Typical of the right-to-work statutes common to these states is the one adopted in Louisiana: "No person shall be required as a condition of employment to become or remain a member of any labor organization, or to pay any dues, fees, assessments, or other charges of any kind to a labor organization."[5]

There is not yet a federal right-to-work law, although such legislation has been introduced in Congress. The map in Figure 12.1 shows the status of state right-to-work laws.

Pro-labor states, such as Illinois, take a different tack. When the owners of a Chicago Spanish-language station, WSNS, resisted organizing efforts among station employees, the state senate intervened. The Illinois lawmakers authorized a resolution that essentially told the Chicago broadcaster to "negotiate in good faith" with its employees, although AFTRA's local executive was blunt about it. "It's time for NBC and Telemundo to recognize the fact that Spanish-language employees have earned the right to the same quality of benefits and working conditions as English-language employees."[6] It should come as no surprise that California and New York, home to a large part of the entertainment industry, are pro-labor states.

This is not the only example of labor negotiations that have encountered friction. Spanish-language media workers began planning for collective bargaining rights at a Miami television station when one of the leading union advocates was dismissed from his job. AFTRA's Executive Director in Miami, Herta Suarez, said others had been threatened with dismissal and their employees had been forced to work without breaks for meals. The union also observed that there were no basic benefits written into employee contracts.[7]

2. D. Patten, "SAG-AFTRA & Studios Set More Contract Talks for Friday; 'Cautious Optimism' Motto of the Day," *Deadline Hollywood*, October 24, 2023. Recognize that when actors and writers strike, others are out of work, too, since there's no need for set builders, makeup artists, catering, transportation, etc.
3. A. Johnson, "Median Income For Actors Is $46,960 – As SAG-AFTRA Fights For Better Residuals And Pay," *Forbes*, July 25, 2023.
4. National Labor Relations Act, 29 U.S.C. at § 157.
5. La. Rev. Stat. Ann. § 22:983 (1976).
6. Roger Feder, "Tracking: Senate Takes Sides," *Chicago Sun Times*, June 8, 2005.
7. Spanish-Language Media Workers Seek Union Representation at Miami's America TeVe Channel 41," *Shoptalk*, newsletter@TVspy.com, August 12, 2005.

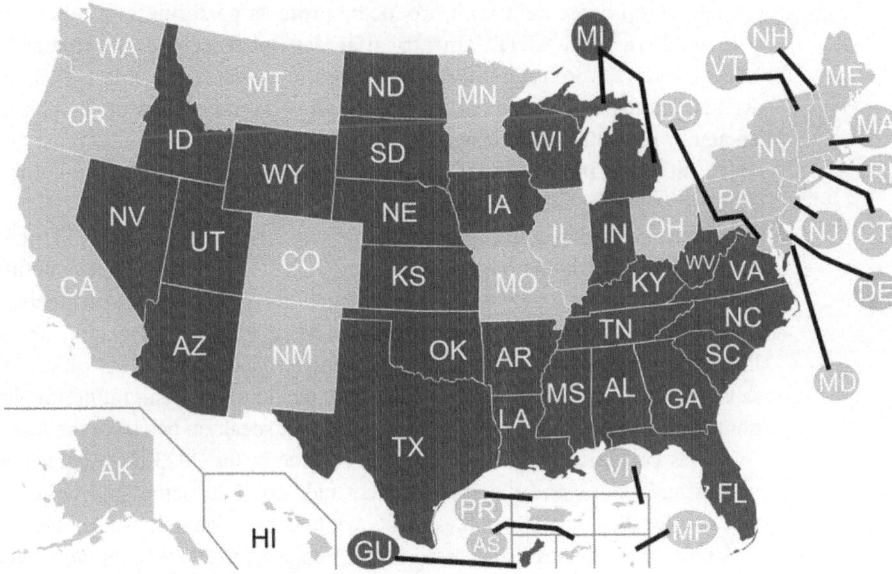

Figure 12.1 Right-to-work states are the dark shaded states

Union groups have been struggling at some major media outlets. In January 2006, NBC News anchors and correspondents voted to sever ties with AFTRA and decertify their representation. It did not take long for the network management to praise the outcome of the vote. "We are grateful for the trust our employees have placed in the company," said the NBC News release. Conceding defeat, the union simply said, "[W]e wish all NBC News broadcasters the best of luck and look forward to the day when they will again be part of the community of AFTRA's broadcast journalists."[8]

At PBS, a majority of the members of the National Association of Broadcast Employees and Technicians-Communications Workers of America (NABET-CWA) approved a separate contract with the network after negotiations reached an impasse. Meanwhile, National Public Radio's largest union, AFTRA, claimed NPR violated its contract by assigning new technical duties to its members without union approval.

Some of the changes were due to the transition to digital editing, which eliminated exclusive union responsibility over audio technician work. Basically, it boiled down to whether union engineers would be the only ones allowed to mix the sounds heard on *All Things Considered* and programs like it. AFTRA leaders argued NPR producers would have to spend more of their time technically mixing and recording the sounds of stories at the expense of writing and reporting them.

The unions often work to establish salaries and benefits for various tasks, and members are given the opportunity to vote on the agreement. These agreements are generally in effect for three years.

For example, in 2016, SAG-AFTRA renegotiated its master contract for commercial work with the advertising industry, and 92% of the membership voted to approve it.[9] SAG-AFTRA also identified the safety concerns of its members. In 2016, the union organized a strike of video game producers, claiming that actors doing video game work were damaging their vocal cords due to the extra demands put upon them.[10]

8. Jesse Hiestand & Paul J. Gough, "NBC News Parts Ways with Union, Hollywood Reporter," republished in *Shoptalk*, newsletter@TVspy.com, August 16, 2006.
9. "SAG-AFTRA Members Ratify Commercials Contract," *Variety*, May 9, 2016.
10. "Voice Actors Strike Against Video Game Companies," *NPR*, October 22, 2016, *at* www.npr.org/sections/alltechconsidered/2016/10/22/498954253/voice-actors-strike-against-video-game-companies.

The union agreement with producers protects performers in other ways. For example, the 2018 SAG-AFTRA theatrical agreement with studios contained provisions for nudity. Actors were required to be notified in advance if a role called for nudity, and a written agreement must exist. In fact, in what would otherwise be a breach of contract, an actor may withdraw consent even after signing, and the studio must honor that agreement, although the studio may use any previously shot material and/or employ a body double.[11]

Unions engage in collective bargaining with employers on behalf of their members. The results are usually in the form of wages and benefits agreements, but sometimes other agreements are struck, and they become contractual obligations for the members.

In 2012, Major League Baseball and the MLB Players Association struck an agreement that included a social media policy. The policy encouraged MLB players to interact with fans, but included ten specific prohibitions, including no denigrating the umpires, no condoning of drug use, and no implying that players speak on behalf of the team or MLB.[12]

It was collective bargaining that was at issue in the 2023 negotiations between screenwriters and actors, and the entertainment industry. Star actors and writers negotiate what they can for their salaries, but lesser-known talent rely on union-negotiated base rates.[13]

Union membership is down as a percentage of the U.S. population, but the need for worker protection still exists. In fact, video game workers asserted claims of sexism; they stated they were being harassed and were expected to work ridiculously long hours without breaks. An industry that had almost no union protection in 2018 now has several unions working with management on their behalf.[14]

In the 1930s, the Supreme Court made clear the laws regulating commerce are applicable to media businesses. The National Labor Relations Act (1935) prohibits businesses from firing or otherwise punishing employees who engage in union activity.

Morris Watson was an Associated Press (AP) employee fired in 1935 for his union involvement. The National Labor Relations Board (NLRB) began an investigation on behalf of Watson, but the AP refused to cooperate, claiming the First Amendment protected it from labor laws. The news wire service argued that subjecting itself to such government scrutiny was a violation of the free press guarantee of the First Amendment. The NLRB even issued a ruling requiring the AP to reinstate Watson, but the news organization ignored it, claiming constitutional protection.

The U.S. Supreme Court did not accept the AP's argument. It was adamant in ruling media are not above laws regulating businesses. The Supreme Court agreed with the assertion "[n]ews and intelligence are, in disregard of the First Amendment, treated as ordinary articles of commerce, subject to federal supervision and control." The decision further held,

> The business of the Associated Press is not immune from regulation because it is an agency of the press. The publisher of a newspaper has no special immunity from the application of general laws. He has no special privilege to invade the rights and liberties of others. He must answer for libel. He may be punished for contempt of court. He is subject to the anti-trust laws. Like others he must pay equitable and nondiscriminatory taxes on his business.[15]

11. SAG-AFTRA Theatrical Agreement can be accessed from their website, *at* www.sagaftra.org/production-center/contract/818/agreement/document. Nudity provisions can be found in Sections 17 and 43 of the Basic Agreement, as modified by the 2020 Memorandum of Agreement.
12. The agreement is online at www.baseball-almanac.com/downloads/mlb_social_media_policy.pdf.
13. For example, in 2024 the base rate for actors in films with budgets of $2 million or more was $1,158/day. Rates are available online at the union websites and also in major trade publications.
14. Wikipedia provides a summary. Search "Game Workers Unite."
15. *Associated Press v. National Labor Relations Bd.*, 301 U.S. 103, 132–133 (1937).

Bedrock Law
Laws regulating commerce are applicable to media businesses as well.

As a result, the AP joined the nation in recognizing the right of labor to organize and enter into collective bargaining negotiations for its employees.

Entire books are dedicated to the subject of business law, and it is well beyond the scope of this text to try to cover all of that. Instead, we focus only on those rules specifically relevant to media businesses.

Contracts

A basic understanding of contracts is essential to communication law. Employees often sign contracts when they start work with a media company. Sometimes those contracts contain clauses affecting the employee's personal life or even that employee's behavior *after* leaving the company.

Motion picture studios sign contracts of all sorts – with actors and other "contractors" for their skills, with distribution companies for carriage of their products, and with investors who contribute sizable amounts for the completion of major films. Some movie producers actually have contracts that require them to be included in *future* projects.[16]

Radio and television stations sign contracts with syndication companies and networks that contain all sorts of stipulations about what will happen if a station does not air a program at the regularly scheduled time, or if the program provider does not deliver the program as promised. What's more, there are occasions when contractual obligations may exist even if there is no written contract.

In 1982, Minnesota reporters promised a source, a campaign associate, they would not reveal the source's identity in a story about a rival candidate for lieutenant governor that featured material about minor offenses involving a petty theft charge of shoplifting.[17] Editors for the *Minneapolis Star* and the St. Paul *Pioneer Press* decided to use the source's name, Dan Cohen, who was subsequently fired from his job.

Promissory Estoppel
A statement may be treated as a promise by a court when the listener relied on the statement to their detriment. *See* § 90 The Restatement (Second) of Contracts.

Incensed, Cohen filed a lawsuit against the newspaper, which was decided by the U.S. Supreme Court in 1991.[18] In the 5–4 ruling, the Court did not find the journalists in breach of contract but instead found they had violated **promissory estoppel**, a doctrine that in essence requires individuals to honor promises they have made to someone if breaking the promise would somehow harm them.

Although not technically a contractual issue, the Supreme Court did endorse the claim such oral agreements do have the force of law, and journalists are not immune to their enforcement. Media professionals also must honor more formal agreements, which means understanding the basic elements of a contract.

Elements of a Contract

Offer
A specific promise, conditional on acceptance, communicated with the intent of forming the terms of a contract.

Three conditions must exist to have a valid, enforceable contract.[19] They are, in order of events,

- offer
- consideration
- acceptance.

16. "'Fast & Furious' Producer Neal Moritz Amicably Settles Lawsuit with Universal," *The Wrap*, September 10, 2020.
17. *See* A.E. Garfield, "The Mischief of Cohen v. Cowles Media Co.," 35 *GA L Rev*. 1087–1128 (2001).
18. *Cowles v. Cohen*, 501 U.S. 663 (1991).
19. It can be argued that there are more than three, and in fact some legal texts list more. USLegal.com, for example, lists six on its website, https://contracts.uslegal.com/elements-of-a-contract/.

Bedrock Law
Three elements define a contract – an *offer* that is based on some form of *consideration* that is *accepted* by at least two parties.

Counteroffer
A conditional promise in response to an offer changing the terms of the original offer and thus requiring acceptance.

Revoke
Withdrawal of the offer by the offeror or offeree before acceptance.

Consider-ation
Each party must receive something of value for the mutual promises to be enforceable as a contract. Money, goods, and services are the most common form of consideration, but it can take other forms of exchange and need not have any monetary value.

Breach of Contract
A legal cause of action based on damages resulting from the failure of a party to fulfill the agreement to perform according to its terms.

An offer is simply when one corporation or individual of sound mind voluntarily agrees to provide goods or services to a second party. Note there are a couple of qualifications. A person must be mentally capable of entering into a contract for it to be binding.

Suppose a friend offers to sell you his car for a certain amount of money. So long as that person is mentally capable (not drunk or a child) and has not been forced to make the offer, the first condition of the contract has been met. Now you may not like the offer, in which case you'd simply ignore it or explicitly reject it.

Perhaps you think the price is too high and instead offer a lower amount. You have made a **counteroffer**, which in effect is a new offer. Now it is up to your friend to decide whether to accept or refuse your offer. Either of you might choose to **revoke** the offer before the contract is completed.

If someone, for example, came along and offered more money for the car before you had accepted the offer, they would be able to retract it. Now if someone offered them more money *after* you accepted the offer, it would be too late to retract the offer. Once all three elements are met, both parties would have to agree on the retraction, or the terms of your contract could be enforced.

Consideration involves some sort of compensation for the goods or services provided. If the offer is to buy his car with cash, money is the consideration. Money is the most common form of consideration in contracts, but there are other exchanges that can take place. They might offer to give you the car and in exchange you mow their lawn for one year.

Regardless, there must be some kind of consideration exchanged. Otherwise, if that party simply promises to give you the car and then changes their mind, there has been no **breach of contract** because there was never a valid contract to begin with. The worst you can say is that their word to you was broken, but *not* that they violated a contract.

Acceptance is your agreement to accept their offer. Acceptance can be **express** (signing the written contract, shaking hands, or saying "It's a deal"), **implied** (as would be the case if you said something like "I'll bring the money tomorrow"), or **conditional**. Conditional acceptance means you accept the offer if certain other conditions are met. This happens in real estate contracts where people agree to buy a home so long as they can sell their current home or provided certain repairs are made to the property.

Once a contract is accepted, it may be tough to get out of it, even if conditions change. The well-known actress Brooke Shields found that a contract her mother signed when she was a minor was still enforceable, even though Shields had become an adult and wanted to rescind the contract.[20]

Shields's mother had signed a contract with a photographer granting him the use of photos taken of her as a child. When she became a young woman, Shields tried to stop the use of her photos through repeated legal actions. Although successful in preventing use of her image in pornographic pictures, she failed to fully invalidate the existing agreement.

Sometimes people enter into legally binding agreements without even being aware of it. Perhaps the best example of this is the user agreements people accept when signing up for "free" services, such as social media accounts. In exchange for free use of the service, users consent to all sorts of conditions, including allowing the platform to use any postings.

Facebook felt the backlash when it started using people's photos in ads they were placing on friends' newsfeeds. Although Facebook eventually stopped its Social Ads program, it did in fact have the legal right to do it.[21]

20. *Shields v. Gross*, 58 N.Y.2d 338 (1983).
21. "How to Stop Facebook from Using Your Name and Photo in Ads," *Business Insider*, March 21, 2011.

Contests are another way you might enter into a legal agreement without realizing it. Contests often require the winner to allow personal publicity for the sponsoring company, but some companies require even those who lose to give their consent.

In 2019, National Geographic was celebrating 100 million followers on Instagram by offering a free photo safari trip to Tanzania for one lucky person who posted a photo in their Instagram contest. Only one person won the trip, but everyone who posted gave consent to National Geographic to use their photos and identity for publicity purposes, forever, for free.[22]

Acceptance
An offeree's assent to the terms of an offer by the means specified or expected by the offeror.

Not all contracts are enforceable. A contract that's agreed to by someone who "lacks capacity" to understand or accept its terms cannot be enforced. Minors, people with mental illnesses, or someone under the influence of alcohol or drugs cannot agree to a legally binding contract.

A contract also may be invalid if someone signs it under duress, as would be the case if someone was threatened with violence or blackmail. Similarly, contracts that require either party to engage in illegal activity are unenforceable, including labor contracts signed by company employees.

Again, we note the three elements: *offer*, *consideration*, and *acceptance* constitute a legally enforceable contract. The contract need not be written, although it is in both parties' interest to see the terms of the agreement in writing.[23] If it's not written, how does anyone prove exactly what the terms of the contract are?

A court battle is likely to involve a number of allegations about what each person was thinking with little evidence to prove all those claims. A vivid example of this occurred with the children's video series *VeggieTales*. Lyrick Studios was licensed by Big Idea to distribute the cartoon.

A series of telephone conversations and faxes went back and forth but no formal signed contract existed. When Lyrick tried to sue Big Idea for issues including rights to DVD distribution (Lyrick had been distributing VHS tapes) and stuffed animals, a federal appeals court ruled no contract existed.[24] There's a joke among lawyers that an oral contract is not even worth the paper it's not written on.

Express Acceptance
Agreement to a contract's terms based on the explicit statements of the offeree.

In the copyright chapter of this text (Chapter 7), we explain how ideas shared only in conversation cannot be copyrighted. Does that leave anyone pitching a story idea for television or film with no legal recourse? Contract law may provide the needed protection. An aspiring producer might pitch an idea by claiming the studio must pay if it chooses to use the idea and might get some sort of affirmation from the studio executive.[25]

Without the formality of a contract, either side can argue there was an understanding between the parties, but without the proof of evidence courts are unlikely to be sympathetic. The Huffington Post was founded in 2005 as a news and opinion website. A lot of the content it used was provided for free by bloggers.

Implied Acceptance
Agreement to a contract's terms only evident due to the context of communication rather than an explicit agreement made by the offeree.

In 2011, when the website was sold to AOL for $315 million, a group of bloggers filed suit claiming they were entitled to a portion of the money, as much of the site's value came from their efforts. A federal appeals court dismissed their claims for unjust enrichment and deceptive trade practices since there was no evidence they should have expected payment.[26]

22. "Celebrating 100M Everyday Explorers," *Vox*, February 20, 2019.
23. The Statute of Frauds does require that some contracts be written. This common law concept has been codified in most states with varying contracts covered. Most states require written contracts for the sale of real estate, the sale of any goods above a certain threshold (often $500), or commitments that would extend beyond one year (such as a two-year employment contract). For a brief explanation, *see* The Statute of Frauds and Contract Law, *at* www.thelaw.com/law/the-statute-of-frauds-and-contract-law.247/.
24. Brooks Boliek, "VeggieTales 'Off Justices' Menu," *Hollywood Reporter*, April 4, 2006, at 4.
25. For a detailed explanation of this process, *see* M. Litwak, *Contracts for the Film and Television Industry* (Los Angeles: Silman-James Press, 2012), *at* 4.
26. *Tasini et. al v. AOL, Inc.*, 505 Fed. App'x. 45 (2d Cir. 2012), *aff'g* 851 F. Supp. 2d 734.

Conditional Acceptance
Consent to an offer qualified by a change in the terms, and so is not an acceptance but instead a counteroffer.

A breach of contract occurs if one of the parties does not fulfill the agreed-to terms. A breach doesn't always result in legal action, though. Sometimes it might be considered so trivial as to be immaterial.

If the contract for selling your friend's car stated his mileage was 100,000 miles and the car was delivered with 100,001 miles on the odometer, then that would be considered an immaterial breach. Strictly interpreted, your friend would be violating the agreed-to conditions of the contract, but the breach would be so inconsequential it would not invalidate the deal.

A material breach of contract might result in a legal order. If your friend refused to sell the car because of a better offer, the court might require its sale to you at the agreed-to price. If the contract was breached by selling you the car with 200,000 miles on it rather than the stipulated 100,000 miles, the court might require your friend to hand the money back or adjust the price appropriately.

Rather than spend all the money on taking a breach of contract to court, the dispute may be resolved by a mediator or through arbitration. Essentially, these alternative solutions require an independent third party to negotiate with the people involved to find the necessary resolution. Professional arbitrators can be found and consulted in most major cities.

CBS settled out of court with five members of the *Happy Days* TV show cast who claimed CBS breached their contract by not paying royalties to the actors for merchandising uses, including putting their pictures on slot machines.[27] Amazon and Woody Allen also settled a breach of contract claim out of court for an undisclosed amount.

Amazon had canceled a $68 million contract for four films, asserting that statements the filmmaker made regarding Harvey Weinstein's sexual misconduct rekindled allegations about Allen's own alleged sexual misconduct. Amazon knew about the allegations against him when it agreed to the contract was Allen's response.[28]

Offer, consideration, and acceptance may be all that's required in a legally binding contract, but they are only the basic elements required. All sorts of terms and conditions are added to contracts to prevent untoward events. Some are clear and simple, such as a clause voiding a contract if one of the parties dies, while others are more obscure and subject to interpretation.

The estate of author Harper Lee and the producers of the Broadway adaptation of her book *To Kill a Mockingbird* fell into a legal dispute over whether the play's script was "faithful to the spirit of the book," which had been stipulated in the contract.[29] The dispute ended amicably when both parties reached an agreement, albeit without disclosing their terms.

It's easy to see how a contract's language can lead to a sticky situation. Ariana Grande sparked quite a controversy over her photographic stipulation requiring all photographers covering her concerts to turn over the rights to any photos they took of her. To get access to her concerts, photographers would have to agree to give her company every image, then request permission from the company to use those images.[30]

From the Trenches: Introduction to Movie Contracts

By Jay S. Kenoff

When Dom Caristi asked me to submit a few paragraphs to provide a short introduction to the scope and complexity of contracts required for motion picture production, my first thought was that I could easily take care of this assignment by copying the

27. "CBS, 'Happy Days' Cast Settle Royalties Lawsuit," *Hollywood Reporter*, July 6, 2012.
28. "Woody Allen Settles $68 Million Suit against Amazon," *Variety*, November 9, 2019.
29. "Broadway 'Mockingbird' Is Back on Track, as Court Dispute Ends," *NY Times*, May 10, 2018. The case was settled out of court.
30. "Ariana Grande's Tour Photo Agreement Prompts Protest by News Outlets," *Billboard*, March 26, 2019.

Table of Contents from my two volumes on "Motion Pictures" that are part of the ten-volume set of *Entertainment Industry Contracts: Negotiating and Drafting Guide* published by the renowned law book company, Matthew Bender.

After a glance at the Table of Contents, I realized that I needed a different approach. So the following paragraphs, while not a comprehensive contract list, will, I hope, by identifying a selection of essential motion picture contracts along with critical steps involved, provide an idea of the scope of legal requirements for motion picture production.

Since an experienced motion picture producer knows the myriad contracts and steps involved in motion picture production and distribution, at the outset the producer hires an experienced entertainment attorney to provide "production legal services." Such services are often provided by an attorney with the assistance of associates who are prepared to work virtually full-time on a movie from the first steps of literary property acquisition until delivery of the completed movie for distribution.

Motion pictures, whether fictional, nonfictional, or documentary, and whether low- or high-budget, will involve a series of contracts, usually starting with the acquisition of a story that may come from a variety of sources, ranging from best-selling books to short stories to magazine articles, and even amusement park rides ("Pirates of the Caribbean").

Once a producer identifies a story (or literary property) as the basis for a movie, the producer will involve an attorney to secure and clear rights. Critical steps will involve reviewing the chain of title to ensure rights are being acquired from the rightful owner of the property. It may be necessary to perform a copyright search of pertinent documents in the U.S. Copyright Office.

With rights secured by an option or purchase agreement, the producer will embark on the process of creating a viable screenplay, and the hiring of a writer will usually signify the start of "development." Depending on whether the producer has already lined up financing, the producer may need to pursue various avenues for obtaining financial backers. Often, the producer will form a single purpose company for the purpose of producing the movie, and the producer's attorneys will be involved in ensuring that fund-raising efforts comply with federal and state securities laws.

The option/purchase agreement will provide the producer with a time window to assemble financing and elements for production. Besides hiring a writer, the producer will enter agreements with a director and cast performers (probably with the assistance of a casting director), and the producer will scout locations. Depending upon guild affiliations, the producer's company may have to become signatory to agreements with the Writers Guild of America, the Directors Guild of America, and SAG-AFTRA. The terms of such agreements will depend on the projected budget of the movie.

The script will be broken down into scenes, and a production budget and schedule will be prepared by film industry specialists contracted by the producer. An attorney will review the script (termed "clearance") for possible infringement and other legal problems. Further contracts will be required for special effects and processes that are added after completion of principal photography.

During a pre-pre-production phase that will commence between a few weeks and several months before actual pre-production starts, contracts will be entered with production staff and crew members. Depending on multiple factors, such as genre, budget, historical period, and locations of the movie, the producer will enter contracts with makeup artists, costume designers, set craftspeople, and so on.

Once pre-production commences for the movie, a rigid timetable has to be followed, especially because key personnel (such as stars) have other commitments that start when their filming of the current movie ends.

Bedrock Law

Oral agreements can be as binding as a written contract but proving the conditions can be challenging.

More contracts are also required for post-production and music services after principal photography ends. Then, after the movie is completed and ready for delivery for exhibition and exploitation, there will be contracts for distribution in theaters, home video, all forms of television, nontheatrical venues, and so forth.

Producing a movie is a collaborative effort. To get a visual idea of all the people who participate, just sit through the lengthy end credits of a theatrical feature motion picture. Virtually all people whose names appear in the credits will need to have signed contracts so that the producer can then confidently seek its distribution.

A founding partner of Kenoff & Machtinger, LLP, Jay Kenoff practices law principally in the area of entertainment transactional matters providing services to individuals and companies in the fields of motion pictures, television, music, concerts, post-production services, publishing, and new media.

Releases as a Contract

Most people are familiar with a simple release form. As a child, you probably had to bring one home for your parents to sign so that you could participate in a class field trip. It was intended to release from liability the school, teacher, and bus driver should anything happen to you on the class trip. The release served two different functions – it assured the school that your parents knew and approved of your going with the class, and it also prevented any lawsuits should anything unexpected occur on the trip.[31]

Bedrock Law

If one of the participants does not fulfill the obligations of a contract, then a breach has occurred that can result in a court order.

Release forms are used by motion picture studios, advertisers, and video producers to obtain permission for the use of people's images in their work. Someone shooting a television commercial at a grocery store must be certain to have a release form signed by everyone who appears in that commercial; otherwise, people later may be able to claim that they were used without their consent and as such have a right to compensation or even the right to have the commercial removed from the air.

To prevent this type of misapprehension, producers have everyone sign a release form that specifically states their willingness to appear in the commercial. In the typical release form, offer, consideration, and acceptance are easy to see. The producer invites the participation of those who appear in the commercial, their acceptance is in writing on the release form, and consideration is offered in the form of a payment.

But what about those occasions when individuals agree to appear in an advertisement or some other commercial use of their image without getting any compensation? Does this mean the signed release form is not a contract? Not necessarily.

Frequently, student filmmakers will involve friends, family, and other volunteers as actors in their films without any payment. While some universities pay students for the use of their images in brochures, on websites, and in other promotional material, others do not. The University of Texas Talent Release Form, for example, begins "For valuable consideration."[32]

Implied Consent

An agreement reached not apparent from a person's express statements, but from circumstances. For example, all licensed drivers in the United States have implied their consent to a field sobriety test.

It can be legitimately argued there is a value in having one's image used in an advertisement. A student with no modeling experience can gain portfolio examples by being included in advertisements. Aspiring actors can add lines to their résumés.

There are actually times when a signed release form may not exist, but a producer or photographer can show an individual did give **implied consent**. In other words, the person whose image is being used obviously knew the image was going to be used and voiced no objections.

31. These releases are limited in protecting the school from liability. If the bus driver had an accident in which you were injured and it was determined that the driver had been drinking, the release would not likely protect the school from a lawsuit given the extenuating circumstance of his actions.
32. https://deanofstudents.utexas.edu/sa/downloads/UTTalentReleaseForm.pdf.

For example, if you were making a video about your university and interviewed fellow students about the reasons why they chose to attend your school, you might assert that by voluntarily sitting down in a video studio and answering your questions, they were giving their consent to appear in the video.

Obviously, they knew they were being recorded. It might be arguable whether they knew how the video would be used, but that's why a signed release form outlining the use of the video, even providing blanket permission to use the video in any way, is always better than trying to assert implied consent.

Bedrock Law

The use of a person's image or persona for commercial purposes requires either implied or stated consent, as in a written release.

If you had told students that you were making a video for use in the classroom and then the video ended up in a national TV commercial, your claim of implied consent would not work because what they consented to and what you used it for were two different things.

It's a lot easier to assert implied consent for a situation such as recording a television talk show, where the actual use of the video is well-known. Members of the studio audience for *Ellen*, for example, know before going in that they may appear on television. They could not later claim that the producers did not have their permission to use their image.

Employment Contracts

Creative Accounting in Hollywood

While many of the people who work on major motion pictures have a specified salary, some prominent figures choose to include a share of the film's profits as part of their payment. Some studios have been accused of "hiding" a film's profits so that they don't have to pay as much to stars, writers, or directors who contracted for a share of the profits, which has resulted in some high-profile lawsuits over the years. Here are just a few:

- Writer Art Buchwald sued Paramount when the film he wrote, *Coming to America* with Eddie Murphy, showed no profit, despite grossing more than $280 million (in 1980s dollars). The studio settled the suit for $900,000.[33]
- The stars and executive producers of long-running TV series *Bones* settled with Fox in 2019 for an undisclosed, "substantial" amount.[34]
- Eight years after starring in *Olympus Has Fallen*, actor Gerard Butler sued claiming he was not receiving his fair share. Finally in 2023 (10 years after the film's release), they announced an undisclosed settlement.[35]

It's good to remember that contracts are important, but they don't eliminate the possibility of legal disputes.

It can be very intimidating to be given a multipage contract when being hired for your first job after college, but this is the situation many graduates find themselves in when joining media corporations. This is especially true for those people who will have on-air positions in large markets, and it is becoming more the norm in smaller markets, as well as for news producers and people in sales and advertising. There are several clauses in particular that are of special interest in media employment contracts.

33. "Buchwald, Partner Win $900,000 From Studio," *Los Angeles Times*. March 17, 1992.
34. "'Bones' Profit Battle Ends As Fox & Disney Settle With Stars Emily Deschanel, David Boreanaz & Eps," *Deadline*, September 11, 2019.
35. "Gerard Butler's $10M 'Olympus Has Fallen' Profits Lawsuit Settles," *Hollywood Reporter*, October 12, 2023.

Noncompete Clauses

Noncompete Clauses
Provisions in a contract preventing a person, often an employee who has learned trade secrets or practical skills from a company, from competing against them after termination of services. Federal Trade Commission regulations made most of these unenforceable after 2024.

Earlier editions of this textbook devoted several pages to **noncompete clauses**, which prevented many media employees from leaving a company to work for a competitor. The rules were rooted in the principle of protecting businesses from unfair competition.[36] On-air talent couldn't take their audiences with them to a competing station, and salespeople couldn't take their clients with them to the competing newspaper or station. The Federal Trade Commission flipped 180 degrees in 2024, asserting that almost all noncompete agreements were unfair competition, in addition to often being exploitative.[37] The FTC claimed companies could use other tools such as trade secrets laws and nondisclosure agreements instead of noncompetes. As of this writing, a federal court in Texas has set aside the FTC rule, and a decision is likely from the Fifth Circuit Court of Appeals.[38]

Nondisclosure Clauses

Nondisclosure Agreement
Clause in a contract that requires the signer to remain silent about company secrets, confidential information, or other designated matters.

Perhaps an employee might be allowed to take a job with a competitor but must agree not to disclose any company secrets. **Nondisclosure** clauses in contracts bind the parties to maintain secrecy. Violations can be costly. In 2017, ZeniMax, a virtual reality company, was awarded $200 million for violation of a nondisclosure agreement by Oculus's cofounder.[39]

In addition to protecting trade secrets, nondisclosure clauses are a part of reality and game show contestant contracts. Shows would naturally lose viewers if everyone knew in advance who won, so participants are obligated to remain silent until their episode airs.[40] The hit reality TV show *Survivor* requires contestants to sign an agreement for nondisclosure of any trade secrets or disclosing anything about the show prior to broadcast.[41]

Nondisclosure agreements (NDAs) that prevent disclosure of a game show winner or secret formula are generally seen as necessary, but what happens when a nondisclosure clause is used instead to hide wrongdoing? In the wake of the #MeToo movement, it seems some sexual assault victims were paid settlements involving NDAs.

In 2017, when allegations of sexual misconduct began surfacing about film producer Harvey Weinstein's professional relations, a former assistant wanted to come forward to disclose how Weinstein's alleged behavior fit a pattern she knew, but the NDA she signed as part of a settlement prohibited her from speaking with anyone about her experiences.[42]

When allegations of sexual misconduct surfaced regarding NBC News host Matt Lauer, some accused the network of using NDAs and out-of-court settlements to keep the viewing

36. A good survey article is "Note: Switching Stations: The Battle over Non-Compete Agreements in the Broadcasting Industry," 27 *Okla. City U. L. Rev.* 693 (2002).
37. "FTC Announces Rule Banning Noncompetes," *Federal Trade Commission*, April 23, 2024.
38. https://www.whitecase.com/insight-tool/white-case-global-non-compete-resource-center-ncrc
39. J. Fingas, "Oculus to Pay $500 Million after ZeniMax Lawsuit Ends," *Engadget*, February 1, 2017, *at* www.engadget.com/2017/02/01/zenimax-partial-win-oculus-lawsuit/.
40. An important detail is that contestants can be restrained, but not people who have no connection to the show. After settling two lawsuits with ABC, website operator "Reality Steve" no longer offers cash to contestants for leaked information but still manages to provide devout readers with lots of juicy tidbits. "'Bachelor' Spoiler Alert! How Reality Steve Still Gets Away with Ruining the Show," *Hollywood Reporter*, May 25, 2016.
41. Sheri Burr, *Entertainment Law in a Nutshell* 49, 3rd ed. (Eagan, MN: West Publishing, 2012). For an in-depth look into reality TV show contracts, the *Village Voice* provided an entire 30-page *Real World* contract. "We Have Obtained a Copy of MTV's Standard Real World Cast-Member Contract," *at* www.villagevoice.com/news/we-have-obtained-a-copy-of-mtvs-standard-real-world-cast-member-contract-6724278.
42. "#MeToo Law Restricts Use of Nondisclosure Agreements in Sexual Misconduct Cases," *Los Angeles Times*, December 31, 2018.

public, and possibly other victims, unaware of the accusations. NBC announced it would release any former employee alleging sexual assault from any NDA, upon request.[43]

In 2018, 16 states considered legislation to prevent enforcement of NDAs in cases involving sexual misconduct.[44] At least eight states (Arizona, California, Maryland, New Jersey, New York, Tennessee, Vermont, and Washington) passed bills along those lines.[45]

At the federal level, a congressional bill known by the acronym EMPOWER – Ending the Monopoly of Power Over Workplace harassment through Education and Reporting – was introduced in 2019. It would make it illegal to enforce NDAs or non-disparagement clauses in alleged workplace harassment complaints, but the bill did not make it out of committee.[46]

Morals Clauses

We have a celebrity-smitten culture, and the elevated status of personal fame is worth a fortune to the stars of sports and entertainment. There are some athletes who actually earn more money from endorsements and personal appearances than they do from the sport itself. In 1999, Tiger Woods signed a five-year deal with Nike for $100 million. That was only *one* of his endorsement deals.

Whenever a new motion picture is released, the stars will appear on TV talk shows to promote the film, and it's often the *only* time some stars will agree to do talk shows. The studios know the promotional value of their personal appearances will boost the box office revenue.

Radio and television personalities attract audiences to parades and local charity events. Because the image of these individuals is so important to the media companies they represent, most of them have a **morals clause** in their contract.

Morals Clause
A provision to prohibit a party's personal behavior from tarnishing a contractor's image.

Morals clauses in contracts hold individuals responsible for behavior that is damaging to their reputation and thus tarnishes the brand of the media outlet or product they represent. In 2003, when basketball star Kobe Bryant was accused of sexually assaulting a hotel worker, he lost $11.5 million in endorsement deals, including $5 million from Coca-Cola.

It's important to recognize that morals clauses require only that a reputation be damaged without a finding of guilt, so even before a trial occurs or even if someone is found innocent of any supposed wrongdoing, the company can claim public allegations were enough to result in a canceled contract. Celebrities accused in public of wrongdoing are "damaged goods" and less likely to attract consumers to the products they endorse.

Broadcast companies are especially concerned about the images of their high-profile employees. NBC fired famed sports announcer Marv Albert in 1997 after he pleaded guilty to sexual assault charges. Michael Nader was an actor on the soap opera *All My Children*. In 2001, he was arrested for selling cocaine, and ABC terminated his contract. Nader attempted to have his contract reinstated claiming discrimination, but the court upheld the morals clause applied against him.

Actor Charlie Sheen was fired from the successful CBS sitcom *Two and a Half Men* in 2011 after CBS and Warner Brothers alleged Sheen had engaged in erratic behavior. Sheen did *not* have a morals clause in his contract, but CBS and WB claimed they were able to dismiss the actor because his behavior rose to "a felony offense involving moral turpitude."[47]

43. "NBC Agrees to Release Sexual Assault Accusers from NDAs," *The Daily Caller*, October 26, 2019.
44. "States Move to Limit Workplace Confidentiality Agreements," *CBS News*, August 27, 2018.
45. "Bag the Gag Provision: New Jersey Is the Latest State to Restrict Non-Disclosure Agreements in Settlements," *Lexology*, May 14, 2019.
46. H.R. 1521, 116th Congress, *at* www.congress.gov/bill/116th-congress/house-bill/1521.
47. Mike Fleeman, "Why Charlie Sheen Was Fired from Two and a Half Men," *People*, March 7, 2011, *at* http://people.com/crime/charlie-sheen-fired-the-inside-story/.

Sheen filed suit for breach of contract, but a clause in his contract required arbitration to settle disputes and so he reached a confidential settlement.[48]

On a local level, U.S. broadcast stations often have morals clauses in the contracts with their on-air staff. If a newsperson gets drunk at a bar and causes a disturbance, stations argue that the audience will lose respect both for the person involved and the station for which that person works. Celebrities (and local broadcast talent) must recognize that their actions are subject to scrutiny, even while not at work, and even if miles away from home.

In 2003, a Youngstown, Ohio, newscaster was vacationing in the Florida Keys after recovering from a serious illness. In celebration, she participated in a wet T-shirt contest and eventually was photographed completely naked. She resigned when pictures of her started showing up on the Internet.

Morals clauses may even lead to a contract being terminated. In 2016, a Pittsburgh television station fired a news anchor over a single social media post. No illegal behavior was alleged; instead, the station severed ties with them over attention the station wanted to avoid.[49]

> The clause in Michael Nader's contract that resulted in his termination from *All My Children* is fairly typical. It read:
>
> If, in the opinion of ABC, Artist shall commit any act or do anything which might tend to bring Artist into public disrepute, contempt, scandal, or ridicule, or which might tend to reflect unfavorably on ABC, any sponsor of a program, any such sponsor's advertising agency, any stations broadcasting or scheduled to broadcast a program, or any licensee of ABC, or to injure the success of any use of the Series or any program, ABC may, upon written notice to Artist, immediately terminate the Term and Artist's employment hereunder.[50]
>
> Sample Morals Clause

Inclusion Rider

Before 2018, very few people had heard of an "**inclusion rider**" in a contract. At the Oscars ceremony that year, Frances McDormand's acceptance speech included the phrase, and suddenly the Hollywood creative community started to discuss it.[51] The rider requires studios commit to inclusiveness (whether by race, sex, age, etc.) on a film or television project.

Artists and actors who wield some power are able to insist on such considerations while others just starting out would never be able to make such demands. Actors Brie Larson, Michael B. Jordan, and Ashley Judd all publicly stated their commitment,[52] but the inclusion rider is far from universally accepted.

Hold-Harmless Clauses

In certain outlets of the media – advertising and public relations, for example – an employment contract can make a discernible difference in terms of how vulnerable the employee is

48. Charlie Sheen, "Warner Brothers Settle Contract Dispute," September 28, 2011, *at* www.watkinsfirm.com/charlie-sheen-warner-brothers-settle-contract-dispute/.
49. "Wendy Bell, Fired over Her Controversial Facebook Posts, Says She Didn't Get a 'Fair Shake'," *Pittsburgh Post-Gazette*, March 30, 2016. The anchor filed a discrimination suit against the station for her firing, which was apparently settled out of court.
50. *Nader v. ABC Television*, Inc., 330 F. Supp. 2d 345, 346 (S.D. N.Y. 2004), *aff'd* 150 Fed. Appx. 54 (2d Cir. 2005).
51. "A Year after Frances McDormand's Oscars Speech, Are Inclusion Riders Making Progress?" *Los Angeles Times*, February 27, 2019.
52. "7 Hollywood Stars to Add Inclusion Riders to Their Projects, from Michael B. Jordan to Brie Larson," *The Wrap*, March 13, 2018.

Hold-Harmless Clause

A provision in a contract in which one party agrees not to hold the other party responsible for damages. This is usually a unilateral indemnification, but it can be reciprocal among multiple parties.

to a corporate lawsuit. In the realm of public relations, there are safeguards – indemnification, or hold-harmless clauses – that essentially free the professional from personal responsibility should a press release that harms a client be approved by higher executives.

Such fine print in an employee's contract relies on mutual and informed assent by both the boss and the practitioner. The contract also will not be worth the paper it is printed on if the terms shift the burden of responsibility to the weaker party in the deal.

Multiple Contracts

Anyone who has ever bought a house knows that a transaction can require *multiple* contracts, not just one. The same can be said for media transactions. Imagine a contestant on a reality TV show where music is performed. The contestants might be asked to sign any of the following:

- Management Agreement
- Merchandising Agreement
- Music Publishing Agreement
- Recording Agreement
- Touring Agreement
- "All Rights" Agreement

Those are in addition to the standard employment contract containing morals clauses, nondisclosure agreements, and the list goes on.

Media and Antitrust

Nothing in the U.S. Constitution says anything about the ownership of media, but there are federal regulations controlling media ownership. Issues of media ownership and concentration became contentious in the twentieth century as media conglomerates grew, and some people feared undue control of the marketplace of ideas by only a few voices. As noted at the beginning of this chapter, media are subject to the laws of commerce, which include prohibitions against antitrust violations.

Sherman Act

U.S. federal law enacted in 1890 to prohibit monopolistic behavior by businesses. It's been used to break up powerful monopolies or near-monopolies, such as Standard Oil.

In 1890, Congress passed the **Sherman Act** in order to curb the growing concentration of economic power. It attacked monopolistic activity by businesses and was used to break up powerful monopolies or near-monopolies, such as Standard Oil in the early twentieth century.

Today, the Sherman Act and its progeny, the Clayton Antitrust Act of 1914, prohibit activities that encourages the monopolization of a market but not all activities. For example, if there are three newspapers in a community, one of them may be able to drive out the other two newspapers by doing a better job of covering the news, by lowering the price of their newspaper, or by providing superior customer service. It is accepted these forces might drive out competition, but none of them would be illegal.[53]

On the other hand, if two of the newspapers colluded to lower their prices, that would be illegal. It might appear at first that the consumer would benefit – after all, two of the three newspapers would decrease in price. Competitors, however, are prohibited from colluding with one another because the result is likely to be less competition. By lowering their prices, the two newspapers could drive out the third competitor, at which time the conspiring papers could then raise their prices, and profits, with no existing competition. Agreements among

53. In fact, lowering the price of the newspaper could be a violation of antitrust regulations if the price drop were determined to be predatory pricing. But that discussion is beyond the scope of this text.

competitors to fix prices are illegal "per se," and no evidence of harm or other effects is needed.[54]

Collusion and Codes

The National Association of Broadcasters used to have both a Television Code and Radio Code to encourage members to follow certain principles the NAB considered to be ethical and awarded the "seal of good practice" to those stations. Standards were applied for journalists to keep editorial opinions to themselves; stations were asked to air religious programming; the maximum number of minutes of allowable commercial time was established.

The Justice Department saw these prescriptions as collusion between competitors, and in 1983 the NAB consented to do away with its codes.

More recently, the Department of Justice has questioned the Academy of Motion Picture Arts and Sciences, claiming its proposed rule changes might be an antitrust violation. The Academy was considering changing the length of time that a film would have to be shown in theaters, as opposed to online, from one week to four weeks to be eligible for the Oscar for Best Picture. Many in the industry saw the proposed change as a clear attack on Netflix, which in 2019 released *Roma*, nominated for ten Oscars and winner of three.[55] However, with the arrival of the coronavirus pandemic restrictions in 2020 and corresponding drop in theater showings, the proposed rule change was quickly forgotten.

Cross-Media Competition

Throughout much of the 1930s and 1940s, the *Lorain Journal* was the only daily newspaper in Lorain, OH. The mere fact it operated a monopoly was not illegal. The paper had done nothing to cause the single-newspaper market in which it found itself. In 1948, a new radio station, WEOL, entered the market and threatened to be a true competitor for the *Journal*.

The newspaper decided to take drastic action. It instituted a policy of refusing to accept advertising from anyone who also purchased advertising from WEOL. The *Journal* hoped to force advertisers to choose between the two competitors, and as the dominant medium in the market, the newspaper expected to be the overwhelming choice.

It should be recognized there is no law against refusing to accept advertising. In most cases, the result is a loss of revenue for the medium, and there may be more harm to the medium than the advertiser. The *Journal* attempted to defend itself in court with this very argument because it had the right to decide whether to sell advertising to anyone.

In this situation, however, the purpose of refusing to sell the advertising was to encourage the monopolization of the market. In court, several Lorain County businesses testified they stopped advertising on WEOL or never started due to the policy. When the case was appealed to the Supreme Court, the unanimous decision held the actions of the newspaper were a violation of antitrust law because it was a blatant effort to monopolize the market.[56]

Sports Franchises

Congress created antitrust regulation, so it has the authority to create exemptions from the laws. National television broadcasts of sports were still in the early stages in 1961 when Congress passed an antitrust exemption to allow professional sports leagues to enforce blackouts on telecasts.[57]

54. "Antitrust Guidelines for Collaborations among Competitors," *Federal Trade Commission and Department of Justice*, April 2000.
55. "As Academy Confronts Netflix Question, Streamer Has Many Friends With a Vote," *Hollywood Reporter*, April 22, 2019.
56. *Lorain Journal v. United States*, 342 U.S. 143 (1951).
57. 15 U.S.C. § 1291.

Without this exemption, the NFL would not be able to dictate that neither television stations nor cable operators could provide a live telecast of a game within that market unless that game was sold out by 72 hours before game time. The FCC enforced sports blackout rules through 2014 but now no longer gets involved. It's a completely contractual agreement between teams, leagues, and media outlets, all through their respective contracts.

Online Competition

Google is a pretty well-known Internet player. Its parent company, Alphabet, is one of the world's most valuable companies. The company is best known for its search engine, which had over 91% of the global market share in January 2024.[58] In 2017 the European Commission fined Google $2.7 billion for antitrust violations involving online shopping, contending it made it so Google searches favored its own product over those of competitors.

The following year, the EC fined Google $5 billion for unfairly favoring its own Android products by forcing phone makers to pre-install exclusively Google apps. Then in 2019, Google was fined again, this time for $1.7 billion for alleged exclusive contracts with publishers using AdSense, restricting them from showing competitors' ads.

In 2023, Google settled a lawsuit with all 50 U.S. states for $700 million. The state attorneys general claimed the company engaged in anticompetitive behavior in its Play Store and Android apps. Had the case gone to trial and Google lost, the judgment could have been as much as $10 billion.[59]

The company continues to face antitrust lawsuits, including one filed by the U.S. Department of Justice in 2024 contending that the company used anticompetitive mergers and bullying to advantage its advertising technology. Google claims the market is competitive.[60]

Global View: Aggressive European Antitrust Enforcement

Companies are attentive to more than just U.S. law when they do business abroad. Google is not alone; the number of European antitrust claims against other tech companies has increased.

Facebook and Apple faced European antitrust wrath in 2020. Amazon is being investigated by the European Union, accused of anticompetitive behavior by exploiting the data it collects from sellers on its platform.[61] Microsoft, which the European Union found guilty of antitrust violations in 2004 for bundling Windows with its Media Player, had a suit filed against it by Slack alleging that by tying Teams to Office, Microsoft was violating European antitrust law. Clearly, the U.S. and European antitrust systems differ,[62] and multinational companies need to act accordingly.

You Paid What for Concert Tickets?

There are no federal laws regulating the price of concert tickets, and that lack of regulation may be impacting the soaring prices. Late in 2022, tickets went on sale for the

58. Search Engine Market Share Worldwide, Statcounter, *at* https://gs.statcounter.com/search-engine-market-share.
59. "Google to pay $700 million to US states, consumers in app store settlement," Associated Press, December 19, 2023.
60. "DOJ Antitrust Case Targeting Google's ad-Tech Business Will Go to Trial in September, Federal Judge Rules," *CNN*, February 5, 2024.
61. "Amazon Faces Antitrust Charges from European Regulators," *NPR*, November 10, 2020.
62. "The European and U.S. Approaches to Antitrust and Tech: Setting the Record Straight: A Reply to Gregory J. Werden and Luke M. Froeb's Antitrust and Tech: Europe and the United States Differ, and It Matters," *CPI Europe*, May 4, 2020.

highly anticipated Taylor Swift "Eras" tour, and Ticketmaster's website crashed within an hour from the high demand. Swift's company worked diligently with Ticketmaster (the largest ticket sales company in the world) to prevent resellers (aka scalpers) from buying up tickets and reselling them for two or three times their face value.

There is also no federal law against ticket scalping, but seven states require ticket resellers to have a special license.[63] With limited resale tickets available, ironically Taylor's fans found they could sell their tickets for as much as **ten** times what they paid, creating a whole new secondary market.[64]

Some see the concert venue/ticketing process as problematic. In 2023 the Senate Judiciary Committee began an investigation into Ticketmaster, which along with parent company Live Nation, controls more than 70% of live event sales and ticketing. With so much market power, abuses are always a possibility, and there is a history of complaints against the company.[65]

Trade publication *Billboard* stated, "if the Live Nation-owned platform didn't have such market dominance, greater competition would force the company to innovate and improve its services."[66] Though no antitrust regulations were imposed, new regulation prevented ticket companies from adding "junk fees" to the total price of tickets.[67]

Employment Laws

Professional media careers can be defined either in terms of full employment or part-time help. It is into this space that the self-employed journalist, broadcaster, or content producer enters the picture. Predictions are that by 2026, 25% of those working in the arts, design, entertainment, sports, and media industries will be self-employed – the highest concentration of any occupational group.[68] They often work as freelancers who are hired on for specific jobs.

Most of the people who work on a motion picture, for example, are not employees of the studio but are either employees of the companies subcontracted for effects, graphics, and other production tasks, or are freelance workers specifically hired on for the one film. This includes everything from minor production assistants up to the film's director. And they are not the only ones.

When you watch a sporting event on a broadcast or cable network, most of the production crew likely consists of freelancers. Entire print and web publications can be produced largely by freelance workers. Rather than hire full-time employees, who must be provided with paid vacation, sick days, insurance, Social Security, and fringe benefits, using freelance labor saves a lot of money. Companies use freelance contracts like the one shown in Figure 12.1 to be certain there are no doubts the company is not an "employer" required to provide employment benefits.

63. Alabama, Georgia, Illinois, Massachusetts, New Jersey, New York, and Pennsylvania.
64. "Taylor Swift's Biggest Scalper for the Eras Tour: Her Fans," *Billboard*, November 17, 2023.
65. Scott Andrzejewski, "Antitrust Complaints Filed Against Ticketmaster and Live Nation in California: An Overview and Analysis," *Univ. Chicago Bus. L. Rev.*, 2023, *at* https://businesslawreview.uchicago.edu/online-archive/antitrust-complaints-filed-against-ticketmaster-and-live-nation-california-overview.
66. "Taylor Swift Is the Least of Ticketmaster's Worries after Senate Hearing," *Billboard*, January 26, 2023.
67. Though Ticketmaster did agree not to add extra "surprise" fees to ticket prices, they later stated this only applied to situations in which Live Nation controls the venue, i.e., they would still add fees to some sales. M. Kelly, "Ticketmaster's Still Hiding Ticket Fees, Senator Says," *The Verge*, October 26, 2023.
68. U.S. Bureau of Labor Statistics, "Small-Business Options: Occupational Outlook for Self-Employed Workers," May 2018, *at* www.bls.gov/careeroutlook/2018/article/self-employment.htm.

BTN BIG TEN NETWORK

CREW DEAL MEMORANDUM	Business Use Only:

NAME: ______________________("Freelancer") DATE: ______ PHONE: ______________

ADDRESS: ____

E-MAIL: ______________________ RATE: $__________/ HOUR DAY WEEK

POSITION / SERVICES:______________________("Services")

TERM OF SERVICES:START DATE: ____________ END DATE: ____________ ("Term")

1. RATE: Services are only guaranteed for the Term and no payment will be made where additional services are provided by Freelancer without prior approval from Big Ten Network, LLC ("Network").

2. COMPENSATION: In full and complete consideration of Freelancer's performance of the Services, the grant of other rights hereunder and all of Freelancer's representations and warranties, and provided Network receives an executed copy of this Crew Deal Memorandum and all other required documentation, Network will pay Freelancer the rate set forth above. The foregoing applicable rate shall be payable less applicable withholdings and deductions as required by law, after Network's receipt of a properly submitted time card(s) from Freelancer. Time cards must be submitted to Network's production accountant on a weekly basis. Any time card submitted late may result in late and/or incomplete paychecks. All time cards submitted must reflect hours worked, with proper start and end times for each day that Freelancer actually rendered Services. Freelancer will not be paid for any day(s) that Freelancer does not actually render Services for any reason (e.g., not scheduled by Network for any reason, including, but not limited to, sickness, dark days, force majeure, etc.).

Network will not provide Freelancer with any benefits (beyond the rate set forth above), including, but not limited to, medical, dental or vision benefits, pension or retirement benefits (including 401k), vacation, stock or stock options. Network will provide Freelancer with Worker's Compensation and unemployment insurance. Network will withhold from the compensation it pays to Freelancer all applicable taxes. Freelancer understands and agrees that Freelancer is responsible to pay all other applicable taxes on all compensation paid to Freelancer.

3. PURCHASES/RENTALS/EXPENSES: Any purchase, rental, or expense must be pre-approved by Network in writing. Network will reimburse only those pre-approved purchases, rentals or expenses accompanied by original receipts.

4. OWNERSHIP: All products, results and proceeds of the Services, including the idea, concept, materials, and format therefore, in whatever stage of completion (collectively the "Works"), are "works-made-for-hire" for Network, and Network is deemed the author thereof. As "works-made-for-hire," at such time as fixed in a tangible medium of expression, the Works will be Network's sole and exclusive property, in perpetuity, throughout the universe, in all media, together with all licenses, rights of every kind and nature, privileges, ancillary rights, copyrights and rights to renew and extend copyrights in and to any or all of the Works. If the Works or any part of the Works are not deemed "works-made-for-hire," Freelancer hereby transfers and assigns all copyrights and all intellectual property or other claim Freelancer may ever have in any of the Works to Network. Freelancer expressly waives any personal or proprietary rights and any "moral rights of authors," now or hereafter recognized, in and to any and all of the Works. Network's rights to the Works include, without limitation, the exclusive and unlimited right to exhibit, perform, display, change, alter, revise, edit, dub, add to, subtract from, combine with other material, distribute, merchandise, market and otherwise exploit any and all of the Works. All rights to the Works granted to Network in this Crew Deal Memorandum are irrevocable and will immediately vest and remain vested in Network, its successors, and assigns.

5. NON-UNION ENGAGEMENT: Freelancer acknowledges that the production of the Show/Event referenced herein, and all of Network's productions are non-union productions and that Network is not a party to, and has no present intention of becoming a party to any guild, collective bargaining or similar agreement that might apply to Freelancer's Services.

6. PUBLICITY RESTRICTION: Except as expressly permitted under this paragraph, under no circumstances and at no time, either during or after the Services, will Freelancer directly or indirectly, disclose, divulge, render or offer any knowledge or information to any other person or party concerning matters relating to the Services or any Series episode or Network's affairs and plans of which Freelancer has knowledge, including, but not limited to, the compensation of the personnel and performers, all past, present, or future production budgets, story ideas, story content, works in progress, confidential or exclusive information, story leads and tips (collectively "Confidential Information"). Any disclosure of Confidential Information by Freelancer will constitute a material breach of this Crew Deal Memorandum and a cause for termination of it and Freelancer's engagement. Notwithstanding the foregoing, the following will not constitute a prohibited disclosure: (i) disclosure to the extent required by law, including by a valid governmental order or regulation, provided Freelancer notifies Network of said government order or regulation; and (ii) disclosure of the contents of this Crew Deal Memorandum to Freelancer's lawyers, accountants, lenders and other business representatives upon condition that Freelancer secures said representatives' agreement to keep all Confidential Information confidential.

7. MISCELLANEOUS TERMS.

(a) Freelancer voluntarily assumes all risks of loss or damage to personal property by participating in the production of the Show/Event or being otherwise present on the specific work premises or work location.

(b) Freelancer acknowledges receipt of, and agrees during the Term to abide by the provisions of Network's Freelancer Work Rules, a copy of which is attached hereto as Exhibit A and incorporated herein by this reference.

(c) Freelancer understands and agrees that Freelancer's employment is on a day-to-day, "at will" basis, and that Network has the right to terminate Freelancer's employment at any time and for any reason upon notice to Freelancer.

(d) Governing law: This Crew Deal Memorandum and all matters collateral hereto will be governed by the laws of the State of California, U.S.A.

(e) Entire Agreement: This Crew Deal Memorandum supersedes and cancels all prior negotiations and understandings between the parties and contains all of the terms agreed to by the parties with respect to the subject matter hereof. No officer, employee or representative of Network has any authority to make any representation or promise not contained in this Crew Deal Memorandum, and Freelancer has not executed this Crew Deal Memorandum in reliance on any such representation or promise.

AGREED TO BY FREELANCER: **BIG TEN NETWORK, LLC**

______________________ ______________________

Figure 12.2 Typical example of a contract for freelance video work

Interns

Media companies have gone back and forth in recent years over their commitment to the proper use of interns. Internships are intended to be educational opportunities where students learn more about a selected career through "shadowing" or working as assistants to employees at the company. Internships are *not* supposed to be simply free labor provided by students. The issue is complicated because students who work for "free" for a media company are likely to be learning while working.

In 2011, a lot of scrutiny was placed on media internships after a lawsuit involving interns working the motion picture production of *Black Swan* raised concerns about their duties. Two interns sued the film's producers, claiming they were made to do menial work that was not educational – work that should have been done by paid employees.[69] Fox Searchlight settled that case in 2016 with interns who worked on the film.[70]

During the intervening years, a variety of similar lawsuits were filed. In 2012, talk news program *Charlie Rose* settled a lawsuit with unpaid interns on that show.[71] In 2017, MGM settled a class action filed by unpaid interns working on their productions.[72]

Obviously, there is some confusion among media companies and interns about what is an acceptable learning at work experience. The U.S. Department of Labor provides guidelines for internship programs under the Fair Labor Standards Act.[73] It specifies six criteria to determine whether unpaid internships for for-profit companies are acceptable. One criterion requires the internship must be for the benefit of the intern. This is often the issue – and if an intern is benefiting, does the company benefit even more? If so, it might be viewed as unpaid labor rather than an internship.

Another important criterion holds the intern should not displace any regular employees. This factor considers whether the intern is doing the job of a regular employee, and if the intern was not there, would the employer have to hire someone else. After a spate of lawsuits filed since 2011, some entertainment companies started to rethink their internship programs.[74] Unpaid internship programs still exist, but not to the extent they once did, and those that do welcome interns are much more careful about their educational nature.[75]

Employee or Independent Contractor?

Gig workers are those independent contractors who move from job to job (*gig* defines a short-term job). Companies hiring independent contractors do not have to pay benefits as they would for employees, and the workers are free to accept or refuse jobs. The entertainment industry regularly hires freelancers to work on productions. A background actor (also known as an extra) who works only an hour or a director who might spend six months on a film could both be independent contractors.

An interesting case involving the horror classic *Friday the 13th* judged whether the screenwriter was an independent contractor or an employee providing a work for hire.

69. "Interns, Unpaid by a Studio, File Suit," *New York Times*, September 28, 2011.
70. "Judge Grants Preliminary Approval of Fox Interns Settlement," *Hollywood Reporter*, August 12, 2016.
71. "Charlie Rose Interns Settle Unpaid Wages Suit," *Hollywood Reporter*, December 20, 2012.
72. "MGM Settles Class Action over Unpaid Internships," *Hollywood Reporter*, January 9, 2017.
73. See Fact Sheet #71, *at* www.dol.gov/whd/regs/compliance/whdfs71.htm.
74. "How All Those Intern Lawsuits Are Changing Hollywood," *Hollywood Reporter*, November 6, 2014.
75. "Appeals Court Considers Importance of 'Friday the 13th' Screenwriters Union Membership," *Hollywood Reporter*, February 14, 2020.

A federal district court ruled that writer Victor Miller was an independent contractor and, as such, retained a copyright in the original work.[76]

The decision had far-reaching implications, and so it was appealed to the U.S. Court of Appeals for the Second Circuit. Attorneys for the producer claimed Miller *was* receiving benefits through membership in his union, the Writers Guild of America.[77] At this writing, a final decision had not been handed down, but the outcome could influence other similar disputes.

Child Actors

What about using underage children in movies and television shows? Why doesn't that practice violate child labor laws? The simple answer is some states create special rules just for child actors. And because employment law is created at the state level, you might expect states where movies are frequently produced would be the ones enforcing such laws. California undoubtedly has the most extensive guidelines regarding the use of children in movies and TV. The laws specify the working hours and conditions that are permissible.

In most cases, special permission must be granted from the state to employ especially young children, those too young to obtain work permits. The hours a child may work are usually set on a sliding scale because older children are permitted to work longer hours. In California, for example, infants (six months of age or less) may only be allowed to be present at the work site for two hours and *work* no more than 20 minutes per day. Older children can work as long as eight hours per day.

This is one reason why identical twins are hired for film and television production. When production began in 1987 on the TV series *Full House*, Mary-Kate and Ashley Olsen shared the acting duties for their character, Michelle Tanner. This rotation enabled the producers to use each girl the allotted amount of time yet double the amount of time they were able to shoot with "Michelle." In addition, school-aged children must be provided with a teacher at the work site.

One other employment law specific to children in entertainment was enacted in California in the late 1930s. Jackie Coogan was a famous child actor who appeared in short films and features with major stars like Charlie Chaplin. By the time he was an adult, he had appeared in more than 20 films and would have had a handsome bankroll for his on-screen work except that his parents had taken the money.

A court decision upheld the right of the parents to keep his earnings. An outraged California legislature passed a law requiring any producer using child actors to pay at least 15% of the child's fee to a trust account that can be accessed only by the child actor once they reach adulthood. The law is referred to as "Coogan's Law" by the Hollywood community, but it lacks a monitoring mechanism, and prominent child stars including Gary Coleman, Macauley Culkin, and Jena Malone have all sued their parents, alleging their earned income had been squandered.[78]

Another state law geared to punish the entertainment industry's exploitation of talent is California's Krekorian Talent Scam Prevention Act. Created in 2009, this law attempts to prevent "talent agents" from taking advantage of people hoping to be cast in television or movie roles.

76. *Horror Inc. v. Miller*, 335 F. Supp. 3d 273 (D. Conn. 2018), affirmed, *Horror Inc. v. Miller*, 15 F.4th 232 (2d Cir. 2021).
77. "Appeals Court Considers Importance of 'Friday the 13th' Screenwriters Union Membership," *Hollywood Reporter*, February 14, 2020.
78. "When Young Stars Sue Their Parents: Whose Money Is It, Anyway?" *Hollywood Reporter*, August 13, 2018.

Aspiring actors or, more often, *parents* of juvenile actors, have been enticed to sign up for expensive acting workshops with the promise that doing so would lead to lucrative acting contracts. There's nothing illegal about charging people to attend a workshop but exchanging money (usually thousands of dollars) for the prospect of employment is illegal in California.[79] The so-called "pay-to-play" contracts have been a Hollywood staple for years, but indications are they are vanishing since the law took effect.[80]

Equal Employment Opportunities

Congress created federal legislation so that employers would provide equal employment opportunities (EEO). As a practical matter, this law prohibits businesses from making hiring or firing decisions based on race, gender, color, creed, or national origin, and there are regulations that exist governing electronic media.[81]

EEO laws are *not* quota requirements for diversity purposes. No court would allow a law requiring a percentage of employees to be of a certain gender or race to stand. EEO is about *opportunities*, and what was critical in cases involving broadcasters was whether there had been opportunities available to learn about job openings and apply for them.

Broadcasters and multichannel video providers like cable and satellite TV systems were required to take affirmative action to be certain that information about vacancies in their business was widely disseminated. It was not enough to simply post a job on a general jobs site because the law required being more proactive by reaching out to underrepresented persons through minority channels. For example, Hispanics might be more likely to read a Spanish-language publication than a general circulation daily newspaper website.

Until 2017, the FCC also advised electronic media to provide notice of all full-time job openings to recruiting organizations and *widely* distribute the information, which would include multiple publications, local educational institutions, and on-air announcements. The FCC expected broad dissemination and fined stations in 2011 for recruiting only by word of mouth and online.[82]

In 2017, a group of broadcasters petitioned the FCC to allow online-only announcements of job openings.[83] The broadcasters claimed in that environment, online ads adequately reach a broad, diverse segment of the population. What's more, employers are expected to conduct "recruitment initiatives," including job fairs, internship programs, and other community events. In 2017, the FCC relaxed its rules and allowed online-only postings of job openings because "Internet usage has become sufficiently widespread."[84]

Beyond ethnic concerns, media enterprises must be aware of other legal issues regarding employee discrimination. There have been a few high-profile cases in which on-air talent at television stations claimed they were discriminated against because of their age. The case that received global attention was that of Christine Craft, a TV news anchor at KMBC in Kansas City. The station removed her from the anchor chair, allegedly because she was "too old, too unattractive and not deferential to men."

79. "L.A. City Attorney Files Charges against 5 Casting Workshops in Pay-to-Play Scam," *Hollywood Reporter*, February 9, 2017.
80. Between 2017 and 2020, a few casting associates entered plea deals or pleaded no contest for community service, but only one casting director was found guilty at trial. "Casting Director Found Guilty in Pay-to-Play Audition Scam," *Hollywood Reporter*, January 31, 2018.
81. *See*, for example, 47 C.F.R. § 22.321.
82. "Web-Only, Word-of-Mouth-Only Recruitment Not Enough," *CommLawBlog*, December 31, 2011, *at* www.commlawblog.com/2011/12/articles/broadcast/eeo-web-only-word-of-mouth-only-recruitment-not-enough/.
83. "Broadcasters Ask FCC to Allow Online-Only Recruiting," *Radio World*, February 1, 2017.
84. FCC 17–47. In the matter of Petition for Rulemaking Seeking to Allow the Sole Use of Internet Sources for FCC EEO Recruitment Requirements, April 21, 2017.

Discrimination Litigation

Craft filed a discrimination suit against the station and was originally awarded $500,000 by a federal district court jury.[85] A federal district court judge set aside that award, and a second jury reduced the figure to $325,000.[86] However, the Eighth Circuit Court of Appeals overturned the verdict, and Craft received nothing.[87] The Supreme Court refused to hear the case letting the lower court's ruling stand.[88]

Craft's suit may have been the most publicized, but it is certainly not the only example. Deserved or not, television news has a reputation for being more accepting of "mature" looking men than it is of older-appearing women. In most cases, as Metromedia argued with Craft, stations provide research data to show the women being removed or demoted have lost some of their appeal to audiences.

Is it discrimination for a station to remove an anchor who has lost the ability to attract an audience? There have been instances in which women have won discrimination suits against stations. Sara Lee Kessler won a $7 million judgment against WWOR-TV in New York in 1999.[89] In some instances, stations and anchor women have reached settlements without having to go to court, reducing the embarrassment and legal costs for both sides.

In 2019, Vice Media faced a class action suit from female workers who claimed the company paid women staff members less than their male counterparts. Vice denied the assertion that it used prior salary history in setting wages, which would automatically result in lower wages for the female workers. The company agreed to settle for $1.87 million, which experts believe was significantly less than their potential liability.[90]

Corporate Speech

The First Amendment was drafted well before the marketplace of ideas became the province of large media corporations, so today the obvious question is how much free expression is owed to businesses seeking to get their viewpoint across to influence voters. The question of corporate speech beyond product promotion has a direct bearing on the role public relations practitioners play in our society.

The key question in a 1978 case was whether a state law that would ban banks and businesses from influencing voter approval of referendum issues might be considered unconstitutional. The Supreme Court decision in *First Nat'l Bank of Boston v. Bellotti* (1978) affirmed First Amendment rights for corporate entities based on the belief not in the seller's interests but in the free exchange of ideas.[91]

It was a close vote of 5–4, which held as unconstitutional the Massachusetts criminal statute prohibiting the funding of messages designed to influence the political process at the ballot box. Those opposed to the ruling criticized its rationale based on listeners' rights as opposed to an analysis of the speaker's rights in light of corporate power.

85. William MacDougall, "Ahead: Rising Role for Women in TV News," *U.S. News & World Report*, August 22, 1983, at 56.
86. "In the News," 5 *Entertainment Law Reporter*, December 1983.
87. *Craft v. Metromedia*, 766 F.2d 1205 (8th Cir. 1985).
88. *Craft v. Metromedia*, 475 U.S. 1058 (1986), cert. denied.
89. Kessler's suit includes charges of discrimination based on age, gender, religion, and disability. Ann Beck, "An Age-Old Problem," *Broadcasting & Cable*, October 31, 2005, at 12.
90. "Vice Media Agrees to $1.87 Million Settlement for Paying Female Staff Members Less Than Men," *Hollywood Reporter*, March 27, 2019.
91. *First Nat'l Bank of Boston v. Bellotti*, 435 U.S. 765 (1978).

Corporations as People

The doctrine of corporate personhood was adopted early in the nineteenth century. The case involved Dartmouth College and an attempt to convert the private school into a state university. The ruling held that even though the word *corporation* is nowhere to be found in the Constitution, a corporate charter is a contract that cannot be reshaped by government.[92] The ruling limited the government's power to control corporations, so states began to write controls into the charters they granted, defining the rights of individuals and industry.

In the case of *Kasky v. Nike, Inc.* (2002), a California activist, Marc Kasky, sued Nike for publicity issued about its use of overseas manufacturers.[93] Nike appealed the case to the Supreme Court, but the justices decided to dismiss the appeal.

The limited rules influencing corporate political speech had a wider berth than what consumer advocates like Kasky felt were warranted. Those who disagree point to constituents and investors, whom corporations must address, and how the Securities and Exchange Commission (SEC) plays a role in the process.

Investing in Media

It's easy to understand why large media conglomerates depend on the capital generated by stock investments. Securities brokers dealing in publicly traded securities have a sharp impact on not only who owns the media but ultimately on what we see, hear, and read over television, radio, and Internet channels.

If you were to take over the media conglomerates of just six companies, you would own close to 90% of the nation's news and entertainment outlets. That reality places the packages of stocks sold for these companies squarely on the radar screen of federal regulators. It also means Congress minds how the game of securities is played on the frontier of American investment. Capitol Hill gave its sternest look at stock sales more than 70 years ago.

During the depths of the Great Depression, the Securities Act of 1933 changed the way Americans invest in their businesses. First and foremost, that law defined what facts should be disclosed and which ones are to be kept quiet until securities are ready for sale.

Even before media stocks are sold, the corporation must file a registration statement with the SEC and wait a certain period before promoting the stock sale. If word leaks out during the 20-day waiting period, *gun-jumping* is the term used by SEC agents for §5 of the 1933 Act to stop this sort of priming the pump for stock sales before the government has approved them.

Stock Sales and Safe Harbors

The strict law against promoting stock sales before their time is not quite so cut and dry. Some believe loopholes do exist, or as the government likes to call them, "safe harbors." Media corporations seek shelter under Rule 134, for example, which is called the "tombstone advertising" safe harbor – allowing a report of the simple facts involved in the potential sale. While this rule forbids providing a full prospectus or supplement to potential stock buyers, sellers can offer information on how investors can sign up to participate in the offering once it begins.

Another safe harbor falls under Rule 168, where forward-looking information in press releases is allowed without penalty due to its factual business nature. A good example would be the report on the business wires by Raycom, Inc., which sold 12 of its television stations to Barrington Broadcasting. Since the transaction had not yet been blessed by the government, press releases carefully referred to the Private Securities Litigation Reform Act of 1995, where the safe harbor of Rule 168 is written.

92. *Dartmouth College v. Woodward*, 17 U.S. 518 (1819).
93. *Kasky v. Nike, Inc.*, 27 Cal. 4th 939, 969 (2002).

Normally, lawyer language accompanies advance press releases warning investors of "risks and uncertainties" involved, including changes in interest rates, advertising sales, taxing authorities, and other financial conditions that might have an impact. What remains are restrictions against announcing the initial public offerings (IPOs) before the media firm files its prospectus.

Most of these offerings are managed by investment banks, which act as underwriters. Not all media companies are publicly traded firms, but those that are fall under the registration requirements to be filed with the SEC along with the annual forms and quarterly reports that keep the company's business fully disclosed to its investors. Publicly traded media impart loads of data to their investors, a lot of statistics to be sure, but also corporate reports to indicate just how healthy their businesses are each year.

Netflix nearly ran afoul of Securities and Exchange Commission rules in 2012, when CEO Reed Hastings posted on Facebook that Netflix had crossed the mark of one billion hours of video watched. That may not seem like anything too troubling, but the Securities and Exchange Commission's Regulation Fair Disclosure Rule[94] requires material information be disclosed to all investors at the same time and not just to a select few.

In 2013, the SEC announced that it was not going to initiate any action against Netflix and instead announced that such public disclosures on social media by publicly traded companies would be fine so long as investors were made aware of the normal channels a company would use to make such announcements.[95] In other words, publicly traded companies can make announcements that might affect a stock's price in a medium of their choosing, provided shareholders know where they will be able to find those announcements.

Stock Prices and Preferences

Media corporations are legally bound to be vigilant in rooting out "misrepresentation, deceit, and other fraudulent acts and practices" that might influence the sale of securities.[96] It also is a matter of case law that media corporations guard their investors from fraud, while promoting honesty and fairness. Yet the focus remains on certain types of fraud and deception. Rule 10b-5 under the Securities Exchange Act of 1934 says if a stock seller makes an untrue or a misleading statement of a material fact, they will be subject to liabilities resulting from anyone acting on that misinformation.[97]

Leslie Moonves was the CEO of CBS in 2017 when accusations of sexual misconduct were made against many prominent figures in media, including CBS newsman Charlie Rose. While speaking at a conference, Moonves said, "There's a lot we're learning. There's a lot we didn't know."[98] In July 2018, *The New Yorker* published an article alleging sexual misconduct by Moonves, and he chose to resign in September.

Changes in the chief executive of a company often affect the stock price of that company, especially when it's a high-profile executive. Stockholders filed a lawsuit alleging that Moonves's 2017 statement was fraudulent because he did know more than he was revealing. The shareholders pointed to $200 million of stock sales made by people who were insiders and had access to privileged information.[99]

94. 17 CFR Parts 240 and 249., 243,
95. "SEC Says Social Media OK for Company Announcements if Investors Are Alerted," *at* www.sec.gov/News/PressRelease/Detail/PressRelease/1365171513574.
96. The Securities and Exchange Commission, *The Work of the Securities and Exchange Commission* (Washington, DC: The Securities and Exchange Commission, 1974).
97. *See* Rule 10b-5 – Employment of Manipulative and Deceptive Devices under General Rules and Regulations promulgated under the Securities Exchange Act of 1934: It shall be unlawful for any person . . . a. To employ any device, scheme, or artifice to defraud; b. To make any untrue statement of a material fact or to omit to state a material fact necessary to make the statements made, in the light of the circumstances under which they were made, not misleading, or c. To engage in any act, practice, or course of business which operates or would operate as a fraud or deceit.
98. "Judge Allows CBS Shareholder Lawsuit Over Leslie Moonves and #MeToo to Proceed," *Variety*, January 15, 2020.
99. "CBS Shareholders Point to $200M in 'Suspicious' Insider Stock Sales Prior to Les Moonves Exposé," *Hollywood Reporter*, February 12, 2019.

Insider Trading

Perhaps the most famous case of stock trading gone wrong is that of Martha Stewart, the homemaking maven who spent five months in prison for lying to federal investigators about why she sold her stock in Imclone Systems Inc. in December 2001, just two days before the price of the stock fell. Stewart first had been convicted of a criminal charge in 2004, but she also suffered liabilities in civil court for **insider trading**, and she ended up paying a fine of $195,000 – four times the amount of the loss she avoided in her sale of stock.[100]

Insider Trading
An illegal business practice where market participants base their buying and selling decisions on facts known to be confidential and not generally available to the market. For example, officers of a company buying stock in the company at a price below what they know will be announced in the future as a buyout price.

Reporters also can run afoul of SEC rules when they become involved in reporting on publicly traded companies. When reporting on business matters, a reporter who makes a negative comment about a publicly traded company can cause the stock to drop. The announcement of a major discovery or development can cause a company's value to rise. An unscrupulous reporter who acquires this information could have a tremendous advantage in buying or selling stock in the time between learning of the news and reporting on it.

The *Wall Street Journal* is well-known and well-respected for its business reporting. In 1987, R. Foster Winans was found guilty of securities fraud. He was not a stockbroker, but as one of the journalists contributing to the *Journal*'s "Heard on the Street" column, he had the ability to influence investors. He took advantage of this position by buying and selling stock before the stories that affected their price appeared in the paper. Winans's conviction for securities fraud was upheld by the Second Circuit Court of Appeals.[101]

The whole system is based on fairness. If a company is publicly traded, then anyone who invests in that company, or others who might invest in that company, ought to have the same opportunity to decide to buy or sell stock based on reliable information. People who have "insider" information (whether because of their own access or if they have been tipped off by an insider) are not allowed to trade on that information because they have an unfair advantage.

People who are very good at reading markets, who follow companies closely and can often predict when a publicly traded company is on the verge of something big, do nothing wrong because they are accessing information that's available to everyone.

Merger Mania

The urge to merge media enterprises has prompted the government to ask for reports from the company that seeks to take control of one of its competitors. If the takeover is a tender offer, then the buyer must disclose who the target company is, how many shareholders are involved, the reason for the bid, and where the buyer wants to take the newly acquired company.

The SEC rules on what constitutes the beginning time of the tender offer. The tender offeror must submit financial statements to the government or face sanctions. SEC Rule 14(d) declares publicity about the purchasing of the company must include the identity of the bidder and information about how stockholders can find more about the pursuing firm. If anything is found to be false or deceptive, it is not out of the question for the SEC to sue the lawyers and the company. There are both civil and criminal penalties for violating the security laws.

The Securities and Exchange Commission is not the only federal agency involved in overseeing mergers. The Federal Trade Commission and the Department of Justice can both get involved in the process. Even the FCC gets involved if the companies involved affect

100. Mike Moffatt, "Martha Stewart's Insider Trading Case," *ThoughtCo.*, January 30, 2020, *at* www.thoughtco.com/martha-stewarts-insider-trading-case-1146196.
101. *Carpenter v. United States*, 484 U.S. 19 (1987).

electronic communication. A text on communication law can't possibly cover all the intricacies of mergers, but we should make it clear that publicly traded companies involved in mergers have strict reporting obligations.

Microsoft's deal with Activision in 2022–2023 was the subject of antitrust investigation in multiple countries. Microsoft paid nearly $70 billion to acquire the gaming company, making it the largest video gaming acquisition in history, but it first had to be approved by government authorities on every continent except Antarctica. In the United States, the Federal Trade Commission challenged the merger in court but was unable to prevent it.[102] Throughout the yearlong process, Microsoft made certain concessions to appease regulators, including assurances that popular games would be available on competing platforms.

Summary

- A contract is an agreement between two parties that must contain three elements to be legally binding: an offer, consideration, and acceptance. Oral contracts are legally enforceable but most of them are written to prevent disputes about what was promised and by whom. Sometimes consideration is in the form of money, but not always.
- A release form is a variant of a contract often used by media companies. Production companies often require people appearing in their videos to sign talent releases stating the producers can use the video in a variety of ways.
- Not everyone who has a job signs a lengthy legal contract, but in media industries many people do have contracts, and those contracts contain a lot more than just salaries and job descriptions. Some media contracts include morals clauses that prohibit employees from engaging in any activity *off the job* that might reflect badly on the employer. Media employees' contracts sometimes contain noncompete clauses that prevent them from taking jobs with a competitor for 6 to 12 months.
- Antitrust laws prevent businesses from engaging in anticompetitive practices, and those laws apply to media companies just like any other business. There are a couple of notable examples of legislation that has exempted certain activities that would otherwise run afoul of antitrust law, such as competing newspapers sharing facilities or sports blackout rules.
- Employment laws are also applicable to media companies, but like antitrust exemptions, special niches have been carved out, allowing media to employ children and have permitted television stations to remove anchors because of their ages without losing age discrimination suits.
- Corporations have *some* rights of free expression but not to the same extent as individuals.
- Corporations that sell stocks have a special obligation to protect their stockholders (i.e., "owners"). People within corporations who have access to insider information could take advantage of their positions by buying company stock just before announcing a great discovery or selling the stock just before news about their losses is announced. The laws prohibit insiders from trading on such knowledge, and journalists who have access to these facts before the public can be held similarly responsible.

102. "Microsoft Closes $69 Billion Acquisition of Activision Blizzard after Lengthy Regulatory Review," *CNBC*, October 23, 2023.

Ethical Dilemmas: Commitment to Inclusiveness?

Media industries claim they want to be more inclusive, but do the systems in place truly operate to ensure diversity? UCLA's 2020 Hollywood Diversity Report shows that while the diversity of actors on the screen is improving, senior studio executives are still largely white (93%) and male (80%).[103] Then there is the question of internships.

Unpaid internships are legal if the students are receiving academic credit and are legitimately learning a skill, but the ones most likely to be able to accept such an internship are students who are financially stable enough to work for no pay. Most students must work to pay for a portion of their schooling, so unpaid internships, even those that really are worthwhile, end up going to students who are already advantaged.

The system isn't much better for Hollywood assistant positions: writers' assistants, showrunners' assistants, or production assistants of all sorts who hope to use those positions to get promoted in the industry. Many work more than 40 hours per week and don't earn enough to live in an expensive city like Los Angeles without some outside income.

Screenwriters John August and Craig Mazin assert the low wages hurt the industry's push for diversity.[104] Writer Liz Alpert, who started #PayUpHollywood in 2019 to bring pressure on the industry for better pay, sees it as a "class privilege" to be able to work in the industry. Pay disparity between male and female actors is well-known. In 2018, *Forbes* reported women earned about 25 cents for every dollar earned by men. Things aren't any better for streamers – only one of the top ten highest paid YouTubers in 2020 was female.

People have been saying, "things are better than they were" for decades, but how long before we find a way to say, "things are as they should be"?

103. 2020 Hollywood Diversity Report, *at* https://socialsciences.ucla.edu/initiatives/hollywood-diversity-report/.
104. "Entertainment Biz Comes under Fire for Assistants' Low Wages, Working Conditions," *Variety*, October 14, 2019.

13

Media and Courts

LEARNING OBJECTIVES

After reading this chapter, you should know

- how pretrial publicity could affect the fair trial rights of a defendant
- how the Supreme Court attempts to strike a balance between the fair trial rights of the accused and the rights of the free press
- how a contempt of court citation can be used by judges to get what they want
- what "gag orders" are and how they can be used to silence the media
- how the judiciary attempts to compel reporters to testify in court or before grand juries
- what shield laws are and the sorts of protections they afford
- the rules governing warrants and subpoenas for information held by news media
- whether cameras are allowed in courts and who decides based on what criteria
- if courtrooms can be closed to observers

Courtroom Drama

The 2024 trial of former president Donald Trump by a New York court on 34 felony charges of falsifying business records was not televised. Unlike other high-profile court cases like O.J. Simpson's murder trial in 1995, Lindsay Lohan's 2010 drunk driving probation violation trial, or the Johnny Depp/Amber Heard libel trial (civil, not criminal) in 2022, New York did not permit camera coverage of the Trump trial.

While the trial may not have been televised, it's wrong to think it was held "in the dark." News media coverage was extensive, including live updates of events as they unfolded. Social media activity was constant. For those interested in this area of law, the trial raised important questions to be answered by balancing the right to a fair trial and the right to free expression:[1]

- Can any celebrity be tried by an impartial jury? Past high-profile cases have raised this question, but never has there been a defendant with such recognition, at a time when

1. "Trump Trial Illustrates Jury Challenges in the Social Media Age," *Reuters*, April 22, 2024.

DOI: 10.4324/9781003462989-13

technology makes disseminating information (and misinformation) so easy. So much information is available to potential jurors, how could anyone avoid hearing about it?

- Trials are usually open to the public, especially criminal trials. When should a trial be televised? Should that decision be left to just one person? Does the fact that some trials are not televised imply there is a potential danger in camera coverage? Rules are different in each jurisdiction, which means the trials watched by viewers in one state might not be televised in another state.
- Potential jurors have their social media accounts examined to determine whether they are capable of being impartial. Does this intrusion further deter citizens from wanting to serve as jurors, already seen as burdensome by most Americans?
- Jurors' identities were not made public by the court to protect them from outside intimidation from those wanting to influence their decision. If juror identities are kept secret, though, there's a risk the jury could be "stacked" for or against a defendant and no one would know. If this anonymity is justified to protect jurors, should it also be extended to others involved including witnesses or even the judges themselves?
- Trial participants, including the defendant (a former president), had their speech outside the courtroom restricted. The prosecution repeatedly accused the ex-president of making prohibited statements outside the courtroom. When should "gag orders" be imposed, on whom, and for how long?
- The judge imposed sanctions on defendant Trump for gag order violations, which included fines and removal of certain statements from his social media. Once the statements were made and further promoted by news media, does requiring their removal accomplish anything? The Streisand Effect[2] suggests such attempts only draw more attention to them.

The Trial of the Century[3] . . . at the Time

In the early hours of July 4, 1954, Marilyn Sheppard was brutally murdered in her Bay Village, OH, home. Her husband, Sam, claimed that an intruder attacked his wife while he slept on the couch downstairs. He asserted that he awoke to the sounds of the attack but did not see the attacker because he was hit from behind. He pursued someone escaping the house but did not catch up with him. Sam called the neighbors and the police to the scene.

The murder case was big news. For the next month, Cleveland media ran a story every day, regardless of whether there were new developments in the case. At first, the news stories were sympathetic to the 30-year-old doctor who, along with his father and two brothers (all doctors), worked at Bay View Hospital in Bay Village. However, suspicion quickly turned away from the intruder Sam claimed to have pursued, and media attention refocused on him.

From the outset there was reason to suspect the doctor, but the Bay View police resisted suggestions by the Cleveland police to arrest him. The investigation had all sorts of problems. The morning of the murder, the Sheppard home was filled with people, including neighbors, who had unlimited access to a crime scene while the police were trying to collect evidence, much of which was contaminated by the fingerprints of others. "Dr. Sam" (as he was known in Bay View) was whisked from the murder scene to the hospital the morning of the crime. It was days after the crime before authorities were able to question him to any extent.

2. In 2003, singer Barbra Streisand sued a photographer for an aerial photo he had taken of her home, which she claimed was a violation of her privacy. The picture received a lot more attention due to the lawsuit than it ever would have gotten, and the term "Streisand Effect" came into the vocabulary. It's attributed to *Techdirt*'s Mike Masnick. *See* Wikipedia or Pop Culture Dictionary.
3. "Trial of the Century" is a rather dramatic term used to attract attention. As Wikipedia points out, at least 30 trials in the twentieth century were called "The Trial of the Century."

The case contained all sorts of twists and turns raising gossip about those involved: a woman who claimed to have had an affair with Dr. Sam and suspicions that the mayor of Bay View (the neighbor Dr. Sam first called) may have been the murderer, among others. No wonder two television series and a motion picture were loosely based on the case.[4]

Sam Sheppard was arrested July 30, 1954, and his trial in the Cuyahoga County, Ohio, Court of Common Pleas began in mid-October, just weeks before presiding judge Edward J. Blythin, 70, would face reelection. The chief prosecutor in the case was also a judgeship candidate. Reporters from across the country wanted to cover the trial, so Blythin accommodated some by seating them behind the bar – an area reserved for trial participants. The judge rejected motions to postpone the trial or move it to another location due to the publicity. Jurors were selected, and their names and addresses appeared in the paper.

The jury was finally sequestered for deliberations after six weeks of hearing testimony, but they were still permitted to make phone calls. Shortly before Christmas, Dr. Sam Sheppard was found guilty of second-degree murder. His attorney began immediate efforts to appeal or have the case reheard. Ohio appellate courts and the state supreme court affirmed his conviction.

The sequence of events after the trial was almost as bizarre as those during it. Less than two weeks after the conviction, Dr. Sam's mother committed suicide. His father died from a hemorrhaging ulcer 11 days later. Ten years after his conviction, a judge ordered him released from prison, citing five violations of Sheppard's constitutional rights. Three days later, he married a wealthy German divorcee who had been corresponding with him in prison for seven years. In 1965, an appeals court reinstated his conviction.

The U.S. Supreme Court was petitioned to hear the Sheppard case in 1956 but turned it down. After a second request, the Court chose differently, and Dr. Sam's case was heard in 1966. The Court was asked to determine whether Sheppard was denied a fair trial due to all the prejudicial publicity. The Court even referred to the "editorial artillery"[5] the local news media used against Sheppard. Five volumes of Cleveland newspaper clippings from before the conviction were provided strongly suggesting the defendant's guilt. Despite the flagrant media bias, the Court's strongest criticism was not of the news media but of the judicial officers.

Justice Tom Clark wrote the opinion for an 8–1 decision that strongly took to task Judge Blythin's lack of action to protect the due process rights of the accused. The Court remanded the case, and after a new trial was held in 1966, Dr. Sam Sheppard was acquitted.

The Supreme Court's *Sheppard* Decision

The following is taken directly from Justice Clark's opinion for the Court:

> A responsible press has always been regarded as the handmaiden of effective judicial administration, especially in the criminal field. Its function in this regard is documented by an impressive record of service over several centuries. The press does not simply publish information about trials but guards against the miscarriage of justice by subjecting the police, prosecutors, and judicial processes to extensive public scrutiny and criticism. This Court has, therefore, been unwilling to place any direct limitations on the freedom traditionally exercised by the news media for "what transpires in the court room is public property." The "unqualified prohibitions laid down by the framers were intended to give to liberty of the press . . . the broadest scope that could be countenanced in an orderly society." . . . And where there was "no threat or menace to the integrity of the trial," we have consistently required that the press have a free hand, even though we sometimes deplored its sensationalism.[6]

4. *The Fugitive* television show of the 1960s starring David Janssen, the short-lived TV series in 2000 starring Tim Daly, and the 1993 movie starring Harrison Ford were all loosely based on the story of Dr. Sam Sheppard.
5. *Sheppard v. Maxwell*, 384 U.S.333, 339 (1966).
6. *Id.* at 350 (1966) (citations omitted).

Then citing an earlier decision, he added,

> [W]e believe that the arrangements made by the judge with the news media caused Sheppard to be deprived of that "judicial serenity and calm to which [he] was entitled."[7] The fact is that bedlam reigned at the courthouse during the trial and newsmen took over practically the entire courtroom, hounding most of the participants in the trial, especially Sheppard. At a temporary table within a few feet of the jury box and counsel table sat some 20 reporters staring at Sheppard and taking notes. The erection of a press table for reporters inside the bar is unprecedented. The bar of the court is reserved for counsel, providing them a safe place in which to keep papers and exhibits, and to confer privately with client and co-counsel. It is designed to protect the witness and the jury from any distractions, intrusions or influences, and to permit bench discussions of the judge's rulings away from the hearing of the public and the jury.
>
> Having assigned almost all the available seats in the courtroom to the news media the judge lost his ability to supervise that environment. The movement of the reporters in and out of the courtroom caused frequent confusion and disruption of the trial. And the record reveals constant commotion within the bar. Moreover, the judge gave the throng of newsmen gathered in the corridors of the courthouse absolute free rein. Participants in the trial, including the jury, were forced to run a gantlet of reporters and photographers each time they entered or left the courtroom.
>
> The total lack of consideration for the privacy of the jury was demonstrated by the assignment to a broadcasting station of space next to the jury room on the floor above the courtroom, as well as the fact that jurors were allowed to make telephone calls during their five-day deliberation.[8]

Pretrial Publicity

The Sixth Amendment states,

> In all criminal prosecutions, the accused shall enjoy the right to a speedy and public trial, by an impartial jury of the State and district wherein the crime shall have been committed, which district shall have been previously ascertained by law, and to be informed of the nature and cause of the accusation; to be confronted with the witnesses against him; to have compulsory process for obtaining witnesses in his favor, and to have the Assistance of Counsel for his defense.

Right to Impartial Jury
The Sixth Amendment guarantees defendants the right to be judged by jurors, who will not be swayed by publicity surrounding the case.

The Sixth Amendment guarantees our constitutional right to a fair trial, which requires an **impartial jury**, but it does not require an ignorant jury (Figure 13.1). It is not a modern phenomenon to have celebrities like Johnny Depp and Amber Heard stand trial before jurors who have already heard some information (right or wrong) about the case. For hundreds of years, there has been a great deal of pretrial publicity surrounding notorious trials, and the jurors very likely already knew something about the case before the trial began.

Former U.S. Vice President Aaron Burr was tried for treason in 1807 with a great deal of publicity surrounding the case, and Supreme Court Chief Justice John Marshall stated that simply being exposed to pretrial publicity did not necessarily prejudice a juror.[9] In 1961 (long before the modern Internet or 24-hour cable news channels), the Supreme Court made it clear that knowing about a case is not the same as pre-judging the defendant:

> In these days of swift, widespread and diverse methods of communication, an important case can be expected to arouse the interest of the public in the vicinity, and scarcely any

7. *Id.* at 355 (citations omitted).
8. *Id.*
9. *U.S. v. Burr*, 25 F. Cas. 49, 51 (C.C.D. Va. 1807).

Figure 13.1 A jury box: Key to the accused's right to a fair trial is empaneling an impartial jury

> of those best qualified to serve as jurors will not have formed some impression or opinion as to the merits of the case. This is particularly true in criminal cases. To hold that the mere existence of any preconceived notion as to the guilt or innocence of an accused, without more, is sufficient to rebut the presumption of a prospective juror's impartiality would be to establish an impossible standard.[10]

Bedrock Law

Judges are responsible for maintaining decorum in their courtrooms and safeguarding the jury from outside factors to protect the defendant's right to a fair trial.

Publicity's role in the outcome of trials is uncertain. As might be imagined, it's impossible to know for certain the effect since we cannot conduct an experiment with real trial litigants where we compare the results in the same case conducted with and without publicity. In the most comprehensive collection of research to date, Jon Bruschke and William Loges concluded there is not a pretrial publicity effect so powerful that it would withstand all remedies. There is even some evidence that pretrial publicity might help defendants. If a pretrial publicity effect exists detected with strict control in laboratory conditions, then that effect will emerge under certain conditions in actual courtrooms.[11]

Legal scholars generally conclude it depends on what sort of pretrial information reaches the jury since some items are more prejudicial[12] than others. We can see how publishing only a suspect's name and address would not be prejudicial, but other types of material may be "presumed" to be prejudicial. On various occasions, the Supreme Court has declared the pretrial publication of the following categories to be prejudicial:

- confessions or admissions of guilt[13] or other sorts of "evidence" that would be considered inadmissible at trial

10. *Irvin v. Dowd*, 366 U.S. 717 (1961) at 722–723.
11. J. Bruschke & W. Loges, *Free Press vs. Fair Trials 136* (2004).
12. The term *prejudicial* itself implies the problem. It is publicity that occurs before the judicial process and causes judgment to occur before the trial. It is not only publicity that can be prejudicial, but that will be discussed later.
13. *Rideau v. Louisiana*, 373 U.S. 723 (1963).

- prior criminal record, although the Court softened this stance by saying that reporting the defendant's criminal record *alone* was not enough to be prejudicial[14]
- attribution of serious character flaws or epithets such as "Mad Dog"[15]

News media are not prevented from releasing any of this information, but they could conceivably result in claims by defendants the impartiality of the jurors was compromised so holding a fair trial would be difficult, if not impossible to do.

Protecting Fair Trial Rights

Prior to *Sheppard*, some may have thought the only option when faced with the possibility of prejudicial pretrial publicity was to restrict the rights of a free press or risk the possibility of violating the defendant's right to a fair trial. The Supreme Court decision offered American courts a variety of ways to protect the fair trial rights of the accused without treading on the free press rights of the media.

Change of Venue

Change of Venue
Moving a trial to a different geographical location.

Change of Venire
Importing jurors from a different geographical location.

If a judge is concerned a jury could be swayed by too much pretrial publicity, the judge can move the trial to another location. **Change of venue** operates under the assumption most publicity is likely to occur in the locale where the offense was committed and moving it away will yield jurors less familiar with the case.[16] Similar to a change of venue is the **change of venire**, wherein jurors from another locale are transported to the court. Both remedies accomplish the goal of obtaining a jury pool of citizens less familiar with the crime.

Change of venue raises other difficult questions, including a constitutional one. The Sixth Amendment to the Constitution promises the accused shall enjoy the right to a trial in "the State and district wherein the crime shall have been committed." It also states the "district" shall be defined, so conceivably it could be as large as a state's boundaries. Even so, the jury pool may not be broad enough to provide an impartial trial.

Imagine a trial for a heinous crime in the state of Rhode Island. It's hard to imagine that anywhere in the state – or possibly the country – would be outside news media coverage, yet the Constitution requires the trial be conducted in the state and district of the crime. Is changing the venue a viable option if every prospective juror is exposed to news coverage of the crime?

Another cause for concern with the change of venue remedy is the cost involved. It is not cheap. Of course, legal scholars are quick to point out that fair trials are costly, but that should not be a basis for denying fair trial protections.

Continuance

Trials can be delayed. Even trials that are not delayed can occur months after the crime was committed. In Sam Sheppard's case, more than three months had passed. If pretrial publicity is a concern, perhaps a delay would help those prospective jurors who heard prejudicial information to forget it. But there is a constitutional concern there as well. That same Sixth Amendment requires a *speedy* trial, and while that term may be vague, it clearly argues against any intentional delays.

14. *Murphy v. Florida*, 421 U.S. 794 (1975).
15. *Irvin v. Dowd*, supra note 10.
16. *Id.*

Continuance
Postpones legal proceedings until a later date.

If a **continuance** dulls the memory of potential jurors, it must also dull the memories of witnesses. Courts try to address this problem by having witnesses provide depositions. These statements can be given back to the witnesses, so they can read what they said earlier, as a means of refreshing their memories. There is always the possibility that a question can arise at trial that was not covered in the deposition, and a witness may not recall the detail.

Sequestration

Sequestering a jury is the process of keeping the jurors secluded so no one talks with them about the trial outside of court. Typically, jurors are housed at a local hotel where they can be watched and supervised. Officers monitor the jurors and keep them from reading newspaper accounts of the trial or watching television newscasts. The jury in the *Sheppard* trial was sequestered only for deliberation. During the testimony, jurors were able to talk with anyone about the trial, read newspapers, and otherwise receive prejudicial information.

Sequestration
The process of keeping jurors secluded to prevent exposure to outside information about the trial potentially affecting their judgment.

In addition to the tremendous expense of **sequestration**, it may cause jurors undue stress to be kept away from their loved ones. With each passing day, pressure to end the trial increases, prompting some jurors to rush the deliberation process or, worse yet, give in to the majority opinion during deliberations just to get the trial over with. In 2020, a judge denied a request by the defense in media mogul Harvey Weinstein's trial for sequestration, which would have isolated the jurors for eight weeks.[17] In the long term, the more often juries are sequestered, the more difficult it becomes to impanel a jury, as fear of possible sequestration would cause more people seeking to be excused from jury pools.

Voir Dire

Sequestration may be an effective tool for keeping jurors from hearing prejudicial information during the trial, but how much has news coverage of the case already formed an impression about the defendant's guilt or innocence in a prospective juror's mind?[18] This is a question best answered during the ***voir dire***, a legal term referring to the jury selection process from the literal French translation, "to see to speak."

Voir Dire
The pretrial process of jury selection.

The lawyers in the *voir dire* have a chance to *see* jurors before *saying* if they are acceptable. Attorneys on both sides in a civil or criminal trial have a chance to interview prospective jurors to determine their truthful knowledge and biases regarding the case. They can reject jurors for cause and explain why the juror is not suited to render a fair verdict, or they can simply issue a peremptory challenge, which requires no explanation.

Judicial Admonition
Judges' statements, direction, or advice to jurors, or anyone, at trial.

Attorneys have a limited number of peremptory challenges, meaning they generally try to explain the reason for challenging a juror (for cause) to preserve their peremptory challenges for ones the judge might not accept. Jury selection is a controversial process, in part due to the research informing trial lawyers about the tendencies of prospective jurors to vote a particular way based on their age, ethnicity, gender, education, income, religion, and other profile elements.[19]

17. "Harvey Weinstein Trial: Judge Rejects Request to Sequester Jury," *Variety*, January 6, 2020, https://variety.com/2020/film/news/harvey-weinstein-rape-trial-begins-1203458014/.
18. Two First Amendment scholars have suggested that the issue is not whether prospective jurors have opinions, because they likely will have them. What is most important is selecting jurors who are capable of setting aside their opinions in deciding the case. *See* N. Minow & F. Cate, "Who Is an Impartial Juror in an Age of Mass Media?" 40 *Am. U. L. Rev.* 631 (Winter 1991).
19. Some legal scholars assert that trials are won or lost based on *voir dire*. Attorneys who are most successful at empaneling jurors sympathetic to their side will win. For a collection of critiques, *see* R. Jonakait, *The American Jury System* (New Haven, CT: Yale University Press, 2003).

Judicial Admonition

The Supreme Court also pointed out to the trial judge in the *Sheppard* case he did not do all that he could in **admonishing the jury**, that is, giving them strict rules about what they could and could not do. Instead, the senior judge's instructions were more in the form of "suggestions" or "requests" to avoid media coverage rather than ordering them not to read newspapers, watch television news, or listen to radio newscasts. Judge Blythin asked jurors during the trial if they had seen or heard a newscast reporting Dr. Sam's purported mistress was pregnant with his child. Two of the jurors stated they had. Obviously, his order to avoid news reports went unheeded.[20]

Control of Courtroom

Bedrock Law
Judges can be forceful in asserting a fair trial *requires* the jury's full cooperation, not just in their attentiveness to the testimony but also in their avoidance of external influences.

Unrelated to pretrial publicity yet highly relevant to Sheppard's due process rights, the Court pointed to the importance of the judge's exercise of authority to maintain courtroom decorum. The location of reporters, their ability to overhear confidential discussions, and their access to evidence and jurors all played a role in corrupting the judicial process. Reporters might have behaved badly, but only because Judge Blythin allowed them to do pretty much whatever they wanted to do. We'll never know if his pending election caused him to cater to the news media, but critics have speculated that it did.

Judges have a tremendous amount of authority in maintaining the decorum of the courtroom. Much of this comes from the British legal tradition. Hundreds of years ago, judges were the crown's representatives. They settled disputes even if they were not schooled in law. The judge's robe is a vestige of the king's royal robe. The fact that all rise when the judge enters the court is a sign of the respect paid to the king.

As representatives of the king, judges were also given wide latitude in coercing those in the courtroom to behave. **Contempt of court** gives the judge the authority to deal with disruptive people by removing them from the court, fining them, or even temporarily imprisoning them. Contempt of court can be a major concern for free press advocates, as judges have also used the power to control the behavior of people outside the courtroom.

Contempt of Court

Black's Law Dictionary defines contempt of court as follows:

> Any act which is calculated to embarrass, hinder or obstruct court in administration of justice, or which is calculated to lessen its authority or its dignity. Committed by a person who does any act in willful contravention of its authority or dignity, or tending to impede or frustrate the administration of justice, or by one who, being under the court's authority as a party to a proceeding therein, willfully disobeys its lawful orders or fails to comply with an undertaking which he has [been] given.[21]

The easiest example to understand of a contempt citation is when a person in court is repeatedly disruptive. Even people who have never been inside a courtroom have seen plenty of movies and TV shows where a judge bangs the gavel and calls for order in the court, threatening or actually holding someone in contempt. This type of contempt is known as **direct contempt** because it takes place in court or close enough to be disruptive, such as being noisy outside the courtroom door.

20. Today there are a plethora of samples that judges can choose from for admonishing the jury. An online search of "model jury instructions" provides hundreds of results, state and federal, for a variety of civil and criminal cases.
21. *Black's Law Dictionary* 319 (6th ed. 1983).

Direct Contempt
Acts of disrespect or disobedience occurring inside the courtroom, such as being disruptive during court proceedings.

There is also **indirect contempt**, which involves activity away from the courtroom but also results in a disruption of the legal process. When a court issues a **subpoena** – an order for someone to appear in court to testify, and the person does not appear at the appointed date and time, the judge may find the person in indirect contempt. If a judge instructs trial participants not to speak to anyone about the case outside the courtroom and one of the attorneys appears on the evening news discussing the trial, the judge may find the attorney in contempt.

Judges are given latitude in doling out punishments for contempt, but they don't quite have absolute power. A judge might slap a fine on someone for being disruptive in court or order a reporter to stop writing notes because it's distracting. However, if a judge's punishment is excessive or a demand is inappropriate, the contempt citation can be appealed. Like any appeal, an appellate judge will review the facts to reach a determination on the merits. In the case of contempt citations, the review is often expedited because of the First Amendment implications. However, any judicial order must be obeyed until an appellate court approves the appeal or grants a stay of that order.[22]

Indirect Contempt
Acts of disrespect or disobedience occurring outside the courtroom, such as failure to appear in court when subpoenaed.

Subpoena
An order by a court that compels the production of evidence or the testimony of a witness.

Bedrock Law
News reporters covering trials should follow the judge's orders until they can be appealed, even if those orders appear to be unconstitutional.

It's important to understand that a judicial order must be followed until an appeal has been heard and granted. Officers of the court recognize if everyone who disagrees with a judicial order can simply ignore it the rule of law would be upended. In 1972, a Baton Rouge, LA, judge prohibited reporters in his court from publishing reports based on public testimony given in court. Two reporters violated the rule, and the judge held them in contempt and issued a fine.

On appeal, the Fifth Circuit Court of Appeals held the judge's order to be a violation of the First Amendment rights of the reporters. But in spite of that decision, the court still upheld the contempt citation. The court opinion explained how reporters should have appealed the order rather than simply violating it, leaving it for the court to decide whether the order was justified, and not the reporters' will.[23]

There is a little wiggle room if reporters make a good-faith effort to appeal what appears to be an unconstitutional order and the appeal is not decided quickly. In such cases, *some* courts in *some* jurisdictions have been willing to invalidate the contempt citation. Still, that has yet to be settled by the U.S. Supreme Court and remains shaky ground for journalists.

One settled area of law recognizes that maintaining order in the court does not require people to silence their criticism of judges *outside* the courtroom. In two separate decisions from the 1940s, the U.S. Supreme Court ruled that calling a judge's decision "outrageous"[24] or stating that judges protect criminals more than the public[25] is unlikely to cause judges or courts to lose respect or cause damage to the process of justice. Saying such things to a judge inside the courtroom might result in contempt, but outside of court, such statements are protected.

In addition to distinguishing between *direct* and *indirect* contempt, there is also a distinction between **civil contempt** and **criminal contempt**. The court uses civil contempt sanctions as a tool to enforce court orders. It is used, for example, to get an uncooperative party to show up for a hearing or respond to a court order. Civil contempt is invoked as the remedy when a reporter refuses to testify in a legal proceeding or when a television station refuses to provide videotape subpoenaed as evidence.

On the other hand, an order of criminal contempt is punitive. There's no attempt to get a particular response from the person; the judge is just invoking a penalty for misbehavior as when a defendant disrupts the trial with an emotional outburst. Some actions can actually

22. A stay is a court order, usually a temporary one, to block a legal action or proceeding.
23. *United States v. Dickinson*, 465 F.2d 496 (5th Cir. 1972).
24. *Bridges v. California*, 314 U.S. 252 (1941).
25. *Pennekamp v. Florida*, 328 U.S. 331 (1946).

provoke both civil and criminal citations for contempt whenever the rules of the court are ignored, and the subject engages in a public display of disobedience.

For example, in 2004, two *San Francisco Chronicle* reporters published a book dealing with the use of steroids in sports. The book contained facts about the investigation into BALCO (Bay Area Laboratory Co-Operative), the company purported to be supplying steroids to athletes. That information was allegedly leaked from grand jury testimony.

In 2006, the reporters were called to testify before a grand jury to explain how they obtained this information, which should have been kept confidential. The reporters refused to testify. The court was prepared to fine the newspaper $1,000 per day that the reporters refused to testify, as if each day they refuse is a new act of contempt. The reporters also faced the possibility of spending up to 18 months in prison. While the orders were being appealed and before the reporters were imprisoned, a source voluntarily came forward revealing his identity and ending the grand jury's need to pressure the journalists.

In some cases, judges can coerce trial participants to cooperate with requests for information without the threat of a contempt citation. In 1979, the Supreme Court ruled CBS's refusal to provide information during the pretrial discovery process would allow the judge to presume the claims made by the plaintiff about the journalist's state of mind were correct.[26]

Since public figure plaintiffs must prove the defendant had a knowledge of falsity or reckless disregard for truth, one way to make that argument is by asking the reporter what they knew and when. If reporters opt not to answer the question, the court may be forced to accept the plaintiff's assertions. When *60 Minutes* producers would not provide hours of videotape requested by the plaintiff in discovery, the Supreme Court said it was reasonable for the judge to assume that the plaintiff's claims about what the tape contained were accurate. The defense had the right to refute the claims by providing the evidence.

Civil Contempt
Court-ordered sanction issued to elicit a particular response, such as compelling reporters to testify or pay a penalty.

Criminal Contempt
Court-ordered citations issued for courtroom offenses, such as an outburst during a trial.

Bedrock Law
Contempt of court citations are used by judges to ensure compliance with their orders such as when trial participants are asked to obey a gag order.

Gag Orders

One of the many things Judge Blythin did not do to protect Sam Sheppard's right to a fair trial was to constrain the behavior of the trial participants: the attorneys, jurors, and witnesses. They were free to talk with anyone, including reporters, outside the courtroom. Of course, doing so would result in news media coverage, which could be read or heard by other trial participants.

Gag orders are edicts issued by judges for people to keep their mouths shut and not discuss anything about a trial with anyone outside of the proceedings. It evolved from the centuries-old practice of controlling unruly people in the courtroom by literally binding and gagging them to keep them quiet. Today, those people would more likely be removed from court, but in the famous 1968 trial of the "Chicago Seven," radical protesters during the Democratic National Convention in Chicago, Black Panthers leader Bobby Seale was bound and gagged to try to prevent his outbursts (it didn't work, and he was later removed). Physical binding and gagging may be outmoded but insisting trial participants not speak about the case even outside the courtroom is still a familiar remedy imposed by judges.

Gag Order
An act by a judge restricting trial participants from discussing the case outside the courtroom.

Gag orders – also known as suppression or restraining orders – may be challenged, and in some cases the orders have been upheld, while in others they have been overturned. Gag orders involve the balancing of two constitutional rights: the First Amendment right of the trial participants to freedom of speech and the Sixth Amendment right of a fair trial.

Among other guarantees of the Sixth Amendment is the right to a trial "by an impartial jury." In determining whether a gag order may be imposed, judges must balance the First and Sixth Amendment rights involved. There is no magic formula for deciding which one wins; each decision is made by weighing the likelihood that a jury will be impartial at the expense

26. *Herbert v. Lando*, 441 U.S. 153 (1979).

of trial participants losing their free speech rights. However, the Supreme Court has called such an order when aimed at journalists "the most serious and least tolerable infringement on First Amendment rights."[27]

The fact the same court has both upheld and overturned gag orders demonstrates the ad hoc nature of each decision. In 1988, the U.S. Second Circuit Court of Appeals found a gag order for trial participants to be constitutional.[28] The federal district court in southern New York imposed a gag order in a bribery and racketeering trial, and the appellate court upheld the order believing there was a "reasonable likelihood" a fair trial would be prejudiced by the publicity.

In a case the very next year, the same southern district court of New York issued another gag order, and the challenge again went to the Second Circuit Court of Appeals. This time, however, the gag order was vacated. One of the reasons given was the lack of information would have threatened the defendant's fair trial rights.[29]

Exactly what standard will be applied? Unfortunately, the answer varies by jurisdiction. Research by the Reporters Committee for Freedom of the Press shows how rules vary by federal circuit, and by states.[30]

One settled area of the law regarding gag orders shows the Supreme Court's distaste for imposing gags on individuals who are *not* trial participants, including the media. The seminal case in this area comes from Sutherland, a small town in Nebraska. In 1975, six family members were murdered. The following day, their neighbor confessed to the police.

Pretrial publicity was rampant, and the judge was asked by the county attorney to impose a gag order on the media to ensure a fair trial. The judge issued the order, and the Nebraska Press Association appealed. The Nebraska Supreme Court modified the gag order slightly but otherwise left it in place. The press association appealed to the U.S. Supreme Court.

The highest court was unanimous in finding the gag order was an unconstitutional limitation on free expression.[31] A majority of the Court held there might be instances when gag orders are warranted and provided three issues a court must examine before gagging the media. They must weigh the nature and extent of the pretrial news coverage; consider alternatives to a gag order for a fair trial; and show the likelihood the order would ensure a fair trial.

The judge in the murder case, like the judge in Dr. Sam Sheppard's trial, never considered the litany of available alternatives. What's more, in a town of just 850 people, rumors spread about their local crime of the century posing a greater threat to a fair trial than responsible media reporting would have done.

The 1976 ruling would make it seem the door was left open for gag orders on news media; however, this is not true. Appellate courts have repeatedly struck down gag orders on non-trial participants. As a result of the *Nebraska Press Association* ruling, which was reinforced in another unanimous ruling the following year,[32] there is a nearly insurmountable hurdle when trying to gag anyone other than trial participants.

One notable exception occurred in 2004, when reporters were gagged while covering basketball star Kobe Bryant's rape case. A court reporter mistakenly emailed transcripts from a closed hearing to major news media outlets. The trial judge ordered the networks and press receiving them to destroy the emails and not disclose their content concerning evidence of Bryant's sexual behavior.

27. *Nebraska Press Ass'n v. Stuart*, 427 U.S. 539 (1976).
28. *In re Dow Jones & Co.*, 842 F.2d 603 (2d Cir. 1988).
29. *In re New York Times Co.*, 878 F.2d 67 (2d Cir. 1989).
30. A comprehensive list can be found *at* www.rcfp.org/open-court-sections/c-gag-orders-on-participants.
31. *Nebraska Press Ass'n v. Stuart*, supra note 27.
32. *Oklahoma Publishing Co. v. District Court*, 430 U.S. 308 (1977).

The press appealed the gag order but the Colorado Supreme Court, in a 4–3 decision, upheld the gag order.[33] It was understood as an attempt to correct an error made by the court's own clerks that made public information available that should never have been disseminated. Viewed that way, it can be understood as an exception to an otherwise firm prohibition of gag orders on nonparticipants in trials.

When it comes to gag orders on trial participants, the hurdle is a much lower one and there are countless examples of gag orders that either were upheld on appeal or never challenged in the first place. Trial participants include everyone formally connected to the trial, including the attorneys for either side, the defendant, witnesses, and the jurors. Judges may elect to gag some of the participants and not others (attorneys are more often gagged than jurors), but once the order is issued, those affected must abide by the gag order until the trial is over. It should be noted that the Supreme Court has ruled in cases *in which the media serve as trial participants*, they can be subjected to gag orders just like any other trial participant.[34]

While gagging trial participants usually does not directly affect journalists, such orders always indirectly affect the ability to gather news. Reporters trying to cover noteworthy trials can be frustrated by gag orders preventing potential sources for a story from speaking to them. There have been instances in which trial participants have violated gag orders and spoke confidentially to the news media, but those who publish such information face another risk.

Imagine this hypothetical example: Judge Pompous issues a gag order in a murder trial. Sharon Seekrits is a witness who is sure that defendant Freddie Badguy committed the crime. She confidentially speaks to WINO-TV reporter Hugh Bagawind. The next day, Bagawind reports an "unnamed source" told him about some evidence. Judge Pompous sees the newscast and immediately realizes the only way Bagawind could have gotten that information was from one of the trial participants, which means whoever spoke to the reporter violated the gag order. The only way Judge Pompous can find out who violated the gag order is to question the reporter. But can reporters be made to disclose their confidential sources? If so, under what circumstances? The next section examines these perplexing questions.

Compelling Reporters to Testify

One of the most frequent conflicts between the rights of a free press and the right to a fair trial is the court's need to gather evidence. Without evidence, a trial obviously lacks the most basic elements for arriving at the correct outcome. Courts have extensive tools to gather evidence. As noted, courts can and do subpoena people to testify in a trial and bring their evidence.

A subpoena in no way implies a person has done anything wrong. If you receive a subpoena, it means the court believes you have information necessary to investigate an offense. For that reason, when an attorney requests a subpoena, a court is likely to grant it. A judge is not going to expect an attorney to prove beyond a reasonable doubt a witness has important evidence, but a subpoena can be quashed (canceled) when the request for evidence is unreasonably burdensome or not legally proper. Unless a witness must travel a great distance, the subpoena is a relatively minor burden in most cases.

When a reporter is called to testify, the situation is considerably different. The media have claimed confidential sources need to be protected to keep a free flow of information to the public. If confidential sources are divulged by reporters, those sources may stop providing information or, in some cases, be subjected to harm.

The reasons sources give for providing information to news media vary greatly. In some cases, a disgruntled employee may want to blow the whistle on an employer. In other

33. *People v. Bryant*, 94 P. 3d 624 (Colo. 2004).
34. *Seattle Times v. Rhinehart*, 467 U.S. 20 (1984).

situations, it could be an adversary in a political battle who provides some dirt about an opponent. Still other sources could be government employees who disagree with policy decisions and want to see a change in direction.

In many cases, confidential sources speak on the condition of anonymity because they face personal or professional retaliation if their identity is revealed. Perhaps the most famous anonymous source in newspaper history is "Deep Throat," a crucial source for *Washington Post* reporter Bob Woodward, who, along with Carl Bernstein, wrote the series of articles credited with breaking the Watergate scandal that toppled the Nixon presidency in 1974.[35]

Despite the value of anonymous sources, media critics claim journalists are too quick to grant anonymity, suggesting they may be hiding a litany of sins behind their veil of secrecy. In 1981, reporter Janet Cooke of the *Washington Post* won a Pulitzer Prize for "Jimmy's World," a story about an eight-year-old heroin addict. Cooke later revealed there was no Jimmy; she concocted him as a composite of many people. Cooke kept the sources for the story anonymous, even from her editors, because she said she vowed to protect their identities.[36]

When her reporting on "Jimmy" was revealed to be a fictional portrayal, Cooke resigned her position at the *Washington Post* and returned the Pulitzer Prize. Apart from the journalistic debate about how and when to use anonymous sources in news reporting, the larger legal question is how and when journalists can be compelled to reveal their sources' names to law enforcement officers. For the seminal case in this area, we go back in time to the turbulent era of the late 1960s to early 1970s, when illegal drug use and civil disorder were hot topics.

***Branzburg* Test**

To compel a reporter to testify, the government must show 1) probable cause to believe a reporter's information is clearly relevant to a specific probable violation of law; 2) the information sought cannot be obtained by alternative means less destructive of First Amendment rights; 3) a compelling and overriding interest in the information.

The *Branzburg* Test

What is referred to in legal circles as "the *Branzburg* case" is actually three cases heard together by the Supreme Court. The cases involved three different journalists working for three different news media. The common thread in all of them was their refusal to disclose the identities of their sources. Paul Branzburg was a reporter for the Louisville, KY, *Courier-Journal*. In 1969 and 1971, he wrote two articles about drug use for his paper that caused law enforcement officials to take notice.

In one story he explained how marijuana was refined to make the much stronger drug hashish. As part of his research, he observed people who made hashish. For another story about drug use, Branzburg interviewed several drug users and observed some pot smoking. Law enforcement officials subpoenaed Branzburg after reading both stories because in each one, he was a witness to the commission of a crime. Branzburg refused to identify his anonymous sources to a grand jury.

In 1970, Paul Pappas was working out of the Providence, RI, office of a Massachusetts television station when he was sent to cover some civil disorder activities involving "fires and other turmoil." He met with leaders of the local Black Panthers and was allowed inside their headquarters for about three hours on the condition he did not disclose anything he saw or heard except an expected police raid, which never occurred. Pappas was later called before a county grand jury seeking to know what he learned during his time at the Black Panthers headquarters, but Pappas refused to answer.

35. Deep Throat's identity was protected by Woodward, Bernstein, and the *Washington Post* for more than 30 years until Deep Throat's family revealed his identity in 2005. W. Mark Felt was serving as assistant director of the FBI when he had the late-night meetings to provide Woodward with information. D. Von Drehle, "FBI's Number 2 Was Deep Throat," *Washington Post*, June 1, 2005, A6.
36. The Associated Press provides rules for the use of anonymous sources, *at* https://www.ap.org/about/news-values-and-principles/telling-the-story/.

Indictment
A formal accusation against someone that is suspected of committing a felony (a serious crime). After a grand jury hearing, the grand jury issues either a true bill, in which case the person is charged, or a no bill, in which case the person is not charged.

A third journalist asked to testify was Earl Caldwell, who was working for *The New York Times*. Caldwell had also been covering the Black Panthers and was subpoenaed to appear before a grand jury to testify about the operations of the militant group. Caldwell complained the subpoena was overly broad and because of the damage it would do to his relationship with his sources he did not want to appear. The grand jury responded by explaining it was investigating several serious crimes, including a conspiracy to assassinate the president. A court ordered Caldwell to testify, but he still refused and was found in contempt.

The importance of the *Branzburg* case should not be underestimated. Since 1972, more than 2,000 cases have cited *Branzburg* (including 58 at the U.S. Supreme Court), and the case has been mentioned in more than 1,700 law journal articles. Because of the variation in cases using the *Branzburg* test, there is a great deal of variation in the "rigor" with which the test is used in various jurisdictions. Regardless of the degree of support, no jurisdiction grants journalists an absolute right to refuse to testify.

It is important to remember how volatile the late 1960s and early 1970s became in the United States. In addition to U.S. involvement in Vietnam, drug use and race relations were subjects often stirring public controversy and protests, sometimes ending in violence. There was a lot of fear at the time. The drug stories by Branzburg and news coverage of militant racial organizations by Pappas and Caldwell helped to fuel that fear.

In 1972, the U.S. Supreme Court heard the appeals of Branzburg, Pappas, and the government in the Caldwell case (Caldwell's contempt was overturned by the Ninth Circuit). The ruling in the *Branzburg-Pappas-Caldwell* trilogy would provide the test applied by courts when determining whether to require a journalist to testify. One might think that such a solid basis for law came from a unanimous Court, but in fact the decision was 5–4. It might also be natural to assume the basis would be derived from the majority opinion, but in fact that is not the situation. The majority held Branzburg, Pappas, and Caldwell did not have the right to refuse to testify before the grand jury.

Yet it is the concurring opinion of Justice Lewis Powell, combined with the dissent by Justice Potter Stewart, that provides the criteria for the test. While the other members of the majority were prepared to turn away any protection for journalists called to testify, Powell was prepared to allow such protection provided conditions that were not present in the *Branzburg* trilogy were met. Combined with the dissent's belief the reporters should not have been made to testify, Powell's swing vote set the stage for the test, provided in Stewart's dissent.

Justice Powell said the freedom of the press and the citizen's obligation to provide testimony must be "balance[d]. . . on a case-by-case basis."[37] The precise criteria for the balancing were then provided in Justice Stewart's dissent. Despite his claim that "all of the balancing was done by those who wrote the Bill of Rights"[38] and that "any test which provides less than blanket protection to beliefs and associations will be twisted and relaxed so as to provide virtually no protection at all,"[39] Stewart provided the three-part test. To compel a reporter's testimony, the government must

- show that there is probable cause to believe that the newsman has information that is clearly relevant to a specific probable violation of law
- demonstrate that the information sought cannot be obtained by alternative means less destructive of First Amendment rights
- demonstrate a compelling and overriding interest in the information.[40]

37. *Branzburg v. Hayes*, 408 U.S. 665, 710 (Powell, J., concurring).
38. *Id.* at 713 (Stewart, J., dissenting).
39. *Id.* at 720 (Stewart, J., dissenting).
40. *Id.* at 743 (Stewart, J., dissenting).

In plain language, the first point prevents law enforcement from going "fishing" for any possible information a journalist might have. To subpoena the reporter, law enforcement ought to know exactly what information the reporter has that is needed.

The second part of the test requires that the journalist be the *only* person who has the information. If other non-media sources have the information, then the journalist need not testify. It also implies that coercing reporters' testimony cannot be a substitute for the law enforcement investigation. If a journalist has information that police could discover through their own resources, the reporter should not be made to testify, even if it costs time and money for law enforcement. The expense of an investigation is not as important as protecting First Amendment rights.

The third prong of the test requires the information being sought is crucial for the investigation. Plenty of testimony is gathered during a grand jury proceeding and the subsequent trial, but much of it is not of "compelling and overriding interest." Of course, critics assert that sometimes it is impossible to know whether testimony is critical until it is heard.

The Grand Jury Process

A grand jury is not like the jury in a trial court. It is a group of citizens brought together to hear evidence and decide whether the government ought to go forward in the prosecution of a crime.[41] There are both federal and state grand juries, and both consist of 12–23 members. The term *grand* jury comes from the group being larger than a common jury, known in legal circles as a *petit* jury.

Grand juries are not called just for one individual case but are impaneled for a period of from one month to three years. Trial juries are drawn from random pools, while members of grand juries come from the same potential pool of registered voters or drivers but are often not random selections, and some grand jurors may serve multiple terms. In some states, grand jurors volunteer for the role.

Grand juries investigate; they do not conduct trials of guilt or innocence. Rather than the standard of "beyond a reasonable doubt" required for a criminal conviction, grand juries are only looking for "probable cause," which is a significantly lower standard. If the grand jury determines there is a probable cause, it will order an **indictment**, a formal written accusation of a crime. Only after there is an indictment does a suspect become a defendant. The grand jury investigation is not conducted by a judge; it is conducted by a law enforcement official, such as a sheriff or county prosecutor.

It surprises many Americans who are unfamiliar with the legal system that grand juries are conducted in complete secrecy. No one else is allowed into the proceedings. Witnesses can't even bring attorneys with them when they provide testimony. This is one reason why journalists don't even want to appear before a grand jury. A journalist who enters a grand jury chamber might refuse to answer any questions about a confidential source, but no one can know whether the journalist told everything because the proceedings are secret. So if a journalist appears before the grand jury for any reason, could it be jeopardizing the source's anonymity?

In 2023, the owner-publisher of a weekly newspaper in Alabama was indicted by a grand jury for allegedly "revealing evidence." The matter was complicated because Sherry Digmon was both a publisher and a school board member. She was accused after her newspaper reported the local district attorney was investigating the school system's use of COVID funds. After lots of media attention over six months, all charges against Digmon were dropped.[42]

41. While there are some "civil grand juries" (in California, for instance) that serve as government oversight bodies, the term grand jury is usually used in connection with criminal charges.
42. "Charges Dropped Against Atmore Journalists Accused Of Revealing Grand Jury Secrets," *North-Escambia.com*, April 21, 2024.

The prosecutors have a great deal of control over the whole process. They decide who will be the witnesses, they ask the questions, and they draft the charges. In Digmon's case, charges were dropped when the local district attorney recused himself, and the state's assistant attorney general decided not to pursue legal action. Critics have called modern grand juries little more than a "rubber stamp" for the prosecutor.[43]

Shield Laws

Shield Laws
Statutes in 40 states afford a *privilege* to journalists to not disclose information (i.e., notes and other materials) obtained during the course of their newsgathering.

One attempt to try to afford journalists a greater degree of protection has been the enactment of **shield laws** in most states. Shield laws are "state statutes which afford *privilege* to journalists to not disclose information (i.e., notes and other materials) obtained during course of their newsgathering."[44]

Shield laws are not a new phenomenon. The first one was passed in Maryland in 1896. Forty states have enacted their own shield laws with varying degrees of protection.[45] There are many differences among the statutes depending on how the terms are defined. For example, exactly who is protected by a state statute? There is no "license" for a journalist, so who qualifies for the privilege?[46]

It might be easy to say a full-time reporter for a newspaper or television station qualifies, but what about a freelancer who is not employed by a news outlet and hopes to sell an article to a magazine? How about bloggers?

Consider Indiana as an example, where the state statute would protect freelancers who have already sold articles to news media but not someone working on a first-time submission.[47] There are no Indiana cases involving bloggers, and the law's language appears to exclude them, unless their blog is "issued at regular intervals and having a general circulation." In contrast, a California court extended the state's shield law to include bloggers when it "decline[d] to embroil [itself] in questions of what constitutes 'legitimate journalism.'"[48]

Privilege
A benefit, immunity, or exemption extended to a specific group of people. In journalism, it is often immunity from being forced to reveal sources.

Privilege

The word *privilege* has many meanings. When used in the law, it refers to a specific power or exemption someone has which others do not. Diplomatic immunity is a form of privilege afforded to foreign officials to exempt them from prosecution. In defamation law, privilege is the immunity legislators have from defamation suits while conducting legislative business.

Other classes of people use privileged communication, and in such cases, the protected person does not have to divulge the content of certain communications.

43. "6 of Your Questions about Grand Juries, Answered," *MSNBC*, December 5, 2014, *at* https://www.msnbc.com/msnbc/6-your-questions-about-grand-juries-answered-msna473536.
44. *Black's Law Dictionary* 716 (5th ed. 1983).
45. The Reporters Committee for Freedom of the Press maintains an online database of reporters' privilege *at* www.rcfp.org/reporters-privilege. Check it for the specifics of your state.
46. At least one scholar suggests anyone can qualify as a journalist since we are all able to publish our observations online to a worldwide audience. Such a position would render a definition of journalists obsolete. *See* S. Gant, *We're All Journalists Now: The Transformation of the Press and Reshaping of the Law in the Internet Age* (New York: Free Press, 2007).
47. The relevant portion of the statute reads as follows: (1) any person connected with, or any person who has been connected with or employed by (A) a newspaper or other periodical issued at regular intervals and having a general circulation; or (B) a recognized press association or wire service; as a bona fide owner, editorial or reportorial employee, who receives or has received income from legitimate gathering, writing, editing and interpretation of news; and (2) any person connected with a licensed radio or television station as owner, official, or as an editorial or reportorial employee who receives or has received income from legitimate gathering, writing, editing, interpreting, announcing or broadcasting of news. Ind. Code § 34–46–4–1 (1998).
48. *O'Grady v. Superior Court*, 139 Cal. App. 4th 1423, 1457 (2006)

"Executive privilege" exempts the president and the White House staff from having to provide information to other branches of government that could jeopardize the executive's ability to do their job.

It also applies to both foreign and domestic communication, although executive privilege is not without its limits. President Richard Nixon discovered that fact when trying to claim a privilege to protect tape recordings made in the Oval Office.[49]

Most people are aware of the confidence that exists in the attorney/client privilege. Any conversation between a lawyer and their client can be kept confidential; otherwise, clients might not be forthright with their own lawyers.

Doctors also have the same sort of privilege in communicating with their patients.[50] Most states provide married couples with a privilege protecting them from having to testify against their spouses. Priests have a privilege in communications with penitents who confess their sins. Opinion is mixed on whether the penitent must be involved in a formal process of confession (such as practiced by the Catholic Church) for that privilege to apply.

The claim of a journalist's privilege not to disclose confidential information has been raised by virtually every journalist subpoenaed to testify who promised his sources secrecy. It is based primarily on the claim that freedom of the press *must* include the right to gather news without government interference; otherwise, the right to publish news is eviscerated.

Excepting spousal privilege, all others are based on the premise the professional given the privilege needs to be protected to successfully do their job. Just like journalists, they learn the important confidential information during their professional activity. As Branzburg, Pappas, and Caldwell learned, the Supreme Court does not recognize such a constitutional privilege for journalists, hence the proliferation of shield laws.

Shield laws also differ in exactly what they cover. Some are specific to the protection of the names of sources of information, while others also include any notes or other work reporters have produced. Some states require sources to specifically request anonymity for the journalist to be protected, while others do not. Some states are clear the shield law does not apply if the journalist is a witness to the commission of a crime; then they must testify.

Many states distinguish between requests made by grand juries, civil trial courts, and criminal trial courts. For example, Hawaii protects journalists rather thoroughly when it comes to grand jury requests but affords less protection in felony prosecutions or in defamation claims.

Ironically, reporter Paul Branzburg was subpoenaed in Kentucky, which had (and still has) a shield law. The Supreme Court was not persuaded the First Amendment provided him a privilege to refuse to testify, and the Court similarly did not accept the argument the Kentucky state law protected him.

New Jersey is thought by many to have one of the most protective shield laws in the nation. One of the early adopters, it has had a statute on the books since 1933. And yet when Myron Farber invoked the shield law in 1978, the Supreme Court of New Jersey did not accept the argument. Farber was a *New York Times* investigative reporter whose crime reporting was a primary reason New Jersey indicted Mario E. Jascalevich for murder.

Farber refused to testify or to provide material for *in camera*[51] inspection by the judge and was held in contempt of court. Farber's attempt to defend himself based on the state's shield

49. *United States v. Nixon*, 418 U.S.683 (1974).
50. Even doctor/patient privilege is not absolute. In many jurisdictions, doctors are required to disclose instances of child abuse, sexually transmitted diseases, gunshot wounds, or other conditions considered to be risks to the public at large.
51. *In camera*, from Latin for in-room, refers to action that occurs in the judge's chambers, away from public view.

law was rejected by the court on the premise the accused's right to a fair trial, a constitutional right, outweighed his use of the shield law, a state statute.[52]

This is, in fact, one reason why even some journalists oppose state shield laws. As they see it, any attempt to rely on a statute is bound to fail on any occasion where it conflicts with the Sixth Amendment rights of the accused in a criminal trial. A shield law may offer protection in civil cases, perhaps even grand jury hearings, but is less helpful in criminal trials.

A journalist of no less renown than the late Ben Bradlee (who as *Washington Post* editor oversaw the Watergate reporting and its use of anonymous sources) opposed shield laws on the premise that if legislatures have the power to give something, they also have the power to take it away.[53] This position holds the First Amendment must be the source of a reporter's privilege, putting it on the same level in the legal hierarchy as the Sixth Amendment right to a fair trial.

Given the fact a majority of the U.S. Supreme Court has not accepted a reporter's privilege as inherent in the First Amendment, others assert the best possible protection should come from a *federal* shield law.

A Federal Shield Law's Fate

When former Vice President Mike Pence was representing his Indiana district in Congress, he proposed federal shield law legislation multiple times. U.S. Rep. Pence, also a former broadcaster, co-sponsored the Free Flow of Information Act in 2011, which was in essence the same bill that failed to pass both houses of Congress in 2005, 2007, and 2009.

Fast forward to the 2024 legislation, co-sponsored by 20 legislators (ten Republicans/ten Democrats). The PRESS (Protect Reporters from Exploitive State Spying) Act removed the stipulation a journalist had to be employed professionally by a news organization. Instead, it defined a "covered journalist" as anyone who "regularly gathers, prepares, collects, photographs, records, writes, edits, reports, investigates, or publishes news or information that concerns local, national, or international events or other matters of public interest for dissemination to the public." This change made it a functional role rather than a professional determination and encompassed more of the digital community of online communicators.

The PRESS act unanimously passed the U.S. House of Representatives early in 2024, although its future seemed far less assured in the upper chamber. Powerful voices in the U.S. Senate have made attacking the news media a pillar of their political careers. Any PRESS act favoring the "enemy of the people," as the 45th president described journalists, would only motivate those senators to kill a federal shield act before the president can sign it into law.

Realizing the uncertainty of a promise of secrecy, the best practical advice for any journalist is to be cautious about accepting confidential information. Before accepting any request to protect the identity of a source, the reporter needs to decide if keeping that promise is worth the risk of going to jail. If the desired information is important to the story and the source faces harm once identified, then a promise of confidentiality is in order.

In states with shield laws, a court could determine it violates an accused person's right to a fair trial and as such the shield law cannot be upheld. *The New York Times* reporter Judy Miller spent 85 days in jail in 2005 for refusing to provide the name of her source in the

52. *In re Myron Farber*, 78 N.J. 259 (1978).
53. "The First Rough Draft of History," 33 *Am. Heritage Mag.* 6 (October/November 1982).

investigation of leaks leading to the disclosure of a covert CIA agent's name (Valerie Plame). It took place during the controversial news coverage surrounding the U.S. invasion of Iraq. Miller had been reporting on disputed evidence Iraq was building weapons of mass destruction justifying the White House's position.

Newsroom Searches

In addition to protecting sources of confidential information, journalists want to protect the materials they gather. As in the argument for protecting sources, journalists need to protect their notes, tapes, photographs, digital files, and computers from intrusive eyes to continue gathering news without jeopardizing sources. Imagine how frightening it would be to reporters if law enforcement officers stormed into their newsroom and rummaged through their files. That is precisely what happened to one university student newspaper in 1971.

The *Stanford Daily* covered some Vietnam War protests involving student demonstrators. Unfortunately, some of the protesters attacked police officers, who had been sent to evict them from the Stanford University Hospital's administrative offices, which demonstrators had taken over and occupied for a day. Two days later, a special edition of the paper included an account of the fracas with photos. Believing the paper might have other photographs revealing the identities of students who struck the officers, the Santa Clara County District Attorney's Office obtained a warrant to search the paper's offices for evidence.

A search warrant differs significantly from a subpoena. As stated earlier, a subpoena is the traditional manner by which evidence is requested. Had the Santa Clara County authorities followed the normal procedures, they would have appeared at the *Stanford Daily* offices with a subpoena ordering the paper to bring all the relevant material to court by a certain date to be examined. The paper would then have time to gather the material or, if it chose to do so, file a legal request to *quash* (legal term for voiding) the subpoena.

Up until this time, the legal community considered a subpoena appropriate when the party being served was not suspected of any wrongdoing, whereas a warrant was preferred for the ones suspected of a crime. Certainly, if a suspected drug dealer received a subpoena inviting them to come to court and bring the illegal drugs with them, it would have little effect, so a search warrant is appropriate.

The Fourth Amendment to the Constitution declares "no warrants shall issue, but upon probable cause, supported by oath or affirmation, and particularly describing the place to be searched, and the persons or things to be seized." Probable cause is not required for the issuance of a subpoena.

Despite the *Daily* not being accused of any wrongdoing, Santa Clara County asserted it needed a warrant to negate the possibility the student publication would destroy evidence it might have. The *Daily* filed suit claiming both rights of a free press under the First Amendment and Fourth Amendment rights against unreasonable searches were violated. Although the federal trial court and the appellate court both found in favor of the student publication in *Zurcher v. Stanford Daily*,[54] the U.S. Supreme Court overturned the rulings and found the police had not violated the paper's constitutional rights. As might be expected, law enforcement officials praised the decision, while media advocates condemned it.

Less than two years later, police searched the offices of a printer in Flint, MI, where a muckraking paper was printed. They also searched the newsroom of KBCI-TV in Boise for videotapes providing information about a prison riot in Idaho. They, too, were issued a warrant rather than a subpoena, knowing the Supreme Court authorized such action.

The criticism of the use of warrants was loud and strong. In 1980, Congress passed the Privacy Protection Act, which called on the attorney general to create guidelines restricting

54. 436 U.S. 547 (1978). James Zurcher was the Palo Alto, CA, police chief.

the issue of search warrants to a "disinterested third party." The result was a set of rules allowing law enforcement officials to obtain a warrant to search a newsroom; however, the rules make obtaining a warrant considerably more difficult. Law enforcement agencies are not to search and seize "work product" or "documentary materials" presumably gathered or produced for "public communication."

Work product includes notes, tapes, or other material used in gathering information. Documentary materials would typically be considered finished work, such as a tape recording for air. Other materials may be seized with a warrant if

- The subject of the warrant is suspected of a crime and not just an "innocent bystander." For example, if a reporter is suspected of selling drugs, a warrant may be used.
- There may be injury or loss of life if the material is not immediately seized. For example, if the reporter's notes contain the location of a time bomb.
- There is a possibility the documentary materials would be destroyed if subpoenaed. It's unclear how much proof is needed to demonstrate the material's destruction is imminent.
- Earlier subpoenas for the material have been ignored.

Journalists can appeal subpoenas, but they cannot ignore them. Journalists in California, Connecticut, Illinois, Nebraska, New Jersey, Oregon, Texas, Washington, and Wisconsin have their own state statutes that afford even more protection than the Privacy Protection Act of 1980.[55]

Cameras in the Courtroom

We live in a video world. Surveillance cameras are almost everywhere. YouTube has all sorts of videos, including moments the participants had no clue would be made available worldwide. Official Iraqi video of Saddam Hussein's execution in 2006 ended before showing the actual moment of execution, but someone with a cell phone camera uploaded a complete version of the hanging online where it could be seen by millions (albeit poor quality).

One part of our world where cameras have been tightly controlled is in the American courtroom (Figure 13.2). Some states allow no cameras whatsoever, while those allowing photography or videography impose a variety of rules limiting a camera's use. The impact of photographic coverage on a trial's outcome has been the subject of debate for years.

American Bar Association (ABA)
The professional organization for lawyers in the United States.

Long before the Dr. Sam Sheppard case, judicial decorum was lacking in another high-profile trial. The controversy began in New Jersey in 1935. Bruno Hauptmann was charged with kidnapping and killing the baby of American icon Charles Lindbergh. Photographers were even permitted to take flash pictures in the courtroom. The fallout from the chaos of this murder trial produced an addition to the Canons of Professional and Judicial Ethics of the **American Bar Association (ABA)**.

The new recommendation was that cameras should be banned from all courtrooms. In 1952, the ABA amended the recommendation to include television cameras in the ban. When the Bar Association makes a recommendation, it does not have the force of law; however, it does have more weight than an ordinary suggestion. For nearly 30 years, the ABA recommendation was followed with nearly no public comment or criticism and was accepted as a given for courtroom decorum.

The situation changed with a U.S. Supreme Court decision in 1965.[56] Financier Billie Sol Estes was indicted by a Texas grand jury for swindling through a fraudulent fertilizer and

55. Electronic Privacy Information Center, The Privacy Protection Act of 1980, *at* https://archive.epic.org/privacy/ppa/.
56. *Estes v. Texas*, 381 U.S. 532 (1965).

Figure 13.2 Typical courtroom; note the separation between trial participants and spectators

cotton business. Due to his association with politically well-connected Texans, including then-Vice President Lyndon Johnson, the *Estes* trial gained a lot of press attention, and the court decided to change the venue of the trial (as suggested in the *Sheppard* case).

Despite the ABA Canon, a similar one from the State Bar of Texas, and over objections from the defense, the judge agreed to allow television cameras in the trial court. During the pretrial hearings, there were as many as 12 cameras in the courtroom. It was extremely disruptive. By the time the trial began, a booth had been constructed in the back of the courtroom, and all cameras were moved inside it. Only certain portions of the trial could be televised live, and most of the rest could be only silent video, which was used in portions during regularly scheduled newscasts.

Estes claimed on appeal of his conviction his right to due process was violated by the presence of the cameras. The Supreme Court agreed, finding them to be a distraction to the jury, the witnesses, and the judge. The Court used the construction of the camera booth, the restriction on what portions could be televised live, the requirement for silent footage during most of the trial, and the prohibition on shooting the defense's closing testimony as evidence it all caused a distraction in violation of the defendant's rights.

The majority opinion concluded with this prophetic statement: "It is said that the ever-advancing techniques of public communication and the adjustment of the public to its presence may bring about a change in the effect of telecasting upon the fairness of criminal trials,"[57] but these words did not apply to the present situation. The Supreme Court's position in 1965 was that the mere presence of cameras in a court could, and in this case did, result in a violation of the defendant's constitutional right to a fair trial.

In 1972, the American Bar Association replaced its Code of Judicial Ethics with a new Code of Judicial Conduct and included the recommendation to ban all cameras from the

57. *Id.* at 551–552.

courtroom.[58] Television technology was rapidly improving. Cameras became smaller, quieter, and capable of shooting in low light conditions. The prevalence of cameras in society was increasing concurrently, making it less extraordinary to see someone videotaping an event.

In 1978, the ABA's Committee on Fair Trial-Free Press proposed experimenting with cameras in local courtrooms, provided the cameras were unobtrusive and the judge maintained strict control. There were mixed reactions to the proposal among ABA committees and governing bodies, but the Conference of State Chief Justices overwhelmingly approved a resolution allowing each state's supreme court to establish the rules for cameras in their respective states.

Florida established a one-year experiment with cameras in the courtroom beginning in July of 1977. At the end of 12 months, the Florida Supreme Court scrutinized reports and comments from the testing period, surveyed trial participants of every kind, and examined the record from six states that had adopted new rules about cameras in court and from ten other states considering adopting rules.

The Sunshine State was satisfied cameras in the courtroom and a fair trial could peacefully coexist, provided safeguards were in place ensuring decorum. Florida permitted no more than one camera and one operator. The camera had to remain stationary for the entire trial. No extra microphones other than those already in the courtroom were allowed. The videotape equipment had to be kept outside the courtroom. The jury could never be photographed, and the judge had the authority to exempt any witness from television coverage.

The same month the state of Florida began its experiment, two Miami Beach police officers were charged with grand larceny for their allegedly breaking into a well-known Miami Beach restaurant. Officers Noel Chandler and Robert Granger tried to prevent cameras at their trial, asserting the experiment violated their fair trial rights. Their motions were denied, and cameras were present.

Notably, Florida was one of the few states permitting camera coverage over the objection of the defendant. Less than three minutes of the actual trial were broadcast, but the material used was all from the prosecution's side of the case. Chandler and Granger were found guilty. They appealed their conviction, again claiming they were denied a fair trial; however, they did not present evidence proving the trial was unfair. The Florida appellate and supreme courts rejected their appeal.

In *Chandler v. Florida*,[59] the U.S. Supreme Court unanimously ruled that Chandler and Granger's right to a fair trial had not been violated. Chandler attempted to argue the *Estes* case provided all the proof necessary that cameras were a violation of fair trial rights, but the Court asserted that a close reading of the decision could not conclude that the intent in *Estes* was to ban all cameras from all courts indefinitely. Estes's rights had been denied, but it was not the same as saying all cameras in all courts were unconstitutional.

> An absolute constitutional ban on all broadcast coverage of trials cannot be justified simply because there is a danger that, in some cases, prejudicial broadcast accounts of pretrial and trial events may impair the ability of jurors to decide the issue of guilt or innocence uninfluenced by extraneous matter.[60]

The Court took the firm position that the presence of a camera alone, without any other evidence, will not result in a violation of due process.

Following the *Chandler* decision, more states allowed cameras in their courts, but each state established its own set of rules.[61] As with shield laws, the rules vary dramatically, and

58. In the Code of Judicial Ethics, the admonition had been Canon 35, but in the new Code of Judicial Conduct, the same rule was Canon 3A (7).
59. 449 U.S. 560 (1981).
60. *Id.* at 574–575.
61. RTDNA provides a comprehensive guide of the states' varying rules, *at* https://courts.rtdna.org/

Radio Television Digital News Association (RTDNA)

The largest professional organization for electronic journalists in radio, television, and all digital media, as well as journalism educators and students.

Bedrock Law

Most states allow some camera coverage at either the trial or appellate court level, but it is rare for federal jurisdictions to do so.

media professionals must know their own state's rules. Some states allow cameras in appeals courts and not trial courts, while it's vice versa in other states, and still others allow both. The District of Columbia prohibits cameras in both trial and appeals court hearings, while other states allow it on a permission basis. One state, Oklahoma, suspended its rules on cameras in the courtroom.

Some states prohibit focusing on jurors while others prohibit any depiction of jurors whatsoever.[62] Almost all states allow the presiding judge to be the final arbiter. Donald Trump's 2024 trial in New York was not televised because state rules require news media to apply for the judge's approval, and the judge in the case rejected the request.[63] The **Radio Television Digital News Association** maintains an up-to-date database online.[64] Most states have some form of electronic media coverage, but not all states allow cameras in trial courts.

Unlike state courts, federal courts are loath to allow cameras. While the American Bar Association's Canons have *suggested* limiting camera access, the U.S. Judicial Conference has explicitly prohibited them in federal trial courts. The 1946 Federal Rule of Criminal Procedure 53 prohibited any cameras or recording in federal criminal trials. The rule was expanded in 1972 to include all federal civil cases as well.

The Conference recommended a federal experiment with cameras in 1988, and a three-year pilot was conducted in six district and two appellate courts. After analyzing the results, the Conference decided to ban cameras in trial courts but allow appellate courts to decide for themselves. Cameras are banned in all but two appellate courts, the Second and Ninth Circuits.

After a four-year experiment in 14 of the 94 federal district courts, the 2016 Judicial Conference of the United States decided to continue the ban on cameras in federal courts, despite nearly two-thirds of surveyed judges agreeing with camera use in courtrooms if federal rules allowed.[65] The Ninth Circuit has been allowed to continue its limited pilot program in three district courts. Since 2011, only one jury trial has been recorded.[66]

Chief Justice John Roberts has shown no interest in allowing cameras in the U.S. Supreme Court.[67] Bills have been introduced in Congress as recently as 2007 to require the Supreme Court to permit cameras, but so far none has passed. When the subject came up in 1996, Justice David Souter told the House Appropriations Committee that there would be cameras in the Supreme Court "over my dead body."[68] Souter may be gone from the Court, but that attitude is not. Despite the repeated efforts of newsgathering trade associations and public interest groups, the nation's federal trial courts, an overwhelming majority of the appellate courts, and the highest court in the nation are closed to cameras.

In 2010, a federal trial judge in northern California was going to allow audio and video to be streamed from his court to other federal courtrooms across the country. The trial court was going to hear a legal challenge to Proposition 8, an amendment to the state's constitution that would recognize only marriages between a man and a woman as valid. Chief Judge Vaughn Walker was prepared to allow the broadcast of the trial to other federal courtrooms but was blocked by appeals. The Supreme Court ruled 5–4 that proper procedures had not been followed to allow for the broadcast.[69]

62. A Nebraska court declared a mistrial when a Kearney TV station showed video of potential jurors. "Nebraska Station Unwittingly Causes Mistrial," *Broadcasting & Cable*, October 27, 2016.
63. "Can You Watch the Donald Trump Trial Live? No, Here's Why," *USA Today*, April 15, 2024.
64. Until 2009, the Radio Television Digital News Association (RTDNA) was the Radio Television News Directors Association (RTNDA).
65. "Courtroom Camera Pilot Program Grounded," *at* https://www.rcfp.org/journals/news-media-and-law-spring-2016/courtroom-camera-pilot-prog/.
66. The federal courts provide a list of court videos, *at* www.uscourts.gov/about-federal-courts/judicial-administration/cameras-courts.
67. However, audio of oral argument is made available by the Supreme Court, *at* www.supremecourt.gov/oral_arguments/argument_audio/2023.
68. On Cameras in Supreme Court, Souter Says, "Over My Dead Body," *New York Times*, March 30, 1996, 24.
69. *Hollingsworth v. Perry*, 130 S. Ct. 705 (2010).

From the Trenches: Cameras as Seen From the Judge's Bench

By Judge Louis H. Schiff

For most of the last century, courts were concerned that bringing in cameras and electronic media into trials would be the kryptonite of the judicial system.

The Florida Supreme Court in 1975 boldly began a pilot program whereby cameras and electronic media were allowed in state courtrooms under the condition that journalists follow a strict set of rules designed to open the courts to the public, while protecting the rights of the litigants. The Florida Supreme Court said in *In re Petition of Post-Newsweek Stations Fla., Inc.*, 370 So.2d 764 (Fla.1979), cameras in the courtroom did not inherently violate the constitutional rights of a defendant. These standards remain in effect today.

The Supreme Court of the United States held the Constitution did not prohibit states from permitting cameras in the courtroom and upheld the Florida Supreme Court in *Chandler v. Florida*, 449 U.S.560 (1981). Florida courts at every level have cameras in the courtroom, with its supreme court broadcasting sessions live on television and over the Internet.

Critics have argued that cameras in the courtroom tend to pose some sort of irreparable harm upon an individual's right to a fair and impartial trial; or they create a "spectacle" like the Hauptmann or the O.J. Simpson trials.

However, under strict rules and guidelines, cameras and electronic media serve to inform a citizenship and pull away the curtain of secrecy in the courtroom. As a trial court judge, I have always welcomed journalists using electronic media and cameras into the courtroom. Our system of democracy demands our citizens not only be informed of the goings on in court, but they should see and hear them as well.

Today, judges and media in Florida participate together in forums that educate the third branch of government and the fourth estate on the rules regarding media in the courtroom.

While I am not so naive to believe judges, lawyers, and litigants have not "showboated" while cameras have been in the courtroom, I can say the overwhelming majority of judges, lawyers, and litigants are not affected by electronic media in the courtroom, and their behavior is not altered or affected by it. As a judge, I am always aware of the presence of the cameras. I realize, whether a camera is there or not, the courts are a very public place with a very solemn purpose, and that purpose is to ensure that justice is carried out. Electronic media can assist the courts in carrying out their duty.

Florida Supreme Court Justice Alan Sundberg said in *Post-Newsweek*, "We have no need to hide our bench and bar under a bushel. Ventilating the judicial process, we submit, will enhance the image of the Florida bench and bar and thereby elevate public confidence in the system." Electronic media and cameras can bring responsible change to courts and the justice system, and they can add an air of confidence to the public at large that the third branch of government is competently operating in the open.

The Honorable Louis H. Schiff served as a Broward County (FL) judge 1997–2024. In addition to his law degree, he also has an undergraduate degree in journalism.

Global View of Cameras in Court

The struggle over whether to allow cameras in courts is not unique to the United States. A *Brigham Young University Law Review* article from 2012 examined the climate for courtroom cameras and found Canada to be a "pioneer" in broadcasting its Supreme Court.[70]

The Supreme Courts of Brazil and the United Kingdom were also found to be camera-friendly, even though lower courts in those countries might not be as permissive. Australia makes its high court recordings available online and proudly touts that full court hearings in Canberra are available the next business day.[71]

When people think of open courts, they are unlikely to think of Ukraine, but they should. The country has allowed recording in courts since 2014 – and they don't require a judge's permission to do so, just that the rules be followed.

The Open Court project has resulted in thousands of trials being recorded by independent experts, and advocates claim it helps maintain standards in courts. Videos containing "flagrant violations" of protocol by any party can result in 100,000 views and affect a person's reputation.[72] Since 2017, the project uses 360-degree cameras to capture all the court activity,[73] providing an immersive viewing experience.

Other Electronic Coverage in Court

Large cameras used by television stations are easy to identify, but what about other devices? Smartphones can take pictures, shoot video, or provide instant commentary. Courtroom rules for cameras apply whether the camera is large or small, and different rules apply in each of the states. Although there might be a rare state court judge who allows it, most are unlikely to allow trial spectators who do not represent media companies to take pictures or video, whether streamed live or not.

The greatest conflict in recent years has arisen over the use of smartphones to provide live commentary. People using X (formerly Twitter) or other social media to provide their followers with instant updates about what is happening in court have angered numerous judges, and some tweeters have been punished. In 2015, a Fort Smith, AR, television reporter was found in contempt of court when he tweeted the verdict of a murder trial from the courtroom.[74] The judge had specifically ordered that all devices be turned off in the courtroom. As such, the reporter disobeyed a court order: a sure path to a contempt citation.

Rules vary tremendously among states. Pennsylvania's Supreme Court rejected a proposed statewide ban on "real time" reporting, leaving it to the discretion of judges in each courtroom to decide.[75] Federal Rule of Criminal Procedure 53 prohibits "the broadcasting of judicial proceedings from the courtroom," but is tweeting broadcasting? Something as simple as a definition dramatically affects interpretation of the statute. A Georgia court

70. Kyu Ho Youm, "Cameras in the Courtroom in the Twenty-First Century: The U.S. Supreme Court Learning From Abroad?" 2012 *BYU L. Rev.* 1989 (2012), *at* https://digitalcommons.law.byu.edu/lawreview/vol2012/iss6/9.
71. www.hcourt.gov.au/cases/recent-av-recordings.
72. "Expert: Open Court Creates Professional Standards for All Participating Sides of Trial," *Ukraine Crisis Media Center*, *at* https://uacrisis.org/en/38966-proekt-vidkritij-sud.
73. "Open Court Project Launches 360-Degree Videos of Court Hearings," *Kyiv Post*, July 10, 2017, *at* www.kyivpost.com/ukraine-politics/open-court-project-launches-360-degree-videos-court-hearings.html.
74. "KFSM's Henry Admits to Tweeting during Murder Trial," June 10, 2015, *at* www.arkansasonline.com/news/2015/jun/10/kfsm-s-henry-admits-to-tweeting-during-/.
75. "Tweeting from Courts Still Slow in Catching On," *at* https://www.rcfp.org/journals/news-media-and-law-spring-2015/tweeting-courts-still-slow/.

determined Twitter is broadcasting and prohibited its use in court, while in Kansas, a judge determined the opposite and allowed it.[76]

A 2015 study of various rules from across the United States showed 14% of the sample courts allowed real-time reporting, 19% banned it, and 31% explicitly left it to the judge's discretion. That means roughly one-third of the sample did not address the question of real-time reporting at all.[77] As with many areas of the law, technology advances much faster, and laws do their best to "catch up." In Indiana, the Judicial Conference of the Indiana Community Relations Committee and the Hoosier State Press Association worked for more than three years to try to develop guidelines for in-court social media use.[78]

Some states have modified rules about smartphone use. Michigan provides a good example. Prior to 2020, courts had the authority to dramatically restrict the devices, but rules now allow phones to be used for notetaking, Internet browsing, or text messaging. Devices must be silenced and can't be used for photography, recording audio or video, or live streaming.[79]

The use of social media by trial participants has caused problems at times. Jurors are supposed to base their decisions only on evidence presented in court, but in a world where people search any subject out of curiosity, jurors can run afoul of court rules. Reuters reported,

> A Florida appellate court . . . overturned the manslaughter conviction of a man charged with killing his neighbor, citing the jury foreman's use of an iPhone to look up the definition of "prudent" in an online dictionary. . . . the West Virginia Supreme Court of Appeals granted a new trial to a sheriff's deputy convicted of corruption, after finding that a juror had contacted the defendant through Myspace . . . the Nevada Supreme Court granted a new trial to a defendant convicted of sexually assaulting a minor, because the jury foreman had searched online for information about the types of physical injuries suffered by young sexual assault victims.[80]

Jurors, who either don't know or don't care about rules of court procedure, sometimes act irresponsibly. A juror sent a Facebook friend request to the defendant in the trial for which he was empaneled. When the judge found out, he was removed from the jury – someone who wants to be the defendant's friend can't be expected to be impartial. The ex-juror then bragged on Facebook about getting dismissed. The judge sent him to jail for three days for criminal contempt.[81]

Judicial admonition, as noted earlier, can help, and guidelines for judges to admonish jurors about social media use were devised in 2012.[82] Yet even admonition may not be enough. A New York juror was fined $1,000 for posting to Facebook during a trial, even though she was aware of the restriction. Because she posted information about the jury deliberations, a mistrial was declared. The judge pointed out the expense behind declaring a mistrial.[83]

76. "Litigation in Twitter Nation: When You Can and Can't Tweet in #Court," February 6, 2017, *at* www.law.com/sites/almstaff/2017/02/06/litigation-in-twitter-nation-when-you-can-and-cant-tweet-in-court/.
77. Tweeting from Courts, supra note 75.
78. "Tweeting Reporters Allowed in Court?" *Ind. Lawyer*, September 21, 2016, *at* www.theindianalawyer.com/articles/41483-tweeting-reporters-allowed-in-court.
79. Michigan Rule 8.115 Courtroom Decorum; Policy Regarding Use of Cell Phones or Other Portable Electronic Communication Devices, *at* https://www.courts.michigan.gov/4a7b65/siteassets/court-administration/standardsguidelines/operations/cell_phone_use.pdf.
80. "As Jurors Go Online, U.S. Trials Go Off Track," December 8, 2010, *at* www.reuters.com/article/internet-jurors-idUSN0816547120101208.
81. "Juror Jailed over Facebook Friend Request," February 16, 2012, *at* www.heraldtribune.com/news/20120216/juror-jailed-over-facebook-friend-request.
82. "Federal Judges Given More Leeway to Discourage Social Media Use by Jurors," *Network World*, August 24, 2012, *at* https://www.networkworld.com/article/2222997/federal-judges-given-more-leeway-to-discourage-social-media-use-by-jurors.html.
83. "Juror Fined for Facebook Posts about Criminal Court Case," November 4, 2015, *at* https://www.abajournal.com/news/article/juror_is_fined_1k_for_posting_on_facebook_and_causing_mistrial.

Must Courtrooms Be Open?

If state and federal courts have the authority to determine rules to govern the use of cameras in court or ban them altogether, do they likewise have the authority to close courtrooms to any and all observers? While the general rule is that trials are presumptively open to the public, not all trials are public, and for trials that are public, a portion of the trial may be closed.

The Supreme Court presumes criminal trials are open to the public, a right that was made clear in 1980. The Sixth Amendment to the Constitution promises "*the accused shall enjoy* the right to a speedy and public trial." If it's the right of the accused to a public trial, might the accused waive that right and ask that a trial be closed? If the Sixth Amendment were the only word on the matter that just might be the case, but history and the First Amendment also come into play.

In *Richmond Newspapers v. Virginia*,[84] a murder suspect's counsel wanted his client's fourth trial – following several mistrials – closed, and the judge consented. Richmond Newspapers appealed, and the Supreme Court agreed the closure was unconstitutional. The Court's reasoning on behalf of due process is unambiguous: "Open trials assure the public that procedural rights are respected, and that justice is afforded equally. Closed trials breed suspicion of prejudice and arbitrariness, which in turn spawns disrespect for the law."[85]

Implicit in the Constitution is the right to attend criminal trials, and the history of the United States bears this out. Allowing defendants to close trials could result in deal making between the participants or the *perception* that something inappropriate happened behind closed doors, resulting in a loss of public trust in the legal system. The Supreme Court did not assert *all* criminal trials must *always* be open, but left for another day the question of precisely what criteria need to be met to close a courtroom.

Juvenile trials used to be closed to the public, and most of them still are. The rationale is that juveniles deserve a higher level of protection than adult suspects. This concern also drives similar laws about nondisclosure of juvenile records – discussed in Chapter 14 – and the media's voluntary nondisclosure of the names of juvenile suspects or victims. In recent years, the presumption that juvenile trials must be closed has been revisited. The National Council of Juvenile and Family Court Judges stated, "Traditional notions of secrecy and confidentiality should be reexamined and relaxed to promote public confidence in the court's work."[86]

Almost half of the states open a juvenile trial if the charges would be felonies in "regular" court. Illinois and California open the trial if the charge is related to "street gang" activity. Some states, such as Pennsylvania, distinguish between younger and older juveniles, opening the trials of the older ones but not the younger. In Michigan, juvenile proceedings are presumptively open, though parties can petition the court for closure.[87]

Minors might also be protected when they testify in criminal or civil courts by closing the court, but in those situations, there must be a compelling reason for closing the courtroom, and only the portion of the trial that protects the compelling interest is closed.

Courts have become less inclined to automatically accept such requests for closure. In 2007, the D.C. Court of Appeals ruled against the closure of a courtroom for the testimony of a 12-year-old victim of sexual assault because it was a violation of the defendant's Sixth Amendment right to a public trial. The defendant objected to closure and the appeals court ruled the judge in the case did not consider alternatives to closure nor demand enough of a

84. 448 U.S. 555 (1980).
85. *Id.* at 595.
86. D. Oddo, "Removing Confidentiality Protections and the 'Get Tough' Rhetoric," 18 *B.C. Third World L. J.* 105 (1998).
87. Michigan Court Rules 3.925, *at* https://casetext.com/rule/michigan-court-rules/michigan-court-rules/chapter-3-special-proceedings-and-actions/subchapter-3900-proceeings-involving-juveniles/rule-3925-open-proceedings-judgments-and-orders-records-confidentiality-destruction-of-court-records-setting-aside-adjudications.

showing that closure was necessary. At the time of the request, the only nonparticipants in the courtroom were supporters of the defendant.[88]

While closing courts when minors testify may be allowed, it is *not* constitutional to *require* closing the courtroom for minors who testify. The Supreme Court ruled in 1982 that a Massachusetts statute requiring judges to close trials during the testimony of minors who were victims of sex crimes was unconstitutional.[89]

The Supreme Court did not say the testimony had to be public; in fact, closure might be warranted. On the other hand, it might be appropriate for the testimony to take place in an open court and then the *requirement* to close the trial would be an unconstitutional infringement. In either case, the court should make clear exactly what the compelling reason for trial closure is.

The Supreme Court interpreted the Sixth Amendment right of the accused to a public trial in *Waller v. Georgia* in 1984.[90] The defendants were charged with gambling, and they attempted to suppress evidence the prosecution had obtained by wiretapping. The court conducted a closed suppression hearing, which the defendants wanted open to the public.

The Supreme Court ruled the defendant's Sixth Amendment right to a public trial included pretrial hearings and these could only be closed with a clearly demonstrated "overriding interest." The Court rejected an unsupported claim of a privacy violation to non-trial participants as rising to the level required to close the hearing.

Earlier in the same term, the Supreme Court ruled the *voir dire* jury selection process is also part of the trial and therefore subject to the same openness as trials. A California judge closed the courtroom for the entire six weeks of jury selection to journalists from the *Riverside Press-Enterprise* in a trial for the rape and murder of a teenage girl. The trial court was acting in response to claims that the questioning of prospective jurors in an open court for such a sensitive case would violate the privacy of the jurors and risk the fair trial rights of the accused.

In an 8–0 decision, the Supreme Court held the *voir dire* to be part of the trial process and as such should be presumptively open under the First Amendment because of the right of access rather than the public trial provision of the Sixth Amendment. The Court observed a narrowly tailored closure might be permissible where there are specific threats to a fair trial or privacy rights. But even in those instances, alternative means for protecting those rights first must be explored.[91]

In those instances, closure could be no longer than absolutely necessary to protect the jeopardized rights. Two years later, the same California newspaper asked for Supreme Court direction for other pretrial events besides jury selection in an "angel of death" case, where a nurse was charged with killing 12 patients with an overdose of heart medicine. The newspaper won that case for openness as well as the right to be present during these pretrial proceedings.[92]

Presumptive Right of Access
The rule in criminal trials (including the pretrial hearings) is that they are presumptively open to the public and press.

While we have standards of access established by the Supreme Court for criminal courts, there is no such definitive opinion for civil trials. As with many of the other fair trial issues discussed in this chapter, the answer differs according to the jurisdiction. Most states recognize there is a **presumptive right of access** even to civil trials, but the conditions under which they allow closure vary. Some are quite clear while others are less so.

California, for example, clearly provides a right of access to civil trials. The California Supreme Court decided the issue in 1999 during a celebrity case involving actor/director

88. C. Zarek, "Appeals Court Reverses Sex Abuse Case for Court Closure," October 9, 2007, *at* www.rcfp.org/appeals-court-reverses-sex-abuse-case-court-closure.
89. *Globe Newspaper Co. v. Superior Court*, 457 U.S. 596 (1982).
90. 467 U.S. 39 (1984).
91. *Press-Enterprise Co. v. Superior Court of Cal.*, 464 U.S. 501 (1984).
92. *Press-Enterprise Co. v. Superior Court of Cal.*, 478 U.S. 1 (1986).

(and mayor) Clint Eastwood and Sandra Locke, a former lover who claimed Eastwood was attempting to destroy her career. California's highest court ruled closing the trial violated the First Amendment, and it also violated a century-old California law providing "the sittings of every court shall be public."[93] California's standards for civil trials follow exactly the rules for criminal trials: closure only under extraordinary circumstances and only if all the requisite criteria are met.

Bedrock Law

Excepting some juvenile hearings, trial judges can only close the courtroom to the public under extraordinary circumstances when an overriding interest is at stake.

One federal appeals court supported both a First Amendment right and a common-law right of access to civil proceedings. The case in point stemmed from a proxy battle between stockholders seeking control of a publicly traded company making liquor and industrial alcohols at a Philadelphia plant.

The parties involved asked the judge to close the proceedings, which he did, asserting the question was not what information should be made public but who decides. The court felt it should be a matter for the judge to decide rather than the news media. The Third Circuit Court of Appeals ruled instead the judge had not conducted an adequate review, specifically because the closure was based on speculation rather than evidence.[94]

North Carolina's Supreme Court also recognized a presumptive right of access to court proceedings, but it did so in a case that upheld the complete closure of a civil trial.[95] In the case, a doctor took legal action against a hospital for revoking his medical staff privileges following his peer review. North Carolina relied on a statute keeping peer reviews confidential. Based on this protection, the North Carolina high court found in favor of the trial court's closure.

A federal court in Texas allowed for the partial closure of a civil trial to protect the identities of minor plaintiffs. Three adults and three minors filed suit against the Santa Fe, TX, school district for policies they believed created an unconstitutional endorsement of religion. To protect them from public retribution, the plaintiffs' identities were kept secret. Because it would be easy for anyone attending an open trial to identify the plaintiffs, they requested closure. The federal district court ruled it would uphold closure for the testimony of the minor plaintiffs but would not uphold it for the adult plaintiffs.[96]

Closing Criminal Court

The rule in criminal trials (including pretrial hearings) is they are presumptively to be open. For a judge to close any portion to the public, including media, the following points must be met:

- A fundamental right, such as privacy or fair justice, must be at risk if the proceeding is held in public.
- There must be convincing evidence (not mere speculation) that the right at risk will be compromised if the proceeding is not closed.
- No alternative exists that would be less restrictive of constitutional rights. The accused has a Sixth Amendment right to a public trial, and the public has an implied First Amendment right to an open trial.
- The closure must be limited to the specific content that causes problems for the fundamental right being protected.

The state of Florida declared all hearings to terminate parental rights must be closed. Florida has a statute that declares it so, and the Florida Supreme Court upheld as constitutional

93. *NBC Subsidiary v. Superior Court*, 86 Cal. Rptr. 2d 778, 788 (Cal. 1999).
94. *Publicker Indus. v. Cohen*, 733 F.2d 1059 (3d Cir. 1984).
95. *Virmani v. Presbyterian Health Servs.*, 350 N.C. 449 (1999).
96. *Doe v. Santa Fe Indep. Sch. Dist.*, 933 F. Supp. 647 (S.D. Tex. 1996).

that law closing parental rights proceedings, asserting that juvenile proceedings are not presumptively open and that the state had the right to close the proceedings.[97]

While there are some exceptions, such as those that apply strictly delineated criteria, courts are open. As one nationally renowned legal scholar, Arthur Miller, wrote in 1991,

> By long-standing tradition, the American public is free to view the daily activities of the courts through an expansive window that reveals both our criminal and civil justice systems. Through this window, people can watch an endless panoply of lawsuits, litigants, judges, juries, sometimes garishly illuminated by television lights and dramatized by graphic, occasionally lurid, press reports.[98]

Summary

- The Constitution guarantees a criminal defendant the right to an impartial jury. Juries may be aware of some facts of a case and still be impartial, but outside the courtroom information may have a prejudicial effect on jurors or potential jurors.
- Courts are inclined to do whatever is within their power to protect the rights of the accused in a criminal trial. The *Sheppard* case in the 1950s outlined the Supreme Court's response. When necessary, courts should safeguard the right to impartial justice using the tools of change of venue, continuance, sequestration, rigorous *voir dire* process, stern admonitions to the jury, and maintaining courtroom decorum – all tools that can help to ensure a fair trial without impinging on the First Amendment rights of access.
- Judges have the power to find people in contempt of court to punish them for their misbehavior in court. The threat of contempt can be used to coerce someone to do what the court wants, such as reveal the name of a source. Though not a daily occurrence, there are famous instances of journalists having been jailed for refusing to name a source.
- Sometimes judges issue gag orders to protect the rights of the accused in a criminal trial. A gag order means no one involved in the trial may discuss the proceedings. While these orders limit the information trial participants can share about a case, they are usually constitutional. On the other hand, attempts by judges to gag non-trial participants, especially journalists, must be obeyed until an appeal can lift the suppression order.
- A balance of sorts has been struck between the court's desire for testimony and the journalist's desire not to testify. The Supreme Court's *Branzburg* 1972 case provides a three-part test in the dissent that recommends when reporters can be compelled to testify.
- Partly in response to the threat of compelled testimony, a majority of states created shield laws to protect journalists from having to reveal information, most notably the names of anonymous sources. Shield laws are far from guarantees for communicators – even in states where they exist, reporters have been ordered to testify or face contempt charges, and some have been jailed. There have been repeated efforts to pass a federal shield law.
- News media are sometimes subpoenaed when law enforcement believe they have evidence (often pictures or video) necessary for an investigation. Media can move to quash the subpoena, and a judge will decide whether to require the media to comply and produce the evidence. A federal statute prohibits law enforcement from using warrants rather than subpoenas to obtain evidence from news media, except in rare instances.
- States decide for themselves whether to allow cameras in courts, and different rules adopted by each state determine which courts can have cameras and microphones

97. *Natural Parents of J.B. v. Florida Dept. of Children & Family Servs.*, 780 So. 2d 6 (Fla. 2001).
98. A. Miller, "Confidentiality, Protective Orders, and Public Access to the Courts," 105 *Harv. L. R.* 428 (1991).

recording, what may be televised or streamed, and how it is all to be maintained. A few federal courts have experimented with cameras, but the Supreme Court, which sets rules for the federal courts, has refused live camera coverage but is more open to microphones.

- Criminal trials are presumptively open, and so are pretrial activities considered part of the process, such as the *voir dire*. Court closure is rare; when it does occur, it is restricted to the least possible amount of time necessary. More states appear to be moving toward openness for civil trials, but there is no constitutional provision requiring open courts, but the Supreme Court has ruled such access is part of the First Amendment's protection.

Ethical Dilemmas From the Trenches: Can Pretrial Publicity Prevent a Fair Trial?

"Theft by Press Conference: Stealing a Defendant's Presumption of Innocence With Prejudicial Pretrial Publicity"

Huffington Post, January 27, 2017

By Steve Drizin

Making A Murderer, Netflix's smash documentary series was a revelation, opening my eyes to many things about Steven Avery's case that I did not know before. As one of Brendan Dassey's attorneys, I had reviewed Mr. Avery's trial transcripts and some of the media coverage of his case. But there's a huge difference between reading a trial transcript or an online news article and seeing events unfold on film. Of all the shockers in the film, the most disturbing to me was Calumet County District Attorney Ken Kratz's press conference on March 2, 2006. I saw, for the first time, how Mr. Kratz destroyed both Mr. Avery's and my client's "presumption of innocence."

On March 2, 2006, the afternoon after Brendan was arrested, Mr. Kratz addressed a throng of reporters whom he had assembled in a press conference that was carried live on many local television and radio stations. Mr. Kratz first issued a warning to viewers and listeners not to let children under age 15 hear what he was about to say. And then he proceeded to narrate Brendan's "confession" over the air. Merely mentioning that Brendan confessed was prejudicial enough, but Mr. Kratz went further. He vouched for the truth of the confession, speaking with certainty with phrases like "we now know what happened" to Teresa Halbach. The release of these gory details coupled with his confidence in their truth all but sewed shut any chance that Brendan or Steven could get a fair trial.

The press conference was such a disturbing spectacle that it traumatized many who heard it, including grown men and reporters like Aaron Keller, the NBC26 Reporter from Green Bay, who told *Rolling Stone* that "it was the single most shocking thing I ever heard as a human being." Mr. Keller, dubbed the "Silver Fox" for his good looks and thick gray hair by *Making a Murderer* fans, had to shut himself in the news truck for an hour afterwards to decompress. He told *Rolling Stone* that he felt the need to reach out to some "decent human beings" who were his loved ones. Keller called his parents.

Other reporters who covered the conference have told me that they could not sleep or eat for days afterwards and one television producer from nearby Fond du Lac told me that she remembered exactly where she was when she heard the news. It was the kind of indelible memory – like Kennedy's assassination or the Twin Towers falling on 9/11 – that people still couldn't shake.

What makes Mr. Kratz's conduct especially galling is that he had to know he was breaching both ethical rules governing pretrial publicity and special rules which expect an even higher duty of prosecutors in criminal cases. He just didn't care.

There's no wiggle room in these rules. Wisconsin Rule of Professional Conduct 3.6(2) (a) prohibits lawyers from making public statements that the lawyer "knows or reasonably should know will be disseminated by means of public communication and will have a substantial likelihood of materially prejudicing an adjudicative proceeding in the matter." Rule 3.6(2)(b) is more specific, prohibiting attorneys in a criminal case, from publicizing "the possibility of a plea of guilty to the offense *or the existence of the contents of any confession*, admission or statement by the defendant or suspect." The Comments to Rule 3.8 which concern "the special responsibilities of a prosecutor" state that "a prosecutor can, and should, avoid comments which have no legitimate law enforcement purpose and have a substantial likelihood of increasing public opprobrium of the accused."

Mr. Kratz violated these rules. He knew that the contents of Brendan's confession would be disseminated widely throughout the Manitowoc area, the entire state of Wisconsin, and soon enough to the world via the Internet. As Mr. Keller can attest to, the manner in which Mr. Kratz read the contents of the confession only served to add to the trauma of those listening to it. The remarks also inflamed the public's scorn of Avery, Dassey, and the entire Avery family.

There is a special reason why the rules prohibit discussing the "contents of a confession." It is because there is no more powerful piece of evidence in a court of law. Former Supreme Court Justice William Brennan once wrote:

> No other class of evidence is so profoundly prejudicial . . . Triers of fact accord confessions such heavy weight in their determination that the introduction of a confession makes the other aspects of a trial in court superfluous and the real trial, for all practical purposes, occurs when the confession is obtained.

The reason for this is because most jurors naively think that they would never falsely confess to a crime. They also believe that only an insane person would falsely confess to a murder. When prospective jurors heard Brendan's confession, Brendan's presumption of innocence morphed into an almost irrebuttable presumption of guilt.

In the wake of Mr. Kratz's press conference, few in the media questioned his conduct. They printed the contents of his confession and played clips of the conference on the air over and over again. State and local prosecutors (and former prosecutors turned talk show hosts) were equally mum about the ethics of Mr. Kratz's behavior. It's only now, in the wake of the film's release, that some prosecutors are publicly condemning Mr. Kratz's conduct and some members of the media are second-guessing their decision to blindly follow Mr. Kratz's lead. At the time, however, their silence made them complicit in Mr. Kratz's ethical breaches.

Mr. Kratz has never paid any price for his theft of Brendan and Steven's "presumption of innocence." Apparently, no disciplinary complaints citing misconduct during the press conference were ever filed against Mr. Kratz before the Wisconsin Office of Lawyer Regulation. But unless prosecutors like Mr. Kratz face serious sanctions for such rule violations in the future, there will surely be others who will follow in his footsteps.

Disciplining prosecutors, however, may not be enough to curb such abuses. In the late 1950s and early 1960s, the United States Supreme Court reversed several convictions due to prejudicial pretrial publicity. But today, this remedy is disfavored. Instead, courts grant continuances, change venues, bring in juries from other counties, give extended *voir dire* to lawyers to pick a fair and unbiased jury, or instruct jurors to disregard information gained from outside the courtroom. Studies have shown that these "solutions" do little to erase the taint of prejudicial publicity. Even the most conscientious jurors may be unable to suppress the biasing effects of hearing that a defendant gave a confession, especially one as graphic as the one described by Mr. Kratz.

In the not so olden days, jurors got their information from newspapers or from nightly news. Such news had a short shelf life. In the Internet age, however, prejudicial information takes on a life of its own; it spreads like a virus, and it lives forever, only a click away. In this day and age, more serious sanctions may be necessary to deter prosecutorial misconduct. When prosecutors deliberately breach the ethical rules in order to contaminate the jury pool, trial courts may have no option but to dismiss indictments and appellate courts may have no choice but to grant defendants new trials. No court likes to use these "nuclear options" but these remedies may be the only way to prevent further abuses and to protect a defendant's fair trial rights.

Steven A. Drizin, one of Brendan Dassey's appellate lawyers, is a clinical law professor at Northwestern Pritzker School of Law's Bluhm Legal Clinic and the cofounder of the Clinic's Center on Wrongful Convictions of Youth.

14

Freedom of Access

LEARNING OBJECTIVES:

After reading this chapter, you should know

- how to know when a record or meeting should be open or closed
- when and where confidential records can be accessed in the U.S. government
- how to balance needs for security and how withholding access affects it
- what the Freedom of Information Act's exemptions mean as interpreted by the courts
- where to begin in making a FOIA request for response from federal officers
- how new technologies changes in FOIA's terms have made items more accessible
- the landmark cases defining the boundaries between openness and secrecy

Sword and Shield

There is a difference between the right to gather information and the right to express it in public. That distinction became clear in the 1960s, when the Cold War between the Soviet Union and the United States placed Cuba beyond the foreign itinerary of curious travelers in the United States. An American citizen by the name of Louis Zemel wanted to go to Cuba, he said, to "satisfy my curiosity about the state of affairs there and to make me a better-informed citizen."[1] Permission was denied, and Zemel challenged Secretary of State Dean Rusk's refusal to grant his passage.

The Supreme Court's ruling in his case underscores the contrast between freedom of expression and access to information. "[T]he right to speak and publish does not carry with it the unrestrained right to gather information," stated Chief Justice Earl Warren.[2] The U.S. Constitution protects freedom of expression, while the dictates of democratic governance require information sharing among voters for the purpose of electoral decision-making. These needs create an unavoidable tension between officials who resist disclosure and

1. *Zemel v. Rusk*, 381 U.S. 16–17 (1965).
2. *Id.* at 17.

DOI: 10.4324/9781003462989-14

citizens who need to know about their government's activities and records. The metaphor to describe this struggle between the right to know and its opposition is *Sword and Shield.*

Origins of Access

The chief framer of the Constitution, James Madison, famously declared democratic governance without access to government information is "the prologue to a farce or tragedy."[3] Madison believed "the right of freely examining public characters and measures and free communication among the people thereon, is the only effectual guardian of every other right."[4] American policy makers secure public records and guard public meetings with regulations that citizens must sometimes strive to overcome to learn more about how tax dollars are spent and their government functions.[5] Despite the rules and procedures that vary from state to state and county to city, the underlying object of a democratic system is to balance freedom of access with specific necessities for withholding disclosure. Two associate justices described this dilemma in their opinions on the rights of investigative reporters and confidential sources.

Justice Lewis Powell concluded the "right to gather news, of some dimensions, must exist" because without the freedom to acquire information, the right to publish would be impermissibly compromised.[6] Justice Potter Stewart argued conversely, "The press is free to do battle against secrecy and deception in government. But the press cannot expect from the Constitution any guarantee that it will succeed." Stewart saw the public's interest in access to be a valid one but only indirectly protected by the free press guarantee of the First Amendment. "The Constitution itself is neither a Freedom of Information Act nor an Official Secrets Act."[7]

Before There Was FOIA . . .

Before the FOIA was signed into law, the 1953 case of *United States v. Reynolds*[8] showed how a state secrets policy carries a special privilege to exclude relevant evidence for a lawsuit if it would reveal information posing a threat to national security (See also Chapter 3). The issue arose after a military plane crash killed three civilian engineers aboard, and the U.S. Air Force's refusal to give their widows the accident reports by maintaining to do so would reveal classified material to the detriment of national security. The Supreme Court took the case knowing that a U.S. B-29 Superfortress had crashed in 1948, and the accident reports were kept in secret. The justices also understood the plaintiff widows sought relief under the Federal Tort Claims Act.

The Court affirmed the military privilege to keep those documents sealed under the national security rationale. Although the widows seeking damages received a reported aggregate sum of $170,000 in exchange for freeing the government of their claims of liability what was left unresolved were how a state secrets privilege could be used by the U.S. government to avoid embarrassment in such circumstances. Some 50 years

3. This quote of Madison's is excerpted from a letter he wrote in 1822 to a Kentucky lawmaker, William T. Barry, about the necessity of funding public education for the good of the people: "A popular government without popular information or the means of acquiring it is but a prologue to a farce or a tragedy, or perhaps both."
4. See "The Report of 1800" from Founders Online, *at* https://founders.archives.gov/documents/Madison/01-17-02-0202.
5. Ironically, Madison himself was an advocate for utmost secrecy during the constitutional convention, fearing that leaks threatened the passage of the new constitution.
6. *Branzburg v. Hayes*, 408 U.S. 665, 728 (1972).
7. Potter Stewart, "Or of the Press," 26 *Hastings L. J.* 631, 636 (1975).
8. 345 U.S. 1 (1953).

later, the daughter of one of the victims was able to obtain the declassified details and discovered how poor maintenance of the plane was involved in the crash.[9]

While the Supreme Court majority sided with the government, the dissenting justices endorsed the appellate court's decision warning of the potential abuse of

> a sweeping privilege against any disclosure contrary to a sound public policy. . . . Indeed it requires no great flight of imagination to realize that if the Government's contentions in these cases were affirmed the privilege against disclosure might gradually be enlarged by executive determinations until, as is the case in some nations today, it embraced the whole range of governmental activities.[10]

The Constitution and the Common Law

Historically speaking, laws governing openness to information were used to promise only access to pertinent records dealing with one's personal affairs and not necessarily to information going beyond that interest. Although courts traditionally protect individual rights to uncover government information of personal relevance, facts about administrative agencies were subject to secrecy and confidentiality that led to abuses of power. That was until a law was passed to deal with the administrative agencies created during the New Deal era.

The Administrative Procedure Act (APA) of 1946[11] arrived in the early days of the Cold War, when secrecy and security interests empowered gatekeepers from the lower bureaucratic offices up to the White House. The APA gave the right to inspect federal agency paperwork only to those who had "good cause" and who were "properly and directly concerned" with information held by the U.S. government. The law lacked a time limit for responding to citizen requests for public records, and it allowed agencies to establish whatever fee they deemed necessary for dispensing public documents. Some felt this law did more to prevent disclosure than to grant access to government-held information, and something more was needed.

The Freedom of Information Act (1966)

The mood of the nation shifted during the 1960s, when civil rights advocates made compelling arguments for more openness in the federal government. President Lyndon B. Johnson signed the first federal **Freedom of Information Act (FOIA)** on Independence Day, 1966.[12] This bill addressed the earlier law, the APA's most awkward language, especially the timid public disclosure section that could forestall press access to documents because the requesting party had failed to justify their need to know beforehand.[13] This language gave extraordinary custodial power to employees of the government and that needed to be changed.

When it comes to the basic purpose of FOIA, the opinion of Justice John Paul Stevens writing for the majority in *Department of Justice v. Reporters Committee for Freedom of Press* (1989) has been quoted: "Official information that sheds light on an agency's performance of

9. I. Glass, "The Secret Life of Secrets," *This American Life*, NPR (2009), *at* www.thisamericanlife.org/383/origin-story-2009/act-two-1.
10. *Reynolds v. United States*, 192 F.2d 987 (3d Cir. 1951)
11. Pub. L. No. 79–404.
12. President Johnson was not an enthusiastic champion of this legislation, possibly because he feared the law could be used against his administration in an adverse manner.
13. The Supreme Court underscored the government no longer required that level of disclosure on the part of the requestor in *NARA v. Favish*, 541 U.S. 157 (2004) "[A]s a general rule, when documents are within FOIA's disclosure provisions, citizens should not be required to explain why they seek the information."

its statutory duties fall squarely within that statutory purpose." More recently, U.S. Attorney General Merrick Garland expanded on FOIA's purpose when he proposed executive branch offices should become proactive in posting essential records online that are likely to be of interest to the public. Garland declared new digital technology is needed to aid in the search and response to official record requests; the U.S. government should invest in the hardware and software necessary to respond more efficiently to FOIA requests.[14]

Freedom of Information Act (FOIA)
U.S. law requiring federal agencies, on request, to disclose agency records unless the information is to be kept confidential based on the provisions of nine exemptions.

The FOIA (pronounced "FOYA") is meant to expedite the access process. Government agencies in general, and federal bureaus in particular, can be tediously slow in responding to citizen requests for records. The length of time it takes for handling requests and making documents ready for dissemination discourages some requestors, but not all.

The Reporters Committee for Freedom of the Press views gaining release of public information on major news events to be a priority. For example, after discovering how FBI agents impersonated employees of the Associated Press and members of a documentary film crew to investigate alleged crimes, the RCFP requested records from the FBI to learn more information about this practice implicating their members and other journalists. The FBI refused, but the U.S. District Court for the District of Columbia ruled the agency needed to find and release those documents to show how the FBI carried out these impersonations.[15]

Requests for information are growing as more individuals – and businesses in particular – seek out all sorts of information from the government, including items to give them a competitive advantage. In *Food Marketing Institute v. Argus Leader Media* (2019), a South Dakota newspaper wanted to know more about the money retail stores received from the Supplemental Nutrition Assistance Program (SNAP), formerly known as the food stamp program. ALM argued taxpayers had a right to know where federal tax dollars were going and the claim by FMI that FOIA's Exemption 4 allowing for nondisclosure was wrong. This provision protects "trade secrets and commercial or financial information obtained from a person and privileged or confidential." The Supreme Court held the law's concern with confidential and substantial competitive harm exempted SNAP information from disclosure.[16]

FOIA Policies and Amendments

In 1976, Congress amended the FOIA with an eye toward speeding up the response time, giving government custodians between 10 and 30 days to respond to record requests. These consumer-friendly provisions met with objections from ranking members of the White House. Nonetheless, the U.S. Congress prevailed and adopted FOIA amendments over President Ford's veto. The law has been changed repeatedly since then, but two amendments in 1986 and again in 1996 seem relevant. In 1986, the exemption for law enforcement records was expanded and the fee structure for obtaining documents modified. Congress, notably in 1996, ordered executive branch agencies to post instructions on their websites about how to use the Electronic Freedom of Information Act (E-FOIA). This act created a digitally accessible approach.

E-FOIA requires federal agencies to use digital indexing, electronic searches of data banks, and "electronic reading rooms." The digitalizing of the FOIA compliance process allowed citizens to specify the format of the information desired. It also gave journalists a

14. Office of Public Affairs, U.S. Dept. of Justice (March 15, 2022). "Attorney General Merrick B. Garland Issues New FOIA Guidelines to Favor Disclosure and Transparency," *at* https://www.justice.gov/opa/pr/attorney-general-merrick-b-garland-issues-new-foia-guidelines-favor-disclosure-and: Attorney General, "Memorandum for Heads of Executive Departments and Agencies" (March 15, 2022), *at* https://www.justice.gov/ag/file/1208711-0/dl?inline.
15. *Reporters Committee for Freedom of the Press v. Federal Bureau of Investigation*, No. 20–5091 (D.C. Cir. 2021).
16. See *Food Marketing Institute v. Argus Leader Media*, 139 S. Ct. 2356 (2019). Exemption 4 of the Freedom of Information Act (FOIA), 5 U.S.C. § 552(b)(4) (2012 & Supp. V 2017)

Bedrock Law

The FOIA opens access to government records without making citizens prove beforehand that they have a right to know based on their personal interest.

Bedrock Law

The identity of the person requesting a public record, or the reason for needing it, should not determine whether it is released, but it could affect whether there is a charge involved.

Presumption of Disclosure

Under FOIA, requests for records are generally approved unless the government can show the information requested falls under one of its nine exemptions.

chance at having their requests expedited. It should be noted, however, journalists have no special privilege beyond those granted to the public.

The U.S. Supreme Court proclaims the goal of the Freedom of Information Act (FOIA) "is to ensure an informed citizenry, vital to the functioning of a democratic society."[17] Government agencies are directed by the FOI law to make available to the public certain classes of information. Under section 552 (a)(1), federal agencies must define their rules, their policies, what functions they serve, and how they are organized.

The second section, 552 (a)(2), requires a disclosure of any final opinions the agency issues in the cases it decides and the interpretation of the law it is enforcing. The third section requires all records be made available to the public, and those records should be copied if they are likely to become the subject of an anticipated request. So basically, any person, not just American citizens, has the legal right to access public documents that have not been exempted, based on the fees required and procedures to be followed.

The assessment of the fees is somewhat controversial though, and the agency should not ask for them in advance unless it will cost more than $250 dollars to copy the document requested. There are times when federal agencies can and do deny requests for records, and in response, the requester can file a complaint to address this refusal.

Policy Shifts

The Freedom of Information Act was reformed in 2016 when Congress passed the FOIA Improvement Act. It codified the *presumption of openness* and made the request process somewhat simpler.[18] What that meant for federal agencies was they must narrowly interpret the law's exemptions to show how disclosure would produce "reasonably foreseeable" harm by the release of government records.[19] The FOIA Improvement Act also created a chief FOIA officers council and gave the office of ombudsman more responsibility.

In 1993, U.S. Attorney General Janet Reno signed an order declaring a **presumption of disclosure**, *not confidentiality*, should be made when government agencies respond to FOIA requests. She specifically encouraged the Department of Justice employees to lean toward transparency rather than concealment. Unless an executive agency "reasonably foresees that disclosure would be harmful," the requested documents should be released.[20]

That policy of openness shifted toward concealment after the terrorist attacks of September 11, 2001. White House policymakers advised federal agencies to maintain closed records whenever there was a "sound legal basis" for doing so. Critics charged this shift in policy gave preference to secrecy over openness; "leaks" could result in the firing of federal employees. Attorney General John Ashcroft orchestrated this shift in policy widely departing from the Reno standard. Ashcroft's policy placed a premium on national security, privacy, and the U.S. government's interests. He declared the DOJ would do its utmost to defend agency gatekeepers that withheld documents under FOIA's nine exemptions; that was temporary.[21]

After President Obama took office in 2009, Attorney General Eric Holder signaled a new shift in policy based on openness, transparency, and accountability. "In the face of doubt, openness prevails . . . an agency should not withhold information simply because it may do

17. *NLRB. v. Robbins Tire & Rubber Co.*, 437 U.S. 214, 242 (1978).
18. "Obama Signs FOIA Reform Bill," *Politico*, June 30, 2016, *at* www.politico.com/blogs/under-the-radar/2016/06/obama-signs-foia-reform-bill-225010.
19. FOIA Improvement Act, Pub. L. No. 114–85 (2016).
20. Memorandum from Janet Reno, Attorney General, to Heads of All Federal Departments and Agencies re: The Freedom of Information Act (October 4, 1993).
21. See J. Ashcroft, "Memorandum for Heads of Executive Departments and Agencies," (October 12, 2001) *at* https://www.justice.gov/archive/oip/011012.htm.

so legally."[22] Holder affirmed the maximum disclosure principle with reliance on discretionary exemptions to ensure executive agencies would release records subject to FOIA requests.

Black Hole Awards

The Society of Professional Journalists applauds openness supported by public officials who possess the courage of conscience to stand by it. When politicians show a contrary attitude and deny access to government documents or meetings, SPJ wants the world to know about it. Each year, a dubious accolade is awarded to public gatekeepers in the United States to bring their shady practices to light. The "Black Hole Award" is celebrated during Sunshine Week each year to shame those people in power who hold obvious contempt for the public's right to know.

Although nominations come from across the nation, SPJ specifies three criteria that should be met to qualify for of this celebrated derision. First, there should be a violation in law that has stifled access to information at the state, federal, or indigenous tribal levels. Second, that openness violation should be egregious showing certain evidence that personal or political interests were placed above the public's good. Finally, the black hole created must be capable of swallowing up not just one person's interests but the public's interests at large.

Consider the merits of Louisiana Governor Jeff Landry's award. He held the office of attorney general in 2021 and moved to block one reporter's Freedom of Information Act request. Andrea Gallo asked for records of sexual harassment implicating a state official. She was denied access since those harassment files were held to be part of an ongoing investigation.

Landry may have thought the journalist needed to be taught a lesson because he sued Gallo, claiming that her open records request would harm state employee rights and lead to further litigation. A court ruled in her favor and ordered the harassment records be released. In addition, Louisiana had to pay Gallo and her newspaper attorney's fees for defending the lawsuit. There are other SPJ winners of noteworthy distinction.

After the Associated Press tracked the Trump administration's response to records requested under the Freedom of Information Act, he became the first president to win the Black Hole Award. The AP calculated 78% of the 823,222 requests made of the executive branch met with disappointment since the government either could not locate the desired information or had to censor the records. In addition, the White House spent a record $40.6 million to defend its decisions to withhold requested files. Keep in mind 386 FOIA cases were recorded during the Trump administration, more than all the cases combined over the Bush and Obama years.

FOIA Exemptions
Nine reasons the government can deny a FOIA request and keep information secret if the requested material falls within one of the qualifying conditions.

FOIA Exemptions

According to FOIA policy, a federal agency should fulfill the requirements of the document seeker but at the same time protect sensitive government information. The nine exemptions are found in Title 5 of the U.S. Code, § 552.[23]

The government's interest in protecting records pertaining to national defense and foreign policy is the number one priority for keeping documents confidential. Exemptions are also made for personnel practices and for routine housekeeping rules, such as parking lot spaces or sick leave policies. If executive agencies are forced to create and dispense such records

22. See E. Holder, "Memorandum for Heads of Executive Departments and Agencies," (March 19, 2009), *at* https://www.neh.gov/sites/default/files/inline-files/foia_memo_attygen_20090319.pdf.
23. *See* 5 U.S.C. § 552(b) (FOI Advocates 2008).

National Defense
FOIA exemption for national defense or foreign policy information properly classified pursuant to an executive order. 5 U.S.C. § 552(b)(1).

Personnel Rules
FOIA exemption for documents "related solely to the internal personnel rules and practices of an agency." 5 U.S.C. § 552(b)(2).

Statutory Exemption
FOIA provision prohibiting release of documents "specifically exempted from disclosure by statute" other than FOIA, but only if the other statute's disclosure prohibition is absolute. 5 U.S.C. § 552(b)(3).

Trade Secrets
FOIA exemption "[t]rade secrets and commercial or financial information obtained from a person" that is privileged or confidential." 5 U.S.C. § 552(b) (4).

for public inspection, it might distract the civil servants from more important items of federal business. The legal exemptions to the Freedom of Information Act include the following areas:

1 **National defense** – *National defense or foreign policy information properly classified pursuant to an Executive Order. 5 U.S.C. § 552(b)(1).*
According to this exemption, the agency has the right to decline the request for a record that pertains to national defense or foreign policy if that record is classified by an executive order of the president. This first exemption classifies certain types of sensitive data necessary for the welfare of the republic, which are established and updated by the White House. An agency will still review the requested documents to make sure that they legitimately require some protection from public viewing.[24]

2 **Personnel rules** – *Documents "related solely to the internal personnel rules and practices of an agency." 5 U.S.C. § 552(b)(2).*
There are two safeguards that fall under this exemption. The first one serves to relieve agencies from assembling and creating access to trivial internal documents and activities, which are generally of no legitimate interest to the public. In *Department of the Air Force v. Rose* (1976),[25] the Supreme Court defined this exemption as "any matter in which the public could not reasonably be expected to have an interest" (425 U.S. at 369–70). This exemption also serves to safeguard internal agency documents such as internal administrative manuals, disclosure of which "would risk circumvention of law or agency regulations" (FOI Advocates 2008, ¶8). In 2011, the Supreme Court voted 8–1 to limit Exemption 2 to "routine" internal personnel practices and not a broader definition that would extend beyond personnel to items such as maps or the handling of dangerous materials.[26]

3 **Statutory exemptions** – *Documents "specifically exempted from disclosure by statute" other than FOIA, but only if the other statute's disclosure prohibition is absolute. 5 U.S.C. § 552(b)(3).*
This exemption allows a federal agency to withhold information if it is prohibited from disclosure by another statute. Generally, the courts make three determinations over whether the disclosure can be reasonably denied. If replies to the three questions are yes, then disclosure can be legally denied. The first criterion is the correct application of a specific statute that authorizes or requires the withholding of information. The court also must determine what specific kinds of information the law in question forbids from release. Finally, the agency must ask if the record or information that is sought properly fits the definition of prohibitive information under this exemption.

4 **Trade secrets** – *Documents that would reveal "[t]rade secrets and commercial or financial information obtained from a person and privileged or confidential." 5 U.S.C. § 552(b)(4).*
Exemption 4 serves to secure the competitive practices of business firms that willingly provide reliable commercial and/or financial information to the U.S. government. The federal service or agency can decline any requests under the FOIA for data if it finds that the request would hurt the competitive position of a business or commercial enterprise in the future. "Trade Secrets," according to the ruling in *Public Citizen Health Research Group v. FDA* (1983) are defined as "a secret, commercially valuable plan, formula,

24. The current executive order on security classification is listed as Exec. Order No. 12958, signed by President Clinton in 1995.
25. 425 U.S. 352 (1976). In this case, the U.S. Supreme Court ordered the release of records of Air Force Academy ethics hearings and held that Exemptions 2 and 6 did not apply.
26. *Milner v. Dept. of the Navy*, 562 U.S. 562 (2011).

process, or device that is used for the making, preparing, compounding, or processing of trade commodities and that can be said to be the end product of either innovation or substantial effort."[27]

Agency Memoranda
FOIA exemption for "inter-agency or intra-agency memorandum or letters," which would be privileged in civil litigation. 5 U.S.C. § 552(b) (5).

5 **Agency memoranda** – *Documents that are an "inter-agency or intra-agency memorandum or letters," which would be privileged in civil litigation. 5 U.S.C. § 552(b)(5).*

Documents falling under this exemption are working papers and records to be shielded from the discovery process in a court-of-law proceeding. Examples cover commissioned studies, reports, and memoranda employed to reach a decision and the elements of deliberation essential to policy recommendations.[28] These data naturally draw upon confidential notes between a client and attorney and other types of privileged information.

There is a special priority granted to the president's office for privacy and frank advice from special agencies. Exemption 5 affords an executive privilege for the president to protect from disclosure inter-agency or intra-agency memoranda and letters that are part of this decision-making process. This exemption also prevents any premature disclosure of policies under review (FOI Advocates 2008, ¶24).

Privacy
FOIA exemption for "personnel and medical and similar files the disclosure of which would constitute a clearly unwarranted invasion of personal privacy." 5 U.S.C. § 552(b) (6).

6 **Privacy** – *Documents that are "personnel and medical and similar files the disclosure of which would constitute a clearly unwarranted invasion of personal privacy." 5 U.S.C. § 552(b)(6).*

This exemption shields the privacy of patients and public employees whose data might be disclosed from their personnel and medical files. Only private files of employees qualify for exemption 6; not records of corporations and private organizations. This exemption safeguards a federal employee from an entirely unwarranted incursion of personal privacy.

Law Enforcement
FOIA exemption for "records or information compiled for law enforcement purposes" but limited to certain cases where specified types of harm would result. 5 U.S.C. § 552(b)(7).

7 **Law enforcement** – *Documents that are "records or information compiled for law enforcement purposes," but only if one or more of six specified types of harm would result. 5 U.S.C. § 552(b)(7).*

To qualify under the seventh exemption, federal agencies must first make sure the FOIA records sought draw upon facts and details useful for law enforcement purposes. Requests for criminal records are exempted only to the extent the distribution of these records would reasonably be expected to interfere with the prosecution of justice and deprive the individual of their right to a fair trial or constitute an unwarranted invasion of privacy.

Two additional elements are involved in this seventh exemption. If the requested record could be reasonably expected to disclose the identity of a confidential source, including a state, local, or foreign agency, or any private institution furnishing law enforcement authorities requested criminal information on a confidential basis, then that record would be exempt. Finally, this provision protects from disclosure the crime-solving techniques and procedures used in law enforcement investigations, especially if their disclosure could be used to circumvent the law or endanger the life and/or physical safety of any individual.

Financial Records
FOIA exemption for documents related to specified reports prepared by, on behalf of, or for the use of agencies that regulate financial institutions. 5 U.S.C. § 552(b) (8).

8 **Financial records** – *Documents related to specified reports prepared by, on behalf of or for the use of agencies that regulate financial institutions. 5 U.S.C. § 552(b)(8).*

This exemption prevents the disclosure of sensitive financial information to the public, including records that would affect the business of banks, the Federal Reserve, trust companies, insurance agencies, and the like.

27. 704 F.2d 1280, 1288 (D.C. Cir. 1983).
28. Such documents might be working papers and tentative drafts, needing protection so that the deliberative process can take place freely and function.

Oil Field Data
FOIA exemption for documents revealing natural gas and petroleum reservoirs, drilling sites, and related information. 5 U.S.C. § 552(b)(9).

9 **Oil field data** – *Documents revealing oil well data. 5 U.S.C. § 552(b)(9).*

This exemption prevents the disclosure of geological, geophysical, and topographical information, including maps and locations, of oil wells that would be of interest to other drillers. It is analogous in some ways to the protection of trade secrets.

FOIA Steps to Access

When government officials refuse to provide requested records, courts are left to decide the legal challenges filed in response. In such disputes, the first step is to agree on the legal terms. The law defines *public records* as those materials used, prepared, or kept by government agencies that represent some transaction with the public. Obvious examples would include transcriptions, bills, photos, or electronic records. A record is generally considered to be any information maintained by the executive branch agency in any format, including digital versions. Of course, this definition cannot apply to public documents that the government has yet to produce, although requests are still sometimes denied for that very reason.

Agency
Under FOIA, "any executive department, military department, government corporation, government-controlled corporation or other establishment in the executive branch of government."

Access requests to national records go to a federal **agency**, which is defined as "any executive department, military department, government corporation, government-controlled corporation or other establishment in the executive branch of government."[29] Thus, the terms **record** and **agency** are central to the interpretation of access, but these apply to any materials the government office has created, has control over, and holds in its possession. In other words, a "record" can be a letter, map, photograph, or audio or video recording; it can be figures, tables, or data used by an agency to keep track of its activities. But it cannot be something that the agency would have to create just to fulfill the FOIA request. It is useful to know that Congress and judicial branches are not subject to FOIA access; only executive branch agencies and bureaus fall under its purview.

Record
For the purposes of the Freedom of Information Act (FOIA), "any information that would be an agency record . . . maintained by an agency in any format, including an electronic format."

When citizens seek to gain access under Title 5 of the U.S. Code, §552, several steps are taken before federal agency records are called up for review. First, the government employee charged with fielding FOIA requests is contacted. This individual is maintaining the materials under their jurisdiction, and they must determine if any FOIA exemptions apply. After those steps are accomplished, the release of the requested documents might be granted. Even if confidentiality appears warranted, some response is recommended within 20 days. Anyone denied access might receive what is known as the "Vaughn Index," an official list of withheld records accompanied by the reasons for their secrecy.[30]

FOIA law obviously demands some judgment on the part of the record holders, who must first look to see whether the information is classified to determine how accessible it is. The government custodian cannot decline to release an entire record just because a single sentence, a single page, or even an image is exempted. If a request is denied in whole or in part, and the reasons for the denial are not quite clear, then the requester's next step is to seek the agency's head for an opinion. If that fails, the last resort would be to go to court.

Once a lawsuit challenges the validity of government claims for secrecy, federal judges inspect the classified documents and rule on the correctness of their status under the FOIA. Obviously, it would take a powerful argument for any judge to rule against a particular agency's authority and question the official's discernment for securing potentially damaging information that has the potential to harm American citizens, property, and other public interests.

29. See Appendix A, Text of the Freedom of Information Act (f)(1) 551(1).
30. *See Vaughn v. Rosen*, 484 F.2d 820 (D.C. Cir. 1973).

Bedrock Law
FOIA only affords access to agencies of the executive branch and does not entitle citizens to inspect court records or congressional proceedings.

Glomar and FOIA

There are times when an affirmative response by a government office to an FOIA request can be invasive of someone's privacy or even damaging to their reputation. The U.S. Office of Information Policy asks agencies fielding such sensitive requests to see whether the subject involved is alive, and then determine if the public interest would compel the disclosure of a criminal record that would override privacy interests.

If a FOIA requestor asks for criminal investigation records, the agency may choose to respond with the reply that it can "neither confirm nor deny" whether such records even exist; that is if it is covered by a FOIA exemption. That is what's called the Glomar response. The name comes from a recovery ship owned by Howard Hughes that was used to recover a sunken Soviet submarine in the Atlantic seaboard. A *Los Angeles Times* reporter wanted the CIA to confirm the deep-sea project and admit its efforts to censor the story.

The FOIA response to neither confirm nor deny existence of sensitive records has been affirmed by courts since the secretive nature of federal criminal investigations requires it under Exemption 7(c), so long as the government provides necessary details to justify the exemption.[31]

FOIA Initiatives

There is no government form required for making an FOIA request. A letter, with the envelope clearly marked as "Freedom of Information Act Request," should be sent to the agency whose records are sought (see Figure 14.1). It is also a good idea to include a daytime phone number. Perhaps the most important item in the request is a clear and specific statement identifying the desired record. Vague or generalized requests take up more time and generally meet with negative or inefficient responses.

Once the request has been submitted to the government, the agency will send an acknowledgment stating the date of the request's receipt, the case number assigned to it, and whether the records desired are available. Obviously, the time taken for each search or review bears on the success of the retrieval, and that, too, depends on a variety of factors, including the complexity of the search and sensitivity of the materials requested.

FOIA Responses

If an unreasonable number of records are requested, the agency can advise limiting the materials and call for a resubmission of the request (Figure 14.2). The agency reviews FOIA requests on a first-come, first-served basis and often chooses one of three responses: 1) fulfill the request, 2) deny the request in part, or 3) deny the request in full. Interestingly, the two federal agencies most besieged by FOIA requests are the Federal Bureau of Investigation (FBI) and the Central Intelligence Agency (CIA), both of which have had to hire additional employees and spend large sums to lawfully comply with FOIA requests.

If the executive branch agent responds positively to the FOIA request, it means the agency has jurisdiction over the information, and it has the practical means for recovering it. There are times, however, when the agency deletes information from its records. Once that happens, the government's responsibility is to indicate exactly why it did so. Either the request is simply denied, or the department fails to find the right information to satisfy

31. Exemption 7(C) shields personal information uncovered in law enforcement records. This provision corresponds with another FOIA Exemption 6, which is used to protect the privacy of individuals.

Agency Head [or Freedom of Information Act Officer]

Name of Agency

Address of Agency

City, State, Zip Code

Re: Freedom of Information Act Request

Dear _____________:

This is a request under the Freedom of Information Act.

I request that a copy of the following documents [or documents containing the following information] be provided to me: [**identify the documents or information as specifically as possible**.]

In order to help to determine my status to assess fees, you should know that I am [**insert a suitable description of the requester and the purpose of the request**.]

[**Sample requester descriptions**:

- a representative of the news media affiliated with the _______________ newspaper (magazine, television station, etc.), and this request is made as part of a news gathering and not for commercial use.
- affiliated with an educational or noncommercial scientific institution, and this request is made for a scholarly or scientific purpose and not for commercial use.
- an individual seeking information for personal use and not for commercial use.
- affiliated with a private corporation and am seeking information for use in the company's business.]

[**Optional**] I am willing to pay fees for this request up to a maximum of $____. If you estimate that the fees will exceed this limit, please inform me first.

[**Optional**] I request a waiver of all fees for this request. Disclosure of the requested information to me is in the public interest because it is likely to contribute significantly to public understanding of the operations or activities of the government and is not primarily in my commercial interest. [**Include a specific explanation**.] Thank you for your consideration of my request.

Figure 14.1 Sample FOIA letter

the request. If the government does not respond satisfactorily, the sender can appeal to a review panel depending on how it was handled. Requesters have 60 days after receiving this refusal from the agency to submit their appeal.

Expeditious Handling
Freedom of Information Act (FOIA) requests are given expedited treatment if the requester can demonstrate a compelling need for speedy dissemination of that information.

Accelerating the FOIA Response

There are times when the government can move swiftly to fulfill requests, particularly for journalists. The term used to describe this special efficiency, **expeditious handling**, indicates a compelling need exists for quickly getting the data to the sender, such as "an imminent threat to someone's life or physical safety," to maintain due process, or because the information can prevent substantial harm to some humanitarian interest. There are times when urgent information about actual or suspected federal activities must be rapidly dispensed to the public. The expedited request must be accompanied by reasons stating the urgent need for such handling, after which the government decides whether it is truly warranted.

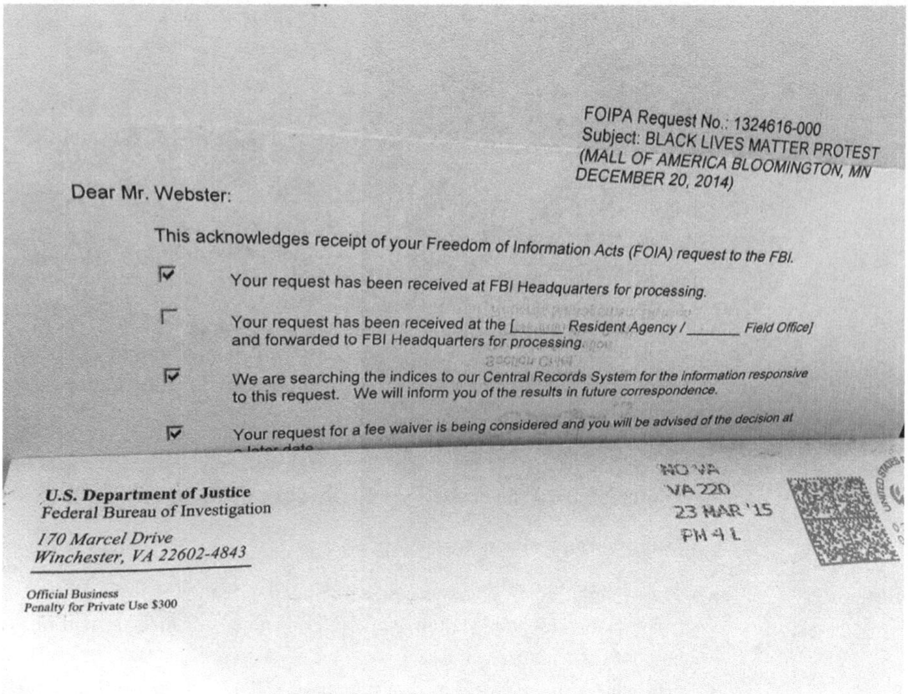

FOIPA Request No.: 1324616-000
Subject: BLACK LIVES MATTER PROTEST
(MALL OF AMERICA BLOOMINGTON, MN
DECEMBER 20, 2014)

Dear Mr. Webster:

This acknowledges receipt of your Freedom of Information Acts (FOIA) request to the FBI.

☑ Your request has been received at FBI Headquarters for processing.

☐ Your request has been received at the [______ Resident Agency / ______ Field Office] and forwarded to FBI Headquarters for processing.

☑ We are searching the indices to our Central Records System for the information responsive to this request. We will inform you of the results in future correspondence.

☑ Your request for a fee waiver is being considered and you will be advised of the decision at

U.S. Department of Justice
Federal Bureau of Investigation
170 Marcel Drive
Winchester, VA 22602-4843

Official Business
Penalty for Private Use $300

NO VA
VA 220
23 MAR '15
PM 4 L

Figure 14.2 FOIA Response Letter

Assessment of Fees

The question of fees involved for access to public information is addressed in this law. U.S. officials handling an FOIA request will not act upon it unless requesters are willing to pay the fees. Another option is to provide suitable reasons for why a *fee waiver* should be warranted. The **fee categories** assigned to each request will vary based on the information desired, the reason for requesting it, and the number of requests submitted. This gives requesters the variables to estimate how much they think the retrieval will cost. If the public interest is involved, such as reports needed for news releases or academic research, the fee might be zero. Three categories by which the requests are organized are *commercial trade*, *educational and scientific institutions*, and *the news media*.[32]

Fee Category
Every Freedom of Information Act (FOIA) request is grouped in a classification to determine the cost to the requester for the retrieval.

- *Commercial Use Requests*: Ones that serve to advance the commercial, trade, or profit interest of the person on whose behalf the request is made (22 CFR § 171.11(l)).
- *Educational Institution Requests*: An educational institution means "a preschool, a public or private elementary or secondary school, an institution of undergraduate or graduate higher education, an institution of professional education, or an institution of vocational education that operates a program or programs of scholarly research" (22 CFR § 171.11(m)).
- *Noncommercial Scientific Institution Requests*: Noncommercial scientific institutions are ones whose sole purpose is to advance scholarly research, not just to achieve commercial gain (22 CFR § 171.11(n)).
- *Representatives of the News Media Requests*: Requests made by journalists who collect news for a news organization, whose mission it is to distribute the information to the

32. *See* Department of State, Information Access Manual (2008).

public. Information refers to news that is of public interest. News media can mean television stations, radio stations, or publishers of periodicals (22 CFR § 171.11(o)).

- *Freelance Journalist Requests*: Freelance journalists must show proof of publication or likelihood of publication through a representative of the news media, even though they are not actually employed by one (22 CFR § 171.11(o)).
- *All Other Requests*: These are requests that do not fall under the previous categories (22 CFR § 171.11(p)). Fees will not be charged for the first 100 pages and the first two hours spent on the searching process for all except the requests pertaining to commercial use.

Removing FOIA Barriers

Compounding the frustration for the advocates of openness in government is the relatively recent phenomenon of outsourcing federal tasks to private businesses. It took a court fight in Georgia to see that a private school bus contractor would let the public know of details about the school district's selection of drivers and their records.[33] The National Freedom of Information Coalition argued that as more government bodies delegate to private contractors, citizens and the media need to be persistent in asking for a freedom of information clause in the local contract to avoid delegating away this information.

Other stifling inhibitions to the quest for public information are the privacy statutes that discourage disclosure of public information because they are confusing either to users, to administrators, or both. Even though frustration reigns over denials and procrastination in response to FOIA requests, there are citizen groups dedicated to gaining more efficient access to the mechanisms of government.

The National Freedom of Information Coalition proposed that federal offices should adopt an approach comparable to what some state governments have done, which is to establish an FOI Commission or Government Records Council to help petitioners by saving them the trouble of having to go to court to resolve their differences. Informal resolutions either authorized by a committee or a public official obviously would be preferable to tying up judicial bodies with access petitions.

Key to opening government meetings and records is the creation of a culture of openness established by the political officers overseeing the various agencies involved. If those administrators hold in contempt the public's right of access, the policy of disclosure written into the law can be easily compromised or ignored. There is also support from public interest groups. One not-for-profit collaborative, Muckrock, was created to keep track online of public records requests, both state and federal, and the agencies' responses to those requests. The database is searchable and includes lots of valuable information to anyone – not just journalists – who hopes to obtain some government information.[34]

The Supreme Court Rulings

The U.S. Supreme Court has ruled many times on FOIA cases and usually shown an inclination toward openness unless important privacy issues became involved as was the case in 1988. FOIA requests were filed with the FBI by CBS News and the Reporters Committee for Freedom of the Press seeking to learn more about the Medico brothers who were under investigation for federal contracts arranged by Pennsylvania congressmen. The Supreme

33. *Hackworth v. Board of Educ. for City of Atlanta*, 214 Ga. App. 17, 447 S.E.2d 78 (1994).
34. The site, www.muckrock.com, tracks requests but also assists anyone wanting help in generating a request.

Court ruled the FBI could turn down the journalists' FOIA petitions because the release of their "rap sheets" would constitute an "unwarranted invasion of personal privacy."[35]

In 1991, the U.S. State Department withheld notes by government personnel on the treatment of Haitian refugees forced to return to their home country. The request on their behalf was made by an immigration attorney, named Ray, who believed the Haitians were subject to political persecution and needed to be interviewed by a human rights activist. The Court, however, held the government could withhold the information to protect their identities, even though the agent was trying to help them to gain asylum.[36]

In 1993, the Supreme Court ruled against the FBI when that agency wanted a blanket exemption to prevent disclosure of an informant's identity. The Court said, rather than a broad exemption, the FBI must present on a case-by-case basis an explanation of why an informant's identity must remain a secret.[37]

In 2001, the Supreme Court reversed an agency order refusing to disclose records of communication with certain Indigenous American tribes. The Court rejected the argument that the Department of Interior served as a trustee of the tribes and could not release an intra-agency memorandum regarding their water rights.[38]

In 2011, CompTel won its battle with AT&T Inc. over an FOIA request for documents held by the Federal Communications Commission. The FCC was looking into whether the telecom company overcharged the federal agency for work performed on an education project. AT&T claimed those records were protected as part of its corporate privacy under Exemption 7(c), but the Court ruled that was a *personal right of privacy* under FOIA, not a corporate one.[39]

That same year, the Supreme Court noted a FOIA exemption had been misconstrued. This case related to a request for maps near Puget Sound where Naval training exercises had used explosive materials. The Navy based its refusal to release those maps under Exemption 2, but the Supreme Court held that one applies only to employee relations or human resources and not to maps detailing where explosives had been used.[40]

A more recent case involves the secrecy allowed under Exemption 5 of FOIA used to shield from public inspection biological opinions applicable to federal regulations. In *United States Fish and Wildlife Service v. Sierra Club, Inc.* (2021) environmentalists wanted to see documents concerning the impact of cooling water intake structures on aquatic wildlife. In her first majority opinion, Justice Amy Coney Barrett ruled for the Supreme Court those documents could be kept from disclosure under a privilege allowing in-house drafts deemed to be pre-decisional and deliberative as confidential materials to be withheld from public release.[41]

The Price of Sunshine

A popular aphorism in the discourse of American politics is simply stated, "freedom is never free," which also applies to certain materials under the Freedom of Information Act. The price paid for government records comes in terms of both the time and money required for researching, reviewing, and responding to requests submitted from the public. Fees vary according to the requester's identity and purpose for searching and reviewing the government records and the charges for photocopying or duplicating materials electronically.

35. *DOJ v. Reporters Comm. for Free Press*, 489 U.S. 749 (1989).
36. *Dept. of State v. Ray*, 502 U.S. 164 (1991).
37. *Dept. of Justice v. Landano*, 508 U.S. 165 (1993).
38. *Dept. of Interior v. Klamath Water Users Protective Assn.*, 532 U.S. 1 (2001).
39. *FCC v. AT&T Inc.*, 562 U.S. 397 (2011).
40. *Milner v. Department of Navy*, 562 U.S. 562 (2011).
41. *U.S. Fish and Wildlife Service v. Sierra Club*, 592 U.S. 261 (2021).

Congress decided the news media would *not* be charged for researching and reviewing records, but non-journalistic groups felt their work in the public's interest was also worthy of such favorable terms. In 1989, the National Security Archives expanded the FOIA terms. Custodians of federal records were advised to decide if the request was coming from someone who publishes or broadcasts news about current events of interest to the public, but in *Department of Defense v. National Security Archives*, a federal appeals court held the professional description should encompass anyone who "gathers information of potential interest to a segment of the public, uses its editorial skills to turn the raw materials into a distinct work, and distributes that work to an audience."[42]

In 2007, Congress stepped in to codify those terms in the Openness Promotes Effectiveness in our National Government Act, which also included the online world of bloggers, freelance journalists, and columnists. The problem is that not all custodians of those federal records have read the terms or are willing to enforce favorable rates for FOIA users, and for those who lack the funds to mount a legal appeal, this fact is more than troubling – it is illegal.

Sunshine in Government Meetings

Government Accountability Office (GAO)
The Government Accountability Office is a congressional federal agency assisting Congress in the oversight of budget expenditures.

Federal Advisory Committee Act (FACA)
The U.S. law that mandates transparency, reporting, and viewpoint diversity when private citizens give advice as part of a commission, committee, or advisory body established or used by the president or federal agencies in making policy.

Alabama law in 1907 prevented closed-door meetings for commissions and boards unless someone's reputation was at stake. Today, all states have laws that govern access to public meetings, but they vary widely in terms of their procedures and penalties. Effective state open meetings laws have strong legislative declarations in support of public sessions, specifically defining each one by listing the number of members who must gather to constitute a meeting and declaring void actions taken during a meeting someone improperly closed to the public.

Most statutes provide for exceptions to open sessions to discuss such matters as personnel actions, real estate transactions, and pending litigation. Florida adopted its open meeting law in 1967, which became a model for others in requiring advance notice, published minutes, and affirmation that only public decisions held in open meetings would be official.

The 1976 U.S. Government in the Sunshine Act amounts to what might be considered a federal open meetings law. This law covers about 50 agencies in the executive branch, including regulatory commissions. Members of such government organizations are not permitted to hold secret meetings unless they intend to discuss material that falls into one of ten categories. These categories mirror the FOIA exemptions and include provisions that permit closed-door meetings to discuss attempts to arbitrate or adjudicate a specific set of legal issues. The law requires the agencies to provide advance notice of meetings and publish an agenda.

FACA's Openness

Citizen groups often want to know more about advisory committee deliberations and membership, but the White House typically resists demands for a full disclosure. Advocates for openness in government seized upon the **Federal Advisory Committee Act** in their efforts to illuminate policymaking activities. The law defines *advisory committee* as "any committee, board, commission, council, conference, panel, task force, or other similar group" that dispenses "advice or recommendations" to the president of the United States.[43]

42. *Department of Defense v. National Security Archive*, 880 F.2d 1381 (D.C. Cir. 1989).
43. The Federal Advisory Committee Act (FACA) (U.S. Public Law, 92–63, 86 Stat. 770, enacted Oct. 6, 1972).

This "FACA" law enacted in 1972 was designed to stop lobbyists from shaping policy behind closed doors in what some sources described as "locker room" conversations, once business employees or private citizens gain membership to an executive advisory committee. There is too much informal conversation in administrative decisions, it was felt, so FACA declared that all administrative procedures and hearings would become available to the public. The law restricts how such committees can be created and limits their terms of operation.

The **Government Accountability Office (GAO)** asked for meeting records as part of its congressional oversight. If a private citizen acts secretly as a member of the task force, the group would be in violation of FACA because the Act was designed to open advisory committee meetings and records to the public.

Access to the President

Whenever the president travels, a group of reporters follow. Many more would like to accompany the president, but for security and logistical reasons, the number is restricted. The White House usually handles this by allowing a rotation of White House correspondents to serve as pool reporters, providing information to their colleagues who are not able to secure a spot in the press pool. Sometimes it's not possible for everyone who wants to attend a "public" meeting to do so. The president conducts press conferences that can only be attended by those who have credentials, and even then, only by a limited number. But can a president decide to deny access to certain reporters or media for ideological reasons?

In *Sherrill v. Knight*,[44] a federal appeals court determined that denial of press credentials implicates the First Amendment and that the reasons for denying access must be based on some *compelling* government interest. The court pointed out that the president is under no obligation to grant an interview to every reporter who wants one, or even to have a press conference. Calvin Coolidge averaged more than six press conferences per month while in office: Ronald Reagan averaged less than one.[45] Just one month into his presidency, Donald Trump made news when he excluded major media outlets, including CNN and *The New York Times*, seemingly because of the president's association with Russia.[46]

Since Richard Nixon's presidency, press access to the president has been more tightly controlled than in earlier times. Ronald Reagan's staff carefully crafted media events that showcased the president without affording the press an opportunity to ask questions. George W. Bush used national security and the threats following 9/11 to remain inaccessible. Barack Obama received a letter signed by 38 news organizations claiming that his administration was obstructing journalists.[47]

President Trump, however, took White House access to an even higher level of obstruction by relieving CNN reporter Jim Acosta of his press credentials – a move prompting lawsuits from CNN and the PEN America Center, a society for authors and artists. PEN sought an injunction against the president from directing any officer in his administration from retaliating against journalists critical of him. Under President Biden's Department of Justice, lawsuits were settled with those litigants.

44. 569 F. 2d 124 (Ct. Appeals DC Circ. 1977).
45. The American Presidency Project, *at* www.presidency.ucsb.edu/data/newsconferences.php.
46. "Press Excluded from White House Briefing Have Been Harshest Critics on Trump's Alleged Russia Ties," *Fortune*, February 25, 2017.
47. "Nixon Is Gone, But His Media Strategy Lives On," *The Atlantic*, August 4, 2014.

State Government Access

The first open records law is attributed to the state of Wisconsin in 1848, but in the wake of the Watergate scandal of the 1970s, all states approved some form of legal access to their government records. The provisions of state laws vary according to which offices must comply and how long they may take to respond. States also have different standards for assessing fees and for determining how each request is to be categorized. Statutes around the country have been generous in defining the types of documents that can be dispensed to the public, but enforcement is often weak, especially if the penalties carry no civil or criminal punishment and the prosecuting attorney sees no reason to pursue actions under the law.

Bedrock Law
All states have some type of access law for records and meetings, but these laws vary widely in terms of their procedures, penalties, and enforcement.

All 50 states have some version of a **FOI statute**, and five states have written it into their constitutions, so it is worth considering some similarities and differences. Florida adopted a constitutional amendment governing access to all its state government offices. Throughout the nation, openness is often based on the interpretation of exemptions regularly used to close certain government meetings and prohibit access to public records. Exemptions include material specifically excluded by other statutes, law enforcement investigatory information, working papers, and highly personal documents.

Even though each state has laws governing access to documents and meetings, they each vary in the degree of access they grant to civic boards, commissions, and public records. Thus, what the laws require in their criteria for access and the costs involved delineate the balance between public disclosure or withholding for each jurisdiction. Most states provide for a right of appeal when and if an open records request is refused, and some states like New York and Connecticut have established commissions that act as arbiters in deciding such matters.

In online applications, the government can wield a sword of access if it wants to find out from social media platforms users who are suspected of criminal activity. Social media companies afford a shield of privacy to their members based on terms and conditions. The online influencers who circulate gossip, spread rumors, and amplify conspiracy theories are subject to flagging, blocking, and "deplatforming" for violating policies of their social media.

The Florida legislature responded to "censoring" acts in 2021 by drafting a law, the Transparency in Technology Act, directing social media sites with notes of how to respond to objectionable content with "detailed definitions" that could be deemed acceptable. Under this law government authorities did not directly engage in "political censorship," but it specified the consequences for denying access, which involved certain penalties and procedures:

- fines of up to $100,000 per day if companies banned political candidates, until their access to the social media site was restored
- grounds for consumers to file suit against their social media platforms if they felt the terms of service had been violated, or they could ask the attorney general to sue the company
- provide a means to opt out of content curators that directed political content to users by means of algorithms

The Florida law took effect on July 1, 2024, but it met with criticism from the Electronic Frontier Foundation (EFF) and others who compared it to another Florida law struck down by the U.S. Supreme Court in 1974.[48] That law would force newspapers to afford politicians the right (sword) of access to its free space to reply to criticism by its editorial writers.

In defense of one teacher's union leader's right of newspaper access, the Florida Supreme Court defended the teacher's use of a right of reply law since it gave him a rebuttal opportunity following public editorial criticism. Ultimately, the U.S. Supreme Court held the law

48. *Miami Herald Publishing Co. v. Tornillo*, 418 U.S. 241 (1974).

to be unconstitutional as a form of government coercion since "press responsibility is not mandated by the Constitution and like many other virtues, it cannot be legislated."[49]

The sensational examples of public record disclosure showing police arrests recorded by body cameras are familiar to American television viewers. Access to this footage, however, is subject to legal challenges that may keep the images out of sight for some time. It took over a year for the Associated Press to obtain Louisiana highway patrol's video footage of body cameras showing the beating death of one suspect. Under that state law, police video recordings were required by a court order.[50] After 474 days the AP journalists obtained footage[51] of Ronald Greene's violent arrest as he was punched, dragged, and repeatedly stunned by state police who left his prone body dying on the ground.[52]

There are states where authorities object to the release of police body camera footage, and in some cases move against citizens who use their own cameras to record arrests. A photographer who showed police officers making an arrest in New England was charged under Massachusetts law with aiding the escape of a prisoner. In the case of *Glik v. Cunniffe*,[53] the photographer was found to be within his rights as a citizen to video record officers apprehending a person in public. Although the U.S. Supreme Court has yet to directly address the question, a federal appeals court ruled the "First Amendment protects the act of photographing, filming, or otherwise recording police officers conducting their official duties in public."[54] Several states have chosen to discourage photographers from recording police activity by making it a crime for citizens to move closer than 25 feet of a law enforcement officer after being asked to stop. Failure to obey the Louisiana law could mean 60 days in jail.[55]

Body Cam Footage – Twenty-First-Century Records

A U.S. survey revealed 95% of large police departments nationwide either have implemented or intend to implement police body cameras.[56] That's a lot of videos being collected daily, and every second of them is potentially a public record. Cincinnati alone estimates it records about 90 hours of video daily.[57] From a public access perspective, this raises lots of issues.

The value of body camera video has already been documented. Both officers and members of the public with whom they interact, knowing their actions are being recorded, may be on their best behavior. Individuals who previously might have accused officers of inappropriate action may not make outlandish claims. In those instances when police behavior is unprofessional, a video record is useful in determining the extent of disciplinary action needed.

Despite the value of body camera video, there must be a balancing of public and private interests. An officer executing a search warrant enters someone's private property.

49. *Id.* at 256.
50. Louisiana Revised Statutes 44:35.
51. J. Mustian, "'I'm Scared': AP Obtains Video of Deadly Arrest of Black Man," *AP News*, May 19, 2021, *at* https://apnews.com/article/ronald-greene-death-louisiana-eca021d8a54ec73598dd72b269826f7a.
52. Police body camera recordings of Ronald Greene's death near Monroe, LA, showed him being dragged, beaten, tased, choked, and left bound in a prone position until he died.
53. 655 F.3d 78 (2011).
54. *Fields v. City of Philadelphia*, 862 F.3d 353, 356 (2013).
55. See C. Jan-Lim, "New Louisiana Law Will Make it Harder for Bystanders to film Police Misconduct," *ACLU Louisiana*, May 30, 2024, *at* https://www.laaclu.org/en/news/new-louisiana-law-will-make-it-harder-bystanders-film-police-misconduct#:-:text=House%20-Bill%20173%20makes%20it,the%20need%20to%20protect%20police.
56. Michael Maciag, "Survey: Almost All Police Departments Plan to Use Body Cameras," January 22, 2016, *at* www.governing.com/topics/public-justice-safety/gov-police-body-camera-survey.html.
57. Aleszu Bajak, "In Police Body Camera Footage, Tech Companies See a Niche," January 25, 2017, *at* https://undark.org/article/as-police-body-cameras-proliferate-companies/.

Should video of that search be accessible by anyone? Making video of the inside of someone's home available online might make a thief's job easier. Imagine if the video includes images of minor children in the home or someone partially dressed. Even on a public street, civilians uninvolved with any police activity might be recorded. Should their images be visible, or should their faces be blurred, as their appearance in the video might imply some kind of wrongdoing?

How accessible should the video be? Arrest reports are public records, but police departments are not obligated to put those records online and make them searchable electronically. Should law enforcement be expected to upload body cam video so it can be accessed by any interested party?

Access to government documents has always had a cost, but the costs associated with body cam footage can quickly get out of hand. How long must video footage be kept? Rules strictly govern the length of time that paper records must be kept, and similar rules need to be in place for video, keeping in mind the massive amounts of storage space necessary for video.

Delaware vaguely states that body cam video must be kept "such time as is necessary for training, investigation or prosecution," while other states more specifically direct storage of police body cam video from 60 to 90 days, or longer if the footage is likely to be used in evidence.[58]

Laws about the use of body cams and what happens to the video are plentiful, and the laws are changing. Muckrock cofounder Michael Morisy describes it this way: "Eventually the public records laws become like Swiss cheese. Nobody really knows how many exemptions are in a given state's public records laws because they're buried in other unrelated laws."[59]

In South Carolina, body cam video is not subject to the state's open records law.[60] The videos are public records in Oklahoma, but police are required to redact any video that shows the death of a person, a dead body, a nude body, or anyone under 16.[61] Not only do states have laws in place, but some cities and counties have also enacted laws. Some law enforcement agencies have recommended practices and procedures that do not rise to the level of law but are recommendations for best practices.

Hundreds of different jurisdictions are involved. The Reporters Committee for Freedom of the Press tries its best to keep current.[62] The Urban Institute, a Washington, DC, think tank, also attempts to keep track of all the various rules.[63]

State laws govern all records kept by their agencies, but few apply only to records that are required by law. Some states have a policy that allows exemptions on broad categories of documents, while others finely parse the limits on records or meetings. Some states include email records within the definition of accessible documents. In states where no such access is granted, it is hard to predict where a particular agency will draw the line. The guiding principle is that government carries the burden of proof for denying disclosure, but in fact

58. "New Castle County Police – Body-Worn Camera Policy," January 20, 2017 https://www.nccde.org/DocumentCenter/View/17200/Appendix-41-B-Body-Worn-Camera-Policy-Revised-1-20-17-PDF?bidId=.
59. Chava Gourarie, "The Public Records Process Can Be Messy: Muckrock Hopes to Tidy It Up," *Columbia Journalism Review*, July 14, 2016, *at* www.cjr.org/analysis/foia_muckrock_public_records.php.
60. "The First Statewide Police Body-Cam Law Comes with a Major Caveat," *Columbia Journalism Review*, June 16, 2015, *at* www.cjr.org/united_states_project/south_carolina_police_camera_public_records.php.
61. "Bodycams: Seeing, But Not Being Seen," *The News Media and the Law*, Spring 2015, *at* www.rcfp.org/browse-media-law-resources/news-media-law/news-media-and-law-spring-2015/bodycams-seeing-not-being-s.
62. www.rcfp.org/bodycams.
63. https://apps.urban.org/features/body-camera-update/.

it is usually the *custodian* of records who arbitrarily restricts access. Where the rule of law is silent on such matters, agencies may speak loudly and forcefully – although usually not affirmatively – in favor of citizen access to their records and meetings.

Texas Reporter's Inquiry

How states view freedom of information varies from state to state; in some places public officials even try to discourage journalists from seeking public records for whatever reason. Along the southern border of Texas, a dispute arose between police and a citizen journalist that made news when an obscure statute was used to take her into custody for seeking information.

In 2017, Priscilla Villarreal, known to her online followers as *La Gordiloca* (crazy fat lady) desired to learn more about a local suicide case and a family involved in a car accident. Texas police familiar with her online reporting resisted her probing these items and arrested her using a statute that deemed it a felony in Texas to "solicit" information that is not a public record.

The case against Villarreal involved not just an alleged violation of the vaguely worded statute, but whether police had qualified immunity when they arrested her for allegedly violating it. After criminal charges were dismissed by a district judge, Villarreal decided it was her turn and filed suit against the city and county for violating her constitutional rights.

At first, a federal district court ruled against Villarreal, saying police have a qualified privilege in such cases. She appealed that point to a panel of the Fifth Circuit in New Orleans, which overturned the lower court's ruling 2–1. That placed the ball in Texas's legal court, and the attorney general was granted a rehearing before the Fifth Circuit Court of Appeals, which *en banc* ruled against her, although seven dissenting opinions went her way.

Villarreal was not about to quit and asked for one more hearing before the Supreme Court. Thirteen journalism organizations, civil rights groups, and individuals filed *amicus curae* briefs on her behalf, citing the dangers of enforcing a seldom-used law that had nothing to do with investigative journalism but much to do about curbing freedom of information.

Laws That Restrict Access

As noted, all states and the federal government have laws that specifically exclude certain types of information from public scrutiny. Today, the right to privacy has expanded as a substantial barrier to access information held by government agencies.

The federal government has adopted a law protecting the privacy of student records, for example. Congress passed a federal privacy law, which may conflict with the provisions of the Freedom of Information Act. The federal government also insisted that states pass statutes controlling access to criminal history records. As a result, the right to privacy is frequently used to block access to public records at the state and federal levels.

Privacy Act of 1974

This law was designed to protect individuals from the willful disclosure of personal information found in government records to third parties. The 1974 law calls for the consent of the citizen before such records can be made public or even transferred to another agency. It further allows for people to review agency records and correct any mistakes they may find. The Privacy Act of 1974 does provide for legal recourse in terms of damages available to Americans who discover their records were mishandled by the government, but it also allows for certain exemptions to permit law enforcement officers to prosecute crimes, census takers to gather data, or Congress to conduct investigations.

The move to privacy means that public access is faced with threatened lawsuits or litigation over actions that involve intrusion or misrepresentation, through laws such as the Family Educational Rights and Privacy Act, the Health Insurance Portability and Accountability Act, and the Driver's Privacy Protection Act.

State Driver's License Records

Driver's Privacy Protection Act (DPPA)
Driver's Privacy Protection Act of 1994 is a federal law protecting the privacy of state driver's license information.

There are times when state and federal bodies come into conflict regarding the types and kinds of confidentiality granted to the public. The U.S. Congress, for example, moved to protect innocent victims of stalkers when it passed the **Driver's Privacy Protection Act (DPPA)** in 1994. That law was the direct result of the stalker murder in 1989 of Hollywood actress Rebecca Schaeffer who was gunned down at the front door of her California home. The murderer was able to discover where Schaffer lived after gaining access to her personal records from driver's license data held by the California Department of Motor Vehicles.

The federal law was designed to protect innocent victims from such violent intrusions, but it was less well received by many states that collected revenue from the sale or release of driver's license data. South Carolina considered the DPPA to be an affront to the Tenth Amendment, which it held was the "legal and spiritual guardian" of states' rights.[64] The U.S. Justice Department, however, argued DPPA was valid under the **commerce clause**. The U.S. Supreme Court unanimously agreed, thus affirming the act.[65] Chief Justice William Rehnquist held that states should not be compelled to disclose certain records if the federal government determines a legitimate reason for keeping them private.

Family Educational Rights and Privacy Act (FERPA)

Family Educational Rights and Privacy Act
The Family Educational Rights and Privacy Act of 1974 is a federal law designed to protect the privacy of children's school information.

The **Family Educational Rights and Privacy Act** (1974) was intended to prevent schools from releasing academic information about children without consent. Sen. James L. Buckley of New York sponsored it so that schools could keep confidential academic records once they receive federal funding from the Department of Education. Before a student becomes an adult, the law protects parental discretion over academic records, but that right shifts to the students at the age of 18 in nearly all 50 states.[66]

FERPA also gives students and parents the right to inspect personal school records and recommend corrections to them if they find information that is inaccurate or misleading. The law also requires their signature before any academic authority can release their records to third parties. Posting grades by any easily identifying means (names, initials, or Social Security numbers) is a violation of the Act.

FERPA has provisions guiding state agencies on the transmission of testing data, but they are not airtight. For example, the law does not prevent law enforcement officers on school grounds from obtaining information regarding criminal activities in student files. Whether an honest mistake is made or there is a malicious attempt to obfuscate, universities have sometimes mistakenly believed that FERPA prevents them from releasing information about

64. Carrying its principle over from the Articles of Confederation, federal constitutional framers felt it prudent to prevent the government from encroaching upon state rights: "The powers not delegated to the United States by the Constitution, nor prohibited by it to the States, are reserved for the States respectively, or to the people."
65. *Reno v. Condon*, 528 U.S. 141 (2000).
66. The age of majority in Alabama and Nebraska is 19.

criminal activity.[67] It also gives accrediting agencies and other academic authorities the right to inspect data in student files. Other reasons for disclosing student records include health concerns, financial aid, and compliance with judicial orders.

Privacy of Health Records

Health Insurance Portability and Accountability Act (HIPAA)
Health Insurance Portability and Accountability Act is a federal law that protects the privacy of individuals' health information.

Protected Health Information (PHI)
The class of individual health care information protected by the Health Insurance Portability and Accountability Act (HIPAA).

A federal law protecting personal medical information seemed like a good idea at first – it would keep medical records private and require patients to decide whether such information should be made public. This was the intent of language in the **Health Insurance Portability and Accountability Act (HIPAA)**, first enacted by Congress in 1996. Title 1 served to protect health care coverage for employees after leaving or changing jobs.

Seven years later, Congress added a provision requiring healthcare providers to ensure confidentiality of medical care records and communications unless they are released from doing so by the patient's signature. Title 2 is known as "AS" for "administrative simplification," where new rules regarding access to patient records have created difficulty for those hoping to gather information.

Unfortunately, many hospitals have broadly interpreted the Privacy Act and have not allowed patient information or condition reports to be released to the families of the hospitalized over the telephone, even if the patient is critically ill and the family member lives out of state. Additional penalties have been implemented for those (mostly nurses) who unknowingly violate HIPAA; some even have been terminated from their positions for accidental blunders that violated their employers' interpretation of the law.

The stringent rules of disclosure apply to materials classified as **protected health information (PHI)** and are an effective ban on the release of details about a patient's health status, financial arrangements, or other provisions of health care. Problematically, liberal interpretations of HIPAA rules can conceal any part of a patient's files or medical history.

Journalism and academic organizations have fought for changes in the law to more effectively inform the public on major health issues. The University of Michigan demonstrated how HIPAA's enforcement drastically reduced their survey results (96% to 34%) in terms of heart disease research. Another study detailing the effects of HIPAA enforcement on cancer research showed an even greater decrease in data collection. The informed consent forms required under HIPAA are rife with legal jargon that tends to discourage researchers and patients alike. The result is a poorer data pool that produces less well-informed decisions about healthcare management and public health policy.

FERPA – A Cloak for Athletic Violations?

An Ohio newspaper used the Freedom of Information Act to discover how colleges were treating their star football athletes and to obtain records about possible violations of rules. The paper simply asked the nation's top football programs for public records including travel reports, flight manifests, and reports of NCAA violations. A majority of the schools provided some records, but many moved to censor part or most of the records.

The Columbus Dispatch reported that three schools refused to release any records of NCAA violations while others heavily censored student violation reports. U.S. Sen. James L. Buckley (N.Y.), one of the architects of the FERPA legislation, saw that its intent was to maintain students' privacy in grading and not to cloak infractions. Schools that were less than compliant with the newspaper's request had added their own interpretation to the law, the senator said.

67. *See* "Same Game, Different Rules," in *Student Press Law Center Report* (Spring 2004).

Press Freedoms to Gather Information

The news media's position as the *Fourth Estate* implies a responsibility to gather information and report truthfully on the workings of the branches of government. However, there remains a legal distinction between the right to publish information and the right to access it.[68] There exists a greater right of the press to defend itself against government encroachment than there is a guaranteed right to claim access. One area where government is less friendly to the public in general and journalists in particular are the grounds and facilities housing prison inmates.

Estimates vary, but states generally spend more money on housing criminals than any other single budget item, and with a million people incarcerated in state penitentiaries each day, the workings of the prison are significant to many Americans. Nonetheless, prisons grant only limited access to the public, and this restriction on public property has been upheld by three rulings of the U.S. Supreme Court.

The decisions came at a period when the news media was growing concerned with the living conditions faced by inmates. Lawyers sued to compel states to end inhumane and often violent conditions and to help improve the prison's sanitation, fire safety, health care, and exercise facilities. In some cases, public action groups succeeded, but access eventually was curbed in the 1970s due to three decisions handed down by the U.S. Supreme Court.

The major rulings – known as *Pell*, *Saxbe*, and *Houchins* – ultimately denied the implied right of access to prisons and saw no valid one under First Amendment guarantees.[69] In the California case of *Pell v. Procunier*, the Court upheld a penal code rule that refused to grant "press and other media interviews with specific individual inmates." In the second case, *Saxbe v. Washington Post Co.*, Justice Stewart delivered a majority opinion that concluded that even though government cannot interfere with a free press, it also cannot necessarily "accord the press special access to information not shared by members of the public generally."[70]

In a prison access landmark, *Houchins v. KQED*, the Supreme Court bolstered Sheriff Houchins's decision when he stopped a TV news crew from visiting a part of the Santa Rita jail where an inmate appeared to have committed suicide.[71] Here the Court seemed even more determined to reject any First Amendment interpretation granting greater access to the news media than the public at large. Three major cases have left it up to each state's regulatory and penal code to draw the lines on just how far they should go in terms of allowing prison access, but it would be a mistake to suppose U.S. prison authorities have grown more liberal toward the news media due to the holdings of the courts in *Pell*, *Saxbe*, and *Houchins*.

Requests for face-to-face interviews create potential conflicts, but there is no outright ban on media–prisoner interactions. The best way to interpret the three precedents is to say that prison administrators are expected to grant individual permission for inmate communications if there is no loss of security and the orderly administration of justice is well served.

The popularity of *celebrity* inmates has inhibited officials from granting greater access to the public or news media. Even attempts to claim a right of access to prisoner executions has failed. When prisons invite witnesses to be present, and prison-run closed-circuit television is available,[72] there is still no legal right of access to executions at the state or federal level.

68. C. Edwin Baker, "Press Rights and Government Power to Structure the Press," 34 *U. Miami L. R.* 819 (1980).
69. *Pell v. Procunier*, 417 U.S. 817 (1974); *Saxbe v. Washington Post Co.*, 417 U.S. 843 (1974); *Houchins v. KQED, Inc., 438 U.S. 1* (1978).
70. 417 U.S. 843, 848.
71. *Houchins*, supra note 70.
72. Infamous Oklahoma City bomber Timothy McVeigh was executed at a federal penitentiary in Terre Haute, IN. Rather than travel from Oklahoma to witness the execution, family members were allowed to view a closed-circuit transmission in Oklahoma City, but its use for any other purpose was prohibited.

Summary

- There is ongoing tension between the government's desire to keep secrets and the media's desire to uncover as much of the public's business as possible through freedom of information laws. This "Sword and Shield" struggle can produce a healthy adversarial relationship to ultimately serve the public's interests. But when the need for confidentiality and secrecy comes in conflict with the citizen's right to know, especially at the federal level, then the judicial branch is called upon to resolve the controversy.
- Under the Freedom of Information Act, public records cover materials and items necessary for a federal agency to deal with the public, and include documents and recordings kept by the agency pertaining to official business.
- Any individual (not just citizens or media professionals) may request records from federal agencies under the FOIA. The Act does not apply to Congress or the judiciary, only the executive branch.
- Once a formal request is received, a federal agency must respond to it in a timely fashion. If a request is denied, the reason for the denial should be made explicit, referring to the specific exemption in the law. Denials may be appealed, and if the denial is determined inappropriate, the government official who refused access is subject to disciplinary action.
- Analogous to freedom of information, official meetings under sunshine laws require that elected leaders open their meetings to the public and provide advance notice of these sessions, including agenda items for consideration. As with the FOIA policies, a list of exemptions allows room for some confidential discussions to occur behind closed doors.
- Every U.S. state affords some level of access to information and government records, comparable to rights protected at the federal level. Differences exist, but the underlying premise – that openness is the goal of good governance – is at the core of these laws.
- Specific records have been identified as ones where the right of access is outweighed by an individual's privacy interest. Driver's license data, educational records, personal health data, and medical records are all protected under federal statutes so that they may not be released, even in states where a more open climate of disclosure is preferred.

Ethical Dilemmas: Mug Shots as Public Records

When a person is arrested for a crime, the booking process often includes taking fingerprints and mug shots. Guilty or not, a criminal arrest is a stressful experience with lasting implications; suspects photographed at their booking usually do not look their best, and most people would prefer not to share their image at that time for wide distribution. What's more, the release of a mug shot, even one that's acceptable in appearance, suggests to suspicious and unknowing onlookers that individual surely must be guilty of something!

Mug shots are state government records, so they are not subject to the federal Freedom of Information Act. In 2016, however, the Sixth Circuit Court of Appeals overruled a decision from 20 years earlier that individuals have no right of privacy to protect their booking photos. The new ruling relied on Exemption 7(c) of the Freedom of Information Act, which prevents disclosure if it "could reasonably be expected to constitute an unwarranted invasion of personal privacy." The court stated,

> Booking photos – snapped in the vulnerable and embarrassing moments immediately after [an individual is] accused, taken into custody, and deprived of most liberties – fit squarely within this realm of embarrassing and humiliating

> Information. . . . In 1996, this court could not have known or expected that a booking photo could haunt the depicted individual for decades. . . . Experience has taught us otherwise.[73]

So then is the photo of a suspect substantially different from the mere fact of an arrest?

Anyone can go into any police department in the United States and request to see the previous day's arrest reports, which is the officer's account of events leading to an arrest. The information found in those documents is public record to be reproduced and published. If the criterion for nondisclosure is the mug shorts are "embarrassing and humiliating," then can't the same argument be made for arrest reports, especially suspects who are never found guilty?

Another factor complicating the mug shot issue are the websites posting mug shots purportedly as a public service that then beckon the victims to have their pictures removed . . . for a fee, of course. The states of Georgia, Illinois, Oregon, Texas, and Utah have enacted statutes to stop this predatory practice. Another tactic is to legally claim mug shots are not public records and only become such when the suspect has been found guilty.[74] A change occurs when someone is found guilty at trial but later found not guilty on appeal.

All these issues lead to several key questions.

Should mug shots be public records or not? Even if a personal visual image is a public record and can be legally published, is it ethical to do so given the abject humiliation it conveys? After all, a suspect is to be presumed innocent until proven guilty, and the dissemination of their mug shot obliterates that ideal to the detriment of people charged with but not convicted of a crime.

73. *Detroit Free Press v. Department of Justice*, 829 F. 3d 478 (6th Cir. 2016).
74. A list is maintained by the National Conference of State Legislatures, *at* https://www.ncsl.org/technology-and-communication/mug-shots-and-booking-photo-websites.

Table of Cases

Index

Note: Page numbers in *italics* indicate figures, **bold** indicate tables in the text, and references following "n" refer notes.